Hallensleben, Zwahlen, Papanikolaou, Kalaitzidis (Eds.)
Building the House of Wisdom
Sergii Bulgakov and Contemporary Theology:
New Approaches and Interpretations

EPIPHANIA

Herausgegeben von
Barbara Hallensleben, Guido Vergauwen, Nikolaus Wyrwoll
in Zusammenarbeit mit
dem Zentrum für das Studium der Ostkirchen
der Universität Freiburg Schweiz

Band 19

Building the House of Wisdom

Sergii Bulgakov and Contemporary Theology:
New Approaches and Interpretations

Edited by
Barbara Hallensleben, Regula M. Zwahlen,
Aristotle Papanikolaou, Pantelis Kalaitzidis

Aschendorff
Verlag

Münster
2024

Die Druckvorstufe dieser Publikation wurde vom Schweizerischen Nationalfonds
zur Förderung der wissenschaftlichen Forschung unterstützt.

© 2024 Aschendorff Verlag GmbH & Co. KG, Münster

www.aschendorff-buchverlag.de

Printed in Germany

ISBN Druck: 978-3-402-12060-6
ISBN Gesamtband OPEN ACCESS: 978-3-402-12061-3
DOI Gesamtband: DOI 10.17438/978-3-402-12062-0

TABLE OF CONTENTS

SOPHIOLOGY

CREATION AND ONTOLOGY

ECUMENICAL PERSPECTIVES

Building the House of Wisdom
DOI 10.17438/978-3-402-12520-5

Building the House of Wisdom.
Editors' Introduction

Barbara Hallensleben, Regula M. Zwahlen, Aristotle Papanikolaou,
Pantelis Kalaitzidis

Ten years ago, the Orthodox theologian Sergii Bulgakov (1871–1944) was called an "awakening giant" to whom "much of contemporary Orthodox God-talk can be traced."[1] Today, the giant seems very much awake. Renewed interest in Bulgakov appeared in the 1970s in the Soviet Union[2] and turned into a genuine revival in the 1990s.[3] Thoroughly annotated new editions of Bulgakov's works sprouted everywhere and sparked a new general interest in Russian religious thought and Orthodox theology in Europe and the USA. Above all, the publications and English translations by Catherine Evtuhov and Rowan Williams, as well as those by Boris Jakim and Thomas Allen Smith, have triggered a real

---

1 Brandon Gallaher, "Antinomism, trinity and the challenge of Solov'ëvan pantheism in the theology of Sergij Bulgakov," *Studies in East European Thought* 64, no. 3–4 (2012), 222.

2 Of crucial importance were Elena Kazimirchak-Polonskaia's lectures at the Spiritual Academy in Leningrad ("Monakhinia Elena", one of Bulgakov's spiritual daughters). Dimitri Sizonenko, "L'héritage du père Serge Boulgakov dans la Russie actuelle," *Le Messager Orthodoxe* 158 (2015), 22; Dimitrii Sizonenko, "Bor'ba za istinu i retseptsiia naslediia Bulgakova v Rossii," *Vestnik RKhD* 203 (2015), 43.

3 Important international conferences on Sergii Bulgakov with the participation of several contributors to this volume (in brackets): "S. N. Bulgakov: Economics and Culture", Moscow, October 11–13, 1994 (B. Hallensleben); "S. N. Bulgakov' Religious-Philosophical Journey (on the occasion of his 130th birthday)", Moscow, March 5–7, 2001 (A. Arjakovsky, C. Evtuhov, A. Kozyrev); "Russian Theology in European Context: S. N. Bulgakov and Western Religious-Philosophical Thought", Moscow, September 29–October 2, 2004 (B. Gallaher, R. Zwahlen); "Sergii Bulgakov's Heritage in Contemporary Social and Humanitarian Sciences (on the occasion of his 140th birthday)", Kyiv, May 12–13, 2011 (B. Gallaher, R. Zwahlen); "Serge Boulgakov, un père de l'église moderne", Paris, June 27–28, 2014 (A. Arjakovsky, B. Hallensleben, A. Mainardi, R. Zwahlen).

boom in the study of Bulgakov in the English-speaking world in the last decade, and more translations are still being published.[4]

Sergii Bulgakov—A Preeminent Theologian of the Twentieth Century

A famous rival of Lenin in the field of economics, and, according to Wassily Kandinsky, "one of the deepest experts on religious life"[5] in the so-called "Silver Age" of Russian art and culture, Bulgakov, professor of national economics, publicist, politician, and later Orthodox theologian and priest, became a significant "global player" in both the Orthodox diaspora and the ecumenical movement of the 1920s and 1930s. Today we discover him as one of the most important theologians of the twentieth century: Sergii Bulgakov, Karl Barth, and Hans Urs von Balthasar have been called "sort of [a] triumvirate over modern systematic theology in Orthodoxy, Protestantism, and Roman Catholicism."[6] After him, "upon the branches of Orthodoxy young shoots" grew,[7] many insights by well-known Orthodox theologians like Vladimir Lossky or John Zizioulas trace their roots back to Bulgakov,[8] and he prepared the ground for ecumenical encounters to this day.

---

4   For translations into other languages, mainly into French, Italian, and German, see Sergei N. Bulgakov, *Bibliographie. Werke, Briefwechsel und Übersetzungen*, vol. 3, ed. Barbara Hallensleben and Regula Zwahlen, Werke (Münster: Aschendorff, 2017). Updates are published on the website of the Sergii Bulgakov Research Center at the University of Fribourg: https://www.unifr.ch/sergij-bulgakov (access 2024/01/26).

5   Andreas Hüneke, ed., *Der Blaue Reiter. Eine Geschichte in Dokumenten* (Stuttgart: Philipp Reclam jun., 2011), 48. On Kandinsky and Bulgakov, see Regula M. Zwahlen, "Sergij Bulgakov und Vasilij Kandinskij, 'über das Geistige in der Kunst'," in *Veni, Sancte Spiritus! Festschrift für Barbara Hallensleben zum 60. Geburtstag*, ed. Guido Vergauwen and Andreas Steingruber (Münster: Aschendorff, 2018), Russian version: Regula M. Zwahlen, "Blagoslovenie. O dukhovnom v iskusstve. Pereklichka idei protoiereia Sergiia Bulgakova i Vasiliia Kandinskogo," *Dary* (2021/2022), 18–31; Antoine Arjakovsky, "Sergii Bulgakov and Wassily Kandinsky: Two Visionaries of the Wisdom of God," *The Wheel* 26/27 (2021), 50–59.

6   Brandon Gallaher, *Freedom and Necessity in Modern Trinitarian Theology*, Oxford Theology and Religion Monographs (Oxford: Oxford University Press, 2016), 11.

7   Sergii Bulgakov, "O tsarstvii Bozhiem [1927]," in *Protoierei Sergii Bulgakov. Put' Parizhskogo Bogosloviia*, ed. Maksim Kozlov (Moscow: Chram sv. Tatiany pri MGU, 2007), 134.

8   Aristotle Papanikolaou, "From Sophia to Personhood. The Development of 20th Century Orthodox Trinitarian Theology," *Phronema* 33, no. 2 (2018), 1–20: 19.

Yet, tragically, or perhaps dialectically, Bulgakov's most prominent younger colleagues Georges Florovsky (1893–1979) and Vladimir Lossky (1903–1953) established the polarizing narrative of their "neo-patristic turn" mainly against Bulgakov's "sophiology."[9] This standard narrative requires serious and thorough revision as Rowan Williams', Paul Gavrilyuk's and other works have shown.[10] The insinuation that "modernist" theologians like Bulgakov and Vladimir Soloviev[11] have altogether abandoned the Church fathers, and that the "neopatrists" are not indebted to modernity at all is simply false.[12] On the contrary, the "neopatristic" theologians owe their rediscovery and the "return to the Church fathers" to the "modernists," if not altogether to the "patristic revival" in the Orthodox Church of imperial Russia in the nineteenth century, often accused of being entirely in "Western captivity." At that time, the Church's clerical academies were translating thousands of patristic texts into

9   Florovsky, for most of his life, refused to criticize Bulgakov and sophiology openly—in his view, their positions were opposed, but they were not enemies: "the encounter of different poles of thought has always been native to theology itself." See Paul Ladouceur, "Georges Florovsky and Sergius Bulgakov: 'In Peace Let Us Love One Another'," in *The Living Christ: The Theological Legacy of Georges Florovsky*, ed. John Chryssavgis and Brandon Gallaher (London: T&T Clark, 2021), 69–85.

10   Rowan Williams, "The theology of Vladimir Nikolaievich Lossky: an exposition and critique" (PhD thesis, University of Oxford, 1975), http://ora.ox.ac.uk/objects/ uuid%3A15b86a5d-21f4-44a3-95bb-b8543d326658 (access 2024/01/26); Paul L. Gavrilyuk, *Georges Florovsky and the Russian Religious Renaissance* (Oxford: Oxford University Press, 2013); Aristotle Papanikolaou, "Why Sophia? Bulgakov the Theologian," *The Wheel* 26/27 (2021), 15–16; Nikolaos Asproulis, "La réception de la sagesse dans la sophiologie russe. Rôle et controverses dans l'orthodoxie," *Revue des Sciences Religieuses* 108, no. 2 (2020), 27–48. The entire double issue of *The Wheel* 26/27 (2021), with guest editor Nikolaos Asproulis, is devoted to a critical overview of Bulgakov's legacy.

11   Jeremy Pilch has convincingly demonstrated that Soloviev's "own teaching about deification was rooted in Chalcedonian Christology [...] and in the spirit and teachings of the Church Fathers." The conclusion that the same is true for Bulgakov is obvious. Jeremy Pilch, *"Breathing the Spirit With Two Lungs": Deification in the Work of Vladimir Solov'ev*, Eastern Christian Studies (Leuven: Peeters, 2018), 19.

12   See Pantelis Kalaitzidis, "From the 'Return to the Fathers' to the Need for a Modern Orthodox Theology," *St. Vladimir's Theological Quarterly* 54, no. 1 (2010), 5–36. See also Marcus Plested, *Wisdom in Christian Tradition. The Patristic Roots of Modern Russian Sophiology* (Oxford: Oxford University Press, 2022); Nikolaos Asproulis, "Georges Florovsky and Sergius Bulgakov in Dialogue: The Church Fathers, the God-world Relationship and Theological Method," in *Ex Patribus Lux: Essays on Orthodox Theological Anthropology and Georges Florovsky's Theology*, ed. Nikolaos Asproulis and Olga Sevastyanova (Volos: Volos Academy Publications, 2021), 101–16.

the vernacular.[13] Paul Gavrilyuk argues that "the debate [...] was not *whether* patristic theology was foundational [...] but rather *how* to engage the patristic tradition this side of modernity."[14] The Orthodox theologian Metropolitan Kallistos Ware (1934–2022) concluded that one of the "chief tasks of Orthodox theology will be to transcend the dichotomy between the 'Neo-Patristic' and the 'Russian' schools, considering how the two may be combined, and at the same time to reach out beyond both trends to a fresh vision of theology that combines what is best in both without being limited to either."[15] Correspondingly, one of the chief tasks of theology in general is, according to Bulgakov, to reach out to a fresh vision of Christian unity beyond confessional boundaries,[16] to build a common "House of Wisdom," as it were.

The House of Wisdom

What is "the Wisdom of God" all about? In his booklet on *The Wisdom of God*, written for a Western public in 1937, Bulgakov brings to mind that his development of sophiology in the 1930s was not an old pre-revolutionary project over which he brooded as an isolated Russian emigrant; rather, he boldly pre-

---

13   Patrick Lally Michelson, *Beyond the Monastery Walls: The Ascetic Revolution in Russian Orthodox Thought, 1814–1914* (Madison, WI: University of Wisconsin Press, 2017), 59. Rather ironically, the somewhat "Protestant" endeavor to translate and popularize ancient Christian texts in order to combat "protestantization," led to the "patristic turn" of both "modernist" and "neopatristic" thinkers.

14   Gavrilyuk, "Georges Florovsky and the Russian Religious Renaissance," 3. Kristina Stoeckl made the same point in: Kristina Stoeckl, Community after Totalitarianism. The Eastern Orthodox Intellectual Tradition and the Philosophical Discourse of Political Modernity (Frankfurt, Berlin, Bern et al.: Peter Lang, 2008), 103–04.

15   Kallistos Ware, "Orthodox theology today: trends and tasks," *International Journal for the Study of the Christian Church* 12, no. 2 (2012), 114. One of the first recent attempts is Marcus Plested's *Wisdom in Christian Tradition. The Patristic Roots of Modern Russian Sophiology* (Oxford: Oxford University Press 2022).

16   Sergej N. Bulgakov, "U kladezja Iakovlja. O real'nom edinstve razdelennoi tserkvi v vere, molitve i tainstvakh," in *Khristianskoe Vozsoedinenie. Ekumenicheskaia problema v pravoslavnom soznanii. Sbornik statei*, ed. YMCA-Press (Paris: YMCA-Press, 1933), 9–32; Sergei N. Bulgakov, "By Jacob's Well. On the actual unity of the apparently divided Church: in prayer, faith, and sacrament," in *A Bulgakov Anthology*, ed. James Pain and Nicolas Zernov (London: SPCK, 1976), 100–13; see also Barbara Hallensleben, "Ökumene als Pfingstgeschehen bei Sergij N. Bulgakov," in *Ökumene. Das eine Ziel—die vielen Wege.*, ed. Iso Baumer and Guido Vergauwen (Freiburg im Üechtland: 1995), 147–80.

sented it alongside and in dialogue with, for example, contemporary Catholic "Modernism" and "Barthianism," as a modern theological conception which, in his view, does nothing less than to link *all* the current "dogmatic and practical problems of modern Christian dogmatics and ascetics," and indeed the problems of Christian theology and culture as whole.[17] But

> as a result of the atmosphere of sensation or scandal [...] for [Western readers], of course, [the words 'Sophia' and 'sophiology'] are tinged with the peculiar exotic Oriental flavour of 'gnosis', and, indeed, smack of every sort of rubbish and superstition. No one seems to suspect that in fact we are talking about the very 'essence of Christianity' [["Das Wesen des Christentums"]], that is a problem which is even now being discussed by the whole of Western [["academic"]] Christendom [[Harnack, Schleiermacher, Barth etc. etc.]].[18]

Bulgakov located the essential problem of contemporary Christian theology in a one-sided focus on God *or* the world, transcendence *or* immanence, God *or* man. Therefore he, together with some of his colleagues, criticized Karl Barth's "non-acceptance of the world" in the early 1930s,[19] because in his view "in Christianity is born the new sense of life that one should not flee the world but that Christ is coming into the world for the marriage feast of the Lamb, the feast of Divine-Humanity."[20] For Bulgakov, the essence of Christianity is expressed above all in the dogma of Chalcedon on God-humanity, which defines the complex relationship between divine and human nature that are united unconfusedly, unchangeably, indivisibly, inseparably, according to the Chalcedonian *Horos*: "The roots of this dogma penetrate to the very heart of heaven and earth, in the inmost depths of the Holy Trinity and into the creaturely nature of human beings."[21]

---

17 Sergei Bulgakov, *Sophia. The Wisdom of God. An Outline of Sophiology* (Hudson, N. Y.: Lindisfarne Press, 1993), 3, 13, 25 ff.

18 Bulgakov, *Sophia*, 12–13. The double brackets contain words in Bulgakov's original manuscript that are not rendered in the English translation. Bulgakov's Russian text and a new German translation will be published by Barbara Hallensleben and Regula M. Zwahlen: Sergij Bulgakov, *Sophia. Die Weisheit Gottes* (Münster: Aschendorff, forthcoming).

19 Regula M. Zwahlen, "Over a Beer with Barth and Bulgakov," accessed July 20, 2023, *Public Orthodoxy* (2022). https://publicorthodoxy.org/2022/07/18/over-a-beer-with-barth-and-bulgakov-cosmodicy/ (access 2024/01/26).

20 Sergius Bulgakov, *The Lamb of God* (Cambridge, 2008), xv.

21 Bulgakov, *Sophia*, 18.

According to Paul Valliere, it was no surprise that Bulgakov, as author of a *Philosophy of Economy* (1912) with its main question "of man in nature and nature in man,"[22] ended up with dogmatic theology, because "what is the dogma of the incarnation of the Word, after all, if not a bridge to the world?"[23] To this extent, by answering the question "Why Sophia, why is it necessary?" we see "the dogmatic theologian, the thinker for whom thought begins and ends with the incarnation of the Logos in Christ."[24]

But why should anyone bother to build a House of Wisdom, "since Wisdom found no place where to dwell, a dwelling was made for her in the heavens. When Wisdom came to make her abode among the children of men, and found no habitation, Wisdom returned to her place, and took up her abode among the angels" (1 Enoch 42:2)?[25] By engaging in the pre-revolutionary political turmoil of his country, always trying to establish or support Christian politics above party lines, Bulgakov experienced the homelessness of wisdom on earth and the impasses of political policy. It was not the external lack of success of his political efforts that drove him to change direction and become a priest. Rather, the fundamental limitations of human political efforts shaped Bulgakov's insight that politics is only possible by recognizing its limitations. And in his view, the one "institution" able or even called to prevent overconfidence or even self-deification of human politics,[26] was the Church—simply because it is not only a human institution (which as such should, in Bulgakov's view, remain self-critical and in strict separation from the state[27]), but also the divine-human

---

22   Sergej N. Bulgakov, *Philosophy of Economy: the World as Household* (New Haven, CT: Yale University Press, 2000), 35; Sergei N. Bulgakov, "From Marxism to Sophiology," *Review of Religion* 1, no. 4 (1937), 364.

23   Paul Valliere, "The Theology of Culture in Late Imperial Russia," in *Sacred stories*, ed. Mark D. Steinberg and Heather J. Coleman (Bloomington, IN: Indiana University Press, 2007), 391. See also Bulgakov, "From Marxism to Sophiology," 364.

24   Papanikolaou, "Why Sophia? Bulgakov the Theologian," 16.

25   Sergii Bulgakov mentioned the text in his lecture "Apocalypticism and Socialism. Religious-Philosophical Parallels" in 1910 and published it later in his anthology "The Two Cities. Studies about the Nature of Social Ideals" (Moscow 1911, in Russian), see also fn. 27 below.

26   Regula M. Zwahlen, "Sergii Bulgakov's Reinvention of Theocracy for a Democratic Age," *Journal of Orthodox Christian Studies* 3, no. 2 (2020), 193.

27   Sergii Bulgakov, *The Apocalypse of John. An Essay in Dogmatic Interpretation*, trans. Mike Whitton (Münster: Aschendorff, 2019), 98. The discernment of "the difference between a political community and *ecclesia*" (see Aristotle Papanikolaou, *The Mystical as Political. Democracy and Non-Radical Orthodoxy* (Notre Dame, IN: University of Notre Dame Press, 2012), 161) is at the very core of Bulgakov's political reflections, es-

Body of Christ, the house of wisdom among men.[28] In this sense, in a Chalcedonian relationship to homeless Wisdom, Bulgakov's vision of Wisdom that "has built her house, hewn her seven pillars" (Prov 9:1) grew stronger: Wisdom, who found a place to dwell in creation (Prov 8:26–31). The Church "is in the world, without being of this world; it lives and moves within history, without drawing its roots from history, but rather from the eschaton, inasmuch as it constitutes an 'icon' of the eschaton and a 'symbol' of the Kingdom."[29] Moreover, in Bulgakov's vision of Christian union,

> in the Father's house there are many mansions, and the gifts of the Holy Spirit are different, and so are the ministries. There are undoubtedly very strong differences between [different] types of Christian piety, which perhaps make mutual understanding difficult, but one must be patient and wise in order to be able to learn from the other and not to persist in one-sided and vain arrogance. This is what our Christianity demands of us.[30]

Thus, the title of this volume, and of the conference "Building the House of Wisdom. Sergii Bulgakov 150 Years After His Birth" (September 2–4, 2021, University of Fribourg, Switzerland), from which it emerges, honors Bulgakov as an architect of the "house of wisdom" with "many mansions," which is also a synonym of the "city that is to come" (Hebr 13:14).[31] In doing so, we go beyond the reverent commemoration of his 150th birthday and take on the task of co-designing a "house of thought" within the human city that the community of authors symbolically represent in their linguistic, cultural, and confessional

pecially in his book *Dva Grada* (The Two Cities) (1911). To date, the work has only been translated into German: Sergij Bulgakov, *Die zwei Städte. Studien zur Natur gesellschaftlicher Ideale*, ed. Barbara Hallensleben and Regula M. Zwahlen, *Sergij Bulgakov: Werke* (Münster: Aschendorff, 2020).

28 Barbara Hallensleben, "Die Weisheit hat ein Haus gebaut (Spr. 9,1). Die Kirche in der Theologie von Hans Urs von Balthasar und Sergij Bulgakov," in *Wer ist die Kirche? Symposion zum 10. Todesjahr von Hans Urs von Balthasar* (Einsiedeln: Johannes Verlag, 1999), 33–61; Barbara Hallensleben, "La sagesse a bati sa maison (Pr 9, 1): l'église dans la théologie de Hans Urs von Balthasar et Serge Boulgakov," in *Visage de Dieu, visages de l'homme* (Paris: Parole et silence et Éditions du Carmel, 2003), 345–66.

29 Pantelis Kalaitzidis, *Orthodoxy and Political Theology* (Geneva: WCC Publications, 2012), 123.

30 Sergej N. Bulgakov, "Die Wesensart der russischen Kirche," *Internationale Kirchliche Zeitschrift* 3 (1930), 181.

31 Bulgakov, *Die zwei Städte*, 13.

diversity. Indeed, Bulgakov's sophiology is a daring attempt to reconcile God and the world, religion and secular thought.

Sergii Bulgakov—A Theologian for the Twenty-First Century

In a text about „Orthodox theology in the twenty-first century," the English bishop and Eastern Orthodox theologian Metropolitan Kallistos Ware expressed his view „that there will be a *shift in the central focus of theological inquiry from ecclesiology to anthropology.* [...] The key question will be, not only, „'What is the Church?' but also and more fundamentally, *'What is the human person?'*"[32] Bulgakov addressed both questions because, in his view, they are intertwined. Human persons are inescapably relational and „each man enlarges itself infinitely into the life of others, 'the communio sanctorum'," and „humanity is one in Christ" and the Church is the Body of Christ.[33]

Bulgakov's influence on Orthodox ecclesiology of the twentieth century is indisputable, but in view of Ware's assessment, we are happy that this volume—alongside topics such as personhood, ecology, political theology, and trinitarian ontology—prominently contributes to Bulgakov studies with regard to theological anthropology. This does not come as a surprise, since we asked our speakers to critically correlate Bulgakov's thought with current theological and philosophical, political, social, and economic issues. Some thirty-three authors, both established Bulgakov researchers and competitively chosen young researchers, have brought forth a wide arrange of new creative ways to critically engage with Bulgakov's work. Their chapters are arranged in five large parts:

- *Personhood and Anthropology*—with chapters on Christology (Rowan Williams, David Bentley Hart), on Bulgakov's concepts of deification (Mark

---

32 Kallistos Ware, *Orthodox Theology in the Twenty-First Century*, ed. Pantelis Kalaitzidis, Doxa & Praxis (Geneva: WCC Publications, 2012), 17, 25 (emphasis added).

33 Sergius Bulgakov, *The Orthodox Church* (with a foreword by Thomas Hopko) (Crestwood, New York: St Vladimir's Seminary Press, 1988), 1, 5; see also Michael A. Meerson, "Sergei Bulgakov's Philosophy of Personality," in *Russian Religious Thought*, ed. Judith Deutsch Kornblatt and Richard F. Gustafson (Madison, WI: University of Wisconsin Press, 1996), 139–53; Regula M. Zwahlen, "Different concepts of personality: Nikolai Berdiaev and Sergei Bulgakov," *Studies in East European Thought* 64, no. 3–4 (2012), 183–204; Konstantin M. Antonov, "Problema lichnosti v myshlenii protoiereia Sergiia Bulgakova i problematika bogoslovskogo personalizma v XX veke," *Khristianskoe chtenie* 4 (2017), 178–206.

McInroy), faith and prayer (Ivan Ilin), kenosis (Sarah Livick-Moses; Jack Pappas), creativity (Deborah Casewell), and mangodhood (Justin Coyle);

- *Politics, Economics, and Ecology*; with chapters on Bulgakov within intellectual history (Catherine Evtuhov and Regula Zwahlen, Nikos Kouremenos, Alexei Kozyrev), and his contributions to modern Political (Antoine Arjakovsky, Nathaniel Wood), Economic, and Ecological Thought (Dionysios Skliris, Tikhon Vasilyev, Austin Foley Holmes);
- *Sophiology*; with chapters on the philosophical and theological roots of Bulgakov's Sophiology (Liubov Petrova, Natalia Vaganova) and its implications for contemporary questions of theological anthropology (Joshua Heath, Dario Colombo, Paul Gavrilyuk);
- *Creation and Ontology*; with chapters on Bulgakov's examinations of Marx's materialism (Caleb Henry) and Schelling's „positive Philosophie" (Taylor Ross), and on the relationship of his Chalcedonian Ontology to Trinitarian Theology (Brandon Gallaher, Antonio Bergamo, Nikolaos Asproulis, John Milbank).
- *Ecumenical Perspectives*; with chapters on Bulgakov's thought on Augustine (Pavel Khondzinsky) and on his (possible) contributions to Liberation Theology (Graham McGeoch), Protestant Theology (Oliver Dürr), and Ecumenical Theology in general (Paul Ladouceur, Adalberto Mainardi).

All chapters resonate well with Metropolitan Kallistos' suggestion to develop a theological anthropology that focuses on the human being as a mystery, image and likeness of God, and mediator between heaven and earth ("priest of creation").[34] With regard to the latter, Bulgakov's work is about "our true relation as human beings to the material world"[35] and about "a more positive relationship between person and nature."[36] If, in Ware's view, the Greek Fathers' emphasis on negative theology requires a "negative anthropology" with a focus on the indefinable character and dignity of the person,[37] we

---

34 Ware, *Orthodox Theology*, 31–32, 43.

35 Ware, *Orthodox Theology*, 27. On the "importance of the material world and collective Christian social action," see Mark Roosien, "The Common Task: Eucharist, Social Action, and the Continuity of Bulgakov's Thought," *Journal of Orthodox Christian Studies* 3, no. 1 (2020), 71–88.

36 Papanikolaou, "From Sophia to Personhood," 20: "rather than the diametrical opposition that is implied especially in the theologies of Lossky and Zizioulas."

37 Ware, Orthodox Theology, 33.

would add that it requires a "negative cosmology" as well.[38] An "ecological turn" based on Bulgakov's view of an anti-positivist but not anti-scientific, apophatic dimension of creation is represented by several contributions to this volume.[39]

Metropolitan Kallistos also points out that "anthropology is a chapter or subdivision of Christology."[40] In this sense, it seems to be no coincidence that the first chapter in this volume, by Rowan Williams, the former Archbishop of Canterbury (2002–2012), considers "Sergii Bulgakov's Christology and Beyond" and is based on Williams' keynote as patron of our conference. At the same time, it reminds us of one of his recent books, *Christ the Heart of Creation*, in which he argues that Christ restores

> a lost or occluded capacity in humanity, the capacity to be a mediatorial presence
> in creation, a priestly vocation to nurture the harmony and God-relatedness of the
> finite order overall and to articulate its deepest meaning in terms of divine gift and
> divine beauty.[41]

In this sense, "Bulgakov in effect claims that hypostatic existence is intrinsically a form of life characterized by *care*: to exist hypostatically is to be in a relationship of 'nurture' towards the world that is encountered."[42] This is only one example of a fresh reading of Bulgakov's sophiological theology presented in this volume. However, readers might miss the odd subject that could have been examined while dealing with Bulgakov's immense work, such as the abovemen-

---

38   Barbara Hallensleben, "Kosmodizee. Das Böse im apokalyptisch-geschichtstheolo-
     gischen Horizont bei Sergij N. Bulgakov," in *Das Böse in der russischen Kultur*, ed.
     Bodo Zelinsky (Cologne, Weimar, Vienna: Böhlau Verlag, 2008), 21.

39   See also John Chryssavgis, Creation as Sacrament. Reflections on Spirituality and
     Ecology, London 2019; Laura Marie Hartman, The Christian Consumer, Oxford 2011;
     Gayle Woloschak, "Ecology, Evolution, and Bulgakov," in: Daniel Buxhoeveden, Gayle
     Woloschak, eds., *Science and the Eastern Orthodox Church* (London: Routledge, 2011),
     53–64; Willis Jenkins, Ecologies of Grace, Oxford 2013; Bruce V. Foltz, *The Noetics
     of Nature: Environmental Philosophy and the Holy Beauty of the Visible* (New York:
     Fordham University Press, 2013), 88–112 (chapter "The Resurrection of Nature: Envi-
     ronmental Metaphysics in Sergei Bulgakov's Philosophy of Economy").

40   Ware, Orthodox Theology, 39.

41   Rowan Williams, *Christ the Heart of Creation* (London: Bloomsbury Continuum, 2018),
     223.

42   Rowan Williams, "Sergii Bulgakov's Christology and Beyond," see below, p. 25.

tioned ecclesiology,[43] the theology of language and the name,[44] his theology of history,[45] the social dimension,[46] and other topics. Therefore, we hope that the present volume will inspire other scholars to carry the field of Bulgakov studies forward by exploring further dimensions.

Lastly, Bulgakov would certainly subscribe to Kallistos Ware's final suggestion to replace Descartes' principle *Cogito, ergo sum* with the principle *Amo, ergo sum* ("I love, therefore I am") or even *Amor, ergo sum* ("I am loved, therefore I am"): "If we can make love the starting-point and the end-point in our doctrine of personhood, our Christian witness in the twenty-first century will prove

---

43 See Paul Valliere, *Modern Russian Theology: Bukharev, Soloviev, Bulgakov: Orthodox theology in a New Key* (Edinburgh: T&T Clark, 2000), 347 ff.; Robert F. Slesinski, *The Theology of Sergius Bulgakov* (New York: St Vladimir's Seminary Press, 2017), 207 ff.; Hallensleben, "Die Weisheit hat ein Haus gebaut (Spr. 9,1). Die Kirche in der Theologie von Hans Urs von Balthasar und Sergij Bulgakov," 33–61; Pavel Khondzinskii, "The Personalistic Ecclesiology of Archpriest Sergey Bulgakov, Archpriest Georges Florovsky and V. N. Lossky (in Russian)," *Nauchnyi zhurnal Sankt-Peterburgskoi Dukhovnoi Akademii Russkoi Pravoslavnoi Tserkvi* 5 (2020), 177–200; Brandon Gallaher, "L'action eucharistique catholique: l'ecclésiologie du père Serge Boulgakov," *Contacts. Revue Française de l'Orthodoxie* 279–80 (2022), 323–40; Yulia Antipina, "The Ecclesiological Foundations of Fr. Sergius Bulgakov's Project for Partial Intercommunion," *The Quarterly Journal of St. Philaret's Institute* 45 (2023), pp. 29–44.

44 See e.g.: Joshua Heath, "Sergii Bulgakov's Linguistic Trinity," *Modern Theology* 37, no. 4 (2021), 888–912; Research will be certainly enhanced by the recent translation of Bulgakov's *Philosophy of the Name* by Thomas Allen Smith (Northern Illinois University Press 2022).

45 Bulgakov, *The Apocalypse*; Myroslaw Tataryn, "History Matters: Bulgakov's Sophianic Key," *St Vladimir's Theological Quarterly* 49, no. 1–2 (2005) 203–18.

46 Sergej N. Bulgakov, "Social Teaching in Modern Russian Orthodox Theology," in *A Bulgakov Anthology*, ed. James Pain and Nicolas Zernov (London: Westminster Press, 1976); reprint, Orthodoxy and Modern Society, ed. Robert Bird. New Haven, Conn.: Variable Press, 1995. 5–25); Sergii Bulgakov, "The Soul of Socialism," in *Sergii Bulgakov: Towards a Russian Political Economy*, ed. Rowan Williams (Edinburgh: 1999); Katharina Anna Breckner, "Vladimir Solov'ev as the Mentor of Anti-Marxian Socialism: Concepts of Socialism by S. N. Trubetskoj, S. N. Bulgakov and N. A. Berdiaev," in *Vladimir Solov'ev, Reconciler and Polemicist*, ed. Wil van den Bercken, Manon de Courten, and Evert van der Zweerde (Leuven, Paris: 2000), 447–60; Josephien van Kessel, "Sophiology and Modern Society. Sergei Bulgakov's Conceptualization of an Alternative Modern Society" (PhD dissertation, Radboud Universiteit Njimegen, 2020); Regula M. Zwahlen, "The Revolutionary Spirit of Revelation: Sergii Bulgakov's Personalist Sociology," *The Wheel* 26/27 (2021), 60–64; Roosien, "The Common Task: Eucharist, Social Action, and the Continuity of Bulgakov's Thought," *Journal of Orthodox Christian Studies* 3,1 (2020), 71–88.

altogether creative and life-giving."[47] Metropolitan Kallistos was probably not aware that Bulgakov made the same suggestion almost exactly a hundred years ago in a piece on "Nature in the Philosophy of Vladimir Soloviev" (1910): "One can also adopt the metaphysical formula: *amo, ergo sum*, because in love life finds its most sublime manifestation."[48] That is why Bulgakov was and is a theologian of both the twentieth and the twenty-first centuries.

***

The conference on the occasion of Bulgakov's 150th birthday would not have been possible without the support of the Swiss National Science Foundation (SNSF), the Orthodox Christian Studies Center at Fordham University, New York, and the Volos Academy for Theological Studies, Greece. The conference was also funded by grants received from the Centenary Research Fund, the Theological Faculty, and the Institute of Ecumenical Studies of the University of Fribourg. Special thanks go to the "deacons" of the conference organization: Dario Colombo, Dr. Stefan Constantinescu, Dr. Mihail Comanoiu, Dr. Adrian Craciun, Timon Schneeberger, and Désiré Ngwene.

We are particularly grateful for the generous Open Access funding for the publication of this volume by the SNSF. Thanks also go to Paul Valliere for his thoughtful review of all chapters, our copy-editor John Heath and to our editor at Aschendorff Verlag, Bernward Kröger, for their conscientious work on the manuscript.

---

47 Ware, *Orthodox Theology*, 49. This is exactly what the late Metropolitan of Pergamon John D. Zizioulas has suggested in his very influential *Communion and Otherness. Further Studies in Personhood and the Church* (London: T&T Clark, 2006), 89.

48 Sergej N. Bulgakov, "Priroda v filosofii Vl. Solov'eva," *Voprosy filosofii i psikhologii* 105 (1910), 1911; Sergij Bulgakov, "Die Natur in der Philosophie Vladimir Solov'evs," in *Die Philosophie der Wirtschaft*, ed. Sergij Bulgakov (Münster: Aschendorff, 2014 [1910]), 271. See also Andrew Louth, "Sergii Bulgakov and the Task of Theology," *Irish Theological Quarterly* 74 (2009), fn. 19. For Bulgakov on love, see Michael A. Meerson, *The Trinity of Love in Modern Russian Theology* (Quincy, IL: Franciscan Press, 1998), 169 ff.; Johannes Miroslav Oravecz, "Sergei Nikolaevich Bulgakov: God's Love-Humility for His Creation," in *God As Love. The Concept and Spiritual Aspects of Agape in Modern Russian Religious Thought* (Grand Rapids: W. B. Eerdmans, 2014), 292 ff.

PERSONHOOD AND ANTHROPOLOGY

Building the House of Wisdom
DOI 10.17438/978-3-402-12172-6

Sergii Bulgakov's Christology and Beyond

Rowan Williams

1.

Vladimir Lossky's notorious attack on Sergii Bulgakov in his 1936 pamphlet *Spor o Sofii* (The Sophia Controversy) addresses a range of topics, from the nature of canonical authority to the status of angels, but one of the central points of contention is a set of concerns about Bulgakov's doctrines of the person and work of Christ—not surprisingly, since the publication in 1933 of the first volume of Bulgakov's 'major trilogy', *Agnets Bozhii* (*The Lamb of God*), primarily an extended treatment of Christology, was the trigger for the series of critical discussions culminating in the dramatic public exchanges of 1936.[1] Lossky—echoing to some extent the criticisms of Bulgakov made by Metropolitan Sergii, deputy *locum tenens* of the Patriarchate of Moscow—challenges Bulgakov's emphasis on the eternally determined character of the Incarnation of the Word, questions the apparent Apollinarianism of Bulgakov's account of the person of Christ, and concludes that Bulgakov allows no real place in the economy of salvation for the free and personal agency of Christ's humanity. 'The Christology

---

1   Lossky's pamphlet *Spor o Sofii. 'Dokladnaia zapiska' prot. S. Bulgakova i smysl ukaza Moskovskoi Patriarkhii* was published by the Confrerie de saint Photius, Paris, 1936, as a response to Bulgakov's defense of his position against the condemnation of his views issued by the deputy locum tenens of the patriarchate, Metropolitan Sergii (Stragorodskii). For a brief summary of the controversy, Sergii Bulgakov, *Towards a Russian Political Theology*, ed. Rowan Williams (Edinburgh: T. and T. Clark, 1999), 173–75; cf. Antoine Arjakovsky, *La génération des penseurs religieux de l'émigration russe. La revue La Voie (Put'), 1925–1940* (Kiev-Paris: Duh i litera, 2002), 433–44, a thoughtful and well-documented discussion of the controversy with some critical perspectives on Lossky's theological assumptions (cf. Antoine Arjakovsky, *The Way. Religious Thinkers of the Russian Emigration in Paris and Their Journal, 1925–1940* (Notre Dame: University of Notre Dame Press, 2013, trans. Jerry Ryan).

of Father Bulgakov diffuses itself in a cosmic "panchristism," swallowing up both the Holy Spirit and the Church, and in the same way annihilating human personhood in a "sophianically-natural" process of divinization.[2] In Lossky's judgement, what is most conspicuously lacking in Bulgakov's theology is any vision of the Church as a genuinely plural and interactive human community of unique subjects called into communion by the Spirit, realizing in their countless free and distinctive ways the single reality of a human nature renewed in Christ. Instead of this, according to Lossky, we have a suprapersonal process in which the restoration of the human as such disappears: the incarnate Christ becomes the embodied sign of a non-temporal drama of intra-trinitarian relations and a vehicle of the nebulous activity of divine 'Sophia,' whose ontological status remains obscure.[3] And the result of this is a cavalier attitude to the actual historical and social constraints of the Church on earth as the God-given context for each finite self to discover its true uniqueness in the form of a personal discipleship that is worked out collaboratively in a flesh and blood community.

Lossky's essay sketches many of the concerns that were to animate his own later writing as a dogmatic theologian, and these foreshadowings are well worth a longer discussion in themselves. But my aim in this paper is to look at some of the specific criticisms he makes of Bulgakovian Christology and to suggest that some points have been missed. Briefly, what I want to argue is that Lossky does not ask what questions Bulgakov is actually trying to answer. He does not engage with the metaphysical hinterland of what Bulgakov was writing about theology, and so misses something very central to what the older man has to say about humanity and its transfiguration, and, as I shall suggest, there are elements here that are of very particular pertinence to contemporary theological discussion. The toxic ecclesiastical politics of the Russian emigration in the '30s certainly intensified Lossky's polemic, and his later discussions of Bulgakov in the lectures of his last years in the 1950s are more measured. But—ironically—he misses some of the ways in which Bulgakov could have been an ally in his own project; and his characterization of Bulgakov's thinking has done a good deal to set in stone a view of his system—especially his mature treatment of Sophiology—that continues to cast long shadows over his legacy. It may well be time to see if some of these can be lifted.

---

2   Lossky, *Spor o Sofii*, 61.
3   Ibid., 27–28, 71–77. Lossky insists (p. 28) that divine 'wisdom' is never treated in classical Orthodox theology as anything other than one among the divine *energeiai*.

One of the points insistently made in *Agnets Bozhii*[4] is that the Chalcedonian Definition provides only a *negative* account of the mystery of the incarnation, a set of cautionary protocols rather than a real theological account of what is entailed in confessing the Logos in flesh.[5] It is tempting to conclude from the Definition that what happens when the Word takes flesh is that divine omnipotence simply brings together two separate substances to attach them to a single subject or *hypostasis*; and the refinements of the centuries that followed do not add up to much more than a set of clarifications of detail within the 'negative' framework. But if that *is* how we read it, we are left with at least two problems. There is a certain arbitrariness about the event of incarnation, the danger of reducing it to a display of divine power (the kind of distortion that came to dominate a lot of late mediaeval Western treatments of the subject[6]), and there is a conceptual problem in that the terms of the Definition seem to deny the inseparability of nature and hypostasis, implying that we can some-

---

4   Sergii Bulgakov, *Agnets bozhii: o bogochelovechestve. Chast' I* (English translation [ET] by Boris Jakim, Sergius Bulgakov, *The Lamb of God* (Grand Rapids: W. B. Eerdmans, 2008); references are both to the original and to this translation), 73–81, 205–06, 219–24, 235–39, 137 (ET 56–63, 182–84, 193–96). Bulgakov begins his book with a lengthy and provocative account of patristic Christology, announcing that it is time for Orthodox theology to do what neither Catholic nor Protestant histories of doctrine have done, which is to clarify the 'dogmatic dialectic' underlying the development of doctrinal formulae. In this introductory account (pp. 79, ET, p. 61) and later (e. g., pp. 235–39, ET 209–11), Bulgakov suggests that the Chalcedonian formula is a sort of providential anticipation of a fuller theological understanding that is still to come: the generation that produced the Definition was theologically unadventurous, but nonetheless by divine guidance kept open the conceptual space which theology would need to fill out in due course.

5   It is worth comparing Bulgakov's account of Chalcedon with that of another brilliantly innovative reader of the tradition at almost exactly the same time, Dietrich Bonhoeffer, whose Christology lectures of 1933 (text in vol. 12 of *Dietrich Bonhoeffer Works in English* (Minneapolis: Fortress Press, 2009), 299–360) also characterize Chalcedon as providing no more than a 'negative' Christological schema. The presence of Harnack in the background is a factor here for both theologians; Harnack and the doctrinal history associated with his influence had considered the vocabulary of Chalcedon to be a sign of conceptual barrenness or even 'bankruptcy.'

6   This is the model associated with the Christology of William of Ockham and other nominalists, for whom God's freedom to become incarnate in any created substance obscured the interweaving of Christology with the doctrine of the divine image in humanity and its restoration by Christ. As we shall see, a major focus of Bulgakov's Christology is precisely that human nature is created in order to be capable of incarnating the Logos; see especially Bulgakov, *Agnets*, 191–205 (ET, 168–82).

how think of them in abstraction from one another, in defiance of any metaphysical intelligibility.[7] Bulgakov wants, in contrast, to present the incarnation as miraculous but not absurd, and the balanced counter-claims of Chalcedon are, he emphasises,[8] not flat contradictions but 'perspectival' truths capable of being held together in a synthesis. Of course, the doctrine of the divine image in humanity is an element which qualifies any apparent arbitrariness, but the chief resource in rethinking Chalcedon in positive terms is Sophiology—not (as Lossky feared) as a system directing our attention away from the concrete relations of finite agents to infinite, and to each other, but as a metaphysical reinforcement for the valuation of the personal/hypostatic which becomes ever more significant in the works that compose the major trilogy.

To understand what is going on in this respect, we need to look at what Bulgakov had been saying about the concept of 'hypostasis' in the period leading up to the publication of *Agnets Bozhii*, especially the forbiddingly complex and compressed discussion in the 1925 essay for Petr Struve's *Festschrift*, *Ipostas i Ipostasnost'* (*Hypostasis and hypostaticity*),[9] with its attempt to clarify a notion of 'hypostaticity' or' perhaps 'hypostatic actuality.' When we speak of the disjunction between hypostasis and 'nature,' we are not designating two *components* of some ontological hybrid: we are simply describing the grammar of *being a subject*: the life of self-reflexive intelligence is what happens as the subject's engagement with the world becomes itself a matter for engagement. In the light of this, we can say that this process of engagement is the core of hypostatic existence and activity—*ipostasnost'*. This makes some sense of the way in which the earlier Bulgakov writes about divine Sophia as the 'love of love':[10] Sophia is not some kind of ontologically intermediary reality between God and

---

7   It is part of the contribution of Leontius of Byzantium to the development of Christology that he rules out any such misreading of the terminology. Bulgakov devotes some detailed attention to Leontius (pp. 81–94, ET, pp. 63–74), but reproduces (again like Bonhoeffer!) some of the current misunderstandings of his schema. For a more sympathetic reading of Leontius, see Rowan Williams, *Christ the Heart of Creation* (London: Bloomsbury 2018), 92–99.

8   Bulgakov, *Agnets*, 206–07 (ET, 183–84).

9   Bulgakov, 'Ipostas i ipostasnost': Scolia k Svetu nevechernemu,' in Sbornik statei posvyashchennykh Pyotru Berngardovichu Struve, Prague 1925, 353–71 (cf. 'Hypostasis and hypostaticity: scholia to the unfading light,' in *St Vladimir's Theological Quarterly* 49, 1–2 (2005), 5–46, trans. Brandon Gallaher, Irina Kukota). The reference is to Bulgakov's 1917 *Svet nevecherni:sozertsaniia i umozreniia* (ET by Thomas Allan Smith, *Unfading Light: Contemplations and Speculations* (Grand Rapids: W. B. Eerdmans, 2012)).

10   Bulgakov, *Svet nevechernii*, 212 (ET, 217).

creation, but the sheer actuality of divine engagement with *both* the divine life as such *and* the finite reality which is posited by God as the other in which God realises love 'externally' just as ceaselessly as he does 'internally'. So whether in finite or infinite reality, what 'hypostasis' actually means is the concrete and continuous activity of engaging with what can and must be embraced, loved, understood, connected with, transfigured. 'Nature' is ultimately just that: a world, an environment, in the process of being perceived lovingly and brought into sustainable, mutual relationality. So *ipostasnost'* is in no sense a 'thing' or even a quality or property among others; it is a name for divine actuality in rela-tion—in the eternally stable relation of the Trinitarian life and in the unfolding relatedness of God at work in the created order.[11] And when we speak of 'So-phia,' 'divine' or 'created,' we are speaking of this 'actualization-in-relationality' of the world, the defining environment or defining conditions, of the life that particular hypostases are living. Divine Sophia is simply *what God actualizes*; in eternity, this is the timeless reality of the shared Trinitarian life, in time it is the interdependent order of a creation which God allows to be other than the divine. Creaturely Sophia, accordingly, is what humanity, made in God's image and exercising God's likeness, actualizes when it is restored to its proper hypo-static liberty, and is drawing and holding together the created environment in its maximal harmony, its optimal state of reflecting God.

But this already makes it plain that 'hypostatic' life is one of the ways in which finite subjecthood reflects infinite life: we are made to be hypostatic— that is, to extend a loving, 'sense-making' welcome to the world in which we exist, to learn to see its hypostatic potential and make that real. Our subjectivity is intrinsically 'sophianic' in that sense. And this means that our engagement with our environment is always already caught up in the divine action of mak-ing space and making sense, allowing the otherness of the created order to unfold in time and engaging with it so as to serve the mutual life-giving that anchors its stability and well-being.[12] This is typically God's action in making the universe both genuinely other to the divine and also genuinely invited into unitive relation (and so into harmony). But our human calling is to reflect this and realise it in the specific circumstances of our own existence. And in the light of all this, it is possible to see how we can speak of the divine Logos *acting as* the hypostatic centre of a continuum of human 'hypostatizing' agency:[13] it is not that some alien subject has inhabited the shell of a created nature but that

---

11   See, e. g., Bulgakov, 'Ipostas …,' 361–62.
12   Ibid., 368, and cf. Bulgakov, *Agnets*, 158–62 (ET, 136–40).
13   Bulgakov, *Agnets*, 208–10 (ET, 185–87).

the mode in which human nature is routinely activated (that is, the 'hypostatic' mode of the awareness of the self in relation) remains unchanged even when that activation originates directly in the divine hypostasis of the eternal Word, since all humans have the capacity to act 'theanthropically'—in the sense that they are always already in some degree involved in the hypostatic transformation of their ambient reality. All human subjects are ultimately defined by their 'sophianic' gift and vocation. Humanity is, from its first beginnings, disposed towards the culminating realization of sophianic transformation that appears in Jesus of Nazareth. Thus the mystery of union between divine and human which the Chalcedonian Definition points to is no arbitrary matter, nor is it (so to speak) an opportunistic solution to a problem; it is the crown of the divine purpose in creation, the fulfilment of humanity's vocation to personalize and humanize the world in alignment with what divine love purposes for it.

Bulgakov says that every human hypostasis is therefore in some sense already 'supernatural,'[14] and even 'uncreated.'[15] But it should be clear from our discussion so far that this is not a claim that there is some *part* of human nature that is uncreated: there is strictly speaking no such *thing* as a hypostasis, just as there is no such quality as *ipostasnost'*, in the sense of some identifiable and circumscribable characteristic which we can scrutinise. The human subject is activated at its fullest by a relation with the creator that frees it to behave 'hypostatically' in relation to its environment—i. e. to act in a way that releases the world it is part of to be fully and harmoniously itself. From the point of view of the activating energy in this context, we can say that the reality of a finite hypostasis is not an item among created substances but a configuration of finite life such that the infinite agency of God brings about certain liberating and transforming relations within the finite order; from the point of view of the unbroken continuity of the finite world, we can say that the hypostatic agent is unequivocally a created being. Bulgakov undoubtedly pushes the envelope in his terminology, but it is hard to convict him of material heresy here—though his argument[16] that the language of Chalcedon permits a distinction between the human *psyche* of Christ and the divine/uncreated principle of noetic rationality which in Jesus is supplied directly by the Logos is completely unsus-

---

14   Bulgakov, *Agnets*, 211 (ET, 188).
15   Ibid., 197–98 (ET, 174), 211 (ET, 188), where the hypostasis of Adam is described as 'uncreated-created'; and cf. 160 (ET 137–38).
16   Ibid., 262–63 (ET, 235). This was one of the ideas which was singled out for criticism in the *ukaz* issued by the Patriarchate, and which Bulgakov had attempted to clarify in his response.

tainable; patristic theologians were determined to rule out the idea that any specific aspect of human existence, including the nous, was lacking in Jesus. Bulgakov's sympathy for Apollinaris,[17] as someone who at least saw as no-one else did a question in need of an answer, repeatedly pushes him to defend the idea that the supreme controlling reality in Jesus, that which constitutes him as 'spirit,' is not any created presence. This is at best an ambiguous and misleading emphasis in the context of the traditional insistence on the unequivocal human completeness of Jesus' humanity. Bulgakov himself is clear enough that there is nothing *lacking* in the humanity of Jesus, but this seems to be on the grounds that every created hypostasis is similarly open to the direct action of the divine. Christ's incarnate reality is undoubtedly unique for Bulgakov, but it is also true that Christ fully realizes what all human agents are called to, so that the hypostatic presence of his divinity is in no sense alien to the common pattern of human nature.

2.

We noted that Lossky understands Bulgakov as effectively denying a role for genuinely human agency in Christ's redemptive work: in what sense can we think of the incarnate Lord as acting freely, being tempted and so on? In fact, Bulgakov's discussion of the consciousness of the incarnate is one of the most original and interesting features of his Christology, and should qualify any suspicion that he gives insufficient weight to the actual liberty of Jesus as a human subject. It is, however, undeniable that Bulgakov sees hypostatic life as almost identical with self-awareness, and Lossky's challenge has a point. To exist hypostatically is certainly, for Bulgakov, to appropriate a calling to relate consciously to the surrounding reality, and to one's own being as subject. Yet, this being said, it is not quite accurate to think of Bulgakov as identifying 'hypostasis' with a purely psychological reality, the process of the self-realizing of consciousness—which is, I think, what Lossky is (rightly enough) worried about.[18] Bulgakov is certainly not proposing that the human self-awareness of Jesus is replaced by the 'divine Mind,' as if the cognitive limitations and moral

---

17 Provocatively, he begins his introductory essay on patristic thought in *Agnets* with a substantial discussion of Apollinaris, arguing that he anticipates something like the Russian idea of 'divine humanity' (20–29, ET, 11–18).

18 Lossky was still teasing out his objections in the lectures he gave in Paris for the Institut Saint Denis in 1955, three years before his untimely death, especially the lectures for 10/11/55 and 17/11/55.

or spiritual acts of questioning and discernment ascribed to Jesus were fictive. The detailed discussion[19] of Jesus' 'theanthropic' consciousness in *Agnets*—one of the most sophisticated speculations on the subject in twentieth century theology—attempts to tease apart the divine 'self-consciousness' as such (which the Word must retain in the incarnation, as the loss of this would be the destruction of the Word's hypostatic existence) from the specific actuality of the self-awareness of a human individuality within particular finite conditions. The Word's divine self-consciousness, we could say, is not and cannot be the awareness of a set of conditions, and so is not in any competition with the self-aware individuality of Jesus the first-century Jew; it does not intrude items of 'divine' knowledge into a human setting. But it is irreducibly a *filial* consciousness, and this is expressed in the fact of Jesus' prayer to the Father. 'Divine Sonship is precisely what the divine "I" in Jesus is, his self-consciousness as divine consciousness.'[20] Follow this through a little further, though, and it implies that we are not in fact looking at any simple identification of hypostasis with self-awareness, and so (as Bulgakov's sections on obedience and temptation[21] make plain) we are not looking at any kind of evacuation of human freedom and finite agency in the incarnate life, of the sort that Lossky most deplores. Bulgakov asserts that *all* human subjectivity includes a tacit connection with the infinite reality of God: it is the immediate effect of our existence in relation to God and our bearing of the divine image. What it is not is an element in our conscious psychological processes, an *item* of consciousness. It could better be described as something grounding or conditioning consciousness; not in fact an idea wholly alien to the mature Lossky's theological account of the personal.[22]

So we might attempt to sum up Bulgakov's concept of hypostasis and the nature of 'sophianic' existence and action along these lines. To exist hypostatically is to exist in a certain relation to a 'world,' an ensemble of life or activity. This relation is not precisely the same as that of a conscious subject to the content of its own perceptions or sensations, though this is the most familiar expression of it; it is certainly to have (in the broadest sense) an 'intelligent' relation to it, i.e. a relation of understanding, even if this is not systematized in concepts, a capacity to respond consistently and creatively to what engages the subject

---

19 Bulgakov, *Agnets*, 291–350 (ET, 261–320).

20 Ibid., 293 (ET, 264; the translation in the text is my own).

21 Ibid., 316–34 (ET, 286–303).

22 See especially the essays in Lossky, *In the Image and Likeness of God* (Crestwood, NY: St Vladimir's Seminary Press, 1974), especially 'The Theological Notion of the Human Person,' 111–23.

from 'outside.' In the context of speaking about God, the 'world' on which divine hypostatic action works is simply the divine life itself, the life that is eternally and irreducibly a life of dispossession or self-displacement for the sake of another. This is fundamentally the life of the trinity in itself, but it is also the life of the divine trinity *in toto* oriented towards the otherness of what it brings into existence out of nothing. 'Sophia' is the content of what divine action acts upon—reflexively in the Trinitarian life, 'dialogically' in relation to creation as it generates the vast scheme of coherent interaction that is finite reality. Within the created order, human subjects stand in a special relation to the divine: they are sustained in their particular form of life by a fundamental connection with the hypostatic action of God such that they are enabled to be vehicles of that action in relation to what lies around them in the finite universe. In this respect, they can be said to stand on the frontier between created and uncreated; to use a rather different idiom, their relation with God is 'non-dualistic,' they do not relate to God as one determinate substance to another. For certain limited purposes, we can refer to their spiritual/hypostatic life as 'uncreated.' They exercise their vocation as hypostatic creatures by acting so as to allow or direct or release sophianic energy in the world, so that the world's coherence and beauty, its character as 'cosmos,' are sustained and intensified. Our human fallenness is our turning away from hypostatic accountability: we have erected our subjectivity as an object of knowledge in itself, ignoring the fact that this subjectivity is always already by nature turning towards the world—the human other as well as the entire ecology of a material universe. Salvation is the restoration of that accountability, the recognition of an already-existing relation to our world which requires us to accept the calling to care and make sense of what engages us. And so the incarnational restoration of our humanity is the re-formation of authentic hypostatic existence—a radical self-emptying (*kenosis*) that permits human subjectivity to recognize anew its already given 'investment' in and definition by its world, and to be released from the fiction that the basic ontological truth is a plurality of atomistic and abstract subjects of consciousness and desire.

Divine hypostatic existence in this context is the originating act on which the existence of a world summoned into intelligent, conscious and developing harmony is grounded. God as (threefold) hypostatic existence embraces the unconditioned love and gift that is the actual shape of divine life; in the language Bulgakov uses especially in *Svet nevechernii* (*Unfading Light*), God loves God's loving,[23] and God's 'Wisdom' is that love of loving. God loves what is not

23   Above, n. 10.

God, refusing (as it were) to be God 'alone' but creating a world to share in the love that is God's; so Sophia is God's love of the love God has *for creation*. Finite subjects realizing their hypostatic life are already 'sophianic' in that they are taken up into relation with this love, but they are also called to make it active in finite particulars; the hypostatic/sophianic vocation of human subjects is to love God's love for creation and to be effective conduits of that love. And of course their love for God's love is already itself an aspect of God's love; they are brought into being as lovers by the love God has for the world that God kenotically allows to be.

Bulgakov brings us back repeatedly to the non-duality of hypostatic life/ sophianic agency/ transfiguring love as these appear in God and in creation, and this is what makes sense of some of what seem to be the more problematic aspects of his Christology. Nothing in human nature is supplanted or replaced in the incarnation of the Word, because all finite hypostatic existence is at some level in the same non-dual but distinct relation with the eternal hypostatic act of God as Word and Son. Nor is he suggesting that hypostatic life is self-conscious subjectivity ('personality'); it is what makes self-consciousness possible, but is operative at a deeper level as grounded in the finite subject's status as the image of God, activated precisely by the hypostatic life-giving reality of the eternal Other, the Word answering to the Father.

How exactly we are to think about the divine Word/Son—or indeed about the interrelation of the three divine hypostases as such—is an issue about which Bulgakov has a number of diverse and complex ideas. The implication of what we have just outlined is that each of the divine hypostases is what it is in virtue of its activation of the same divine substance, the *ousia*/Sophia which is ultimately self-abandoning gift. But—in the wake of the patristic tradition of distinguishing the three persons on the basis of their 'mode of origination'[24]— Bulgakov offers two schemata for understanding the differentiation of the divine hypostases. They cannot be three co-ordinate instances of divine life (Bulgakov is critical of the degree to which even theologians as sophisticated as the Cappadocians give hostages to fortune on this); they have to be configured in a set of specific and non-transferable relations. So, in *Ipostas*, we have a model that owes something to Fichtean philosophy, though it takes this in a very distinctive direction: the subject is always the subject engaged in/invested

---

24 *tropos huparxeos*; the formulation is used by Basil and Gregory of Nyssa in their polemical works against Eunomius (the distinct names of the Trinitarian persons are ascribed on the grounds of their distinct 'modes of origination'—being unbegotten, being begotten, proceeding).

in the object or datum that actualizes it *as* a subject, but at the same time is inseparably bound up in the perspective of the other 'I,' which guarantees that the first subject is not caught in a simple binary relation with what it sees or grasps. There is always an excess beyond the binary of subject and object, an excess constituted by the 'co-ego,' whose presence both establishes the 'I' as what it is (a unique nodal point of relation) and prohibits the reduction of the shared world to what the 'I' is encountering or negotiating. Elsewhere, notably in *Glavy o troichnosti* (Chapters on the Trinity), this is supplemented by the 'linguistic' account of Trinitarian ontology so well explored recently by Joshua Heath.[25] Communicative or meaningful reality has the propositional form of 'x is f':[26] there is a 'this' specifying a unique substantive point of orientation, a 'thus' specifying a continuous or coherent *form* of existing, and the copula which directs us to the actuality of *this* existing *thus* in actuality. Relating this to the earlier Trinitarian model, we can see that the 'thus' of the interhypostatic life of the Godhead is a version of what that model presents as the primordial 'object' which makes the primordial subject what it is, while the copula announces that the relation between subject and predicate is not an abstract or context-free identity, but a living non-equivalence that is at the same time an inseparable interdependence and mutual definition. As Bulgakov argues in *Glavy*, the propositional form 'x is f' has as its paradigm the first-person 'I am A'—the subject's recognition of being constituted in and by otherness, existing in and only in a state of relatedness, an active *mode*; the copula establishes the related and self-reflexive subject as both living and productive of life. The form of predication mirrors the form of subjectivity.

Lossky and other critics worried that Bulgakov's Trinitarian thought reduced the divine life to the self-realization of a single subject—the Fichtean pattern that haunted a good deal of Idealist-inflected theology and philosophy in the nineteenth century.[27] But this is to ignore the subtlety of Bulgakov's models: early on in *Agnets*, he goes to some pains to clarify what he does and does not accept in Fichte, and to warn against any assimilation of divine life to the unfolding of human selfhood.[28] From one point of view, he can indeed affirm that the divine life is a single 'consciousness', not a fusion or co-operation of

---

25 Joshua Heath, "Sergii Bulgakov's Linguistic Trinity," *Modern Theology* May 2021, 888–912; I must record my indebtedness to him for countless illuminations of Bulgakov's texts.

26 To use the most common logical notation rather than Bulgakov's own idiom.

27 Lossky develops this point in his lecture of 10/11/55.

28 Bulgakov, *Agnets*, 113–15, 119–20 (ET, 90–92, 96–97).

three subjectivities; from another, it is clear that what it means for God to be a 'subject' entails the irreducible plurality of the points of orientation set out in the two models of hypostatic diversity we have just considered, and that each point in the triadic life is fully 'hypostatic' in the sense that it exists eternally and actually, and is both wholly implicated in and wholly distinct from both other points. So the entire life of the three persons of the trinity is 'hypostatic' action, and we can also rightly say that the Father, the Son and the Holy Spirit are equally hypostases; but because they are hypostases in the fullest and most perfect sense, we cannot enumerate them as three comparable or co-ordinate agents. They act hypostatically only *in* their differentiated relation to one another—and this is an aspect of their 'kenotic' reality, the fact that they have no reality *en soi*, no reality that is not constituted by their unrestricted gift of life to each other: a 'self-sacrifice' that would seem to us a tragic self-destruction is in God the plenitude of productive love and bliss.[29] Infinite spirit and finite spirit are alike in that both are hypostatic agencies realized in the embrace of generative love towards what is other; but what is always *to be* realized in finite spirit (the coincidence of hypostasis and nature, of subjectivity and content) is eternal and simultaneous in God.[30]

3.

Bulgakov's Christology cannot be understood without this distinctive approach to hypostatic existence. It is this that enables us to see that his ambiguous—and often lyrically transgressive—language about the 'uncreated' character of hypostatic spirit does not amount to a denial of the concrete humanity of Jesus, just as his conception of sophianic transformation does not subordinate created freedom to a collective or supra-personal cosmic process. Lossky's engagement with this hinterland is sketchy at best; and, as already noted, the irony is that his own insistence on the unfathomable singularity of the hypostasis and its freedom from the determinism and repetition of the merely 'natural' addresses some of the same concerns. But one aspect of Bulgakov's scheme which finds no echo in Lossky—or indeed in other theological 'personalists' of the twentieth century—is the point noted at the end of the preceding section, and is a theme of particular pertinence to current theological and practical discussions. Bulgakov in effect claims that hypostatic existence is intrinsically a form of life characterized by *care*: to exist hypostatically is to be in a relationship of 'nur-

---

29   Bulgakov, *Agnets*, 122–24 (ET, 98–101).
30   Ibid., 117–18 (ET, 94–96).

ture' towards the world that is encountered.[31] To put it still more strongly, any account of subjecthood that ignores the responsibility to nurture and include the environment in the construction of human meaning is illusory and destructive. For Bulgakov, God's 'sophianic' existence is the continuity of a form of life, an 'essence,' that is ceaselessly productive of and affirming of *otherness*: as we have seen, this is primarily the internal differentiations of the Trinitarian life and derivatively the creation and sustaining of the finite world. Earlier, I used the summary formulation that Sophia is 'what God actualizes': the hypostatic agency of God eternally exercises the life of self-emptying 'bestowal' which is the divine reality. Translated into the terms of finite subjecthood, what is significant in the analysis of how the created subject emerges into actuality is that its analogy with the divine subject, the divine 'I,' implies a necessary link between self-awareness or self-recognition and the generative gift of self in nourishing otherness.

Bulgakov's phenomenology of subjectivity is distinctive (and markedly un-Fichtean) in that the object whose co-presence establishes the subject as a subject is not simply an object to be *known*: the sophianic analogy—to use a rather shorthand expression—implies that self-reflexivity is at the same time 'the love of loving.' What is encountered as other is that which has an immediate claim to our love; what I know myself *as* if I know myself truthfully is a subject whose life is constituted by offering or sharing life with the other. In the hypostatic life that is God's, this life is literally generative of the other—the Father's birthing of the Son, the creation of the finite cosmos: we do not and cannot originate 'otherness' in this way, but our role in creation is quite specifically to bring the environment more fully alive in its sophianic interdependence. Bulgakov's already richly developed anthropology in *Svet nevechernii* related the sophianic to art and politics as well as liturgy; it is the transformative vocation of the human in all these diverse contexts that Sophia grounds and enables. What the protracted wrestling with concepts of hypostasis and subjectivity does is to refine this insight by arguing that the hypostatic is necessarily bound up with loving the world in such a way as to enrich and reinforce its beauty, its orderly mutuality, its character as the context of transfiguring reciprocal gift. God as hypostatic knows the divine self as generatively loving; our hypostatic existence is always already given in the bare fact of our creation in the divine image, and so our realizing of the hypostatic calling of our humanity is an 'owning' of the generative loving that is at the root of what we are.

---

31   The Heideggerian allusion in this phraseology is deliberate, though Bulgakov seems never to have read Heidegger.

Bulgakov's deepening focus on a strictly theological agenda in the late 1920s and early '30s allows a more detailed Christological reflection to complete these speculations. The incarnation of the Word is the point at which we see with greatest clarity the continuity between divine and finite hypostatic life. If what is affirmed about Jesus in the Chalcedonian Definition is true, *and* (a key point for Bulgakov) if the Incarnation of the Word is more than a display of arbitrary omnipotence, what makes incarnation possible and thinkable is simply that the hypostatic actualization of humanity (including its vocation of transforming and 'personalizing' its material environment) is always a process in which the divine hypostasis of the Word is active: the unique presence of the Word in Jesus as the 'hypostatizing' energy of his human nature is both miraculously and unrepeatably singular *and* in accord with the logic of human existence from the beginning. In that sense certainly, the incarnation is prepared from 'before the foundation of the world.' The questions as to whether the incarnation would have happened without the Fall of Adam or (one of Lossky's anxieties[32]) and whether the eternal determination of the incarnation implies the inevitability of the Fall misunderstand what Bulgakov is trying to say. He is clear[33] about the fact that the work of Christ heals and releases a fallen humanity, restoring the possibility of authentic hypostatic life. But it is possible to say that the incarnation is fully congruent with what has been prepared from before the foundation of the world while also saying that its actual historical and ontological effect *in the circumstances of fallenness* is redemption from sin and release from captivity. It is important not to read his discussion through the lens of a late mediaeval Western debate about the atonement. His aim is manifestly to set out a model for thinking about the incarnation that takes with full seriousness the creation of humanity in God's image and thus allows us to understand the incarnate Word as completing rather than displacing the finite order.

And it is this connection with the divine image that offers decisive insight into what needs saying in a Christian anthropology for our own context. It is almost commonplace for theologians (and others) to complain about individualistic models of human selfhood; it is increasingly common to note

---

32   See Lossky, *Spor*, 46–66; Arjakovsky, *La génération*, 438, n. 42, observes that Lossky has to defend some views—or at least, some turns of phrase—in Metropolitan Sergii's critique in this area which do not sit well with the theological tradition.

33   The exhaustive section on 'Redemption' in *Agnets* (372–401) (ET, 342–72) should be read alongside the earlier section on 'The Foundations of the Incarnation' (191–205, ET, 168–82) to clarify Bulgakov's understanding of the nature of the Fall and what exactly needs redeeming or healing in human life.

that many aspects of inherited Christian anthropology have reinforced the illusion of a human destiny detached from the world to which humanity belongs. What Bulgakov's discussion of hypostatic existence achieves—for all the over-complex idioms and loose ends—is a way of connecting non-individualist conceptions of selfhood not only with the givenness of interpersonal relations, but with a pre-existing relation to a world whose fulfilled meaning requires the human hypostasis to be itself and to enact its vocation to responsibility. Not only are we always already connected with the material and temporal universe we inhabit, through the countless natural processes we are part of; we are always already called to love the world that is ours as God loves—that is, to make space for its freedom and integrity and to animate and enrich its interconnection and balance; to serve its beauty and its justice. The self that we become conscious of in reflexive human activity (at any level, not just in 'canonically' sophisticated forms of self-awareness) is a self which *would not exist* except as capable of and summoned to care, because its foundation is the prototypical self-giving identity of God in whose image the finite self exists. There is no other way of being self or 'spirit'; the attempt to create and sustain a culture in which investment in and nurture of our environment is an option irrelevant to the integrity and well-being of our selfhood is an exercise in dangerous fantasy. It is an aspect of the dangerous fantasy that seduces us into trying to think of our selfhood independently of human others or of the transcendent Other; like those doomed enterprises, it will make us less fully human—no less in the divine image, no less embodying a summons to love, but persistently frustrating the expression of that image.

Bulgakov's Christology remains a complex and controverted area of his theology, but it is a strikingly bold development of his sophiological thinking. During the '20s, he radically recasts his theories about Sophia to purge away any trace of the 'mythical,' personified Sophia who had haunted the systems of some of his predecessors; in one sense, it could be said that he abandons 'Sophiology' as a direct metaphysical thesis and uses the *imagery* of Sophia in the service of a different kind of metaphysic, centrally preoccupied with language and the conditions for the creation of meaning: 'Sophia' is a helpful shorthand for the increasingly dense package of ideas to do with this 'creation of meaning' that he explores in the two theological trilogies, especially the notion of 'that upon which God acts' in time and eternity, that which is passive to a divine activity pervading and fulfilling it by self-surrendering love. Fundamental in this development is the elaboration of the meaning of 'hypostatic' existence as the locus for a sophianic actuality that is in some way continuous or analogous between the divine and the human: just as God *is* concretely God only in the

reflexive exercise of love towards God's own act of generating and sustaining
the Other, so humanity is human only in its alignment with and participation
in this act. The phenomenon of human language is to be understood not merely
as the creation of shared meaning and communicable purpose among subjects;
it is rooted in a call and capacity within the human that persists even when
it is denied, because it is implied in the foundational fact of finite hypostatic
existence, its relatedness as image to the divine hypostatic action. It is a call
and capacity to make sense of the world by renouncing the seductive fictions
of self-containment or self-legislation or the generation of reality out of the
individual will, or any of the other myths that shore up the fragile illusion of
subsistent individuality.

It is what I have called a basic relation of 'care,' but it could equally well be
read in the light, say, of Dostoevsky's affirmation of the universal 'answerabil-
ity' of the self for the healing of the world, not as an individual achievement,
a manifestly absurd picture, but as the grace-prompted readiness to exercise
care and serve the processes of reciprocal life-giving in whatever situation the
self finds itself in. Bulgakov presents his readers with a sometimes disorienting abundance of insight about art, politics and discipleship in their interdependence, and our current social and intellectual context is badly in need of
that level of integrated reflection, if we are adequately to resist the dominant
myths of a reductive market ideology even more ambitiously destructive than
the varieties identified and attacked by Bulgakov in his day. His Christology,
I suggest, deserves further unpacking to draw out an anthropology in which,
quite simply, what makes us human is a shape or direction of involvement in
the making of meaning which is prior to all our choosing or self-positing. Bulgakov's friend and spiritual daughter, St. Maria Skobtsova, argued with passion
that Christianity needed an ethic that went beyond an ideal of loving action
that was somehow added on to the basics of discipleship and was anchored in
connections that pre-existed our moral dispositions.[34] For her, this was symbolized above all in the love of motherhood, where the bare fact of physical
involvement entailed a kind of love that went beyond choice and policy, and
this symbol provided a key to grasping what love in the Body of Christ actually meant. Bulgakov works in a different idiom entirely, but some of the same
concerns are in view—the recognition above all that the self, in order to be
a self in any robust sense, must recognize the *givenness* of its investment in

---

34   See especially the essays 'The Second Gospel Commandment' and 'On the Imitation
     of the Mother of God' in Mother Maria Skobstova, *Essential Writings*, trans. Richard
     Pevear and Larissa Volokhonsky (Maryknoll, NY: Orbis Books, 2003).

the service of the world's ecology, in the embodied meaningfulness of a fully reciprocal pattern of life for human society and for the 'society' of the finite cosmos. Bulgakov's efforts to spell out what life as hypostatic spirit entails are laboured and not always clear; but in their Christological setting it is possible for us to see them as guidelines for imagining the 'spiritual' as essentially the intentional giving of life and building of mutuality and solidarity which runs analogically through the whole pattern of the life that God unveils to us in the narrative of the divine action and supremely in the self-emptying act of new creation that is the Paschal mystery.

Building the House of Wisdom
DOI 10.17438/978-3-402-12173-3

Masks, Chimaeras, and Portmanteaux:
Sergii Bulgakov and the Metaphysics of the Person

David Bentley Hart

I.

It seems to me that Sergii Bulgakov demonstrated as thoroughly and convincingly as one could that, if there is such a thing as a distinctively Christian concept of the person, and if that concept is coherent, then it can be adequately expressed only as, at once, a metaphysics of being, a philosophy of subjectivity, and a theology of the one divine Person who is, in the end, the one Person of all persons. Needless to say, however, I cannot *prove* this to be so within the narrow confines I have set for myself here, but I do feel obliged to try to indicate why I make the claim. And I hope it will not be taken amiss if I begin by registering a few disagreements with a scholar of whose work I have a high opinion—not for the sake of disagreement as such, but solely because I am trying to find my way into and out again of something of a labyrinth and, not having the hermeneutical equivalent of Ariadne's thread readily at my disposal, I am grateful to anyone who has already explored and marked out apparent routes of escape that in fact will not get me where I want to go.

In two recent articles,[1] Joshua Heath calls attention to what he takes to be a tension or even contradiction in Bulgakov's transcendental account of personal subjectivity, and so also in his theological account of the intratrinitarian relations. The inconsistency appears, Heath suggests, if fleetingly, as early as *The Tragedy of Philosophy*, where it constitutes only an occasional and incidental discordant note. It recurs, however, in the much later epilogue of *The Comforter*, "The Father," where it swells into a crescendo of sustained disso-

---

1   Joshua Heath, "On Sergii Bulgakov's The Tragedy of Philosophy," *Modern Theology* 37:3 (2021), 805–22; ibid., "Sergii Bulgakov's Linguistic Trinity," *Modern Theology* 37:4 (2021), 888–912.

nance. In the earlier treatise, Heath believes, the contradiction is easy enough to isolate from the rest of the argument: Throughout that text, Bulgakov frequently affirms that "the transcendent is always linked to the immanent" and that "the subject, the hypostasis, always reveals itself, always expresses itself, in the predicate";[2] moreover, he explicitly insists that "the plurality of the *I* is a fundamental axiom of thought and life" and that any attempt to think the *I* without any *you* renders the former unintelligible.[3] And yet, even so, at other times he speaks of an abiding transcendence within subjectivity, and does so in terms of "hidden depths" or of "self-enclosure," or even of a "realm hitherto unknown to light"[4]—language that according to Heath threatens to depict that transcendence as some inaccessible, private *quantum* of subjectivity only secondarily externalized in its predicate.[5] This, he believes, would appear to be irreconcilable with the insight that the "transcendent subject is [...] not merely an *I*, but a *we*." As Heath puts the matter, "we can say that what is 'hidden' in the subject, that which lies 'beyond' the predicate, is not a mysterious *quantum*. Rather, the subject's 'noumenal quality' is the *act* of the subject's self-positing in relation to other subjects."[6]

Here is where I must register my disagreement. I believe we are being confronted at this point with a false either-or, and I would in fact argue the reverse: that it is precisely because Bulgakov understands the transcendence of the subject as *in itself* an undisclosed depth, always in some sense logically prior to its manifestation or predicate, that his account of the subject's total self-disclosure and self-realization in outward relation does not become vacuous; for it is precisely that inexhaustible and indispensable *in itself* that is always also given as *in and by another* and only in this way also given *to itself*. That is to say, what is revealed and thereby constituted in the relation of any personal subject to its predicate by way of the copula is not some process by which an original interiority is somehow always already dissolved in its own exteriority, but rather the imperturbable and abiding structure of personhood, which is of necessity a structure of the hidden and the manifest at once. When Bulgakov says that what is transcendent in the subject is inseparable from what is immanent, he is necessarily asserting the reverse as well. What he is talking about, after all, is a

---

2   Sergii Bulgakov, *The Tragedy of Philosophy*, trans. Stephen Churchyard (Brooklyn: Angelico Press, 2020), 12.
3   Ibid., 111.
4   Ibid., 10, 14.
5   Heath, "On The Tragedy of Philosophy," 814.
6   Ibid., 814.

single source of subjectivity that is never effaced, exhausted, or negated as the one and only source of the person even in being poured out in its revelation in another: a hidden depth that is always already manifest, but manifest also *as* a hidden depth. The *we* that is implicit in the *I* is not a social concord that yields a subject or that simply dispels the hiddenness of subjectivity; it is still always the hierarchy of the hidden and the manifest in their essential convertibility *with*—rather than their opposition *to*—one another: a hierarchy in which the *I* of the subject is forever constituting itself in the *we* out of its (so to speak) "ingenerate" ground of subjectivity. Simply enough, Bulgakov's is a structural—not a genetic—account of personhood.

The issue, I think, becomes clearer when one turns to Bulgakov's account of the intratrinitarian relations in that famous or infamous epilogue, and then to Heath's criticisms of it. In one sense, Heath is taking Bulgakov to task for claims that are actually inevitable from the very logic of classical Trinitarian theology. In fact, if Bulgakov is wrong in his reasoning in these pages, so arguably is the entirety of post-Nicene theology. But, more to the point, in accusing Bulgakov of contradicting his own earlier insistence that divine personhood is always already interhypostatic and convertible with God's act of self-manifestation,[7] Heath is clearly misconstruing the metaphysical content of that claim. The reality is precisely the opposite: far from constituting a contradiction, Bulgakov's argument in the *Comforter*'s epilogue confirms and renders fully coherent the picture of divine personhood that, say, *The Tragedy of Philosophy* (as well as writings from the same period, such as his "Chapters on Trinitarity")[8] expressed in somewhat more inchoate form. True, certain themes—the Father's silence, his hiddenness and interiority, his life within himself,[9] his transcendence in remaining forever outside of revelation, as its absolute subject rather than its object[10]—assume a dominance in the epilogue that they had not previously enjoyed. And, perhaps more explicitly than had previously been the case, all of these themes apply there no less to the Father's self-outpouring in the life of the immanent Trinity than to his self-outpouring in the economic Trinity. Heath is wary, I suppose understandably, of any concept of divine transcendence—as well as any apophatic reserve in speaking about that transcendence—that

---

7   Heath, "Linguistic Trinity," 911.

8   Sergii Bulgakov, "Glavy o troichnosti" (Chapters on Trinitarity), in ibid., *Trudy o troichnosti*, ed. Anna Reznichenko (Moscow: OGI, 2001).

9   Sergii Bulgakov, *The Comforter*, trans. Boris Jakim (Grand Rapids: W. B. Eerdmans, 2004), 379.

10   Ibid., 188.

seems to rest not on the mutual inherence of the divine Persons, but instead on the intratrinitarian distinctions of hypostases. He finds it all but impossible to make sense of this in terms of Bulgakov's claim that the real revelation of a subject in its predicate is not merely the disclosure of who that subject already is, but is rather the very act by which that subject is anyone at all; nor does it seem to him to accord with the attendant claim that, of course, in the divine life there is a perfect adequacy of both predicate and copula to the subject they manifest.[11] Thus, where Bulgakov asserts that, even within the immanent life of the Trinity, the Father reveals himself to the Son and Spirit not only as Father, but also as *God*, Heath glimpses a troubling specter: "a ghostly separation of the Person of the Father from the single act of generation and spiration, from the particular kenotic act that is constitutive of Fatherhood."[12] And this he sees as incongruous with Bulgakov's earlier, explicitly linguistic Trinitarian reflections, and as a deviation from Bulgakov's own most important insights of such violence that it threatens to overthrow those insights, and to reinstate the idea of a subject already possessed of an interiority prior to relation.[13]

Again, I take these worries to rest upon a misunderstanding. To begin with, considered simply as theologoumena rather than as a metaphysics of personhood, many of Bulgakov's assertions regarding the relations of the divine Son and Spirit to the Father follow necessarily from the one indispensable maxim of all Trinitarian theology and dogmatics: to wit, that the *taxis* of the economic Trinity is the *taxis* of the immanent Trinity, and that only by virtue of that identity is it possible to affirm anything about God as Trinity. Inasmuch as the Trinity is not a confederation of three individuals, but rather the very order of relations whereby God is God, one cannot conceive of the economy of revelation as in any way dissembling that eternal order without effectively denying the reality of the Incarnation. The divine Son is also a man only if his identity as the eternal Son, in relation to Father and Spirit, is also who he is *as* that man. Thus, in the kenosis of God in Christ, all that is not accidental to the humanity of Christ as Son *ad extra* must have its premise in the identity of the Son *ad intra*. By this logic, Bulgakov is quite correct, it seems to me, when he asserts that even the absolute transcendence of the Father to creation has its premise in the intra-divine life,[14] if only because Jesus addresses the Father both as Father and as God, and this reality—the very possibility of Jesus's human prayer

---

11   Heath, "Linguistic Trinity," 910–11.
12   Ibid., 911.
13   Ibid., 911–12.
14   Bulgakov, *The Comforter*, 361.

to God being fully compatible with and expressive of the Son's eternal relation
to the Father—cannot be attributed solely to the economy: "The kenosis refers
to the *life* of the God-Man's Personality, to its state, but it does not refer to His
Personality itself; on the contrary, according to the Chalcedonian dogma, the
entire power of the Incarnation consists in the unchanging nature of the God-
Man's Personality."[15] Had the Son's prayer to his God and Father been *only* a
temporary arrangement, this would have introduced a change into the very
personality of the Son.[16] The Logos is, after all—and here Bulgakov is drawing
not only on the Letter to the Hebrews, but on one of the very oldest continuous
motifs of high Christology—the eternal and Heavenly High Priest, the Great
Angel or Angel of Mighty Counsel, in whom the whole of creation is forever
turned toward the mystery of the Father in adoration.[17]

If, moreover, the revelation of the Absolute in the world presupposes the
self-revelation of the Absolute "in itself," as Bulgakov claims,[18] then he is certainly correct also to claim that it is a revelation not of natural or ontological
differences among the divine hypostases, all of whom are equally God in his
fullness, but of hierarchical distinctions within the one "trihypostatic Person."[19]
In that hierarchy of relations, the Father is forever, at one and the same time,
both God revealing himself in the eternal kenosis of his love *and also* the un-
searchable depth of that self-manifesting abyss of love, the divine ἀρχή from
whom the Son and Spirit receive themselves, and whom they know as their
own inexhaustible source in knowing themselves.[20] In his own proper idiom,
however, the Father is not the object of that knowledge, but rather the subject
who is being made known in the objective manifestation of Son and Spirit.
Again, it is vital to recall here that when Bulgakov speaks of the interhypostatic constitution of the divine life, he is speaking not of three discrete persons
poured out in one another as though from three distinct sources of personhood; nor is he speaking of a dynamic exhaustion of transcendence in kenosis,
or the exhaustion of the interior life of the Father in the absolute exteriority of
either the divine or the created order. Rather, he is speaking of one source of
all that is, one *fons deitatis*, constituting itself as one trihypostatic Person: not a
threefold intersubjectivity, that is, but a single subject in three hypostases who

---

15 Bulgakov, *The Comforter*, 372.
16 Ibid., 372–73.
17 Ibid., 74.
18 Ibid., 361.
19 Ibid., 379.
20 Ibid., 376–77.

are one in essence, and three only as distinct moments within the structure of divine personhood. And this must always remain a structure of the hidden and the manifest at once—subjective depth and objective revelation—if God is both one and truly personal. In that life of love, none of the divine hypostases can be deprived of his own proper idiom, his own mode of subsistence—not the Son or Spirit as completely revealing the Father, and not the Father as the transcendent mystery that the Son and Spirit reveal. Hence, again, Bulgakov speaks of the identity of—not the contradiction between—the Father's inner Word, restrained in silence, and the uttered hypostatic Logos,[21] in seeing whom one has seen the Father. This was, after all, the most notable advance that the Nicene-Constantinopolitan settlement made over earlier theologies that presumed an absolute disproportion between the Father in himself and the Son and Spirit: the transcendent hiddenness of the Father (which was axiomatic for all theologies, Nicene no less than ante-Nicene) was now understood as also made fully manifest in the Father's co-equal Son, in the light of his co-equal Spirit. And yet, still, the Son in that theology is not the hidden Father, and the Father is not the revealed Son.

Anyway, Heath need not fear that Bulgakov's argument in the epilogue will lead back, as he says, to some kind of "self-positing of the Father apart from and prior to his kenosis,"[22] analogous to the metaphysics of subjectivity that Bulgakov himself found to be so disappointingly truncated in Fichte's thought.[23] On the contrary, Bulgakov is speaking of that depth of subjectivity that is constituted precisely *as* unified subjectivity—as, that is, a living "I"[24]—in the generation and procession of its predicate and copula. This remains clearly the case, and perhaps especially so, even if one sets Bulgakov's explicitly theological reflections somewhat aside and considers his account of personhood in the abstract. To use the linguistic scheme that he so favored in the 1920's and never thereafter abandoned, in any act of personal existence there is a subjective depth that is becoming *someone*, so to speak, through its outward expression in its predicate, as accomplished by the mediation of real being, in the copula—the "am" or "is"—of that predication. In that very act, however, the subject becomes true subjectivity, which must of its nature be constituted inwardly as what is withheld even in being given outwardly in its predicate. In

---

21   Bulgakov, *The Comforter*, 364.

22   Heath, "Linguistic Trinity," 911.

23   Bulgakov, *The Tragedy of Philosophy*, 218–19.

24   Sergii Bulgakov, *The Lamb of God*, trans. Boris Jakim (Grand Rapids: W. B. Eerdmans, 2008), 89.

becoming a personal subject, that is, I become an object at once to you and to myself; in fact, my own subjectivity, as *pure* subjectivity, remains invisible even to me, and is known to me only in the act of reflecting upon what has been made manifest. To you, however, I am known as the object of *your* subjectivity, which is of its nature withheld from me. Conversely, whenever you reveal yourself to me in words—even if it were possible that the words you speak should be not only perfectly true, but also miraculously wholly expressive of the full depth of your subjectivity—what you disclose to me still remains, in itself, a necessary hiddenness; what I know in the idiom of expressed words you still possess also in the idiom of an interior Word. Were this not so, the event of personhood would be the dissolution of the subject. And, in that exchange whereby each of us is yielded up as the object of another's subjectivity, we are each engaged in the other's constitution as persons, each allowing the other to come to himself or herself as the distinct and personal subject of revelation. Still, the structure of personhood abides. As Bulgakov writes (in that in fact alarmingly clarifying epilogue), "Revelation of the noumenon in phenomena presupposes a subject, a predicate, and the copula between them. It presupposes that which is revealed, that which reveals, and a certain unity or identity of the two: a mystery and its revelation."[25]

This was always, I submit, the logic of Bulgakov's earlier, more purely linguistic accounts of the Trinity and of personhood. Yes, in his "Chapters on Trinitarity" (for instance) Bulgakov speaks of the life of spirit as the dynamic identity of subject, predicate, and copula;[26] he speaks also of the ontological love by which the "I" lives never only in itself, but always also in the you and the he or she and so forth;[27] he speaks of the subject as knowing itself only in and through otherness.[28] But, even so, he is quite clear that this self-revealing subject is also expressed out of an unrevealed "state of depth,"[29] and that in that self-expression the subject is at one and the same time a certain silence, a certain express Word, and a certain concrete life.[30] The "I" that grounds itself by expressing itself as I, you, we and so forth all the while remains "I."[31] Once again, what is at issue here is not a process—not even an eternal and timeless

25 Bulgakov, *The Comforter*, 360.
26 Bulgakov, Chapters, 34.
27 Ibid., 60, 89.
28 Ibid., 66–67.
29 Ibid., 93.
30 Ibid., 64.
31 Ibid., 80.

process—of interiority being converted into exteriority or exteriority being converted into interiority; rather, it is the eternal coinherence of inner and outer, the hidden and the manifest, the ingenerate source and its generated and "breathed" (that is, living) disclosure.

So, then, if indeed this is the structure of personhood, divine and human, what is its ground?

II.

It is something of a commonplace in a great deal of modern theology to speak confidently and even a little proudly of something called Christian "personalism," or to assert that Christianity, in its understanding of the shape and foundation of reality, uniquely elevates and ennobles and grants special eminence to the concept of "personhood" as such; supposedly, as a result of its Trinitarian and Christological dogmas, and of its language of the Fatherhood of God and of humanity's filiation to God in Christ, Christianity has produced an understanding of and concern for the person that surpasses that of any other creed or tradition. I take such claims to be false. Quite apart from the silly cultural triumphalism in pronouncements of that sort (inevitably born of ignorance), there is the not inconsiderable reality that, throughout most of theological history, the very language of "persons" has been something of a protean presence in Christian thought that has never assumed the stable form or conceptual clarity or even moral centrality we would like to imagine it has. If we reconstruct the history of its doctrinal usage with sufficient care, and then its theological sequels, what we really find is not so much the story of a lucid and specific idea naturally emerging from earlier epochs of Christian discourse and thought and developing consistently, but rather something more like the tale of an uninvited dinner guest who, by virtue of a tenuous connection with one of his host's distant relations, insinuated himself into the household and then, by sheer tenacity, somehow established himself as heir to the family fortune.

The Latin word *persona*, after all, entered the Christian lexicon at first as something of a cipher, called upon to discharge the roles of two distinct Greek terms of art in Trinitarian theology, πρόσωπον and ὑπόστασις: in the former case as a more or less literal rendering, in the latter for want of any better way in the Latin of the fourth century for representing the distinction between the two terms ὑπόστασις and οὐσία, which were themselves already hazily amphibologous ciphers whose principal usefulness lay in their syntactic—rather than strictly semantic—distinction from one another. All that these words established within the dogmatic grammar of the faith was that in God there is an "essential" whatness, οὐσία, of which the Father and the Son, and in time the Spirit, could each be regarded as a "subsistence", ὑπόστασις. In general, in fact, all the Trinitarian terms proper to the Nicene settlement were not so much names for clear and precise concepts as semantic tokens distinguished from one another only in order to exclude alternative semantic economies. And, in their being translated from Greek into Latin, the range of those distinctions was, if anything, slightly impoverished. What little concrete meaning might have seemed naturally to inhere in the word ὑπόστασις—*subsistentia*, if one were to make a literal transposition into Latin—was progressively diminished; and the same is true of the term πρόσωπον or *persona*, which gradually ceased to carry the connotation of an "aspect" or "expression" of a nature or essence, and began instead to mutate into something else. Down the centuries, in consequence (accidental or natural), the language of "person" (or its equivalent in other tongues) has not only assumed a position of special prominence in Christian discourse; it has come successively to acquire, even within theological usage, all the attributes and connotations with which we have invested it in any given epoch—ethical, legal, psychological, social, what have you—and all the while we have been constantly, retroactively, and largely unconsciously altering our understanding of its usage in the tradition as a whole. In a sense, the very concept of the "person" in any given epoch of Christian thought is like a quantum potentiality wave (in the standard Copenhagen interpretation, at least) that, in being observed, collapses into one particular history, thereby in a sense creating its own past.

Perhaps the most popular and frequent claim regularly made for Christianity's uniquely "personalist" view of reality is that, for Christian thought, "person" is a concept transcendent of and logically prior to any concept of "nature" or φύσις. This, after all, at least seems as if it must in some sense be true. Orthodox Christology clearly appears to elevate the hypostasis of the divine Son over the difference between his two natures when it proclaims that the single person of the incarnate Logos is at once entirely human and entirely divine; and orthodox soteriology seems also to elevate the human hypostasis over that same difference when it proclaims the deification of human beings in Christ. The logic here appears almost banal in its obviousness. Of course, it is also a logic that gives license to some perilously extreme formulations, as when Maximus the Confessor assures his interlocutor Pyrrhus that the natures hypostasized in Christ share nothing in "common," κοινόν, other than the one hypostasis by which they are joined in a single activity.[32] And extreme formu-

---

32 *Disputatio cum Pyrrho* 28–31, PG 91: 296C–297A.

lations require careful exegesis. What Maximus is saying here is true if one takes κοινόν to mean one or another *univocum*, some "property" univocally resident in both the divine and the human natures considered in the abstract; for, manifestly, the infinite and simple God possesses nothing under the form of discrete properties or accidents or qualifications, whereas creatures possess their natures always in finite, composite, and diverse fashion, divided between substance and accidents (and so forth and so on). If, however, Maximus were taken as saying that the being and nature of the creature are alien and extrinsic to the being and nature of God, without analogy, and that these otherwise unrelated or even mutually repugnant realities are reconciled to one another in Christ only by virtue of an ontological indifference to the properties of any nature on the part of the hypostasis of the Logos, he would be saying something absurd and somewhat atrocious. For one thing, obviously it would be foolish to imagine that God and creation could be posed over against one another equivocally, within some more capacious context of existence, or that finite beings could possess any real natural properties or perfections that are anything other than participations in the being of God. Clearly the absence of any univocal commonality between Christ's two natures must not be understood as the absence of an analogous commonality.

More to the point, though, what could it possibly mean to say that "person" or "hypostasis" transcends nature, or is prior to nature, or (in the cases of the God-man and of deified human beings) is indifferent to the differences between the natures it instantiates? Surely, for this to be intelligible, one must also grant the reciprocal claim that any "personal" hypostatic realization of a nature is the realization of a nature that is intrinsically personally hypostatic—which is to say, capable of actuality *only* in and as "personhood," whatever that means—and that this capacity, which clearly lies at the ground of both natures, is already an essential unity, and can in fact be no less a unity than is the full expression of that capacity in the one indivisible personhood of Christ. Only an intrinsic orientation toward personhood in the divine and human natures at once makes it possible for them to be fully actual in and as the same person, in such perfect unity that those natures are not merely juxtaposed, but truly coinherent one in the other. Otherwise, Christ would not be truly the God-man, but only a kind of chimaera composed of eternally juxtaposed but unreconciled properties, part human, part divine, and wholly *unnatural*; and personhood—far from being the uniquely exalted and integral principle we so keenly desire it to be—would be vacuous to the point of monstrosity. If personhood is not understood as essentially the instantiation and subsistence of the nature it makes actual, and so as rooted in that nature as its own innermost potential, then it becomes an oddly nihilistic concept: a kind of ontological portmanteau within which potentially any collection of disparate natures and abstract properties might somehow magically be contained together. This would conceptually sever those natures from their own intrinsic modes of expression and manifestation, thereby evacuating the very category of nature of any real meaning, and deprive personhood of the power of truly *expressing* any nature at all. At that point, the words πρόσωπον and *persona* would seem to revert to their most "superficial" meaning—a "mask," either dramatic or funerary—as though they indicated only a kind of sterile haecceity, a unity superimposed only as an *outer* aspect upon what in itself is a mere confluence of divergent forces, as much a rupture as a union, in an almost Deleuzo-Guattarian way: the ever repeated univocity of "person," the unrepeatable equivocity of "persons." At that point also, logic would become impotent, and one would be forced simply to rely on affective rhetoric: to speak, say, of the "dynamic" power of personality to unite incompatible things in a single activity, or (once again) to speak of personhood meaninglessly as something that always somehow transcends nature, precisely by being nothing in itself as such.

Yes, of course, the person of Christ is in one sense prior—at least, logically—to the union of natures he comprehends; and, by reciprocal necessity, the persons of creatures enjoy that same logical priority over that same union of natures within themselves when they are deified. Even so, it is not enough to assert that the concept of person transcends the concept of nature in order to explain how it is that Christ's one divine hypostasis is able to comprehend both his divine and his human natures without confusion or separation. It may be tempting to regard this as the proper "neo-Chalcedonian" solution to the Christological paradox; but, viewed dispassionately, it soon turns out to be no solution at all. It is instead only a repetition of the initial problem, but with the superaddition of a category so scrupulously purged of intrinsic content that it is no longer resistant to even a total contradiction. This is a useless approach to the issue. By this logic, the Logos might just as well have become incarnate as a lettuce. To say that the miraculous coinherence of human and divine natures in Christ without either confusion or separation is "explained" by a concept of "hypostasis" or "person" that is indifferent to the difference of natures in Christ is to say nothing at all, but to do so with a redoubled emphasis in the hope that it will sound like a positive assertion. In the end, this is simply the invention of a category so barren as to be infinitely capacious, and then an attempt to pretend that the problem in question is somehow—magically—its own answer. It may be very dramatic to assert that there is some mysterious quantum called "personality" that possesses the dynamic power of uniting incompatibles, but nothing has that power; not even God can unite the truly incompatible. True union between disparate realities—and this includes disparate natures—occurs only by way of their reduction to a wider, more encompassing, simpler, and more primordial commonality.

Hence, while it may be necessary to assert the priority of hypostasis over nature in the actual union of human and divine in Christ or in us, it is no less necessary to affirm that personhood is also the subsistence of—and so onto-logically dependent upon—the nature it expresses. Hypostasis and nature must remain the two indissoluble sides of a single metaphysical principle: as ontic actualization and ontological axiom. There is nothing wrong, needless to say, in taking all the later developments of the concept of "hypostasis" or "person" into account in one's Christological speculations; but one can do so to a purpose only so long as one does not render the concept vapid by severing those devel-opments from their most fundamental, original, and indispensable ground: the concept of a subsistence. And so one still must ask what it is about the divine and human natures—what primordial commonality or point of indistinction, that is, that exists between them, at a level presumably more fundamental than any merely univocal properties could occupy—that allows for them to come to full expression in one and the same person. The properly essential question of Christology, then—the only one that can yield an answer that is more than a rhetorical gesture toward some *quantum ignotum* or *persona ex machina*—is not: "How are two incompatible natures reconciled in a single hypostasis?" Rather, it is: "How is it that a full subsistence of the divine nature and a full subsistence of the human nature can be one and the same subsistence, without contradiction?" Only one answer is possible (or interesting).[33]

III.

Much of the obscurity in Christian talk of the "person," of course, lies in the simple and rather trivial reality that, under ordinary conditions, the first ques-tion one asks of any person *as* person is who he or she is. But, then, in regard

---

33   It is probably as well to note that, in the entirety of section II, I am taking exception not only to a certain well-established articulation of Christian "personalism," but also to many of the Christological premises espoused at present by a small school of young theologians who see themselves as "New Neo-Chalcedonians." The current manifesto of the movement is a book by Jordan Daniel Wood entitled *The Whole Mystery of Christ: Creation as Incarnation in Maximus Confessor* (South Bend: University of Notre Dame Press, 2022). It is an impressive text, I should note, even if I regard its arguments as defective in numerous crucial respects.

to God, that is a question that has to be qualified by the additional specification of whether it is being asked about "God" as addressed by creatures, and then whether God so addressed is to be understood (as by Jesus) as the Father or rather as the Trinity, and then whether in the latter case this is to be understood as an address to what Bulgakov calls the one trihypostatic Person or to each of the persons according to their distinct idioms … and so forth. To inquire after the "who" of a human being, by contrast, is to seek not a simple answer, perhaps, but at least one whose subject is more or less precise (or, at the very least, local). So one might legitimately wonder whether an analogical rupture occurs within the very concept of personhood when we attempt to apply it both to God and to creatures. And here too we happen upon a certain seemingly irresoluble ambiguity in the way the language of "person" operates across the analogical interval between the economic and immanent Trinities. Jesus of Nazareth was none other, says dogma, than the person of the divine Son, while at the same time being wholly human in his very personhood; conversely, the whole hope of the creature's deification in Christ depends on a genuine proportional equivalence between the exchange of divine and human natures in his divine person and that same exchange within created persons. This, however, creates something of a difficulty in defining how the hypostasis of the Son is distinguished as one of the Trinitarian persons, as opposed to the other two. After all, when tradition says that only "one of the Holy Trinity suffered" on the cross of Christ, surely this cannot mean that Jesus's sufferings belong to only one of the divine persons as a private subjectivity, in a way that simply excludes the Father and Spirit as separate private subjectivities; to say that the Father did not suffer on the cross is not like saying that it does not hurt you when I cut my finger. Originally, of course, all this claim was intended to convey was the real divinity of the one who (by kenosis) suffered in Jesus of Nazareth. Today, we often hear it instead as an assertion that the divine Son was the psychological subject of the passion, and that his was one of three such subjectivities within God. But God does not have a psychology, of course, except by condescension; the psychological self of Jesus—the soul or ψυχή—belonged to no one other than the Logos, just as his flesh and blood did, as something assumed by the Son's self-emptying. Neither, moreover, does God possess three separate subjectivities, psychological or otherwise. To imagine that he does would simply be to embrace tritheism.

As Bulgakov notes, the Cappadocian fathers who secured the vocabulary of Nicene orthodoxy maintained that it is the divine οὐσία that in a sense "founds" the deity of the Trinity, and is (so to speak) concretized as a true "triune I," in whom the three divine hypostases are distinguished by relations of origin, rather than as three distinct subjects.[34] By virtue of this essential oneness, "God, as the Absolute Person, is thereby also the trihypostatic Person, truly One in Three and Three in One. He is not Three in one, but the *triunity* of the Divine Person and of His Life."[35] We can then say at one and the same time, perhaps, that the divine simplicity is the "result" of the self-giving transparency and openness of infinite persons, but also that the distinction of the persons within the one God is the "result" of the infinite simplicity of the divine essence. Else we trade in mythology: speaking of God *either* as an infinite psychological subjectivity possessed of plural affects *or* as a confederacy of three individual centers of consciousness, in either case reducing God, the transcendent source of all being, to a composite being in whose "subjectivity" there would remain, even within the immanent divine life, some sort of unexpressed interiority (or interiorities), some surfeit of the indeterminate over the determinate, some reserve of self in which identity is constituted simply as what is withheld by each of the persons for that "person" alone. God is one because each divine hypostasis, in the circle of God's knowledge and love of his own goodness (which is both wisdom and charity), is a "face," a πρόσωπον or *persona*, of the divine essence that is—as must be, given the infinite simplicity of God—always wholly God, in the full depth of his "personality." Each hypostasis is fully gathered and reflected in the mode of the other: as the one and as other, as at once I and we. Obviously, for us this is not the case, except in the most tenuously analogous sense. Even our presence to ourselves as discrete persons is in this life an incomplete and always inadequate revelation of our subjective depths to ourselves, in an always incomplete expression or predicate, which is only partially actualized. As has already been said, we must also come to ourselves in and through others beyond ourselves, and can fully come to ourselves only in God; our personhood is always as much beyond us as within us.

In God, then, the intratrinitarian distinctions among hypostases are distinctions not among separate subjectivities, but among distinct moments within the one "subjectivity" or Personhood of the God who is Trinity. Each of the divine hypostases is the one God in his fullness according to one specific idiom; but the one God nonetheless remains always the one trihypostatic Person who is at once the hiddenness of the Father, the express image of the Son, and the living reality of both together in the Spirit. The alternative to this view of the matter is, once again, simply tritheism. To say that, of the Trinitarian hypostases, it was the Son who suffered on the cross is not to say that the Son alone,

---

34 Bulgakov, *The Comforter*, 29–31.
35 Ibid., 44.

in the interiority of his own discrete subjectivity, experienced what the other two hypostases, in the interiorities of their separate subjectivities, did not. The purely subjective interiority of the Son, in its full depth, simply *is* the Father; the Father's fully expressed exteriority simply *is* the Son; the perfect life and ac- tuality of the Father and Son as personal simply *is* the Spirit. Thus Christ names himself as the Son in saying, "He who has seen me has seen the Father." But to say the reverse would be meaningless; it is not a statement about a reciprocal relation between two selves, but rather a structural description of the divine personhood. For the same reason, it would be meaningless to suggest that some other of the three hypostases could have become incarnate. The Trinity is God as the hierarchy of the hidden and the manifest. Where God is disclosed, there is the Son. One ought to say, for instance, not that the Son is the divine per- son who "appropriated" the incarnation, but rather that God incarnate—God manifest—is of necessity the Son, and that incarnation is therefore always and uniquely a filial *proprium*. Thus, the assertion that "one of the Trinity suffered in the flesh" is an idiomatic or even modal claim, not a claim about the sub- jective identity of the particular divine agent of the incarnation. God suffered, so to speak, in the mode of the Son, as the only proper mode in which God is reflectively present to himself and objectively present to us who live, move, and exist within the life of love and knowledge that he is. The Father is that mode of being God that, as unexpressed and unmanifest in itself, is present to itself and to creation only in the Son, and so does not suffer in itself. The Spirit is the living presence of Father and Son to one another in the one divine life of love that, so to speak, eternally overcomes any abstract opposition of hiddenness and manifestation—such as that between the not-suffering of the Father and the suffering of the Son.[36] Or let us put it this way: when you experience pain, the always unmanifest source of your personal existence (we may call it *nous* or *intellectus* if we like, or the transcendental or even apperceptive "I" if we prefer, or even *Atman* or *Sakṣi* if we are feeling a little daring and exotic) is not in itself either the agent or patient of that experience; the empirical or psycho- logical self, however, is; and your existence as a rational spirit is the living unity of these truths that, in being made actual, constitutes you as a real subject. A distant, defective, wholly inadequate analogy of what happened in Christ, no doubt, as all analogies must be; even so, the not-suffering of the Father is more like that than like your not-suffering when I cut my finger.

All of which is to say that the language of "person" in Christian thought, to the degree that it possesses sufficient analogical scope to make sense si-

---

36   Bulgakov, *Chapters*, 59.

multaneously of Trinitarian theology and of creaturely personhood, must be
a language grounded not simply in the threeness of the divine hypostases, but
also, and no less securely, in the oneness of the divine essence *understood as* the
"hypostasible" oneness of the divine Person who God is.[37] It is only in terms of
that same unity that one can make sense of the claim that in the one person of
Christ both the divine and human natures in their wholeness are present and
fully expressed, and of the reciprocal claim that created persons are called to realize both natures in themselves in like manner. If, as I have asserted, "person"
and "nature" cannot be separated from one another as extrinsic principles, the
explanation of how it is that human nature is not an impediment to union with
the divine in one person, or how it is that the divine nature is not the destruction of the human in that union, is not simply some ontological indifference on
the part of the principle of hypostasis to the difference between the two natures,
but rather, more originally, the primordial indistinction of those natures in
their divine source. Yes, the principle of personhood is neither, as such, divine
nor human, but that is only because it is always already both. There must be,
Bulgakov insists, some prior commonality in the human and divine natures,
mediating and serving as the unalterable foundation of their union in Christ;
and this he chooses to call Sophia, or Sophianicity,[38] or Divine Humanity, or
the pre-hypostatic "hypostasibility" of the divine essence as it is possessed in
the Father—all of which is to say, that intrinsic movement of personhood that
is always already the essential going forth of the Father, in the immanent divine
life and then also in creation. The possibility of the incarnation, says Bulgakov,
is not merely the correspondence of the divine and human natures to one another, but is rather something still more radical: "even their primordial identity
in Sophia, Heavenly and creaturely," inasmuch as, "with regard to personality,
the Son of God is *kindred* with the sons of God by grace."[39] This is one of those
delightfully exorbitant formulations, so abundant in Bulgakov's writings, that
scandalously combine wanton audacity with absolute logical inevitability. Conversely, moreover, the human being must always already be capable of receiving
and encompassing the divine hypostasis; "by his initial essence man must already be divine-human in this sense," such that one must postulate that same

---

37   See David Bentley Hart, "The Mirror of the Infinite: Gregory of Nyssa on the Vestigia
     Trinitatis," in ibid., *The Hidden and the Manifest: Essays in Theology and Metaphysics*
     (Grand Rapids: W. B. Eerdmans, 2017), 113–21.
38   Bulgakov, *The Lamb of God*, 196–97.
39   Bulgakov, *The Comforter*, 372.

"primordial identity between the Divine I of the Logos and the human I."[40] That is an extraordinary formulation, obviously; it is also necessarily correct if the Christian story is more than a beguiling fantasy. The Logos is the "pre-eternal God-man as the Proto-Image of the creaturely man";[41] thus all human beings are called to deification by their very nature, and the incarnation is the natural fulfillment of the human essence.[42] All personhood, whether divine or human, is born of the same divine-human hypostasibility, and so the perfect inherence of the divine and human in the one person of Christ is not an accidental jux-taposition of natures that, as they share no univocal properties, must merely coexist when contained within some kind of ontological portmanteau without any nature of its own; rather, it is the wholly *natural* expression and enact-ment of both divinity and humanity in the always already divine and human principle of personhood. (Here too, I might note, is the ground of the natural compatibility, noted above, of Christ's address to the Father as "Father" and his prayer to the Father as "God": all personhood belongs to this divine Person-hood that is at once the perfect filial manifestation of its source and also the "obedient" mission of the self as turning back in spiritual love to its source.) And, once again, given that aforementioned "primordial identity between the Divine I of the Logos and the human I," it is not only licit, but necessary, to say that the same Logos that is the ground of the self of Jesus of Nazareth is also the ground of every self; but in Jesus the self's subjectivity—his psychologi-cal ego—is so perfectly transparent to that ground that there is no interval of otherness, no distance between the human I and the divine I. Thus he is truly God incarnate. But thus too all human beings, who exist only as participating in that divine source of the I, are called to have their "selves" transformed into that very same transparency before their one shared divine ground. Sophia, hypostasibility, Divine Humanity—what have you: it is that original common-ality of the divine and the human logically prior to any differentiation of the two natures that is also the perfectly concordant commonality of those natures in act, even to the point of identity in one and the same person.

---

40   Bulgakov, *The Lamb of God*, 186.
41   Ibid., 187.
42   Ibid., 189.

IV.

Where then to bring these reflections to an end?

There are a number of conclusions I might draw. The first might simply be that, for Bulgakov, the category of "person" spans not only the difference between the divine and human natures, but also the difference between God and creation as a whole. In his thought, with its creative appropriation and Christian repristination of German idealist thought, the structure of personhood is also an ontology, a description of the structure of being as such. As he notes, to say that "I am x" already expresses the ontological architecture of *all* reality: any "substance" exists not merely "in itself," as a subject, but also "for itself," as a predicate, and so "in and for itself," in the copula that joins subject and predicate in the act of real existence.[43] Every "who" and every "what" becomes manifest as "he" or "she" or "this" or "that" in the living unity of an "am" or an "is." Hence Bulgakov's impatience with Kant's Cartesian assumption that there exists some gulf of alienation between the "nomological" realm of the phenomena and the "pathological" realm of the noumena, and that the subjective apparatus of perception is of its nature denied all access to the *Ding an sich*. All being is personal expression, personal communion, and so the conditions of human knowledge and experience are the same conditions as allow for the existence of the known and experienced. The whole of being is an image of the divine life. The whole of being is language, and is *personal* communication of its depths to another.

My second conclusion is a little more radical. For finite beings, as I have noted, our reality as persons is both something given and something never as yet wholly realized in us; our very nature is always also a project for us, one in which we are dependent on and responsible for those outside ourselves. Each of us is, and yet is ever seeking to become, truly the "I" who truly says "I am." Part of this dynamism I have already described above, as the reciprocity between the way in which we become objects of our own reflective subjectivity by becoming also objects of the subjectivity of the other, and vice-versa. And yet the entirety of humanity by itself, and even the entirety of creation, still does not exhaust the depth of the possibility of that subjectivity, and cannot bring that "I" fully to light. As Bulgakov says, God alone, in his infinite Spirit, overcomes the mere "ipseity" of subjectivity in perfected love, and therefore alone is entirely truly personal.[44] Only in God is the full depth of personhood fully known and fully

---

43   Bulgakov, *The Tragedy of Philosophy*, 9–11.
44   Bulgakov, *The Comforter*, 180–82.

loved and loving. Each of us is in transit; each of us is always as yet becoming a person; and the "I" that we are always seeking to become is the "I" who the incarnate Logos always already is: the human being who is wholly human in being wholly God, and who thereby entirely realizes the divine-human essence of our nature. We truly become persons only in his person, as his person is the full expression of the one trihypostatic Person of God. When that dependence on others that constitutes us as living subjects becomes an ultimate dependence on the person of the incarnate Logos, making his manifestation of the Father the object of our own subjectivities, we are transformed into what he is. Gregory of Nyssa described this miraculous commerce of divine and human identity within us with exquisite loveliness as a kind of inverse and transfiguring reflection—in the "mirror" of the soul's own structure of hiddenness and manifestation—of the Trinitarian order of God's self-revelation;[45] and Bulgakov echoes Gregory when he says that one becomes a true and actual "I" only in gazing upon the divine "I," and thereby knowing oneself as the image and reflection of that divine sun.[46]

My final conclusion, however, is more radical still, and somewhat exceeds any formulation I am aware of Bulgakov having ever explicitly ventured. Yet, if one follows the metaphysical and theological principles he espoused and developed with such indefatigable and somewhat repetitive resolve, it seems difficult to avoid the conclusion that there must be a point in his vision of things where the distinction between the language of image and archetype and that of a yet more original identity begins to seem at most merely formal, and even rather arbitrary. After all, if the Father predicates himself in the Son, by the existential copula of the Spirit, and if this is the very structure of being itself, and if all of creation lies in the infinite predication of the Logos in all the logoi it contains, and if all creatures become themselves only in fully realizing the content of that predication through union with the Father in the Son by way of the Spirit—where, precisely, is the demarcation to be drawn between the intrinsic economy of the divine life and its secondary expression in creation? Obviously, creation is a contingent expression of that divine fullness, while that fullness in its absolute nature is unqualified by a relation to anything contingent; otherwise, it would be merely the reciprocal and hence extrinsic relation of two distinct "things." But it seems clear as well that this is not a distinction that encompasses any actual possible counterfactual ("If God had not created …"), but only one that indicates a modal definition of creation as

---

45　Hart, "Mirror," 122–33.
46　Bulgakov, *Chapters*, 66.

wholly contingent in relation to the plenitude of content and expression that is the divine life. Bulgakov's is, by any just characterization, a monistic metaphysics. This is not in itself surprising, inasmuch as any coherent metaphysics is a monism in some sense, grounded in some primordial, irreducible, and universal principle: "Being," "act," "the One," "God," "infinite substance in infinite modes," "the *Begriff*," even perhaps "difference" (as pronounced in a strangely transcendental register). What is astonishing and new in Bulgakov's monism, given its Christological foundation, is the discovery that it is not merely possible and coherent but perhaps also necessary to say that, among the privileged names for this most original of principles, the highest of all is "person," or even "*the* Person": he, that is, in whom all personhood has its existence and in which all things have their ground *as personal*—the one divine Person who is all that is, who shall in the end be all in all, and who alone is forever the "I am that I am" within every "I" that is.

Building the House of Wisdom
DOI 10.17438/978-3-402-12174-0

Bulgakov and Lot-Borodine as Shapers of Deification in the West

Mark McInroy

This chapter maintains that Sergii Bulgakov shaped twentieth-century percep-tions of deification in the West through a frequently overlooked route, namely Myrrha Lot-Borodine's seminal studies of the doctrine published in 1932 and 1933 in the *Revue de l'histoire des religions*.[1] At a time when deification was primarily known in the West through Adolf Harnack's withering denuncia-tion of the doctrine, and at a moment when many Russian theologians' works remained untranslated, Myrrha Lot-Borodine's groundbreaking articles pre-sented the first sustained Orthodox defense of deification widely accessible to Western readers. This paper maintains, however, that in key regards Lot-Boro-dine's studies in fact functioned as a conduit through which Bulgakov's version of the doctrine was made known in the West, even though Bulgakov's influence on Lot-Borodine has often gone unrecognized.

Myrrha Lot Borodine: An Influential Figure in the Russian Diaspora

After a lengthy period of neglect, Myrrha Lot-Borodine (1882–1957) is at last beginning to receive sustained scholarly attention, as indicated by the recent upsurge of publications on her work.[2] Although she made contributions in

---

Presented at "Building the House of Wisdom: Sergii Bulgakov—150 Years After His Birth," International Conference hosted by the University of Fribourg, Switzerland– September 2–4, 2021.

1   Myrrha Lot-Borodine, "La Doctrine de la 'déification' dans l'Église grecque jusqu'au XIᵉ siècle," *Revue de l'histoire des religions* 105 (1932): 5–43; 106 (1932): 525–74; 107 (1933): 8–55, 245–46.

2   Teresa Obolevich's recent monograph is the most substantial treatment to date: *Mirra Lot-Borodina: istorik, literator, filosof, bogoslov* (Saint Petersburg: Nestor-Istoriia, 2020).

a number of different academic arenas, her most enduring legacy will likely involve her treatment of the Christian doctrine of deification. Her articles on the doctrine played a pivotal role in making deification widely known in the West; particularly significant in this connection are the prominent French Catholic theologians who took note of her studies. Yves Congar, for instance, endorsed her depiction of deification in a review article in *La Vie Spirituelle* in 1935,[3] and Jean Daniélou proclaimed in his preface to the republished edition of Lot-Borodine's studies, "Reading these articles was decisive for me. They crystallized something I was looking for, a vision of man transfigured by the divine energies."[4] Later in his preface Daniélou remarks that he was led to the articles by either Henri de Lubac or Hans Urs von Balthasar (he cannot recall which one), giving further indication of the enthusiasm for deification Lot-Borodine generated among figures associated with *la nouvelle théologie*. Marie-Dominique Chenu also credits Lot-Borodine with his own turn to the Christian East; he openly acknowledges that it is to her "that I owe much of my appetite for Eastern theology."[5] Other luminaries of French Catholicism influenced by Lot-Borodine include Étienne Gilson (a colleague of her husband, Ferdinand

---

See also Teresa Obolevich, "Myrrha Lot-Borodine: The First Female Orthodox Theologian," *European Journal of Science and Theology* 16, no. 3 (June 2020): 119–27; I.-M. Morariu, "Myrrha Lot-Borodine et la redécouverte de la théologie orthodoxe dans l'espace français," *Studia Monastica* 60, no. 2 (2018): 413–19; Andrew Louth, "Apophatic theology and deification: Myrrha Lot-Borodine and Vladimir Lossky," in *Modern Orthodox Thinkers: From the Philokalia to the Present* (Downers Grove, IL: InterVarsity Press, 2015), 94–110; Michel Stavrou, "La Démarche néopatristique de Myrrha Lot-Borodine et de Vladimir Lossky," in *Les Pères de l'Eglise aux sources de l'Europe*, ed. Dominique Gonnet and Michel Stavrou (Paris: Cerf, 2014), 200–25; Heleen E. Zorgdrager, "A Practice of Love: Myrrha Lot-Borodine (1882–1954) and the Modern Revival of the Doctrine of Deification," *Journal of Eastern Christian Studies* 64 (2012): 287–307; Fedor Poljakov, "Myrrha Lot-Borodine: Wegzeichen und Dimensionen des west-östlichen Dialoges in der russischen Diaspora," in *Festschrift für Hans-Bernd Harder zum 60. Geburtstag*, ed. Helmut Schaller (Munich: Verlag Otto Sagner, 1995), 401–13.

3   Yves M.-J. Congar, "La déification dans la tradition spirituelle de l'Orient, d'après une étude récente," *La Vie Spirituelle*, Supplement (May 1, 1935): 91–107. ET: "Deification in the Spiritual Tradition of the East (in the Light of a Recent Study)," in Yves M.-J. Congar, *Dialogue between Christians: Catholic Contributions to Ecumenism* (Westminster, MD: The Newman Press, 1966), 217–31.

4   Jean Daniélou, "Preface," in Myrrha Lot-Borodine, *La doctrine de la déification dans l'Église grecque jusqu'au XIᵉ siècle* (Paris: Cerf, 1970), 9–18, at 10.

5   Marianne Mahn-Lot, "Ma mère, Myrrha Lot-Borodine (1882–1954). Esquisse d'itinéraire spirituel," *Revue des Sciences Philosophiques et Théologiques* (2004): 745–54, at 752.

Lot), whose examination of Bernard of Clairvaux appeared shortly after her studies and treats deification at several points, with Lot-Borodine cited in the bibliography.[6]

Although mention of Lot-Borodine by name tends to wane as the twentieth century progresses, central features of her characterization of deification only grow more prominent.[7] Most influential is her claim that Western theology cannot espouse deification because of its fundamentally different model of the God-world relation, particularly as displayed in its theological anthropology and view of grace. The notion that deification is not part of Western theology had been introduced—for different reasons—by Albrecht Ritschl and amplified by those in his "school," especially Adolf Harnack.[8] However, whereas the Ritschlian school had been highly critical of the doctrine, Lot-Borodine celebrates deification, upending the negative judgment among German liberal Protestants and provoking enormous positive interest in the doctrine.

For all of Lot-Borodine's influence, however, what remains largely unrecognized is that the particular version of deification that she puts forward shares deep affinities with that of Sergii Bulgakov, so much so that in key regards she effectively serves as a spokesperson for his model of the doctrine.[9] Those familiar with Myrrha Lot-Borodine may be surprised—if not deeply skeptical—at the claim that Bulgakov so significantly influenced her views. Scholars have tended to place Lot-Borodine firmly within the "neo-patristic" movement of Georges Florovsky and Vladimir Lossky rather than the "modernist" approach of figures such as Bulgakov and Pavel Florenskii. As overstated as this opposition often is, such a characterization of Lot-Borodine has not arisen without reason. In an important account of her own theological inclinations, she mentions "the instinctive mistrust that all heresy inspired in me," and she even specifies the targets of her suspicion as the "Gnosticism" of Soloviev and

6   Étienne Gilson, *The Mystical Theology of Saint Bernard* (London: Sheed and Ward, 1940).

7   Although Vladimir Lossky's *The Mystical Theology of the Eastern Church* would not appear for over a decade after Lot-Borodine's articles, its significance for Western attitudes toward deification should not be overlooked.

8   See Mark McInroy, "How Deification Became Eastern: German Idealism, Liberal Protestantism, and the Modern Misconstruction of the Doctrine," *Modern Theology* 37/4, 934–58.

9   Congar is one of the few figures who detects the significance of Bulgakov for Lot-Borodine's view of deification.

Bulgakov.[10] Similarly, Antoine Arjakovsky notes that Lot-Borodine attacked the "gnosis" of Dimitrii Merezhkovskii, and Arjakovsky also reports that Nicolai Berdiaev regarded Lot-Borodine as "too orthodox and very right wing."[11] Perhaps most instructively, in 1938 Lot-Borodine published a defense of Florovsky's *The Ways of Russian Theology* in which she signaled her support for a return to the "narrow way of the fathers."[12] There would seem to be good reason to cast Lot-Borodine as a thoroughgoing traditionalist who deeply opposed figures such as Bulgakov.

Concerning Lot-Borodine's treatment of deification in particular, there are even clearer reasons to suppose that she would stand with Florovsky. It was, after all, Florovsky who prompted Lot-Borodine to pursue deification in the first place. She reports that she heard him lecture on the topic at the Berdiaev Colloquy in 1928,[13] and she even corresponded with him as she was composing her articles. She expresses her desire to consult him "in order to clarify some points which are still doubtful for me," suggesting that he had a shaping influence on her studies.[14] As one would expect based on these biographical details, Lot-Borodine's articles mention Florovsky's works at several junctures, and she additionally draws from a treatment of Pseudo-Dionysius published by Vladimir Lossky, seemingly cementing her place among neo-patristic figures.[15] And yet, as will be shown by an examination of Bulgakov's account of deification and its telling echoes in Lot-Borodine's studies, it is neither Florovsky nor

10 Mahn-Lot, 748. The passage is complex. In spite of her concern about his alleged Gnosticism, Lot-Borodine describes Bulgakov as a "true genius of our diaspora." Heleen Zorgdrager appears to have taken this positive assessment as an endorsement of Bulgakov's position, but such an interpretation is questionable; Andrew Louth and Michel Stavrou both understand Lot-Borodine's remarks as expressing concern about Bulgakov (in spite of some degree of admiration), not attraction to his views.

11 Antoine Arjakovsky, *The Way: Religious Thinkers of the Russian Emigration in Paris and their Journal* (Notre Dame, IN: University of Notre Dame Press, 2002), 278, 411.

12 Myrrha Lot-Borodine, "Prot. Georgii Florovskii. 'Puti russkogo bogosloviia,'" Sovremennye zapiski 66 (1938), 461–63. Cf. Paul L. Gavrilyuk, *George Florovsky and the Russian Religious Renaissance* (Oxford: Oxford University Press, 2013), 197.

13 Georges Florovsky offered a brief treatment of deification published in Russian in 1928 as "Tvar' i Tvar'nost."

14 Myrrha Lot-Borodine, Letter to G. Florovsky from of 24 July, 1931, Princeton University Library, Rare Books and Special Collections, Georges Florovsky Papers, Box 27, F. 30. Quoted in Obolevich, 121.

15 Vladimir Lossky, "La Notion des 'analogies' chez Denys le Pseudo-Aréopagite," *Archives d'histoire doctrinale et littéraire du Moyen Age*, 5 (1930): 279–309.

Lossky whom Lot-Borodine most decisively follows on the deification of the human being, but rather Bulgakov.

Sergii Bulgakov on the Sophianic Structure of Deification

Florovsky was not the only Orthodox theologian with an interest in deification in the early twentieth century. In fact, one can regard the doctrine as something of a contested topic within the Russian émigré community in Paris. Whereas Florovsky focuses on patristic models of deification, Bulgakov reformulates the idea through a critical appropriation of the identity philosophy of F. W. J. Schelling and the thought of Jacob Böhme. These interlocutors lead Bulgakov to advance a stunningly bold model of deification that centers on the "sophianicity" of humankind. Our examination begins with Bulgakov's treatment of the topic in *The Burning Bush*, as this volume had a particularly powerful impact on Lot-Borodine.[16]

In that text, which was published in Russian in 1927, Bulgakov opens his discussion of deification with what he contends is the Orthodox understanding of the relationship between God and creation: "God in His love for creation abolished the abyss lying between Him and creation and made humankind for divinization. In its primordial condition, before sin, humankind had that power of divinization as the direct consequence of the harmonious structure of its spirit."[17] In this brief formulation Bulgakov makes two controversial points, each of which will be challenged by Florovsky. First, deification to Bulgakov involves *eliminating* the gap between God and creation. Second, human beings at their creation had the capacity for deification as a result of the very structure of their being.

Similarly bold remarks can be found in other works by Bulgakov. For instance, in *Philosophy of Economy*, he explains, "In their freedom people are gods, creatures potentially intended for divinization, capable of merging into the ocean of divine being—and fusing and merging are possible only for what is like and *of one substance* in the first place."[18] Along equally provocative lines, in *The Lamb of God*, Bulgakov claims, "Man has not a creaturely origin, but a

16 Lot Borodine also published a review of Bulgakov's *L'Orthodoxie* in *Revue de l'histoire des religions*, 107 (1933): 209–13.

17 Sergii Bulgakov, *The Burning Bush: On the Orthodox Veneration of the Mother of God*, ed. and trans. Thomas Allan Smith (Grand Rapids: W. B. Eerdmans, 2009), 36.

18 Sergii Bulgakov, *Philosophy of Economy: The World as Household*, trans. Catherine Etuhov (New Haven, CT: Yale University Press, 2000), 207 (emphasis added).

divine origin. He is a created god. [...] Man [...] has within himself an uncreated, divine principle."[19] In *The Bride of the Lamb*, too, Bulgakov claims that man
"in a certain sense is already divine according to creation."[20]

The careful reader will note that the above passages do in fact display re-
straints—even if they are subtly conveyed—on Bulgakov's seemingly soaring
anthropology. Competing with what appears to be an assertion of consubstantiality between divine and human nature in the first quotation is the notion that
deification is merely a possibility, not an already present actuality.[21] The same
passage arguably specifies that human beings are gods only "in their freedom,"
leaving open the possibility that other aspects of human beings are not divine.
Along similar lines, in the final quotation above, Bulgakov holds that human
beings are divine only "in a certain sense"; the human being is not God *tout
court*.

Also important in this regard is the fact that—at certain moments, at least—
Bulgakov maintains that deification is not based in human nature alone. As he
puts this point in *The Burning Bush*, "Adam was, so to say, naturally blessed [...]
He was not separated from God, and thus there was not even a place for opposition of the natural and the graced in their indivisibility, in the power of divinization of humankind which began with his creation."[22] Bulgakov maintains
that nature and grace should not be contrasted with one another, and in fact
he suggests that nature is always already graced, and that deification therefore
occurs through the operation of both working in harmony with one another.

These nuanced qualifications will assuage some, but a striking vision of deification nevertheless remains. A number of Bulgakov's readers express concern
that the ontological distinction between God and humanity has been uncom-
fortably blurred if not entirely eliminated, an issue that intensifies as we turn
to the sophiological aspects of Bulgakov's anthropology.

Although the role of sophiology in the anthropology described thus far
might not be apparent, in the discussion of Adam as "naturally blessed," Bulgakov makes the connection clear: "This blessedness is not something arising
from the outside, which could even not exist, but is rather interiorly, imma-

---

19   Sergii Bulgakov, *The Lamb of God*, trans. Boris Jakim (Grand Rapids: W. B. Eerdmans,
     2008), 137.
20   Sergii Bulgakov, *The Bride of the Lamb*, trans. Boris Jakim (Grand Rapids: W. B. Eerd-
     mans, 2002), 115.
21   Ruth Coates identifies this tension, too. See her *Deification in Russian Religious Thought:
     Between the Revolutions, 1905–1917* (Oxford: Oxford University Press, 2019), 166.
22   Bulgakov, *The Burning Bush*, 37.

nently grounded in humankind by a creative act, as by creaturely Sophia."[23] Within humanity one finds creaturely Sophia, which with divine Sophia establishes a bridge between God and the world. Not so much a hypostasis herself as a means of "hypostaticity," Sophia is that through which the divine is able to be manifested in the world.

Sophia, then, allows for the union of God and human in the incarnation, but also in additional "creaturely hypostases" that bear the divine image. As Bulgakov explains elsewhere in *The Burning Bush*, "The human being is created by God according to His image and likeness. This means that God imprinted on the human being His tri-hypostatic image and placed him in the world as if in His own place, and made him a creaturely god. [...] He was a personal bearer of Divine Wisdom, of creaturely Sophia."[24]

Crucially for Lot-Borodine, Bulgakov holds that Catholic theology, from medieval scholasticism to the present day, "annihilates the Sophianicity of humankind" through its doctrine of the *donum superadditum*.[25] This doctrine maintains that humanity in its originally created state possessed "neither immortality nor freedom from lust," in Bulgakov's characterization, but instead needed God's grace to be superadded onto to its "pure nature," which is in truth merely an impoverished shell of what human nature should be.[26] According to Bulgakov's critique, the vulnerability of human nature to death and lust in Catholic theology means that human beings do not in fact bear the divine image within their nature. Bulgakov instead emphasizes the importance of *"an ontological link*, an internal necessity."[27]

From here Bulgakov goes on to insist that sophiology is the only way to develop the anthropology required for deification. He holds that "such a basis for anthropology can only be the doctrine of Wisdom as the pre-eternal foundation of creation, pre-eternal humanity, by virtue of which the earthly human is created according to the image of Christ the heavenly human."[28] It is only through Sophia that human beings have the image of God within their nature. To Bulgakov, then, a sharp divide can be observed between the anthropologies of the Orthodox and Catholic churches, and the sophianic structure of humanity is the key marker of difference.

---

23 Bulgakov, *The Burning Bush*, 37.
24 Ibid., 15.
25 Ibid., 37.
26 Ibid., 15.
27 Ibid., 16.
28 Ibid.

Florovsky's Corrective: Deification despite Non-Consubstantiality

Florovsky's "Creation and Creaturehood" has been viewed as an implicit challenge to Bulgakov, and it is not difficult to grasp the reasons for such a characterization. Immediately after broaching the topic of deification, Florovsky explains that, as the human being is deified, an "immutable, unchangeable gap"[29] remains between the human and the divine, and he next emphasizes the "impossibility of created nature's transubstantiation into the divine."[30] Along similar lines, elsewhere in his article he insists on the "non-consubstantiality" between God and the world.[31] In contrast to Bulgakov's suggestion that one must be of the same substance as God in order to merge into the divine being, Florovsky unequivocally holds that we cannot be changed in our substance into God.

Driving home the difference between the divine and human natures, Florovsky quotes Macarius of Egypt, noting that although "the divine Trinity inhabits the soul, which through God's grace keeps itself pure, she only does so to the extent of everyone's ability and spiritual measure, *not as the Holy Trinity is in herself* […] for God cannot be contained by a creature."[32] With this text as crucial support, Florovsky maintains that "from the outset it was understood that there is an insurmountable divide between the two natures, and a distinction was made between divinity by nature (*kat' ousian* or *kata physin*) and divinity by communion (*kata metousian*)."[33] In clear opposition to Bulgakov's sophiologically grounded version of deification, Florovsky holds that the distinction between God and humanity remains even as human beings are drawn into the divine life.

Additionally crucial for our examination, Florovsky emphatically holds that deification occurs not on the basis of human nature, but instead through divine grace. In this effort, he marshals considerable textual evidence from Maximus the Confessor, who will emerge as the key patristic figure in Lot-Borodine's studies. The following passage is worth quoting at length:

---

29   Georges Florovsky, "Creation and Creaturehood," in *Creation and Redemption: Volume 3 of the Collected Works of Georges Florovsky* (Belmont, MA: Nordland, 1976), 43–78, at 74. Newly translated as "Creation and Createdness," trans. Alexey Kostyanovsky, with assistance from Olena Gorbatenko, in *The Patristic Witness of Georges Florovsky: Essential Theological Writings*, ed. Brandon Gallaher and Paul Ladouceur (London: T&T Clark, 2019), 33–63.

30   Florovsky, "Creation and Createdness," 60.

31   Florovsky, "Creation and Creaturehood," 46.

32   St. Macarius of Egypt, *De amore*, 28, PG 34.932A. Florovsky, "Creation and Creaturehood," 61.

33   Florovsky, "Creation and Creaturehood," 62.

In the writings of St. Maximus, "Those who are saved receive salvation *by grace, not by nature* [Eph 2:5],"[34] and if "in Christ the whole fulness of the Godhead dwelt *by nature*, in us God dwells *not fully, but only by grace*."[35] Therefore the future deification for St. Maximus means *becoming like God by grace*; in his words, "we will appear like him, in virtue of deification by grace" (*kai phanōmen autōi homoioi kata tēn ek charitos theōsin*).[36] However, even as the creature partakes of divine life "in the union of love," "wholly and completely co-inhering with the whole God" (*holos holōi perichōrēsas holikōs tōi Theōi*) and sharing in his divine attributes, it still remains outside God's nature (*chōris tēs kat' ousian tautotēta* [without identity according to essence]).[37]

Florovsky goes to significant lengths in his use of this material to *contrast* nature and grace; he does not describe deification as the result of nature and grace working together, and he instead suggests that deification occurs through grace without nature playing a noteworthy role.

In sum, then, Florovsky's account of deification emphasizes the distinction between God and creatures, the enduring non-consubstantiality between God and the world (even in the face of any change that God might effect within created nature), and the notion that we are deified by grace to the exclusion of nature. Lot-Borodine, as we shall see, puts forward a view of deification that opposes each of these points.

Lot-Borodine's Bulgakov-Inspired Version of Deification

It is unlikely that Lot-Borodine would have missed the challenge Florovsky issued to Bulgakov. And yet, with the points of distinction clearly outlined, Lot-Borodine unexpectedly opts for Bulgakov's version of the doctrine rather than that of Florovsky. One observes instructive departures from Florovsky's position in three interrelated aspects of Lot-Borodine's presentation: she advances a competing interpretation of Maximus the Confessor that suggests one is deified on the basis of one's nature; she contests Florovsky's view that grace could operate on the human being to the exclusion of nature; she blurs

---

34 St. Maximus the Confessor, *Capita Theologiae et Oeconomiae Centuria*, I, 67, PG 90.1108B.

35 Ibid., *Cap. theol. et oecon. cent*, II, 21, PG 90.1133.

36 Ibid., Ep. 43: *Ad Ionannem cubicularium*, PG 91.640C.

37 St. Maximus the Confessor, *Ambigu*. 41, 222b. Florovsky, "Creation and Createdness," 62.

the distinction between God and creatures so assiduously upheld by Florovsky, most clearly in her explicit challenging of the non-consubstantiality between God and creation. Lot-Borodine's preference for Bulgakov can also be observed in her mention of him at one of the most decisive interpretive junctures in her treatment, and his influence can be detected elsewhere, especially surrounding Lot-Borodine's critique of the *donum superadditum* in Western theology.

Concerning Maximus, whereas Florovsky had used him in order to demonstrate that deification occurs through grace, and not on the basis of nature, Lot-Borodine deploys Maximus in order to advance the opposite claim. According to Lot-Borodine, "Maximus considers the *noûs* [...] this cap of the intellectual soul, as naturally deiformed. [...] St. Maximus, as well as other Fathers of the Eastern Church, does not hesitate to call the man 'the created god' (*le dieu créé*). That in all the strength of the term, without mitigating anything."[38] Lot-Borodine sees a robust deiformity *within* human nature, and in this context she explicitly gestures toward Bulgakov's importance for her interpretation of Maximus. Immediately following the above quotation, she explains that the human being is, "as will be said by a prominent representative of the Russian doctrine of Sophia, Father Bulgakov, a true 'terrestrial hypostasis of God' (*une véritable 'hypostase terrestre de Dieu'*); according to St. Maximus, of the Word 'through whom all things are.'"[39] In this quotation, Lot-Borodine moves from a claim for natural deiformity to the significantly bolder view of the human being as a *hypostasis* of the Word.

Complicating matters, however, Lot-Borodine does at other points dutifully convey that deification occurs through grace. And yet, close scrutiny of her model of the nature–grace relation reveals that she blurs the line between the two, often to the point of entirely collapsing grace into nature such that it is a part of the constitution of human beings at their creation. For instance, she claims that "Adam should have been a participant, by right of birth, to glory. In other words, *the supernatural would have been the true nature of man in earthly paradise*."[40] To Lot-Borodine, humanity as initially created has the supernatural within itself as its "true nature." The elision of the distinction between nature and grace is most marked in the following, near-paradoxical formulation: "The grace of divine adoption is *native*, incorporated in man."[41] As a result, it cannot be that we are deified by grace and not by nature, as Florovsky claims.

---

38   Lot-Borodine, "La doctrine de la déification," I, 23.
39   Ibid.
40   Ibid., 21 (emphasis added).
41   Lot-Borodine, "La doctrine de la déification," II, 546.

Lot-Borodine's reliance on nature itself (i. e., without mention of grace) grows more prominent as she deploys her anthropology to insist that the West completely lacks a doctrine of deification. Interweaving key points from Bulgakov's critique of the *donum superadditum* and Étienne Gilson's then-recent work on Augustine, Lot-Borodine launches a criticism of Augustine's view of human nature that renders deification entirely impossible, in her estimation. In so doing, however, she is moved to insist more clearly on the distinctiveness of the East's view of human nature as such. She seizes on a remark in Gilson's *The Christian Philosophy of St. Augustine* in which the author explains, "There is in the creature a kind of original lack (*manque originel*)."[42] From this starting point she further claims that, within his or her nature, the human being to Augustine has a "predisposition to imperfection, if not to sin."[43] The fact that the human being is "drawn from nothingness" implies an "idea of decay" within his model of human nature.[44] In fact, according to Lot-Borodine, under Augustine "our decay became the trademark of the human species."[45] This could not contrast more sharply with "the ideal divinity of our species" upheld by "the Greeks."[46]

Having drawn from Gilson, Lot-Borodine next widens the scope of Bulgakov's critique of the *donum superadditum* (which for him is limited to medieval and modern Catholicism) such that it also applies to the *ancient* Western church. She insists that in Augustine "the immortality of the first man consisted only in not having to, and not being unable to die; nor did Adam's rectitude and *amor imperturbatus* belong to man's own nature."[47] Although she does not mention Bulgakov by name at this particular juncture, her criticism closely follows his appraisal of the *donum superadditum*, and the strong suggestion of her remark is that human beings need immortality and *amor imperturbatus* in their nature as such.

Lot-Borodine similarly betrays her desire for a robust view of human nature in a comment on Augustine's account of pre-lapsarian humanity. She explains, "The state of 'justice' where our ancestors were in paradise was not, strictly speaking, natural to them in the Augustinian system: it was a *donum superadditum*, a gratuitous privilege of God."[48] Adam was able to remain in paradise not

42 Étienne Gilson, *The Christian Philosophy of St. Augustine*, trans. L. E. M. Lynch (New York: Random House, 1960), 148. Lot-Borodine, "La doctrine de la déification," I, 29.
43 Lot-Borodine, "La doctrine de la déification," I, 29.
44 Ibid.
45 Ibid.
46 Ibid., 29, n. 1.
47 Ibid.
48 Lot-Borodine, "La doctrine de la déification," I, 29.

through his nature, but only through the gift of God's grace, indicating that primordial humanity is bereft of justice and immortality in Augustine's thought. Later Lot-Borodine suggests that, because human nature in itself is possessed of this deep deficiency, the image of God for Augustine is but a distant reflection. "Once removed by the fact of the fall, the *donum superadditum*—which is a supernatural grace, from the beginning—the mystical resemblance to God darkens and disappears: no more direct communication with the Creator."[49] In sharp contrast to Maximus' "deiform nous," Augustine advances an anthropology in which human nature is profoundly alienated from God.

Lot-Borodine does not explicitly insist that deification be developed through sophiology; however, like Bulgakov, she suggests that the doctrine of deification demands an anthropology in which human beings have the supernatural within themselves at their creation, and she even holds that human beings are created in their inmost structure as hypostases of God. In fact, in what is surely the most instructive moment in her treatment of the doctrine, Lot-Borodine proposes that deification requires a view of the human being as *consubstantial* with God. In a remark that goes considerably further than the earlier blurring of the distinction between the supernatural and the natural, she explains that Augustine cannot espouse a doctrine of deification, "since there can be no consubstantiality (*consubstantialité*), and therefore interpenetration, of divine nature and human nature."[50] Although one might be tempted to view this remark as an infelicitous moment of excess, I would suggest that Lot-Borodine's formulation is better understood as a telling echo of Bulgakov's model of deification, which as we have seen suggests that the human being must be of the same substance as God in order to be deified.

Conclusion

Myrrha Lot-Borodine effectively defined what deification is for several generations of theologians in the West. In claiming that hers is in key respects a Bulgakovian version of the doctrine, this paper establishes a largely unappreciated facet of Bulgakov's significance, as his model of deification ultimately shaped perceptions of the doctrine at a crucial moment in modern Western scholarship. Evidence for Bulgakov's formative influence in this regard can be found in Congar's 1935 article, in which he reiterates without criticism the most controversial point that Lot-Borodine draws from Bulgakov. Congar explains,

---

49   Ibid., II, 547–48.
50   Ibid., I, 20.

"The East speaks of 'deification'. It consists in realizing the likeness to God in becoming 'consubstantial' with God."[51] Shortly thereafter, Congar even drops the scare quotes around the contentious term: "Deification [is] the realization of the soul's consubstantiality with God in virtue of a progressive illumination of being."[52] Congar rather surprisingly accepts, then, that deification does indeed involve consubstantiality between God and the human being, and his endorsement of this characterization performs significant work in disseminating the view in modern Western theology.

Concerning characterizations of Lot-Borodine in contemporary scholarship, it is certainly true that patristic figures play a crucial role in her work. However, inasmuch as Lot-Borodine reads a figure such as Maximus through Bulgakov, this paper demonstrates that mere use of ancient Christian theologians does not itself signal alignment with a "neo-patristic" approach. Instead, what becomes clear is that the patristic materials are a contested site that is being claimed by both neo-patristic and modernist figures. As a result, Myrrha Lot-Borodine emerges from this study a considerably more complex figure than she is often made out to be, one who cannot be tidily encompassed with classifications such as "neo-patristic," much less "traditionalist" or "right-wing." She appears as a highly intriguing, even enigmatic theologian who merits further examination for a full grasp of her subtle and often unexpected views.

Finally, these findings prompt contemporary scholars to trouble yet further the dichotomy often drawn between neo-patristic and modernist circles in the Russian diaspora in the early twentieth century. This chapter suggests noteworthy influence and borrowing across that divide, and it therefore demonstrates that advocates of the two approaches were not by any means cordoned off from one another. Instead, one observes here the kind of exchange one might expect of a vibrant (if frequently contentious) intellectual community in which ideas are perpetually proposed, tested, and in some cases adopted even when one might otherwise oppose the views of the individual in question. In this regard it is surely significant that Lot-Borodine conducted her investigations of deification in the early 1930s (before distinctions between positions hardened in 1935), but it suggests that, for a time at least, there was greater intellectual exchange across lines of difference in the Russian émigré community than is often thought to have taken place.

---

51   Congar, "Deification," 224.
52   Ibid., 226.

Building the House of Wisdom
DOI 10.17438/978-3-402-12175-7

"*Transcende te ipsum*": Faith, Prayer and Name-Worship in Bulgakov's *Unfading Light*

Ivan Ilin

Introduction: Overcoming „Immanentism"

Anyone who begins to read Sergei Bulgakov's philosophical magnum opus, *Unfading Light*, will immediately notice its strong emphasis on the proclamation of divine transcendence. Continuing his struggle with anthropolatric *Zeitgeist* that started in his earlier writings, Bulgakov opens the book straightaway with a critique of Western "immanentism" (or onto-theology, to use the Heideggerian-Kantian neologism). The key characteristic of immanentism, as Bulgakov defines it, is an almost complete disappearance of the distance between the Creator and the creation.[1] There is a variety of immanentist manifestations— Bulgakov applies this label to a whole range of philosophical, religious, and social currents—but for all of them God is ontologically immanent within this world. He is sort of "pulled" into being by and on the terms of human reason, which claims to have full access to God's nature. Epistemological immanence here is inextricably linked with ontological immanence, and the *otherness* of God is put into question. This process is marked, in particular, by the emergence of proofs of the existence of God; after all, they mean exactly that God "possesses" existence, depends on it, and does not condition it as its Creator and giver.

This chapter is the result of a research project implemented as part of the Basic Research Program at the National Research University Higher School of Economics (HSE University).

1   Sergei Bulgakov, *Svet Nevechernii* (Moscow: Respublika, 1994), 5. English translation (henceforth ET): Sergius Bulgakov, *Unfading Light. Contemplations and Speculations*, trans. Thomas Allan Smith (Grand Rapids: W. B. Eerdmans, 2012), xl.

Bulgakov realized that to reaffirm transcendence only ontologically would not be sufficient to overcome immanentism. For the immanentist way of thought is not merely the ontological assertion that there is the Highest Being who gives unity to the whole of being; it is above all the epistemological claim that with reference to this Highest Being it is possible to render the whole of being fully intelligible to human understanding. Therefore, it must be the rejection of both epistemological and ontological claims together that will complete the task of deconstructing "bad transcendences".[2] In view of this, in *Unfading Light* Bulgakov is seeking to reaffirm divine transcendence in both dimensions. I think that Bulgakov's ontological configuration that upholds God's epistemological alterity, can be presented as a set of several concentric circles: he consistently moves from a more general concept to a more specific, exploring their nature in a transcendental aspect. So, Bulgakov begins with the broadest phenomenon—religion, which is understood as a bond with reality beyond our empirical world. At the center of religion lies faith, which is considered a way (Bulgakov wouldn't call it a method) of approaching the transcendent. Then, at the center of faith lies prayer, which is understood as an act of transcending. And at the center of prayer lies *imyaslaviye*—"name-worship", an act of naming the Divine in prayer—treated in this case not as a doctrine but as a "transcendental condition of prayer". Such a transcendental "ascending" analysis of these phenomena allows Bulgakov not only to display the limitations of speculative reason, but also to show gradually and in detail the ways in which the cognition of the Divine is achieved, or in other words, how transcendence opens to immanence at "the intersection of two worlds".[3]

In the remainder of this chapter, I shall briefly analyze said phenomena—faith, prayer, and "name-worship"—and note the distinctive features of Bulgakovian "philosophy of revelation", to use Paul Valliere's expression[4]. I will argue that its main feature is its orientation towards the transcendent. My thesis is that for Bulgakov's transcendent-oriented philosophy of religion, the affirmation of divine transcendence is intrinsically intertwined with the practice of human self-transcendence, or kenotic/ascetic decentering of the self, achieved in acts of faith and prayer. In defining self-transcendence, Merold Westphal's book on the subject might be of use; there he describes it as "the movement

2   Cf. Michael Frensch, *Weisheit in Person: das Dilemma der Philosophie und die Perspektive der Sophiologie* (Schaffhausen: Novalis, 2000), chapter II.
3   Bulgakov, *Svet Nevechernii*, 26 [ET 24].
4   Paul Valliere, *Modern Russian Theology: Orthodox Theology in a New Key* (Edinburgh: T&T Clark, 2000), 268.

that draws us away from our natural preoccupation with ourselves."[5] Self-transcendence, as Westphal puts it, is that crucial dimension of the religious life in which through the love of God we are drawn out of our usual preoccupation with the question of what is in it for us. It displaces us from the center in our relations with God. In terms of epistemology, self-transcendence has a negative/apophatic side, i. e., epistemic humility, and a positive/cataphatic side, which begins with praise or doxology.[6]

Both of these sides are present in *Unfading Light*, the former however being much more explicit. Affirmation of epistemic humility is precisely one of the reasons why Bulgakov explicitly uses (at least at the beginning of the book) the Kantian methodology of transcendental criticism. For Kant's critical turn represented for Bulgakov a philosophical version of the *via negativa* approach that provided a means for human reason to limit the claims about metaphysical knowledge.[7] Developing Kant's apophatic lines of thought, Bulgakov points out that since the transcendental condition of religion is the disclosure of the transcendent in the immanent, human reason is unable to grasp the divine reality with its own efforts: "there are not and cannot be any naturally determined, methodical paths to him, but precisely therefore he in his condescension becomes infinitely close to us."[8] Thus, all intellectual efforts to approach God are futile if they ignore or lack the disclosure of the Divine manifested in religious experience:

> The decisive moment remains the encounter with God in the human spirit, the contact of the transcendent with the immanent, the act of faith. God exists. This is what resounds in the human heart, the poor, little, puerile human heart; God exists, sing heaven, earth, and the world's abysses; God exists respond the abysses of human consciousness and creativity. Glory to him![9]

Therefore, only living religious experience is considered the real way to gain certain knowledge of Divine truth, and proofs of the existence of God are viewed as attestations to an approaching *crisis* in theology. Here we come to

---

5   Merold Westphal, *Transcendence and Self-Transcendence: On God and the Soul* (Bloomington & Indianapolis: Indiana University Press, 2004), 2, 10.

6   Westphal, *Transcendence and Self-Transcendence*, 119 f.

7   See Jonathan R. Seiling, *From Antinomy to Sophiology: Modern Russian Religious Consciousness and Sergei N. Bulgakov's Critical Appropriation of German Idealism* (PhD dissertation, Toronto: University of St. Michael's College, 2008).

8   Bulgakov, *Svet Nevechernii*, 24–25 [ET 23].

9   Ibid., 25 [ET, 24].

one of the central points of Bulgakov's philosophy of religion: the epistemological (*ergo*, ontological) importance of religious experience.[10] Here, Bulgakov is
in line with Russian religious thought, with its dominance of religious experience over abstract knowledge (specifically, proofs of the existence of God)[11]—in
other words, with its "primacy of the spiritual" (Maritain's formula): doxology
("Glory to Him!") comes ultimately before speculative theology:

> How is one to think this revelation of Mystery, this abstraction of the absoluteness
> of the Absolute, such as the revelation of the Absolute to the relative is? No answer
> in human language can be given to this. Not everything is understandable, but God
> is in everything and in this is the great joy of faith and submissiveness. We draw
> near to the abyss where the fiery sword of the archangel again bars to us the further
> path of cognition. It is so—religious experience tells us about this entirely firmly;
> even religious philosophy needs to accept this as the original definition—in the
> humility of reason, for the sacrifice of humility is demanded from reason too, as the
> highest reasonableness of folly. The unutterable, unnameable, incomprehensible,
> unknowable, unthinkable God is revealed to creation in a name, a word, a cult,
> theophanies, incarnation. Glory to Your condescension, O Lord![12]

***

Like many other theologians in Germany[13] and in Russia at that time, Bulgakov was preoccupied with the problems arising from the post-Kantian situa-

---

10   The influence of Florensky, who begins his *The Pillar and the Ground of the Truth* with
     similar reflections.
11   See Christina M. Gschwandtner, "The Category of Experience: Orthodox Theology and
     Contemporary Philosophy," *Journal of Eastern Christian Studies* 69, nos. 1–2 (2017),
     181–221. In relation to Florensky and Bulgakov, Gschwandtner notes (pp. 182–83), "This
     insistence on experience as 'showing' Orthodoxy (and the rejection of proof) might also
     be a slogan to introduce almost all subsequent Orthodox theology in the 20th century.
     Although many Orthodox theologians are either quite critical of Florensky and his
     student Sergius Bulgakov or ignore their work altogether, this emphasis on experience
     as an essential or even the prime characteristic of Orthodox theology is evident in the
     work of most of them."
12   Bulgakov, *Svet Nevechernii*, 136 [ET 159].
13   See Mark D. Chapman, *Ernst Troeltsch and Liberal Theology: Religion and Cultural
     Synthesis in Wilhelmine Germany* (Oxford: OUP, 2001), esp. the chapter "Struggles over
     Epistemology: The Religious A Priori." For a comparison of German and Russian at-
     tempts to apply Kant's transcendental methodology to philosophy of religion see Kirill
     Ukolov, "Problema religioznogo apriori v zapadnoj i russkoj religioznoj filosofii," *Vest-
     nik PSTGU I: Bogoslovie. Filosofija* 29, no. 1 (2010), 25–42.

tion in thought about religion. Those concerns include: unsatisfaction with reductionist—i. e. positivist, psychological and ethicist[14]—accounts of religion and, consequently, justification of religion as a *sui generis* and independent reality. That is why in addition to the above-mentioned emphasis on divine transcendence, *Unfading Light* has a second strong emphasis—on declaring the objective character of religion and faith. To claim their objective nature for Bulgakov means to highlight their direction towards the transcendent, beyond this immediate reality. Two important consequences arise here. First, *pace* Vladimir Soloviev, Sergei Trubetskoi and Nikolay Lossky, Bulgakov distinguishes faith from a "mystical intuition" which remains entirely within the empirically given reality. For those thinkers (as well as for Semen Frank), faith means an "intuitional, pre-discursive perception of the primordial ontical relation between subject and object which Soloviev expressed by the formula: 'we believe that the object *is*.'"[15] Bulgakov is critical towards such a broad use of the term that undermines the objective and transcendent-oriented nature of faith. And it is plausible that Bulgakov had seen in the intuitions of totality, embedded in some of these all-unity projects presupposing the subordination of all spheres of culture to mystical intuition, a mode of thinking which would not be much better than the equally totalizing claims of immanentism that he had struggled with.

Secondly, for the very same reasons Bulgakov doesn't oppose faith and reason/knowledge. According to Bulgakov, faith in God and knowledge of finite beings are qualitatively different acts: faith is transcendent in its orientation while knowledge deals with empirically given reality. Thus, there is no mutual exclusion between faith and knowledge in the sense that faith is epistemically deficient in comparison to knowledge. There is "neither an epistemic hierarchy nor an opposition"[16] between knowledge and faith. Faith, as Bulgakov argues, "is a function not of some individual aspect of the spirit but of the whole human person in its entirety, in the indivisible totality of all the powers of the

14 Such as found, for instance, in the theology of Albrecht Ritschl and his school. Cf. Bulgakov, *Svet Nevechernii*, 42 [ET 43].

15 Teresa Obolevitch, "Faith as the Locus Philosophicus of Russian Thought," in *Faith and Reason in Russian Thought*, ed. Teresa Obolevitch and Pawel Rojek (Krakow: Copernicus Center Press, 2015), 7–23, 15. See Vladimir Soloviev, "Kritika otvlechennyh nachal," in: ibid., *Polnoe sobranie sochinenij i pisem v dvadcati tomah*, vol. 3 (Moscow: Nauka, 2001), 296. Emphasis in the original.

16 Christoph Schneider, "Faith and Reason in Russian Religious Thought: Sergei Bulgakov, Pavel Florensky and the contemporary debate about ontotheology and fideism," *Analogia* 8 (2020), 131–42, 140.

spirit".[17] It has a unitive character and directs all human powers—reason, desire and will—towards their ultimate τέλος, which is God. Thus, Bulgakov sought to recognize the role of faith in all forms of knowledge and the legitimacy of religious experience and language that expresses the data of revelation. And that is why, as it has been noted by scholars,[18] Bulgakov's theological method considers human person in its entirety and has several dimensions: intellectual, spiritual, psychological and ethical. In the framework of this holistic methodology and its unitive character, faith provides a basis for Bulgakov's Sophiology, for it is faith that unites the sophiological system by allowing human beings to grasp a key sophiological characteristic that is not grasped by the rationality of reason—the difference between the Absolute and God the Creator. As a philosophical position, faith made it possible to talk about religious knowledge that did not accept reason, but went beyond it.[19] As Bulgakov puts it,

> There is no logical bridge between the transcendent or the Absolute and the immanent or God: here there is an absolute hiatus, a bottomless abyss. This has to be recognized simply as a fact in all its triumphal obviousness, but also in its definitive incomprehensibility: it is so [...] Although unsolvable, it [the antinomy of religious consciousness] is resolved constantly in religious life, being experienced again and again as the source of religious illuminations in the flame of faith. For the sake of faith, it does not have to be understood to the end; faith is the child of mystery, the spiritual striving of love and freedom. It need not fear the rational absurd, for here eternal life is revealed, the boundlessness of Divinity.[20]

Recognition of this logical hiatus necessarily leads to accepting one's own epistemic humility and consequently to passing from constructing immanentist totalizing systems to a more faithful mode of living and theologizing. "Where divine transcendence is preserved in its deepest sense, the affirmation of God as Creator is not merely the attribution of a certain structure to the cosmos but above all the commitment of oneself to a life of grateful striving."[21] Or in Bulgakov's own poetic words: "The sophianic soul of the world is covered with many veils like the goddess of Sais, and these veils are themselves worn thin ac-

---

17   Bulgakov, *Svet Nevechernii*, 30 [ET 30].
18   Pierro Coda, *L'altro di Dio. Rivelazione e kenosis in Sergej Bulgakov* (Rome, 1998), 58.
19   Seiling, *From Antinomy to Sophiology*, 247.
20   Bulgakov, *Svet Nevechernii*, 93 [ET, 110].
21   Westphal, *Transcendence and Self-Transcendence*, 231.

cording to the measure of the spiritual ascent of humankind."[22] There is a direct relationship between how we describe divine being and what is prescribed for our becoming: these are flip sides of the same coin.[23] Thus, faith in its spiritual and ascetic dimension is closely related to the kenotic decentration of the self, or self-transcendence. As Bulgakov puts it, faith

> is the highest and final sacrifice of a human being to God—himself, his reason, will, heart, his whole essence, the whole world, all evidence, and is a completely disin-terested exploit, giving away everything and demanding nothing. It is the love of humankind for God exclusively and for the sake of God himself; it is salvation from the self, from one's givenness, from one's immanence; it is hatred of the self, which is love for God. It is a mute, imploring, searching gesture, it is a single aspiration: *sursum* corda, sursum, sursum, sursum, excelsior! […] Here a sacrifice is offered by oneself and the world (which here signifies one and the same thing) for the sake of the supramundane and supernal, for the sake of the Father who is in heaven.[24]

Here the self is called away from satisfaction with its earthly preoccupations, its autonomy and egoism. This kenotic account of faith points us in the direction of ways in which a deeper appreciation of divine *otherness* might be gained. One needs to sacrifice everything—and most of all, one's ego—so that God can be properly addressed in an act of faith. This needs to be done so that God as the Other can enter our experience on His own terms and not ours.

Later in the book Bulgakov will once again return to the figure of God as the Other (this time speaking specifically about Christ) and about the necessity of self-transcendence, while asserting the intersubjective—i. e., ecclesial—dimension of religious consciousness:

> One must hate oneself for the sake of Christ and love him more than oneself, and then in his universal face will be revealed for each one their own face. Each will find themselves in the Other, and this Other is Christ. And finding themselves in the Other, being aware of the source of life in love for them, people will communicate in the mystery of the Holy Trinity, the mutual emptying of the Divine Hypostases in reciprocal love, the blessedness of life in the Other and through the Other. The

---

22 Bulgakov, *Svet Nevechernii*, 196 [ET, 229].
23 Westphal, *Transcendence and Self-Transcendence*, 2.
24 Bulgakov, *Svet Nevechernii*, 33 [ET, 33]. Bulgakov's emphasis.

human spirit is lifted up to unattainable heights and the human person shines in the beauty of that image after which and for the sake of which it is created.[25]

The place where such a Trinitarian experience is possible, which has not only a soteriological, but also an epistemological nature, is the Church. This experience is possible thanks to living in the Church, but living inasmuch as "they themselves become Church, men and women receive Christ into themselves."[26] And there is only one condition under which a person becomes the Church: to voluntarily sacrifice his personality, to lose his soul "in order to save it from selfishness and impenetrability, to open to it the joys of love-humility. That sick, Luciferian I which is aware of itself in opposition to every other I as to Not-I, must acquire compatibility with it and through it receive a positive and not only a negative definition."[27] Thus, it becomes clear why any conscience that seeks to establish itself on the foundation of true and absolute truth transcends the world; this is a uniting and conciliar event, according to the words spoken before the Creed during the Divine Liturgy: "let us love one another and confess with one mind."[28]

This sacrificial, dynamic nature of faith finds its culmination in prayer, "the fundamental form of religious achievement κατ'ἐξοχήν".[29] Bulgakov remarks in a footnote that the works of church asceticism are filled with a doctrine of prayer, but "the phenomenological analysis of prayer is entirely lacking."[30] So, what he sketches further can indeed be called an "outline of the phenomenology of prayer".[31] Answering the question as to what prayer represents according to its "transcendental makeup," Bulgakov highlights that its transcendental

---

25   Bulgakov, *Svet Nevechernii*, 300 [ET, 358].
26   Ibid., 299 [ET 357]. See Lubomir Žak, "L'attualità della teologia di Bulgakov in dialogo con l'Occidente," in *La teologia ortodossa e l'Occidente nel XX secolo. Storia di un incontro*, ed. Adriano Dell'Asta (Bergamo: La Casa di Matriona, 2005), 92–111.
27   Bulgakov, *Svet Nevechernii*, 300 [ET 357].
28   Žak, "L'attualità della teologia di Bulgakov," 138. See Bulgakov, *Svet Nevechernii*, 300 [ET 357] and 53 f. [ET 58 f.]. Antonov argues that Bulgakov draws here on Sergei Trubetskoy and his concept of conciliarity of consciousness (*sobornost' soznanija*) and his understanding of consciousness as an intersubjective "universal process." Konstantin Antonov, *Kak vozmozhna religija? Filosofija religii i filosofskie problemy bogoslovija v russkoj religioznoj mysli XIX-XX vv*. In two pts. Pt. 1 (Moscow: PSTGU, 2020), 396. See Sergey Trubetskoy, "O prirode chelovecheskogo soznaniya," in ibid., *Sochineniya* (Moscow: Mysl', 1994), 495–98.
29   Bulgakov, *Svet Nevechernii*, 25 [ET 24].
30   Ibid., 26 [ET 443].
31   Antonov, *Kak vozmozhna religija?*, 391.

content includes "the striving of all the spiritual forces of a human being, of the whole human person, for the Transcendent".[32] Prayer for Bulgakov is thus an act of human self-transcendence *par excellence*. As in the case of faith, it connects human beings to the divine, to something beyond themselves and beyond immediate reality: in prayer, the transcendent becomes an "object of human aspiration as such, precisely as God, as something absolutely other, and not the world, not a human being." And it is precisely this connection that distinguishes prayer from its "theosophical surrogates"—"concentration, meditation, and intuition"—that "do not deal with God but with the world."[33] (Note the same "transcendent-directed vs. empirically-oriented" argumentation as in the case of faith.)

Any prayer, says Bulgakov referring to Augustin, calls on: *transcende te ipsum*.[34] Praying, one thus makes an effort to come out of oneself, to rise above oneself. Bulgakov uses Augustin's expression—inherited from the symbolist poet and philosopher Vyacheslav Ivanov[35]—twice in the book, in different parts but both times while speaking about prayer. Transcending, coming out of oneself, necessarily implies emptying a space within oneself. To speak phenomenologically, emptying a space within ourselves allows us to prepare a space for the appearance of the Divine. In the words of Pseudo-Dyonisios: "We should be taken wholly out of ourselves and become wholly of God, since it is better to belong to God rather than to ourselves."[36] Or, as Westphal puts it, prayer "is a deep, quite possibly the deepest decentering of the self, deep enough to begin dismantling or, if you like, deconstructing that burning preoccupation with

32 Bulgakov, *Svet Nevechernii*, 25 [ET 24].
33 Ibid., 26–27 [ET 25].
34 Augustin of Hippo, *De vera religione*, XXXIX, 72. Bulgakov also uses this Latin expression in an article on Tolstoy, "Chelovek i hudozhnik" [The Man and the Artist] (1912).
35 Ivanov has a poem with such a title (1904), where one may uncover references to Augustine's idea of *transcensus sui* as an early Platonic concept of self-transcendence. See Maria Cymborska-Leboda, "O ponjatii 'transcenzusa' u Vjacheslava Ivanova: k probleme 'Vjacheslav Ivanov i Blazhennyj Avgustin'," in *Sub Rosa. Köszöntő könyv Léna Szilárd tiszteletére*, ed. Denise Atanaszova-Szokolova (Budapest: ELTE BTK Irodalomtudományi Doktori Iskola, 2005), 123–32. On Ivanov's concepts "transcende te ipsum" and "YOU ARE," which are so influential in *Unfading Light*, see Michael Aksionov Meerson, *The Trinity of Love in Modern Russian Theology: The Love Paradigm and the Retrieval of Western Medieval Love Mysticism in Modern Russian Trinitarian Thought (from Solovyov to Bulgakov)* (Quincy, Il.: Franciscan Press, 1998), 63–78.
36 Pseudo-Dionysius, *The Divine Names*, in ibid., *The Complete Works*, trans. Colm Luibheid (Mahwah, N.Y.: Paulist Press, 1987), 106.

myself".[37] Practicing self-emptying, we find ourselves open and receptive before
the Divine, which can incarnate itself in our behavior and bodily being. Or, to
speak with more traditional patristic metaphors, "the purified soul becomes
a mirror of divine perfection" (Gregory of Nyssa). Sharing in the divine is a
"disorienting experience, where we lose all our familiar bearings as we mingle
with a reality which is so close as to be almost part of us and yet at the same
time utterly transcendent."[38]

Bulgakov highlights the kenotic/sacrificial nature of prayer once again
when speaking about the theurgic dimension of sacraments. But what is more
interesting is that he also speaks about the creative or even artistic nature of
prayer:

> Prayer itself is always a sacrifice to God, a sacrificial giving back of the human ele-
> ment, but to that extent it is also a creative act. Here the straining of all the powers
> of a spiritual being in a single burst to God is creative effort: *transcende te ipsum.*
> If sophianic creativity strives for some insight, for artistic achievement, and thus is
> expressed in *creation*, then prayerful creativity, 'spiritual artistry,' 'noetic doing,' is
> realized fully in the *act* itself, in prayer and communion with God.[39]

Creative essentially means transformative. There is no doubt that praying we
find ourselves in the process of change. It has a transformative effect on our
passions, so that we learn to love and live differently.[40] In the prayerful words
of St. Paul: "May the God of peace himself sanctify you entirely; and may your
spirit and soul and body be kept sound and blameless at the coming of our Lord
Jesus Christ" (I Thess. 5:23). Prayer inspires and structures human life so that
it becomes true and faithful. And as a transformative force, prayer is to be the
most basic and daily activity. That is one of the reasons why Bulgakov mentions
the "Jesus prayer" as the very exemplification of prayer. "A religious genius,"
Bulgakov writes, "is necessarily an adept of prayer and in essence the whole of

---

37 Merold Westphal, "Prayer as the Posture of the Decentered Self," in *The Phenomenology of Prayer*, ed. Bruce Ellis Benson and Norman Wirzba (New York: Fordham University Press, 2005), 13–31, 15. See also James Mensch's "Prayer as Kenosis" in the same volume, 63–74.

38 Norman Russell, *Fellow Workers with God: Orthodox Thinking on Theosis* (Yonkers, N. Y.: Saint Vladimir's Seminary Press, 2009), 87.

39 Bulgakov, *Svet Nevechernii*, 323 [ET 389]. Smith's translation modified.

40 Bruce Ellis Benson and Norman Wirzba, "Introduction," in *The Phenomenology of Prayer*, ed. Bruce Ellis Benson and Norman Wirzba (New York: Fordham University Press, 2005), 1–9, 2.

Christian asceticism only teaches the art of prayer, having as its highest goal unceasing ('automatic') prayer, the 'Jesus prayer,' or 'noetic activity,' i. e., the unceasing striving towards the transcendent Divinity by immanent consciousness".[41] All that we do needs to become part of prayer. Or, as the Benedictine motto has it, *laborare est orare.*[42]

Prayerful self-transcendence is directed towards the union with God, and this union is achieved according to Bulgakov in the central element of prayer, which is invocation of the Name of God. "The Name of God," Bulgakov writes, "is, as it were, the intersection[43] of two worlds, the transcendent in the immanent, and hence beside its common theological sense 'name-worship' is in a certain manner the transcendental condition of prayer that constitutes the possibility of religious experience."[44] For God is experienced through prayer, the heart of which is the *naming* of Him, and He, as Bulgakov argues, "confirms this name, recognizes this name as His own, not only responding to it, but also being really present in it."[45]

Here one finds the outlines of the theme that Bulgakov will be developing in his *Philosophy of Name*: the real presence of God in His name invoked by the praying person. According to Bulgakov, God reveals Himself in human consciousness, so that the Divine Names come from God through man. They are not just human concepts, but are the result of συνέργεια, of divine and human activity together: "the naming of God is accomplished in man and through man; it is his act, an awakening of his theophoric and theophanic potential, a realization of the image of God contained in him, a realization of his primordial divine-humanity."[46] Thus, prayerful kenotic posture witnessing of human finitude finds its *Aufhebung*, to use the famous Hegelian concept, in disclosure of human sophianic potentiality. In calling God's name human beings start their journey on the way to theosis, "in the process burnishing their likeness or similitude with their Creator."[47]

---

41 Bulgakov, *Svet Nevechernii*, 26 [ET, 25].

42 Benson and Wirzba, "Introduction," 2.

43 It should be noted that Slesinski modifies Smith's translation: "suppression" (*presechenie*) instead of "intersection" (*peresechenie*). Robert F. Slesinski, *The Theology of Sergius Bulgakov* (Yonkers, N. Y.: Saint Vladimir's Seminary Press, 2019), 219.

44 Bulgakov, *Svet Nevechernii*, 26 [ET 25].

45 Ibid., 26 [ET 25].

46 Sergius Bulgakov, "The Name of God," in ibid., *Icons and the Name of God*, trans. Boris Jakim (Grand Rapids: W. B. Eerdmans, 2012), 116.

47 Slesinski, *The Theology of Sergius Bulgakov*, 237.

Prayer thus appears in Bulgakov's thought "as the starting point of religious life in general, occupies the place that cult occupies in the thought of the later Florenskii, and revelation in Berdiaev's thought."[48] Or, as Robert Slesinski puts it, "it is thus in prayer, according to Bulgakov, that human beings truly transcend themselves, thereby *fulfilling their vocation qua humans* in a *lived encounter with the Divine.*"[49]

Conclusion: Reuniting Theology and Spirituality

Bulgakov's "struggle for transcendence" in *Unfading Light* led him to outline a holistic philosophy of religion that would combine insights into the nature of religious consciousness provided by German idealism with the distinctive features of Orthodox theology,[50] including its contradictory unity of mystical and rational-discursive aspects, and thus would be able to form the premise of an antinomian representation of the contents of revelation without falling into immanentist/onto-theological modes of thinking.

Recognizing the fundamental role of faith, prayer—both communal and personal—and kenotic self-transcendence for theology, Bulgakov takes us back as if to the first centuries of Christianity, to its very nature, while at the same time trying to preserve our post-Kantian and postmodern consciousness. As Andrew Louth notes, Bulgakovian thought intrinsically combines both

> a systematic account of the objective truths of revelation with the root question of the anthropological approach: how do we know any of this? and also: how does this make sense of my human experience? This leads him to be concerned for the *place, as it were, from which we behold the revelation of the glory of God: standing before God in prayer*, fundamentally in the Divine Liturgy. The human being stands before God in prayer and beholds the revelation of God, participates in it, and is caught up with it—and, in particular, for Bulgakov, is drawn towards the fulness of the revelation of God at the end of time.[51]

---

48 Antonov, *Kak vozmozhna religija?*, 392.
49 Slesinski, *The Theology of Sergius Bulgakov*, 219. First emphasis mine.
50 Paul Gavrilyuk stresses four distinctive features of Orthodox epistemology: ontologism, apophaticism, holism and theosis. All of them are present in Bulgakov's works. Paul Gavrilyuk, "Modern Orthodox Thinkers," in *The Oxford Handbook of the Epistemology of Theology*, ed. Frederick D. Aquino and William J. Abraham (Oxford: Oxford University Press, 2017), 578–90.
51 Andrew Louth, "Sergii Bulgakov and the Task of Theology," *Irish Theological Quarterly* 74 (2009), 243–57, 252. Emphasis mine.

Striving to reunite speculative theology with the living experience of faith, Bulgakov symbolizes a spirituality that is premodern, but at the same time he also anticipates many insights of postmodern philosophy with its attention to the theme of alterity and critique of onto-theological thinking. From this living unity arises his perception of the experience of faith as the true foundation of a theological act. For Bulgakov, theology is an act that cannot be understood as a reasoning about some givenness or some kind of experience that one might approach "from the outside," without having the intellect filled at the deepest level with the novelty of the experience of faith.[52] This experience of faith is gained daily in the transformative act of prayer. One thus might recall in this regard the famous formula of Evagrius: "If you are a theologian, you will pray truly. And if you pray truly, you are a theologian." This clearly shows how Bulgakov saw the task of doing theology: if one is to inquire about God's essence, then this essence is to be the essence of an interlocutor.[53] This indissoluble link between theology and spirituality would later find its peak in Bulgakov's major theological writings, but the seed is planted already in *Unfading Light*. For this is what Bulgakov comes to when he points out that the fundamental content of religion is not an abstract "God exists" but a personal "YOU ARE."

---

52 Coda, *L'altro di Dio*, 58.
53 Westphal, *Transcendence and Self-Transcendence*, 97.

Building the House of Wisdom
DOI 10.17438/978-3-402-12176-4

The Kenotic Iconicity of Sergii Bulgakov's Divine-Humanity: Doctrinal, Anthropological, and Feminist Considerations

Sarah Elizabeth Livick-Moses

> *In the art of antiquity this icon creation attains true heights of sublimity.*
> *This icon creation is direct artistic testimony about [humanity's] likeness*
> *to God, a testimony that religiously justifies its general task.*
> *In antiquity's icon veneration two questions were clearly posed:*
> *What does the image of God in [humanity] consist in,*
> *and if this image of God is portrayable, how is it portrayable?*
> (Sergii Bulgakov, *Icons and the Name of God*, 56)

Introduction

In her article on the gendered dimensions of Hans Urs von Balthasar's theology, Jennifer Newsome Martin comments on "the 'subterranean lines of filiation' between Balthasar and the emigré 'Russian School' of Russian Orthodoxy, particularly Sergii Bulgakov, whose highly gendered sophiological commitments are inseparable from his protology, anthropology, and kenotic trinitarianism."[1] Martin's comments on Bulgakov are made in her consideration of Balthasar's understanding of gender and cosmological anthropology, and the alleged inseparability of this understanding from his larger theological project. This paper will provide a partner piece to Martin's that evaluates the same set of questions along Bulgakovian lines. It will treat Bulgakov's liturgical context and iconographic hermeneutics, address his notion of Image and Proto-Image in

---

1   Jennifer Newsome Martin, "The 'Whence' and the 'Whither' of Balthasar's Gendered Theology: Rehabilitating Kenosis for Feminist Theology," *Modern Theology* 31, no. 2 (2015), 213.

his doctrine of Divine-Humanity, and trace the implications of this doctrine for his anthropology. The consequences of Bulgakov's iconicity for a feminist retrieval will be demonstrated in the last part of the paper while we consider the intersection of Bulgakov's doctrine of God, the icon, and current concerns regarding gender and sexuality, essentialism, and theological anthropology. While his protology reveals an undesirable complementarity between the sexes, Bulgakov's more fundamental iconology illustrates a liberative anthropology to be found in the doctrine of Sophia. It is this which I seek to retrieve.

Theology from the Bottom of the Chalice: Liturgy and Icon

In his article, "Sergii Bulgakov and the Task of Theology," Fr. Andrew Louth argues that the entire cosmological vision of Bulgakov's systematic theology can be best understood through the ritual observation of the liturgy.[2] He writes especially about Bulgakov's fundamental belief in the mutual influence of the life of prayer and the development of systematic theology. The liminal nature of liturgical celebration well reflects Bulgakov's own antinomic methodology. Liturgy is both temporal and always already participating in the eternal liturgy of the Heavenly Kingdom in the presence of the angels and the choir of saints. It is "together with these blessed powers" that worship is repeatedly offered in the liturgy of St. John Chrysostom.[3] Although a critic of Bulgakov's more contentious theological statements, Fr. Alexander Schmemann remained an admirer of Bulgakov, most especially inspired by his deeply liturgical disposition. It is liturgy which informs Bulgakov's perception of all things—including his theological inquiry.

> For the theology of Fr. Sergii, at its most profound, is precisely and above all liturgi-
> cal—it is the revelation of an experience received in divine worship, the transmis-
> sion of this mysterious 'glory,' which penetrates the entire service of this 'mystery' in
> which it is rooted and of which it is the 'epiphany.' The liturgy is the manifestation
> of God in the world as God created it, revealing the divine roots of creation and
> transfiguring it to become that in which God is 'all in all.'[4]

---

2   Andrew Louth, "Sergei Bulgakov and the Task of Theology," *Irish Theological Quarterly*, 74, 3 (2009), 243–257.

3   Greek Orthodox Archdiocese of America, "The Divine Liturgy of Saint John Chrysostom," https://www.goarch.org/-/the-divine-liturgy-of-saint-john-chrysostom (access 2024/01/26).

4   Alexander Schmemann quoted in Louth, "Sergei Bulgakov and the Task of Theology," 249.

Serving as a priest in the Russian Orthodox Church certainly informed Bulgakov's liturgical vision. Bulgakov consistently held the duality of memorial and eschatological hope throughout his theological works. Indeed, one of the "strongest features [liturgical theologians] note about the liturgical temporality is the paradox or tension evident in its texts and practices between anamnesis (memory) and eschaton (anticipation)."[5] At the heart of the cosmological import of liturgy lies the iconographic imprint of divinity in the world according to the kenotic nature of the Trinity and the correlativity between Creator and creation. The icon fully represents the incarnational mediation of this ontological reality and while it remains true that he drew the whole of this theological vision "from the bottom of the eucharistic chalice,"[6] it is also true that he communicates this theological reality through an iconographic construction.

The preeminence of liturgy in the Eastern Orthodox context is intimately associated with the devotional practice of icon veneration; liturgy and icon are inextricably bound. In his review of Bulgakov's *Icons and the Name of God*[7] and C. A. Tsakiridou's *Icons in Time, Persons in Eternity*,[8] Rowan Williams comments on the iconographic mediation of divine presence in the liturgical space. "The icon in some sense stops being a human artefact when it is blessed for use: every icon is—as far as liturgical use is concerned—acheiropoietos, 'not made with hands,' like those legendary images imprinted directly by divine action; every icon is 'wonderworking,' a site of divine intervention."[9] Already we can see the centrality of Bulgakov's doctrine of Divine-Humanity in his theological

---

5 Christina M. Gschwandtner, *Welcoming Finitude: Toward a Phenomenology of Orthodox Liturgy* (New York: Fordham University Press, 2019), 35. This work is particularly important in the current discourse of liturgy at the intersection of theology and phenomenological analysis. Gschwandtner offers an excellent and insightful philosophical study of liturgical practice, ritual, space, time, and sensuality. For more of her comments specifically relevant to the work of Bulgakov, see especially her first chapter, "Temporality," 31–56.

6 Quoted in Louth, "Sergei Bulgakov and the Task of Theology," 249: Sister Joanna Reitlinger, "The Final Days of Father Sergius Bulgakov: A Memoir," in Sergius Bulgakov: *Apocatastasis and Transfiguration* (New Haven, CT: The Variable Press, 1995), 31–53; Boris Bobrinskoy, *La compassion du Père* (Paris: Éditions du Cerf, 2000), 160, and see also 173; Boris Bobrinskoy, *La mystère de la Trinité* (1986; repr. Paris: Éditions du Cerf, 1996), 149.

7 Sergius Bulgakov, *Icons and the Name of God*, trans. Boris Jakim (Grand Rapids: W. B. Eerdmans, 2012).

8 C. A. Tsakiridou, *Icons in Time, Persons in Eternity* (London: Routledge, 2013).

9 Rowan Williams, Review: "Icons and the Name of God/Icons in Time, Persons in Eternity." *Art & Christianity*, no. 76 (Winter 2013): 12–13.

corpus. The dogmatic significance of icons established at the Seventh Council of Nicaea (AD 787), and its inherent Christologic,[10] remains for Bulgakov both a fundamental part of tradition and a means of theological innovation.

> No pre-established forms are prescribed for the tradition of the Church: the Holy Spirit that lives in her "bloweth where it listeth." In this respect, as sources of the sacred tradition, the canons, the patristic writings, the liturgical texts, and the icons are of equal value. All this—not in isolation but in its living and organic totality—expresses the truth of the Church.[11]

Unafraid to approach the tradition in a constructive and incorporative method, Bulgakov finds in the liturgical veneration of icons an untapped resource for considering the "eternal correlativity"[12] of divinity and humanity. To understand the unified personhood of the Son, and his position as the cosmic embodiment of Divine-Humanity, it is pertinent to also comprehend Bulgakov's language of Image and Proto-Image.

---

10 Sergius Bulgakov, *The Lamb of God*, trans. Boris Jakim (Grand Rapids: W. B. Eerdmans, 2008), 88.

11 Sergius Bulgakov, *The Friend of the Bridegroom: On the Orthodox Veneration of the Forerunner*, trans. Boris Jakim (Grand Rapids: W. B. Eerdmans, 2003), 137.

12 On correlativity: "Eternity and temporality are correlative, without intruding into each other or interfering with each other. In no wise and in no sense can temporality diminish or limit eternity, for it belongs to a different ontological plane. One can say that eternity is the noumenon of time and time is the phenomenon of eternity. They are linked by a relation of foundation and being, but there can be no mixture or confusion between them, and they cannot limit one another. The imprint of God's eternity therefore lies upon all of creation, for it is the revelation of His eternity." "God, as the Creator who is correlated with time, does not stop being the eternal God; on the contrary, it is precisely His eternal Divinity that is the foundation for His creation. If He were not the Absolute in Himself, God would not be the Creator, just as, conversely, since He is the Absolute, He is revealed in the relative—that is, He creates the world." *The Lamb of God*, 135. "The Lord is always creator, now and forever and unto the ages of ages. Consequently in some sense the creature is co-eternal with the Creator, as light coexists with the sun, although eternity is realized for it in temporality." Sergius Bulgakov, *Unfading Light: Contemplations and Speculations*, trans. Thomas Allan Smith (Grand Rapids: W. B. Eerdmans, 2012), 210.

Kenotic Impressions: Proto-Image, Image, and Divine-Humanity

A fundamental insight into Bulgakov's entire systematic theology is that there is more to be positively developed about the *interrelation* between divinity and humanity than has been accomplished in the history of dogmatic theology. While this is considered primarily in the Christological vein of Bulgakov's work, it is also a question which already presupposes a certain theology of creation and Trinity. Christ is the eternal Image of the Proto-Image, that is, the Father. The Father's love pours forth from himself towards an Other who can receive and return it in full. This is the eternal begetting of the Son.

In his essay in *The Oxford Handbook of the Trinity*, Aristotle Papanikolaou argues, "The Son, therefore, is the Image of the Father, the Word of the Father in which is contained all words; the 'objective self-revelation' (Bulgakov 1993: 43) of the Father, the Truth of the Father, and, as such, the divine content (Bulgakov 2008: 111)."[13] It should be noted that Papanikolaou's comments on the Son here do not address the sophiological context of the passage which he cites from *Sophia: The Wisdom of God* (Bulgakov 1993: 43), though he later addresses the complexity of Sophia as God's *ousia* of revelation.[14] While it is not the central point of reflection for our study, mention should be made of how Bulgakov develops his comments on the Son's imaging of the Father precisely within the sophiological register. "The imprint of the self-revealing hypostatic love of the begetting Father and of the begotten Son, of the Proto-Image and of the Image, lies also on the Divine world, in the Divine Sophia."[15] Sophia plays a vital role in Bulgakov's systematic theology, *particularly* in his discussion of Divine-Humanity and his non-contrastive theological grammar.[16] The connection here between Sophia and Bulgakov's language of Proto-Image and Image within the Trinitarian relations emphasizes that his language of icon and image already

13   Aristotle Papanikolaou, "Contemporary Orthodox Currents on the Trinity," in *The Oxford Handbook of the Trinity*, eds. Emery, Gilles, and Matthew Levering (Oxford: Oxford University Press, 2011), 329.

14   Ibid., 330.

15   Bulgakov, *The Lamb of God*, 111. For more on the role of Sophia in Bulgakov's doctrine of God, see the chapters, "The Divine Sophia" and "The Creaturely Sophia" in *The Lamb of God*. Additional resources include Bulgakov's *Sophia: The Wisdom of God* and Andrew Louth's article "Father Sergeii Bulgakov on the Doctrine of the Trinity," in *A Transforming Vision: Knowing and Loving the Triune God*, ed. George Westhaver (London: SCM Press, 2018), 183–91.

16   For more on non-contrastive grammar, see Kathryn Tanner's *God and Creation in Christian Theology: Tyranny or Empowerment* (Oxford and New York: Blackwell, 1988).

presupposes his doctrine of God's kenotic love. The imprint of this sophianic and iconographic lens in Bulgakov's anthropology might helpfully contribute to contemporary theologies of the body which seek to avoid the polarities of materialism and angelization.

The Son's knowledge of the Father is the self-objective understanding of the divine Icon, a relationship of "mutual mirroring" which is ultimately accomplished in the Incarnation.[17] The mirroring of the Son as the Image of the Proto-Image (Father) is characterized most formally by the sharing of intra-Trinitarian kenotic love. The Father's begetting is itself a kenotic act.

> The Father acquires Himself as His nature, not in Himself and for Himself, but in proceeding out of Himself and in begetting, as the Father, the Son. Fatherhood is precisely the form of love in which the loving one desires to have himself not in himself but outside himself, in order to give his own to this other I, but an I identified with him.[18]

The Holy Spirit, too, participates in the Trinity as the very reality of the Son and the Father's love, and it is only by the Holy Spirit that "the *reality* of this nature [of kenotic mutuality] is experienced."[19]

The kenosis of the Son in the Incarnation is thus grounded in the nature of his divine essence and is not his exclusive personal property. The particularity of the Incarnation is maintained, however, as the full manifestation of God's relationship to humanity; this is what Paul Gavrilyuk terms the "kenosis *par excellence*" in Bulgakov's system.[20] "The Proto-Image and the Image are united by a certain identity that establishes between them a positive interrelation and announces the Incarnation to come."[21] The kenosis of the Incarnation is distinct, though never separate, from the kenotic character of the intra-Trinitarian relations and its subsequent outpouring into creation. It reveals the preeminent desire of divinity to be in full communion with humanity and motivates Bulgakov's confidence that the Incarnation is necessary regardless of the Fall.

---

17   Papanikolaou, "Contemporary Orthodox Currents," 329.
18   Bulgakov, *The Lamb of God*, 98.
19   Ibid., 100.
20   Paul L. Gavrilyuk, "The Kenotic Theology of Sergius Bulgakov," *Scottish Journal of Theology* 58 (2005), 253.
21   Bulgakov, *The Lamb of God*, 138.

According to the direct testimony of Scripture, the coming of Christ into the world, the Incarnation, is predetermined before the creation of the world [...] God's pre-eternal design manifested His love for creation, which did not stop at the creation but went beyond it; as the act of the new creation of the world, it determined the descent into the world of God Himself, that is, the Incarnation.[22]

I diverge from Papanikolaou when he writes that Bulgakov holds a "striking affinity" with Barth's assertion of "the Father as the revealing hypostasis, the Son as the revealed hypostasis, and the Holy Spirit as the revelation." Indeed, Bulgakov explicitly rejects the statement that the Father is the revealing person of the Trinity.[23] Bulgakov is clear that, "In the Holy Trinity, the Father is the revealed hypostasis, not a revealing hypostasis, and He is revealed in the Son."[24] And again, "A fundamental difference also exists between the First hypostasis on the one hand and the Second and Third hypostases on the other: the First hypostasis is the revealed hypostasis, whereas the Second and the Third are the revealing hypostases."[25] This understanding of revelation is contingent on Bulgakov's assertion that the immanent and economic Trinity must be identified as one and the same divine reality.[26] If the Incarnation of the Son, and the Holy Spirit's participation therein, is the fulfillment of God's kenotic nature, then it is precisely in the economy that God's immanence is revealed. This has major implications for Bulgakov's iconographic anthropology.

---

22 Bulgakov, *The Lamb of God*, 168–69.
23 Papanikolaou, "Contemporary Orthodox Currents," 329. Papanikolaou does acknowledge that the Son and Holy Spirit are the revealing hypostasis earlier on the same page, primarily with the Father's revelation to Godself through the other persons. His connection to Barth's axiom still does not seem tenable, however, given Bulgakov's explicit comments to the contrary, though his observations about the revelation of God to Godself do pair well with some of Barth's notions of revelation and divine knowledge. Andrew Louth also identifies Bulgakov's emphasis on the Son and the Holy Spirit as the revealing hypostases in "Father Sergei Bulgakov."
24 Bulgakov, *The Lamb of God*, 166.
25 Bulgakov, *The Lamb of God*, 304.
26 Note that the famous Rahnerian *Grundaxiom* seems to first appear in the work of Bulgakov, *The Lamb of God* being originally published in 1933, thirty-four years prior to the publication of Karl Rahner's essay on *The Trinity* ("Der dreifaltige Gott als transzendenter Urgund der Heilsgeschichte," in *Die Heilsgeschichte vor Christus*, vol. 2 of *Mysterium Salutis, Grundriss heilsgeschichtlicher Dogmatik*).

Image and Likeness

As much as the Son is the eternally begotten Image of the Father as the Proto-Image of divinity, so too is humanity made in the image of the eternally kenotic Trinity. To be made in the image and likeness of God is already to anticipate the Divine-Humanity accomplished by Christ in the Incarnation. The "spiritual being [humanity] is rooted in Divine eternity; the creaturely spirit has an eternity that is analogous to the Divine, and it is uncreated."[27] This is not to say that there is a pre-existent humanity in heaven, as if it might operate from its own ontological foundation. Instead, the divine origins of humanity work in Bulgakov as a form of exemplarism, the fullness of all images grounded in the Proto-Image and eternally "rooted in divine life."[28] The manifestation of the Proto-Image in creaturely hypostases, however, remains distinct from the revelation and accomplishment of humanity's divine image by the Son and the Holy Spirit.

Bulgakov does not argue for a simple outline of the human person as created in the image of the Trinity. While he claims that "Man is an uncreated-created, divine-cosmic being, divine-human in his structure by his very origin," and "is the living image of the trihypostatic God in His Wisdom,"[29] Bulgakov's distinction between the Proto-Image (Father) and the other Trinitarian persons introduces a complication which requires further interrogation. The previous emphasis on Father's role as the *revealed* hypostasis is essential here.

The Paternal Hypostasis, as the eternal and divine Proto-Image, is not revealed to creation "in its own countenance, but through the Son and the Holy Spirit," and thus cannot be the direct Proto-Image of humanity's divine imprint. Rather, the Incarnation of the Son in the economy eternally precedes the creation of the world. Christ is the Lamb slain before the foundation of the world,[30] and thus acts as the image in which the first Adam is made. "Man is created in the image of God, but this means that he is created in the image of Christ; for man, Christ is the revelation and accomplishment of this image."[31] The natures in Christ are not arbitrarily related; it is not divinity's taking on of something external to God (for there is no 'inside' or 'outside' of God), but instead "the ontologically grounded and pre-established union of the Proto-Image and the

27   Bulgakov, *The Lamb of God*, 91.
28   Ibid., 139.
29   Ibid., 140.
30   Rev. 13:8, Eph. 1:4, NRSV.
31   Bulgakov, *The Lamb of God*, 139.

image, of the heavenly Man and the earthly man."[32] This incorporates the bodily connotations to Bulgakov's understanding of image. The image is given not only to either spirit or body, but to the singular hypostasis of the spiritual-psycho-corporeal human.[33] The whole human person (body, soul, and spirit) is made as the image of the Divine-Human content of the Son, "worthy of veneration and portrayable on icons."[34]

Despite his decisive statement that humanity is made in the image of Christ, to read Bulgakov's anthropology only on a Christological level would be to contradict the earlier citations concerning the Trinitarian image of humanity. The significance of Bulgakov's identity between immanent and economic Trinity is once again relevant.

Because the entire Trinity is revealed in the Incarnation, and the Incarnate Word is fully divine, the entire content of the Trinity is revealed in Christ, although the Father and the Spirit are revealed differently than the Son Himself. Because the Father is only revealed by the Son and the Spirit, "the image of the human hypostasis can only come from the hypostases that *reveal* the Father, both in his proper divine world and in the creaturely world."[35] Humanity thus has a "double Proto-Image, which belongs to the heavenly humanity in its two countenances: the Logos and the Holy Spirit."[36] Notice here that the language of Proto-Image is used not in relation to the Father as the Proto-Image of the Son, but according to the Son and Spirit as the Proto-Images of humanity. Sophia is the proper content of the world's Divine-Humanity, the creaturely Sophia existing as the image of the Divine Sophia. Because Sophia is hypostasized as both the Son and the Spirit, "All *iconicity* is based on this relation between the trihypostatic God and His Image, the Wisdom [Sophia] of God, which is the world's Proto-Image in Divinity Itself, and on the relation of the world's Proto-Image to the world as its creaturely image."[37] It is this same Divine Sophia which holds as its content the eternal Divine-Humanity, which is fully realized in the Son's Incarnation and the Spirit's resting upon him.[38]

Sophia is to be understood as being that eternally hypostasizable *ousia* of God, disclosed in revelation by the Son and the Spirit but not exclusive to any

---

32   Bulgakov, *The Lamb of God*, 17.
33   Ibid., 139.
34   Note that for Bulgakov the body is not equivalent with flesh or matter. Bulgakov, *Icons and the Name of God*, 61.
35   Bulgakov, *The Lamb of God*, 140.
36   Ibid., 140.
37   Ibid., 54.
38   Ibid., 55.

one divine person. As much as Divine-Humanity is made manifest and brought to completion in the person of Christ, there is something about Divinity Itself which already includes the Heavenly Humanity.

> One can say that the very Image of God in God [the Son] is the Heavenly Human-
> ity, and that the Proto-Image according to which the anthropocosm was created
> is precisely this Heavenly Humanity. And man is the image of this Proto-Image;
> the earthly Adam is the image of the Heavenly Adam, as the creaturely Sophia, the
> living Icon of Divinity.[39]

Therefore, to say that humanity is made in the image of Christ, while holding a double Proto-Image from the Son and the Spirit, and also maintaining that humanity is made in the image of the Trinity, is to express in varying accounts the same divine sophianic reality.

Having treated the major themes that Bulgakov develops in his understanding of the "image," we will turn briefly to how "likeness" is understood in light of this image. The likeness of which humanity is capable is found most foundationally in the kenotic reflection of divinity. It is the acknowledgement of humanity's kenotic roots in the life of the Trinity. The idolatry of sin takes the divine image found in humanity as God in Godself, using the capacity for self-positing for "solitary I-ness."[40] This is what allows for humanity's self-deception in which "he considers himself to be his own source and proto-image, [transforming] his creaturely I into a pseudo-divine I."[41] This subsequently extinguishes the love which should more naturally be the content of the image divinized by the grace of God. The alternative for the self-positing I is for the creaturely self to acknowledge in humility her existence as an image of her Proto-Image—she can only "be understood in all the sublimity and absoluteness of its calling."[42] Human desire is thus fundamental to its divine ground, intimately intertwined with the gift of God's image and oriented by kenotic love towards an Other. The Son loves the Father, and humanity, in loving God, sees herself only as an image of her Creator, from whom she has being. Humanity freely posits herself as an image; she accomplishes the act of the kenosis of love.[43] The accomplishment of this kenotic act is to develop a disposition of self-emptying

---

39   Bulgakov, *Icons and the Name of God*, 55.
40   Bulgakov, *The Lamb of God*, 143.
41   Ibid.
42   Ibid., 91.
43   Ibid., 143.

love towards the Other, the very content of what it means to become like God. This is the same disposition which the Father holds in the kenosis of His eternal begetting of the Son—the same which the Son and Spirit hold in their kenotic response to the Father, to each other, and towards creation.

Gender, Sexuality, and Kenosis

The essential characteristic of humanity's divine image and likeness is to eternally turn towards the Other, both divine and human, in self-emptying love. Bulgakov's treatment of image, icon, divinely ordered anthropology, and humanity's ontologically kenotic foundation raises questions of gender and sexuality which will be the focus of the following section.

Art is itself a kenotic phenomenon. In his work on the Orthodox veneration of icons, *The Art of Seeing: Paradox and Perception in Orthodox Iconography*, Fr. Maximos Constas writes:

> It therefore seems churlish to protest that the image is somehow "less authentic" than the archetype, or that the surface acquires meaning only through depth, for it is these very "limitations" that enable creation to share in the life of God. The perceived "weakness" of the icon is precisely its "strength."[44]

If all bodies are considered to be equally made in the image of God, then it is also true that every body authentically reflects its Christological archetype, even if the historical body of Jesus Christ was one marked by X and Y chromosomes. In his descriptions of the double Proto-Image of humanity, Bulgakov seems to essentialize sexual difference by identifying a "masculine" principle with the Logos and a "feminine" one with the Holy Spirit.[45] He maintains that these "two distinct images of man, bear, in their unity, the fullness of humanity and, in this humanity, the fullness of the image of God."[46] Bulgakov's greater vision of Divine-Humanity and Sophia seems to elide any kind of essentialism; he comments elsewhere that both men and women hold within them the fullness of the image in their distinctive subsistence as hypostases.[47] Still, it remains

---

44 Maximos Constas, *The Art of Seeing: Paradox and Perception in Orthodox Iconography* (Alhambra: Sebastian Press, 2014), 29.

45 Bulgakov, *The Lamb of God*, 140.

46 Ibid., 140.

47 Sergius Bulgakov, *The Burning Bush: On the Orthodox Veneration of the Mother of God*, trans. Thomas Allan Smith (Grand Rapids: W. B. Eerdmans, 2009), 82.

difficult to parse Bulgakov's meaning in his more problematic comments. It is, at best, ambiguous where gender and sexuality fit into the iconographic model presented by Bulgakov.

We will once again rely on Martin's work on Balthasar to serve as our companion. She comments that the "whence" of Balthasar's gendered language draws heavily on Bulgakov, but also suggests that the "whither" of potential development draws equally from his use of Russian kenotic theology.[48] While the language of kenosis and self-sacrifice is already looked upon with suspicion by many feminist critiques of the Cross,[49] Bulgakov's Trinitarian and iconographic model of kenotic love opens up possibilities for critically conceptualizing desire, gender, and sexuality within the doctrine of Divine-Humanity.

Bulgakov's theology was not concerned with the specific questions of gender and sexuality now raised, but instead with demonstrating the intimate and full presence of the Second and Third Hypostases in the world through the sophianic Divine-Humanity of the Word and world. The creaturely principles in the world exist as images and reflections of the divine hypostases not because of a literal essentialized character in God, "and it is of course self-evident that anything having to do with sex or, in general, with sensuality must be excluded [in imaging God],"[50] but in a symbolic way which, like the icon, provides a new mode of perception. Even as Bulgakov addresses the "male" and "female" principles of humanity and their reflections in the persons of the Son and Spirit, respectively, he is always attempting to undermine any kind of idolatrous positing of gendered language about God.[51] He sometimes evades this kind of idolatry by omitting sexuality completely from the deified state, describing sex as an introduction of the Fall and suggesting an integral virginity present in the sophianic state. "The male and the female in and of themselves, outside of the fall, are in no way already *sex*."[52] He maintains that humanity is, in its fullness, that which includes both male and female as "*spiritual* principles,"[53] and identifies them in a symbolic way to the Son's "truth in beauty" (m) and the

---

48 "Here is the whither: informed specifically by the Russians, kenosis itself is construed in a broader context that is robustly Trinitarian and not simply Christological self-sacrifice, preserving kenotic theology both for and from traditionally feminist concerns." Martin, "The 'Whence' and the 'Whither'," 214.

49 Ibid., 214.

50 Bulgakov, *The Lamb of God*, 115.

51 Ibid., 114–15.

52 Bulgakov, *The Burning Bush*, 82.

53 Ibid., 82.

Spirit's "beauty in truth" (f).[54] As much as he remarks that sex is non-essential to humanity, this does not exclude "the spiritual distinction between the male and female essences," both of which are fully imbued with the image of God.[55]

The question of women's subjectivity is one to which there is no clear solution. Toril Moi, commenting on the work of Simone de Beauvoir, wrote: "Torn between their existence as women and their existence as human beings, women under patriarchy are obliged either to deny their specificity or obsessively focus on it."[56] Bulgakov's comments on gender seem to do both: excluding the physical reality of sexual differentiation from humanity's universal and divine origin while simultaneously re-inscribing the gender binary in his symbolic order of creaturely spiritual principles. The work of de Beauvoir attempted to dismantle the gender binary, providing insightful developments in the feminist understanding of gender construction, wishing to see both men and women liberated from their obsession with sexual difference. "Only then will she be able to attempt to discover in her life and her works all of reality and not only her own person."[57] Despite the difficulties of Bulgakov's comments concerning gender, his fundamental theological desire was oriented towards the discovery of humanity's iconicity. This does not, of course, uncomplicate Bulgakov's treatment of sexuality, but it does open new points of consideration in his work for the contemporary theologian.

Rather than take Bulgakov's essentialism at face value, it is important to maintain the kenotic character of his language as it constructs and shapes his symbolic understanding of the icon. It is here that a third way possibly emerges. Rather than a denial of sexuality or an obsession with it, the layering of the two may allow for a kind of fluidity within the universal-particular, divine-human, subject. This is simply to say that as a *symbol*, the work of essentialism in Bulgakov is not itself essential to retrieving other dimensions of his dogmatic theology, but merely depicts the givenness' of bodies present in a world imbued with divine creativity.

Bulgakov comments that "humankind is not only a male or only a female principle, but contains in itself the one and the other, and besides *not as sex*, i. e., half-and-half, non-fullness, but precisely as *the fullness* of its own exis-

---

54 Bulgakov, *The Burning Bush*, 82.
55 Bulgakov, *The Lamb of God*, 299.
56 Toril Moi, *Simone de Beauvoir: The Making of an Intellectual Woman* (Cambridge, MA: Blackwell, 1994), 209–10.
57 Simone de Beauvoir, *The Second Sex* (New York: Vintage Books, 2011), 845.

tence."[58] Both male and female are the full image of the kenotic Trinity, but Bulgakov also maintains the necessary union of both as the singular icon of Divine-Humanity embodied in the Son. Christ's body encompasses the entirety of humanity (both male and female principles, perhaps even somewhere in between the two) while maintaining the particularity of his historical body. The implication is that the kenotic nature of human love and desire are fully realized in the reception of Christ's body into the life of the Trinity—male, female, and non-conforming bodies. This fundamental insight in Bulgakov's theology undermines any literal reading of the 'male' Logos and 'female' Spirit, although those categories continue to operate symbolically in his work.

The difficulty with Bulgakov's symbolism, of course, is that it does not eschew the patriarchal and possibly abusive assumptions which can be inferred therein. Sarah Coakley reminds us of Paul Ricœur's axiom that "the symbol gives rise to thought," in her analysis of Trinitarian iconography and gender.[59] Without proper care, the antinomy which Bulgakov seeks to maintain can be easily compressed into an unnuanced binary which already pervades so much of the Christian tradition, but this need not be one's only option.[60]

By pursuing a Bulgakovian anthropology through a critical lens, contemporary theologians may resist the idolatry of essentialism by following his emphatic conclusion that the true essence of humanity is found only in the kenotic iconicity of the God who has already incorporated all things into himself. Of course, the tricky reality of Sophia's own potential essentialism as a divine 'feminine' principle warrants further critical reflection, though it is not possible to address it adequately in this essay.

Bulgakov's doctrine of Divine-Humanity antinomically maintains both transcendence and immanence, understanding each to be characteristic of divinity's kenotic love for creation, without completely eliding all conceptions of transcendence. A feminist retrieval of kenosis, as proposed by Martin and Coakley and read through the iconographic hermeneutic outlined in this study, would allow gender, sexuality, bodiliness, and desire to become significant points of reflection in Bulgakov's theological anthropology and doctrine of God. Coakley argues for the significance of kenosis on feminist grounds,

---

58   Bulgakov, *The Burning Bush*, 82.
59   Sarah Coakley, *God, Sexuality, and the Self: An Essay 'On the Trinity'* (Cambridge: Cambridge University Press, 2013), 191.
60   Coakley makes a similar critique of the Freudian-Lacanian school of psychoanalysis and symbolic philosophy, which seems to re-inscribe the very categories which they seek to overcome. Ibid., 1–31.

commenting that kenosis is "vital to a distinctively Christian manifestation of [feminism], a manifestation which does not eschew, but embraces, the spiritual paradoxes of 'losing one's life in order to save it.'"[61] The kenotic mode of humanity's sophianic state, orientated always towards the Other, is, as Martin argues, not a denial of the self so much as "a move toward flourishing, whole human persons participating in the mysterious life of the divine Trinity."[62] The feminist retrieval of kenosis can thus be centered on our own iconographic approach towards the deified anthropology which Bulgakov manifests in the image of the Trinity.

The passionate, kenotic love of divinity shared within the Trinity, poured forth in creation, and perfected at Golgotha is the very Proto-Image of humanity's sophianic telos. Bulgakov may not fully draw forth the liberating dimensions of this iconicity for a feminist project, and indeed this paper serves only as an introduction. Paired with the work of Martin and Coakley, however, a feminist theology of Divine-Humanity which accounts for the complexities of gender and sexuality begins to emerge within the space of liturgy, icon, and kenotic prayer.[63]

61 Sarah Coakley,"Kenosis and Subversion: On the Repression of 'Vulnerability' in Christian Feminist Writing," *Powers and Submissions: Spirituality, Philosophy and Gender* (Oxford: Blackwell Publishing, 2002), 4.

62 Martin, "The 'Whence' and the 'Whither'," 231.

63 This final point invites dialogue especially with the following works: Emmanuel Falque, *The Wedding Feast of the Lamb: Eros, the Body, and the Eucharist* (New York: Fordham University Press, 2016); Luce Irigaray, *An Ethics of Sexual Difference* (New York: Cornell University Press, 1993), Virginia Burrus and Catharine Keller, eds., *Towards a Theology of Eros Transfiguring Passion at the Limits of Discipline* (New York: Fordham University Press, 2007), Sara Ahmed, *Queer Phenomenology: Orientations, Objects, Others* (Durham and London: Duke University Press, 2006), and Michel Henry, *Incarnation: Une philosophie de la chair* (Paris: Éditions du Seuil, 2000)—there is an excellent translation of this work of Henry's by Karl Hefty published with Northwestern University Press in 2015).

Building the House of Wisdom
DOI 10.17438/978-3-402-12177-1

Sergii Bulgakov's Fragile Absolute: Kenosis, Difference, and Positive Disassociation

Jack Louis Pappas

Introduction

A specter is haunting contemporary philosophy and theology, the specter of Kant's transcendental subject. To be sure, according to long-prevailing consensus, we have been assured that Kant's abstracted apperceptive self is but an anachronism belonging to a long-discarded epoch, displaced by subsequent developments in phenomenology, (post)structuralism, and the more liminal discourses of so-called "postmodernity." And yet, the question must be raised as to whether these allergies to Kant and the tradition of post-Kantian idealism themselves betray a residually Kantian dogmatism, presupposing the dependency of knowledge upon the range of possible "lived experiences" of a historically situated, irreducibly finite self. Have we really moved beyond Kant's insistence that the reach of speculative reason terminates only in the scission of insurmountable antinomy, a scission marked by the irreconcilability of a spontaneous subject with an inaccessibly noumenal-Real [*Ding an sich*]?

These questions have been posed with renewed urgency by thinkers such as Slavoj Žižek, Alenka Zupančič, Adrian Johnston, Todd McGowan, and S. J. McGrath, who have each sought to interrogate the traces of transcendental philosophy beneath the surfaces of contemporary theory. Moreover, they have sought to recover the contributions of the speculative idealists J. G. Fichte, F. W. J. Schelling, and G. W. F. Hegel, who attempted not only to overcome the strictures of Kant's transcendental philosophy, but to radicalize its antinomic tensions by enacting a parallax shift that would integrate it within a more comprehensive account of the Absolute as such. Such a retrieval of these idealist sources does not, however, represent an uncritical return to a dogmatic exposition of German idealism. Rather, these theorists have instead offered a reading

of the idealists through the lens of Lacanian, Jungian, and broadly psychoana-
lytic metapsychology to elaborate what may be called a "meta-transcendental"
theory of subjectivity. Whereas the Kantian fracture between phenomenon
and noumenon is often taken in purely epistemic terms to be a mere descriptor
of the inevitable incompleteness of thought, contemporary metapsychological
theorists instead interpret this fracture to be constitutive of reality itself, acting as the underlying condition which shapes human personality and identity
formation. The speculative philosophies of Fichte, Schelling, and Hegel, thus
in turn read as diagnostic accounts of the psyche and its emergence.

My wager is that the theology of Sergii Bulgakov at once anticipates this
parallax shift in contemporary thought and articulates what may be interpreted as its own unique mode of metapsychology and theory of personality. Like
many of the aforementioned contemporary theorists, Bulgakov's reading of
idealist sources (especially Hegel and Schelling) is marked by a distinctive emphasis on the positive and meta-transcendental significance of antinomy as an
underlying precondition of (both human and divine) personhood. The aim
of this paper therefore is to at once demonstrate how these features of Bulgakov's theology might be clarified by a metapsychological reading, as well as to
explicate how Bulgakov's theology might provide a crucial intervention within contemporary metapsychological theory more broadly. To this end, I will
proceed by placing Bulgakov's theology in conversation with Slavoj Žižek's
interpretation of Schelling and Hegel. While Žižek may initially appear to be
something of a surprising interlocutor for Bulgakov, his metapsychological
reading of idealist authors is noteworthy insofar as it foregrounds the explicitly
theological aspects of German idealism and directly correlates them to metapsychological accounts of personality formation. Indeed, for Žižek as much as
for Bulgakov, antinomic fracture does not simply name a negative aporia which
finite thought cannot exceed, but is taken to be reflective of the irreducibility
of self-diremption as constitutive of both the Absolute and the human subject.
Like Bulgakov, Žižek engages Schelling and Hegel to interrogate how the theological categories of kenosis and self-differentiation operate within a broader
diagnostic of the self and its agency. As such, I will initially examine Žižek's
metapsychological interpretation of Schelling and Hegel, before explicating
how Bulgakov's own critical appropriation of these sources might provide the
possibility of a different approach to speculative metapsychology than that
proffered by Žižek.

Schelling's Hysterical God

In Žižek's reading, Schelling's middle period represents an effort to radically invert Kant's Copernican revolution, a refusal to accept the constitutive opposition between the transcendental subject (ideal-phenomenon) and the noumenal-Real.[1] Schelling instead conceives of the noumenal-Real as the anterior Ground [*Grund*] from which subjectivity itself arises. That is, the excessive opacity of the *Ding an sich* not only transcends and resists subjectivity, but also founds and underwrites it. Precisely because the noumenal-Real is the condition of possibility for both subjectivity and discursive reason, Schelling understands it to be an "indivisible remainder" [*der neu aufgehende Rest*], a pre-subjective and pre-logical foundation "which can never be grasped 'as such,' but only glimpsed in the very gesture of its withdrawal."[2] The subject is therefore derivative of the noumenal-Real, parasitic upon its aboriginal Ground, which it cannot comprehend except in the mode of a limit-concept excluded from the domain of possible experience. However, Schelling's identification of the primordial Ground with Kant's *Ding an sich* poses difficulties. First, insofar as Schelling posits an ontogenetic Ground underlying the antinomic scission between the ideal and the real, he is forced to account for how differentiation could possibly emerge from a unitary Absolute. Second, Schelling is confronted with the question of how any significance can be assigned to the Ground at all, given that it is both pre-subjective and pre-discursive.

Schelling confronts these difficulties by way of a speculative theogony which correlates the ontogenesis of subjectivity with the emergence of a personal God from an impersonal Ground. As Žižek summarizes, "[for Schelling] the becoming of the world is the becoming of God himself, his self-creation and self-revelation, such that the human subject's awareness of God is the subjective self-awareness of God himself."[3] Schelling admits that if the Ground is conceived in terms of a self-identical unitary substance, then any subsequent process of division or self-differentiation would be impossible. Following Fichte, Schelling recognizes that if the Ground is identified with a selfsame totality, it would be incapable of positing itself as an "I" because it would have

---

1   Slavoj Žižek, *Less Than Nothing: Hegel and the Shadow of Dialectical Materialism* (New York: Verso, 2014), 12.
2   Slavoj Žižek, "The Abyss of Freedom" in *The Abyss of Freedom/Ages of the World* (Anne Arbor: University of Michigan Press, 1997), 1–104, 7.
3   Slavoj Žižek, *Absolute Recoil: Towards a New Foundation of Dialectical Materialism* (New York: Verso, 2014), 256–57.

no exterior other ("Not-I") against which it could determine itself. "Were the first nature in harmony with itself it would remain so. It would be constantly One and would never become two."⁴ As such, at least in Žižek's reading, Schelling does not conceive of the Ground as a primal origin [ἀρχή] but rather as an *anarchic* indeterminacy, a pre-ontological black hole of potential being. That is, for Žižek, Schelling's Ground is ultimately a sheer groundlessness [*Ungrund*], "a chaotic impersonal abyss of blind drives in rotary motion,"⁵ an unconscious libidinal economy in conflict with itself. To the degree that the impersonal longing of the groundless Ground is an enclosed feedback loop of indeterminate volatility, it is also on account of its own undifferentiated excessiveness capable of recoiling from itself.

The transition from the horrific unconsciousness of the Ground to self-conscious subjectivity is enacted via what Schelling calls an "un-prethinkable" [*unvordenklich*] "decision" [*Ent-scheidung*], a repression of conflicting drives that serves as the foundational moment of self-determination. The scission between ideal-subject and noumenal-Real is thus symptomatic of a primal diremption, an unconscious (or, better, pre-conscious) *de*-scission, whereby the libidinal chaos of the Ground is ejected into an immemorial past, and consciousness assumes itself in the form of a self-positing subject. The emergence of the subject then coincides with a displacement of drives, a self-sundering of the aboriginal abyss which excretes an "I" in recoil from the condition of its own genesis. Consciousness is predicated of a subject only to the extent that the subject has at once posited itself as grounded and differentiated from its contracted Ground. Žižek writes, "A free subject has to have a Ground that it is not itself; it has first to contract this Ground and then to assume a free distance toward it via the act of primordial decision [*Ent-scheidung*] that opens up time."⁶ That is, the primal undifferentiated Ground is assigned to the unconscious, becoming a noumenal-Real whose opacity imposes the limitation which sustains the personalized consciousness [*Selbstheit*] of the subject itself.

In theological terms, Schelling explicates the pre-conscious act of disassociation as the pre-eternal moment in which the unconscious Absolute represses its conflicting potencies and determines itself over and against a true other. The indifferent Ground atemporally "becomes" the personal God, by consciously positing himself [*für sich*] over and against the excremental remainder [*an*

4   F. W. J. Schelling, *Ages of the World: Third Version* (1915), trans. Jason M. Wirth (Albany: State University of New York Press, 2000), 12.
5   Žižek, *The Indivisible Remainder* (New York: Verso Books, 2007), 13.
6   Žižek, "The Abyss of Freedom," 33.

sich] which he has jettisoned into an unconscious past. Self-division therefore constitutes God's personalization, and his diminution [κένωσις] enacts both his own self-revelation and the true "beginning" of historical creation. "There is no God prior to his *kenosis*. God emerges through his loss […] in a case of absolute recoil, the history of God is the story of his loss and the final consummation of this loss."[7] Although this loss is the result of a single decision, it results in a form of divine personality [*Selbstheit*] irreducibly out of sync with itself, fragmented between its self-enunciating entrance into discursive self-determinacy and set in opposition to the excremental fallen world as the residue of its own disavowed past. That is, on the one hand, this self-division constitutes the simultaneous event of the begetting of the Son-Word [λόγος] and the emergence of created materiality. The former acts as the regulative norm which gives the emergent subject its coherence, while the latter remains an irreducible alterity which resists all discursive assimilation, the repressed remainder concealed beneath every semblance of the symbolic order.

Schelling does not simply oppose the dark domain of the pre-ontological drives, the unnamable Real which can never be totally symbolized to the domain of the Logos, of the articulated Word which can never totally "force" it. Rather, the unnamable Unconscious is not external to the Logos, but its obscure background, but *the very act of naming*, the very founding gesture of the Logos […] the act of imposing a rational necessity on the pre-rational chaos of the Real.[8]

Theogony culminates not in a harmonious synthesis between formerly conflicting drives, but rather in their displacement by an act of discursive supplementation. Divine personality is founded on a persistent antagonism between the self-revelatory pronouncement of God through the Son-Word and the excluded noumenal-Real, manifested in a fallen creation.

The perduring chasm between divine self-revelation and the excreted residue returns us to the question of the relationship between the content of Schelling's theory of subjectivity and the narrative theogony which explicates it. According to Žižek's interpretation, the basic contours of the narrative itself betray the very truth of subjectivity which the narrative aims to conceal. "Schelling's move is not simply to ground the ontologically structured universe in the horrible vortex of the Real […] rather this terrifying pre-ontological vortex is itself a phantasmic narrative, a lure destined to detract us from the true traumatic cut."[9] Put simply, subjectivity is inherently pathological, enacted by

7   Žižek, *Absolute Recoil*, 261.
8   Ibid., 185.
9   Žižek, *Less Than Nothing*, 275.

a symbolic repression of the Real which it relegates to an imagined past. More-over, the edifice of personality is founded upon a denial of its own ground-lessness, reinforced through the artifice of a primordial abyss dispelled by a personalized God. For Žižek, Schelling's mythological pre-history—as much as the very Word pronounced by Schelling's God itself—is an artifact of hys-teria, "a comforting fiction which substitutes the horrible truth of constitutive repression."[10] In turn, as with all hysterics, the truth is confessed through the lie: the primal beginning in which the Son-Word is begotten and the Absolute is personalized, in McGrath's words "unwittingly betrays the primal crime of subjectivity, the murder of the Real."[11]

Hegel's Monstrous Christ

Hegel's advance over Schelling, in Žižek's reading, lies in his rejection of the excess of an indivisible remainder altogether.[12] However, in contrast to frequent caricatures of Hegelian dialectics, Žižek maintains that Hegel's thought does not attempt to dispel negativity by resolving in a final unifying synthesis. On the contrary, Žižek's Hegel instead owns up to the persistent contradiction immanent to every identity, including that of the Absolute.[13] Where Schelling attempts to ontologize Kant's antinomic scission for the sake of explicating its genesis, Hegel does the exact opposite. Žižek writes,

> Hegel *de*-ontologizes Kant by introducing a gap into the very texture of reality. Hegel's move is not to "overcome" the Kantian division, but rather to assert it "as such," *to remove the need for its overcoming,* for the additional reconciliation of the opposites, that is to gain the insight into how positing the distinction "as such'" already *is* the looked-for "reconciliation."[14]

In other words, Schelling simply repeats Kant's error, and fails to recognize his own ruse. Rather than reconciling himself to the immanence of contradiction, he projects contradiction into the transcendent "beyond," of a noumenal-Real. He-gel's dialectics, on the other hand, by unfolding the contradictions immanent to thought, enacts nothing less than an unmasking of the repressed truth concealed

---

10   McGrath, *The Dark Ground of Spirit*, 31.
11   Ibid.
12   Žižek, *The Indivisible Remainder*, 103.
13   Žižek, *Less Than Nothing*, 17.
14   Ibid., 267–68.

behind Schelling's fiction: there is no abyss excluded from the grasp of Logos, no chimerical unconscious with which the subject cannot be reconciled. In short, for Hegel, the Real is not a noumenal, pre-discursive substantial Ground, but a break within the symbolic economy which both sustains and constitutes it.

For Žižek, the Hegelian dialectical play of opposites and unfolding negations [*Aufhebung*] represents a form of proto-Lacanian therapeutics. Ultimately, the whole range of possible *an sich* entities are exposed as artifacts of the subject's own self-deception, generated by the repression of negativity. Once unmasked, the presupposed domain of the supersensible is made to appear as *mere* appearance. "To unmask the illusion does not mean that there is nothing to see behind: what we must be able to see is this nothing as such—beyond the phenomena, there is nothing but this nothing itself, nothing which is the subject."[15] The phantasm of the supersensible, which had initially appeared as substantial and real, and acted as the exterior impasse that resisted and constituted symbolization, is therefore exposed to be a product of the innate tensions within the process of the subject's own self-idealization.

Nonetheless, this raises the question which haunted Schelling: how does subjectivity arise in contradistinction with its own negativity if negativity itself is a product of the discursive subject?

According to Žižek's view, Hegel sees this question as an effort to retroactively uncover a logical necessity upon an event of inexplicable contingency. Rather than attempting to explicate this emergence as Schelling does, by retreating from the negative by substantializing it as the very Ground of the Absolute, Hegel instead affirms the Absolute as contradictory, a self-relation of identity and difference, a negated subject without a pre-subjective negative. Hegel's ultimate identification of truth with the recognition of "substance as essentially subject, expressed in the representation of the Absolute as *Spirit* [*Geist*],"[16] is taken by Žižek to mean precisely that "substance is not a pre-subjective Ground but a subject, an agent of self-differentiation which posits otherness and then reappropriates it. 'Subject' stands for the non-substantial agency of phenomenonalization, appearance, 'illusion,' split, finitude, Understanding and so on, and to conceive Substance as Subject means precisely that appearance and split are inherent to the life of the Absolute itself."[17] The recognition of

15   Slavoj Žižek, *The Sublime Object of Ideology* (New York: Verso, 1989), 195.

16   G. W.F. Hegel, *The Phenomenology of Spirit* (Oxford: Oxford University Press, 1977), 14 [§ 25].

17   Cf. Slavoj Žižek, *The Ticklish Subject: The Absent Center of Political Ontology* (New York: Verso, 1999), 88.

self-splitting [*Entzweiung*] as the inherent and constitutive fact of subjectivity, yields a reconciliation with the traumatic negative which Schelling's pre-conscious decision [*Ent-scheidung*] aims to disavow. Yet, this reconciliation does not suture the underlying "cut" of the negative by way of synthesis so much as it "confesses" and "absolves" the crime of the repressed trauma.

Insofar as Hegel's dialectical therapeutics is understood by Žižek to enact a reconciliation with the intractability of contradiction, then by extension Hegel's affirmation of Christianity, as the summit of "revealed religion,"[18] can be said to enact the very inverse of Schelling's hallucinatory theogony. That is, while Schelling's narrative represents a myth that dissimulates the truth of the negative, Hegel's Christianity represents a true myth that dispels every mythology and "gives up the ghost"[19] of the spectral Real. For Žižek, the "perverse core" of Christianity is confessed in the image [*Vorstellung*] of the crucified Christ who is himself the monstrous truth of contradiction—a self-alienated God—whose death reveals sheer negativity to be constitutive of the Absolute.[20] Žižek's Hegelian *theologia crucis* is thus at once Trinitarian and radically theopaschite, a Christian atheism which identifies the crucified God with an exhaustive diminution [κένωσις] of transcendence into sheer immanence. The transcendent God [*an sich*] is unreservedly incarnated in Christ such that Christ's crucifixion is itself the very death of God, the final dissolution of the supersensible.

By way of God's death, the alienation of the subject is made mediate to itself, and through this mediation it is reconciled to the monstrous negativity of contingent being. Žižek observes,

> [The difference of substance and subject] has to reflect/inscribes itself into subjectivity itself as the irreducible gap that separates human subjects from Christ, the "more than human" monstrous subject [...] Christ signals the overlapping of two kenoses: man's alienation from/in God is simultaneously God's alienation from himself in Christ. So it is not only that humanity becomes conscious of itself in the alienated figure of God, but in human religion, God becomes self-conscious.[21]

---

18   Hegel, 456 [§ 754].
19   Slavoj Žižek, *The Fragile Absolute: Why the Christian Legacy is Worth Fighting For* (New York: Verso, 2000), 90.
20   Ibid., 96.
21   Slavoj Žižek, "The Fear of Four Words: A Modest Plea for the Hegelian Reading of Christianity" in *The Monstrosity of Christ: Paradox or Dialectic* by Slavoj Žižek and John Milbank, ed. Creston Davis (Cambridge MA: MIT Press, 2009), 75.

The double-sided figure of the human subject alienated from a supersensible God, and a self-alienated God abandoned unto death are, in turn, reconciled by their being sublated into a virtualized relation between contingent subjects in community. This community, which Žižek identifies with the Holy Spirit, is one liberated from all projected bonds of significance apart from their own immanent mutual association as expressed in common action. The virtualized horizon of meaning is therefore the flipside of absolute negativity and contingency, the exigent presupposition animating the actions of a community of purely finite individuals. "God" is made conscious in a collective of godless partisans who commit themselves to the realization of an idealized possibility.

Bulgakov's Metapsychology of Positive Disassociation

Both Žižek and Bulgakov read the post-Kantian idealist tradition as an effort to challenge the constitutive antinomic scission at the heart of Kant's account of the transcendental subject. This challenge is interpreted, by Žižek and Bulgakov alike, in terms of an interrogation of the underlying "structural scaffolding of [Kant's] fully formed account of transcendental subjectivity,"[22] which comes to identify the rupture at the heart of the subject as derivative of an anterior rupture constitutive of the Absolute itself. This similarity between Žižek and Bulgakov not only reflects their common rootedness in the idealist tradition, but also attests to a shared predilection for what might called a meta-psychological or meta-transcendental interpretation of that tradition. Both Žižek and Bulgakov affirm a continuity between speculative discourse regarding the Absolute and a certain diagnosis of the human personality as such. Indeed, Bulgakov, like Žižek and the idealists, affirms that the Kantian construction of subjectivity remains ultimately incomprehensible on its own terms. The subject [*Ich*] only apprehends itself relative to its other, a predicate which constitutes its limit, but remains unable to exceed the limits of its own identity such that it can know the content of its own predication. Bulgakov writes,

> This antinomical task makes the *I* into a riddle for itself, into an insoluble charade. That which [...] appeared [...] to be the most reliable and most self-evident [...] fulcrum turns out to be situated at the point of an antinomical knife, to be a living paradox, which, obviously, cannot be understood from out of itself.[23]

---

22   Adrian Johnson, Žižek's *Ontology: A Transcendental Materialist Theory of Subjectivity* (Evanston: Northwestern University Press, 2008), 71.

23   Sergii Bulgakov, *The Tragedy of Philosophy: Philosophy & Dogma* (Brooklyn: Angelico Press, 2020), 125.

Moreover, in tandem with Žižek's reading of Schelling and Hegel, Bulgakov approaches this tension not by attempting to dissolve the immanent contradiction at its center, but by affirming polarity itself as his point of departure and ultimate terminus of his thought.

For Bulgakov, the scission between the enclosed field of the subject and the transcendent "Not-I" [*Nicht-Ich*], the *Ding an sich*, is absolute and insurmountable from the standpoint of the subject's own immanence, and can only be overcome by way of the "Not-I"'s own self-disclosure to the "I" by a negation of its own pure exteriority. Conversely, to the extent that the Subject is able to possess itself and know itself, it must always already be presupposed relative to the self-disclosure of its otherwise noumenal predicate. "I" and "Not-I" must somehow be correlated to one another, simultaneously without reserve and without collapse of differentiation. Both the finite subject and its transcendent other must be posited as constitutively split and co-known, with the split in the latter operating as the condition of possibility for the former's own reflexive self-positing:

> The task of the absolute with respect to the relative, or of the relative in light of the absolute, is the unification at once of the absolute and the relative of the immanent and the transcendent—such is the nature of the predicate. The relative-absolute or absolute-relative predicate is an antinomy which reason finds intolerable.[24]

However, it is precisely here that Bulgakov's account of a ruptured Absolute at once most closely approximates but ultimately diverges from those proffered by Žižek's reading of Schelling and Hegel. On the one hand, with Žižek's Schelling, Bulgakov explicates the relationship between the relative-Absolute and Absolute-relative as founded upon a primal decision [*Ent-Scheidung*], an act of disassociative self-sundering and a refusal of totality. On the other hand, with Žižek's Hegel, Bulgakov takes this foundational fracture to be irreducible and immanent to the Absolute itself, and thus refuses to substantialize it into a pre-subjective groundless Ground.[25] And yet, Bulgakov's Absolute cannot be identified with Žižek's traumatized Hegelian subject, condemned to a per-

---

24 Bulgakov, *The Tragedy of Philosophy*, 127.
25 Ibid., "Schelling's error lies in his putting the nature [s. c. *Grund*] of the hypostasis *before* the hypostasis, and deducing hypostasis from that nature. In other words, he takes the predicate, understood as a dark potentiality, *apart from* and *before* the subject, and forces it to engender its own hypostasis from out of itself [...] he does not merely distinguish God's nature from God himself, but directly opposes the two." 99.

verse enjoyment of the symptoms of its woundedness, any more than it can be identified with Žižek's Schellingian hysteric, in repressed denial of its own groundlessness.

According to Bulgakov, the primal decision of the Absolute to enact its own diminution [κένωσις] is indicative neither of a repression of anhypostatic drives, nor of a parasitic subject that derives its personality from self-deception by positing an anarchic noumenal-Real. Rather, for Bulgakov, there is no Absolute "behind" the Absolute-relative, no unconscious Ground which is not always already the predicate of a self-conscious subject. Put theologically, Bulgakov's God is not pure transcendence, but an immanent-transcendence who is eternally and irreducibly sundered, known to himself in being co-known, relative to a genuine other with whom he has placed himself in correlation.

> The Absolute is never thought, never known, never exists in its *abstract* absoluteness [...]. Even abstracting thought must have something from which it might be reflected and thus acquire content; and the transcendent never remains only in its transcendence but has a *trans* which not only conceals but defines it. In other words, the Absolute itself is *relative* in its absoluteness, just as the transcendent is *immanent* in its transcendence.[26]

Bulgakov describes God's aboriginal diremption as the very enactment of the eternal *ad intra* self-revelation of divine personality in the communion of Father, Son, and Holy Spirit, as well as the ultimate foundation of its *ad extra* repetition in the temporal unfolding of created Being.[27]

Even as this self-revelation is constituted by a self-sacrificial Urkenosis, an eternally pre-established "Golgotha of the Absolute,"[28] it is in no way taken to represent an instance of negativity or loss. For Bulgakov, the reality of the Absolute's self-sundering is instead an eternal, atemporal event of loving donation which inscribes difference with the utmost positivity, rather than a mode of dialectical contradiction or antagonism.[29] That is, the Absolute is always already correlated not only to his creation [*ad extra*] but rationally knows and loves himself as the Trinity. The Absolute is pre-eternally the Father who bestows and receives himself through the Son-Word, and who in the mutuality of the Father

26 Sergius Bulgakov, *The Comforter* (Grand Rapids: W. B. Eerdmans, 2004), 360.
27 Ibid., 361.
28 Cf. Sergius Bulgakov, *Unfading Light* (Grand Rapids: W. B. Eerdmans, 2012), 185.
29 Cf. Bulgakov, *The Tragedy of Philosophy*, 61–62.

and the Son-Word is transparent to himself in the "We" of the Holy Spirit, who proceeds from the Father and rests upon the Son-Word.[30]

The ultimate identity of substance with subject is therefore not a product of pure self-mediated immanence which, like Žižek's Hegelian subject, could be said to suffer alienation for the sake of its self-virtualization. Rather, for Bulgakov, substance is identified with a unitary Not-All, a living antinomy that is always comprehended relative to predicate and copula. This antinomic unitary-difference names nothing less than the triunity of Father, Son, and Spirit and their three-fold hypostatization of a singular divine substance. This tri-hypostatized substance is rendered transparent and self-conscious, just as subject, predicate, and copula express an organically self-differentiated whole.

> The hypostasis, the person, the I, exists in so far as it has a nature of its own, that is, an unceasing predication, a revelation of its own, which it can never exhaustively utter. "Substance" exists not only "in itself" [*an sich*], as subject, but also "for itself" [*für sich*] as a predicate, and moreover, "in and for itself" [*an und für sich*], in the copula as existence. And these three beginnings are by no means merely dialectical moments of a unity, negating each other and being sublated into synthesis: no, they are, simultaneously and with equal dignity [...] three [...] which in their joint make up the life of substance.[31]

The life of personality is thus a dynamic movement of donative self-positing whereby the "I" is constituted by its own self-abnegation, its unreserved self-abandonment to the "Not-I." This is illustrated by the self-determination of the Father as subject in relation to his predicate, the donation of his very substance through the begetting of the Son-Word. In turn, insofar as the Urkenosis of the Father's self-donation enacts his self-revelation in the Son-Word, the self-determination of the Son-Word consists in his own self-renunciation and reciprocal self-offering to the Father.[32] As such, the self-positing of each of the co-divine hypostases, while singular in the self-consciousness of their transparent and wholly realized substance, is personally distinguished according to

---

30 Cf. Sergius Bulgakov, *The Lamb of God* (Grand Rapids: W. B. Eerdmans, 2008): "This reality of the divine nature, already revealing itself in an ideal manner in the fatherhood of the Father and the sonhood of the Son, is accomplished by the Holy Spirit, who proceeds from the Father, reposes upon the Son and unites the two of them. This is the mutual love of the Father and the Son [...]; it is the accomplished self-revelation of Divinity in its nature." 100.

31 Bulgakov, *The Tragedy of Philosophy*, 11.

32 Bulgakov, *The Lamb of God*, 97–100.

the manner in which they each enact their donative love in relation to their co-divine other.

The mutual self-sacrificial determination of the Father and the Son is described by Bulgakov in continuity with his affirmation of an aboriginal Golgotha as a "pre-eternal suffering,"[33] but remains differentiated from the mere pathos of tragic, finite limitation, on account of its resolution in the third co-divine other, the Holy Spirit. As copula, the Holy Spirit manifests and actualizes the positive content of divine substance, which he shares in mutually-donative communion with Father as subject and the Son-Word as predicate. The *ideal* revelation of the Father in the begetting of the Son-Word is made *real* in the procession of the Holy Spirit, who in his repose upon the Son-Word, and together with him, forms the "revealing dyad"[34] of predicate and copula which the expresses the substance of the Father as subject. This actualized expression is not merely a virtualized reciprocity of self-identification in self-differentiating love ("I am Thou and Thou art I; I am We."[35]) but is realized *hypostatically* in the Holy Spirit as co-divine person, together with the Father and Son-Word. The content of this triune revelation of the divine personality is identified by Bulgakov with the divine wisdom, Sophia. As Brandon Gallaher summarizes, "as God the Father's revealed nature, Sophia is transparent to the hypostases who reveal her, the dyad of the Son and Spirit, and they live in and by their self-revelation in and as her. Sophia, in this way, becomes hypostatically characterized by the Father as Wisdom (for the Logos) and Glory (for the Spirit)."[36] Putting to one side its obvious idiosyncrasy, Bulgakov's quasi-personal appellation of the divine substance signals the extent to which his speculative theology can be interpreted as a form of metapsychology, albeit in a decidedly different register than the Lacanian approach elaborated by Žižek in his reading of the idealists.

---

33 Bulgakov, *The Lamb of God*, 99.
34 See, Bulgakov, *The Comforter*, 183–86. Bulgakov writes, "This mutuality is expressed in the depths of the Holy Trinity by the Fact that there is a Revealed hypostasis, the Father, and there is a Dyad of Revealing hypostases, the engendered Son and the proceeding Holy Spirit. The inseparability of these two hypostases is based not only on the fact that both of them have a common 'principle' in the Father but also on the fact that both of them *together* reveal Him in the Divine Sophia, by a unified concrete act determined by their interrelation." 183.
35 Bulgakov, *The Lamb of God*, 100.
36 Cf. Brandon Gallaher, *Freedom and Necessity in Modern Trinitarian Theology* (Oxford: Oxford University Press, 2016) 78.

Bulgakov's metapsychological orientation can be interpreted as representing a form of what S. J. McGrath has called "positive disassociation."[37] McGrath sharply differentiates positive disassociation from any form of repression or psychosis. While repression takes any constitutive split within personality to be a mode of psychotic denial, such that self-consciousness is defined in conflict with its unconscious drives, McGrath conversely describes "positive disassociation" as a form of productive self-contraction and relational openness:

> Positive disassociation must be distinguished from negative association. Where the former enlivens personality, the latter encloses it. Negative disassociation is willful unconsciousness [...] [Positive disassociation] affirms that to be a personality is to be involved in disassociation for the sake of re-identification, of dialoguing with difference.[38]

Indeed, for Bulgakov, the split within the Absolute is not taken to be something inherently pathological or an indication of a personality that is constitutively disjointed. Rather it is the loving self-donation of the Father's very substance to the Son-Word and the Spirit, a dynamic upsurge of desire whose *ens realissimum* finds expression in loving relation to others. The outpouring of the sacrificial gift of the Father's substance in no way enacts a self-deceptive ejection of an unconscious abyss but is instead a consummation of his subjectivity in relation to predicate and copula, a completely self-transparent personality in the mode of a "natured nature" [*natura naturata*]. Sophia as the substance of divine self-consciousness is itself the eternal reality of the Absolute in its self-revelation, the identification of the differentiated Father, Son, and Spirit in mutual recognition.

This positive disassociation and virtualized reidentification in otherness is ultimately the basis of human personality, which repeats the personalization and self-revelation of God's own substance as Sophia *ad extra*.[39] Although God's personality is eternally realized in the reciprocal donation of the Trinitarian

---

37   McGrath, *The Dark Ground of Spirit*, 27.

38   Ibid.

39   Sophia is simultaneously the Divine nature ("divine Sophia" or "substance-Sophia") and the fundamental entelechy and fulfillment of creation ("creaturely Sophia"), which by extension is the principle of God's self-revelation both *ad intra* and *ad extra*, as well as the very foundation of created material-historical being and its ultimate fulfillment. In both cases, difference is not dissolved, but rather fulfilled by a fundamental unity and identification. This one Divine-created—or Divine-Human—Sophia ultimately belongs to God, representing a panentheistic rather than pantheistic view. The difference

life, Bulgakov nonetheless grounds creation in the very same unprethinkable event of his self-sundering, gratuitously positing his own substance outside himself in creaturely being.[40] In positing Sophia as the foundation of creation, God's self-bifurcation further extends for the sake of ever greater love and reciprocity. Likewise, in receiving Sophia as its foundation, creation possesses Sophia as a potency to be realized as its own [*natura naturans*], an entelechy to be attained. The realization (i. e. "sophianization"[41]) of this potency is both the gift and the task of the human person.

Conclusion

For Žižek subjectivity is constitutively disjointed, its "substance" consists in the innate contradiction between the wound of the unconscious and the projection of a symbolic-imagined economy. Whether in the Schellingian mode of an unconscious "indivisible remainder" or as the immanent trauma of the Hegelian negative, Žižek perceives the split within personality as inherently pathological, a tragic dissonance of conflicting drives. To speak of any production of a higher standpoint of possible reconciliation, whereby otherness and identity are brought into a dynamic relation, can only inevitably be identified with a kind of ideological artifice. Even if the lie of ideology is exigent and noble—as it is for Žižek's Holy Spirit as the self-consciously godless community-in-solidarity—it is nonetheless a virtualized loss of reality, an alienation from the contingency and brutality of the real that lurks beneath every surface. In the end, the question is posed to us whether we can accept the wound of selfhood and come to abandon ourselves to the pure immanence of a utopian expectation without guarantees.

Bulgakov offers a counterproposal to Žižek's question, one which refuses to identify self-sacrifice with loss and fragility with negation. Indeed, Bulgakov's Sophia indicates that the essential fracture which yields differentiation is not merely an open wound concealed by a veneer of hysterical self-deception, but rather a donative self-offer that produces the possibility of relation and expressive re-identification in otherness. As the "organic image"[42] or mirror of the

---

between "Divine" and "Creaturely" Sophias is not one of being, but one of reception. Bulgakov, *The Lamb of God*, 119–23.

40 Bulgakov, *Unfading Light*, 195–99.
41 Sergii Bulgakov, *Philosophy of Economy: The World as Household* (New Haven: Yale University Press 2000), 145–50.
42 Bulgakov, *The Lamb of God*, 98.

self-differentiated, antinomic identity that constitutes both the Trinitarian God and the relation between Creator and creature, Bulgakov's Sophia is neither a flight into illusory fantasy nor a virtualized projection of a repressed subject. On the contrary, Sophia names nothing less than the self-transparent personality which has disavowed the deluded temptation of solipsism and attained itself by embracing the other as its utmost condition of self-revelation. Bulgakov's metapsychology of positive disassociation, as expressed in his sophiology, thus represents the precise inverse of the psychosis which Žižek aims to alleviate by "unmasking" the truth of negativity. For Bulgakov, the irreducible fracture which bruises the heart of the Absolute is "the life-creating power of trihypostatic love"[43] and as such attains the utmost positivity, serving as the very wellspring of personhood.

---

43   Bulgakov, *Unfading Light*, 217.

Building the House of Wisdom
DOI 10.17438/978-3-402-12178-8

The Authenticity of Creativity:
The Philosophical and Theological Anthropologies of
Nikolai Berdiaev and Sergei Bulgakov

Deborah Casewell

The later thought of Sergei Bulgakov, as opposed to his earlier engagement with German Idealism and political thought, is largely contrasted with his theological fellow travellers, some of whom found fault with his sophiology and his reliance on German Idealism. However, through this relationship to German Idealism, Bulgakov can be better linked to his fellow Russian émigré Nikolai Berdiaev. Although their systems are distinctive enough from one another, there are a number of ways in which it is productive to compare and contrast their thought.

Due to their political and personalist interests, it is done on these grounds rather than philosophical or theological ones. However, considering Berdiaev's link to existential philosophy, there exists another way to compare and contrast their thought. One prominent aspect of existential philosophy concerns the creation or realisation of the self, of being authentic or inauthentic. Authenticity can be a complete self-creation from nothing or it can be the alignment of one's life in a certain way. However, there is a sense in authenticity that one decides for oneself how to exist, that the self has the freedom to make itself in its own image. Thus what can be presented to the world is the *true*, individual self. Both thinkers explored in this essay engage with some key concerns of authenticity: in terms of creativity, freedom, and selfhood.

Bulgakov may not engage in existential philosophy or existentialism as Berdiaev does, but he has an understanding of what it means to be fully and truly human such that a theology of personalist authenticity results from Bulgakov's thought. As a result, Bulgakov can thus be seen as part of a wider theological tradition that contains within it the tools with which to respond to claims that authenticity must always be pure self-creation and self-assertion. Seeing Bulgakov's thought through this lens also provides us with another helpful way to explore the similarities and dissimilarities between him and Berdiaev, who develops his own understanding of authenticity from his own, more radical, account of self-creation.

I will develop this analysis through the concerns of creation, creativity, and how that bears upon the self. Both these thinkers have rich, complex systems, and this is especially the case for Bulgakov, who constructs a particular elaborate theology. However, the focus of this essay is resolutely focused on theological anthropology, and in particular on how to become truly, authentically human. For it is in this area that theology is especially able to interrogate and engage with philosophical concerns and formulae.

Nikolai Berdiaev

I begin with an account of Berdiaev's thought, in particular his understanding of creation and creativity. Berdiaev's existential character emerged independently of the usual genealogy of existentialism, noting that he saw himself as an existentialist 'before I even came to know of Kierkegaard's writings'.[1] His thought is instead shaped by sources that he shares with Bulgakov: Jakob Boehme and Schelling, alongside his engagement with Pascal, Nietzsche, Dostoevsky, Tolstoy, Kierkegaard, and Heidegger.

Berdiaev's key existential concern is to avoid thought he terms "objectivising":[2] that shuts its eyes 'to the mystery of the life of man, of the world, and of God.'[3] This rests on Berdiaev's distinction between the natural and the supernatural, where objectivising philosophy is philosophy that is natural, that remains within the world and works solely within those limits. In contrast, authentic existence and philosophising takes place with a turn towards the supernatural in the natural, beginning its investigations there.

Here, Berdiaev's understanding of creation and creativity is key. Drawing on Jakob Boehme's philosophy, Berdiaev sees that God wills himself into existence from the void of nothingness, the *Ungrund*. From this act of will, God transforms and modulates into the Trinity. This account of God prevents God

---

1   Nikolai Berdyaev, *Dream and Reality: An Essay in Autobiography*, trans. K. Lampert (London: Geoffrey Bles, 1950), 102.
2   Objectification means 'alienation, loss of individuality, loss of freedom, subjection to the common, and cognition by means of the concept' (1953, 11).
3   Berdyaev, *The Divine and the Human*, trans. R.M. French (London: Geoffrey Bles, 1949), v.

from being associated with being, because one cannot say that God *is*. Instead, as Berdiaev comments, the vision is '*nothingness* as distinct from *something* in order of being'. It is a 'primal pre-existential freedom' that precedes being and is beyond the world of causality.[4] The foundation is freedom rather than being, and human freedom and creativity is also drawn from this non-being. Created as we are in God's image and likeness, we also will and create, and are called to this free, spontaneous activity, rather than shaping ourselves to a pre-determined ideal. This creativeness, as the exercise of our freedom, is our own creating out of nothingness. However, we cannot create life or matter from nothing, like God. In this way humanity is fraught: both the riddle of and the solution to the universe.

Strictly speaking, Berdiaev does entertain the concept that a separate principle gives rise to God and humanity. He sources it in the meontic *Ungrund*, arguing that it thus has no 'being' of which to speak which stands as a *concrete* other principle to God. This metaphysical sleight of hand will save him some of the issues that Bulgakov runs into with his account of Sophia, although it does open his thought up to different problems.[5] Turning now to Bulgakov's account of creation, we can see certain similarities: a navigation of nothingness and a debt to mystical German thought, alongside a rather different ontological approach.

Bulgakov on Creation

In Bulgakov's cosmology, God exists originally as the Absolute, 'an unchanging entity, wholly satisfied and wholly blessed, and the world process neither adds anything to him nor subtracts anything from him'. Yet God also chooses to create and therefore bind himself to the world, to become in and through the world, and therefore 'God is not complete insofar as the world is not complete'.[6] Hence Creation is a kenotic act, the sacrifice of the Absolute's absoluteness, a

---

4   Berdyaev, *Spirit and Reality*, trans. George Reavey (London: Geoffrey Bles, 1939), 144–45.

5   This is the judgement of Zwahlen, for example, who in her contrasts of Berdyaev and Bulgakov sees that the former's ontology is too unstabilising, with the world 'always in danger from the negative forces roaring in the *Ungrund*'; Regula Zwahlen, "Different Concept of Personality: Nikolaj Berdjaev and Sergej Bulgakov", Studies in East European Thought 64, 3–4 (2012), 193.

6   Sergei Bulgakov, *Unfading Light: Contemplations and Speculations*, trans. and ed. Thomas Allan Smith (Grand Rapids: W. B. Eerdmans, 2012), 196.

creative sacrifice of love that we are to mirror.[7] In becoming relative the Absolute limits and subjects itself, and in doing so posits nothing outside of the Absolute fullness of God's being.

What form does this nothingness take? Bulgakov distinguishes between *me on* and the *ouk on* of nothingness, one creative, the other sterile. God creates out of the *ouk on*, transforming it into the *me on*, and it is this nothingness that surrounds being. God originates being and non-being,[8] and this creative activity is similar but distinguished from creaturely creativity. God can create out of absolute nothing, whereas we create out of the nothingness that God creates.

The above cosmology is one of the ways in which, as Bulgakov states, his understanding of God's relation to the world is panentheistic, his effort to avoid what he sees as the extremes of immanentism and transcendentism. The first is found in German Idealism, the latter strays into deism and later dualism. The most famous, and controversial, aspect of this panentheism is Sophia. Originally associated in the *Philosophy of Economy* with the world soul and the *natura naturans*,[9] Sophia is described contentiously in *Unfading Light* as a fourth hypostasis.[10] In *The Lamb of God*, Sophia is bifurcated, with the divine Sophia subsumed to the nature of God and the creaturely Sophia continuing the role of the world soul. Sophia mediates between God and creation, and distinguishing yet uniting God and the world.

In the *Philosophy of Economy* Sophia is also the human ideal, as the 'original, metaphysical unity of humanity' that 'is a positive spiritual force acting in the world as a unifying principle'.[11] Bulgakov unites this doctrine with his own stresses on creativity, on transcendental humanity, and on the sociality of that humanity. As the transcendental human subject is linked with the unificatory role of Sophia, Bulgakov is able to avoid what he sees as the atomism of Kan-

---

7   This results in a complex series of antinomies, between the Absolute and the Absolute-relative.

8   Gayrilyuk's 2015 commentary on Bulgakov's account of creation notes that God chooses to posit nothing outside of the fullness of God's being.

9   'the world soul, the divine Sophia, the Pleroma', Bulgakov, *Philosophy of Economy. The World as Household*, trans. Catherine Evtukov (New Haven: Yale University Press, 2000), 13.

10   'And as the love of Love and the love for Love, Sophia possesses personhood and countenance, is a subject, a person or, let us say it with theological terminology, a hypostasis; of course she is different from the Hypostases of the Holy Trinity, and is a special hypostasis, of a different order, a fourth hypostasis' (Bulgakov, *Unfading Light*, 217).

11   Bulgakov, *Philosophy of Economy*, 140.

tian subjectivity. Sophia is also a 'living, organizing force contained in nature'[12] that can overcome brute nature, subject as it is to the laws of necessity. The creativity is also sourced in Sophia and transforms the world out from there, and 'humanity as the soul of the world thus works within nature but is also transcendent with respect to the natural world'.[13]

This underscores Bulgakov's understanding of creaturely creativity presented above: limited as we cannot create from nothing. However, Sophia allows us a form of creativity that we can work towards, for the 'theory of the transcendental subject, the world soul, resolves this question differently'.[14] Sophia allows a relationship to God through the world, where 'Sophia, partaking of the cosmic activity of the Logos, endows the world with divine forces, raises it from chaos to cosmos'.[15] This resolves the puzzle of human creativity, which can then be a free re-creation. Humanity cannot create anything new, metaphysically, but our creative acts are 'flashes of another light in the creaturely darkness'.[16]

Creativity, Self-formation and the Person

What do these comments about creation and human creativity mean for becoming, and being human? The kenotic stress in Bulgakov's thought puts the stress on becoming, on work, asceticism, and development. The personalist stress in his thought sees the image and likeness of God as essential to that development. Humanity creates and melds itself into the divine that is revealed in Christ and grounded in Sophia. In participating in the divine world, in the heavenly Divine-Humanity of the God-Man, the Logos, the divine, trinitarian Godhood is mediated to us through the divine Sophia. The world, as the creaturely Sophia 'exists in conformity with its heavenly Proto-Image and is therefore also the human world, centered on and by man'. Amongst these worlds—of God, of the world itself—humanity is 'a "microcosm", and his imprint therefore lies upon the entire world, the macrocosm'.[17] Or, as he put it earlier in a particularly existentialist statement, 'the nature of humankind is marked by genius and nothingness'.[18]

12 Bulgakov, *Philosophy of Economy*, 132.
13 Ibid., 143.
14 Ibid., 144.
15 Ibid., 145.
16 Bulgakov, *The Lamb of God*, trans. Boris Jakim (Grand Rapids: W. B. Eerdmans, 2008), 124.
17 Ibid., 136.
18 Bulgakov, *Unfading Light*, 187.

This is the shape of Bulgakov's personalism. God grounds and gives us personhood as a 'hypostasis that has its own nature', in which sense 'He is a living personal spirit'.[19] From this 'man is an uncreated-created, divine-cosmic being, divine-human in his structure by his very origin … the living image of the tri-hypostatic God'.[20] The image of God in the human 'is connected not only with the trinitarity of its spiritual composition but also with the hypostaseity of the spirit. *A human being is a hypostasis, a countenance, a person*'.[21] The personality is 'the unknowable mystery inherent to each, an unfathomable abyss, an immeasurable depth'. The image is the foundation of our being and the likeness is what we are to realise 'on the basis of the image, as the task of its life'.[22] Returning to this image is Bulgakov's account of *theosis*, which, as can be seen from his cosmology and ontology, is enjoined to his sophiology. Even in its fallen state, humanity preserves in itself the image of God, even if the entelechic form of it within us is lost. Yet Sophia is manifested in the world and it is the sophianicity of the world that is an 'inexhaustible source of the inspiration of life with the nature that elevates, purifies, strengthens, and saves the fallen man'.[23]

We remain within the world, composed of both the spiritual and the natural. Whilst these are in a sense at odds with each other, Bulgakov saw that brute, deterministic nature could liberate itself. This may only be through 'a cosmic process involving labor',[24] but the end is to become a mediator between this world soul and the world, its 'frozen and distorted reflection'.[25] The spiritual principle spiritualises the natural (as the natural is not shorn from Sophia), and we are called to this path of work, of 'likening oneself to God'.[26] The task and role of humanity, living amongst the tatters of the divine life, is to take these up and patch them together. In doing so we are aided by grace, the reception of which is sophianisation.

Therefore, the process of becoming fully, truly human is the process of shaping the self and the world to the divine. Humanity is always in a process of becoming more what it *should* be: the image of God, not quite what it *could* be,

---

19   Bulgakov, *The Lamb of God*, 89.
20   Ibid., 140.
21   Bulgakov, *Unfading Light*, 290.
22   Ibid., 290–91.
23   Bulgakov, *The Lamb of God*, 153.
24   Bulgakov, *Philosophy of Economy*, 132.
25   Ibid., 133.
26   Bulgakov, *The Lamb of God*, 147.

as the 'I as I can only be a self-positing'.[27] Despite the stress on being shaped into and conforming to the image of God, Bulgakov is keen to preserve humanity's freedom, seeing it as a gift given by God, one included 'in the very creation of this being'.[28] Yet the freedom is only justly and correctly used to restore the image of God in humanity, to attend to the sophianicity of human being. Bulgakov sees that 'all creaturely creativity is imperfect and error-prone'.[29] It is not our own efforts but our sophianicity that 'signifies the universal fullness of his being' that we are to actualise.[30]

That task is both individual and ascetic and realised socially and communally in the Church. Bulgakov attends to the singular man and the transcendental man, where both must thrive but not at the expense of the other.[31] Bulgakov will speak of the importance of the individual labouring and re-creating their existence in the world, but also sees that 'selfness throws its heavy veil over all of life, transforming it into a vale of tears and sorrow, implanting deep melancholy, sadness, and dissatisfaction'.[32] Therefore there is a risk in the mandate to labour and create oneself, not out of and into Sophia but instead as mere self-assertion, for 'to want oneself in one's own selfhood, to lock oneself in one's creatureliness as in the absolute, means to want the underground and to be affirmed in it'.[33]

That tension echoes the antinomies that characterise Bulgakov's ontology. We are to be creative but not too self-creative as a necessary consequence of how the human is both a creature and a non-creature. As a result, we are a constant trouble to ourselves, 'a living antinomy, an irreconcilable duality, an

---

27 Bulgakov, *The Lamb of God*, 142–43.
28 Bulgakov, *The Bride of the Lamb*, 94.
29 Ibid., 144.
30 Ibid., 202.
31 Some of this struggling is present in *Unfading Light*, where he writes that 'Humanity is in truth a single Adam both old and new, both first-made and reborn in Christ, and it is necessary to understand in their full significance the words of the Lord Jesus Christ that he himself is present in those who hunger and in those who thirst, in those imprisoned and in all suffering humanity. But at the same time the individualization, the contrasting of separate people as individuals with the Christ-humanity in them, remains no less real. Christ is a human being as such, the whole idea of the human, and in this sense the genus in the human being; but the latter is realized in being as an indeterminate plurality of individualities in which genus is disclosed. Still, the bases of individuality, namely of the given, and just this, are hidden in genus, are ontologically grounded in it', 236.
32 Bulgakov, *Philosophy of Economics*, 141.
33 Bulgakov, *Unfading Light*, 187.

incarnated contradiction'. However, it is this antinomic quality that is 'an expression of its authentic being', and this potential within us is what is capable of divinisation.[34]

How does this vision of humanity and the person compare to Berdiaev's account of creative freedom? Although it appears that their systems are alien to each other's, there are a number of similarities in their philosophical and theological anthropologies. There is the stress on creativity, a transcendental humanity that we are to become, the navigation of the self in the community, and the antinomic nature of humanity. However, from the above discussions of their doctrines of creation, one key difference is apparent. Although they both place a strong stress on creaturely creativity, in Bulgakov the creativity of humanity can be seen as a form of re-creation whereas in Berdiaev it is sourced more directly in the *Ungrund*. Both the means and the ends of human creativity are therefore different. In Bulgakov authentic human existence is our actualisation of our potential towards sophianicity, whereas in Berdiaev it is our own free action that draws on the primal depths of God.

Thus more so than Bulgakov, Berdiaev's philosophy is a philosophy of freedom.[35] In Berdiaev it is God who is the guarantee of freedom: 'if there is no God then I am the slave of the world. The existence of God is the guarantee of my independence of the world, of society, of the State'.[36] Without God, we remain in the world of necessity, of objectivity and objectivizing, for the meontic freedom of God is primordial, not parasitic. Yet this freedom also gives rise to our feelings of unease in the world, as the world is composed of two irreconcilable realities. These are the 'given world of necessity'[37] and the divine, present in human nature, that stands over and against the world of necessity.[38] Created in freedom, we are both in and of the world, existing in an 'eternal

---

34 Bulgakov, *Unfading Light*, 286.

35 Ana Siljak notes that 'Berdiaev's personalism developed out of his lifelong obsession with freedom'; 'The Personalism of Nikolai Berdiaev' in *The Oxford Handbook of Russian Religious Thought*, eds. Caryl Emerson, George Pattison, Randall A. Poole (Oxford: Oxford University Press, 2020), 309–26, 303.

36 Berdyaev, *The Divine and the Human*, 136.

37 Berdyaev, *The Meaning of the Creative Act*, trans. Donald M. Lowrie (New York: Collier Books, 1962), 11.

38 He writes 'God is immanent in the world and in man. The world and man are immanent in God. Everything which happens with man happens with God. There is no dualism of divine and extra-divine nature of God's absolute transcendence of the world and of man.' (Berdyaev, *The Meaning of the Creative Act*, 15).

antinomy of transcendent and immanent, of dualism and monism'.[39] We are conscious that '*in his essence, man is a break in the world of nature, he cannot be contained within it*'.[40]

This lack of unity is both our disjunction with the natural and the source of our creative action and our freedom. In *Truth and Revelation* Berdiaev talks of the transcendental human, who exists beyond the duality of subject and object, open to the divine with the 'a priori of religion'.[41] That enables humanity to be open to grace, the 'divine element in man, the eternal bond between transcendental man and God'.[42] The transcendental human is the free human: free from static concepts of being, God, nature, society, history, and civilization, amongst others. Full as we are of unresolvable paradoxes and living in a fallen world, we are to exercise our creativity and create our ethical existence, orientated towards the future even as we are involved in history and its failures. We are called on not to follow particular moral laws but to create the good, to exercise our freedom and 'co-operate with God, to create the good and produce new values'.[43] As the break in the natural world, we can reach through that and relate the world back to the supernatural reality that it points to. The self-contradictory, fraught nature of humanity is the spur for our creativity.

Berdiaev's thought is also personalistic: as the image and likeness of God we contain a 'Divine idea which his freedom may realize or destroy',[44] we are persons as we contain that image. This personalism grounds Berdiaev's ethics. Personality is 'eternal, identical and unique' as well as 'permanently in a process of creative change', its content is 'best revealed in love'.[45] This love presupposes another personality to which our personality must relate, and enables an I–Thou relationship that aspires towards communion. That community (*sobornost*) is founded on an ethics which begins 'by opposing the final socialization of man which destroys the freedom of spirit and conscience'[46] grounded in the love of God.

Therefore, our individual creativity opens the infinite up into the finite and points towards God: to being infinite, free, creative, and loving, focused on the

39 Berdyaev, *The Meaning of the Creative Act*, 15.
40 Ibid., 60.
41 Berdyaev, *Truth and Revelation*, 17.
42 Ibid., 23.
43 Berdyaev, *The Destiny of Man* (New York: Harper and Brothers, 1960), 44.
44 Ibid., 53.
45 Berdyaev, *Solitude and Society*, trans. George Reavey (London: Geoffrey Bles, 1947), 122, 128, 146.
46 Berdyaev, *The Destiny of Man*, 58.

concrete and individual. Love, as the content of freedom, leads us to an individuality of the new Adam, not the old freedom of individualism. It calls us to imitate Christ, as both divine and human, who as Absolute Man instantiated a new anthropology that humanity can participate in, redeeming and saving human nature.[47] Berdiaev's ethics underline the priority of the supernatural, indicating 'a set of values outside of the empirical world of necessity [...] giving the individual a place from which to critique what exists and from which to pursue the possibility of reform and transformation'.[48]

Authenticity and Creativity

Over the course of this essay I have explored how both Bulgakov and Berdiaev could understand authenticity. As an existential philosopher, Berdiaev is easier to place in this conversation. However, through Bulgakov's use of concepts such as creativity, freedom, and the antinomic quality of human existence, his thought can be explored with reference to authenticity. Whilst not a philosopher or theologian of authenticity, Bulgakov does not shy away from discussions of how one is, or is not, to make oneself. There is enough in his thought that can stand as a contrast or as way in which to further explore Berdiaev's more existentialist mandate, to create the authentic self. Indeed, the differences sourced in their accounts of creation and creativity are ones that can be used to navigate a self-creation that may be able to avoid the more existentialist pitfalls of subjectivity and self-affirmation, as it espouses a creativity that is not self-creation.

Thus far, the fullest examination of both Berdiaev and Bulgakov's thought together is Zwahlen's analysis, focused on the doctrine of creation. Both Bulgakov and Berdiaev have second first principles that enable them to avoid par-

---

47   As Bodea points out, 'it is in the understanding of humanity from above, from the relatedness of humanity with God that the authenticity and recognition of the dignity of the human person stems. The height of this dignity of humanity, and the meaningfulness of humanity, was revealed in its fullness in Christ. That is why Berdyaev calls Christology the true anthropology' (Raul-Ovidiu Bodea, 'The Task of Authenticity: Martin Heidegger and Nikolai Berdyaev in Dialogue' in *Ex Patribus Lux: Essays on Orthodox Theological Anthropology and Georges Florovsky's Theology*, eds. Nikolaos Asproulis & Olga Sevastyanova (Volos: Volos Academy Publications. 2021) 58). Siljak also sees that 'the person, then, is the partly Divine, partly natural creature who contains within himself pure, unlimited creative potential, who must be free in order to fulfil his divine, creative 'reality''; 'The Personalism of Nikolai Berdiaev', 315.

48   Siljak, 'The Personalism of Nikolai Berdiaev', 310.

ticular metaphysical problems, even as they create others.[49] Whilst attentive to
the issues of Sophiology, Zwahlen sees that Berdiaev's less stable metaphysical
system entails that his personalist work is more troubled. God's freedom is
limited by the *Ungrund* and thus the freedom of humanity is similarly restricted.[50] This then impacts the image of God, whereas Bulgakov's personalism is
fundamentally better grounded, as his Sophiology allows for 'an autonomous
good creation *out of nothing* to be able to be created'.[51]

That system can support the image of God, for both thinkers see that the
image of God is that by which we are to be measured. Bulgakov's structure and
system enables him to put forward a more concrete understanding of human
authenticity. She argues that the 'famous, controversial, and dreaded sophiology is not about drowning human persons in an indifferent cosmos';[52] instead
it is an anthropocentric system that underscores the image of God. She further
argues that Bulgakov's vision of the world is not as dualistic as Berdiaev's, as
Bulgakov seeks to change the world rather than reach beyond it—although
this is only possible because the supernatural is so diffused within the world.

It is this aspect of Bulgakov that complicates the positive vision of his account of human creativity and becoming. To become ourselves in Bulgakov's
theology is to become the cosmos, to become Sophia. The more stable ontological framework that Bulgakov provides is based on an antinomic ontology,
and thus we are still separated from God as Absolute. Even with, and perhaps
because of, the antinomies, bifurcations, human becoming is fundamentally
conformation rather than freedom. Berdiaev remarked on this, and Gavrilyuk
notes his objection that 'the idea that rational creatures freely assent to their
being created by God makes sense only if Bulgakov accepts Berdiaev's postulate
that freedom is uncreated [...] Bulgakov forceably [in the *Bride of the Lamb*]
rejected the idea of uncreated freedom as entailing cosmic dualism'.[53] In the

---

49   Slesinski thus notes that 'at the heart of Bulgakov's sophiological conception is his in-
      tuition of the inherent correlativity of the divine and human worlds, Robert Slesinski
      'Sergius Bulgakov in Exile: The Flowering of a Systematic Theologian' in *The Oxford
      Handbook of Russian Religious Thought*, eds. Caryl Emerson, George Pattison, Randall
      A. Poole (Oxford: Oxford University Press, 2020), 480–94, 481.
50   Regula Zwahlen, *Das revolutionäre Ebenbild Gottes. Anthropologien der Menschenwürde
      bei Nikolaj A. Berdjaev und Sergej N. Bulgakov* (Münster: LIT, 2010), 365.
51   Ibid.
52   Zwahlen, 'Different concepts of personality,' 185.
53   Paul Gavrilyuk, 'Bulgakov's Account of Creation: Neglected Aspects, Critics and Con-
      temporary Relevance', *International Journal of Systematic Theology*, 2015, 17/4. 450–63,
      458.

Philosophy of Economy Bulgakov sees freedom as a gift from God to honour not just humankind but to enshrine the individual,[54] and yet with Bulgakov's understanding of Sophia, creaturely and otherwise, we can only really become the world, and Bulgakov's continued use of the world-soul to refer to Sophia underscores this. For it is mere, flawed re-creation, utilising the stuff of a Sophia-suffused world.[55] Although it is more stable, it also runs the risks of pantheism and of being absorbed into the *natura naturans*.[56]

Although Bulgakov presents, then, a far more stable, and perhaps coherent, ontology, viewing his understanding of authentic human existence through these particular lenses brings out the limits of his navigation of creaturely creativity. Bulgakov may change the world and be more positive towards the world, but the stuff of the world is, fundamentally, God. Even with what Gavrilyuk describes as Bulgakov's more successful kenoticism (2005, 253), it may not quite exorcise the spectre of Spinoza that haunts German Idealism.

The question remains whether Berdiaev's unbridled and primordial freedom is a *better* principle to hold than Bulgakov's more complex understanding of freedom. It is not clear that that is the case. Making that freedom the

---

54 'God as the perfect and absolute Individual, as Freedom itself, wished in his love to honor man with his image, that is, freedom, and therefore freedom is included in the plan of the universe as its foundation' (Bulgakov, *Philosophy of Economy*, 202).

55 Gavrilyuk does seek to defend Bulgakov from pantheism, stressing instead that the mediating figure of Sophia allows some flexibility here. Yet as May states, 'The theological and philosophical first principle that motivates the need for an 'intermediary figure' to unite two 'opposing notions' already undermines the Christian doctrine of creation and the ontological relationship that it establishes between God and the world. Put simply, God cannot be opposed to the world in the manner that Bulgakov assumes, unless God and the world are inhabiting common ontological ground. In other words, in Bulgakov's scheme God is being subsumed under the same mode of being as other created beings.' (Richard May, 'Between God and the world: a critical appraisal of the sophiology of Sergius Bulgakov' in *Scottish Journal of Theology* (2021) 74, 67–84, 78).

56 Richard May's analysis of Bulgakov's Sophiology argues that despite his desire to avoid the German Idealist collapse of God and the world, his use of antinomies does not succeed, for 'in true Idealist style Bulgakov merely demonstrates that what appears to be dialectically opposed is in fact one and the same thing. We are therefore left with an Absolute becoming itself in another that in the end is revealed to be no other at all.' ('Between God and the world', 76–7). Gallaher also notes that the antinomies are not truly antinomic but the same 'simply stated twice but in a different form' (Brandon Gallaher, 'There is Freedom: The Dialectic of Freedom and Necessity in the Trinitarian Theologies of Sergii Bulgakov, Karl Barth and Hans Urs von Balthasar,' Ph. D. thesis., Regent's Park College, Oxford, 2011, 107).

foundational metaphysical principle results in Berdiaev's own sleights of hand: qualifying nothingness into something worryingly substantial at times, and upholding that substantive void as the ideal for humanity. In making freedom ultimate, which he separates from nature, Berdiaev sacrifices the love that Bulgakov makes the key aspect of the supernatural in the natural. His freedom requires a stark dichotomy, as he sees that 'the attempts which have been made to base freedom upon naturalistic metaphysics have always been superficial'.[57] This makes him a powerful critique of atheistic existentialism, but also raises concerns about how God relates to the world. It results, as Pattison comments, in an 'extreme dualism in which the creativity of freedom and spirit are consistently threatened from the side of the material world'.[58]

Conclusion and Possibilities

To resolve the complications of both of these visions, perhaps, in the grand tradition of Hegel, the other great German Idealist, himself, a mediation can be found between these two visions of authentic human existence and their metaphysical foundations. Doing so also sets a laudable goal for both philosophy and theology: to think anew what the fullness of human existence is, how to continuously negotiate freedom and obedience, creativity and limitation, and to see that it is a process of love that these dichotomies are continuously resolved and unresolved.

Therefore, with that in mind, we can think about the further possibilities of Bulgakov's thought. For Bulgakov's sophiology and his understanding of the God–world relationship remain as concepts to be drawn on even as they are to be carefully navigated. Bulgakov's wider project does present a more concrete account of how we become more truly human, and what are to become more human towards. It presents a clearer account of human becoming than that of Berdiaev's, which is more attentive to what, other than freedom, should structure and determine our relationships to others. Bulgakov's particular account of personalism can also be brought into conversation with other, contemporary personalists, whom Berdiaev associated with and which were associated with the philosophies of existence in France. Bulgakov can thus be seen as advancing a particular personalist ethics that resonates with the questions raised by these other contemporary personalists.

---

57 Berdyaev, *Freedom and the Spirit*, trans. O. F. Clarke (London: Geoffrey Bles, 1935), 117.
58 George Pattison, *Thinking about God in an Age of Technology* (Oxford: Oxford University Press, 2005), 43.

Secondly, another aspect of Bulgakov's authenticity that can be a source of further exploration is his use of labour and asceticism. There is now renewed focus on spiritual practice, formation, and asceticism in relation to religion and society. Bulgakov's thought provides an understanding of ascetic authenticity that does not devote itself just to self-formation, but explores how that can and should be realised in community, grounded as it is in the church and in the perichoretic Godmanhood. There can be a revisioning of authenticity—not just as self-assertion from nothing, but as an ascetic practice that incorporates the church and the world. The seeds sown in the *Philosophy of Economy* may, and indeed should, sprout in further and farther fields than originally conceived.

Building the House of Wisdom
DOI 10.17438/978-3-402-12179-5

Bulgakov on Mangodhood—or, Satan after Schelling

Justin Shaun Coyle

I want to draw attention to the satanology of Sergei Bulgakov—and not only because it is so rarely commented upon by his readers.[1] Bulgakov's satanology deserves attention precisely as an instance of modern satanology that refuses neatly and cleanly to distinguish scriptural exegesis from theological specu-lation. One way his readers might learn to admire Bulgakov's refusal is by attending closely to how he adopts and adapts philosophic idioms to interpret scripture's deliverances on Satan. More narrowly: I propose here to measure Bulgakov's oft-noted but rarely examined use of F. W. J. Schelling, particular-ly the latter's satanology.[2] That act of measuring yields three points at which Schelling's Satan stretches his black wings over Bulgakov. I dedicate a section of what follows to each point. Within each section, I not only assay *what* Bul-gakov borrows from Schelling but also consider *how* he develops and refines and burnishes it.

---

1 Tikhon Vasilyev briefly treats Schelling's influence on Bulgakov's *angelology* in "As-pects of Schelling's Influence on Sergius Bulgakov and Other Thinkers of the Russian Religious Renaissance of the Twentieth Century" in *International Journal of Philosophy and Theology* 80.1/2 (2019): 143–59 and more extensively in "Christian Angelology in Pseudo-Dionysius and Sergius Bulgakov" (PhD thesis, Oxford University, 2019).
2 Recently Robert F. Slesinski's *The Theology of Sergius Bulgakov* (Yonkers: St Vladimir's Seminary Press, 2017) argues that Bulgakov's thought "cannot fully be apprized apart from an appreciation of its philosophical roots in German Idealism" (143). But his monograph treats Schelling little—most Anglophone Bulgakov literature runs similar-ly. Jennifer Newsome Martin's *Hans Urs von Balthasar and the Critical Appropriation of Russian Religious Thought* (Notre Dame: University of Notre Dame Press, 2015) offers a bit. The best treatment of Bulgakov that takes Schelling seriously remains Brandon Gallaher's *Freedom and Necessity in Modern Trinitarian Theology* (Oxford/New York: Oxford University Press, 2016).

I.

Bulgakov begins his mature satanology with one of his most controverted doctrines—that is, the self-positing of created hypostases. Let this, then, serve as the first point of Schelling's influence. In *The Bride of the Lamb*, Bulgakov writes of "hypostatic spirits" who derive their origin antinomically both from outside themselves *and* from their own act of "self-positing."[3] If each bears its own "mode"—the former "before time" and thus "original" and the second "temporal" and thus "empirical"—they constitute a single act of "self-determination."[4]

Constitutive of creaturely hypostases, then, is a singular act of self-determination. For Bulgakov, that act comprises two modes: the first transcending the bounds of spacetime, the second falling squarely within it. And both modes together just are for Bulgakov the singular act the self is.

Bulgakov admits that he borrows this concept of radical self-determination from Schelling's 1809 *Freiheitsschrift*.[5] Yet here, Schelling himself develops this concept in response to Kant. Whatever freedom means for Schelling, it cannot entail a capacity to choose among options "without determining reasons."[6] Against this "common concept" Schelling wields Kant's. For Kant, Schelling summarizes, free is only that which "acts only in accord with the laws of its own being and is determined by nothing else either in or outside itself."[7] Of course freedom of this sort for Kant obtains only in the noumenal x of humanity's *intelligible* being.[8] Empirically, however, no such freedom exists or could. So runs Kant's third antinomy.[9]

Schelling admires how Kant discovers an antinomy of freedom's "absolute beginning" but not how he resolves it. Kant imagines that the antimony's thesis and antithesis bear equal claim to truth. Only they apply to different domains. Causal necessity belongs to the realm of appearances. Freedom in turn applies to the noumenal, which Kant tucks safely beyond reason's reach. We must *postulate* human freedom as a practically justified belief to get on with the business

3   Sergei Bulgakov, *The Bride of the Lamb* (Grand Rapids: W. B. Eerdmans, 2001), 87, my emphasis.
4   Bulgakov, *The Bride of the Lamb*, 119.
5   Sergei Bulgakov, *Philosophy of Economy: The World as Household*, trans. Catherine Evtuhov (New Haven: Yale University Press, 2000), 205.
6   I/7, 382/48.
7   I/7, 384/50.
8   I/7, 383/49. See also *KrV* A538/B566.
9   Immanuel Kant, *Critique of Pure Reason* (New York: Palgrave Macmillan, 2007), A444/B472, 409–15.

of ethics. But we cannot and should not confuse this practical postulate with a theoretical account of freedom. To that last reason cannot attain.[10]

Allergic to final contradiction, Schelling refuses Kant's refusal. He does so by denying that freedom and necessity both claim truth in their respective domains. Schelling teaches instead that the very antimony Kant discovered *itself* belongs to the order of appearances. Innocent of spacetime, freedom and necessity brook no antinomy. Rather the intelligible truth of each just *is* their unity. Or, as Schelling has it: "absolute necessity alone is also absolute freedom."[11] For Schelling, then, Kant was right to identify the formal essence of freedom with self-determination absent external coercion. But he was wrong to assume that its opposition to necessity does not itself feature among spacetime's appearances.

Schelling is determined to render Kant's failure his own success. Discovering a speculative identity between freedom and necessity suggests to Schelling a much more radical "absolute beginning" than in Kant's conception.[12] Schelling calls that absolute beginning *die intelligible Tat*: an act of self-positing outside spacetime in which of necessity agents freely determine themselves.[13]

This "deed" beggars the imagination not least because it operates wide of choice, consciousness, and the capacity to act. No choice: this would involve time-dependent deliberation or indecision.[14] No consciousness: this would mean the act follows rather than constitutes consciousness. And no capacity to act: certainly not if "the essence (*Wesen*) of the human being is fundamentally his own act."[15] There is neither actor nor capacity 'before' the act. Rather the act constitutes both actor—she is the doing of the eternal deed—*and* capacity—act precedes potency.[16] Details aside, Schelling's fundamental point is that the human being depends for its existence on its act and not the other way round.[17]

---

10   For Schelling's early criticism of Kant's practical postulates, see his *Philosophical Letters on Dogmatism and Criticism* (1795).

11   I/7, 385/50.

12   In fact, Schelling's thinking here combines two aspects of Kant's: the third antinomy of the first critique and the account of "radical evil" in book 1 of *Religion within the Bounds of Mere Reason*.

13   I/7, 386/51–52.

14   Even if choice did not entail time, Schelling rejects a conflation of decision with choice on the grounds that "if freedom is to be saved by nothing other than the complete contingency of actions, then it is not to be saved at all" (I/7, 382/49).

15   I/7, 385/50.

16   I/7, 385/52.

17   I/7, 387/53.

Schelling judges the cost of the doctrine's difficulty worth its double reward. The first is ethical: we remain on this view radically responsible for our
own acts. Indeed, it is responsibility that causes Schelling to shirk theological
accounts of predestination. If humans are culpable agents, he argues, then it
must be we rather than God who determine ourselves.[18] The second reward is
metaphysical: it allows Schelling to loosen the Gordian knot of freedom and
necessity without Kantian antimony. The eternal deed remains necessary to the
extent that we could not be without it. And it remains free to the extent that
the act alone determines itself. If for Schelling we are essentially an "originary
and fundamental willing," that willing must be ontologically both perfectly free
and unavoidably necessary.[19]

Bulgakov's *Philosophy of Economy* (1911) adopts Schelling's intelligible deed
without adapting it much. Bulgakov variously names its agent the "substantial
I" and "human individuals."[20] He then uncritically correlates both with "man's
ideal preexistence" in the thought of Plato and Origen. By *Unfading Light* (1917),
however, Bulgakov translates the doctrine into a more familiar dogmatic idiom. Here, the subject of the intelligible deed is a "hypostasis" (ипостась), now
explicitly inclusive of Satan.[21] With this last Bulgakov targets Schelling, who
had rendered both the angelic host and Satan "faceless and uncreated."[22] Still,
Bulgakov's position remains underdeveloped. However, insofar as he insists
that the intelligible deed falls wide of spacetime, Bulgakov often lapses into
protological description. The eternal mode of the act almost seems to antecede
its temporal mode both logically and chronologically.[23]

Fast-forward to *Jacob's Ladder* (1928), where Bulgakov theorizes a Satanic hypostasis who attempts metaphysical suicide only to fail.[24] And fail Satan
must, since as a creature his eternal I has always consented to being counted among God's creatures. Thus Bulgakov dares a more structural break with
Schelling. To be a created hypostasis is now not (as for Schelling) to determine
oneself between good *and evil* supratemporally. It is rather to have always already determined oneself for the good alone and so consented to one's own

18   I/7, 385/ 52–53.
19   I/7 385/52.
20   Bulgakov, *Philosophy of Economy*, 202–04.
21   Sergei Bulgakov, *Unfading Light: Contemplations and Speculations* (Grand Rapids:
     W. B. Eerdmans, 2012), 291 and 312.
22   Bulgakov, *Unfading Light*, 312.
23   Bulgakov, *Philosophy of Economy*, 201–05; UL 210, 316.
24   Sergei Bulgakov, *Jacob's Ladder: On Angels* (Grand Rapids: W. B. Eerdmans, 2010), 108
     and 110.

creation outside of time. Good and evil appear as options only in spacetime. By restricting Satan's fall to his temporal mode, Bulgakov renders Satan impotent to place under erasure his own act of co-creation that looms "metaphysically behind" even his depredations here below.[25]

By *The Bride of the Lamb* (1945), Bulgakov has overhauled Schelling's doctrine to form an entire theology. Creaturely hypostases—differentiated now from mere individuals[26]—are still antinomic. But their antinomy is now structured christologically rather than platonically. That is, the antinomy lies between uncreated and created rather than eternal idea and temporal instantiation.[27] This christological turn allows Bulgakov to ground the supratemporal and temporal modes of the one hypostatic act theandrically in the Virgin's fiat and Christ's two wills.[28] It also allows Bulgakov to think the intelligible deed eschatologically—or from the end backward. Where in 1911 Bulgakov alluded to "preexistence" he now denies any temporal seriality.[29] And so by 1945 creation's eternal truth before God becomes less anticipation than incorporation—even enhypostatization—into created Sophia, "the all-man, to whom the incarnation and the redemption refer."[30]

Bulgakov's christological revision of Schelling's intelligible deed affords him another move. It allows him to recast the final judgment synergistically as *self*-judgment. Might we imagine, Bulgakov asks, Judas *the Apostle* as the supratemporal I sitting with Christ in judgment over Judas *the Betrayer* as the temporal I?[31] Bulgakov extends the same logic to Satan. "Even Satan in his madness," Bulgakov claims, "does not have the power to overcome the fact of his own being, its divine foundation, that is, the sophianicity of all creation, by virtue of which God will be all in all."[32] So if "satanism exhausts itself,"[33] it is

---

25   Bulgakov, *Jacob's Ladder*, 108.

26   Bulgakov, *The Bride of the Lamb*, 83.

27   Ibid., 85, 95. See also *The Lamb of God* (Grand Rapids: W. B. Eerdmans, 2008), 140–56 and "The Problem of 'Conditional Immortality'" in *The Sophiology of Death: Essays on Eschatology: Personal, Political, Universal* (Eugene: Cascade Books, 2021), 68.

28   For the former, see Bulgakov, *The Lamb of God*, 179; for the latter, see ibid., 78 and *The Bride of the Lamb*, 143, 496.

29   Sergei Bulgakov, *Judas Iscariot: Apostle-Betrayer* (Mike Whitton, 2017), Kindle edition.

30   Bulgakov, *The Bride of the Lamb*, 113. See also *The Lamb of God*, 187.

31   Ibid., 476. For more, see Bulgakov, *Judas Iscariot*. Satan's function in this text is much more political than metaphysical, however, as "Luciferism" becomes a cipher for Bolshevism.

32   Bulgakov, *The Bride of the Lamb*, 517.

33   Ibid., 512.

only because Satan at time's end yields to *his own* supratemporal act of co-creating himself. At length, it seems, Satan too must become who he is. And that for Bulgakov can be nothing less than who he has always already determined himself to be in Christ.[34]

II.

But time sees Luficer fall into Satan. How Bulgakov thinks Lucifer-Satan's personality, then, is the next point of Schelling's influence. In *The Bride of the Lamb*, Bulgakov distinguishes within the personality (личность) a "little I" (малое я) and the "big I" (Я) it wishes to become. The "hypostatic fall" of the former is "Luciferian" to the extent that it attempts to conceal its ontological dependence on God but lapses only into "all-devouring [...] hypostatic envy."[35] In other places Bulgakov claims that in his fall Satan rages against creation's very purpose, or "overcoming the individual as self-isolating, nonuniversal being in the ongoing sophianization of creation."[36] What does he mean?

Here again Bulgakov develops Schelling, particularly his concept of personalization. In his *Freiheitsschrift*, Schelling wonders why the formal essence of freedom as self-determination should spell a real capacity for good or evil. Because, he discovers, only by dissociating can an agent attain self-consciousness and thus personality.[37] Yet dissociating need not mean repressing—still less fracturing into good and evil.[38] Schelling explains: "personality is founded [...] on the connection between a self-determining being and a basis independent of him."[39] All of reality parses along this scission, the two sides of which Schelling most often calls "that-which-exists" (*das Existierende*) and "ground" (*Grund*).[40] In fact this division rives even God, in whom Schelling locates "two equally eternal beginnings of self-revelation."[41]

---

34 Bulgakov, *The Bride of the Lamb*, 225.
35 Ibid., 98.
36 Ibid., 149.
37 F. W. J. Schelling, *The Ages of the World* (1811) (Albany: State University of New York, 2020), 128.
38 On which difference see Sean J. McGrath, *The Dark Ground of Spirit: Schelling and the Unconscious* (New York/London: Routledge 2012), 126 ff.
39 I/7, 394/59.
40 I/7, 358/52.
41 I/7, 394/59.

And so god-before-God splits into two wills.[42] The "will of the ground"—or First Potency—wills only itself in a negative, undifferentiated solipsism.[43] But by so positing itself (A=A), First Potency betrays its very duality. After all, positing differs from posited (A=B). A second will wills only to reflect First Potency back to itself (A²). As such, it positively and kenotically wills another and so constitutes the "will to love." First Potency wills to save its own life and loses it (A=B), Second Potency wills to lose it for the sake of another and so saves it (A²). The unity of these wills is Third Potency (A³), the "connection of the ideal principle [...] with the independent ground [...] the living unity of both is spirit."[44] For Schelling, Third Potency is nothing less than the Absolute's self-consciousness of itself as the mediation of two wills subordinate one to another.[45] Schelling's conviction throughout is that only a dissociated Absolute forsakes *Selbstheit* to achieve *Persönlichkeit*.[46]

Not so with creatures. Even if they posit their essence in the intelligible deed, they receive their existence from the Creator.[47] Like God, creatures too bear a distinction between ground and that-which-is. Unlike God, for creatures these are not "equally eternal" and so always already subordinate one to another.[48] If "the same unity that is inseverable in God must therefore be severable in man," creaturely dissociation risks repression.[49] Evil appears on the scene, then, precisely when ground's "will to nothing" (*der Wille, der nichts will*) resists that-which-exists's "will to love." The structure of surrender now accommodates seizure and sequestration. When surrender yields to seizure, *Selbstheit* resists *Persönlichkeit* by hoarding its "peculiar life [...] through the misuse of freedom." And so "evil resides," Schelling concludes, "in a positive perversion."[50]

For Schelling, reality just *is* the struggle to wrest personality from undifferentiated selfhood (*Selbstheit*). Thinking evil as a "positive perversion" of this process leads Schelling to notice a "second principle of darkness."[51] About this principle Schelling teaches three points. First, that it is humans who awaken

---

42   "Before" here is logical, not temporal. Cf. *WA* (1811), 76; 132.
43   I/7, 375/42.
44   I/7, 394/59.
45   Schelling, *The Ages of the World*, 121–22.
46   Ibid., 221.
47   See Thomas, "Freedom and Ground," 420.
48   I/7, 365/32–33. Cf. Schelling, *The Ages of the World*, 112.
49   I/7, 365/33.
50   I/7, 366/35.
51   I/7, 378/44, my emphasis.

and activate the "spirit of evil" and not the reverse. Second, that the spirit of evil is not itself created, but rather develops its curious positivity in creation. And third, that this spirit emerges through a nocturnal parody of Second Potency, "self-doubling [...] as the means to an ever-greater intensification of selfhood and not as a means for freeing oneself from it."[52] A later Schelling will name this evil principle *der umgekehrte Gott*—God-in-reverse.

Like Schelling, Bulgakov too thinks reality as process from natural selfhood to personality. Like Schelling too, Bulgakov indexes this process to trinitarian relations. And like Schelling, Bulgakov imagines Satan as parodic antipode to this process. Yet on each point, Bulgakov revises Schelling heavily.

On the first point, Bulgakov insists that the process of personality in question is not a self-overcoming of Schelling's nondialectical, voluntarist sort.[53] For Bulgakov too, this process does not result in a merely individual personality. On the contrary: it is axiomatic for Bulgakov that individuals are *not yet* hypostases.[54] So whatever the hypostasis' becoming in time entails, it terminates not in personalization but in *sophianization*. By incorporation into creaturely Sophia, that is—or Christ's resurrected and so supratemporal human nature— the hypostasis becomes who it always supratemporally is.[55] But for Bulgakov, it does so only in Christ and with the saints. As in the *trinitas quae deus est*, the hypostatic is always "*multi*hypostatic."[56]

On the second point, Bulgakov undertakes even heavier revisions. First, Bulgakov declines subjecting the Absolute to a process of personalization as had the middle Schelling. "Schelling's heresy," Bulgakov reports, "lies in putting the nature of the hypostasis before the hypostasis [...] its being *anhypostatic*."[57] For Bulgakov there is no nature—created or otherwise—that is not enhypostatized (even if it seems otherwise to the creaturely, empirical I). Just as subject grounds predicate and Father Son,[58] so hypostasis grounds nature.

On the last point, Bulgakov agrees that Satan parodies Second Potency's logic by inversion. Satan is variously "mangodhood" and "antichrist." Bulgakov

---

52 Schelling, *The Ages of the World*, 158.
53 Cf. McGrath, *The Philosophical Foundations of the Late Schelling*, 95–101.
54 Bulgakov, *The Bride of the Lamb*, 83 ff.
55 Bulgakov, *Sophia, the Wisdom of God: An Outline of Sophiology* (New York: Lindisfarne Press, 1993), 126.
56 Bulgakov, *The Comforter* (Grand Rapids: W. B. Eerdmans, 2004), 356.
57 Bulgakov, *The Tragedy of Philosophy: Philosophy and Dogma* (Brooklyn: Angelico Press, 2020), 99. See also Bulgakov, *The Lamb of God*, 183.
58 For Schelling, First Potency is object/predicate and Second Potency is subject; Bulgakov intentionally reverses this order.

concedes also to Schelling that the dissonance between Satan's consciousness of his derivative being and his drive to displace God explain his insanity or "hunger."[59] Bulgakov wonders, though, whether Schellingian personalization does not bear its own undoing. If personalization promises only self-overcoming for the self rather than incorporation into creaturely Sophia, then Schellingian personalization risks shading into satanization.

Which is why, incidentally, Bulgakov so often renders Fichte an inadvertent theorist of Satan.[60]

Eclipsed in Fichte are theological distinctions among the temporal, empirical I (likeness), the supratemporal I (image), and the Absolute I (Archetype).[61] Not only does Fichte erroneously and impossibly identify the first with the last.[62] He also renders every other I a *Nicht-Ich*. This in turn indulges an instrumental positing of the *Ich* melting reality's irreducible remainders into a "mirror" reflecting only itself.[63] True, Schelling circumvents the first error by horizontalizing Fichte's *Tathandlung* into a process whose beginning is given. But Bulgakov suspects that the result of Schelling's process—the person as individual, self-determined will—bears striking resemblance to Fichte's *Ich*. Sophianization triply mediates the creaturely hypostasis: it is given to itself by God, by other creaturely hypostases, by its supratemporal I. Without such mediation what distinguishes personhood in Schelling from mere selfhood? Personalization from satanization? Godmanhood from mangodhood?

III.

The last point of Schelling's satanology Bulgakov develops concerns evil's curious positivity. In *The Bride of the Lamb*, he teaches of evil both that "one must also recognize its fatal, destructive force in creation [...] as a *positively* and peculiarly *creative* force"[64] and that it "arises in time [...] *created* by creatures [...]

59　Bulgakov, *The Bride of the Lamb*, 508.

60　Ibid., 232.

61　Bulgakov, *Unfading Light*, 209; *Tragedy of Philosophy*, 232–33; *The Bride of the Lamb*, 43, 86, 127, 512.

62　For Bulgakov on Fichte, see Joshua Heath's "Sergii Bulgakov's Linguistic Trinity," *Modern Theology* (2021): 1–25. Still, recent literature has downplayed or ignored Schelling's influence to focus instead on Fichte's. But we ought to ask whom exactly Bulgakov has in mind when in *Tragedy of Philosophy*, 234 he writes: "Fichte plus Spinoza—that is the task."

63　Bulgakov, *The Bride of the Lamb*, 512.

64　Ibid., 147, my emphasis.

actualized nothing becomes *a reality*."[65] On their surface, these texts seem to contravene two deeply held tenets of Christian theology: that, first, evil is sheer privation and that, second, evil is not a creature. How indeed Bulgakov skirts the otherwise Manichaean becomes clear, however, when we read him against Schelling.

Schelling too found the *privatio* account incomplete. What motivates his critique is as ever his twin preoccupation with freedom and personality. For Schelling the *privatio* account at best cannot explain *why* any person would or could decline the good itself for its lack. At worst it too closely identifies evil with matter and so robs embodied agents of freedom.[66] In its place, Schelling proffers his own theory. That theory begins with a distinction between general and particular evil.[67] General evil exists therefore only as pure potency. To exist actually it must be "aroused to actuality" by humans. But first, whence general evil as pure potency? From a parodic "self-doubling" issues "another spirit"— not the kenotic Second Potency but "the reversed god." As ground becomes "obscenely actual," this reversed god lives as hunger for being that will never be. Its very striving to conceal the givenness of its ground discloses its failure. Seizure of selfhood stymies its process of personalization: ontologically the reversed god is sheer oscillation between being and nothing.

Schelling does not yet name this other spirit 'Satan' until his later *Urfassung der Philosophie der Offenbarung* (1831/32), where he embroiders the *Freiheitsschrift's* latent satanology with scriptural exegesis.[68] Even if he grants that general evil as reversed god is what the tradition calls Satan, Schelling hesitates to hypostatize him. His reasons for hesitating are two. First, Satan's being precisely refuses the process of personalization by seizing (rather than surrendering) selfhood. Second, Schelling denies that scripture anywhere directly teaches

65 Bulgakov, *The Bride of the Lamb*, 153, my emphasis.
66 I/7, 368–70/36–37.
67 I/7, 390/54, my emphasis. Schelling takes the Greek from Plato's *Timaeus*.
68 Schelling, *Urfassung der Philosophie der Offenbarung* (1831/32) vol. 2, ed. Walter E. Ehrhardt (Hamburg: Felix Meiner Verlag, 1992), 615–72. Most of the small literature on Schelling's satanology focuses on his *Philosophie der Offenbarung*, whether 1831/32 or 1841/42. See Walter Kasper, *The Absolute in History: The Philosophy and Theology of History in Schelling's Late Philosophy*, trans. Sr Katherine E. Wolff (New York/Mahwah: Paulist Press, 2018), 391–403; Malte Dominik Krüger, *Göttliche Freiheit: Die Trinitätslehre in Schellings Spätphilosophie* (Tübingen: Mohr Siebeck, 2008), 206–08; Alexandra Roux, "La majesté du diable dans la philosophie de la révélation de Schelling," *Revue philosophique de la France et de l'étranger* 2 (2009): 191–205; and Jason M. Wirth, "Schelling and the Satanic: On *Naturvernichtung*," *Kabiri* 2 (2020): 81–92.

Satan's creation. Neither creature nor Creator, neither personal nor fully existent, Satan lives as an "evil principle," an "eternal hunger and thirst, eternal seeking [...] for reality."[69]

What then renders general evil particular? For Schelling only a human being can reduce evil's pure potency to 'act', as it were. When she does—when she seizes rather than surrenders selfhood—she "opens herself to the spirit of lies."[70] Schelling calls this act "sin." What exactly this sin's anti-personal act emanates can be known, as Plato says of the χώρα, only through "bastard reasonings (λογισμῷ τινι νόθῳ) [...] seeing that it has not for its own [...] but fleets ever as a phantom of something else (ἑτέρου φάντασμα)."[71]

Schelling's discovery of evil's curious positivity through sin also explains his later reversal of Genesis 3. There Satan is neither angelic supernova nor serpent, Schelling explains. Rather he is the divine ground illicitly and perversely "made actual" by our first parents. Being impersonal, Satan's "should-not-be-but-yet-is" from First Potency's *Seinkönnen* can emerge only in and through creatures as a sort of "false life" (*falsches Leben*).[72] And so for Schelling the creation myth depicts externally what always threatens selves internally: the latent dissociation in consciousness gone sideways, the pursuit of a freedom which only enslaves. If Satan be a creature, he is not God's but ours.[73]

All of which, again, Bulgakov reads and refines.[74] He learns from Schelling first to trouble the received *privatio* account of evil. If Bulgakov hardly rejects the account outright, he seeks more.[75] The *privatio* account reckons only evil's *what*—and by abstract negation at that. More often Bulgakov asks after evil's *how*, or its curious positivity. When he does, Bulgakov imitates Schelling in refusing Satan a personality—only for different reasons. If Schelling declines Satan a personality on the grounds that he is no *creature*, Bulgakov declines

69 Schelling, *Urfassung*, 2, 646.
70 I/7, 392/56.
71 I/7, 390/54; *Tim.* 52b–c. For more on Schelling's use of Plato here, see Peter Warnek's "Bastard Reasoning in Schelling's *Freiheitsschrift*," *Epoché: A Journal for the History of Philosophy* 12.2 (2008): 249–67.
72 Schelling, *Urfassung*, 2, 633. By 1831, Schelling has replaced the language of ground/that-which-is/existence-personality for the potencies with Could-Be/Must-Be/Shall-Be.
73 Ibid., 624–34.
74 Though per *Unfading Light* Bulgakov reads the (much shorter) shorter *SW* 1841/42 version.
75 Bulgakov, *Philosophy of Economy*, 307–08; *Unfading Light*, 270–73; *The Bride of the Lamb*, 147–48.

Satan a hypostasis on the grounds that *he* is no creature.[76] No, Satan's hypostatic identity belongs properly to *Lucifer*. Distinguishing as Bulgakov does between Satan and Lucifer does not signal, as Balthasar advocates, forgoing speculation by "simply accept[ing]" scriptural vignettes. On the contrary, by revising Schelling's intelligible deed Bulgakov has lit upon new exegetical possibilities.[77] For Bulgakov, 'Satan' plays temporal I to Lucifer's supratemporal I. Worse: 'Satan' has—"in his insane desire to be God's equal," even to the point of desiring "complete incarnation in humankind"[78]—projected his "little I" into a "cosmic I and considered the whole world its throne."[79] Only this self is not his, and exactly because 'Satan' is not the name he bears from everlasting. 'Satan' is rather the "hypostatic mask" (ипостасная личина) Lucifer erroneously takes himself to be.[80] So construed, 'Satan' exists positively only as "a pose, a grimace, the mask of the fallen angel [...] of pretend genius and self-deification."[81]

As with Satan, so with us. If Satan be a creature rather than a principle, then Bulgakov has no truck with Schelling's 'general evil'. Evil knows only "emanations" by *particular* creatures. And when humans reduce evil to act and so gift it "creative power," "an imaginary, 'bad' infinity of emptiness is thus created, where [...] a multiplicity of illusory forms reign."[82] Ontologically, the disintegration of the temporal I into what Bulgakov calls "the little I" parodies the second person of the trinity even more radically than Schelling imagined.[83] It is not just that evil seizes itself by self-doubling rather than surrendering to the Father. For Bulgakov evil positively seeks a "complete incarnation in humankind," an inverted sophianization—even a false world.

Within this "kingdom of shadows"[84] whose prince is Satan, the self no longer distinguishes its emanations (the little I) from itself (the temporal I), let

---

76   Bulgakov, *Unfading Light*, 312, where Bulgakov explicitly takes issue with Schelling's impersonal angels and demons.
77   Bulgakov, *The Bride of the Lamb*, 154.
78   Ibid., 159; Bulgakov, *Unfading Light*, 320.
79   Bulgakov, *Unfading Light*, 269.
80   Bulgakov, *Jacob's Ladder*, 74; *The Bride of the Lamb*, 155.
81   Bulgakov, *The Bride of the Lamb*, 155.
82   Ibid., 157–58.
83   Bulgakov, *Unfading Light*, 343.
84   Bulgakov, *Philosophy of Economy*, 146. In *Unfading Light*, Bulgakov will attribute the construction of this false world to "sui generis hallucination" (428). In *The Bride of the Lamb*, Bulgakov will call the same a "transcendental illusion, a reified fantasy, a supra-reality" (509).

alone its supratemporal I.[85] Here Bulgakov reminds his readers of the devil's evening call to Ivan Karamazov, who knows not whether he finally speaks to himself.[86] The self can be cleaved from its "works" or "veils of falsehood" only by the consuming fire of judgment (1 Cor 3:13). That judgment belongs properly to Christ first. But it belongs also and by extension to the supratemporal self who is always already sophianized in Christ.[87] Thus Bulgakov's arresting (and controversial) conclusion: Lucifer can be saved to realize his own supratemporal freedom only on the condition that the "hypostatic mask" he confected for himself burns unto the ages after the "final division of light and dark, the ultimate unmasking of this shadowy existence."[88]

IV.

That and how Bulgakov adopts and adapts Schelling's satanology to confect his own has been the argument of this essay. But what does it mean for Bulgakov to remember Christian tradition *through* Schelling?

Suppose we isolate just one point of satanology on which Bulgakov refines Schelling. Suppose too we consider the most speculatively stratospheric with the least reference to the Church Fathers: that evil's curious positivity permits creatures (including Lucifer) to "emanate" a shadow-self or false world. Where is this in the Christian tradition's memory? Among the Fathers on this point Bulgakov sources only St Maximus Confessor.[89] But he might have quoted still more of Maximus's teachings than he does. Maximus's claim that by falling Adam posited "another beginning," for instance.[90] Or that sins form works "not generated by God."[91] But beyond and before Maximus, this practice of reading scriptural images of alternate selves knows a deep history among ascetics. Remember only Evagrius on imagination's phantasmagoria, Cassian on incarnating "the body of sin," Hesychios of Sinai on "mixing" with demonic fantasy to generate sin, Niketas Stetathos on sin as soul-splitting. As examples

---

85 Bulgakov, *The Lamb of God*, 147.

86 Bulgakov, *Unfading Light*, 267.

87 Bulgakov, *The Bride of the Lamb*, 456, 463. At 458: "The judgment of Christ is also every human being's own judgment upon himself."

88 Bulgakov, *Unfading Light*, 146.

89 At least in *Unfading Light*. Pavel Florensky sources more fathers for the same idea in his chapter "Gehenna" in *The Pillar and Ground of Truth* (Princeton: Princeton University Press, 1997), 151–89.

90 Maximus Confessor, *Quaestiones ad Thalassium* 61.7.

91 *QThal* 42.4; 51.19; 61.9.

compound, Bulgakov's speculative Schellingian flights begin to appear rather more like tradition's memories long lost. Determining on what other points of Bulgakov's thought this might also hold true will prove a heavy mantle, if one well worth taking up.[92]

---

92   And made easier, really, by the uptick in translations and scholarship on both Bulgakov and Schelling.

POLITICS, ECONOMY,
AND ECOLOGY

Building the House of Wisdom
DOI 10.17438/978-3-402-12180-1

Seven Days of *Narod*: Sergei Bulgakov's Christian Socialist Newspaper

Catherine Evtuhov and Regula M. Zwahlen

What does it mean for a religious worldview to lie at the foundation of politics? Sergei Bulgakov's politics were as intense, thorough, and passionate as everything else he did; the period of his real political engagement coincides with the Russian Revolution of 1904–7. As we know, he was a founding member of the Union of Liberation, which held its first meeting at Schaffhausen in Switzerland in 1903; he worked together, sometimes in harmony and sometimes in discord, with key figures in the Kadet (Constitutional Democratic) party, then more usually referred to as the Party of Popular Freedom; he was a delegate to the short-lived but important Second Duma before Prime Minister Stolypin shut it down on 3 June 1907 and altered its mandate and composition. In all of these roles, Bulgakov had some very highly developed and clearly defined positions on the burning issues of the day (and to be sure there were many).

Rowan Williams has recently highlighted Bulgakov's continuing engagement with the idea of socialism as late as the early 1930s; here, we return to take another look at his literal "Christian Socialist" period, defined by Williams as "the first dozen years of the twentieth century."[1] It is an overtly political moment, when Bulgakov not only wrote about ideas, but sought explicitly to translate them into practice. In this essay, we turn our attention to a short-lived but astonishingly rich political endeavor: the newspaper, *Narod* ("The People"), published in Kiev in the spring of 1906.[2] In the programmatic article,

---

1   Rowan Williams, *Sergii Bulgakov, Socialism, and the Church* (Volos: Volos Academy Publications, 2023), 17.

2   Kolerov's and Lokteva's important article on *Narod* focuses on the circumstances of the newspaper's publication rather than on its content. M. A. Kolerov, O. K. Lokteva, "S. N. Bulgakov i religiozno-filosofskaia pechat' (1906–1907)," in *Litsa. Biograficheskii al'manakh*, ed. A. V. Lavrov (Moscow: Feniks, Atheneum, 1994), 401–24.

"An Urgent Task," written in autumn 1905 on the eve of the "actual realization of popular government,"[3] Bulgakov proposed to create a *Union of Christian Politics*—not a party—with "five basic aims: to cultivate Christian society, to unite all Christians regardless of denomination, to work for the political and economic liberation of the individual, to oppose Black Hundredism, and to establish a propaganda campaign,"[4] including the creation of a special press organ. In his words, "we should strive to create a daily Christian press, in which life in society would be presented from a strictly Christian perspective."[5] And so he became a main editor of the Kiev newspaper *Narod* published by Vladimir Lashniukov. The paper lasted only seven days—Easter Week of 1906, with the first issue appearing on Easter Sunday. Bulgakov put a lot of energy into the project and was deeply disappointed when he found out about the serious lack of funding only a few days after the first issue.[6]

How could such a short-lived little paper be of any significance? It is worth noting that we are dealing with texts that have hitherto been difficult to access, have never been reprinted, and were only digitized by helpful librarians in 2020. Excited about this newly accessible source with regard to Bulgakov, we found that the paper was so ambitious and full of ideas and projects that it provides a brilliant peephole through which to catch a glimpse not only of the Christian socialist program, but of society both locally in the Kiev region and throughout the Russian Empire. Quite a few of the articles were written by Bulgakov himself and provide productive insight into his perspective as he made critical transitions from radical to practical politics, and from a general defense of religion to a fervent call for Orthodox Church reform.

---

3   Original publication: "Neotlozhnaia zadacha," *Voprosy zhizni* 9 (1905), 332–60. In this paper we cite the more easily available separate brochure: S. Bulgakov, *Neotlozhnaia zadacha (O soiuze khristianskoi politiki)* (Moscow, 1906), 1; English translation by Marian Schwartz: Sergei Bulgakov, "An Urgent Task," in: *A Revolution of the Spirit. Crisis of Value in Russia 1890–1924*, ed. B. Glatzer Rosenthal and M. Bohachevsky-Chomiak (New York: Fordham University Press, 1990), 137–59.

4   Catherine Evtuhov, *The Cross and the Sickle: Sergei Bulgakov and the Fate of Russian Religious Philosophy, 1890–1920* (Ithaca: Cornell University Press, 1997), 101.

5   Bulgakov, *Neotlozhnaia zadacha*, 34.

6   Vasilii Zen'kovskii, "Iz vospominanii,"*Vestnik russkogo khrist'ianskogo dvizheniia* 139, no. 2 (1983), 119.

1. Bulgakov in Kiev. The Newspaper

After the defense of his Master's thesis on *Capitalism and Agriculture* on 1 April 1901 in Moscow, Bulgakov did not get a job there, because he was already considered a "renegade" by his mainly Marxist colleagues.[7] In his thesis he questioned Marxist historical materialism, since "every age introduces new facts and new forces."[8] However, Bulgakov was invited to teach political economy and statistics at the brand new Polytechnic institute and at St. Vladimir's University in Kiev. In a public lecture in November 1901, Bulgakov revealed himself to be an idealist and his fervent appeal to personal responsibility proved to be a huge public success.[9] Bulgakov's elective seminars on the social sciences, in particular, were attended by 100, sometimes up to 400 people, including students, workers, and women.[10] One of his students from 1901 to 1903 was Nikolai Valentinov, who shared Bulgakov's critique of Marxism, but not his interest in religion. When Valentinov told Lenin about Bulgakov's approach—"Truth is attained through the honest, free, and loyal confrontation of ideas"—Lenin answered:

> Isn't it perchance Bulgakov's influence that accounts for your inclination to correct the philosophy of Marx? That's a slippery path. The Social Democratic Party is not a seminar where various ideas are confronted. It is a militant class organization of the revolutionary proletariat.[11]

Neither did the police like Bulgakov's fame. An article titled "Happy New Year" in January 1904 provoked a scandal and the closure of the journal *Iugozapadnaia nedelia* [Southwest Weekly], co-edited by Lashniukov, that promoted "the freedom of the person in the social dimension." Bulgakov had written about the resurrection of Russian life, which the police (correctly) interpreted as synonymous with "down with autocracy." After that, Bulgakov was under strong police surveillance, but he was still allowed to teach. In fact, most professors

---

7 Vladimir Akulinin, "Vekhi zhizni i tvorchestva," in *Khristianskii sotsializm (S. N. Bulgakov)*, ed.V. Akulinin (Novosibirsk: Nauka, 1991), 9.

8 Sergei Bulgakov, *Philosophy of Economy: the World as Household*, trans. Catherine Evtuhov (New Haven: Yale University Press, 2000), 323, n. 9.

9 Evtuhov, *Cross and Sickle*, 57. The famous lecture was entitled "Ivan Karamazov as a philosophical type."

10 Ol'ga Lokteva, "Neizvestnaia stat'ia S. N. Bulgakova (1904)," in *Rossiia i reformy. Vyp. 2*, ed. Modest Kolerov (St. Petersburg: Medved', 1993), 67.

11 Nikolai Valentinov, *Encounters with Lenin* (Oxford: Oxford University Press, 1968), 178.

of the Polytechnic institute were members of the Union of Liberation and later of the local section of the Kadet Party.[12]

Bulgakov's Union of Christian Politics fused with Lashniukov's project to join social-political radicalism with faithfulness to the Orthodox Church, and culminated in *Narod*. Bulgakov was quite successful in attracting authors and poets from St. Petersburg and Moscow for this collaboration, including, first of all, his co-editor Volzhskii (Aleksandr Glinka), Valentin Sventsitskii, and Vasilii Zen'kovskii.[13] This point about it having to be a *daily* paper is interesting: Christian politics (*khristianskaia obshchestvennost'*) had to be part of everyday life. In terms of genre, *Narod* might be compared to the *Gubernskie vedomosti* and at the same time to the mainstream St. Petersburg or Moscow papers—*Rech'* or *Novoe vremia*, perhaps with an admixture of the *Eparkhial'nye vedomosti*. It was a local paper but aimed to be national at the same time. It was anything but narrowly clerical in its focus. The title referred back to the "God and people" ("Dio e popolo") slogan, borrowed from Giuseppe Mazzini, with which Bulgakov concluded "An Urgent Task."[14] But the word "narod" had acquired new layers of meaning by 1906—a moment of reckoning when the intelligentsia had a sudden revelation of the people's "true nature" through the violence of revolution.[15] The editors were at once frightened and inspired, as perfectly expressed in Bulgakov's formulation in the first issue:

> We still share Dostoevsky's and Soloviev's faith that our narod, that beast-like pogrom hooligan (*pogromnyi khuligan zverinogo obraza*), drowning in stinking (*smradnyi*) sin, is nonetheless a narod—God-bearer (*narod-bogonosets*), and has its own important and well-defined task in world history with respect to the salvation of the world.[16]

12   Lokteva, "Neizvestnaia stat'ia," 68–70.

13   Kolerov, Lokteva, "Bulgakov i pechat' (1906–1907)," 406. In fact, the list of collaborators, though it remained largely aspirational, reads like a "Who's Who" of Silver Age writers and philosophers.

14   Bulgakov, *Neotlozhnaia zadacha*, 36.

15   On the problematic nature of the term "narod" see Evert van der Zweerde, "The Rise of the People and the Political Philosophy of the Vekhi Authors," in *Landmarks Revisited: the Vekhi Symposium One Hundred Years On*, ed. Robin Aizlewood, Ruth Coates (Boston: Academic Studies Press, 2013), 104–27.

16   Sergei Bulgakov, "Paskhal'nye dumy," *Narod* 1 (1906), 1; on Bulgakov and Russian messianism, see Sergii Bulgakov, "Easter Thoughts (1906). With Commentary by Regula Zwahlen," *Public Orthodoxy*, April 2022; https://publicorthodoxy.org/2022/04/25/sergii-bulgakov-easter-thoughts/ (access 2024/01/26).

What do we actually find in the newspaper? A brief survey reveals the following key themes: Duma elections, national revival, and tasks that lie ahead; an articulation of Christian politics and its relation to other intellectual currents, including Marxism; the Jewish question (especially the Kishinev pogrom); a summary of the press, and telegrams from *Narod's* correspondents; a chronicle of events compiled from the local, regional, imperial, and international press; church reform and Christianity for modern times; social consciousness: aid to famine victims, the demand for the release of political prisoners and the abolition of capital punishment; workers' movements and unions; and letters "from below," including from provincial clergy and responses to "An Urgent Task." We also find mundane but useful things like train schedules and advertisements (e. g., charity concerts for female students). The first issue contains a classic Silver Age appendix of art and poetry, focusing mostly on Vrubel' in Kiev. Bulgakov's articles primarily deal with Christian politics and are virulently anti-regime.

Not long after the paper ceased publication, Bulgakov confessed that *Narod* had been "a huge temptation and a project of endless impertinence," but at least made him aware of the obligation to "participate religiously in society" himself. Therefore, he decided to engage in politics and moved to Moscow in the autumn of 1906.[17] Bulgakov's wife Elena was not very happy about that.[18] A sister of Maria Vodovozova, Lenin's and Bulgakov's first publisher, in Kiev she participated in the "Union for Women's Equality" and published a couple of articles.[19] In her contributions to *Narod* she criticized the tendency to use historical material about the French Revolution not for enlightenment, but to stir a militant atmosphere.[20] She seemed to share Bulgakov's later impression that in the Russian revolution of 1905, the "creative forces proved far weaker than the destructive ones."[21]

17 Vladimir Keidan, *Vzyskuiushchie grada. Khronika russkikh [...] dvizhenii v chastnykh pis'makh i dnevnikakh ikh uchastnikov, 1829–1923 gg. Antologiia. Kniga III 1905–1906*, ed. Modest Kolerov, *Issledovaniia po istorii russkoi mysli* (Moscow: Modest Kolerov, 2020), 729, 828–30.
18 Keidan, *Vzyskukiushchie grada*, 791.
19 Zen'kovskii, "Iz vospominanii," 117. Modest Kolerov, *Ne mir, no mech: russkaia religiozno-filosofskaia pechat' ot 'Problem idealizma' do 'Vekh' 1902–1909* (St. Petersburg: Aleteia, 1996), 347.
20 Elena Bulgakova, "Frantsuzskaia revoliutsiia v narodnoi literature," *Narod* 7 (1906), 2.
21 Sergei Bulgakov, "Heroism and Asceticism. Reflections on the Religious Nature of the Russian Intelligentsia," in *Vekhi: Landmarks*, ed. Marshall S. Shatz and Judith E. Zimmermann (Armonk: M. E. Sharpe, 1994), 18.

2. *Narod* as an Organ of Christian Politics

In his introductory "Easter thoughts," in the first issue, Bulgakov sincerely hoped for nothing less than the resurrection of Christ in the Russian people.[22] Following in the footsteps of Vladimir Soloviev, Bulgakov believed that *Narod* would fuse progressive, democratic political thought with Christian faith and accused his political liberal allies in the Kadet party of neglecting religion as the most important feature of the Russian people's social life.[23] Therefore, Bulgakov at first cooperated with Valentin Sventsitskii, who, together with Vladimir Ern and Pavel Florenskii had just founded the *Brotherhood of Christian Struggle* and called for a complete religious transformation of society.[24] They did not want to fight for the improvement of life on a personal level; rather, they sought to provide a spirit of social struggle in Christ's name.[25] Likewise, in *Narod*'s stated goals the "revelation of the untruth of capitalist exploitation of today's agrarian relationships" came second after "the people's freedom" and before "the struggle against national hatred." The task of "the all-national religious-social sermon" of *Narod* should be fulfilled in the spirit of "universal (*vselenskoe*) Christianity" (with reference to Vl. Soloviev).[26] In Bulgakov's view, the

> general mission—the emancipation of the person—is provided for by religion [...] [and] the democratic movement strives to embody the purely Christian commandments of love, freedom, and equality in social relations.[27]

The flirtation between Bulgakov and Sventsitskii was however rather short, since Bulgakov soon criticized the Brotherhood's "sectarian dogmatism" as well as their economic agrarian communism advocating the abolition of private property to give it to the Church.[28]

---

22 Bulgakov, "Paskhal'nye dumy," 1.
23 See Evtuhov, *Cross and Sickle*, 95 ff.
24 Evtuhov, *Cross and Sickle*, 102. *Narod* presented several advertisements for the Brotherhood's brochures from the "Religious-social Library" between 1906 and 1911; see Modest Kolerov, "Izdaniia 'Khristianskogo Bratstva Bor'by' (1906–1908)," *Novoe literaturnoe obozrenie* 5 (1993), 299.
25 Moskvich [V. P. Sventsitskii], "'Khristianskoe Bratstvo Bor'by," *Narod* 3 (1906), 4.
26 Sergei Bulgakov, Aleksandr Volzhskii, "Ot redaktsii," *Narod* 1 (1906), 1.
27 Bulgakov, *Neotlozhnaia zadacha*, 16, 25; "An Urgent Task," 145, 151.
28 Bulgakov had argued in favour of private property for farmers—which Lenin did not like either. Vladimir Lenin, "Agrarnyi vopros i 'kritiki Marksa'," in *S. N. Bulgakov: pro*

From Universal Christianity to Orthodox Reform. Yet the emphasis on "universal Christianity" did not really correspond to the "Russian people's faith." Zen'kovskii remembers that in 1906 Bulgakov was not yet openly Orthodox, hidden behind a "religious worldview—'in general,'" and that he seemed to be ashamed, in front of his numerous students, of his return to Orthodoxy.[29] In the "Urgent Task" he called on "people of various denominations and various religious philosophical nuances" to come together and defend "the human person's natural and sacred rights to freedom of speech, freedom of conscience, freedom of association among people […]. These rights must be an axiom of Christian politics."[30] Bulgakov even tried to attract the Polish Catholic scholar Marian Zdziechowski as a contributor. Zdziechowski was one of the promoters of Russian thought and Catholic Modernism in Poland.[31] In his letters to him, Bulgakov claimed that "universal Christianity must win, and universality (*vselenskost'*) is the highest point towards which we are striving," and praised him for his "striving to constantly acquaint the West with our world and thereby contribute to tearing down the walls erected by history."[32] However, Bulgakov changed priorities rather quickly: "The cause of Christian politics must be an interdenominational cause and, in concept, all-national, *although for the time being we are setting purely national, Russian goals* [italics added]," because the task of the "emancipation of the Church by its separation from the state" and the "rebirth of communal church life" must be accomplished *before* it could "approach the realization of the ideas of Christian politics."[33] He did not shy away from harsh condemnations of the current Church institution in passages like these:

> And, it's strange, Russian people attribute to themselves the defense of religion, they turn to the defense of Orthodoxy, they want to act in the name of God. But how do they really treat religious thought, how do they really treat the Orthodox Church? They treat it as a means to a political end, as some kind of patent of trustworthi-

et contra, ed. I. I. Evlampiev (St. Petersburg: Izd-vo Russkogo Khristianskogo gumanitarnogo instituta, 2003), n. 6.

29 Zen'kovskii, "Iz vospominanii," 117.

30 Bulgakov, *Neotlozhnaia zadacha*, 23, 14; "An Urgent Task," 149, 144.

31 Irina Vorontsova, "Stat'ia 'neokatolika' M. E. Zdzekhovskogo 'Modernistkoe dvizhenie v R.-K. Tserkvi' kak istochnik po rimo-katolicheskomu modernizmu: opyt kriticheskogo analiza," *Voprosy filosofii* 2 (2017).

32 Al'vidasa Iokubaitisa, "Pis'ma S. N. Bulgakova M. E. Zdzekhovskomu," *Vil'nius. Litva literaturnaia* 4 (1990), 158.

33 Bulgakov, *Neotlozhnaia zadacha*, 24; "An Urgent Task," 150–51.

ness, they thereby pervert the very idea of the Church, blaspheming it, blaspheming God. The guardians, in clear violation of the commandments of Christ, have long maintained in us an atmosphere of religious warfare and inquisition [...]—this is how the supposed supporters of Orthodoxy have defended it—by completely abandoning it to the whim of the autocracy, thus repeating the sad example of Iscariot.[34]

Hence, Bulgakov's shift from "universal Christianity" to "Orthodox Church reform" was not a change of attitude with regard to his ecumenical vision of universal Christianity. Rather, he wished to begin its practical implementation by preparing the ground for it in Russia.

In keeping with the spirit of universal Christianity, *Narod* reported on a brochure of the World Student Christian Federation (WSCF) founded in 1895. It claimed to unite 11 national unions with 105,000 members (students and professors) by 1905. The author remained sceptical: "Isn't this one of many clerical organizations [...] without any future?"[35] Which is somewhat ironic, since in 1908, Baron Pavel Nicolay, the founder of the (protestant) Russian Student Christian Movement (RSKhD) in St. Petersburg, in a letter to John Mott, the general secretary of the WSCF and leader of the YMCA, suspected Bulgakov of the same: "Professor Bulgakoff,—formerly [...] an extreme atheist, [...] has been drawn to Christianity, [and] is going towards the opposite extreme—clericalism."[36] However, Nicolay praised Bulgakov's striking lecture on "The Intelligentsia and Religion" before 500 students, and the latter was equally impressed by the RSKhD.[37]

In the *Narod* entry, Mott is probably mentioned for the first time in Bulgakov's environment: he would become a major figure in Bulgakov's life, especially in exile. The Orthodox RSKhD, founded in Psherov in 1923, the St. Serge Institute of Orthodox Theology in Paris in 1924, and other Russian exilic institutions were established with the American YMCA's financial support.[38] The new emphasis on the Orthodox confession of the RSKhD in exile in the 1920s reflected the wish to preserve the Orthodox tradition given its persecution in the USSR, but the goals of "establishing a community with the Christians of all

---

34 Sergei Bulgakov, "O zadachakh narodnogo predstavitel'stva v Rossii," *Narod* 3 (1906), 1.

35 "Vsemirnyi khristianskii studencheskii soiuz," *Narod* 6 (1906), 4.

36 Robert Bird, "YMCA i sud'by russkoi religioznoi mysli (1906-1947)," *Issledovaniia po istorii russkoi mysli: Ezhegodnik za 2000g.* (Moscow: OGI, 2000), 83.

37 Bird, "YMCA," 184.

38 Matthew Miller, *The American YMCA and Russian Culture. The Preservation and Expansion of Orthodox Christianity, 1900–1940* (Lanham: Lexington Books, 2013), 159, 201.

confessions in the West"[39] mark a clear continuity with the incipient ecumenical conversations of 1906.

Christian Politics, Individuality, and Activity. One of the most fascinating aspects of *Narod* is that it created a forum for readers' responses to the Christian Socialist project—a genuine exchange of views. "Christian politics (*obshchestvennost'*)," became the journal's only real interchange with readers,[40] with a special column dedicated to the topic. The first entry of this section published a letter by Bulgakov "To my correspondents" related to his earlier article on an "Urgent Task." He mentioned letters "from men and women, priests and students, seminarists and 'kursistki' (female students), doctors and jurists, etc." They revealed the "religious yearning and suffering of spiritual loneliness" of the modern soul, a thirst for "new forms of religious life and social creativity," because they found satisfaction neither in political parties nor in the "impoverished forms of existent Church community." *Narod* would print their letters in order to connect these people.[41]

One of the letter writers was Ivan Vetrov,[42] who called himself an "anarchist-communist" and a "religious metaphysician." In essence, Vetrov wanted to know if the Union of Christian Politics shared his convictions about religious individualism, the abolition of the Church as an institution, and anarchism, because "a religious person can only be an individualist and each form and hierarchy externally forced on him harms the holy of holies of his soul."[43] The *Narod* editors made clear that they did not, since they were committed to Christian politics, church reform, and constitutional-democratic reform. Still, Sventsitskii's and Bulgakov's answers to Vetrov were slightly different. Sventsitskii strongly condemned Vetrov's "antichristian religious individualism" and what he described as an "inward religious 'monastery' common to the majority of believers today." Clerics should be chosen by the church members, and hierarchy need not be about power, but rather a "special form of service." Also, a Christian should not abandon the apostolic teaching about power: "For a Christian the best political structure is one that reflects the notion of the state

39   Nikolai Berdiaev et al., "Dukhovnye zadachi russkoi emigratsii," *Put'* 1 (1925), 6.
40   Kolerov and Lokteva, "S. N. Bulgakov i religiozno-filosofskaia pechat'," 409.
41   Sergei Bulgakov, "Moim korrespondentam," *Narod* 1 (1906), 4–5.
42   Vetrov was a pseudonym of the publicist Izrail' S. Blank. See V. P. Sventsitskii—I. S. Blanku (8.4.1906, in: Keidan, *Vzyskuiushchie grada*, 670.
43   Ivan Vetrov, "K voprosu o 'Soiuze khristianskoi politiki'," *Narod* 4 (1906), 4.

as the Church in process of becoming."[44] The latter point was not shared by Bulgakov, who advocated for a clear separation of church and state.

Bulgakov's answer to Vetrov, entitled "Individualism or sobornost'?," mainly discussed the "eternal antithesis between the person and society," and, in contrast to Sventsitskii's, reflects an unwillingness to condemn "individualism" altogether. Later that year, Bulgakov would prominently criticize Karl Marx's lack of attention to the "the problem of individuality" of each human person,[45] who, in Bulgakov's view, was dignified in the Christian teaching on the image of God.[46] At the same time, he tried to avoid both secular and ecclesial individualism (see below). Bulgakov's rather confusing struggle for a suitable conception of personal individuality is expressed in his contribution: in the process of growing up, he suggests, a human becomes more individualist, yet by acknowledging the new potentials and boundless strivings of his spiritual "I," the "threads that bind individuals to humanity become ever more complex, subtle and strong." Bulgakov reminds his reader of the lonely sufferings of Lord Byron's self-exiled heroes (Child Harold, Manfred) who listen to the sermon of Nietzsche's Zarathustra. Nevertheless, "individualism and sobornost'" are correlating notions" in modern human consciousness that should not fight each other. The fact that "the person awakened and became conscious of its own self," that the child left home and its mother's comfort, cannot and should not be undone. However, the healing of individual suffering by external bonds or even a "Social Democratic Church" will not work, because only "common love, a common religion, i. e., the Church" can overcome individualism, by not annihilating, but confirming the spiritual "I." In this sense, Bulgakov argued that "a religious person by definition cannot be an individualist, he partakes of sobornost', he is in the Church." Religion provides an objective meaning to personal religious experiences, and religious individualism is a "typical misunderstanding of our time," caused by the "anti-ecclesial characteristics of the

---

44 Valentin Sventsitskii, "Otvet g. Vetrovu na pis'mo ego k S. N. Bulgakovu," *Narod* 5 (1906), 2; on the transformation of the state into the Church see Dostoevsky's novel *The Brothers Karamazov*, Book 2, chapter 5.

45 Original publication: "Karl Marks kak religioznyi tip," *Moskovskii ezhenedel'nik* 22, 23, 24, 25 (1906). In this paper we cite the separate brochure. Sergei Bulgakov: *Karl Marks kak religioznyi tip* (Moscow, 1907), 12. English translation by Luba Barna: Sergei Bulgakov, *Karl Marx as a Religious Type* (Belmont, MA: Nordland Publ., 1979), 51.

46 Even from the perspective of the dean of the Moscow Theological Academy, individuality was "one of the most characteristic traits of our time, […] previously strongly suppressed." Cited by Vera Shevzov, *Russian Orthodoxy on the Eve of Revolution* (Oxford: Oxford University Press, 2004), 13.

historical Church" with its rituals and formalism.[47] With regard to Tolstoy's harsh critique of the institutional Church, and since Tolstoy's excommunication in 1901 had been a major event, Vetrov wanted to hear about Bulgakov's position on Tolstoy, and Bulgakov promised to write about him later. He did not in *Narod*, but actually wrote no fewer than nine articles about Tolstoy between 1904 and 1912. In a nutshell, Bulgakov condemned Tolstoy's religion of self-redemption and "moralization of religion," but highly praised his contributions to the "spiritual birth of personality."[48]

Like Bulgakov, Zen'kovskii placed strong emphasis on a free religious individuality. He argued that Marx's call for "unification of workers" had "something liberating and appealing,"[49] but objected that Marx only thought of economic liberation and unification by means of state measures, while liberalism wanted to free individuals from state oppression. Socialism risks becoming oppressive, because "the truth of individualism is more primordial, closer and deeper than the truth of any restrictions of individuals whatsoever"; the tension between both can be resolved only on religious grounds by "religious politics."[50] Yet in this context, both Bulgakov and Zen'kovskii criticized the historical Orthodox Church's "cultivation of individualism:"[51] In "The Social Obligations of the Church," Bulgakov admits that the Church has "deeply known and highlighted the task of personal salvation, personal holiness, [but] should equally deeply know and highlight the task of Christian politics" based on "the pathos of love and holy wrath" against social injustice. It should cultivate social conscience that, in contrast to interests that divide, unites people.[52] This is reminiscent of Bulgakov's groundbreaking article on the moral task of progress from 1902: "It is conscience, the moral law, [...] [that] in application to historical development, commands us to want the good in history, [...] to want *progress*."[53] Now, in 1906, Bulgakov claimed that only the Church, which

47 Sergei Bulgakov, "Individualizm ili sobornost'?," *Narod* 6 (1906), 3–4.

48 Regula M. Zwahlen, "Russische Religionsphilosophie," in *Tolstoj als theologischer Denker und Kirchenkritiker*, ed. Martin George et al. (Göttingen: Vandenhoeck & Ruprecht, 2014), 6, 8; Christian Münch, "'Englischer Tolstoismus'," in *Sergij Bulgakovs Zwei Städte im interdisziplinären Gespräch*, ed. Barbara Hallensleben and Regula Zwahlen (Münster: Aschendorff, 2021), 45, 48.

49 Vasilii Zen'kovskii, "Predchuvstviia marksizma," *Narod* 1 (1906), 2.

50 Zen'kovskii, "Liberalizm i sotsializm," *Narod* 1 (1906), 2–3.

51 Zen'kovskii, "Ob odnom somnenii," *Narod* 7 (1906), 2.

52 Sergei Bulgakov, "Sotsial'nye obiazannosti tserkvi," *Narod* 5 (1906), 1–2.

53 Bulgakov, "Basic Problems of the Theory of Progress," in *The Problems of Idealism. Essays in Russian Social Philosophy*, ed. Randall A. Poole (Yale: Yale University Press, 2003), 111.

must want the good "for all humanity, in which there is neither Greek nor Jew, neither free men nor slaves, neither capitalists nor workers, neither leader nor subordinate, but Christ" (Gal. 3:28), could cultivate such conscience: "the Church is a divine-human institution and demands active human activity, the work of conscience, [...], it demands the fullness of gifts, productive usage of given talents, and not to bury them in the ground."[54] Individual social activity seems to have been Bulgakov's contemporary solution for overcoming the "eternal antithesis between person and society." In a letter to Volzhskii in July 1906 Bulgakov wrote: "Religious politics [*obshchestvennost'*] is a problem, the 'Kingdom of God' is neither here nor there, but within us, and how to find it—in 'isolation' or among people—is hard to say. But religious participation in politics is an obligation before life."[55]

The question of "Christian activity" (*aktivnost'*) received further expression in *Narod*. In his part of "Easter Thoughts," Volzhskii highlighted what Christian activity should strive for: first, a synthesis of religion, philosophy, and science reminiscent of Vladimir Soloviev's,[56] and second, in the words of Dostoevsky's Zosima, an "overcoming of the personal isolation in a human common wholeness that truly cares for the person,"[57] by *active* Christian politics. Zen'kovskii objected to the Marxist claim that religion was intrinsically passive, because "the religion of Christ is a religion of the unwavering value of the person, [...] of religious freedom which is incompatible with 'mental captivity' and decline of creativity." Religious activity engenders cooperation: spiritual life is the source of enormous social energy, which means not that "we appreciate religion on the grounds of its 'social value,' but that we illuminate the social process religiously."[58] Alexander Presniakov, professor of Russian history in St. Petersburg, likewise argued that the Christian ideal of "full inner freedom" of man made in the image of God was the "only way to the realization of the unconditional good of human nature," and therefore it was an ethical ideal as a call for "active love."[59]

---

54   Bulgakov, "Sotsial'nye obiazannosti tserkvi," 2.

55   Keidan, *Vzyskuiushchie grada*, 828.

56   This topic was addressed by Bulgakov's article "Voskresenie Khrista i sovremennoe soznanie," about the compatibility of the theory of evolution and the theology of resurrection: Sergei Bulgakov, *Narod* 1 (1906), 2–3; German translation by Katharina Breckner and Regula Zwahlen, "Die Auferstehung Christi und das moderne Bewusstsein," in Sergii Bulgakov, *Zwei Städte* (Münster 2020), 434–42.

57   Volzhskij, "Paskhal'nye dumy," *Narod* 1 (1906), 1.

58   Zen'kovskii, "Ob odnom somnenii," 2.

59   Alexander Presniakov, "Nash tserkovnyi vopros," *Narod* 5 (1906), 2–3.

Joining the discussion, another letter responding to Bulgakov's "Urgent Task" objected that a rationalist "Union of Christian Politics" was useless, since God could only be found by mystical experience. Bulgakov acknowledged the point, but argued that the union was a first step to gather like-minded people in order to debate what Christian politics really is.[60] This process was necessary, because the official Church was only a state "chancellery of spiritual matters" or an "office of Orthodox confession" which sought to rescue the collapsing autocracy by organizing spectacles like the canonization of Serafim of Sarov (in 1903).[61] In Bulgakov's view, the

> Russo-Japanese war [was] the fruit of a series of criminal mistakes by our government, and the "office" [i. e., the Church], instead of exposing and talking sense into the government, organized prayers to "smash the enemies down," and to hand over icons to [...] generals and admirals.[62]

The Church kept silent in response to Bloody Sunday in January 1905 and the October pogroms in Kiev—a great sin in Bulgakov's view: "All have understood and seen that the Church was enslaved by the state and it did not even recognize the level of its own enslavement."[63] Hence, Russia needed a church reform and Orthodox Christians should strive for it. Bulgakov's comments evoke a series of vital questions vis-à-vis the political role of the Church, though he does not pose them himself. Should the Church merely call for peace? How should it interact with the government? Should it pray for the soldiers? Or demarcate a specific stance vis-à vis particular political and military issues?

Church Reform and the Clergy. "If I were an artist, I would paint a picture of this scene and name it: 'Episode from the resurrection of the Church.'" Bulgakov's scene depicts a girl in prison, tormented by a guard. A priest stands up for her and is admonished by the guard: "And as a priest, you're not ashamed?!"[64] Priests of such strong convictions were invited to write for *Narod*,[65] which re-

---

60 M. L., "Pis'mo intelligenta;" and Sergei Bulgakov, "Post-scriptum," *Narod* 7 (1906), 2.

61 See John Strickland, *The Making of Holy Russia. The Orthodox Church and Russian Nationalism before the Revolution* (New York: Holy Trinity Publications, 2013), 30–32.

62 Bulgakov, "Sotsial'nye obiazannosti tserkvi," 1–2.

63 Bulgakov, "Sotsial'nye obiazannosti tserkvi," 1–2.

64 Sergei Bulgakov, "O zadachakh narodnogo predstavitel'stva v Rossii (Iz rechi, skazannoi pered izbirateliami v Kieve)," *Narod* 2 (1906), 1.

65 Every *Narod* issue contained an advertisement for the journal "Notes from Rural Pastors" (*Otkliki Sel'skikh Pastyrei*), a monthly journal edited by a priest called K. Kmit in Kiev.

ported on the Preconciliar Commission between March and December 1906. The controversies over Russian church reform extend back to 1861; the debate embraced all levels of ecclesial life and ran "the gamut from peasant to patriarch," intellectuals, and churchmen. The Preconciliar Commission exposed strong tensions between an autonomous community-based understanding of the parish and the definition of the parish "as an institution under the direction of the bishop," and the Commission eventually opted for the latter.[66] In *Narod* Sventsitskii and Vladimir Ern appealed to the Commission members first and foremost to abolish spiritual censorship concerning debate groups with regard to the Church Council,[67] but these hopes were soon deceived.[68]

In "Three Letters by a Rural Priest (a modern epos)," a priest told his story about his reading groups for intelligent rural parishioners, their belief that the Tsar's October Manifesto from 1905 brought the kingdom of God to Russia, his efforts to prevent radicalism among workers' unions, and his attempt to find a solution in a conflict between farmers and their landowner. Nevertheless, the priest was arrested, released, and again investigated—"There is nowhere to find the truth, and God only knows where to look for defense." In the end, he received permission to serve, but according to the *Narod* editors this was a rare happy ending in such affairs.[69]

Furthermore, *Narod* published two essays about the situation of Russia's clergy, both of which deplored the suffering of the parish clergy under the knout of archbishops and monks and the Holy Synod, identified as a secular power. These hierarchs both tried to "prevent the significance of the parish as an autonomous, living cell of the great Church body" and built a wall between pastors and their parish by countless prescriptions and instructions. A pastor was expected to be a "clerk of the office of Orthodox confession," with the task of preventing "a development of a conscious relation to the needs of the life around them," because the secular power knew very well that "this would not be favorable for its own views in the end."[70] A similar critique was articulated by Presniakov, who argued that the Eastern Church perverted the ideal of the Church as a guiding principle for society by the bureaucratization of the clergy, and criticized its close union with the political structures.[71]

66   Shevzov, *Russian Orthodoxy*, 4–5, 13–14.
67   Valentin Sventsitskii, Vladimir Ern, "Tserkovnaia reforma," *Narod* 1 (1906), 4.
68   "Pravda-li?" [Seriously?], *Narod* 2 (1906), 3.
69   Sviashchennik N. L., "Tri pis'ma sel'skogo sviashchennika (sovremennaia epopeia)," *Narod* 2 (1906), 2.
70   Iver', "Dukhovenstvo v Rossii i na zapade," *Narod* 3 (1906), 2–3.
71   Presniakov, "Nash tserkovnyi vopros," 2--3.

3. *Narod* as a Prism for Revolutionary Politics

While as noted above, Bulgakov had not fully made the transition to the Church in 1906, this moment does mark the apex of his political engagement. Christian Socialism was not an abstract theoretical construct. The very act of founding this ambitious daily newspaper with his voice arguably the most prominent testifies to an acute desire to translate ideas into practice. *Narod* had a genuine political and social program, and therefore helps us understand what Christian socialism meant in its application to the issues of the day. *Narod*, as an historical document, can also function for us as a glimpse into the political configurations of the city and the country at an extraordinarily tense moment in the unfolding of the Russian Revolution. Indeed, this is how *Narod*'s participants conceived the time they were living in: this was the great Russian Revolution, right now in 1906.[72]

The Political Moment: Elections and Revolution. The spring of 1906 was the moment when the "umbrella" political organizations, no longer illegal, transformed themselves into actual parties capable of canvassing and collecting votes.[73] Without doubt, the single most pressing issue on the minds of *Narod*'s contributors was the elections to the First Duma, held through February and March; the opening session of the Duma loomed just weeks ahead, on 27 April (OS). Bulgakov opened the second issue of *Narod* with an expansive programmatic article, detailing the tasks he envisioned for the newly-elected delegates. He began with an impassioned general description of the overall sociopolitical situation, and appealed to Soloviev's earlier judgment:

> It was expressed about 30 years ago by V. S. Soloviev, who wrote: "One thing we know for sure: if Russia does not fulfill its moral duty, if it does not renounce national egoism, if it does not renounce the law of power and does not believe in the power of law, if it does not sincerely desire spiritual freedom and truth, it can never have lasting success in any of its affairs, either external or internal."[74]

---

72   See esp. M. Plebeiskii, "Blizitsia vremia … [Pis'mo v redaktsiiu], *Narod* 3 (1906), 2.

73   This is the subject of Emmons' classic study. Terence Emmons, *The Formation of Political Parties and the First National Elections in Russia* (Cambridge, MA: Harvard University Press, 1983).

74   Bulgakov, "O zadachakh," *Narod* 3:1.

The article is suffused with the sense of the world-historical significance of the new Duma institution. Unlike Germans or Englishmen calmly proceeding to their established Reichstag or Parliament, Russians would be making their way to an "arena of struggle" where they could potentially be greeted by bayonets and cannon muzzles from one side or hostile mistrust from the other. Nothing less than Russia's salvation was on the line: "And now, those representatives of the people whom we are electing [...] must save Russia, endow it with law and right, and restore the truth that has been desecrated."[75] At the same time, Bulgakov had an extremely ambitious but also very concrete agenda for the Duma. The first task was the proper organization of the organ itself, including the abolition of the curial system of elections. Next was the reform of the State Council, and the rectification of past errors: assigning responsibility for the recent pogroms, proclaiming full amnesty for political prisoners and exiles,[76] and abolishing the death penalty. Once these mistakes of the past had been resolved, the Duma could move on to a positive program: establishing the rule of law and the inviolability of the person, "freeing" the church from the state by abolishing state religion, affirming freedom of conscience and speech, and resolving the national question by legalizing Poland's autonomy. Then one could proceed to more pedestrian matters such as the agrarian question, which Bulgakov saw as increasing the land allocated to the peasants; and then the "workers' question" as well.[77] One can only imagine his disappointment with the actual Duma given these expectations: there was no progress on Bulgakov's agenda, although Prince Urusov did make a scandalous speech accusing the authorities of complicity in the Jewish pogroms.[78]

Narod also addressed the practical issues of party politics. Without any doubt, *Narod*'s participants identified with the center-left Kadet party, which they saw as precariously situated between the stubbornly entrenched autocracy (the "sphinx of bureaucratic love of power") and the equally mysterious peasantry ("also a sort of sphinx").[79] What did "the people" really think and want? Would the workers trust the Kadets? Evidence indicated that they did not, at least at first. Representatives of the Kadet Party were handing out leaflets to

75 Bulgakov, "O zadachakh." On Bulgakov's apocalyptic vision of the Duma see Evtuhov, *Cross and Sickle*, 118–22.
76 The release of political prisoners, a crucial aspect of revolution and post-revolution tumult, appears repeatedly on the pages of *Narod* and is clearly a major concern.
77 Bulgakov, "O zadachakh."
78 Sarah Warren, *Mikhail Larionov and the Cultural Politics of Late Imperial Russia* (Burlington, VT: Ashgate, 2013), 64.
79 Bulgakov, "Narodnye predstaviteli i gosudarstvennaia duma," *Narod* 4 (1906), 1.

workers gathered in front of the municipal duma in Kiev, only to receive the response: "Let's go talk about this, we need to elect our own people and not Jews and professors."[80]

Another incident clearly produced a strong impression, because the newspaper reports it several times: On 4 April at a pre-election meeting for Kiev workers, twenty-seven of forty-one eligible voters showed up, and voted 20–7 to boycott the elections, which they considered unrepresentative of workers' interests. Defying the boycott, five of them appeared the next day and chose two electors anyway. So, whom did they represent? The author speculated that they were most likely on the right of the political spectrum. A similar boycott had also failed in St. Petersburg. The workers, the author insists, should have sided with the Kadet Party. In the fight for political freedom, everyone temporarily needed to ignore factors like class antagonism and the prevalence of bourgeois politics.[81] The centrality of the Duma elections in *Narod*'s authors' consciousness is confirmed by a plethora of short reports, in every issue, detailing local elections in Kiev and across Russia.

In keeping with the importance of reader "feedback" through published letters, an interesting exchange, in the final two issues, takes on the question of autocratic power. A sort of conversation takes place among Lashniukov, an anonymous "Subscriber," and by implication Sventsiskii, Vetrov[82]—and Bulgakov as the shadow presence who initiated the exchange.[83] Lashniukov vehemently argues that the tsar must take an oath of allegiance to the Constitution,[84] only to be chided by the Subscriber that a Christian's (i.e., the tsar's) word cannot be subordinated to a political document. Lashniukov then refers the subscriber back to Sventsiskii's "Answer to Vetrov,"[85] for the proper distinction between autocracy and the tsar's power. "The 'best Christian,' whoever he may be, cannot be an unlimited autocrat,"[86] or as Sventsiskii had put it, the only form of government directly opposed to Christianity is an autocratic one. "Acceptance of Autocracy is already a renunciation of Christ."[87]

80 S. [Bulgakov], "K vyboram po kievskomu uezdu. Kartinki s natury," *Narod* 5 (1906), 4.
81 Bulgakov, "Rabochie i gosudarstvennaia duma," *Narod* 6 (1906), 1. The problem appears to have been less pronounced outside of the big cities. In the district elections, 76 out of 79 eligible electors attended the meeting, and the question of a boycott did not arise.
82 On Vetrov see n. 40.
83 These letters form a sort of coda to the dialogue described in this essay, 9–10 (n. 41).
84 Lashniukov, "O prisiage konstitutsii," *Narod* 6 (1906), 2.
85 Sventsiskii, "Otvet Vetrovu."
86 Lashniukov, "Otvet podpischiku," *Narod* 7 (1906), 2.
87 Sventsitskii, "Otvet Vetrovu."

Pogroms & the Jewish Question. It is perhaps a peculiarity of the Kiev setting
that the "Jewish question" loomed especially large. As Scott Ury has shown, the
Revolution of 1905 proved transformative for Warsaw's Jewish population.[88] A
similar point might be made for Kiev, the second-largest city on the territory
of the Pale of Settlement.[89] Memory of the Kishinev pogrom just three years
earlier remained sharply painful; indeed, Archimandrite Mikhail (Semënov)
noted, on the second page of the first issue of *Narod*, that the pogrom had, like
the new newspaper, begun on Easter Day in 1903.[90] For Mikhail, the link was
more than coincidental: he perceived the Kishinev events as a "second crucifixion" in which Christ's disciples trampled the scrolls of Divine Law with their
own feet, evidently failing to understand that they were crushing not only the
word of God the Father, but also the Gospel of the Son.[91] Jews were mentioned
in each but the last of the seven issues, with Lashniukov, in № 6, lamenting the
exile of Jewish electors from Kiev as a symptom of the continued evil of the
Pale, and the power of the Black Hundreds.[92] Jewish politics was subsumed in
liberal politics, with the presumption that the victory of the Kadet party would
bring Jewish liberation, and corresponding disappointment when it did not. To
return to Mikhail: Easter Day in 1906 was a dual Easter, because "Apart from
the festival of the Resurrected God, we celebrate the Easter of the people in
the process of resurrection," the moment when "we as a people could cleanse
ourselves of the shame of the sinful, Bartholomean days in Kishinev."[93]

There was also, however, a philosophical dimension to the conversation
about Jewishness, which marks it as an integral part of the Christian Socialist
vision. It was articulated by Anna Inozemtseva[94] under the fairly banal title

88   Scott Ury, *Barricades and Banners: The Revolution of 1905 and the Transformation of
     Warsaw Jewry* (Stanford: Stanford University Press, 2012).
89   On the Kievan *fin de siècle* see Irena R. Makaryk and Virlana Tkacz, *Modernism in
     Kyiv: Jubilant Experimentation* (Toronto, 2010), and Michael Hamm, *Kiev: A Portrait,
     1800–1917* (Princeton: Princeton University Press, 1993), ch.7.
90   Mikhail's biography (1873/74–1916) is astonishing, as Zinaïda Gippius noted: a Russian
     Jew, Orthodox archimandrite, professor at Kazan Theological Seminary, Old Believer
     bishop, progressive journalist, *intelligent*, hermit, and religious proselytizer of the "new"
     Christianity. He died at the age of 42 after being assaulted in the street. Zinaïda Gippius,
     Siniaia kniga: peterburgskii dnevnik, 1914–1918 (Belgrade: Tipografiia Radenkovicha,
     1929), 193.
91   Arkhimandrit Mikhail, "U podnozhiia raspiatiia," *Narod* 1 (1906), 2.
92   Lashniukov, "Vse-taki vysylaiut!," *Narod* 6 (1906), 3.
93   Mikhail, "U podnozhiia."
94   Anna Andreevna Inozemtseva (née Zolotilova, 1864–1915 [?]) was a writer and journal-
     ist from Nizhnii Novgorod who published short stories in a variety of local and national

"Christianity and the Jewish Question." And yet, the author took her argument from the far more interesting piece by Vladimir Soloviev, with the title inverted: "Judaism and the Christian Question." Here he proposed (and was feebly echoed by Inozemtseva) that it was Christians who were lacking in a religious perspective, and that by reducing the Jews to a political problem they were betraying their own faith while the Hebrews had a more appropriate, religiously-infused view of Christians. "The Jews always took a Jewish stance towards us, while we Christians have still not learned to take a Christian stance towards the Jews."[95] Soloviev launched a wide-ranging exploration of three questions which he saw as fundamental to this discrepancy. His points were that Christ himself came from the Jewish milieu because Judaism was particularly receptive to the notion of Godmanhood, that the majority of the Jews mistakenly failed to accept Christianity because they did not understand the truth of the Cross (i. e., suffering), and that the Slavic peoples, specifically Russia and Poland, were ideal for coexisting with the chosen people of Israel, because only together could all three unite to pursue the perfect theocracy fusing the Church, the tsar, and prophecy—each of which essential principles was embodied differently by Orthodox Russians, Catholic Poles, and Jews. The current inability to coexist should not be blamed on history. Rather, the problem lay with the secularized, jaded Christians. It was Christians who were not following the Word of their Book, not the Jews.[96] It should be noted that the ultimate end was the conversion of the Jews, because once the Christians had shown them "visible and *palpable* Christianity" they would recognize this superior truth.[97] Inozemtseva echoes Soloviev quite precisely and consciously. We should not apply Christ's words on the cross, "they know not what they do" (Luke 23:34), to the wicked instigators of pogroms, but admit that they are insulting Christ and condemn them for that. Only then will our will be consonant with that of Christ, and "will lead all of humanity, by means of mercy and love, to acknowledge Christianity's truth."[98]

---

journals, and a first volume of collected works (Nizhnii Novgorod, 1899). It is curious that she shared this interest in Soloviev with her fellow Nizhnii Novgorod journalist, Anna Shmidt, who imagined herself as Sophia.

95 Vladimir Soloviev, "Evreistvo i khristianskii vopros" (1884), in: Soloviev, *Stat'i o evreistve* (Jerusalem: "Maslina," 1979), 7.

96 Soloviev, "Evreistvo," 42–43.

97 Soloviev, "Evreistvo," 56.

98 Anna Inozemtseva, "Khristianstvo i evreiskii vopros," *Narod* 4 (1906), 1. On Bulgakov's own "insistence on the ultimate Christological destiny of Israel" and his internalization

Capital Punishment. Possibly the most interesting issue of *Narod* is № 4, Friday 7/20 April—because here the editors published the transcript of Vladimir Soloviev's speech from 13 March 1881, in which, while acknowledging the obvious guilt of the assassins of Alexander II, he urged the new tsar to pardon them and spare them the death penalty. It was a position that cost him his job at the university. The people, says Soloviev, can know only one truth—God's or the tsar's—and God's is "Thou shalt not kill." Capital punishment has a rich history in Russia. Recently, Elena Marasinova has argued that the *de facto* abolition of the death penalty under Empress Elizabeth in the eighteenth century was a reflection not of the Enlightenment (and hence "progress"), but of Elizabeth's profound religiosity: Orthodox principles made capital punishment untenable.[99] As we know, it came back with a vengeance, most famously with the (botched) hanging of the Decembrist conspirators.

Capital punishment was one of Bulgakov's main issues during the years of revolution—one on which he had a very specific practical position, and a considered moral argument to back it up. The practical cases are the following. On 19 March 1906 Lieutenant (Petr) Shmidt (whom many know only as the name of a Neva bridge, now Blagoveshchenskii) and three sailors were executed by firing squad for their leadership of the real Black Sea mutiny of 1905—the revolt on the cruiser *Ochakov* (not the battleship *Potemkin*), joined by a significant part of the Black Sea fleet. The execution was greeted by demonstrations and expressions of "religious horror before the sea of blood in which our poor homeland is drowning," and a controversial memorial service for Shmidt at the St. Petersburg Theological Academy.[100] The second was the case of the SR terrorist Maria Spiridonova (1884–1941), who carried out her mission to kill the Tambov provincial official and leader of the local Union of the Russian People Gavriil Luzhenovskii in January 1906. In an echo of the acquittal of Vera Zasulich three decades earlier, Bulgakov came to the impassioned defense of this "sweet Russian girl" who had killed out of "love and spiritual suffering" and suffered horrendous beatings if not rape (this was discussed at length) at the hands of her captors. The article, placed prominently on page 1 of the last

---

of the "'Jewish question' as a Christian one," see Inga Leonova, "Christianity and the Jewish Question," in *The Wheel* 26/27 (2021), 73–79.

99 See for example Elena Marasinova, "Pochemu imperatritsa Elizaveta Petrovna otmenila smertnuiu kazn'," *Kommersant Nauka* 6 (2017), https://www.kommersant.ru/doc/3396753 (access 2024/01/26).

100 Vasilii Uspenskii, "O smertnoi kazni.—Panikhida po leitenante Shmidt," *Narod* 4 (1906), 2.

issue of *Narod*, exhorted readers not to pass judgment, for "our torpor, our indifference provoked this young girl to commit murder."[101] Spiridonova's death sentence was commuted to exile to a Siberian penal colony.

The theoretical mindset behind these very concrete and to many shocking views was outlined in an essay for a collected volume, *Against Capital Punishment*, published in 1906. Bulgakov's essay posits capital punishment as partaking of that evil which is inevitably embodied in an ill-conceived, godless law that forces individuals to participate in a cold, indifferent execution. In an ironic commentary on the collection itself, Bulgakov noted that any number of pamphlets or edited volumes could be published; this was not important. What was important was the moral position, not because it is "bad" to take another life, but because the actual responsibility for any given execution rests with the public or "narod" as a whole. In other words, it is you and I who are killing this person, not the state. By his own criterion, society as a whole is complicit in the fate of the executed, and also in that of the hordes of political prisoners filling Russian jails. His opposition was a matter of political substance, and his ethical stance is one that regards society and not merely the individual.

But he goes further still. It is not just a matter of collective responsibility, but of passionately and totally putting oneself on the line: "The falsity [of publishing volumes against capital punishment] is that only he can speak with a strong and powerful voice who himself is prepared to be executed, and only when he has internally performed this execution upon himself, has denied his own being. [...] Therefore it is so awful and shameful only to *write* about the death penalty."[102]

Bulgakov's clear position found further expression in his practical activity as a delegate to the Second Duma. He extended his argument to the matter of Stolypin's courts martial, in which frequently innocent peasants or workers were arbitrarily hanged as a radical means of stopping the revolution. This, to Bulgakov, was a case of multiple capital punishments, or the application of the death penalty to hundreds of individuals. In his speech to the 12 March 1907 session, he once again brought a moral position, seeing the courts martial as

101   Bulgakov, "Iz zapisnoi knizhki," *Narod* 7 (1906), 1.
102   Bulgakov, "O smertnoi kazni," in *Protiv smertnoi kazni*, ed. M. N. Gernet et al. (Moscow: Tipografiia Sytina, 1906), 74; and in *Smertnaia kazn'. Za i protiv,* ed. O. F. Shishov, T. S. Parfenova (Moscow: Iuridicheskaia literatura, 1989), 56. The volume includes a list of 612 death sentences between 1826 and 1906 (some not executed, or converted to time in a penal camp).

symptomatic of Russia as an agitated sea, torn by civil war, "in no condition to tell the difference between good and evil," inured to the value of human life.[103]

Working Class & Labor Organization. Nearly every issue included a column, "From the Workers' World," on page four, detailing plans for a labor union or society of one sort or another, from printers to wallpaperers to various artisans.[104] Clearly, the *Narod* editors and authors were very serious both about practical political organization—this was not merely a debating club for theoretical issues—and about the popular (*narodnyi*) aspect of their program. There is no hint of anything specifically Christian in any of these rules and charters, though there was indeed always a provision for the "satisfaction of [members'] spiritual needs and development of their class consciousness."[105] It is interesting to note that, while "a peasant voice" occasionally makes an appearance, and Bulgakov naturally insisted on the agrarian question as the key agenda item for the First Duma,[106] *Narod*'s regular focus was on workers far more than peasants—perhaps because it was, after all, an urban newspaper.

News from Kiev, Russia, and Across the World. The very first sentence of *Narod*'s programmatic agenda proclaimed that it was "an organ that is not only local (Kiev) and regional, but primarily all-Russian." It was time, the editors proclaimed, to move the press outside the capital cities and to the regions.[107] *Narod* echoed its more famous national counterparts in the attention it dedicated to news items across Russia and in the larger world. Reports came in from Europe, Asia, and the United States. The negotiations of the Anglo-French Loan to Russia in Paris, signed on 16 April 1906, figure prominently.[108] On 10 March

---

103 Stenograficheskii otchet Gosudarstvennoi Dumy, 12 March 1907, 397–98.
104 Specifically, the charters printed in *Narod*'s seven days were for printers (the largest union in Kiev, with more than 700 members), suppliers (explicitly, male and female), salespeople, carriage-makers, and wallpaper and drapery workers. These are all "in-between" workers, part artisan and part worker—not like assembly line workers in a factory, for example.
105 E. g., "Iz rabochego mira," *Narod* 5 (1906), 4.
106 "Krest'ianskii golos," *Narod* 1 (1906) 5; Bulgakov, "O zadachakh," *Narod* 3 (1906), 2.
107 Bulgakov, Volzhskii, "Ot redaktsii," 1. This echoes an argument made by Dmitrii Mordovtsev three decades earlier. D. L. Mordovtsev, "Pechat' v provintsii," *Delo* (Sept.–Oct. 1875).
108 See Olga Crisp, "The Russian Liberals and the 1906 Anglo-French Loan to Russia," *The Slavonic and East European Review* 39, 93 (1961), 497–511: 497: "In Russia the political parties in opposition to the government of Nicholas II resented what they considered

(25 February OS) 1906, 1,099 miners perished at Courrières, in France, as the result of a coal dust explosion; the catastrophe was immediately followed by massive strikes protesting against safety conditions in the mines. These events were commented on in nearly every issue. The days of publication followed soon after the eruption of the Vesuvius in Italy on 5 April (23 March OS) and happened to coincide exactly with the major catastrophe of the San Francisco earthquake on 18 April (5 April OS), conveyed in apocalyptic terms. One report described dangerous "torn and ragged electric wires," lack of water, fish "thrown from the bay onto the streets of the city" by the power of the earthquake, and extraordinary heat. "Three hundred head of cattle escaped from a slaughterhouse in flames and ran through the city's streets, trampling everything in their path."[109] Such events surely adumbrate the end of the world. Drawing on these, Bulgakov described the political atmosphere in Russia as "the calm before the storm": "We stand before a yawning abyss, the Vesuvius of popular fury is only beginning to be active. The earthquake is nigh. Save yourselves before it is too late."[110]

4. *Narod* in Bulgakov's Spiritual Evolution

As a hypothesis for further consideration, we can suggest that, while Bulgakov's spiritual development, with its multiple sharp shifts in conviction and worldview,[111] is the result of "events" internal to his consciousness and cannot necessarily be related to events in the material world, nonetheless his extended return (over two decades) to the Church as an organization and his willingness or need to work inside the Church do appear connected to politics. The shift to Orthodox Christianity, fully realized when he launched his new truly theological enterprise in the 1920s in Paris, was completed through politics. A crucial step along the way was the decision to devote his energies to concrete reforms in the Orthodox Church in Russia over the course of 1904–7, which, in his view, were the main precondition for realizing ideas of Christian politics in his

---

to be a hurried bargain with the autocratic government on the eve of the meeting of the newly elected national assembly. They branded the French government's decision to lend money to the Witte-Durnovo government as siding with the forces of reaction against the people."

109   "Telegrammy (Ot S. P.B. Agentstva), *Narod* 6 (1906), 3.

110   "Na groznom rasput'i," *Narod* 5 (1906), 1.

111   See Regula M. Zwahlen, "Sergei Bulgakov's Intellectual Journey, 1900–1922," in *Oxford Handbook of Russian Religious Thought*, ed. Caryl Emerson et al. (Oxford: Oxford University Press, 2020), 277–92.

country. The eventual ordination that followed Bulgakov's work in the Church Council, and the Bolshevik victory, in 1918, might be seen as the logical culmination of this evolution. One of the main obstacles to Bulgakov's becoming a priest earlier was definitely political too—the connection of Orthodoxy with autocracy: "I was unable to overcome this, neither did I want to, nor should I have. This obstacle abruptly vanished with the revolution in 1917: the Church was suddenly free—now persecuted and no longer official."[112]

Who was Bulgakov as a politician? In his once-universally-read essay, Max Weber outlined an inspiring and demanding agenda for a vocation in politics.[113] (The essay was written in 1919, and became ubiquitous in the post-WWII period.) "One can say," Weber proposes, "that three pre-eminent qualities are decisive for the politician: passion, a feeling of responsibility, and a sense of proportion."[114] In the political projects we have examined, Bulgakov begins to look like Weber's ideal politician: the passion and sense of responsibility with which he approached land politics, the question of church reform, a Christian press, and the indiscriminate application of the death penalty are evident. Sense of proportion is a more difficult criterion: a contemporary reader is shocked by the almost casual ease with which he affirms the necessity of land redistribution. But by "proportion" Weber means not so much the content of a program as the ability to convert abstract ideals into practical measures; so it applies as well, in the sense that he was able to reconcile his goals with those of the Kadets, get elected to the Duma (and later the Church Council), and introduce a series of concrete proposals, some of them very significant. In each situation, Bulgakov's position was never instrumental or expedient, but always reflected a deeply-considered moral stance—which does not mean that he didn't make mistakes. Weber's famous formulation in which a "mature man" feels full responsibility for his conduct and "reaches the point where he says: 'Here I stand; I can do no other,'" seems to fit Bulgakov very well, and is characteristic of each phase of his life, no matter how distinct the specific circumstances and projects.

---

112 Sergii Bulgakov, "Moe rukopolozhenie," in *Avtobiograficheskie zametki*, ed. Lev Zander (Paris: YMCA Press 1946), 34–43: 38.

113 For Bulgakov's views on Max Weber, see "The National Economy and the Religious Personality," *Journal of Markets and Morality* 11, 1 (2008), 157–79 (dedicated to Ivan F. Tokmakov, Bulgakov's father-in-law, a wine merchant, not the writer mentioned by the translator); on Bulgakov's correspondence with Weber see Sergii Bulgakov, *Die Philosophie der Wirtschaft* (Münster: Aschendorff, 2014), 295–97.

114 Max Weber, "Politics as a Vocation," in *From Max Weber: Essays in Sociology*, ed. H. H. Gerth and C. Wright (London: Routledge, 1948), 77–128: 115.

Building the House of Wisdom
DOI 10.17438/978-3-402-12181-8

Is It All the Greeks' Fault? Reconsidering the Byzantine Legacy in Sergius Bulgakov's *By the Walls of Cherson*

Nikos Kouremenos

1. Introduction

Fr. Sergius Bulgakov is a prominent figure in the history of twentieth-century Orthodox theology, principally for two reasons: i) his further development of theological reflections on divine wisdom initially expressed by Russian thinkers such as Soloviev and Florenskii, broadly known as Sophiology,[1] and ii) his proposal for a pilot initiative concerning a limited intercommunion between Anglicans and Orthodox within the annual meetings of St. Sergius and St. Alban Fellowship[2]—fruit of his active engagement in the field of inter-Christian dialogue and the ecumenical movement, though still in its infancy. Nevertheless, only little scholarly attention has hitherto been paid to

---

1   In this regard, see Mikhail Sergeev, *Sophiology in Russian Orthoxoxy: Solov'ev, Bulgakov, Loskii, and Berdiaev* (Lewiston: Edwin Mellen Press 2006). Cf. also Karel Sládek, "Sophiology as a Theological Discipline according to Solovyov, Bulgakov and Florensky," *Bogoslovni vestnik* 77 (2017) 109–16. For a critical approach to Bulgakov's Sophiology, see Richard May, "Between God and the world: A critical appraisal of the sophiology of Sergius Bulgakov," *Scottish Journal of Theology* 74, no. 1 (2021): 67–84.

2   On Bulgakov's proposal of a partial intercommunion between Eastern Orthodox and Anglicans, to which Fr. Georges Florovsky was strongly opposed, see Brandon Gallaher, "'Great and Full of Grace': Partial Intercommunion and Sophiology in Sergei Bulgakov" in *Church and World: Essays in Honor of Michael Plekon*, ed. William C. Mills (Rollisford: Orthodox Research Institute, 2013), 69–121; Sergei V. Nikolaev, "Spiritual Unity: The Role of Religious Authority in the Disputes between Sergii Bulgakov and G. Florovsky concerning Intercommunion," *St Vladimir's Theological Quarterly* 49, no 1/2 (2005): 101–23.

one of his lesser-known essays, titled "By the Walls of Cherson,"[3] which has been called, not inaptly, a "Catholic temptation" in his spiritual and intellectual paths.[4]

Four years after his ordination as a priest (June, 1918) and a few months before his irrevocable exile from his ancestral land (December, 1922), while the consequences of the October Revolution profoundly shattered Russia, Fr. Sergius was temporarily settled in Crimea. It was there that he would compose an essay in the form of a multipart dialogue in which his troubled inner world and his critical assessment of the collapsing imperial and Slavophile worldview are uneasily reflected. Be that as it may, the uncertainty of the emerging new reality for Russian society led him to reappraise the pope as a factor of consistency safeguarding the smooth running of the Church. The very history of the transmission and diffusion of said text is of relevance, given that it remained unpublished as a manuscript, almost disowned, in the personal archive of Fr. Sergius, since his student, Leo Zander, typed it up in the 1960s. In this version, the essay enjoyed a limited circulation,[5] up to the early 1990s, when it was published, first in Russian,[6] while a few years later a French[7] and an Italian[8]

---

3   The studies dedicated *ad hoc* to this Bulgakov's essay that I was able to identify are the following: Filippo Cucinotta, "L'VIII Concilio ecumenico: l'ecclesiologia ecumenica di S. Bulgakov", in *La Chiesa tra teologia e scienze umane: una sola complessa realtà*, ed. Rosaria La Delfa (Rome: Città nuova, 2005), 217–60; Agostino Marchetto, "Dalle mura di Chersoneso al pozzo di Giacobbe: Evoluzione del pensiero di Sergii Bulgakov sul primato del vescovo di Roma," *Apollinaris* 73, no. 1/4 (2000): 603–14; Myroslaw Tataryn, "Between Patriarch and Pope: the theological struggle of Sergei Bulgakov," in *In God's Hands: Essays on the Church and Ecumenism in Honour of Michael A. Fahey, S. J.*, ed. J. Skira (Leuven: Peeters, 2006), 137–59. Barbara Hallensleben, "Vom griechischen Russentum zur Universalen Kirche: Sergij N. Bulgakov" in *Russische Religionsphilosophie und Theologie um 1900*, ed. Karl Pinggera (Marburg: Elwert 2005), 109–20.

4   See the introduction to the French translation by Bernard Marchadier, "Les remparts de Chersonèse ou la 'tentation catholique' d'un théologien orthodoxe," in Serge Boulgakov, *Sous les remparts de Chersonèse* (Geneva: Ad solem, 1999), 5–19.

5   In this typewritten form, the text was used in a thesis by Stanislaw Świerkosz, *L'église visible selon Serge Bulgakov: structure hiérarchique et sacramentale*, Orientalia Christiana Analecta, 211 (Rome: Pontificium Istitutum Studiorum Orientalium Studiorum, 1980). I am not aware of any earlier use of this essay.

6   S. N. Bulgakov, "U sten Khersonisa," Simvol 25 (1991), 169–331.

7   Serge Boulgakov, *Sous les remparts de Chersonèse* (Geneva: Ad solem, 1999). In what follows, I cite from this French translation.

8   Sergej N. Boulgakov, *Presso le mura di Chersoneso: per una teologia della cultura* (Rome: Lipa, 1998).

translation appeared, contributing to its dissemination to and reception by a broader audience.

One of the central ideas of "By the Walls of Cherson" could be summarized as follows: the reception of the Christian faith *manu graeca* had a devastating impact on Russia's spiritual development. Byzantine Christianity endowed the new converts not only with the Great Schism between East and West but also with a controversial rhetoric alienating Russia from the Universal Church. Furthermore, Byzantium handed down the political theory of Caesaropapism and the Church's subsequent subjection to the imperial authority. As a result, a *sui generis* ecclesial nationalism or nationalistic ecclesiology was born that sent the Russian Church into a spiraling crisis and a deadlock. The source of all this evil, according to Bulgakov, was the fact that the Russian Church had adopted the Byzantine mentality. How much factual truth can be found in these approaches? How original was Bulgakovs' anti-Byzantine attitude and in what way does this differ from similar ideas expressed by previous Russian religious thinkers, such as Vladimir Soloviev (1853–1900)? How different did Slavophiles on the one hand and Bulgakov in "By the Walls of Cherson" on the other assess the Byzantine tradition in respect to Russian history and culture? Did Bulgakov's rejection of the "Catholic temptation" lead him eventually to reconsider his criticism of the Byzantine heritage? These are some of the issues I will attempt to discuss in this paper, examining mainly but not exclusively the influence Slavophiles and Soloviev exercised on Bulgakov's negative perception of Byzantium.

2. A Multipart Dialogue on the Destiny of the Russian Church

A Refugee, a lay Theologian, an erudite Hieromonk, and a parish Priest are the four personages engaged in a conversation during a full-moon night in front of the ruins of the ancient Tauric city of Cherson. The selection of characters and the very style of a debate should come as no surprise to the reader of the Bulgakovian corpus. Two of them, namely the Refugee and the lay Theologian, are also to be found in the work "At the Feast of the Gods: Contemporary Dialogues," written a few years earlier, in 1918,[9] an essay expressing, as Rowan Williams put it, a strong sense of tragedy and unclarity about the future and criticizing the lack of dynamism and decisiveness in the recent Council of the

---

9   Sergius Bulgakov, "At the Feast of the Gods: Contemporary Dialogues," *Slavonic Review* 1, no. 1 (1922), 172–83; 1 no. 2 (1922) 391–400; 1, no. 3 (1923), 604–22.

Russian Church (1917–1918).[10] The general idea of both essays is the well-known phrase of Dostoyevsky's: "the Russian Church is paralysed," used as an epigraph by Bulgakov for the fifth dialogue of his essay "At the Feast of the Gods."[11] In the same essay, one can find the fundamental references to the Byzantine tradition that would be more comprehensively developed in the "By the Walls of Cherson." It is worth pointing out that according to Fr. Sergius, the impact of the Russian Revolution upon the historical course of the Orthodox Church is of crucial importance. The resignation of Tsar Nicholas marked the end of autocracy, which was a legacy of the Byzantine worldview and mentality and eventually signified the dawn of a new, post-Constantine era. Indeed, through the literary persona of the Refugee, with which Bulgakov expresses his personal views in both essays, one reads:

> Personally, I consider we have actually crossed the boundary of historical Orthodoxy and that church history has reached a new epoch, as different from the preceding one as, say, the pre-Constantine epoch is from the one before it. The Constantine era ended for Byzantium in 1453, and for the entire Orthodox Church on the 2/15 March 1917.[12]

Returning to the "By the Walls of Cherson," one should not be surprised by the dialogue's setting. It is not exclusively the physical presence of Bulgakov in Crimea at that very moment that conditioned that choice. The symbolic meaning for Russian culture carried by this territory is reflected throughout the entire essay. The crucial importance of the Byzantine city of Cherson in the historical understanding and interpretation of the Christianization of Rus' has come to the forefront of scholarly research in recent years.[13] According to the most reliable medieval sources, such as the *Primary Chronicle*, it was there that the baptism of Vladimir took place in 988. While returning to Kiev, the prince of Rus' brought along Chersonite clergy to effectuate the evangelization of his people; even the first bishop of the city of Novgorod at the time of Vladimir's conversion, Joachim, originated from Cherson. As far as the ecclesiastical or-

---

10   Rowan Williams, ed., *Sergii Bulgakov: Towards a Russian Political Theology* (Edinburgh: T&T Clark, 1999), 164.
11   Bulgakov, "At the Feast of the Gods," 604.
12   Ibid., 611–12.
13   Significant in this perspective is the study by Alex M. Feldman, "How and Why Vladimir Besieged Chersōn," *Byzantinoslavica* 73, no. 1–2 (2015), 145–70, in which he attempted to deconstruct more traditional narratives glorifying Prince Vladimir's conversion.

ganization of the early Kievan church and the related jurisdictional issues are concerned, a range of different theories have been expressed over the decades, which, however, remain beyond the scope of this essay.[14] Instead, particular focus will be placed on the reception of Vladimir's conversion and the Christianization of Rus' by the Byzantine missionaries along with the consequences which ensured the alleged attachment of Russian Christianity to the Byzantine tradition, according to the views of modern religious thought, as they are depicted in Bulgakov's work "By the Walls of Cherson." Codifying the Byzantine influences upon Russian culture, Fr. John Meyendorff distinguishes three consistent elements: the Roman political tradition, the Greek literary heritage, and the Orthodox Christian faith.[15] In this specific essay, Bulgakov deals with the first and the third and it is thus these that will be discussed here: Byzantine political theology and the Eastern Orthodox version of the Christian faith.

Against the background of the collapse of the Russian imperial ideology and the very structures of the Russian Church due to the dramatic events of the Bolshevik revolution, the two main characters engaging in dialogue, namely the Lay Theologian and the Refugee, are arguing about who should be considered responsible for that development. While the Lay Theologian, reflecting the Slavophile view, attributes the responsibility to the reforms of Peter the Great and Russia's forced Westernization, the Refugee, more or less expressing Bulgakov's personal opinion, not being satisfied by such an explanation, seeks the origins of said crisis in the distant past, back to the very conversion of the Rus' to Christianity. Cherson, in that sense, as the place of the spiritual and historical birth of Rus', is crucial for Bulgakov's attempt to understand the situation in his contemporary Russia. According to the Refugee, conversion to Christianity signified not only a rejection of their pagan/barbarian past and the acceptance of a new religious faith but, more decisively, the entrance of Russia to the European family of nations. Becoming Christian in the ninth century was interpreted by Bulgakov in the first quarter of the twentieth as becoming European. Moreover, since the Great Schism between East and West had not occurred at the time of Vladimir's conversion, the "Russian" people's baptism signifies for the Refugee their entrance not to a particular local church but to the Universal Church.

---

14   By way of indication, see the study by Andrzej Poppe, "The Christianization and Ecclesiastical Structure of Kyivan Rus' to 1300," *Harvard Ukrainian Studies* 21, no. 3/4 (1997), 311–92.

15   John Meyendorff, *Byzantium and the Rise of Russia: A Study of Byzantino-Russian Relations in the Fourteenth Century* (Cambridge: Cambridge University Press, 1981), 10–28.

At this point, Bulgakov, through the character of the Refugee, identifies the crisis of Cherson with the Byzantine heritage in Russia. Due to the Byzantine influence, the form of Christianity established in Kiev resulted in the separation of Russia from the rest of the world. Byzantium is linked with ecclesial particularism and separatist tendencies towards the Universal Church. To better clarify this view, the Refugee speaks about a crisis of principles:

> La crise des principes de Chersonèse est la crise des principes de Byzance ou, plus exactement, de l'Orthodoxie byzantine en tant que force spirituelle, historique et culturelle [...] En même temps qu'à cette heure fatale et terrible de l'Histoire elle recevait des Grecs la religion chrétienne, la Russie héritait de toute l'étroitesse et du repliement sur soi de Byzance et se voyait séparée de l'ensemble de l'Europe occidentale, et chrétienne, par une véritable muraille de Chine [...] Ici, à Chersonèse, la Russie a été placée sous une cloche de verre et condamnée à la solitude et à la séparation.[16]

It is necessary to stress, at this point, that the idea of Russia's separation from the Universal Church due to the Byzantine heritage of the former is a concept initially found in the philosopher Vladimir Soloviev's well-known book *La Russie et l'église universelle*, published in 1889. Soloviev's anti-Byzantine position was expressed through his contestation of the very Christian quality of the Byzantine Empire. Indeed, the Russian philosopher accused Byzantium of superficial religiosity. According to Soloviev, the Byzantines, emphasizing rituals, forgot to transform the social and political structures of public life according to Christian values and principles. As a consequence, they built an Empire that was more pagan than Christian. Returning to Bulgakov's essay, the reader can find traces of an anti-Byzantine attitude based principally on beliefs according to which certain negative behavioral traits are supposed to be linked with certain national features. Seeking to exempt Russians from any responsibility, due to their lack of sophistication, the Refugee blames the Byzantines—or Greeks as he prefers to call them—for the direction that Christianity took in Russia:

> [...] les sauvages « Rus » ne purent qu'imiter maladroitement les fastes extérieurs du rite byzantin – si somptueux et si beau – et se montrèrent absolument incapables d'assimiler la culture grecque, en adoptant malgré eux les fleurs dans la liturgie. De plus, les Grecs s'avérèrent des pédagogues incapables, indifférents, paresseux et,

---

16 Boulgakov, *Sous les remparts*, 29–31.

surtout, âpres au gain. Ce qui les intéressait, c'étaient le pouvoir et les revenus, non pas les âmes et leur éducation chrétienne.[17]

The Refugee's harsh criticism towards the Greek clergy is not limited only to the period of the conversion and formation of a Christian state in Kiev. It is also extended to the entire course of Russian history, including the period of ecclesiastical and jurisdictional dependence from the Patriarchate of Constantinople and even after the fall of the Byzantine Empire. The Refugee even questions the role of the Eastern Patriarchates in ecclesiastical affairs in modern times, going so far as to wonder what the future would have held for Russia had the Latin clergy been the ones who undertook the Christianization of the land:

> Oui, les Grecs nous ont donné les richesses fabuleuses de leur génie avec le rite liturgique, mais ils ne nous ont pas appris à l'apprécier, et n'étaient pas en état de le faire. Des évêques et des prêtres grecs furent dépêchés en Russie et pendant plusieurs siècles la Russie fut un diocèse byzantin qui avait pour pape le patriarche de Byzance – car c'est bien sûr à une papauté byzantine (qui, d'ailleurs rampait devant le pouvoir impérial) qu'avaient essayé d'aboutir les prétentions de Photius et consorts. Si, au lieu des Grecs, nous avions eu, par exemple, les « Latins », avec leur zèle, leur savoir-faire et leur énergie, notre christianisation aurait bien entendu reçu d'autres traits et la Russie aurait peut-être été véritablement un pays chrétien et civilisé. Mais les Grecs n'en étaient pas capables. Ils sont restés des étrangers en Russie et avec les invasions tatares le lien avec Byzance s'est affaibli, jusqu'à ce que nous parvenions enfin à nous en affranchir. Après la chute de Byzance les patriarches d'Orient, et en particulier le patriarche de Constantinople, se transformèrent en véritables quémandeurs d'aumônes, prêts à tout pour de l'argent, et jouèrent parfois dans les affaires de la Russie un rôle fort affligeant et ambigu (par exemple pendant la crise du Raskol).[18]

3. The Temptation of Caesaropapism

According to the Refugee's literary persona, the greatest sin of Byzantium was neither greed nor the indifference or whatever negative feature of the Greek clergy. In this regard, one can note Soloviev's influence on Bulgakov regarding the Byzantine heritage. Both religious philosophers consider Caesaropapism,

---

17 Boulgakov, *Sous les remparts*, 31.
18 Ibid., 32.

the subordination of the Church to the secular power, to be the most significant Byzantine defect transmitted to Russian culture. Bulgakov discerns not only the concept of *translatio imperii* from the Byzantine to the Muscovite Russian principality after the fall of Constantinople in 1453 but also a *translatio potestatis* from the Byzantine emperor to the Russian tsar:

> Quant au tsar, il adopta dans les faits tous les traits fondamentaux du despotisme ecclésial byzantin. Certes, il n'y eut pas chez les tsars de ces hérétiques qui furent si nombreux sur le trône de Byzance—les souverains russes étaient pour cela trop ignorants et trop primitifs, et ils se bornèrent à la correction des livres anciens et aux disputes sur les vieux rites. Mais ils disposaient de la *potestas juridictionis* pour toutes les questions d'administration de l'Église. [...] De fait, ils étaient les chefs de l'Église russe. Bien plus : sur toutes les questions ecclésiales, même en matière de canonisation des saints, ils manifestaient leur souveraineté, comme chacun s'en souvient bien.[19]

In practical terms, this concept entailed the transplantation of the Eusebian model of the Church's subordination to the state from the Eastern Roman Empire to the Muscovite State and later to the Russian Empire. In this regard, as the Byzantine Emperors were considered to be the Heads not only of the Byzantine Church but also of the Eastern Orthodox Church in the broader sense, in a similar way, Russian tsars were supposed to function as the supreme authority in the ecclesiastic affairs of all the Eastern Orthodox Churches:

> De même que les empereurs byzantins étaient à la tête non seulement de l'Église byzantine mais de l'ensemble de l'Église d'Orient, de même les tsars russes se montrèrent dans les faits les vecteurs de l'unité non seulement de l'Église russe mais de toutes les Églises orthodoxes.[20].

Therefore, it is evident that the role assumed by the tsar as the absolute leader of the Orthodox Church was not a modern innovation but a faithful continuation of the Byzantine model. From Constantinople to Moscow and then to Petrograd, Bulgakov sees the Constantinian period of the Church, in which the Eusebian paradigm in governing ecclesiastic affairs predominated and was eventually abruptly interrupted by the Bolshevik revolution:

---

19   Boulgakov, *Sous les remparts*, 55–56.
20   Ibid., 56.

[…] c'était le tsar qui gouvernait l'Église; *de jure* et *de facto*, il était le chef de l'Église russe – que dis-je, de l'ensemble de l'Église orthodoxe – et en exprimait l'unité. En ce sens, il était l'héritier et le continuateur direct des autocrates byzantins et, dans l'histoire de l'Église, c'est en droite ligne que se succèdent Byzance, Moscou et Petrograd, formant une époque historique unique de césaropapisme indiscutable, déclaré et décidé où le vecteur de l'unité de l'Église a été l'empereur.[21]

It may be of interest to mention, in this context, the first person who attempted in a systematic way to formulate a political theology in Russia, namely Vladimir Soloviev. The religious philosopher based his approach regarding the relationship between Church and state upon a Christological dimension.[22] Reassuming Soloviev's thought, the perfect union of the divine and the human, dogmatically expressed in Chalcedon, reflects Christianity's social and public life, an intimate connection between the Church, representing the divine, and the state, representing the human element. Consequently, the Church should take precedence over the state, for the divine is anterior and superior to the human. Any concept, therefore, seeking to subordinate the Church to the state, as, for example, the Eusebian model does, is for Soloviev a distortion based on pagan principles and undoubtedly leads to heresy.[23] This approach expressed in Russia towards the end of the nineteenth century can be interpreted as a reaction to the official imperial ideology and the exploitation of the Orthodox Church for nationalistic purposes. In this regard, Bulgakov's criticism of the model of Caesaropapism differs from that of Soloviev, for it came at a crucial moment when the Eusebian model had already collapsed, and the future of the Russian church was still obscure.

4. Westernizers' Attitude Towards Byzantium

Tracing the roots of Bulgakov's negative predisposition towards Byzantium in his work "By the Walls of Cherson," one should turn one's attention to the rich literary production of the Russian intelligentsia during the nineteenth century. In fact, it was in that period that while seeking an identity for the Russian nation and the specific feature of Russian civilization in relation to the

---

21 Boulgakov, *Sous les remparts*, 58.
22 On this regard, see Emmanuel Tawil, "Les Relations Église-État dans *La Russie Et L'Église Universelle* de Vladimir Soloviev," *L' Année Canonique* 51, no. 1 (2009), 307–32.
23 See, Vladimir Soloviev, *La Russie et l'église universelle* (Paris: Nouvelle Librairie Parisienne Albert Savine, 1889), xlvi–xlvii.

rest of the world and particularly Western Europe, the interest among Russian intellectuals concerning the influence of the Byzantine tradition upon the formation of the Russian culture and Russianness was reinvigorated. The debate between Westernizers and Slavophiles on the interpretation of the past, the understanding of the present and the future perspectives of the Russian nation, also entailed some value judgments regarding the Byzantine legacy for Russian culture.[24] The cases of Petr Chaadaev (1794–1856) and Aleksey Khomiakov (1804–1860), as representative examples of a Westernizer and a Slavophile respectively, would shed light on the broader cultural and intellectual context that shaped Bulgakov's thinking.

In the first place, the philosopher Pyotr Chaadaev, considered the forerunner of the Westernizers movement in Russian intellectual circles,[25] was aggressive enough regarding the Byzantine legacy's impact on Russian culture. In his work "Premiere lettre philosophique" (First Philosophical Letter), initially written in French, on December 1, 1829, before being published in Russian a few years later, in 1836, in the Muscovite journal *Telescope*, proclaimed in an almost provocative way the essential, inevitable, and apparently irremediable inferiority of the Russian nation.[26] In his pessimistic view, Chaadaev identifies Russia's cultural isolation and its estrangement from Western Europe with its Byzantine legacy. Indeed, the ties of Russian civilization with the Eastern Christendom were seen as a fatal misfortune for the Russian people:

> [...] poussés par une destinée fatale, nous allions chercher dans la *misérable Byzance*, objet du profond mépris de ces peuples, le code moral qui devait faire notre éducation. Un moment auparavant, un esprit ambitieux avait enlevé cette famille à la fraternité universelle.[27]

---

24   On the ideological controversy between Westernizers and Slavophiles in nineteenth-century Russia, see the classical study by Andrzej Walicki, *The Slavophile Controversy: History of a Conservative Utopia in the Nineteenth-Century Russian Thought* (Oxford: Oxford University Press, 1975).

25   Gary M. Hamburg, "Petr Chaadaev and the Slavophile-Westernizer Debate," in *The Oxford Handbook of Russian Religious Thought*, ed. Caryl Emerson et al. (Oxford: Oxford University Press, 2020), 111–32.

26   Regarding the First Philosophical Letter and the intellectual background of its composition, see Pierre Gonneau, "En réponse à Karamzin ... La première *Lettre philosophique* de Čaadaev comme réplique à la préface de l'*Histoire de l'État russe*", *Revue des études slaves* 82, no. 2/3 (2012), 783–92.

27   Ivan A. Gagarin, ed., *Œuvres choisies de Pierre Tchadaïef publiées pour la première fois* (Paris/Leipzig: Librairie A. Franck, 1862), 29.

The aforementioned "ambitious spirit" who cut Eastern Christianity from communion with the Universal Church should be identified as the Patriarch of Constantinople, Photius. It is an uncritical and unquestioning adoption of the Roman Catholic argumentation, according to which it was Photius' ambition that was to blame for the ninth-century schism between Rome and Constantinople.[28] In any case, what impresses in Chaadaev's argumentation is the disparaging reference to Byzantium.

Although promoted a heated debate in literate circles in Russia, the First Philosophical Letter's publication in Russian bore dramatic consequences for its author's reputation. *Telescope* was suspended, its editor was exiled, while Chaadaev was declared insane and put under police supervision. Under these circumstances and to defend himself, a year later he published his work *Apologie d'un fou*. Of particular interest, however, was the reaction of the great Russian writer and poet Alexander Pushkin, who, despite his disagreement with Chaadaev's pessimism, assessed Byzantine tradition in an equally disparaging light:

> Vous dites que la source où nous sommes allé puiser le christianisme était impure, que Byzance était méprisable et méprisée etc. – hé, mon ami ! Jésus Christ lui-même n'était-il pas né juif et Jérusalem n'était-elle pas la fable des nations ? L'évangile en est-il moins admirable ? Nous avons pris des Grecs l'évangile et les traditions, et non l'esprit de puérilité et de controverse. Les mœurs de Byzance n'ont jamais été celles de Kiev.[29]

While objecting to the inferiority complex of the Russian nation emerging from Chaadaev's approach, Pushkin shared with his friend his unfavorable opinion of Byzantium. The brilliant Russian poet attributes to the "Greeks" a spirit of puerility and controversy, which was not transmitted to the Russians through the adoption of the Byzantine form of Christianity. Advocating a moral superiority of Kiev compared to Constantinople, Pushkin tends to neutralize Chaadaev's primary argument against Byzantine tradition. The common denominator of the two intellectuals nevertheless remains the depreciation of the Byzantine culture. Needless to say, their perception of Byzantium relied

---

28 See, for example, the study by abbé Jean-Nicholas Jager, *Histoire de Photius, patriarche de Constantinople: auteur du schisme des Grecs, d'après les monuments originaux, la plupart encore inconnus* (Paris: Vaton, 1845).

29 See Tatiana Wolff, ed., *Pushkin on Literature* (Evanston: Northwestern University Press, 1998), 470.

much on the quite widespread assessments expressed by prominent figures of Enlightenment historiography such as Edward Gibbon and Montesquieu concerning the constant and continuous decline of the Eastern Roman Empire.[30]

5. Slavophiles' Attitudes Towards Byzantium

If the Westernizers' attitude towards the Byzantine heritage was determined by the prejudices bequeathed to the nineteenth-century Russian intellectuals from the historiographic tradition of the Enlightenment, as has been shown in the previous section, the Slavophile's predisposition to Byzantium, although based on different presuppositions, did not differ much. The renowned historian and Byzantinist of the twentieth century Dmitry Obolensky stressed the similarities between Westernizers' and Slavophiles' approach to Byzantium, namely their similar Russia-centered bias, their almost identical penchant for judgments of value, and their ambiguity.[31] In the mid-nineteenth century, perhaps the most representative advocate of the Slavophile movement, Alexey Khomiakov, wrote that "in our opinion, to speak of the Byzantine Empire with disdain means to disclose one's own ignorance,"[32] thereby providing an indirect response to Chaadaev's derogatory assessment. Having said that, one should not expect Khomiakov to be a fervent advocate of Byzantine tradition. His position towards Byzantium was rather muddled. To begin with, the prominent Slavophile suggested that the political life of Byzantium did not correspond to the grandeur of the spiritual one.[33] Moreover, in his essay "O starom i novom" (On the Old and the New), which represents one of the earliest testimonies of the Slavophile movement, published in 1839, Khomiakov pointed out that even though the doctrinal purity of Christian faith was preserved in Byzantium,

30 See Przemysław Marciniak and Dion C. Smythe, "Introduction," in their edited volume *The Reception of Byzantium in European Culture since 1500* (London/New York: Routledge, 2016), 4.
31 Dimitri Obolensky, "Modern Russian Attitudes to Byzantium," *Jahrbuch der Österreichischen Byzantinistik* 15 (1966): 64.
32 Alexei Khomiakov, *"Golos greka v zashchitu Vizantii,"* in Alexei Khomiakov, *Polnoe sobranie sochinenii*, vol. III, Moscow: Universitetskaia tipografiia, 1900), 366, as cited in Alexander A. Vasiliev, *History of the Byzantine Empire 324–1453*, vol. I (Madison: University of Wisconsin Press, 1952), 33.
33 Aleksei Khomiakov, "Zapiski o vsemirnoi istorii, part III," in Alexei Khomiakov, *Polnoe sobranie sochinenii*, vol. VII (Moscow: Universitetskaia tipografia, 1906), 50.

the social implications of the evangelical doctrine scarcely applied.[34] As abbé Pierre Barron noted, Khomiakov was convinced that Byzantium received from ancient Rome both the worship of the State and absolutism as an ideal way of governance.[35] In this regard, Nikolai Berdiaev's remarks on the perception of Byzantium by the Slavophiles movement are eminently enlightening. The religious philosopher observes that one of the main Slavophile principles is the distinction between Russian and the Byzantine Orthodoxy. Although the Eastern Orthodox faith was received by the Russian people through Byzantine missionaries, there are, however, several particular features belonging particularly to the so-called "Russian soul":

> Mais l'âme russe est infiniment distincte de l'âme byzantine : dans l'âme russe il n'y a pas la malignité byzantine, l'obséquiosité byzantine devant les puissants, la culte de l'étatisme, la scolastique, la tristesse byzantine, la cruauté et la morosité byzantines[36]

As one can readily perceive, the adjective *Byzantine* also carries for Slavophiles and partially for Berdyaev negative and pejorative connotations. As has been shown, Westernizers tended to criticize the Byzantine heritage for the regress and the separation of Russia from other Western European nations. Slavophiles, on the contrary, adopted a different approach. They suggested that the grain of Christian faith planted by the Byzantines in the fertile Russian soil was able to bear the unique fruit of Christian principles. In this way, the democratic spirit, the thirst for catholicity (*sobornost*) or the predominance of the unity of love over the unity of authority had shaped Russian Orthodoxy as the purest form of Christianity.

6. Interpreting Prince Vladimir's Conversion: from Soloviev to Florovsky

Supposing one accepts that the debate between Slavophiles and Westernizers in the middle of the nineteenth century established the framework for shedding

---

34 Aleksei Khomiakov, "O starom i novom" , in Alexei Khomiakov, *Polnoe sobranie sochinenii*, vol III (Moscow: Universitetskaia tipografia, 1900), 23.

35 Pierre Barron, Un théologien laïc orthodoxe russe au XIXe siècle Alexis Stépanovitch Khomiakov (1804–1860): son ecclésiologie—exposé et critique, Orientalia Christiana Analecta, 127 (Rome: Pontificum Istitutum Orientalium Studiorum, 1940), 128.

36 Nicolas Berdiaev, *Khomiakov* (Lausanne: L'age d'homme, 1988), 16.

light on the concepts expressed in Bulgakov's aforementioned essay, then the immediate and undoubted influence on Fr. Sergius should be sought in Vladimir Soloviev. It is not only the temporal proximity between the two religious thinkers but rather their content, argumentation, and the pro-Roman Catholic disposition that justify such a remark. In other words, one should legitimately suggest whether Bulgakov wrote this essay in the spirit of Soloviev. In his essay "Byzantium and Russia," published in 1896, Vladimir Soloviev offers an idealized description of Vladimir's conversion to the Christian faith.[37] The Russian philosopher identifies the radical change in the mentality of the Kievan prince in the way the latter took a stand against the practice of the death penalty. Vladimir's Christian consciousness prevented him from embracing the death penalty for felons and criminals. Moreover, Soloviev ingeniously contrasted the behavior of the Russian ruler with the exhortations expressed by the Byzantine clergy in favor of the execution of convicted felons.

It is worth noting, at this point, a couple of interesting observations regarding Soloviev's positions. First, the uncritical adoption of hagiographical motives concerning Vladimir's conversion and subsequently his idealized behavior as a Christian ruler, as shaped and transmitted in medieval chronicles. It remains extraordinarily surprising that Soloviev challenges neither the credibility of the written sources nor the motives of their writers as one might expect of a well-educated Russian scholar of his caliber in the nineteenth century. Secondly, he underestimates, implicitly though quite clearly, the qualitative value of Byzantine Christianity. According to his view, the Byzantine bishops sent to Kiev were not able to influence with their preaching the behavior of Vladimir and infuse him with the moral doctrines of the gospel.

A key aspect of Soloviev's criticism of Byzantium was the question of capital punishment. According to him, a Christian or Christianized society that has accepted the redemptive message of the gospel, preaching the values of forgiveness and reconciliation, could abandon the punitive and disgraceful penalty of death for even the worst criminals. Soloviev's sensitivity in this respect was determined by his Christian identity and his personal experience. In 1881, during a public lecture, he proposed granting mercy to Tsar Alexander II's assassins. Soloviev's sincere, honest but naive conviction concerning the need for complete Christian forgiveness marked the end of his professorship and led

---

37   Vladimir Soloviev, "Vyzantinizm i rossiia," *Vestnike evropi* 31 (1896): 342–59, 787–808. I base my following remarks on Chapter III of Soloviev's essay.

him to exile in Saint Petersburg.[38] Therefore, it is quite evident that his strict and unequivocal commitment to Christian principles was not without consequences for his own life and his professional and spiritual advancement too. This may explain Soloviev's particular emphasis on the rejection of the death penalty while assessing the degree of authenticity and integrity of Christian principles in Byzantium.

A different approach in this respect was formulated by Fr. Georges Florovsky in his now monumental work *The Ways of Russian Theology*.[39] The prominent theologian stresses that the conversion of Kievan Rus' to Christianity was more of a dynamic operation than a static action that took place in a fixed moment, namely at Prince Vladimir's baptism. Extending his thought on the influences upon a pre-Vladimirian diffusion of Christianity in Rus', Florovsky suggests a double non-Byzantine impact; the Bulgaria of Tsar Symeon on the one hand and the kingdom of Great Moravia on the other. Thus, he continues, the most important and decisive Byzantine influence upon the medieval kingdom of Rus' was indirect, coming through the missionary activity of the brothers Cyril and Methodius. Tellingly, Florovsky referred, with a certain degree of probability, to a competitive conflict in ancient Kiev between impacts and elements emanating from the Bulgarian Christianity and others derived directly from the Byzantine realm,[40]

---

38   On these events, see Manon de Courten, "The Prophet Intervenes: Solov'ëv's Lectures after the Murder of Tsar Alexandrer II," in *Vladimir Solov'ëv: Reconciler and Polemicist*, ed. Wil van den Bercken, Manon de Courten, and Evert van der Zweerde (Leuven: Peeters, 2000), 297–312. As Paul Valliere notes, these events marked a turning point in Soloviev's intellectual paths, as it was then that he began to reassess the concept of theocracy and turn to the West and the Roman Catholic Church with a positive perspective. See, Paul Valliere, "Vladimir Soloviev: Faith, philosophy, and law" in *Law and The Christian Tradition in Modern Russian*, ed. Paul Valliere—Randall A. Poole (London/New York: Routledge, 2022), 200–01.

39   This work first appeared in Russian as *Puti russkogo bogoslovia*, Paris: YMCA Press 1937. Several decades later, a second revised edition was published in two volumes in English translation; see *The Ways of Russian Theology*, trans. Robert L. Nichols, ed. Richard S. Haugh (Belmont Mass: Nordland Publishing 1978 and 1987 respectively). On this work, see the chapter "Georgii Florovkyi and The Ways of Russian Theology" by Kåre Johan Mjør in his book *Reformulating Russia: The Cultural and Intellectual Historiography of Russian First-Wave Émigré Writers* (Leiden: Brill, 2011), 153–201. Cf. also Paul Gavrilyuk, *Georges Florovsky and the Russians Religious Renaissance* (Oxford: Oxford University Press, 2014), 159–71.

40   Florovsky, *Ways of Russian Theology*, vol. I, 5.

For medieval Kievan Rus', receiving Christianity was thus not a one-dimensional procedure that was directly and exclusively connected to the Byzantine Christian tradition. Moreover, Christianization did not result in a severance of Kiev from the rest of the European context, as Soloviev suggested and Bulgakov later faithfully repeated in a rather unhistorical manner. Besides, Florovsky pointed out that during the tenth century, Byzantium was the only state possessing a genuine spiritual and intellectual culture within the whole "European" family.[41]

7. Conclusion

Bulgakov's anti-Byzantine attitude in his essay "By the Walls of Cherson" seems to depend to a high degree on the concept of his great master, Vladimir Soloviev. Nevertheless, Bulgakov's approach is not based on particular or external aspects of Byzantine civilization such as the death penalty or the institution of slavery. Contrary to Soloviev, the Russian thinker attempts to reconsider the spiritual history of the Russian Church and the Russian people, highlighting that the current crisis of Russian culture has its roots in the origins of its Christian existence. For this reason, he placed the narrative in the geographical context of the Crimean Peninsula. It was in Cherson that the conversion of Prince Vladimir to Christianity took place. Bulgakov referred in this respect to the spiritual and historical birth of the Russian Church, which was grafted into the Universal Church, given that the definitive schism between Western and Eastern Christianity had yet to occur.

Two factors appear to determine the dispraise of the Byzantine heritage to the thought of both religious philosophers: the prejudices towards Byzantium and its legacy inherited by the intellectual processes of the Enlightenment and an idealized view of the Russian nation in accordance with the principles of nineteenth-century Romanticism. The appropriation of Byzantine tradition by the Imperial Russian propaganda for secular purposes also played an essential role in this respect. However, needless to underline, these attitudes reflect the intellectual tendencies of the period in which they were produced. After the renaissance of Byzantine studies in the course of the twentieth century, shedding more light on Byzantine–Russian relations in a more historical-critical approach—it might suffice to mention the names of John Meyendorff, Dimitri Obolenski or Alexander Soloviev in this regard—one can easily discern the one-sided and unhistorical feature of these anti-Byzantine tendencies.

---

41   Florovsky, *Ways of Russian Theology*, vol. I., 2.

Building the House of Wisdom
DOI 10.17438/978-3-402-12182-5

"The Sophia Dispute" in the Context of Political Ontology

Alexei P. Kozyrev

The political context of the sophiological argument is both very simple and very confusing. We propose analysing it using the concept of "political ontology" which was employed by Pierre Bourdieu to analyze Heidegger's thought.[1] Thought always takes place in time, is immersed in processes which have temporal reality, even when aligned with eternal entities such as God, Sophia and being. Theological disputes—no less than philosophical and political disputes—are a product of the *Zeitgeist* ("spirit of the age"). To a significant degree, Archpriest Sergius Bulgakov recommends himself as a "hero of the age" in which he lived; the *Zeitgeist* necessarily gives birth to heroes, in whom the spirit of the age is most successfully embodied. Oswald Spengler characterizes the interwar "Zeitgeist" in this way, which is distinguished by an emphasized desire to create complex intellectual theories:

> Strong and creative talents [...] are turning away from practical problems and sciences and towards pure speculation. Occultism and Spiritualism, Hindu philosophies, metaphysical inquisitiveness under Christian or pagan colouring, all of which were despised in the Darwinian period, are coming up again. It is the spirit of Rome in the Age of Augustus. Out of satiety of life, men take refuge from civilization [...].[2]

Was Bulgakov's embrace of the priesthood and return to the church a flight from history? After all, Bulgakov had formerly been a political economist and member of the 2nd State Duma. It is unlikely that we will be able to fully de-

---

1   Pierre Bourdieu, *L'ontologie politique de Martin Heidegger* (Paris: Minuit, 1988).
2   Oswald Spengler, *Man and Technics. A Contribution to a Philosophy of Life* (1932), trans. Charles F. Atkinson (New York: Alfred A. Knopf, 1932), 97.

cipher Bulgakov's personality here, though we can say that it generated a very unique and remarkable life trajectory and made it possible for him to refrain from betraying himself, whilst retaining a certain integrity and a rare personal dignity, not to mention the breadth of his intellectual, and then spiritual quests. Mikhail M. Prishvin sees in Bulgakov "a sort of 'ideologue of the gaps' who learned theory in the library from Marxism to idealism, from idealism to realism, and from realism to theurgy."[3]

Bulgakov's Changing Ideas on Power

In his autobiographical text on "My Godlessness" Bulgakov speaks of "the idea of sacred power, which has acquired [...] the character of a political apocalypse, the ultimate metahistorical manifestation of the Kingdom of Christ on earth."[4] "Freedom-loving" and "royal-loving" ideas grow together in his mind to form a complicated antinomic complex. Recalling the meeting with the tsar in Yalta in 1914, he writes:

> I then fell in love with the image of the Sovereign and since then I have carried it in my heart, but it was—Alas!—a tragic love: the 'white king' was in the blackest environment, through which he could not break through until the very end of his reign.[5]

In exile, Bulgakov will be tormented by the thought of who should erect a cross on the Hagia Sophia. It seems to him that the gates of Constantinople will open to the "White Tsar,"[6] and not to the "political conqueror and all-Slavic Tsar," and that the cross should be erected "not by Rasputin's protégé, but by the Ecumenical patriarch, the Pope,"[7] and, after Bulgakov's estrangement from Catholicism, by "the universal hierarch in his consciousness."[8]

---

3   Mikhail M. Prishvin, _Dnevniki. 1926–1927_ (Moscow: Russkaia kniga, 2003), 257 (on April 20, 1927).
4   Sergii Bulgakov, "Moe bezbozhie," in ibid., _Avtobiograficheskie zametki: Posmertnoe izdanie_ (Paris: Put', 1946), 25–33: 28–29.
5   Ibid., 29.
6   According to Russian folk legends, the White Tsar outshines all tsars not with regard to power or wealth, but to true faith and justice. Aleksandr L. Dobrokhotov, "Belyi Car' ili metafizika vlasti v russkoi mysli," in _Izbrannoe_, ed. Aleksandr L. Dobrokhotov (Moscow: 2008), 126.
7   Sergii Bulgakov, "Iz 'Dnevnika'," _Vestnik RKhD_ 129 (1979) 237–68; 130 (1979) 256–74, reprint in: _Tikhie dumy_ (Moscow: Respublica, 1996), 351–88: 360.
8   Sergii Bulgakov, "V Aia-Sofii: Iz zapisnoi knizhki," _Russkai mysl'_ 6/8 (1923), 229–37: 233, reprint in _Avtobiograficheskie zametki: Posmertnoe izdanie_ (Paris: Put', 1946), 94–102: 99.

Bulgakov's political orientation in exile can hardly be called monarchist. In a 1927 course on "Christian Sociology," he says:

> The church should not impose certain tasks on the people or the state. The politi-
> cal form of government cannot be the subject of church teaching. It is necessary
> to separate what is God's and what is Caesar's [...]. The monarchist state has the
> advantage from the Christian point of view that it is single-handed, like a spiritual
> principle in general. But one should not lay the unbearable burden on one person.[9]

Belief in the church people, ruled by the Providence of God—this is how Bulgakov's political creed could be described. It is no coincidence that after February
1917, Bulgakov was obsessed with thoughts of reforming the church parish,
which could become the basis of church democracy. Distrust of the monarchy
is caused by anthropological pessimism:

> Each person, to the extent of his weakness, can bear only a small share of responsi-
> bility, and he must bear responsibility with the help of others. Power is a common
> task of the Christian people, everybody is responsible. It is not right to overestimate
> the charismatic character of royal power.[10]

Fundamentally different in respect to monarchy was the position of the rep-
resentatives of the Sremski Karlovtsi jurisdiction, whose separation from the
"Eulogians,"[11] to whom Bulgakov belonged, was due not so much to their atti-
tude to monarchy as to the essential form of Orthodox authority. Archbishop
Serafim (Sobolev), who condemned Bulgakov in his book entitled *The New
Doctrine of Sophia* (1936), believed that

> the 'holy of holies' of the Russian people has nothing in common with constitu-
> tional and/or republican forms of government, in which the human personality
> cannot find the support it requires for the achievement of its highest religious and
> moral demands.[12]

---

9   S. N. Bulgakov, "Khristianskaia sotsiologiia," in id. Trudy po sotsiologii i teologii, t. 2
    (Moscow: Nauka, 1999), 542.
10 Ibid.
11 Metropolitan Evlogii (Georgievskii) (1868–1946), from 1931 on head of the Patriarchal
    Exarchate for Orthodox Parishes of Russian Tradition in Western Europe.
12 Seraphim (Sobolev), *Russkaia ideologiia* (first ed.—1939) (St. Petersburg: Izdatel'stvo
    imeni A. S. Suvorina, 1992), 66.

The bishop's conviction with regard to monarchy as *the* Russian form of government was intertwined with his cherished dream of the ratification of a law introducing the death penalty for atheistic propaganda and blasphemy.

Defending the Freedom of the Church in Paris

We shouldn't lose sight of the fact that Bulgakov was an active participant in the Ecumenical movement and political issues were high on the agenda at Ecumenical meetings and conventions. In June 1937, both he and Georgii P. Fedotov, another professor at the St. Sergius Orthodox Theological Institute in Paris, attended the Second World Christian Congress on *Life and Work* in Oxford; the same year, the English translation of Bulgakov's *The Wisdom of God* was published. Fedotov published a report on the work of the Congress in *Sovremennye zapiski* (Notes of the Fatherland): Fascism had already taken root at the centre of Europe and was leading the European ship headlong toward a wreck. The hope remained that Christians of different confessions, by rallying together, would be able to stop the catastrophe from coming to fruition. Stating that there was not a single absolute monarchy left in the world, that capitalism was a chaotic wreck, that democracy was facing a formidable crisis, and that socialism—which had "won in one country"—had nevertheless revealed deep contradictions at its core, Fedotov concludes:

> the secular, totalitarian state is a completely new fact within world history, [and] theological theories created by the 'German Christians' in some respects suspiciously resemble Russian Slavophilism and Messianism. Not surprisingly, Oxford's response to these theories in places resembles Vladimir Soloviev.[13]

For this reason, in Fedotov's view, it was improper for the Church to remain in its atmosphere of rarefied prayerful spirituality: "Never before in her heroic past has the Church been so bound up with dominant groups and forms of social life as in this age of spiritual individualism."[14]

However, during the 1939 controversy surrounding Fedotov's journalistic activities in support of the Spanish Republicans, the professor's employer, the St. Sergius Institute (Paris), openly declared its *apolitical* stance. Fedotov had been accused of pro-Soviet agitation by the right-wing daily newspaper *Voz-*

---

13 Georgii P. Fedotov, "Posle Oksforda," in ibid., *Sobranie sochinenii v 12 t*, vol. 7 (Moscow: Sam, 2014), 156, 159.
14 Ibid., 151.

rozhdenie (Renaissance),[15] and Vasilii V. Zen'kovskii and Georgii V. Florovskii wrote to him:

> If we all, as members of the Institute, defend freedom for ourselves in church and public work, then it is precisely in the sphere of politics that we believe that it is very difficult for active and especially 'fighting' political work to be compatible with the responsible service of the Church through participation in the Theological Institute. This is especially harmful for the Russian emigration, in which the task of the Church is to free the consciousness of the Russian people clouded by passions from everything that spiritually lowers and weakens them in the political struggle.[16]

Metropolitan Evlogii called a meeting of the board of directors: it demanded "that Fedotov sign a written promise not to publish any more political articles," and, in a private letter by Evlogii, "socialist declarations."[17] Bulgakov did not object to the board's decision. In February 1939, he turned to Fedotov with an appeal to stop newspaper journalism for the benefit of the Institute. After surgery for throat cancer, six months later, he asked Fedotov for a "mutual amnesty."[18] Although disappointed that Bulgakov "did not dare to open his mouth" in his defense, Fedotov still considered him "a like-minded friend."[19]

A few years earlier, responding directly to the condemnation of Bulgakov's teaching, Fedotov wrote that Bulgakov's "sophianic cosmology" was an example of "a clogged Orthodox inspiration in the Russian church."[20] In his book *Spiritual Verses* of 1935, Fedotov positively evaluated sophiology: "In modern theological sophiology the prophetic premonitions and millennial dreams of

---

15 Antoine Arjakovsky, *The Way. Religious Thinkers of the Russian Emigration in Paris and their Journal* (Notre Dame 2013), 409. For more on the affair see pp. 405–15.

16 D. Bon, "K 110-letiiu Georgiia Fedotova. Dokumenty i pis'ma po povodu raznoglasiia, voznikshego mezhdu profesorom G. P. Fedotovym i Pravleniem Pravoslavnogo bogoslovskogo instituta v Parizhe," *Zvezda* 10 (1996), 135.

17 Arjakovsky, *The Way*, 409.

18 Bon, "K 110-letiiu Georgiia Fedotova," 151.

19 Anton A. Voytenko, "'Napishu, chto ia otnyne ne uvazhaiu svoikh kolleg.' Deistvuiushchie litsa konflikta G. P. Fedotova s pravleniem bogoslovskogo instituta v Parizhe (1939)," *Vestnik Volgogradskogo gosudarstvennogo universiteta. Serija 4* 22, 4 (2017), 56–65: 61, 63 (in Russian). Voytenko concludes that Bulgakov "probably remained neutral."

20 Georgii P. Fedotov, "K sovremennym bogoslovskim sporam" in *Vestnik RSKhD*. Dec. 1935 – Feb. 1936, 19–24: 24.

a slumbering people's soul await expression."[21] In his personal diary of the war years, in an entry dated February 14, 1941, Fedotov returned to events six years earlier ("Six years have passed, and the world is still the same") and asserted the "collapse of humanism" in the world and the breakdown of his own ideas about God and traditional church Christianity. In this context, Fedotov once again returned to an assessment of Bulgakov:

> When one is aware of the power and gravity of tradition, one begins to respect Fr. Sergius more. Confront it with your own thought, your own position! And at the same time be aware that you are not destroying tradition, but developing it. Yes, you have to be strong for that. And what did he pay for his impudence? With shaggy hair and an ugliness of speech [because of the throat cancer surgery—A. K.]. A truly cheap price for great inner freedom.[22]

The Political Aspects of the Condemnation of Sophiology

The political aspect of the Moscow Patriarchate's condemnation of sophiology via Deputy Patriarchal Locum Tenens, Metropolitan Sergius (Stragorodskii) (1867–1944) is a topic in its own. Metropolitan Sergii was Chairman of the Religious-Philosophical Assemblies in St. Petersburg (1901–1903), and well acquainted with the Russian philosophical and literary milieu. In 1904 he blessed Fr. Gapon's labor movement, and in 1905, as bishop of Finland, he welcomed the Tsarist manifesto of October 17, which legalized freedom of conscience in the Russian Empire. As an author of the 1927 Declaration who had publicly declared the church's loyalty to Soviet power, he gave an interview to foreign correspondents in 1930, in which he stated that in the USSR believers were not persecuted for their religious beliefs and that any persecution of priests was a result of their illegal activities. Two decrees about Bulgakov's doctrine of Sophia, dating from September 7 (No. 1651) and December 27, 1935 (No.

---

21 Georgii P. Fedotov, *Stikhi dukhovnye. Russkaia narodnaia vera po dukhovnym stikham* (Moscow: Gnozis, 1991), 123. However, Georges Florovsky, a staunch opponent of sophiology and appointed to the commission "on Bulgakov's case" by Metropolitan Evlogii, claimed many years later in a letter of 1966 to his brother that among Bulgakov's "friends" "others had a very negative attitude toward sophianism, such as the deceased G. P. Fedotov and especially Kartashev, who considered sophianism to be mere nonsense and fantasy." Prot. Georgii Florovskii, *Pis'ma k bratu Antoniiu* (Moscow: PSTGU, 2021), 182.

22 A. V. Antoshchenko "Neopublikovannyye stranitsy dnevnika G. P. Fedotova," *Vestnik Omskogo universiteta. Seriya "Istoricheskiye nauki,"* 283–89: 286.

2267) and addressed to Metropolitan Eleutherius of the Moscow Patriarchate in Western Europe, are sometimes seen as part of the metropolitan's conciliatory, pro-Soviet activity; at the end of his life, Metropolitan Sergii received his patriarchal ministry directly from Stalin's hand. This is how the first decree was perceived in the milieu of the Russian exile which was close to Father Sergii. A parishioner of the Moscow church, Maria Kallash, who wrote under the pseudonym "M. Kurdyumov," wrote to Father Sergius: "It has come to the point where the decree is attributed to the GPU, and the consideration of your theological works is given over to the KGB, headed by Yagoda."[23]

However, the decrees were not the expression of the sole opinion of Metropolitan Sergius; they were based on definitions signed by eleven bishops, and were a conciliar judgment of a small ("incomplete") council of "arrived bishops." On June 22, 1934, Metropolitan Sergius and the Synod, which had not yet been dissolved, fulfilled the demand of the Soviet government and declared the Karlovites schismatics, with the ensuing ban on serving all those who found themselves in a different jurisdiction. Since the final division between the "Karlovites" and the "Eulogians" had not yet taken place, this prohibition can be considered extended to Parisian parishes as well. The first condemnation of Bulgakov's sophiology occurred in 1927 in the Epistle of the Synod of Bishops of the Russian Orthodox Church Abroad. About the upcoming new, now conciliar, definition of the Karlovites of October 17/30, 1935, Metropolitan Sergius and his staff in Paris most likely knew. It can be assumed that the Decree of September 7 should have pre-empted it.

A special role in the preparation of these decrees was played by the Brotherhood of St. Photius, which was created in Paris around 1924 and had as its goal spreading Orthodoxy in France. Its members hoped that France would become the center of the rebirth of the Christian spirit in the West. Characteristically, they chose Photius I, the ninth-century Byzantine patriarch, as their patron, under whom the split between the Patriarchate of Constantinople and the See of Rome in 863–867 had occurred. The first head of the Brotherhood (1925–1931) was Alexei V. Stavrovskii (1905–1972), who was educated at the philosophical and theological faculties in Sofia and Berlin, at the philological faculty at the Sorbonne and at the Sergius Theological Institute. As Lidiia Berdyaeva testifies in her diary entry of October 26, 1935, "it was certainly not for him, of course, to denounce the heresies of Father Bulgakov, from whom, by

---

23   Aleksei P. Kozyrev, Aleksei E. Klimov (eds.), "Materialy k 'Sporu o Sofii'," *Transactions of the Association of Russian-American Scholars in the USA* 39 (2014–2016), 27.

the way, he failed his exam as a student of the Theological Institute."[24] Vl. Lossky became his deputy in the Brotherhood of St. Photius. The decree was issued on the basis of a "Report" sent from Lithuania by Stavrovskii which contained a critical analysis of Bulgakov's book *The Lamb of God* (1933), which the metropolitan had not seen by the time the decree was issued. Hence, the "Report" was initiated not by Metropolitan Eleutherius, but by the "Photievites." Maria Kallash wrote to Bulgakov:

> Metr<opolitan> Eleutherius not so much ordered as agreed to Stavrovskii's proposal to send extracts from your work to Moscow. The simplest thing would be to send your book 'The Lamb of God' to Metropolitan Sergius, who did not know that sending was possible. It is obvious to me that Stavrovskii did not limit himself to rigged excerpts, but composed his own 'review' and not only of your teaching, but likely of the 'fact' that the teaching is persistently preached by you everywhere, that all Orthodox abroad and even part of the heterodox, attracted to Orthodoxy, 'are infected with Sophianism.'[25]

Stavrovskii had been forced to leave Paris for Kovno (Kaunas) after embezzling money, Metropolitan Eleutherius took him in as a church reader, and Kallash wrote that he was "not loved by the clergy in Kovno," mentioning his "self-righteous criticism of everyone and everything" and a "spirit of gendarmerie in the Church of Christ." Vladimir Lossky, who needed to explain himself to Bulgakov in writing after the scandal broke out, also bore witness to Stavrovskii's authorship:

> We took the task of systematically criticizing your teachings upon ourselves, though this could never have been accomplished in full in less than several months, after which we had intended to deliver our main theses. The decree of Metropolitan Sergius, however, appeared before we could finish our work. It was based on extensive quotations from 'The Lamb of God', which were collected under the direction of Metropolitan Eleutherius by A. Stavrovskii. To see here any ill will on the part of Stavrovskii would be unwarranted: he was acting, in this case, as Vladyka's secretary.[26]

---

24 Lidiia Berdiaeva, *Professiia: zhena filosofa* (Moscow: Molodaia gvardiia, 2002), 119.
25 Kozyrev, Klimov (eds.), "Materialy k 'Sporu o Sofii'," 28.
26 Ibid., 35.

The figure of Lossky is assessed by Maria Kallash in equally vivid terms: "a man deeply honest, undoubtedly scholarly, but of that absolutely conservative disposition which is defined not only politically, but also by a kind of religious 'fascism,' prone to exaggerate church discipline even to the extreme."[27] His letter to Bulgakov, the pamphlet entitled *Dispute on Sophia* and *Explanations by the Brotherhood*, Lossky signed with the initials B. F., which were short for "Brotherhood of Photius," thus imitating the cryptonyms common in Catholic orders. The Brotherhood existed until the early 1950s.

Let us recall Bulgakov's criticism of "spiritual pedocracy"—the intellectual cult of student youth in *Vekhi* (Landmarks) from 1909[28]—or the words of Nikolai A. Berdiaev that "fascism is the dictatorship of the youth." Nikolai M. Zernov characterizes Alexei Stavrovskii as "a man of imperious and fighting temperament."[29] Being in Lithuania, he survived the occupation there, served as Chargé d'Affaires for the Russian population of the Lithuanian General District, collaborated with the Nazi administration, fled to Italy after the liberation of Lithuania , and took refuge in Rome, in a Catholic monastery with Father Philippe de Régis, the founder of the *Collegium Russicum* in Rome. Many Russian refugees were hiding there; for converting to Catholicism, they received a sum of USD 220, sufficient to obtain a visa to the American continent. In 1948, among the thousands of Russian refugees boarded by Fr. Philippe, Stavrovskii emigrated to Argentina. In Buenos Aires he joined the *Committee of the Russian Colony*, published brochures and collaborated on the newspaper for Russian emigrants *Za Pravdu*! (For the Truth), published by Fr. Philippe.[30] Articles written by him in support of the papal dogma of infallibility[31] testify to Stavrovskii's Catholic denomination after his emigration to Argentina. V. Lossky, on the contrary, played an active part in the Resistance Movement, remaining in France during the occupation.

Metropolitan Sergius had confidence in the Brotherhood of Photius. In his correspondence with the Serbian Patriarch Barnabas, he calls the Russian

---

27   Kozyrev, Klimov (eds.), "Materialy k 'Sporu o Sofii'," 29.

28   See Sergei Bulgakov, "Heroism and Asceticism. Reflections on the religious nature of the Russian intelligentsia," in *Vekhi: Landmarks: a collection of articles about the Russian intelligentsia*, ed. Marshall S. Shatz, Judith E. Zimmermann (London: M. E. Sharpe, 1994), 17–49: 31.

29   N. M. and M. V. Zernovy (eds.), *Za rubezhom: Belgrad-Parizh-Oksford (Khronika sem'i Zernovykh: 1921–1972)* (Paris: YMCX-Press, 1973), 161–62.

30   See: M. A. Kublitskaia, "Russkaia periodicheskaia pechat' v Argentine v XX veke," http://emigrantika.imli.ru/publications/840-kublickaja (access 2024/01/26).

31   See in *Simvol* 14 (1985).

emigration not political, but spiritual; for him, the revolution was a spiritual cataclysm and communism a secular religion:

> He writes that the God-ordained task of the emigration is to reveal to Western Christianity all the richness of the Orthodox faith, and reproaches the emigration for instead being carried away with senseless discord and endless condemnation and harassment both in print and from the pulpit.[32]

A book entitled *Patriarkh Sergii i ego dukhovnoe nasledstvo* (Patriarch Sergii and his Spiritual Legacy), published by the Moscow Patriarchate in 1947 (M. Kallash-Kurdyumov was actively involved in its preparation), includes three letters from Metropolitan Sergius to V.N. Lossky without any indication of the addressee. One of them is entirely about Bulgakov, but from the perspective of the political context, the letter in which the metropolitan shares with Lossky his views on the nature of the Orthodox mission in Europe is more interesting. In a letter dated October 23, 1935, Metropolitan Sergius thanks Lossky: "for sending your pamphlet" (*Spor o Sofii* [The Dispute about Sophia]). The Metropolitan writes in this same letter: "You may safely say that I do not judge this book by its excerpts: I have received it and read attentively."[33] This coincides with M. Kallash's report to Bulgakov that she sent *The Lamb of God* to the metropolitan around the middle of October. "The brethren themselves simply didn't think of doing so." The copy was received fairly quickly.

Hence, it can be assumed that the appearance of the decrees was caused not by pressure from the Soviet authorities, but by a bet placed on young zealots of the faith who came up with the ambitious program of an Orthodox mission among the heterodox. Bulgakov had the experience of the pre-revolutionary intelligentsia who had come to Orthodoxy, and the members of the St. Photius Brotherhood were prepared for liturgical and linguistic innovations to expand the Orthodox mission to the territory of the Latin West. T. Manukhina writes to V. Bunina:

> The Photius boys are young, arrogant people, they believe in their youth that having read the fathers of the Church, one can judge everything, supported by their

---

32 Dmitrii Pospelovskii, *Russkaia pravoslavnaia tserkov' v XX veke* (Moscow: Respublika, 1995), 181.

33 *Patriarkh Sergii i ego dukhovnoe nasledstvo* (Moscow: Moscow Patriarchate, 1947), 75.

authority. But here there is a completely different layout, and therefore other ways of knowing the truth.[34]

Moreover, the style and behavior of the "Photius boys," make it difficult to take the side of the accusers: Mother Maria (Skobtsova) would return Vl. Lossky's book to its author with the words: "I don't read books written by denunciators," even though, in fact, many of their arguments may have been valid.

Political Implications of Sophiology?

The philosopher Vladimir Bibikhin (1938–2004) linked the failure of the dispute over Sophia to the absence of an imperial authority which could have legitimized its results, and sees in the whole situation a parallel with the fourteenth-century Palamite disputes: i. e., Bulgakov lacked his Kantakouzenos: John VI Kantakouzenos was a Byzantine emperor who patronized Gregory Palamas at the Council of Constantinople in 1351, which approved a cathedral tomos in favor of the Orthodoxy of Palamism and had Palamas occupy the episcopal chair in Thessaloniki, the city controlled by his political rival, John V Palaiologos. Bibikhin unequivocally sees sophiology as a development of the Palamite problematic:

> The sophiology of Rev. Sergius Bulgakov, which continues the Palamite dogma, was condemned by the Metropolis of Moscow to a large extent or perhaps solely out of its desire to be politically correct. Because of the Orthodox Church's attachment to power, the dogma of essence and energies extended only into the regions subject to John Kantakouzenos. Similarly, the condemnation of Bulgakov's sophiology did not extend to territories in which autocephaly already actually existed.[35]

In the Byzantine model of royal power, one of its most important functions is the "dogmatic alliance" (Fr. A. Schmemann) with spiritual authority, which makes it possible for the church to be protected from heresies. The decrees of the Moscow Patriarchate did not directly accuse Bulgakov of heresy, and the Decision of the Council of Bishops of the Russian Orthodox Church Abroad

---

34 *Vestnik RSKhD* 175 (1997), 173.
35 Vladimir V. Bibikhin, "Sofiologiia o. Sergiia Bulgakova," *S. N. Bulgakov: religiozno-filo-sofskii put'*, ed. Alexei P. Kozyrev (Moscow: Russkii Put', 2003), 85.

of October 17/30, 1935 decided "to recognize the teaching of Archpriest Sergei Bulgakov on the Sophia of the Wisdom of God as heretical."[36]

In the diary of Archim. Cyprian Kern, we find extracts from the report of Archim. Cassian (Bezobrazov) to the Archbishop's Council, which quotes the opinion of Anton V. Kartashev, one of the members of the commission appointed by Metropolitan Eulogius to examine the justice of charges of heresy against Bulgakov:

> Calling the works of Fr. Sergii [...] "ultra-academic volumes inaccessible to anyone due to their academic complexity," and recognizing that *heresy* is a *tragic* illness and real delirium of *the entire Church*, rather than a typographical fact somewhere in the academic wilds, Anton V. Kartashev has expressed his conviction that all this "business has been contrived by scribes and Pharisical hypocrites" not out of pure striving for the glory of God, but inspired by the tactical malice and petty vindictive passions of petty demagogues, who make use of the morbid irritability of the unfortunate masses of immigrants.[37]

An authoritative historian of the church under Metropolitan Eulogius, Kartashev contrasts the theological judgment of the Archbishop's Council of the Russian Orthodox Church Abroad with a sociological judgment: the modern world is far from Christianity, hence heresies cannot be of concern to the broad masses of people:

> With the deadening of sobornost in the Church, it is now possible only to stylize our academic arguments, which are alien to the people of the Church, under the concept of 'heresy.' There are no living heresies. And it is fruitless and pastorally unpedagogical to stir up people artificially with them.[38]

Does sophiology have any political implications for today? Can sophiology correlate with any political regime? One often encounters references to the philosophy of all-unity as almost a prolegomenon to Stalinist totalitarianism, the Gulag, or at least to authoritarian economic systems built on a model of communality and economic coercion. The Russian ethnographer Oleg Kirichenko sees in Russian philosophy an intellectual parallel to Russian sectarianism and a source that feeds Bolshevism: "The Bolshevik Leninists were clearly carried

---

36 N. T. Eneeva, *Spor o sofiologii v russkom zarubezh'e* (Moscow: IVI RAN, 2001), 111.
37 Diary of Archim. Cyprian Kern, in Archive of St. Sergius Theological Institute in Paris.
38 Ibid.

away to a certain extent by the sectarian ideas not only of Lev N. Tolstoy, as Lenin wrote about, but also by the sophiology of Vl. Soloviev, and the 'common deed' philosophy of Nikolai F. Fedorov."[39] Sophia was personified in the leader, "the leader became the source of tradition, its energy and a special person, pouring this light on his subordinates […] In short, he was the real 'Sophianic being', dreamed of by Vl. Soloviev, A. Blok, S. Bulgakov and Fr. Pavel Florenskii, who died in Lenin's camps."[40] Vasilii Shchipkov sees in sophiology a discourse of modernity by which "Radical Orthodoxy" (Milbank) seeks to re-Christianize the Western world. Speaking of sophiologists, the author writes:

> Their goal was to combine two discourses, Orthodox theology and secular philosophy/science, *to theologically fill and enlighten materialism, positivism and secular science in general* without abandoning its achievements, to reopen Christianity to secularized society, to explain the idea of being as a whole and to connect it with the Church and God in rational philosophical language.[41]

However, let us return to the context in which Bulgakov's sophiology was developed—the time between the two world wars. Martin Heidegger, in a speech delivered on June 27, 1945 to a small circle of listeners in the hunting lodge of Wildenstein Castle in Hausen, refers to the sophiological problems of Russian philosophy:

> The Spirit is the active force of enlightenment and of wisdom—σοφια (sophia) in Greek. This substantial essence of the spirit was thought through in the theological-philosophical speculation of the Christian Church about the [dogma] of the trinity of God; for the Western Roman Church, the work of Augustine *De Trinitate* became fundamental; in the Eastern Church another development took place; thus in Russianness (Russentum), the doctrine of Sacred Sophia became widespread. Even today it still lives in Russian mysticism, taking on forms that we can hardly even imagine. The action of the spirit as an all-pervading force of enlightenment and wisdom (Sophia) is "magical." The essence of the magical is as obscure as the essence of the pneumatic. But we know that the theosophist and philosopher Jakob Boehme—the Goerlitz shoemaker, the quietest of all shoemakers, as he was called—recognized the magical in the light of his shoemaker's lamp and conceived

---

39   O. V. Kirichenko, *Obshchie problemy etnografii russkogo Naroda. Traditsiia. Etnos. Religiia* (St. Petersburg: Aleteiia, 2020), 372–73.
40   Ibid., 393.
41   Ibid., 177.

it as primordial will. Boehme's doctrine of the divine Sophia (Theosophy) became known in Russia as early as the seventeenth century; the Russians then spoke of the holy father of the Church, Jacob Boehme; the renewal of this influence by Jacob Boehme took place in Russia at the beginning of the nineteenth century, coinciding [then] with the powerful influence of Hegel and Schelling (Vladimir Soloviev). Therefore, it will not be an exaggeration if I say: what today is short-sighted and insufficiently thought out is considered only to be something 'political,' crudely political even and is called Russian communism, came from a spiritual world about which we know almost nothing, quite apart from the fact that we forget to think in what sense even crude materialism, the façade of communism, is not something material, but spiritual: we do not think that it is some kind of spiritual world, and experiencing it and determining its truth or untruth is possible only in the spirit and proceeding from the spirit.[42]

At the end of this text, Heidegger says that the outcome of wars is based on spiritual decisions and strengthens them. Understanding what lies in the spiritual

---

42 "Das bedeutet: der Geist ist die wirkende Kraft der Erleuchtung und der Weisheit, griechisch der σοφια. Dieses substanzielle Wesen des Geistes wurde in der theologisch-philosophischen Spekulation der christlichen Kirche über die Dreieinigkeit Gottes durchdacht; maßgebend für die westlich römische Kirche wurde das Werk Augustinus' de trinitate; in der Ostkirche vollzog sich eine andere Entwicklung; zumal im Russentum entfaltete sich die Lehre von der heiligen Sophia. Sie ist noch heute in der russischen Mystik in einer Weise lebendig, die wir uns kaum vorstellen können. Das Wirken des Geistes als der alles durchwirkenden Kraft der Erleuchtung und der Weisheit (Sophia) ist ,magisch'. Das Wesen des Magischen ist so dunkel wie das Wesen des Pneumatischen. Aber wir wissen, daß der Theosoph und Philosoph Jacob Böhme—der Görlitzer Schuster, der stillste aller Schuster, wie man ihn genannt hat,— am Licht der Schusterkugel das Magische erkannte und es als den Urwillen dachte. Böhmes Lehre von der göttlichen Sophia (Theosophia) wurde bereits im 17. Jahrhundert in Rußland bekannt; die Russen sprachen damals vom heiligen Kirchenvater Jacob Böhme; eine Erneuerung dieses Einflusses von Jacob Böhme vollzog sich in Rußland zu Beginn des 19. Jahrhunderts, gleichzeitig mit dem starken Wirken von Hegel und Schelling (Wladimir Solowjoff). Es ist daher weit entfernt von einer Übertreibung, wenn ich sage, daß das, was man heute kurzsichtig und halbgedacht nur ,politisch' und gar grob-politisch nimmt und russischen Kommunismus nennt, aus einer geistigen Welt kommt, von der wir kaum etwas wissen, ganz abgesehen davon, daß wir schon vergessen, dies zu denken, wie selbst noch der grobe Materialismus, die Vorderfläche des Kommunismus, selbst nichts Materielles, sondern etwas Spirituelles ist und eine geistige Welt, die nur im Geist und aus dem Geist erfahren und zum Austrag seiner Wahrheit und Unwahrheit gebracht werden kann." Martin Heidegger, "Die Armut," ed. Friedrich Wilhelm von Hermann, *Heidegger Studies* 10 (1994), 5–11.

essence of the people is required in order to enter into a dialogue. Heidegger's awareness cannot be underestimated: indeed, as early as the seventeenth century, the poet and mystic Pietist Quirinus Kuhlmann came to Russia to preach the teachings of Jacob Böhme to his countrymen in the German Sloboda in Moscow. He was denounced and burned in Red Square in 1689. However, Heidegger's observation that the doctrine of Sophia "even today still lives in Russian mysticism" was made about a year after the death of Father Sergius. The German philosopher's attempt to connect the presence of this doctrine among Russian philosophers and theologians with actual history and political implications suggests that it is legitimate to present Russian sophiology not as an abstract metaphysical doctrine, but as a doctrine that responds to the sharp challenges of its time and thereby has its own political ontology.

Translation by Anna Makarova.

Building the House of Wisdom
DOI 10.17438/978-3-402-12183-2

Sophiology and Personalism, Foundations of the New Political Science in the Twenty-First Century

Antoine Arjakovsky

We observe today, in an increasingly dramatic way, an acute crisis of modern consciousness and of its heir, more worried, post-modern consciousness. The problems of fundamentalism in Afghanistan and elsewhere, the rise to power of China and Russia, or even extremely violent wars in Ukraine or Syria, the dramatic consequences of global warming and the loss of biodiversity, based on a totally non-spiritual vision of the economy, testify to the fact that contemporary political science is absolutely incapable of helping to solve these crises that come at an increasing cost and loss of life: Each year the planet's major powers spend more than 1.7 trillion dollars on armaments but find only 140 billion for development aid. In fact, everything is happening as if the world has entirely lost its moral compass.

There is no need to be surprised by this development, since contemporary political science refuses any association with morality, as John Milbank and Adrian Pabst regret in their 2018 book *The Politics of Virtue*.[1] This situation was already denounced in September 1941 by Jacques Maritain in a lecture given at the University of Chicago on Machiavelli. In his text "The End of Machiavellianism," the French thinker explained how, under the influence of the Florentine thinker, the goal of politics was no longer the implementation of the common good but the sole acquisition of power and the struggle to keep it.[2] For Maritain, the tragedy of Machiavelli was to stop believing that man had an eternal destiny. The drama of modern political philosophy, under the influence of Hegel, has been to transform Machiavellianism into atheistic metaphysics. This is why, for Maritain and his Russian friends Sergii Bulgakov

---

1   John Milbank, Adrian Pabst, *The Politics of Virtue* (London, Rowman & Littlefield Publishers, 2016).
2   Jacques Maritain, "The End of Machiavellism," *The Review of Politics* 4, 1 (1942), 1–33.

and Nikolai Berdiaev, only a renewal of eschatological metaphysics, the real source of justice and moral virtue, was able to refocus politics on justice and on the construction of peace.[3]

But their position was not heard after the war. In France, Raymond Aron rehabilitated Machiavellianism: For him, democracies could not do without using effective means specific to politics, especially when they are threatened by regimes ready to use all means to achieve their ends. This appeared to be common sense after WWII. But the eschatological basis of Maritain's thought was lost and the criticism of Hegelian thought by Russian religious thought was ignored.

1. The Eschatological Metaphysics of Fr. Sergius Bulgakov, the Foundation of a New Political Science

Even before the Russian Revolution, Sergei Bulgakov, in his courses in political and economic science at the Moscow Commercial Institute, had shown the limits of the modern conception of politics. For Bulgakov, it was appropriate to recognize the partial truth of Machiavelli's treatise in the face of the political theology of the papacy in the Middle Ages:

> In contrast to the medieval view, according to which the supreme power belongs to the pope and is only delegated by him to the emperor, a number of writers, beginning with Dante, sought to defend the independence of the state and its interests, the secular nature of the state, and the need for its secularization. Of particular importance here is the literary work of Machiavelli (The Prince), Hobbes, Hugo Grotius, et al.[4]

Bulgakov considered that Machiavelli had been right to criticize, in the continuity of Dante, the theory of the two swords of the papacy. He was bold in breaking away from the Augustinian view of history understood as a long empty corridor where men can only suffer while awaiting their salvation at the

---

3   On Maritain and his Russian friends, see Antoine Arjakovsky, *The Way. Religious Thinkers of the Russian Emigration in Paris and their journal*, 1925–1940 (Notre Dame: University of Notre Dame Press, 2013); Bernard Hubert, ed., *Un dialogue d'exception (1925–1948). Jacques Maritain et Nicolas Berdiaev* (Paris: YMCA Press, 2022).

4   S. N. Bulgakov, "Ocherki po istorii ekonomicheskikch uchenii" [1913] in *Istoriia ekonomicheskikh i sotsial'nykh uchenii*, ed. V. V. Sapov (Moscow: Astrel', 2007), 187 (trans. the editors).

end of time. There was nothing Christian about this vision. But nor was there anything evangelical in Machiavelli's rehabilitation of the Roman conception of the state:

> After Dante came a political thinker, less religious but more courageous, Machiavelli, who in his essay *The Prince* consistently developed his theory of the state, where he considered all means convenient for the service of the state, without being concerned with either ethical or religious requirements. He resurrected the Greek and Roman idea of the state as a self-sufficient principle of life.[5]

The mobilization of *virtu*, comprising skill but also devious blows and manipulations in the name of the prince's interests, had nothing to do with Christian *virtue*. It drew on a pagan Greek background according to which the world was ruled by fortune, that is to say by all that we do not owe to the merit of our own actions.

After the Russian Revolution, the émigré Russian theologian gave a seminar at the Saint Serge Institute in Paris on the notion of the Kingdom of God. He offered an authentic alternative to modern political science, an ecumenical and eschatological metaphysics.[6] His last book, *The Apocalypse of John*, completes all his political thinking by taking the perspective of the Kingdom of God on earth seriously. The last book of the Bible was indeed for him a "book of revelation firstly about the earthly, temporary thousand-year kingdom, and then of the universal and ultimate reign of the saints unto the ages of ages."[7] According to his exegesis, there is a Christian form of interpreting the coming of the reign of Christ and his saints for a thousand years, announced in the Revelation of John in chapter 20 as well as in the description of the descent of the heavenly Jerusalem to the earth described in chapters 21 and 22. The second description

---

5   Bulgakov, "Ocherki," 220.
6   See Sergii Bulgakov, "Khristianskaia sotsiologiia," in *Istoriia ekonomicheskikh i sotsial'nykh uchenii*, ed. V. V. Sapov (Moscow: Astrel', 2007), 814–16. See also his lectures in Prague: Sergii Bulgakov, "Novozavetnoe uchenie o Tsarstvii Bozhiem. Protokoly seminariia professora protoiereia S. N. Bulgakova (po zapisi L. A. Zandera)", ed. and introduced by Anna I. Reznichenko in *S. N. Bulgakov, Religiozno-filosofskii put'*, ed. Alexei P. Kozyrev (Moscow: Russkii Put' 2003), 427–520.
7   Sergii Bulgakov, *The Apocalypse of John. An Essay in Dogmatic Interpretation* (Münster: Aschendorff, 2019), 239–40, trans. Mike Whitton [Serge Boulgakov, *L'Apocalypse de Jean*; traduction française par Anne Kichilov, préface d'Antoine Arjakovsky (Paris: Parole et Silence, 2014), 282].

of the descent from heaven of the Jerusalem, described in 21,10, belongs truly, according to Bulgakov, to the history of this world, unlike that revealed in 21,2:

> It is therefore a divine-human work that crowns the human history—and that is why it is necessary to fully understand this humanity which is his. But in it is also revealed the action of grace, the power of God, manifested in the transfiguration. This is the manifestation of the Kingdom of God on earth, even though still within the confines of earthly possibilities, God's revelation, God's closeness to creation.[8]

This revelation allows us to understand why Christ taught his disciples to pray to the Father that his kingdom come and that his will be done "on earth as it is in heaven." Bulgakov's, but also Berdiaev's, awareness of the historical and political implications of this prayer, beyond the heretical millenarian temptations, brought about a reconciliation between sapiential theology and personalist metaphysics. Neither of them, for example, believed in the coming of a time of the Spirit as a *deus ex machina*. On the other hand, both thought in an eschatological, personalist and sophiological way the relation of the personhood of God to its trinitarian consciousness. The philosopher Nicolas Berdiaev, in his commentary on the *Mysterium magnum* by Jakob Boehme, identified Sophia with the deepest freedom of God and of man. Whereas Bulgakov understood Wisdom not as a new divinity but as the trinitarian self-consciousness of the divine personhood.

Their stroke of genius, to put it in a nutshell, was to think of an intermediate eschatology, between the temporality of participation in ecclesial grace—which recognizes that the Kingdom of God can manifest itself in a community way in this world—and the temporality of the gift of glory, when God will be all in all. Berdiaev, in his *Essay on Eschatological Metaphysics (1947),*[9] insisted on the fact that every creative and ethical gesture makes it possible to complete fallen history and to manifest in this world the Kingdom of the saints. Bulgakov also theorized his eschatology, which combined the time of grace with that of glory:

> None of these aspects of the Kingdom of God—communion with God and eschatology—exhaust the whole meaning of the Kingdom of God. For the Kingdom of God, which is in us, although it inaugurates eternal life, does not exclude life in time. On the contrary, it affirms the meaning of what is happening in time. In

---

8   Boulgakov, *L'Apocalypse de Jean*, 269 (own translation) [Bulgakov, *Apocalypse*, 228].
9   See Nicolas Berdyaev, *The Beginning and the End* (Semantron Press, 2009), trans. Boris Jakim.

time we understand the meaning of the Last Judgment, because in time, in a way, eternity is considered. The aspiration for the second coming does not destroy the feeling that the history exists, even if the time between the first and second coming is longer than originally thought. And this time is not for us an indifferent course of events, but the history of the Church, the authenticity and the content of what is happening in the Church. History finds its justification.[10]

While the modern conception of sovereignty, inspired by Machiavelli and by Jean Bodin, proved incapable in the 1930s of stemming the rise of conspiracy theories, populism and finally totalitarian regimes, Father Sergius Bulgakov proposed a conception of politics connected with a new metaphysics. For him God has not withdrawn from the history of men. God reveals himself to mankind when it is ready to turn to His divine Wisdom, through the reign of the Father, the power of the Son and the glory of the Holy Spirit. Genuine *Dasein* consisted of being aware of both, being thrown into the world and already being able to participate now in the Kingdom of God on earth.

The whole history of humanity is therefore that of the encounter between divine and eternal Wisdom and created and temporal Wisdom. This means, in particular, that the Church, which is both the Body of Christ and the Bride of the Lamb, is called to go through the same stages of divinization as Christ, the passage from a prophetic conscience to a sacramental conscience and *finally to a royal conscience during the millennium announced by Revelation in chapter 20.* If Augustinian a-millenarian political theology is to be condemned, it is because it excludes any participation by humanity in the advent of the Kingdom of God. This is a form of ecclesiological docetism.[11] However, according to Christian revelation, history does have a meaning which *will be* manifested by a period of peace on earth thanks to the action of the Virgin Mary, the saints, and the just, starting *already now*.

This intermediate eschatology is found today in the Catholic Church as it emerges from the work of the catholic theologian Cyrille Pasquier, in the thesis he recently defended at the University of Fribourg. This refers more to the sapiential thought of Louis-Marie Grignon de Montfort than to that of Father Sergius Boulgakov. But his mariology brings him closer to Bulgakov's eschatological, personalist and sapiential metaphysics.

---

10   Bulgakov, "Khristianskaia sotsiologiia," 815.
11   Docetism (from the Greek *dokein*, to appear) is a set of Christological tendencies from the beginning of Christianity for which Christ becoming "flesh" does not mean that he becomes "man."

The parousia will be triggered both by a transcendent principle—the Father who sends his Son, Christ the Head with all the saints, for resurrection, judgment and entry into eternity—and by an immanent principle: The mystical birth of Mary, the new virgin who prepares the Body of Christ for its eternity, through the spiritual resurrection of its elect. (A. A.: my translation.)[12]

2. The Consequences of Eschatological Metaphysics for Political and Moral Science

The new eschatological metaphysics elaborated by Bulgakov, both personalist and sophiological, is neither a return to the theory of two swords nor a new sacralization of public power. For this vision the world is indeed constituted by power relations. But authentic power is not found in the claim to be able to destroy one's adversary, for the soul is an indestructible reality. Genuine sovereignty consists in manifesting over time the just, the true, the good and the beautiful. Some states may spend their fortunes on propaganda, but the recent history of totalitarianism shows that truth always triumphs over lies.

This spiritual metaphysics induces a certain number of developments in political and moral science, which can be briefly sketched out, starting with a new theory of sovereignty and law, an ecumenical conception of political action, and finally a rediscovery by Christians of the sense of their involvement in politics.[13]

Let's start with sovereignty and law. The state is not, as Bodin thought, the secular power capable of imposing, outside any participation in divine life, an absolute power at once unique, indivisible and untransferable. Contemporary authors like Pascal Lamy, the former director of the WTO, have shown the ridiculousness of such a claim in the age of globalization and the advent of multinational powers, especially financial ones. Nor is the state, as Hegel's modern epistemology imagined, the fulfilling People's Spirit that puts law at its service. This vision, which refuses to link any conception of justice to public power, as Ernst Cassirer has shown, was also shattered in the twentieth century.[14]

---

12   Fr. Cyril Pasquier, "Approches du Millénium. Une christologie de l'histoire" (Université de Fribourg, Thèse de doctorat 2018), 545.

13   We can add a sense of renewed ecclesiality within the various Christian denominations: Antoine Arjakovsky, "Les voies possibles de réforme de l'Eglise Orthodoxe à la lumière du livre de la Révélation" ("The possible ways of reforming the Orthodox Church in the light of the book of Revelation"), *Le Messager orthodoxe* 166–67 (2021), 21–34.

14   Ernst Cassirer, *The Myth of the State* (New Haven: Yale University Press, 1946).

Rather, for Bulgakov the state should be understood as a spiritual power, itself subject to divine justice, capable of subjecting society to legal relations. The latter must itself be at the service of the highest conception of justice, both distributive and appreciative, according to the theory today of Michael Sandel, if it wants to prevent the state from dissolving into corruption or anarchy.[15] This is why law itself must be placed at the service of that which transcends it, namely Wisdom, as King Solomon knew.[16]

It is through the Wisdom that God gives that man can recognize divine justice. God answers Solomon's prayer in this way (1K, 3,11): "Since you ask for wisdom to exercise righteousness, behold, I will do according to your word." It is therefore on God that the gift of wisdom depends and it is by this wisdom alone that man can recognize justice. In the Book of Proverbs 2, 6–22, Wisdom makes Justice depend on itself: 'For the Lord gives Wisdom [...] then you will understand justice (*zedek*), equity (*mischpath*), righteousness [...] And thus you will walk in the way of the good people, you will keep the path of the righteous." Human justice can therefore only be understood and followed through the wisdom of God!

The New Testament conception of law is clearly eschatological. The glory of the nations and therefore human rights is preserved in the heavenly Jerusalem, as evidenced by chapter XXI of Revelation (Revelation 21, 24–26). Likewise, Matthew insists on this word of Christ: 'You will be judged as you have judged" (Math 7,2). This means that God chooses to judge a man not the absolute of righteousness, but the righteousness of that man. He judges him according to his own criteria, according to his words, according to his rules of life or law, according to his judgments. And man finds himself condemned not first of all by the absolute holiness of God before whom he is annihilated, and who appears only when God forgives, but above all by his own justice. This eschatological conception of law is hostile as much to positive law as it is to natural law because of their rejection of any transcendent vision of justice.

The French thinker Jacques Ellul, a personalist thinker marked by W. Visser't Hooft and Nikolai Berdiaev, published an important book on this subject in 1946.[17] For Ellul, as for Bulgakov, that which is *just* is that which is in accor-

---

15 Michael J. Sandel, *Justice* (Paris: Albin Michel, 2016).

16 See Sergei N. Bulgakov, "Tserkovnoe pravo i krizis pravosoznaniia," in *Russkaia nauka tserkovnogo prava v pervoi polovine XX veka: Poisk metodologii*, ed. Irina Borshch (Moscow: URSS, 2008), 201–22.

17 Jacques Ellul, *Le fondement théologique du droit* (Paris: Dalloz 2008; Delachaux et Niestlé, 1946).

dance with the will of God. What is ordered in relation to that justice is right. The act of God that establishes law is the covenant, that is, the righteousness of God in motion. Consequently, in this eschatological conception of justice, the legal construction must derive mainly from discernments in concrete situations, from a judgment based on historical facts (more or less *just* according to the justice of God), and from human relations with bringing into play human rights and God-given institutions.

Second, eschatological metaphysics is fully ecumenical and must be investigated in all forms of inter-confessional, inter-religious and inter-convictional dialogues and joint actions. For Bulgakov the advent of the kingdom of God on earth, marked by the advent of the City with 12 gates in the names of the 12 tribes of the sons of Israel, described in Rev XXI, will be the triumph of Judeo-Christianity in the whole world.[18] This ecumenical character (in the trans-religious sense of the term, therefore, both personal and universal) can be actualized today by political science.[19] The state, for sapiential, personalist and ecumenical metaphysics, is the power capable of embodying divine-human Wisdom through its executive, legislative and judicial expressions. According to the Judeo-Christian tradition of wisdom, the state should be able to embody virtues such as wisdom and discernment, counsel and valor, knowledge and fear. Now Wisdom is a gift of the Spirit which belongs to the different spiritual traditions of East and West, as David Bentley Hart has shown very well in his superb book *The Experience of God*. For the sapiential tradition of Asian religions, rediscovered today by the jurist Mireille Delmas Marty, harmony is found in the balance between freedom and security, competition and cooperation, exclusion and integration, innovation and conservation.[20]

The four pillars of religious faith (just glorification and faithful memory, moral uprightness and knowledge of justice) and the four ways of acquiring the truth (as correspondence and as stability, as coherence and as consensus) are found in varying degrees of consciousness within the main religious and convictional traditions.[21] Also, to deprive oneself of the spiritual dimension of faith, as Western democracies do, is as absurd as to deprive oneself of its

---

18   Bulgakov, *Apocalypse*, 230 [Boulgakov, *L'Apocalypse*, 272].

19   Antoine Arjakovsky, *Qu'est-ce que l'œcuménisme?* (Paris: Cerf, 2022).

20   Mireille Delmas Marty, *Sortir du pot au noir. L'humanisme juridique comme boussole* (Paris: Buchet Chastel, 2019).

21   Antoine Arjakovsky, *Essai de métaphysique œcuménique*, Paris, Cerf, 2021. English translation: *Towards an Ecumenical Metaphysics. The Principles and Methods of Ecumenical Science* (Brooklyn, NY: Angelico Press, 2022) (3 volumes).

rational depth, as fundamentalist and dictatorial regimes do. This is why the political and moral science of the twenty-first century will necessarily be based on an ecumenical theology and on an ecumenical metaphysics of politics.

Finally, the new political and moral science also offers a response to the contemporary craze for transhumanism through its eschatological and ecumenical anthropology. There is a vision in transhumanism that we will qualify as Manichean or neo-Cathar. The soul is captured there as a disembodied mind to the point that artificial intelligence researchers and video game designers already imagine that they can download the human mind (*mind uploading*) and transfer it from one computer to the other. Bulgakov, like Berdiaev had the merit not only of criticizing the dualistic or even monistic vision of the human spirit but also of proposing an alternative by re-establishing ternary anthropology. They particularly appreciated the thought of Fedorov, in particular his great project of raising the dead, which was to become the common work of humanity liturgically united to Christ.[22] Both, admittedly, criticized Fedorov for failing to see that there were two possible conceptions of the resurrection, a resuscitation in the material body and a resurrection in the spiritual body.[23] But what was important to them was Fedorov's proposed update of the ternary anthropology of the Church of the first millennium. We know in fact that the apostle Paul addressed the Thessalonians in this way (1 Thes. 5, 23): "May your whole being, spirit, soul and body, be kept without reproach".

Following Bulgakov we can suggest that political science should be associated with a fully eschatological and ecumenical vision of the vocation of man in order to overcome the transhumanist gnosis. Future political and moral science must not be afraid to confront the question of the victory, at least partial, of life (*zoi*) over death. It must question the mystical experiences describing the existing relationships between the Spirit, eternal by definition, the created body and the soul that unites them. According to the gospel faith, Christ brought resurrection power into the world. Indeed, as the evangelist Matthew reports in chapter 10, Christ made it clear to his apostles that they would be concerned

---

22 "For Fedorov, according to Berdyaev: "Liturgy ought to embrace the whole of life, not the spiritual only and inward, but also the external, the worldly, the mundane, transforming it into a deed of resuscitation." Nikolai A. Berdiaev, "Filosofiia obshchego dela N. F. Fedorova," *Russkaia Mysl'* July 1915, 76–120.].

23 Ibid.: "His truth is in this, that he emphasised the activity of man and the immanent character of resuscitation, but this truth cannot be torn asunder from its other side, from the power of the grace of Christ, in which and through which only there is also possible for man both resurrection and resuscitation. Resurrection can only be mystical, in a mystical flesh."

with his disciples as they carried out their mission of resurrection. But this was based above all on an active faith in the proximity of the kingdom of heaven. Christ's words to his disciples are:

> Go, preach, and say: The kingdom of heaven is at hand. *Heal the sick, raise the dead, cleanse lepers, expel demons.* (Mat, 10, 7–8)

When we study the text closely, we see that the orthodoxy of the apostolic faith in the proximity of the Kingdom consists in holding together the two visions of the descent from heavenly Jerusalem, which are intertwined in the perspective of divine humanity. A vertical axis is discerned in the first vision of heavenly Jerusalem. In fact, we find here, on one side, the celebration of the glory of God (namely *the gift of resuscitating* since, as the Apocalypse attests, "of death there will be no more"; Rev. 21, 4). This gift is intertwined on the other side with the work of authentic memory, that is, of the coming Kingdom. This is why it is advisable to accomplish a *work of purification* with regard to the fallen memory. In the gospel of Luke, the leper who is justified is the one who *remembers* that he has been healed by God. This is why it is necessary to accomplish a work of purification of the forgetful memory by the glorification of the divine action. The angel therefore asks John to write because "these words are certain and true" (Rev. 21.5).

But we can also discern a horizontal axis in the second vision of messianic Jerusalem, namely the incarnation in moral law of divine justice (and therefore the *expulsion of demons* from the divine-human City, Rev 21:27). We observe also in the Book of the Revelation the fulfillment of God's righteousness in the political life of the nations that will walk in the light of the Lamb. This allows the ability *to heal the sick* as in the vision of St. John with the trees of life whose leaves can heal the pagans (Ap, 22, 2).

Conclusion

Of course, the rediscovery by Christians of their authentic political vocation requires prior spiritual work.[24] Likewise, the virtuous and harmonious state which could succeed the various figures of the state in the post-modern era,

---

24   Antoine Arjakovsky and Jean-Baptiste Arnaud, "Our global crisis has brought one conception of life to an end — what comes next?" *ABC Religion & Ethics (https://www.abc. net.au)*, July 17, 2020; id., "What comes "after"? Our crisis demands an epistemological revolution", *ABC Religion & Ethics*, August 3, 2020.

from the ultra-liberal state to the mafia state, has no chance of seeing the light of day unless contemporary consciousness manages to free itself from the quite primitive modern doctrine according to which the finality of politics is the conquest and the conservation of power.

The new political science must be able to call on the resources of different religious traditions. Kate Raworth's new economics, respectful of social life as much as of creation, draws on the resources of Buddhism as much as on the Christian vision of the tree of life and its healing leaves.[25] Sophiological thought agrees with personalist thought in recalling that the end of politics is the common good of a people united within just institutions. Only such a metaphysics allows man to be in the world in the mode of being both embodied in this world and participating in a realm which transcends the limits of this world.

Like Berdiaev, Bulgakov refused to sanctify the state and distanced himself from the monarchist circles of the Russian emigration. In the 1920s and 1940s he defended a democratic state on the American model, institutionally separated from religious institutions while cooperating with them and based on the principles of human rights of the human beings understood as divine creatures:

> the insurmountable opposition between the two ideologies of power—"by the grace of God" and "by the will of the people." Christian history knows a power that recognizes itself as approved by the grace of God and is exercised by the people, not by the king: this is the system in America based on the right of man and citizen as the son of God.[26]

But for him, only an in-depth rediscovery of Wisdom, in God and in creation, was able to transform the Modern conception of the solitary state into a new form of personalist sovereignty, virtuous, inclusive and respectful of creation.

---

25   Kate Raworth, *Doughnut Economics: Seven Ways to Think Like a 21st Century Economist* (Vermont, White River Junction, 2017).
26   Bulgakov, "Khristianskaia sotsiologiia," 832.

Building the House of Wisdom
DOI 10.17438/978-3-402-12184-9

Sergii Bulgakov's Chalcedonian Politics of Personhood

Nathaniel Wood

Among the many enduring aspects of Sergii Bulgakov's theology, one of the most important is his integration of the doctrine of *theosis* with political theology. There has always been at least an implicit connection between the two within Orthodoxy, as in the various formulations of church–state *symphonia*, with their focus on formal institutional cooperation between church and empire, Bulgakov stands out as one of the first Orthodox theologians—following on the heels of Vladimir Soloviev—to reflect in more explicit terms on how an Orthodox logic of deification might provide guiding principles for Christian political action in changing modern contexts, including democracy. Although Bulgakov was interested in church–state relations and took various positions on the issue throughout his career,[1] the real heart of his political theology, what gives it continued relevance, is the ethical task standing behind it: namely, to provide theoretical grounding and material protection for the dignity and freedom of the human person.

Bulgakov stands on the front end of the broad stream of "personalist" thought prominent in Orthodox theology of the 20th century. One of the characteristic moves of Orthodox personalists has been to posit an essential link between personhood and *theosis*. Not only does personhood become the main category through which deification is understood, but one of the main roles of *theosis* is to give an ontological foundation for the absolute value of the singular person—the person's irreducible uniqueness, irreplaceability, and freedom from subordination to some impersonal order or whole—while also differentiating the person, *ek*-statically oriented towards communion, from the

---

1   On the historical development of his understanding of theocracy, monarchy, and democracy, see Regula M. Zwahlen, "Sergii Bulgakov's Reinvention of Theocracy for a Democratic Age," *Journal of Orthodox Christian Studies* 3, no. 1 (Spring 2020), 175–94.

self-enclosed individual. These are themes that are most popularly associated with the work of John Zizioulas; yet for Bulgakov, despite the vast differences between his Sophiology and the neo-patristic theology of personalists like Zizioulas, the turn to *theosis* was driven by a similar commitment to personal freedom and irreducibility. Whereas Zizioulas says little about the *politics* of personhood (differing sharply in this regard from his fellow Greek personalist Christos Yannaras[2]), Bulgakov's concern for the person is inseparable from his involvement in the political struggles of his time. In offering a theoretical defense of the person rooted in *theosis*, Bulgakov intended to justify the political and economic defense of human dignity against attacks from both right and left, while also pointing to the more perfect fulfillment of personhood beyond the sphere of worldly politics, in divine-human communion. Thus, his philosophical embrace of *theosis* affirmed this seemingly otherworldly doctrine into the basis of a politics of personal flourishing. Moreover, insofar as deification is accomplished in the person of Christ incarnate, the God-Man, both *theosis* and its politics have an essentially Chalcedonian shape; the politics of *theosis* is a Chalcedonian politics of personhood. This political-theological linking of personhood and *theosis* opens possibilities for Orthodox politics beyond tired reiterations of *symphonia*, possibilities that can inform Christian approaches to liberal democracy. This chapter will briefly examine some of the contours of a Bulgakovian political theology with focus on personhood and Chalcedonian Christology in relation to liberalism.

Progress, Personhood, and Theosis

Bulgakov's personalist impulses preceded his reembrace of Orthodoxy and the start of his theological career, being a catalyst for his transition away from his early Marxism. Like many others at the time, Bulgakov approached the question of personhood in connection to theories of progress, reiterating, with more philosophical precision, aspects of the critiques that had been offered half a century earlier by Russian Westernizers like Alexander Herzen.[3] In his contribution to the 1902 volume *Problems of Idealism*, for instance, he condemns the impersonalism of positivist theories of progress and argues instead for a model

---

2   A helpful short summary of Yannaras's political theology is Jonathan Cole, "Personhood, Relational Ontology, and the Trinitarian Politics of Eastern Orthodox Thinker Christos Yannaras," *Political Theology* 34 (2017): 1–14.

3   Alexander Herzen, *From the Other Shore and The Russian People and Socialism* (Oxford: Oxford University Press, 1979).

of progress centered on the human person: the true aim of progress must be the "creation of the conditions for the free development of the person," which he considers morally axiomatic.[4] Soon, Bulgakov would begin to affirm this commitment in explicitly Christian terms, as in his essay "An Urgent Task," written at the time of the 1905 revolution, which describes the free development of persons as the "absolute ideal" of Christian politics. This was to be the guiding principle of his Union of Christian Politics, to be implemented in the political and economic liberation of the person from Russia's "centralist, autocratic despotism" through a combination of democratic self-government, civil rights, and socialist economics.[5]

Bulgakov's turn to *theosis* would grow out of this commitment to the liberation of the person, motivated, in part, by his disillusionment with positivism. Deification would make up for what he considered lacking in positivist ideas of progress: namely, a metaphysics of personhood. Describing his disenchantment with Marxism in 1906, he cites the failure of positivism to provide an ontological basis for the person as "single, irreplaceable, and absolutely unique." Positivism suffers from a "theoretical disregard for the person,"[6] a refusal to confront the singular person in his or her concreteness; indeed, the "very problem of personhood is altogether absent" from positivism,[7] which instead relies on a crude, deterministic "sociologism" that dissolves the concrete person into "humanity" as an abstract collective, reducing him or her to little more than a "ripple on the wave of society."[8] In other words, positivism is the objectification of the person. Thus, while Bulgakov could praise positivist socialists for their "faithful and courageous defense of oppressed people, [and of] the laboring classes,"[9] he parted company from them on the deeper meaning of liberation.

---

4   Sergei Bulgakov, "Basic Problems of the Theory of Progress," in *Problems of Idealism*, ed. Pavel Novgorodtsev, English edition trans. and ed. by Randall A. Poole (New Haven: Yale University Press, 2003), 104.

5   Sergei Bulgakov, "An Urgent Task," in *A Revolution of the Spirit: Crisis of Value in Russia, 1890–1924*, eds. Bernice Glatzer Rosenthal and Martha Bohachevsky-Chomiak (New York: Fordham University Press, 1990).

6   Sergei Bulgakov, *Karl Marx as a Religious Type: His Relation to the Religion of Anthropotheism of L. Feuerbach*, trans. Luba Barna, ed. Virgil R. Lang (Belmont, Mass.: Nordland Publishing, 1979), 51.

7   Sergij Bulgakov, *The Tragedy of Philosophy (Philosophy and Dogma)*, trans. Stephen Churchyard (Brooklyn, NY: Angelico Press, 2020).

8   Sergii Bulgakov, "The Soul of Socialism," in *Sergii Bulgakov: Towards a Russian Political Theology*, ed. Rowan Williams (Edinburgh: T & T Clark, 1999), 259.

9   Bulgakov, "Urgent Task," 138.

Certainly, he thought that many of the social reforms they advocated were necessary for creating the conditions of personal development: e. g., he argues that the "battle against poverty," against exploitation, etc., "is a battle for the rights of the human spirit."[10] However, positivism itself could not account for that spirit, having instead a one-sided focus on external improvement of social conditions. At its worst, Bulgakov feared, positivism ends up *instrumentalizing* the person, subordinating personhood to the development of the collectivized "humanity" awaiting perfection in the future. Such is his basic critique of progress: cast in positivist terms, it makes an idol out of a dead logical abstraction, which demands the sacrifice of living persons.[11]

Insofar as it resisted this objectification and instrumentalization of the singular person, Bulgakov's political theology is, in a broad sense, a "liberalizing" one. The socialist impulse had to be coupled with the defense of what might be called various "rights of personality," including broadly liberal rights such as freedom of speech, of conscience, of association, and so forth—all crucial for free personal development but which the positivists, in their neglect of personhood, tended to ignore or treat only as means to an end, and thus subject to restriction. However, Bulgakov's political theology, even in its most liberal moments, is by no means liberal without qualification. For one thing, Bulgakov's "person" is not the abstract individual subject often associated with liberalism, nor are his rights of personality based in subjective self-assertion. If Bulgakov's personalism is on the one hand "liberalizing," it simultaneously challenges at least certain iterations of liberal theory.

If politics is about the free development of the person, this raises the metaphysical question: towards *what* is the person developing? Bulgakov would turn to *theosis* for the answer, mainly under Soloviev's influence. Soloviev had also devoted much of his intellectual output to formulating a metaphysics and a political theology centered on the "absolute significance of human personality,"[12] which he grounded in the person's "capacity for deification."[13] Bulgakov carried forward the fundamentals of that project, embracing deification as the basis for the rights of the person. However, as for Soloviev, his turn to *theosis* is

---

10   Sergii Bulgakov, "The Economic Ideal," in Williams, *Sergii Bulgakov*, 43.
11   Bulgakov, "Basic Problems."
12   Vladimir Soloviev, *The Justification of the Good: An Essay on Moral Philosophy*, trans. Nathalie Duddington, ed. Boris Jakim (Grand Rapids: W. B. Eerdmans, 2005), 211.
13   Vladimir Soloviev, "A Note in Defense of Dostoevsky against the Charge of a 'New' Christianity," in *The Heart of Reality: Essays on Beauty, Love, and Ethics by V. S. Soloviev*, trans. and ed. Vladimir Wozniuk (Notre Dame, Ind.: University of Notre Dame Press, 2003), 202.

contrasted explicitly with the immanent *self-deification* of humanity, the seizing of a false absoluteness without reference to God—false because, enclosed within itself, humanity remains trapped in conditional, transitory existence.[14] One form of this "mangodhood" is the Feuerbachian type, the "man-god of the deified predicate, human nature," the idolatrous "humanity" mentioned above. But there is also the mangodhood of the self-enclosed individual subject, an error he associates, in its preeminent philosophical expression, with Fichte.[15] This latter is the "Luciferian" man-god, the closed self-consciousness that absorbs the non-self into itself as its property, leaving no space for encounter with another *I*, and thus no *we*—a "windowless" self, "impenetrably locked," like Leibniz's monad.[16] In ethical-religious terms, this is the sin of individual egoism, the refusal of communion, which Khomiakov had condemned in his writings on ecclesial *sobornost'*,[17] and which Soloviev had denounced in his critique of self-deification.[18] The path of egoism ends in the same place as positivist sociologism: in the *objectification* of the (other) person, in the transformation of the (other) person into an instrument of self-realization. In this way, the two sides of mangodhood collude with each other towards the debasement, the de-personalization, of the human being.

Theosis, the real self-transcendence of humanity, the real union of the human and the divine, is Bulgakov's way past these two faces of the man-god and the answer to the question "towards what is the person developing?" Personal development leads human persons outside themselves; its end is none other than participation in the divine *we*, the triune communion of divine persons, and the realization of a creaturely communion in the divine likeness (the church in its cosmic significance). Moreover, as with Soloviev, Bulgakov understands that such personhood has been realized definitively within humanity in the incarnate God-Man, the one who harmonizes the human and divine wills

---

14   Vladimir Soloviev, *Lectures on Divine-Humanity*, trans. Peter Zouboff, revised by Boris Jakim (Hudson, NY: Lindisfarne Press, 1995), 18.

15   See the "Excursus on Fichte" in Bulgakov, *Tragedy of Philosophy*, 207–36. The quoted text is from page 233.

16   Bulgakov, *Tragedy of Philosophy*, 230. The theme of the Luciferian, empty ego reappears, in a more explicitly theological key, in Bulgakov's various discussions of Satan throughout *Jacob's Ladder: On Angels*, trans. Thomas Allan Smith (Grand Rapids: W. B. Eerdmans, 2010).

17   See, among others, the collected texts of Khomiakov in *On Spiritual Unity: A Slavophile Reader*, trans. and ed. Boris Jakim and Robert Bird (Hudson, NY: Lindisfarne Books, 1998).

18   E. g., throughout Lectures on Divine-Humanity.

and into whose deified body all are called. *Theosis* thus gives a definite Christological shape to social progress: its goal is neither abstract "humanity" nor empty individuality, but the specific person of Christ. Thus, at least as early as 1905, Bulgakov had begun to speak of historical progress as a "process of the God-Man" and to tie political theology to Chalcedonian Christology.[19] History is the progressive realization, in Christ, of the divine *we* in creation—that is to say, of deification.

It is here that possible tensions start to appear between Bulgakov's politics of the person and political liberalism, since the Christological shape of personal development cannot fit within the liberal individualist framework. Deification has a social dimension, because the God who has promised to "be all in all" (1 Cor. 15:28) is tri-hypostatic. The image of the tri-hypostatic God is in humanity "only to the extent that humanity's human, creaturely nature can contain it," Bulgakov argues in *The Tragedy of Philosophy*. Because human persons are finite and mono-hypostatic, they can be an image of God's tri-unity only by going outside of themselves "in the plural infinity of society, in the human *we*." Therefore, the tri-hypostatic God "furnishes the Archetype not only of the nature of an individual human being, but also of human community."[20] Elsewhere Bulgakov articulates a similar idea in relation to the notion of All-Unity he had adopted from Soloviev, which is a projection of Khomiakov's idea of ecclesial *sobornost'* in the world's foundation in God. All-Unity frames the ground of the created order as a cosmic harmony-in-diversity the nature of which is kenotic love. Drawing on Maximus the Confessor's theology of the divine prototypes,[21] Bulgakov posits a unique *logos* for every creature preexisting within the content that is "eternally spoken by the Logos in the depths of Divinity"; the content of creation is an extra-divine repetition of the content of the Father's Word. Eternally differentiated within the Word, the prototypes exist, not in a state of exclusiveness or discord, but in the ontological peace of an eternally-actualized society of love, what Bulgakov calls a "universal cosmic *sobornost'*."[22] Again, however, this likeness to the divine can exist only insofar as the created world can embody it. In the act of creation, the world of the divine prototypes enters the milieu of becoming, and the *sobornost'* of being is

19   Bulgakov, "Urgent Task," 142.
20   Bulgakov, *Tragedy of Philosophy*, 152–53.
21   Sergius Bulgakov, *The Lamb of God*, trans. Boris Jakim (Grand Rapids: W. B. Eerdmans, 2008), 126. In fn 6 on this page, Bulgakov suggests that Maximus's doctrine of the *logoi* anticipated his own thought, that it was "essentially a sophiology."
22   Bulgakov, *The Lamb of God*, 104.

"potentialized" insofar as creatures are spatially and temporally divided along the lines of their finitude, so that what is eternally actual in the Word must be *actualized* in and through this division, as the God "inwardly overcomes" creaturely separateness by enticing creatures towards the sacrifice of kenotic love. Again, deification, as the realization of the divine likeness in the world, is accomplished through the building of community.

Within this framework, "sin" becomes synonymous with egoism, with the isolated positing of the self outside of communion with other selves, binding the creature to its finite separateness. "It can be said that the whole life of that which is evil in the world is built according to the categories of the *I*'s self-love, an *I* rent asunder from the *we* and knowing the *thou* only as its own mirror."[23] As other persons harden in my consciousness into alien objects, into hostile threats to my individual selfhood, egoism fractures the empirical reality of creation along the lines of difference, transforming difference into division and discord, veiling creation's foundation in sobornal peace with the illusory primacy of universal conflict. Therefore, if personal development is understood as progress towards Christ and the perfect personality that Christ has realized in creation, then it entails an ascetic renunciation of egoistic attachment to one's self-enclosed, self-sufficient individuality to grow towards an ever-deepening communion with the world. To perfect *oneself* is to perfect society, to regenerate it in the likeness of the Christological *sobornost'* of all things.

Personhood, Liberal Democracy, and the Church

This way of linking personhood to *theosis*, hence to communion, has significant implications for how one might think theologically about liberal democracy. Deification is a social phenomenon; the perfection of the person is the perfection of relations between persons. It is no surprise, then, that Bulgakov often denounces the "atomization of society," since social atomism runs counter to the whole vision of personal development he defends.[24] Any Bulgakovian politics of personhood would need some response to the problem of atomism; the question is whether liberalism is equipped to provide one. At the *theoretical* level, it is not clear that it is so equipped, even if, at the level of practice, liberalism has made tremendous strides in securing many of those rights of personality Bulgakov had desired for the Russian people (freedom of conscience, speech, and so forth). In his critique of secular socialism, Bulgakov challenged

23 Bulgakov, *Tragedy of Philosophy*, 151–52.
24 Bulgakov, "Soul of Socialism," 261.

not so much the implementation of socialist economic policy but rather social-ism's "soul," its attempt to pass itself off as a comprehensive account of human nature and social relations, becoming a rival pseudo-theology.[25] Contemporary critics of liberalism, such as John Milbank, have likewise depicted the "soul" of liberalism as that of a rival (heretical) theology.[26]

Bulgakov would certainly share this wariness of liberal democracy's threat of becoming a pseudo-church, with the false *sobornost'* of social contract. To the extent that liberal theory tends to treat atomism and self-interest (and, in the Hobbesian strain, universal conflict) not as sin but as the natural condi-tion of humanity, and to the extent that it frames rights within a framework of external contract between these fundamentally separate and self-interested individuals, liberalism risks *reinforcing* the sin of egoism, and the sphere of personal freedom it secures risks cultivating a freedom as the empty satisfac-tion of private desire. Liberalism might at once have both done a great deal to liberate human persons from external oppression *and*, by not directing the development of personal freedom towards its proper end in divine-human communion, created new opportunities for spiritual bondage.

What this suggests is that the liberal democratic community, at the level of its own self-understanding, is insufficient for fostering the sort of personal development foundational to Bulgakov's Christian politics. There is, at the very least, a tension between them, and the liberal principles of individual freedom and rights would need a theological corrective and supplement. The true idea of personal freedom is to be found not in liberal contractual society but in a different kind of community: the church. Bulgakov came to see the church as the authentic basis of social development fairly early in his evolution be-yond Marxism. In "An Urgent Task," for instance, immediately after calling on Christians to cooperate with secular liberation movements, he proclaims that the true idea of personal freedom is not found in democratic or socialist prin-ciples but in "the ideals of anarchic communism we find in the first Christian communes," that is, the *sobornost'* of the church.[27] The church, in a sense, *is* the deification of the person, the creaturely likeness of divine triunity, as a society organized not around the contractual preservation of egoistic self-interest but its free renunciation in sobornal love. Only here does human personality reach

25 This is Bulgakov's critique in "The Soul of Socialism."

26 John Milbank, *Theology and Social Theory: Beyond Secular Reason*, 2nd ed. (Malden, Mass.: Blackwell, 2006); also John Milbank, *Beyond Secular Order: The Representation of Being and the Representation of the People* (Malden, Mass.: Wiley Blackwell, 2013).

27 Bulgakov, "Urgent Task," 158.

the height of its development, become filled with absolute content, and evade the grasp of non-being, as an irreplaceable and inextinguishable member of the whole. For this reason, Bulgakov's politics of personhood calls for a distinctly *ecclesial* social theory, a theory of the church as the foundation and goal of every human social impulse (however distorted by sin), what he calls a "Christian sociology." In Bulgakov's view, "it is only the Church that possesses the principle of true social order, in which the personal and the collective, freedom and social service can be given equal weight and unified harmoniously. It is itself this very principle—living *sobornost'*."[28]

Thus, Bulgakov, while rejecting the clerical domination of the state by the institutional church, also rejects a strict secularist separation between the ecclesial and the political. Instead, he advocates for a "Christianizing" or "churching" of society, an extension of the church's sobornal principles into every nook and cranny of the social order.[29] Social progress involves moving beyond mere liberal rights to the transformation of the social and political spheres in the direction of freedom-as-love. "Social life is to be organized according to the postulates of Christian love," he argues. "We must seek for a state of things in which the Church may penetrate as with inward power the whole of human life."[30] The final endpoint of progress, he argues, is that the secular state and society will be "overcome and dissolved in ecclesial life."[31]

Chalcedon and Politics

All this is to say that the logic of a Bulgakovian political theology moves from a commitment to the absolute value of the human person, through deification, to ecclesiology—and finally arrives at the theoretical question of church–state relations. If secular society, as he suggests, is destined to be dissolved into ecclesial society, it raises the question of how the Christian community should relate, in the sphere of political action, to the liberal order here and now. Here it is crucial to turn back to Chalcedonian Christology, which, as I have argued in more detail elsewhere, becomes in a Bulgakovian key (as earlier in a Solovievan) a framework for thinking about the relationship between the *ecclesia* and

---

28   Bulgakov, "Soul of Socialism," 264.
29   Ibid., 256.
30   Sergii Bulgakov, "Social Teaching in Modern Russian Orthodox Theology," in Williams, *Sergii Bulgakov*, 282.
31   Bulgakov, "Soul of Socialism," 264.

liberal politics.[32] In short, if deification is understood to be a collective incarnation of Christ's personality in and as the communion of created beings, then the doctrine of incarnation offers a model for the "churching" of secular society. The political task of "churching," of "sobornizing," of extending the incarnation into society, should be treated as a continuation of a single incarnational process, a single process of free cooperation between the human and the divine, begun in Mary's womb. Christian politics carries forward Christ's own work of deifying his own particular human nature, his own victory over the Luciferian temptation of egoism. If this is the case, then the manner by which the church overcomes the anti-sobornal forces of the secular order should correspond to the manner in which Christ assumed the humanity of a man from Nazareth, conformed it to his divine personality, and made it into an agent of divine activity. It is chiefly in this sense that Bulgakov's politics of personhood, as a politics of *theosis*, culminates in a *Chalcedonian* politics—or, as Bulgakov might say, a *neo*-Chalcedonian politics, one that attends seriously to the dynamic interplay between the divine and the human within Christ's personal consciousness.[33]

Bulgakov's incarnational Christology offers an important qualification to Vladimir Lossky's statement that Christ's human nature "is a deified nature that is permeated by the divine from the moment of the Incarnation."[34] While of course affirming the divinity of the Christ child, Bulgakov views the incarnation not as something fully accomplished in a single moment, like conception or birth, but as a "ceaselessly continuing process of the attainment of the divine in the human and the human in light of the divine," carried out across Christ's whole earthly life. Building on Soloviev's insight that Christ's *kenosis* of divinity makes possible an *attainment* of that divinity in which his humanity, through its own *kenosis* of egoism, freely cooperates, Bulgakov writes that the Son of God "'comes down from heaven' and abandons, as it were, the divine life. His

32 Nathaniel Wood, "'I Have Overcome the World': The Church, the Liberal State, and Christ's Two Natures in the Russian Politics of *Theosis*," in *Christianity, Democracy, and the Shadow of Constantine*, ed. George E. Demacopoulos and Aristotle Papanikolaou (New York: Fordham University Press, 2017).
33 For Bulgakov's embrace of the term "neo-Chalcedonian," see, e.g., Constantin Andronikof, "Afterword: Philosophy versus Theology in the Works of Father Sergius Bulgakov (with Particular Reference to the Eucharistic Writings)," in *The Holy Grail and the Eucharist*, ed. Boris Jakim (Hudson, N.Y.: Lindisfarne, 1997), 143.
34 Vladimir Lossky, *The Mystical Theology of the Eastern Church*, trans. the Fellowship of St. Alban and St. Sergius (Crestwood, N.Y.: St Vladimir's Seminary Press, 1976), 146.

divine nature retains only the potential of glory, which must be actualized anew."[35] It is actualized "measure to measure" from the manger to the cross.[36]

In other words, the incarnation is accomplished jointly with Christ's ascetic struggle to deify his humanity. Christ's divinity is now expressed—and is now known even in Christ's own personal self-consciousness—through his humanity. Once again, the capacity of the creature to receive and reveal the divine comes into play in Bulgakov's theology; the accomplishment of the incarnation depends on the humanity's power to accept divinity into itself without destroying itself, the power to reveal divinity in and as the human. "The divine-humanity consists precisely in such a *correlativeness* of the divine and the human," Bulgakov writes; the divine does not "exceed" human capacity.[37] In the process of incarnation, Christ "actualizes His divinity for Himself only in inseparable union with the human nature, *as a function of [his humanity's] receptivity*," which is to say, "only to the extent of the deification of His humanity."[38]

The incarnation, then, is a display of divine *restraint* as much as one of divine power—or rather, power through restraint, the power to redeem humanity, to mend the fractures of egoism, from within humanity's own freedom. What does this mean for political theology? In the first place, as the fountainhead of Christian politics, this Chalcedonian "inward overcoming" of egoism would rule out any sort of Eutychian political theology in which the church would simply swallow up the secular, dominating it. This is why Bulgakov would come to realize that the church in the modern world should no longer try to impose its will on the state or society externally or from above, as in theocracies of old, but— here Bulgakov is pushing forward Soloviev's notion of "free theocracy"—should influence society from within, "in a democratic way."[39] Understood in a Chalcedonian key, a Christian politics that strives to "church" a liberal democratic society would not do so in a way that violently exceeds that society's receptivity to ecclesial *sobornost'*. Instead, practicing kenotic restraint, even a Christ-like submersion within the limits of limit democracy, the church would strive to deify democracy from within, nudging it gradually towards clearer expressions of sobornicity. This would mean that, instead of a stance of rejection, the Bulgakovian position is more one of *ambivalence*. It recognizes

35   Bulgakov, *The Lamb of God*, 224.
36   Ibid., 229.
37   Ibid., 251.
38   Ibid., 256.
39   Sergius Bulgakov, *The Orthodox Church*, trans. Lydia Kesich (Crestwood, NY: St. Vladimir's Seminary Press, 1988), 163.

the dual character of liberalism as, on the one hand, an external safeguard of the sphere of personal freedom and dignity but also, on the other hand, as a potential rival pseudo-church offering its own competing vision of freedom and dignity that misdirects the development of persons away from their proper end. The Chalcedonian response to this tension, it seems, is that of creative dialogue, not just with liberalism but also within it—that is, developing the liberal tradition in more authentically Christian directions, working to further unfold liberalism's commitment to freedom and dignity while also challenging the aspirations to redefine the human being and the impulses towards atomization. It is to imagine possibilities for the liberal order one inhabits to be reformed, little by little, in ways that recognize human persons as more than empty and aimless individuals, and in ways that more fully accept the responsibilities of neighbor-love, making this human "flesh" of society more receptive to the divine influence that is drawing creation towards universal *sobornost'*—while recognizing that *sobornost'* itself cannot be implemented through the force of coercive law, but only through the freedom of interpersonal bonds of affection.

Conclusion

Bulgakov thus pointed to potential new paths for Orthodox political theology: political theology centered on the dignity of the human person growing towards sobornal love, and on the incarnational union of the divine and human that makes such growth possible. The task falls to others to follow those paths. The greatest progress towards the sort of Christian engagement with liberalism Bulgakov's theology supports has been made, I suggest, by his contemporary, and fellow heir of Soloviev, S. L. Frank. It is appropriate to end with the Johannine Christological metaphor that structures much of Frank's politics, and which also describes Bulgakov's own: light shining in darkness. The ambivalence of liberal democracy is this: that however much it is darkened by self-interest and egoism, it "can and must receive the rays of Christ's truth" and be illuminated by the light of that ecclesial love in which human personality is deified. Yet within history, liberal society, "like the moon, can shine only with a dim, reflected light, can [...] only indirectly reflect the influence" of divine light.[40] Liberal society will never be the church, and human persons cannot find deification in it; but it can protect and promote the divine significance of the person to greater or lesser degrees. The summons of Bulgakov's political

---

40 S. L. Frank, *The Light Shineth in Darkness: An Essay in Christian Ethics and Social Philosophy*, trans. Boris Jakim (Athens, Ohio: Ohio University Press, 1989), 221.

theology is to take up this personalist task in response to the distortions and degradations of personhood in our time.

This chapter was supported by the author's participation as Senior Fellow in the "Orthodoxy and Human Rights" project sponsored by Fordham University's Orthodox Christian Studies Center and was generously funded by the Henry Luce Foundation and Leadership 100.

Building the House of Wisdom
DOI 10.17438/978-3-402-12185-6

The World as the Household of Wisdom: Political Theology and Philosophy of Economy

Dionysios Skliris

Sergei Bulgakov, an economist, philosopher, politician as well as an important Marxist scholar in the 1890s, had distanced himself from Marxism in the
early twentieth century, after having taken a spiritual path that led him to the
work *Philosophy of Economy* in 1912.[1] The latter includes Bulgakov's critique
of Marxism and his own alternative view of an idealist (i. e., non-materialist)
communism, which he relates to his notion of *Sophia*.

The Ideal of Sophic Communism

For Bulgakov, true philosophy consists in the coordination with life and its
source. It starts from a stance of wonder (θαυμάζειν) toward the miracle of
life, as in Aristotle, and consists in a coordination with life in all its concrete
manifestations. Following the traditional theology of the logoi of beings, Bulgakov considers that the logos, i. e., the logical principle of life, transcends
thought, while life itself is an eminent supralogical synthesis of the logical and
the alogical.[2] Formal thought with its emphasis on limits and boundaries cannot render it fully; however, Bulgakov supports the possibility of ascribing to
an eminent philosophy that could coordinate with life's flow. For Bulgakov, modernity has produced a vicious couple of intellectualism and anti-intellectual-
ism: The former consists in regarding the logical principle as fundamental and
thus considers being as self-developing thought. The latter gives priority to the

---

1   Catherine Evtuhov, "Introduction," in: Sergei Bulgakov, *Philosophy of Economy. The
    World as Household* (New Haven and London: Yale University Press, 2000), 1–2.
2   Sergei Bulgakov, *Philosophy of Economy. The World as Household*, trans. Catherine
    Evtuhov (New Haven and London: Yale University Press, 2000), 48.

unconscious instincts over conscious reason.[3] Bulgakov himself is inspired by
the traditional philosophy of the logoi of beings,[4] as expounded bya variety of
thinkers from Philo of Alexandria to Saint Maximus the Confessor, according
to which the logos signifies a connection of beings with a trans-subjective and
realist meaning.[5] However, Bulgakov does not propose a return to pre-modern
thought. On the contrary, he proposes a transcendence of modern dilemmas
from within the spiritual itinerary of modernity. In this sense, Bulgakov would
propose a reception of modern liberal values in his Sophiological project.[6] He
would also expound a synthesis of the particularly modern types of intellectualism and anti-intellectual scepticism, since thought is for him self-reflecting
life. Concepts could become abstract fossils of living thought in the context of
intellectualism; but they can also be regarded as signs and symbols of living
reality.

Bulgakov's synthesis lies in a modern interpretation of the Christian faith
in the Holy Trinity. Christian Trinitarian theology is viewed as an archetype
of synthesis between interior subjectivity and exterior otherness.[7] Bulgakov
thought that this Trinitarian archetype is reflected in the conciliar structure
of the Church, which synthesizes between an invisible aspect of divine in-
wardness and a visible one of exterior institutional structures.[8] He also linked
this synthesis to the theology of creation *ex nihilo* through the agency of the
Logos: The "void" that precedes creation is formed by the Word thus leading to
a worldly synthesis of the logical and the alogical, which echoes the Trinitarian one through Christ. Bulgakov tries to reformulate the Orthodox theology
of creation in a novel way drawing from Fichte and Schelling,[9] as a synthesis
between the 'I' of subjectivity and the 'not-I' of otherness. The same view is
articulated as a synthesis between being and non-being in the sense of the μὴ
ὄv. It is to be reminded that the term οὐκ ὄv signifies what does not exist in
any way whatsoever, such as the absolute nothingness, the nihil 'before' and
'outside' creation whereas the term μὴ ὄv denotes a relative non-being, a posi-

---

3   Bulgakov, *Philosophy of Economy*, 48.

4   Irénée-Henri Dalmais, "La théorie des "logoi" des créatures chez S. Maxime le Confes-
    seur," *Revue des Sciences Philosophiques et Théologiques* 36 (1952), 244–49.

5   Bulgakov, *Philosophy of Economy*, 53.

6   Aristotle Papanikolaou, *The Mystical as Political: Democracy and Non-Radical Ortho-
    doxy* (Notre Dame, Indiana: University of Notre Dame Press, 2012), 36–43.

7   Bulgakov, *Philosophy of Economy*, 57.

8   Stanisław Swierkosz, *L'Église visible selon Serge Bulgakov. Structure hiérarchique et sa-
    crementelle* (Rome: Pontificium Institutum Studiorum Orientalium, 1980), 195–96.

9   Ibid., 56–57.

tive indefinite, that is, what does not exist in relation to something else. In this sense, creation is seen as a synthesis between on the one hand the subjectivity of the eidetic formation and, on the other, the initial unconscious void that received this formation. Philosophy thus aims at a synthesis between subjectivity and objectivity as well as between necessity and freedom. For this reason, it resembles poetry, which is also characterized by a combination of inner consistency and free creativity, being a "poetry of concepts."[10] The aesthetic activity of poetry is the highest embodiment of philosophy because it synthesizes between free creativity and necessary consistency or, in other words, between the conscious and the unconscious.[11] It is in this sense that in Bulgakov, Kant's vision of aesthetics as a bridge between science and ethics and Schopenhauer's vision of art as a coordination with will that is deeper than formal presentation, are integrated in a Christological vision that, after Dostoevsky, beauty will save the world.

The same antithesis is viewed by Bulgakov as one between life and death. Life is the world of teleology, whereas death is equated with inorganic matter and the realm of mechanistic determinism. But Bulgakov observes the coexistence of both in the universe, thus finding room for both types of philosophy in his worldview. The world of becoming is one of mortal life. The latter constitutes an inherently ambiguous and inconsistent concept that poses a grave problem for thought. Especially after the Darwinian theory of evolution we are accustomed to thinking that life uses death as an instrument for its preservation, but one could also possibly claim the inverse, namely that death, the 'prince of this world,' is strengthened through the reproduction of life.[12] For the human person, the reign of death is tantamount to a reduction to thingness and to alienation. However, in the world of becoming and mortal life, the survival of both the individual and the species is achieved through the satisfaction of material needs: The result is that the teleology of the mortal life paradoxically takes place through the determinism of lower instincts.

The philosophy of economy thus begins as an examination of the struggle for survival that man shares with other animals. However, this is only an initial version of economy. For human life can transcend this primordial level and broaden itself beyond determinism. The definition of economy as a proper philosophical domain is for Bulgakov one of studying humanity's expansion and development as well as its expression through labour. The widening of

---

10 Swierkosz, *L'Église visible*, 59.
11 Ibid., 92.
12 Ibid., 70.

humanity takes place through an encounter with the reality of dead matter and mechanistic necessity. It seems that Bulgakov envisages a confrontation in which humanity is in combat with the forces of death on behalf of all life, since it may be true that humans share life and even some economic features with other animals (for example, one could speak of an economy of bees, ants etc.), but the freely creative life of humanity is the apex of life and the peak of its teleology as a synthesis between freedom and necessity that subdues the latter. For this reason, even though one can envisage an economy of animals, the teleology of economy consists in human expression as the peak of a rather continuous movement of life from animality to humanity. This humanization of nature consists in the organism assuming and transcending the mechanism and intentionality assuming and transcending causality.[13]

What is particularly theological about this vision is that Bulgakov regards economy as a battle with the forces of death, the "prince of this world," the latter including, as we have observed, inorganic matter, necessity, deterministic causality and its reflection in lower instincts. However, the peak of this combat is not mere humanity, but Christ as God-man who is the only one able to conquer death and chase it out of life.[14] This consists in a leap from teleology to eschatology and not in a simple progress from the one to the other. There is thus a first definition of philosophical economy as a necessity to defend life, which turns economy into a "function of death." In this first definition, economy is a self-affirmation of life that is, however, defensive in character, since it aims to avoid or rather postpone death. But this effort is vain: Man remains subject to death and in fact this sort of economy cannot but instrumentalize death for the temporary protection of life. This happens on the one hand because the motivation of this economy is the fear of death. And, on the other hand, Bulgakov seems to refer to an economic equivalent of Darwinism, in which the evolution of the life of the species is achieved through the death of the unfit, which makes possible the progress of life as a whole. In a similar way, progress in this sort of economic life is based on an antagonism that comprises the reality of death and even uses it for the sake of economic progress.

The transformation into a theological understanding of economy thus seems to require this leap from teleology to eschatology: Christ makes possible the final overcoming of death and thus a definition of life that is not dependent on it. But this also means a definition of life in which life has no fear of death. This could arguably be a way to formulate after Bulgakov the mystery of the

---

13   Swierkosz, *L'Église visible*, 72.
14   Ibid., 73.

cross: Instead of founding the economy on the fear of death and consequently on its instrumentalization for the progress of life, Christians can conceive of a life that knows no fear of death and is thus ready for any sacrifice. Thanks to the God-man, this mystery of readiness for sacrifice leads to the resurrection, which constitutes the final victory over death. It is to be noted that the mystery of the cross is not an instrumentalization of death for progress, as in a biological or economic version of Darwinism. One could arguably extend Bulgakov's thought and claim that the resurrection is in a sense the final survival of the unfit, since death is not used to achieve progress. This is an event that is eschatological in character and not teleological, since Christ's resurrection comes as an end from the outside and not as an internal evolution of mortal life. For Bulgakov, the mystery of the cross is after all a mystery of the entire Trinity.[15] However, at the same time, I think that it would also be true to claim that if we follow Bulgakov's thought, then Christ's victory over death could also be characterized as a sort of "economy" and also as a sort of "progress." Thus, in the first place, one could say that what we theologians term "divine economy," i. e., God's plan for the salvation of the world, is regarded by Bulgakov as being the peak of human economy, studied by the philosophers, that is, as the confirmation of life's struggle to expand and develop. Similarly, Christ's victory over death could be regarded as the true ontological progress of life and it could establish a philosophy of progress that would not forget death like secular progressivist theories,[16] but would engulf it as a moment to be transcended. It thus seems that the mystery of the cross is rather integrated by Bulgakov in a narrative of the continuity of life, while Christological eschatology is rather viewed as a confirmation of teleology.

In any case, one could sum up that there are at least three notions of economy in Bulgakov's work, the combination of which consists in a rejection of Marxist political economy.

The first notion is that of a scientific discipline that deals with the contingent aspects of economy, approaching it through analytic scientific methodology.

The second notion is philosophical economy as a speculative observation of the phenomenon of life as a whole in its combat with the forces of death. This combat is considered a battle between, on the one hand, organism, teleology, freedom, creativity, *natura naturans* and, on the other, correspondingly, mechanism, deterministic causality, necessity, lower instincts, *natura naturata*, etc. It

---

15   Sergius Bulgakov, *The Lamb of God*, trans. Boris Jakim (Grand Rapids: W. B. Eerdmans, 2008, 213–46).

16   Aidan Nichols, *Wisdom from Above* (Herefordshire: Gracewing, 2005), 220.

is the task of philosophy to witness this combat as an event of economy, i. e., as an event of the real even if futile struggle of life for expansion. In this notion of particularly human economy, production and consumption play a similar role to that of inhalation and exhalation in biology.[17] This economic metabolism bears witness to the fundamental similarity of the universe, its *sympathy*, if one puts it in Stoic terms, or in Bulgakov's own terms, to the 'physical communism' attested by the philosopher. For Bulgakov, economy as a whole as studied by the philosopher is both logically and empirically prior to separate and contingent economic acts.[18]

The third notion is theological economy as observing the final victory, expansion and progress of life through the mystery of the cross and the resurrection of Christ, as well as the Pentecost in the Spirit, which fulfils the divine plan for salvation.[19] In Christ we find the "divine economy" as the culmination of the human one, be it scientific or philosophical. It is true that this theological economy is eschatological and not teleological in character. It is based on a reversal of terms: Death is not avoided but assumed by Christ and the result is that the unfit for survival ultimately survive together with the fit. But Bulgakov examines this eschatological event in terms both of economy and of the expansion/ progress of life. For Bulgakov, the theological notion of economy constitutes the inevitable debt of the philosophical one, since for him death is "metaphysically unnatural"[20] and life should be able to be defined philosophically by itself and not through an opposition to its opposite. But the latter is only revealed in Christ, who reverses the terms of mortal life and manifests this possibility of defining life itself. At the same time, the Word shows the ultimate synthesis between body and soul or, philosophically speaking, between materialism and idealism,[21] something that was impossible for pre-Christian Neoplatonism.

What is peculiar to Bulgakov's thought is the ultimate valorization of the notions of economy and progress, which even have an eschatological content and are considered part of spiritual life.[22] This might seem a modernist progressive attempt, but one could claim that this is a subject also present in traditional theology. For example, one can refer to the vision of Gregory of Nyssa

---

17   Bulgakov, *Philosophy of Economy*, 95.
18   Ibid., 124.
19   Sergius Bulgakov, *The Comforter*, trans. Boris Jakim (Grand Rapids: W. B. Eerdmans, 2004), 267–84.
20   Bulgakov, *Philosophy of Economy*, 88.
21   Ibid.
22   Ibid., 217.

in whichthe eschatological state is one of perpetual progress (*epektasis*).[23] Or to the patristic notion of divine economy as the caring for the salvation of the worldly house and body of the Word. Bulgakov's originality rather lies in the fact that he considers this perpetual progress and divine economy to be the culmination of a movement of progress and economy that is already present inside history according to the progressive narrative of modernity.

Bulgakov's most interesting difference from Marxism lies in his theory of labour. For Bulgakov, the philosophical notion of economy could also be defined as "the struggle through labour for life and its expansion."[24] Consequently, the world as household is the world as the object of labour. For Bulgakov, labour is "a feeling of outwardly directed effort"[25] that constitutes the expression of life in its direction of expansion. He insists on an expressivist understanding of labour as "man's coming out of himself to act in the external world"[26] and consequently as life's effort to integrate the exterior world in it. Labour also has an epistemological value, since it manifests the subject. The problem of solipsism that is inherent in the philosophy of establishers of modernity, such as Descartes and Kant, is thus solved, since the fundamental act of cognition lies in the manifestation of subjectivity in the external world through labour. The latter arguably also creates a form of intersubjectivity. Bulgakov thus follows the Marxist attempt to raise communion to the level of first philosophy, in order to respond to the objection of solipsism, but, contrary to Marx, he observes the exteriorization of labour as a question of idealism and not of materialism.

It equally has a theological Trinitarian meaning: As an exteriorization of subjectivity, it is like an echo of the synthesis between subjectivity and otherness in the Trinity.[27] The two fundamental versions of labour are modelling and projecting, which are also the two main forms of technology. However, Bulgakov insists that intellectual and scientific activity should also be considered a form of labour. Bulgakov thus finds that the Marxist notion of labour as an expenditure of nervous-muscular energy that constitutes the foundation of economic values is an excessively narrow definition and that in this Marx presents a fundamental continuity with liberal predecessors such as Adam

---

23 Kathryn Rombs, "Gregory of Nyssa's Doctrine of Epektasis: Some Logical Implications," in *Studia Patristica* Vol. XXXVII. *Papers presented at the Thirteenth International Conference on Patristic Studies held in Oxford 1999. Cappadocian Writers. Other Greek Writers*, ed. Maurice Wiles and Edward Yarnold (Leuven: Peeters, 2001), 288–93.

24 Bulgakov, *Philosophy of Economy*, 74.

25 Ibid., 75.

26 Ibid.

27 Ibid., 115. See also Swierkosz, *L'Église visible*, 195.

Smith and David Ricardo. It is to be noted, however, that Bulgakov is closest to Marxism when he considers labour what is particularly human in contrast to the merely natural forces of life and growth.[28] More precisely, production and consumption are regarded by Bulgakov as being the particularly human version of interactions that in mere biology have the form of inhalation and exhalation or of metabolism.[29] In a neo-Aristotelian sense, labour is considered humanity's specific difference in relation to animals.

However, Bulgakov's philosophy is rather one of idealistic vitalism. He considers a natural teleology in which nature's goal is to become an object to herself, the latter finally being achieved by man.[30] For Bulgakov, the teleology of nature is not put merely in terms of a struggle between matter and form, as in Aristotle, but also as one between the unconscious and the conscious, after the modern German idealism of Schelling. The teleology thus consists in the unconscious goal-orientedness of nature, economy in its philosophical notion being the very discipline that can explain this teleological passage from the unconscious to consciousness, or in other words nature's 'achievement' of becoming the object for the labour of human consciousness. Economy is thus considered by Bulgakov in the terms of a philosophy that one could arguably name 'idealistic vitalism.'

The World as Sophia's Household

Even though Bulgakov engages in a harsh criticism of Marxism, at the same time he draws certain important signifiers from the latter, in order to re-interpret them in a very novel and interesting way. After all, Marx is considered an offspring of German idealism, i.e., of thinkers such as Kant, Fichte, Schelling, Hegel and Schopenhauer, and the same is true for Bulgakov. The philosophical strategy of Bulgakov is to read the Marxist ideal of communism through the more fundamental modern project propounded by Kant, Fichte and Schelling[31] and then to achieve a synthesis of the latter with intuitions from the tradition of the Eastern Fathers, which has incorporated elements of Neoplatonism and Stoicism. In this, Bulgakov is significantly inspired by Vladimir Soloviev, as he himself admits. To take a characteristic example, Bulgakov does use the

28   Bulgakov, *Philosophy of Economy*, 76.
29   Ibid., 95.
30   Ibid., 86.
31   Mikhail Sergeev, *Sophiology in Russian Orthodoxy. Solov'ev, Bulgakov, Losskii and Berdiaev* (Lewiston: The Edwin Mellen Press, 2006), 127–30.

signifier 'communism' in his political thought, in many different versions. The first is in the version of the signifier 'physical communism,'[32] which means the fundamental similarity of being in the world in a way that is reminiscentof the Stoic notion of sympathy. This 'physical communism of being' is attested by the philosopher and the metaphysician and is considered to be the ontological foundation of economy, since it makes consumption and thus also production possible in the economic metabolism that is the particularly human sublimation of biological metabolism.

At the philosophical level, one can observe merely a "communism of life and death"[33] which consists in the simultaneous mortality of life and the life capacity of the non-living. This is also formulated as an accessibility of nature to human action that makes technology possible.[34] But the philosopher who observes this identity of life and death has to choose which reality is the most fundamental and either engage in a monism of death or in a monism of life. Bulgakov opts for the latter, following Soloviev, but also Plato, Plotinus, Böhme, Baader and Schelling, and terms his metaphysical philosophy "panzoism."[35] But Bulgakov's panzoism is rather an idealistic vitalism that is contradistinguished from pantheistic hylozoism, the latter being a materialistic monism, not an idealist one like in Bulgakov. For the latter, it is important to note not only that life permeates everything, but also that even material non-living mechanisms are organisms *in potentia*. Bulgakov thus engages in Aristotelian teleology with the significant emphasis that this is a teleology of life's expansion, i. e., leading to a linear temporality of perpetual progress in a modern sense. Bulgakov does include the ancient and even pre-Christian elements in his thought, like the Platonist image of matter as a feminine principle of 'chora' and its interpretation by Plotinus as non-being (μὴὄν), but always reinterprets them through a Judeo-Christian vision of linear development toward the eschaton.

Consumption, the basis for seeing the world as a household, is founded on the similarity of being, its 'communism,' which permits not only biological eating but also every form of reception, such as sensation and even thought. Eating is for Bulgakov, as for Feuerbach and later for Schmemann,[36] the paradigm for every relation with the world. But the philosopher can only witness the 'mortal' version of eating, i. e., an eating through which we kill what we

32   Bulgakov, *Philosophy of Economy*, 96.
33   Ibid., 97.
34   Ibid., 120.
35   Ibid., 98.
36   Alexander Schmemann, *Pour la vie du monde* (Paris: Desclée, 1969), 9.

eat, or, to be more precise, we become what we eat, as Feuerbach would put it, but only through killing other beings, thus remaining ourselves mortal. It is the task of the theologian to evangelize another non-mortal form of eating that is made possible by the resurrection of Christ and the communion of His crucified and resurrected Body in the Eucharist.

The 'cosmic communism' that is attested at the philosophical level is transformed in a 'eucharistic communism' at the theological level, since Christ has integrated in His person the flesh of the world, He has offered it to self-sacrifice without fearing and avoiding death, and has resurrected it in the Father and the Spirit, thus offering it to us as a "medicine of immortality." The "metaphysical communism of the universe," the unity of the living and the non-living, the universality of life, is transformed into a Christological and eucharistic communism which is the only possibleform of communism that can justify the monism of life that is so precious for Bulgakov and consequently reject the monism of death that is for him tantamount to materialism. In Bulgakov's epistemology, the scientific examination of economy with its analytic method is integrated in the philosophical synthetic vision of the metaphysical communism of being and the latter is transformed in its theological justification, namely the 'communism of the resurrection' that guarantees monist vitalism.

A question that arises is whether there is a space for the Aristotelian distinction between economy and politics in the thought of Sergei Bulgakov. The Russian thinker would rather say that economy proper is the preoccupation with universal humanity and that this is what distinguishes man from the animals. Even though many animals have 'families,' only humans have a self-consciousness of the unity of their species. For Bulgakov this distinction between humanity and animality is also one between economy proper and economic acts or one between the merely collective and the social.[37] For Bulgakov, economy proper aims at the universal and is thus different not only from the relative scientific discipline, but also from historiography. But this universal economy stands in need of a transcendental subject. The latter is the theological role of the divine Sophia.[38] The divine Sophia leads economy in a transition from mechanism to organism that has an aesthetic character. For Bulgakov, economy as the discipline that studies the sophic dynamism of life is concluded by aesthetics and it is in this sense that one should understand the famous dictum that "beauty will save the world, which is understood in both a Sophiological and in a Mariological sense, since Mary is considered as the embodiment of

---

37   Bulgakov, *Philosophy of Economy*, 125.
38   Ibid., 130.

sophianic beauty."[39] Thus, the philosophical quest is necessarily complemented by the theological vision of the sophic community of free persons in harmonious love.[40] Even though theology integrates philosophy, which has already integrated science and history, there is also an element of discontinuity, since Bulgakov remarks that the sophic community is the reversal of the *homo homini lupus*. However, the element of continuity and integration prevails in Bulgakov's thought, since the divine Sophia partakes in the cosmic activity of the Logos and thus endows the world with divine forces that transform it from chaos to cosmos.[41]

Conclusions

For Bulgakov, the event of life has an ontological character of radical birth that is different from formation through labour, art and technology. Life is a sophic event, whereas man can only recreate. At the same time, Bulgakov insists that the word *natura* in Latin is in the future, thus signifying that nature is always recreated through human synergetic cooperation.[42] The theological ground of the Sophia is the one that makes the economic process possible. For Bulgakov there are two levels: on the one hand, that of Sophia establishing metaphysical humanity and, on the other, that of the human nature of the incarnated Logos. The latter manifests the truth that death is not an indispensable part of life and economy. Thus, there can be an everlasting economic life even and especially after its abolition by Christ. This is not the economy of the *natura naturata*, i.e., of economy's dead products, but one eternally dynamic and creative *natura naturans* that can also take the form of unexpected worldly beauties, like the charm of a child, the enchantment of a flower, the beauty of a starry sky or the flaming sunrise according to Vladimir Soloviev.[43] When appropriated by man through art, this form of artistic labour is a confirmation of the primordial Edenic version of economy as harmonic interaction with nature.[44] Art, mystical intuitions and cognition through symbols have a higher epistemological value, since they constitute insights into the universality of the world

---

39 Walter Nunzio Sisto, *The Mother of God in the Theology of Sergius Bulgakov. The Soul of the World* (London and New York: Routledge, 2018).
40 Bulgakov, *Philosophy of Economy*, 140.
41 Ibid., 145.
42 Ibid., 147.
43 Ibid., 151.
44 Ibid., 154.

as Sophia's household before and after the divisions brought by death, whereas science can only study the fragmentary world.[45] If science isolates itself, then it orients us to the kingdom of death.[46] On the contrary, if science is integrated in philosophy and theology, it can study life as being concluded in love, which is the highest form of divine trinitarian life. This latter is manifested in the world through Sophia, which is the transcendental subject that makes possible the universalization of both humanity and history, i. e., the fact that there is after all one single humanity and one single history.[47] The political result of observing the world as the household of Sophia would thus be a socialism of love that would transcend a version of socialism that is based merely on utilitarianism and rationalism.

---

45 Bulgakov, _Philosophy of Economy_, 155.
46 Ibid., 191.
47 Ibid., 215.

Building the House of Wisdom
DOI 10.17438/978-3-402-12186-3

Rethinking the Language of Economics as a Systematic Christian Response to Economic and Ecological Crises in the Thought of Sergii Bulgakov

Tikhon Vasilyev

Greta Thunberg, in her speech at the United Nations in 2019, voiced the problems that have worried humanity for over a decade. Thinkers of Greta's parents' and grandparents' generation had already called on politicians and economists to change the existing system of the world economy—not only unfair in the distribution of wealth, but also causing serious environmental crises for the entirety of the planet.

In my paper, I would like to analyse Bulgakov's sophiological interpretation of the economy and compare it with how the problems of economics and ecology were approached by some later thinkers. To do this, I first need to resolve the issue of methodology: how one can read Bulgakov's sophiology in general and his economic theology in particular. Secondly, after making necessary methodological remarks I will focus on the sophianic interpretation of economics by Bulgakov. Thirdly and finally, I will turn to the questions raised by economists, philosophers, sociologists, and theologians dealing with the global ecological and economic crisis, relating their thought to the vision of Bulgakov.

A great number of papers dedicated to the analysis of Bulgakov's sociological and economic views have been published recently in Russian.[1] However,

---

1 Nataliia Makasheva, 'Sergei Bulgakov: towards Christian political economy,' *Obshchest-vennye nauki I sovremennost'* = Social Sciences and Modernity 3 (1994): 27–36; N. Matveeva, *S. N. Bulgakov as a sociologist. Analysis of social problems, ideas and processes* (Moscow: Infra-M, 2018); G. Kovaleva, 'Ideas of spirituality in the philosophy of cosmism S. N. Bulgakov,' *Voprosy kul'turologi* = *Questions of Cultural Studies* 2 (2013): 33–37; D. Stozhko, K. Stozhko, 'The Political Economy of S. N. Bulgakov (to the 150th anniversary of his birth),' *Ekonomicheskaya istoriya* = Russian Journal of Economic History 17:2 (2021): 178–90; M. Eloyan, *S. N. Bulgakov: the sophiology and sophianity of economy* (Moscow: Moscow State University, 2005); see also Barbara Hallensleben,

apart from the excellent book by Rowan Williams[2] and the Introduction to the English translation of the *Philosophy of Economy* by Catherine Evtukhov,[3] one can hardly think of any other recent publications dealing with this aspect of Bulgakov's heritage in English. This article represents an attempt at least partially to fill this gap.

1. Bulgakov's Theological Metalanguage

It is impossible to make sense of Bulgakov's sophiology without understanding what kind of logic lies behind it. That is why it is necessary to consider the question of methodology before we approach the subject of Bulgakov's economic theology, which is in fact an incarnation of his sophiology. In this section I argue that sophiology is Bulgakov's theological 'metalanguage,' which he applied to different spheres of theology as well as to economics.

One of the criteria we can use to define a new theological language is the introduction of a new discourse, in other words when a theological talk is appropriated in a non-theological discourse but with an ultimate theological purpose.[4] This can be said about Bulgakov's economic theology.

The terms 'performance' and 'performative' come from analytic philosophy or, to be more precise, from J. L. Austin's theory of speech acts. Russian philosopher Upravitelev applies them to his analysis of the works of Bulgakov. A performative utterance (for instance, 'this meeting is now adjourned') does not describe reality as do other utterances but is an action or a speech act. It is not a description but the creation of reality. A performative utterance enforces the recipient; it causes him or her to enter the reality created by the utterance. It forms the subject of its existence. Upravitelev argues that Bulgakov's deliberations on the economy or religion become the method constructing the

---

Regula M. Zwahlen, *Sergij Bulgakovs Philosophie der Wirtschaft im interdisziplinären Gespräch* (Münster: Aschendorff, 2014) with contributions from Nataliia Makasheva, Hans G. Nutzinger, Matthias Mayer, Karen Horn, Anne Reichold, Lisa Herzog, Guido Vergauwen, Josephien van Kessel, Gerhard Schwarz und Alexander Lorch.

2   Rowan Williams, *Sergii Bulgakov: Towards a Russian Political Theology* (Edinburgh: T & T Clark, 1999).

3   Catherine Evtuhov, 'Introduction' in Sergei Bulgakov, *Philosophy of Economy: The World as Household* (2000).

4   See for example Florenskii's mathematical appendix in his *The Pillar and Ground of the Truth* and Bulgakov's *The Tragedy of Philosophy*, where, in his own words, philosophy is used for theological purposes.

subject of economics or religious action.[5] Bulgakov's texts are not descriptive or explanatory. They establish an ideal; they set a goal and call for change and action. The reality described in Bulgakov's texts is created through the reading of those texts, which are both prescriptive and performative.

Having stated our definition of a theological language and having pointed out the performative function of Bulgakov's texts, we are able to put forward our own argument concerning the understanding of Sophia as a metalanguage in Bulgakov's theology. For the purposes of this paper, I define theological metalanguage as a new and idiosyncratic language introduced by the author. It relies on emerging terms whose meaning is not universally accepted. Initially, this new language is meaningful only to the author, but may later be appropriated by the following generations, and its terms contribute to the set of established ones.[6]

The performative function of sophiology can be seen as the distinctive feature of the metalanguage of Sophia. Thus, Bulgakov's economic theology is performative in its essence.

Indeed, Bulgakov writes concerning the essence of sophiology, and we can see here a clear statement of its performative function:

> The real point at issue [that is, of sophiology] is that of the Christian vocation as it is related to the very nature of Christianity; it is the problem of a dogmatic *metanoia*, nothing less than a change and a renewal of human hearts.[7]

Bulgakov maintains: "I admit and consider obligatory for my theology all the doctrines of the Church."[8] And elsewhere: "My sophiology is a theological doctrine which has been only mine so far [...] I have never had the idea to charge anyone who opposes sophiology with heresy or unfaithfulness to Orthodoxy." Bulgakov speaks of a "sophianic interpretation of the doctrines of the Church"[9]

---

5 Alexander Upravitelev, *Konstruirovanie sub"ektnosti v antropologii S. N. Bulgakova* (Barnaul: Izdatelstvo Altayskogo Universiteta, 2001), 121.

6 T. Vasilyev, *Christian Angelology in Pseudo-Dionysius and Sergius Bulgakov*, DPhil thesis (University of Oxford, 2019), 10–11.

7 Sergei Bulgakov, *Sophia, The Wisdom of God: An Outline of sophiology* [1937], trans. revised by Christopher Bamford from that of Patrick Thompson, O. Fielding Clarke and Xenia Braikevitch (Hudson, NY: Lindisfarne Press, 1993), 13.

8 Sergei Bulgakov, "Dokladnaya zapiska predstavlennaya v oktiabre 1935 Ego Vysoko-peosviaschenstvu Mitropolitu Evlogiyu professorom prot. Sergiem Bulgakovym," in *O Sofii Premudrosti Bozhiey* (Paris: YMCA-Press, 1935), 30.

9 Bulgakov (1935) "Dokladnaya zapiska," 50.

and claims to be fully Orthodox: "I confess all the true doctrines of Orthodoxy. My sophiology relates by no means to the content of those doctrines, but only to their theological interpretation."[10]

2. Sophianic Interpretation of Economics

In the light of the theme of this paper the question arises: how can this interpretation of Bulgakov be useful for us and what does he try to achieve through the application of his metalanguage to economics? One can agree with Nicholas Sakharov, who writes:

"The work of salvation, the work by which God in Christ restores wholeness to the universe, is a work that relates at every point--to the physical world, to the human body, to the material environment. This is something which again comes to light very clearly in the work of Bulgakov. As an economist and as a former Marxist, Bulgakov never loses sight of the practicalities of these relations--between human beings themselves, and then between human beings and the things amongst which they live."[11]

Therefore, the economy is not some kind of separate sphere of life unimportant for salvation. Rather, the economy should be salutary for the body, for the soul, for the whole person.

According to Bulgakov, one of his immediate tasks in writing the *Philosophy of Economy* was, quite surprisingly, the interpretation of the Christian patristic heritage. He wanted to present "the religious ontology, cosmology and anthropology of St. Athanasius of Alexandria, Gregory of Nyssa and others" in the light of modern philosophical thinking. In contrast to materialism and idealism, Bulgakov develops the idea of "religious materialism." Part of this general plan was the substantiation of the "ontology of the economic process."[12] Making a "diagnosis" of his contemporary economy, Bulgakov notes that "economic

---

10   Bulgakov (1935) "Dokladnaya zapiska," 51; N. Vaganova observes that in *The Burning Bush* (1927) and in other later works "*everything is defined through Sophia*: 'man is created Sophia', 'the revelation of the Holy Trinity in the world is Sophia', 'the world is created Wisdom', 'hypostasis is a noetic ray of Sophia', etc." (Vaganova, N. *Sophiologia Protoiereya Sergiya Bulgakova* [The Sophiology of Archpriest Sergiy Bulgakov] (Moscow: PSTGU, 2011), 328) (Emphasis N.Vaganova's.).

11   Nikolai Sakharov, "Essential Bulgakov: His Ideas about Sophia, the Trinity, and Christ", *St Vladimir's Theological Quarterly* 55:2 (2011): 173.

12   Sergei Bulgakov, *Philosophy of Economy: The World as Household.* Trans., ed., and with an introduction by Evtuhov, Catherine (New Haven [Conn.]: Yale University Press, ca. 2000), 38.

materialism" should not be "denied, but overcome from within, explained in its limitations as a philosophical 'abstract principle,' in which one side of the truth is sold as the whole truth."[13]

Bulgakov distinguishes two types of historical eras according to the type of a person's attitude to material wealth:

> the era of asceticism (Buddhism, Franciscanism), when contempt for wealth is commendable; and the modern era that loves and believes in wealth, when life becomes an economic process.[14]

Speaking about the economic theory of his day, Bulgakov makes the following important observation, which is in many ways relevant even today: "In practice, economists are Marxists, even if they hate Marxism."[15]

Bulgakov links the economy with the concept of life as such while providing a preliminary definition of the economy. According to him, "life is the principle of freedom and organicism."[16] The whole world process is a contradiction between a mechanism, a thing, and an organism or life. The economy thus turns out to be a struggle for life. The economy, according to Bulgakov, is not a well-honed mechanism for extracting wealth from nature and the organization of material life. On the contrary, it is aimed at overcoming the mechanism in itself, as the beginning of necessity. Its task is to expand the realm of cosmic freedom, to transform a mechanism into an organism.

Therefore, on the one hand, the economy is actualized in man's defensive-offensive attitude to nature.[17] On the other hand, Bulgakov refuses to separate and oppose nature and spirit. This division and opposition carry death.[18]

In all of Bulgakov's above arguments, two fundamental ideas of Schelling are refracted: 1) the identity of the subject and the object 2) an understanding of nature as a living growing organism.[19] Schelling's philosophy is the starting point for Bulgakov's constructs. The universe is presented, in the light of the philosophy of identity, as a ladder of steps or "potentials," as an evolutionary development, the general content of which is the revelation of the spirit.[20] In

---

13   Bulgakov, *Philosophy of Economy*, 39.
14   Ibid., 40.
15   Ibid., 41.
16   Ibid., 70.
17   Ibid., 74.
18   Ibid., 84.
19   Ibid., 83.
20   Ibid., 85.

Bulgakov's understanding, Schelling's philosophy is an interpretation of Christian anthropology:

> Schelling expressed one of the most fundamental truths of Christianity in the philosophical language of his time. For Christianity is equally far from materialism and subjective idealism; it removes the contradiction between flesh and spirit in its teaching of man as *spirit incarnate*, the living unity of both."[21]

From Schelling Bulgakov also borrows the doctrine of the "world soul." The "world soul" is the highest unity of spirit and flesh, possessing the qualities of a universal (transcendental) subject, a universal spirit, and a universal object, the mother's womb of all creation.[22]

Individual human beings partake in this higher unity of the world soul. Various aspects of unity: embracing the spirit and matter of human nature, the unity of created nature, the unity of creation and the Creator are of paramount importance in Bulgakov's vision. When Bulgakov gives a sophiological definition of the economy, he answers the following fundamental questions: "How is economy possible? What are its a priori premises or preconditions? What is the philosophical significance of the essential functions of the economic process?"[23]

One might ask: what did Bulgakov mean by the sophianic nature of the economy? Above all, the sophianic nature of the economy is revealed in its teleological nature: "Economic activity overcomes the divisions in nature, and its ultimate goal—outside of economy proper—is to return the world to life in Sophia."[24] The beginning of the economy is also outside this world. Man is the natural ruler of the world and the vehicle of sophianism:

> Thus economic activity and investigation ('science'), the labor on a real and ideal object, began in an Edenic state, when the metaphysical essence of man's relation to the world was still unharmed, when he did not fear death or hunger, for the tree of life was accessible to him: the labor of cognition and action could here be performed only in a spirit of love toward God's creation. In this sense we can speak of

---

21 Bulgakov, *Philosophy of Economy*, 87–88 (Bulgakov's italics).
22 Ibid., 88.
23 Ibid., 94.
24 Ibid., 153.

the Edenic economy as the selfless loving effort of man to apprehend and to perfect nature, to reveal its sophic character.[25]

3. Bulgakov's Thought in Conversation with Modern Thinkers

In the 1970s, environmental problems came to the forefront of political debate, with philosophers and politicians discussing them publicly. It was in this decade that terms such as "deep ecology" and "ecological ethics" emerged. While the United Nations Framework Convention on Climate Change was adopted in 1992, it was only in 2015 that the Paris Agreement was signed--the first ever legally binding document on climate change under this convention. The main point of this agreement is that new technologies will be gradually introduced worldwide to minimize CO_2 emissions into the environment, in an attempt to reduce the risks associated with the main problem--global warming caused by the rapidly intensifying industrial activity of the past century.

However, it is difficult to disagree with the German philosopher Vittorio Hösle, who issued a warning back in 1994:

> Those who think that the ecological crisis can be dealt with the help of economic measures alone are mistaken. The ecological crisis is caused by the 'arrows' directing the movement towards specific values and categories, without correcting which we will never be able to start radical changes.[26]

Hösle was right. No radical changes have been considered to date. First of all, because the goals of economic activity remain unchanged: maximizing economic growth, increasing the material well-being of economic entities. No matter how beautiful the words national governments speak about ecology, their main goal is to maximize economic growth, to increase the population's consumption and incomes, or also to increase their own incomes, if we are talking about authoritarian rulers. Such international economic actors as international financial organizations and transnational corporations have economic growth as their priority. Further, economic indicators are used by economists for calculations, mathematical modeling of economic systems, being components of fundamental economic theories. It must be said that this is currently

---

25   Bulgakov, *Philosophy of Economy*, 154.
26   Vittorio Hösle, *Filosofia i ecologia*. [Philosophy and Ecology] (Moscow: AO "Kami", 1994), 7.

the dominant approach, and has been in recent decades. Mathematical modeling reigns supreme here, while philosophy, with ethics and morality, not to mention theology, is extremely marginalized.

In his paper "Central Fallacies of Modern Economics" (2018), Tony Lawson, professor of Economics and Philosophy at Cambridge, argues that "the modern discipline of economics is in some disarray, short on explanatory successes, largely detached from its subject-matter, and seemingly without clear objectives or sense of direction".[27] Lawson opposes mathematical modeling as the only proper or serious "scientific" way of doing economics. He wants to emancipate economics from this domination of mathematics. At the same time, he highlights that criticizing "the current mathematical modelling emphasis does not mean to adopt an anti-mathematics stance, pointing out that in social reality mathematic tools are generally inappropriate and more useful alternatives are available."[28]

He insists that economics should be concerned with questions of philosophy, in particular ontology, for which the Cambridge Social Ontology Group was formed. Hence, together with Tony Lawson, we can say that the main problem of modern economic theory is the methodological problem, the dehumanization of economics, the marginalization of interdisciplinary approaches, the brackets of fundamental philosophical issues. Peter Rona, from Oxford, goes further, arguing that "modern economics is an ideology presenting itself in scientific garment, but, in fact, it is promoting a particular agenda."[29]

We might remember Bulgakov in this respect, who says that all "economists are Marxists, even if they hate marxism" (see full quotation above). Rona questions the scientific status of economics and convincingly argues that at the core of modern economic theory lies a normative choice:

> Although its prescriptions are presented in a form that mimics the form of laws of the natural sciences, it is concerned with identifying the sort of behaviour that is most conducive to achieving its ideological ends, such as maximising efficiency, understood and measured as the return on capital employed. The choice of efficiency as the foundational value and its measurement as the return on financial capital employed, may or may be a "rational", a desirable or laudable choice, but is a normative choice, and not a science. Most importantly, its purported moral

---

27 Tony Lawson, "Central Fallacies of Modern Economics," 51.
28 Ibid., 60.
29 Peter Rona, "Objects of Nature and Objects of Thought," 30.

neutrality--obtained by the claim to scientific status--is a dangerous and destructive deception.[30]

The solution to the current crisis appears thus to have two stages. First, we need to recognize that the state of the world economy is conditioned by values, and therefore ethical, philosophical, and theological discourses should be considered in the global decision making. Only after such a recognition can we be in a position to begin to imagine a new economics. Attempts to offer answers of this kind have been made in various fields of knowledge; ideas about reforming economic theory can be said to be in the air. I do not pretend to cover all such attempts; I name only a few significant instances to set the context for a discussion of Bulgakov's thought relevant to this question.

For their part, economists are looking for ways to bring economics closer to humanitarian knowledge, including philosophy and theology. An outstanding example of this is the aforementioned research led by Tony Lawson at Cambridge. I have already mentioned another economist—Peter Rona, but would like to say a few more words about his "Economy as a Moral Science Project" at Oxford. A group of Catholic economists and theologians at Blackfriars (Oxford) are undertaking "to redefine the domain of economics so as to provide the foundation for reestablishing the spiritual nature of man when acting as economic agent".[31] Peter Rona argues that "free will, intentionality and moral judgement were excluded from economics," which resulted in creating an "unsatisfactory and unjust world." The idea that "facts can be separated from values in individual and group social action" is fundamentally wrong, but this is the foundation of modern economics. Isaiah Berlin wrote along these lines:

> As any description of what is, embodies an attitude, that is, a view of it in terms of what should be: we are not contemplating a static garden; we are involved in a movement with a perceptible direction; it can be correctly or incorrectly described; but any description must embody a valuation, that is, a reference to the goals toward which the movement proceeds, and in terms of which it can be 'understood' ...[32]

---

30   Peter Rona, "Objects of Nature and Objects of Thought," 30-31.
31   Peter Rona and Laszlo Zsolnai (eds.) Preface, *Economics as a Moral Science, Virtues and Economics 1*, Springer International Publishing AG (2017), v.
32   Isaiah Berlin, *The Sense of Reality* (New York: Farrar, Straus and Giroux, 1996), 130. (Peter Rona, "Postscript on Ontology and Economics," 186).

We can see here how the language of sophiology can be helpful in such a description, as indeed it includes a valuation and a reference to the goal, the divine Sophia in Bulgakov's thought.

A few economists and political scientists have questioned the materialistic understanding of economic development. They argue that development is a multi-dimensional phenomenon. It cannot be limited to GDP growth and must "include improvements not only in terms of welfare, but also of social conditions, political empowerment, the cultural foundations of self-esteem and ecological aspects."[33] Others point out that in 'the era of globality' there is an urgent need for complex and transdisciplinary approaches.[34]

At the same time, philosophers and theologians show a tremendous interest in economic knowledge.[35] This interest is evidenced by the many published articles and monographs, and even the emergence of a new subject: economic theology. We can mention here the recently published *Routledge Handbook of Economic Theology* (ed. Stefan Schwarzkopf, 2020) and *the Oxford Handbook of Christianity and Economics* (ed. Paul Oslington, 2014). The value of Bulgakov's *Philosophy of Economy* for modern environmental and ecological research has been pointed out recently.[36]

On considering all these publications, one can see how Father Sergii Bulgakov anticipated many of these problems more than a hundred years ago. An astonishing thing perhaps is that his ideas have not lost their relevance today. It would be more correct to say that his theological thought, including those aspects of it applied to economics, is more relevant than ever. It is striking how Bulgakov's Christian economic theology is resonant with more recent non-religious ethical proposals. For instance, Hans Jonas, the author of "The Imperative of Responsibility: In Search of an Ethics for Technological Age," develops the topic of environmental responsibility. He rejects the traditional ethical "anthropocentrism," which reduced the problem of moral responsibil-

33 Boda Zsolt, "Ethics of Development in the Age of Globalization," 246.
34 Francois Lepineux, and Jean-Jacques Rose, "Transdisciplinarity Governance and Common Good," 253.
35 An Orthodox perspective on economic development and bibliography can be found in: Vasilios Makrides, "Orthodox Christianity and Economic Development: A Critical Overview," *Archives de sciences sociales des religions* (Paris) Année 64, no. 185 (January–March 2019): 23–43.
36 Bruce V. Foltz, *The Noetics of Nature: Environmental Philosophy and the Holy Beauty of the Visible* (New York: Fordham University Press, 2014), Chapter 5; Elizabeth Theokritoff, "Green Patriarch, Green Patristics: Reclaiming the Deep Ecology of Christian Tradition," *Religions* (2017): 8, 116.

ity solely to the relationship between people. Nature, including as the basis of human existence, is considered by Jonas to be a kind of "subject" of morality. Jonas formulated the ethical imperative of responsibility for the "technocratic age," which had a profound influence on the development of environmental ethics: "Act so that the effects of your action are compatible with the permanence of genuine human life."[37] Yet, this kind of non-religious ethics can be called 'the ethics of fear,' which might seem effective for the purposes of pure survival while still being inferior to the Christian ethics of love, which is at the core of Bulgakov's sophiology and is reflected in the "Encyclical of the Holy and Great Council of the Orthodox Church" (2016).[38]

Conclusion

In conclusion, I would like to highlight some key observations regarding the question as to how Bulgakov's deliberations on Sophia can be helpful in tackling the ecological crisis and why it matters theologically. It seems undeniable that Bulgakov inspires Christians not to avoid economics; he urges us to take care of the created world out of love, with this in mind and in heart to translate the language of economics into the theological language. Following this, Christians should become the leaders of the ecological movement, creating and promoting the new global political paradigm. Above all, our hope is confirmed by St. Paul's words about little yeast which "leavens the whole batch of dough". (1 Corinthians 5. 6–8). Bulgakov's idea that "economic materialism" should be "overcome from within" means that when the new sophianic language acquires meaning in the sphere of economics, the old one will necessarily lose its power and attractiveness not only in the eyes of Christians; it can become a powerful missionary tool in converting the world to Christ.

---

37 Hans Jonas, *The Imperative of Responsibility: In Search of an Ethics for the Technological Age* (Chicago: University of Chicago Press, 1984), 11.
38 Cf.: "*The roots of the ecological crisis are spiritual and ethical,* inhering within the heart of each man." "Encyclical of the Holy and Great Council of the Orthodox Church" (Crete, 2016), *Holy Council,* accessed August 18, 2023, https://www.holycouncil.org/-/encyclical-holy-council?_101_INSTANCE_VA0WE2pZ4Y0I_languageId=en_US (access 2024/01/26).

Building the House of Wisdom
DOI 10.17438/978-3-402-12187-0

Bulgakov's Ecology

Austin Foley Holmes

> *Life is a creative activity and therefore history is a creative activity.*
> *(Unfading Light, 362)*

From his earlier *Philosophy of Economy* to the later trilogy *On the Divine Humanity*, Fr. Sergii Bulgakov (1871–1944) developed what amounts to a full-bore theological ecology. The term Ökologie was coined by the German zoologist Ernst Haeckel (1834–1919), whose work was well known to Bulgakov, in order to express the economy-like patterns of exchange and commerce among species living in shared environments (or "households").[1] This biological definition has since been superseded. Ecology now denotes a manifold pattern of thinking which is manifested across disciplines and is particularly at home in the humanities. Ecology attempts to think our ecological crisis of Global Warming/Mass Extinction by thinking its origin and its future. In particular, ecology thinks the relationality of humankind to the nonhuman and attempts constructively to open up new possibilities for that relationality. For a time, the ultimate horizon of ecological thought would rightly have been identified with the political. Today, however, ecology is in the midst of an *ontological* turn—the search for a metaphysics capable of bringing into being a politics and an ecological age of the future. Ecology is *the idea* of all-pervasive interconnectedness, and the thinking of that interconnectedness in and for everything.[2] Ecology, so understood, seeks a relational ontology. To think ecologically is to think relationality without reserve.

---

1   Bulgakov references Haeckel, e.g., in *Jacob's Ladder* (Grand Rapids: W.B. Eerdmans: 2010), 85–86.

2   Drawing on Timothy Morton, *The Ecological Thought* (Cambridge, MA: Harvard University Press, 2010).

This essay reads Bulgakov in concert with the ontological turn in contemporary ecology. Part I explores this ontological turn in three preeminent ecological thinkers: David Abram's animism, Freya Mathews's panpsychism, and the idea of "subscendence" in Timothy Morton's *Dark Ecology*. Then we turn to Bulgakov's own ecological thought. Part II considers the "world" (*mir*) in the God–Sophia relation, especially Sophia's status as the "world soul." Part III investigates Bulgakov's "Nature aesthetics" and his claim that the beauty of the natural world is a specifically *pneumatological* reality. Finally, Part IV assays Bulgakov's idea of the "humanization" of the world. Kenosis, self-creativity, synergy, and "love-humility" emerge as the simultaneous bases of Bulgakovian ecology.

Metaphysics in Recent Ecology

Ecological philosopher David Abram has argued that a sensuous attention to our surrounding environment reveals the fundamental reciprocity of being—the interplay between perceiving and being perceived.[3] His phenomenology of embodiment and language re-envisages human agency as communion with a "more-than-human-world" of other sensorial subjects rather than our unilateral action upon an inert background. This account of human agency is, for Abram, inseparable from "animism": a metaphysics which recognizes the communicative agency of every encountered being, from celestial bodies to blue herons; everything is ensouled and expressive.[4] Freya Mathews has argued for the coherence of a particular form of panpsychist metaphysics in which the universe is a "psychophysical unity," one whole bound together by the *sympatheia* of its disparate parts.[5] Like Abram, Mathews sees such a metaphysics as capable of eliciting a new kind of human agency in the world. The "blind matter of classical physics" becomes perceptible, in its truth, as a "subjectival matrix" in which the scientific order of manipulation is replaced by an erotic order of "dialogical engagement with a communicative world."[6] Whereas Abram grounds the communion of human and nonhuman subjects in reciprocal per-

---

3   David Abram, *The Spell of the Sensuous* (New York: Penguin Random House, 1997, 2017), 278. Abram draws especially on Merleau-Ponty, who underwent an ecological turn at the end of his life, shifting from an emphasis solely on the human body to the "flesh of the world" in the unfinished and posthumously published *Le visible et l'invisible* (Paris: Gallimard, 1964).

4   E. g., Abram, *Spell*, 262 f.

5   Freya Mathews, *For Love of Matter* (Albany: SUNY, 2003).

6   Ibid., 4–11; 45–69.

ception (the "reversibility of flesh"), Mathews articulates a formal monism: "This universal system or subject (the One) realizes itself through its creation, via self-differentiation, of a manifold of conative subsystems that possess a relative unity of their own, and hence qualify as derivative subjects (the Many). By following their own conative desire, the unself-conscious Many perpetuate the self-realization of the One."[7] Such a metaphysics may be compatible with Christian Neoplatonic thought.[8] What Abram and Mathews share, fundamentally, is a rhetorical habit of insisting on the primacy of re-immersing oneself in the natural world and cultivating attunement with one's environment. Each basically recommends, to borrow a term from ancient philosophy, a program of *theōria physikē* or "natural contemplation"—a concept now equally central to the field of Christian ecology.[9]

Timothy Morton's *Dark Ecology* treads another path. According to Morton, the widespread tendency of ecologists to narrate in their writing the experience of becoming re-immersed in Nature (e.g., "As I write this," followed by rich sensorial detail) actually perpetuates a version of Romantic consumerism: "a consumption of transformative experiences that presumes a liquid subjectivity akin to (indeed co-derived with) that generated by capitalism [...] the Romantic subject who aesthetically yearns for an impossible reconciliation with the alienated object (Nature)."[10] We rather need an ecology *without Nature*: an ecology which thinks *not* in terms of a harmonious natural whole that humankind can choose either to embrace (through re-immersion) or recklessly destroy, but rather an ecology which begins with the reality of the Anthropocene's ecological truth—i.e., the recognition of humankind's radical "loop-like" relationality to everything else, such that there is neither a pre-given nonhuman Nature nor a reified pure humanity disentangled from the nonhuman.[11] However, such an ecology should resist the temptation to simply replace the idea of humanity and Nature as two isolated entities with their combination into one larger whole, such as James Lovelock's "Gaia," since such a holism

7   Mathews, *For Love of Matter*, 9.
8   E.g., Eric Perl, *Theophany: The Neoplatonic Philosophy of Dionysius the Areopagite* (Albany: SUNY, 2007), 17–34.
9   E.g., Douglas Christie, *The Blue Sapphire of the Mind: Notes for a Contemplative Ecology* (Oxford: Oxford University Press, 2013).
10   Mick Smith, "Dark Ecology," *Environmental Politics* 20.1 (2011), 133–38 (136). See the use of Hegel's concept of the "beautiful soul" in Timothy Morton, *Ecology without Nature* (Cambridge, MA: Harvard University Press, 2007).
11   There is an intriguing isomorphism between Morton's rejection of pure humanity/pure nonhuman Nature and the twentieth-century Catholic debate concerning *natura pura*.

(plagued by a "theistic hangover") tends to regard the whole's parts as ontologically inferior and expendable.[12] The axiom that "the whole is always *greater* than the sum of its parts" must be inverted: "the whole is always weirdly *less* than the sum of its parts."[13] By thinking the interconnectedness of everything first, there then appears to be strangely less of everything in itself: rather than thinking of things in themselves as grandiose wholes (which Morton indexes to Aristotelian "substance" ontology) we should therefore think in terms of "*collectives*."[14] As Morton concedes, this is not to abandon wholes entirely but to think wholes differently through the primacy of multiplicity and relationality—the "subscendence" of the whole into its parts, which are suspended over the "first darkness" of their irreducible alterity. Thinking this *difference* as absolute, mediated by relation but never coalescing into identity—difference as the dark void which is first depressing, then uncanny, then sweet—is the thought of *Dark* Ecology.[15] Rather than humanity *and* Nature, or their monistic sublation, Morton opts for an ecological collective called the "symbiotic real" (a whole, to be sure, but an "implosive whole" which elicits its own subscendence into its ontologically greater parts). The Anthropocene is the contingent historical unfolding of the supra-relationality which humankind inherently *is*. A genuinely ecological politics, for Morton as for Slavoj Žižek, will declare that "the regeneration of the earth obviously does not depend upon our smaller and more mindful role—it depends on our gigantic role."[16] The paradox of the Anthropocene is that we are now confronted by our capacity to severely damage nature and feel the need to don sackcloth and go into exile precisely at the point where a human-led response is the only foreseeable salvation.

Each of these ecologies are more complex and compelling than this brief survey allows them to appear. For our purposes, Abram, Mathews, and Morton each represent interpretive lenses which, borne in mind, will enrich the following attempt to trace Bulgakov's ecological thought.

12 Morton, *Humankind* (London: Verso, 2017), 105–09.
13 Morton, *Dark Ecology* (New York: Columbia University Press, 2016), 12.
14 N. B.: Morton takes subscendence to mean simply that parts are *ontologically greater because numerically greater* than the whole they comprise—a claim which depends implicitly on a univocity of being and a negation of any ontological hierarchy.
15 See Morton's "object-oriented ontology," a form of modern realism "developed from a deep consideration of the implications of Martin Heidegger's version of modern Kantian correlationism" (*Dark Ecology*, 16).
16 Slavoj Žižek, "Last Exit to Socialism," *Jacobin* (July 7, 2021).

Bulgakov's Ecological Metaphysics

Bulgakov's idea of the "world" (*mir*) is ecological insofar as "world" is Bulgakov's primary category for thinking interconnectedness, with respect to both God and humankind. For Bulgakov, neither monism nor the dualism of some classical Christian models of creation are sufficient for elucidating the sophianic character of the God–world relation.[17] Dualism at least "recognizes the world's createdness," but it fails profoundly insofar as it thinks of the nothing out of which God creates as some sort of positive, non-divine reality (a "something" existing alongside of but alien to God). Creation has absolutely no ontological foundation other than God's own life. This eternal "foundation of the world in God" is essentially what Bulgakov means by the "sophianicity of the world." The Platonist doctrine of emanation is venerable insofar as it sees in its Absolute principle "the inexhaustible source of super-abounding being which is the outpouring of its wealth and fullness[.]"[18] The non-possessive love of God for creation, which makes possible the autonomy and freedom of creaturely life, involves the kenotic self-limitation of the Absolute:

> Creation is therefore an act of the measureless humility of the Absolute [...] *love-humility* is the ultimate and universal virtue of Christianity. It is the ontological basis of creation. By giving a place in itself to the world with its relativity, the Absolute in its love humbles itself before the creature—in truth the depths of divine love-humility are unsearchable![19]

To imitate this "love-humility," by which divine Love brings into being and loves what is non-divine (such that creaturely *difference* from and *unity* with God is guaranteed by one and the same divine loving), is the goal of Christian asceticism and also, as will become clear below, encapsulates Bulgakov's vision for how human agency should be operative in relation to the world.

Bulgakov thinks of Sophia as a demiurgic principle but is always very careful to distinguish Sophia's creative activity from the creative activity which is proper only to the Trinity. The conversion of absolute non-being into the primordial waters of cosmic potency, the dark void of *meonal* nothing, is accomplished by the "submergence" of Divine Sophia into non-being, her kenosis or

---

17 Sergii Bulgakov, *The Bride of the Lamb* (Grand Rapids: W. B. Eerdmans, 2002), 3–78.

18 Sergii Bulgakov, *Unfading Light* (Grand Rapids: W. B. Eerdmans, 2021), 183.

19 Ibid., 186.

diffusion into the multiplicity, temporality, and relativity of particular being.[20]
The fecund *meonal* nothing of the unformed world just is the light of Sophia
shining in the darkness of non-being. And it is her illumination of non-being
that makes God's creative activity not, properly speaking, one of cause and
effect. Rather, divine creativity is—by virtue of Sophia's presence—a dialogical
activity: "This is not creation out of nothing [since *creatio ex nihilo* describes
only that initial conversion of *ouk on* to *mē on*] [...] It is birth from the pro-
to-mother who is summoned to participate in her own way in creation: The
earth *responds* to the creative summonses of the Creator that are addressed
to her."[21] Scripture bears a direct witness to this collaboration: "Let the waters
bring forth abundantly the moving creature that hath life"; "Let the earth bring
forth the living creature" (Gen. 1:20, 24). This synergy between divine creativity
and the birthing power of the earth is what Bulgakov calls "God-creatureliness." The term is potent because analogous to the more commonly appearing
"God-manhood," a shorthand for the theandric interrelation and perichoresis
of Christ's divinity and humanity which, under Bulgakov's Neo-Chalcedonian
lights, involves a real mutuality that rules out the pure passivity of the human
nature in relation to the divine. Bulgakov insists that in Christ, the archetype
and source of God-manhood, "the human nature puts its imprint on the life
of the divine nature."[22] In the case of the Incarnation the basis for the created
principle's penetration of divinity can be attributed to Christ's human freedom,
which suggests that by "God-*creatureliness*" (assuming that God-creatureliness
has a meaning analogous to God-manhood) Bulgakov intends to signal that
even *nonhuman* created nature imprints itself on the life of the divine—i.e.,
is made a partner with divinity through an exercise of its own finite agency.

Sophia relates to creation as the "world soul," as both the vital force that fills
the world with a diversity of species and the foundation of the world's integrity.[23] "She is the life of the world." No part of the world, as such, is devoid of
Sophia's animative life-giving power. Bulgakov adds a qualification to this idea:
Sophia is "the soul of the world, *not* its spirit." This is because spirit is hypostatic
and Sophia is not a hypostasis: "The soul corresponds to the spirit's *nature*. The
soul lives and is hypostatized by the spirit (and, in this sense, the soul is not the
spirit's hypostasis but its hypostatizedness, or more precisely, its hypostatizability)." A consequence, therefore, of Bulgakov's doctrine of Sophia as the world

20   Bulgakov, *The Bride of the Lamb*, 79.
21   Ibid., 66.
22   Sergii Bulgakov, *The Lamb of God* (Grand Rapids: W. B. Eerdmans, 2008), 256–59.
23   Bulgakov, *The Bride of the Lamb*, 79–80.

soul is a recognition of the world's universal hypostatizability—the intrinsic connection of the world of nature (soul) to person (spirit) as the source and content of its actualized hypostatic life. This distinction between hypostatizability and hypostasis is, of course, Bulgakov's way of distinguishing divine Sophia and the divine Trihypostatic Person. In the case of *creaturely* Sophia (the world soul), her nature is hypostatized precisely by *creaturely* hypostases. Yet this hypostatization cannot be actualized by the demiurgic activity belonging to Sophia "who cannot communicate to creation what is not proper to her" (i. e., her vitalization of the world as its *soul* is not capable of positing its *spirit).*[24] "The creation of hypostases is therefore a special, additional or parallel act, alongside the creation of the world [...] if the world is created 'out of nothing,' that is, 'out of' the Divine Sophia [...] then the creaturely hypostases, the spirits that hypostatize the world, are directly created by God out of Himself[.]"[25] The creaturely Sophia is hypostatized by the human person whom the Trihypostatic Person creates "face to face."[26] The relation between the non-human natural world and human beings is therefore a finite repetition of the relation between Sophia ("the divine world") and the Trinity, which is why the relation of human beings to the world is Bulgakov's way of addressing what it means that human beings received the image of God: "The fullness of the divine image given to man, his nature, that is, *the world as belonging to man*, is sophianic, and this sophianicity of *the world in man* belongs, of course, to the fullness of the divine image."[27] The human person is a living icon of God, indeed a "creaturely god," precisely insofar as she actualizes a world as her own. This is why the image of God in humankind is known explicitly in their "dominion over the earth" (Gen. 1:26–28). What the image images is nothing other than the relationship between God and Sophia, the divine Persons and the divine nature or world. And for this reason, the human person's actualization of the world as her own cannot possibly denote a crude ownership of, or even a unilateral power over, the world as such. Humankind and the natural world, as creaturely hypostases and creaturely hypostatizedness, are mutually determining.[28] Their relation is one of genuine synergy (a Bulgakovian equivalent to Morton's "symbiosis") in which the nonhuman world, no less than humankind, is characterized by a

---

24 Bulgakov, *The Bride of the Lamb*, 84.
25 Ibid., 83–84.
26 Ibid., 87.
27 Ibid., 86.
28 Ibid., 100.

regal freedom, spontaneity, and its own peculiar creativity.[29] There are many levels of will and mind proper to the nonhuman: "one must completely eliminate the idea that the domain of non-hypostatized, natural being is completely alien to hypostatization, is a kind of dead matter [...] God did not create death. There are only different degrees of life on the way to its complete triumph and the complete hypostatization of being."[30]

We are now prepared to consider the Human-World relation which, according to Bulgakov, is the creaturely icon of this God–Sophia relation.

The Beauty of the World

Bulgakov seems to have been something of an amateur naturalist, generally spellbound by *flora* and *fauna* (especially birds) and eagerly up to date with the zoological science of his day (e. g., Haeckel). And it should not be overlooked that Bulgakov first encountered Sophia in the azure glow of the Caucasus Mountains.[31] Certain aspects of Bulgakov's idea of "Nature," obviously indebted to Romantic *Naturphilosophie*, are susceptible to Morton's critiques and undesirable for a future ecology. However, it would be a mistake to write off Bulgakov's account of the beauty of the natural world (his "Nature aesthetics") as naive sentimentality.

Nature's beauty bears a pneumatological signature. Bulgakov refers to the Holy Spirit as "the hypostasis of Beauty" who "clothes nature in beauty."[32] Bulgakov thinks Beauty is a pneumatological reality not only in the creaturely world but, eternally, in the divine world: i. e., Beauty as the proper life of the Third hypostasis. The Father's begetting of the Son is an exhaustive self-sacrificial kenosis which, on its own, cannot realize its self-revelation ("it is as if the dyad of the Father and the Son exhausts itself in this birth of the Word").[33] It is completed only "by *another* form of the self-revelation of the Father: by the procession of the Holy Spirit upon the Son."[34] The Holy Spirit is "the triumph of life-giving Love [...] the hypostatic movement of Love," i. e., the Love of the Father and the Son. In the Spirit's life as the hypostatic *unity* of the Father and

---

29   Ibid., 103: "The animal world is already called to build the world, and insofar as it is individual, this world is called to freely follow and actualizes its own laws in nature."

30   Ibid., 100.

31   Bulgakov, *Unfading Light*, 8–9.

32   Sergii Bulgakov, *The Comforter* (Grand Rapids: W. B. Eerdmans, 2004), 202.

33   Ibid., 179.

34   Ibid., 180.

the Son, as *their* Love, lies the Spirit's "*own* kenosis, which consists precisely in hypostatic *self-abolition* [...] the Third hypostasis loses itself, as it were, becomes only a *copula*, the living bridge of love between the Father and the Son, the hypostatic *Between*."[35] The Spirit's "hypostatizedness is [...] a non-hypostatizedness, a complete transparence for the other hypostases, a non-selfhood."[36] Or, as Bulgakov says in summary, this kenotic self-abolition of the Spirit, in which the divine life acquires its perfection, reveals that "Love is *Humility*," which Bulgakov again indexes to the "impersonality" of the copula disappearing in its linkage of subject and predicate. In the act whereby the Father begets the Son, God *knows* Himself as "the absolute Truth or Word," which is to say He reveals himself as "ideality" or "content."[37] In the act whereby the Father breathes the Spirit upon the Son, God *feels* Himself "as the actualized *reality* of this content, as *beauty*." Beauty is the *reality* of ideality; truth as *felt* distinct from truth as known; the pneumatic *actualization* (self-depleting unification) of subject and predicate. The dyadic unity of the Father's self-revelation, in the Word (Truth) and the Spirit (Beauty), grounds the circumincession "of the logical and the alogical, of ideality and reality" in God's own life, which Bulgakov identifies with divine self-positing—the artistry of God's self-creation.[38] "By the Spirit the Father inspires Himself in His own Word, and this self-inspiration is divine life, Beauty." Beauty is the Spirit accomplishing the Word. Beauty is God being made.[39] All of this pertains to the supra-eternal interrelation of the Trihypostatic life in its sacred order: the Word is the *Second* hypostasis, the *theme* of divine self-creation, the Art of the Father; the Spirit is the *Third* hypostasis, the Father's self-inspiration, which *realizes* the theme of divine self-creation ("In God, all things are actual and actualized in the Holy Spirit").[40] The beauty of the created world, too, radiates from the kenotic life of the Spirit (its cosmic Pentecost): "Life with nature and the joy of nature are accessible to every human being, even to the unbeliever if the breath of the spirit touches him. This mystery of love for nature and its effects on the soul, the joy of nature, attests to the spirituality of nature, to the grace of the Holy Spirit that inheres in it."[41]

---

35 Bulgakov, *The Comforter*, 181. See Joshua Heath, "Sergii Bulgakov's Linguistic Trinity," *Modern Theology* 37, 4 (2021), 888–912.
36 Ibid., 182.
37 Ibid., 180–82.
38 Ibid., 183–84.
39 This last phrase borrowed from my friend Terence Sweeney's insightful gloss on Beauty in Eriugena.
40 Bulgakov, *The Comforter*, 184.
41 Ibid., 202.

Bulgakov pairs this role of the Spirit with the angels, the "servants of Beauty."[42] The angels are the helmsmen of the natural world's poetic order: "The elemental life of the world [...] is protected and directed by the hypostatically conscious guidance of the angels," "Is it not by the angelic power implanted in them that flowers blossom? Is it not by their guardians that all forms of beauty, from the lowliest animal to the human body, are robed with beauty?"[43] The angels possess a uniquely *pneumatological* ontology: "Love does not seek its own [...] in their voluntary love they renounce *being in themselves*: they live only outside themselves, not *their own* life, in metaphysical self-kenosis."[44] Beauty, again, is the realization of the theme of the divine life: Beauty is the Spirit's kenotic "self-abolition" (as "Love-Humility") accomplishing the Word of the Father. The angels are the "artists of the world" because their lives, poured out into the creaturely Sophia, hymn an antiphon to the Spirit's kenosis. The beauty of the natural world *is* the manifestation of this Love for the creaturely Sophia. Yet we can be more precise, for the pneumatic movement of hypostatic Love is, in an absolute sense, *love for the Logos.*[45]

The Idea of „Humanization"

The creaturely Sophia receives its *logos*—its thematic center or captivating idea—in humankind.[46] The "mystery of human love for nature" is preempted by nature's love for humankind: to perceive the world's *beauty* is not to encounter an aesthetically pleasing series of passive objects; it is rather the sensorial experience of an attractive force which Bulgakov identifies with the outpouring of pneumatic-angelic love. This dyadic relationship between the natural world and humankind suggests, at a minimum, their mutual determination of one another (world–human *perichoresis*, Bulgakov might say). There are, for example, many texts in which Bulgakov describes a genuine synergy between humans and nonhuman animals: "The ability of animals to enter into communion with man [...] shows that animals participate in the world soul not only in its necessity but also in its creaturely freedom"; "The bounds that separate human from animal are not unconditional, but relative and constant-

---

42   Bulgakov, *Jacob's Ladder*, 84–86.
43   Ibid., 85.
44   Ibid., 162.
45   Bulgakov *The Comforter*, 180–81.
46   E. g., Bulgakov, *Unfading Light*, 293: "The human being is the logos of the universe in which the universe recognizes itself."

ly shifting."[47] We noted above that for Bulgakov the human person is a living icon of God insofar as she actualizes a *world* as her own. This intrinsic relation between the human person and the world is, however, not predetermined in its actuality. "Dominion" names a historical process in which the human relation to the world is open to the possibility of severe deterioration (N. B.: dominion itself is *not* optional—humankind cannot elect to abdicate; there is only the question of how humankind will rule).

The shape which humankind's relation to the world should take is what Bulgakov refers to as "humanization."[48] As Bulgakov developed the concept in his mature treatise on history; *humanization* refers broadly to the activity of personal creative spirit in the world, including "the entire domain of culture and civilization [...] no nations or epochs are excluded from this common human task in the world[.]"[49] And this creative history of humankind is not, properly speaking, at the service of any particular institution or authority ("humanity is not an *ancilla*, an obedient instrument [...] it is a goal for itself"), nor is the final content of humanization in any sense pre-determined.[50] Bulgakov often connects humanization to the meta-history of Eden. The naming of the animals and keeping of the Garden are paradisal expressions of humankind's capacity for elevating the self-creativity which is proper to nonhuman life.[51] This Edenic relationality (*dominion* in its true form) was not really a world "under man's rule" at all, but rather "the development of creation *with* man."[52] Earthly rulers inevitably govern by subjugation and a degree of coercion whereas gods—and human beings are called to become "created gods"—are not so limited in their exercise of power. But humankind abandoned this synergy with the world as its gods, opting to pursue instead "the conceit of gnosis before humbly believing love."[53] The ecstatic divine love once characteristic of humankind was supplanted by lustfulness for a possessive, anti-divine mode of dominion: "proprietorship" emerges here as part of the cursed reality of the world under the influence of Luciferian egoism.[54] Bulgakov describes this distorted mode of humankind's relationality as a "magism" that aspires to mastery and control, antithetical to

---

47 Bulgakov, *The Bride of the Lamb*, 103; 294.
48 Bulgakov, *The Comforter*, 202.
49 Bulgakov, *The Bride of the Lamb*, 320–23.
50 See Bulgakov's cautions against the "clericalization of history" at *The Bride of the Lamb*, 331 f.
51 Ibid., 102–03; 177 f.
52 Ibid., 179.
53 Bulgakov, *Unfading Light*, 322.
54 Ibid., 325.

the activity of humanization.[55] With humankind having abandoned its divine communion with the world, Nature drifts toward elemental chaos or enslavement to "blind instinct" rather than growing in Edenic intelligence and freedom. Nothing seems so basic to the world now as a constant chain of "natural disasters" and a necessary cycle of death and predation (evidence that "the forces of nature" are capable of becoming demonic).[56]

And yet, humanization remains an imminent possibility for the unfolding life of humankind and the world. It will require becoming free from the practices of ownership and impulses to mastery, i. e., Luciferian dominion, that have tended to characterize humankind's relation to the world. Economics can be systematically rethought, ecologically, as a vehicle for human creativity "to defend and spread the seeds of life, to resurrect nature."[57] As it is, the most powerful economies in the world today depend instead on a functional necromancy (the burning of carbon-dense "fossil fuels") presided over by an oligarchic class.[58] The path to another economic reality, according to Bulgakov, begins in the recognition of economy's compatibility with *art*. In our experience, economy and art seem related only by a natural antagonism: "art treats economy haughtily and contemptuously for its thrifty utilitarianism and lack of creative inspiration […] economy looks patronizingly on art for the impotence of its reverie and the involuntary parasitism."[59] Economy and art are two kinds of relation to the beauty of the world, two methods for unifying the real and the ideal (the latter of which only humankind can actualize as the *logos* of the world). Economy tends to attempt this unification, again, by magism. Art operates through elicitation, "the artist wants to *convince*" rather than master the world, to illuminate matter with beauty through poetic addition.[60] Art, properly conceived, is a practice of non-mastery and dispossession. But even art can be tempted toward mastery ("artistic magic"), and economy always contains an aesthetic minimum. Before their separation as "two perceptions of the world," in economic materialism and idealistic aestheticism, economy

---

55   Bulgakov, *Unfading Light*, 363.
56   Bulgakov, *The Comforter*, 206.
57   Bulgakov, *Philosophy of Economy*, 153. On the ecological importance of Bulgakov's economics, see Bruce V. Foltz, *The Noetics of Nature* (New York: Fordham University Press, 2013).
58   On "Necrosphere," see Enric Sala, *The Nature of Nature* (Washington, DC: National Geographic Partners, 2020), 123 f.
59   Bulgakov, *Unfading Light*, 367–69.
60   I am influenced here by Rowan Williams, *The Edge of Words* (London: Bloomsbury, 2014).

and art converged in a seamless Edenic life of human creativity ("efficacious," "life in harmony," "free of compulsion").

What we find in Bulgakov's meditation on art, at the end of *Unfading Light*, is his vision of a future humankind which, having suffered the divine pedagogy, has made its own that quintessentially godly *love-humility*. Artistic agency is a Bulgakovian way of thinking about ecological agency: the "humanization of the world" describes the task of creative human synergy with the world, that *kenotic* mode of creativity peculiar to art (and originating in the artistry of the self-creative life of God). This kenotic love-humility is what distinguishes humanization (understood as *Edenic* dominion) from the various tyrannical modes of human relation to its world. Kenotic love-humility, however, does not imply any degree of retreat from the world. As Bulgakov often insists, true Christian asceticism (which has the cultivation of this divine love-humility as its goal) is not an "acosmism"; it is rather an *angelic* mode of life: rapturous love in and for the world, "metaphysical self-kenosis," self-renunciation for the sake of absolute engagement with the creaturely Sophia. Love for the world, and creative synergy *with* (not over) nonhuman life, are not peripheral aspects of human personhood: for Bulgakov, these are our highest calling and our very path to deification. For this reason, humankind's ecological task is not less than, nor even other than, our very salvation.

SOPHIOLOGY

Building the House of Wisdom
DOI 10.17438/978-3-402-12188-7

The Reception of Palamite Theology in the Sophiology of Sergii Bulgakov

Liubov A. Petrova[1]

The primary concern of the sophiological theme in philosophy is the inter-relationship between God and the world, and the Sophiology of Sergii Bulgakov is no exception. The problem of the connection between God and the world is dominant and determinant in his work, and is connected with his basic philosophical and theological intuitions.[2]

It is common to consider *Philosophy of Economy* to be the first sophiological work of Sergii Bulgakov. Sophia is mentioned here only in the cosmological sense, as the principle of the overworldly unity of the empirical world, as the "single essence" of the world and the image of its extra-temporal being. Subsequently, Bulgakov developed his teaching on the connection between the world and God, the conceptual core of which was Sophiology.

As a teaching on the participation of the world in God, Sophiology in its various versions has the same foundation—the idea of the ideal prototype of the world in God, analogous to Plato's "noetic cosmos." Accordingly, the connection between the world and God within the frames of the Platonic paradigm is considered the connection of the empirical world with this ideal prototype, which manifests the principle of the unity of plurality in a rather Classical (Platonic) way. In this sense, from the very outset the sophiological disposition sets

---

1   The research was conducted with the support of the RSF, project № 18-18-00134, "The Heritage of Byzantine Philosophy in Russian and Western European Philosophy of the 20th–21st Centuries."
2   See Irina B. Rodnianskaia, "Chtitel' i tolmach zamysla o mire," in Sergii Bulgakov, "Svet nevechernii," in: *Pervoobraz i obraz: sochineniia v dvukh tomakh. T. 1.* (St. Petersburg: Inapress, Moscow: Iskusstvo, 1999), 12: "Bulgakov began to justify metaphysically such a strategy of Christianity, which [...] would save the world, taking on itself the responsibility for the sprouts of eternity granted to it which have the Divine genealogy. Here is the source of the sophiological topic which Bulgakov lifts upon his shoulders."

a rather concrete system of ontological coordinates, which fit into the Platonic philosophical tradition very well. Analogies to Platonic ideas and the "noetic world" are present in all sophiological constructions.[3] As for the attempts to create a Christian Sophiology, a comment by Sergei Khoruzhii seems quite fair: "each Christian Sophiology is from the very outset constructed within the line of Christian Platonism and is, in its philosophical essence, an attempt to combine, to unite the impersonal Platonic ontology of all-unity and the sharply personal Christian ontology of the trihypostatic God."[4]

These words can also be applied to Sergii Bulgakov, for whom Sophia is "the world of intelligible ideas," "the Divine world, existing in God "before creation," "primordial humanity in God" and so on. Let us quote a passage from Bulgakov:

> The world of ideas, the ideal *all*, which is actually contained in Sophia, exists for the creaturely world not only as foundation or causality (in the above-indicated sense) but also as the *norm*, the maximum task, the law of life, Aristotelian entelechy with respect to the potential state of being. Every entity has its idea-norm; it searches for and creates itself in keeping with a definite image that is proper to it alone, to its idea, but this is because it has in its supratemporal nature this idea as its single genuine being, τὸ ὄντως ὄν, as its unrepeatable individuality that cannot be confused with anything.[5]

However, a distinct feature of sophiological intuitions is the thesis that Sophia is not only the world of ideas and the principle of unity of plurality, but in some sense also possesses independence, acting as a separate entity or, as in Bulgakov's version, is personified and endowed with the attributes of a personal being (which does not prevent the formulation of the sophiological conception within the circle of Platonic notions). Sergii Bulgakov's texts, starting with the

---

3   See Sergei S. Khoruzhii, "O filosofii sviashchennika Pavla Florenskogo," in Pavel A. Florenskii, *Stolp i utverzhdenie istiny*, vol. 1 (Moscow: Pravda, 1990), xii: "Some kind of soil for sophiological ideas was always preserved in the Christian picture of being and first of all within the line of the tradition of Christian Platonism, where the analogies of Platonic notions of idea-eidos of each thing and the 'noetical world,' the gathering of ideas-eidoses of all things are present."

4   Sergei S. Khoruzhii, *Posle pereryva. Puti russkoi filosofii* (St. Petersburg: Aleteyya, 1994), 81.

5   Bulgakov, "Svet nevechernii," 201 (English translation [ET]: Sergius Bulgakov, *Unfading Light. Contemplations and Speculations*, trans. Thomas Allan Smith (Grand Rapids: W. B. Eerdmans, 2012), 227.

Philosophy of Economy and ending with such later works as *The Bride of the Lamb*, are rich in Platonic terminology and direct analogies between Sophia and "the world of ideas," which allows us to conclude that his metaphysical system as a whole has a tendency to be constructed within the tradition of Christian Platonism.

Gradually, in the course its development, the theology of Gregory Palamas acquires ever more significance in the sophiological conception of Sergii Bulgakov. We can see a transition from the Platonic to the Palamite language in his Sophiology. Externally, such a transition is conditioned by Sergii Bulgakov's closer acquaintance with the Palamite texts, which started some time before his writing of *Unfading Light*.[6] Internally, it is apparently conditioned by the fact that Sergii Bulgakov was not quite satisfied with some elements of the Platonic language, while the Palamite terminology corresponded to his sophiological intuitions to a greater degree. Indeed, in combining Christian dogmatic with Platonism, it is inevitable that some difficulties of both philosophical and dogmatic character appear, and the more straightforwardly such combining is pursued, the stronger the resistance of the two ontologies to one another; they are essentially incompatible. This circumstance seems to be sufficient ground for Sergii Bulgakov to include elements of the Palamite discourse in the scope of his theology.

We can judge the significance of Gregory Palamas' theology for Bulgakov's sophiological conception on the basis of his own statements. For instance, in a letter to Pavel Florenskii (1914) Bulgakov writes that he studies Gregory Palamas' texts and considers the publication of a translation of some of his major treatises "necessary and timely."[7] More than ten years later, in *The Burning Bush* (1927), Bulgakov states that the development of the positive teaching about Sophia is only possible on the basis of Gregory Palamas' teaching "on the energies

---

6   See Anna I. Reznichenko, "Genezis i artikuliatsionnye formy iazyka russkoi filosofii (S. L. Frank, S. N. Bulgakov, A. S. Glinka-Volzhskiy, P. P. Pertsov, S. N. Durylin): Istoriko-filosofskii analiz" (doctoral diss., Moscow, 2013), 127: "It is known that Bulgakov first became interested in Palamas' work as early as the mid-1910s. This interest became stable in the period of writing 'The Philosophy of Name,' the main portion of the text of which was created in 1918–19, and during the period of the writing of 'Hypostasis and Hypostaticity' (i. e., 1924) it became the foundation for the formation of the new model of correlation between God and the world."

7   *Perepiska sviashchennika Pavla Aleksandrovicha Florenskogo so sviashchennikom Sergiiem Nikolaievichem Bulgakovym*. Arkhiv sviashch. P. A. Florenskogo, vol. 4 (Tomsk: Vodoley, 2001), 78.

of God in their distinction from the hypostatical essence of God,"[8] and also that Palamas' teaching on Divine energies refers "in its inner meaning to the teaching on the Wisdom of God."[9] Finally, in *The Bride of the Lamb*, published in 1945, Bulgakov unequivocally states that "by accepting Palamism, the Church has definitely entered onto the path of recognizing the sophiological dogma."[10]

These evaluations of Gregory Palamas' theology by Bulgakov are reflected in the conceptual structure of his sophiological ontology, in the gradual change of its conceptual tools. In *Philosophy of Economy*, the first sophiological work by Bulgakov of 1912, Palamas is not mentioned at all and Sophia is interpreted predominantly in the Platonic vein as "primordial ideas," the "soul of the world," "κόσμος νοητός," and so on. In *Unfading Light* (1917) "Bulgakov uses Palamas' texts studied by him in the context of his deliberations and quotes Palamas' works, apparently, in his own translation."[11] However, Bulgakov applies the results of his studies not in the sophiological, but exclusively in the theological context, using the notion of "energy" to draw the distinction between the transcendental essence of God and his manifestations in creation: "By revealing himself to the creature, God is divested of his absolute transcendence and is manifested in his operation for the creature, in grace or (to use the expression of the dogmatic disputes of the fourteenth century) in his energies."[12] At the same time, the language of Sophiology in *Unfading Light* remains predominantly Platonic ("Ideal intelligible world," "eternal prototype of creation," "ideal seeds of all things," etc.).[13]

If in "Philosophy of Economy" Sophia is interpreted exclusively in a cosmological sense, the sophiological ontology of *Unfading Light* is essentially different. As Vasilii Zenkovskii notes, "the notion of Sophia, remaining a cosmological notion, bifurcates: Sophia is partly still within the confines of the

---

8   Sergii Bulgakov prot. *Malaia trilogiia* (Moscow: Obshchedostupnyi pravoslavnyi universitet, 2008), 162, note (ET: Sergius Bulgakov, *The Burning Bush*, trans. Thomas Allan Smith (Grand Rapids: W. B. Eerdmans, 2009).

9   Ibid., 182.

10 Sergius Bulgakov, *The Bride of the Lamb*, trans. Boris Jakim (Grand Rapids: W. B. Eerdmans, 2002), 19.

11 Dmitrii Biriukov, "Tema ierarkhii prirodnogo sushchego v palamitskoi literature. Ch. 2. Palamitskoe uchenie v kontekste predshestvuyushchei traditsii i ego retseptsiia v russkoi religioznoi mysli XX veka (Filosofiia tvorchestva S. N. Bulgakova)," *KONŠTANTÍNOVE LISTY* 12, 2 (2019), 7.

12 Bulgakov, "Svet nevechernii," 192 (ET, 215).

13 Ibid., 207: "The ontological basis of the world consists precisely in the continuous, metaphysically uninterrupted sophianicity of its foundation."

world, but partly already out of it."[14] "Two centers" are discovered in Sophia, which correspond to the Divine Sophia and the cosmic Sophia.[15] The first is Sophia addressed to God, which pertains to the inner-Divine life, while the second (in the Platonic vein) is directed towards the world, and is, in this sense "the world soul, i. e., the principle that links and organizes the world's plurality,"[16] "the beginning of a new, creaturely multi-hypostaseity."[17] The theological lens of *Unfading Light* introduces new motives into Bulgakov's sophiological intuitions, and it is not accidental that in a special excursus devoted to Palamas as an apophatic thinker Bulgakov pays attention to Palamas's drawing a sharp boundary not only "between the concept of οὐσία and the concept of the Holy Trinity, as that which is in God himself," but also between the "uncreated energies (ἄκτιστος) and creaturely, created being."[18] In this way Bulgakov emphasizes the cosmological aspect of Palamas' teaching and, as Natalia Vaganova notes, "finds the correspondence to his own sophiological positions in his teaching about the distinction of essence and energy in God."[19] In *Unfading Light*, Bulgakov considers Sophia a boundary between God and the world, uniting and separating them, μεταξύ in the sense of Plato,[20] at the same time imparted with hypostatical, personal attributes ("the fourth hypostasis"[21]).

Bulgakov's work *Hypostasis and Hypostaticity* (1925) can be considered a borderline between the Platonic and the Palamite ways of description of the reality of Sophia, as Bulgakov's mastering of "new logical and language space."[22] "Bulgakov seeks to think of Sophia, which had previously been understood in a Platonic way (as 'noetic essence', the 'perfect organism of Divine ideas') and, following Soloviev (as 'all-unity'), now in the Palamite way. He wants to 'translate' her into the energetic basis, presenting her as the unfolding world of Divine energies, distinct from the nature of the Divinity."[23] The Palamite notion of "energy" is now used by Bulgakov not only in the purely theological context,

---

14   Vasilii V. Zen'kovskii, *Istoriia russkoi filosofii* (Moscow: Akademicheskii proekt; Raritet, 2001), 849.

15   Bulgakov, "Svet nevechernii,"215 (ET, 245).

16   Ibid., 203 (ET, 229).

17   Ibid., 194 (ET, 217).

18   Ibid., 124 (ET, 134).

19   Natalia A.Vaganova, *Sofiologiia protoiereia Sergiia Bulgakova* (Moscow: Izdatel'stvo PSTGU, 2011), 109.

20   Bulgakov, "Svet nevechernii," 193 (ET, 217).

21   See in more detail in: ibid., 195 (ET, 218).

22   Vaganova, *Sofiologiia*, 318.

23   Ibid., 319.

but enters the conceptual structure of his Sophiology too. According to Bulgakov, Sophia is the revelation of the transcendental Divine essence in the same
sense as energy for Gregory Palamas is an act of God, in which his essence,
unknowable and unparticipatable in itself, is manifested. Such identification of
Sophia and energy turned out to be incompatible with understanding Sophia
as "the fourth hypostasis" (even if "of another order" than the hypostases of
the Trinity), which is probably connected to the fact that in Gregory Palamas'
treatise "Theophanes," which Bulgakov relies on,[24] energy is equally distinct
from both the essence and the hypostasis.[25] As a consequence—in *Hypostasis
and Hypostaticity* Bulgakov tries to revise this definition of Sophia, defining
Sophia not as a hypostasis, but as a special state of being—"hypostaticity,"[26] at
the same time not ceasing to think of it as a "living intelligent reality."[27]

Subsequently, in the course of ripening and detailed elaboration of Bulgakov's teaching on Sophia, Palamite motives in her interpretation grow stronger
and stronger. Thus, in *The Burning Bush* (1927) Sophia is presented as "*energy
of God's energies* which alone are accessible to the creature, given the complete
inaccessibleness ('transcendentalness') of God's very essence,"[28] "energy,' [...]
God's operation in creation."[29] Unlike the Sophia of *Unfading Light*, the Sophia
of *The Burning Bush* "is not a Divine Hypostasis, she is the life, action, revelation, 'energy' of the Divinity, which is worshipped in the Holy Trinity."[30]

However, in Bulgakov's later works the line of identification of energies with
Sophia is interrupted. In *The Lamb of God* (1933), the notion of "energy" is used
almost exclusively in the historical-theological context in the discussion of the
formation of the Christological dogma about the two wills and two natures.

24   Biriukov D. Tema ierarkhii prirodnogo sushchego ..., v palamitskoi literature. Ch. 2. Pa-
      lamitskoe uchenie v kontekste predshestvuyushchei traditsii i ego retseptsiia v russkoi
      religioznoi mysli XX veka (Filosofiia tvorchestva S. N. Bulgakova)," *KONŠTANTÍNOVE
      LISTY* 12, 2 (2019), 7.
25   See Gregory Palamas, *Theophanes*, 12.10: οὐδεμία γὰρ τῶν τοιούτων ἐνεργειῶν
      ἐνυπόστατος, τουτέστιν αὐθυπόστατος ("none of the energies is not en-hypostatic,
      that is, self-hypostatic").
26   Reznichenko, *Genezis i artikuliatsionnye formy iazyka russkoi filosofii (S. L. Frank, S. N.
      Bulgakov, A. S. Glinka-Volzhskiy, P. P. Pertsov, S. N. Durylin)*: Istoriko-filosofskii analiz":
      (doctoral diss., Moscow, 2013), 89.
27   Protopresbyter Sergii Bulgakov, "Hypostasis and Hypostaticity: Scholia to The Unfad-
      ing Light," trans. Anastassy Brandon Gallaher and Irina Kukota, *St Vladimir's Theolog-
      ical Quarterly*, 49, no. 1–2 (2005), 27.
28   Bulgakov. *Malaia trilogiia*, 137 (ET, 118).
29   Ibid., 159 (ET, 138).
30   Ibid., 164 (ET, 142).

As for the theology of Gregory Palamas, Bulgakov expresses in passing his hesitation regarding the adequacy of his terms οὐσία and ἐνέργεια.[31] At the same time, the way of thinking about the reality of Sophia changes: firstly, it is identified with the Divine essence, and secondly, the distinction between "the created Sophia" and "the Divine Sophia" is pursued by Bulgakov in a more definite and sharp way than in the previous periods. As Anna Reznichenko notes, "the ontological status of Sophia in relation to the persons of the Trinity in Bulgakov's system of the 1930 is more fixed and distinct: Sophia is *ousia*, i. e., that which is common to all hypostases, by the relation to which their personal character is defined."[32] These changes are very serious in comparison with the version of Sophiology presented in *Hypostasis and Hypostaticity*, where Bulgakov emphasized that Sophia must be strictly distinguished from the essence or nature of God and understands her as energy and "the revelation of the Tri-hypostatic God about himself"[33] par excellence.

The device of referring to Gregory Palamas in Bulgakov's last work, *The Bride of the Lamb* (published posthumously in 1945), points to the distancing of Sophiology from the Palamite discourse. Sophia is no longer defined as "energy"; the most we can find here is speaking about the "energies" of Sophia with reference to the Palamite language.[34] There are also some analogies with Palamas' theology of rather secondary character, which does not add anything to the basic conception. At the same time, we see Bulgakov's multiple critical judgments about Palamism. In one passage, Bulgakov notes that "Palamas considers the energies primarily in the aspect of grace, the supracreaturely 'light of Tabor' in the creaturely world," while these energies have, first and foremost, "a world-creating and world-sustaining power which is a property of Sophia."[35] At other junctures Bulgakov formulates what he sees as the main shortcoming of Palamist theology—the lack of clarity in his description of the relation between the Divine hypostases of the Trinity and energies: "Palamas' doctrine of essence and energies is not brought into connection with the dogma of the Trinity, in particular with the doctrine of the three hypostases as separate persons and of the Holy Trinity in unity."[36] The applicability of Gregory Palamas' ideas within the confines of Sophiology is limited by his "fundamental idea" of the "multi-

---

31   Sergius Bulgakov, *The Lamb of God* (Grand Rapids: W. B. Eerdmans, 2008), 122, note 2.
32   Reznichenko A. I. *Genezis i artikuliatsionnye formy iazyka russkoi filosofii …*, 91.
33   Bulgakov, "Hypostasis and Hypostaticity: Scholia to The Unfading Light", 25.
34   Bulgakov, *The Bride of the Lamb*, 63.
35   Ibid., 18–19.
36   Ibid., 18.

plicity and equi-divinity of the energies in God," which "discloses 'the manifold wisdom of God,'" while he proclaims the rest of Palamism to be "an unfinished sophiology"[37] which awaits its future interpretation and sophiological application—the same way Platonism is characterized in *Unfading Light*.

So, speaking about Bulgakov's Sophiology, we cannot speak about its passage from the Platonic to the Palamite language, but only about the temporary convergence of its ontological model with the Palamite one, which later, in the course of the development of Sophiology, revealed its limits.[38] The reasons for Bulgakov's refusal to follow the Platonic model fully are understandable: Platonism satisfied his tendency to establish a solid connection between the world and God, to justify the world, to ground it in Sophia. However, establishing the correlation between the world and God, it was necessary to preserve their essential difference, fixed dogmatically, while the Platonic model tends towards the idea that the cosmos and its beginning have the same nature and towards understanding creation as an act subdued to necessity. For Bulgakov, none of these perspectives was acceptable, at least if judged on the basis of his critique of the conceptions of emanation. As Irina Rodnianskaia notes,

> it is not very easy to unite the Platonic 'noetic place,' where, according to the Hellenic thinker, 'ideas' are placed, with the theistic notion of God. For the intelligible world of ideas, according to Classical thought, belongs to the cosmos and cannot be painlessly 'reassigned' to the God of theism, because there is an ontological abyss between him and the cosmic, 'created' being.[39]

Moreover, within the confines of Platonism the connection between the world and the Divine reality is realized in its "ideal" aspect, while the "material" aspect remains in the shadow of non-being. But for Bulgakov it was fundamental to justify the actual, becoming world, the world as history, and not only its ideal prototype. This is the basis of his characterization of Plato's and Plotinus' cosmologies as "unfinished" and "defective": their matter is empty, they "are entirely ignorant of sophianic earth, the mother Demeter."[40] On the other hand,

---

37   Bulgakov, *The Bride of the Lamb*, 18.

38   This is one of the reasons why Natalia Vaganova speaks about the "unfinished project" of re-orienting Sophiology from the Platonic to the Palamite ontological model. See Vaganova, *Sofiologiia*, 370.

39   Rodnianskaia, "Chtitel' i tolmach zamysla o mire," 12–13.

40   Bulgakov, "Svet nevechernii," 216 (ET, 246).

Palamism allowed the connection with God to include the material historical actuality of the world.

What was, then, the obstacle for the complete and consistent reformulation of Bulgakov's Sophiology in terms of the Palamite ontological model? Apparently, Bulgakov's critique of Palamas' theology for the lack of connection between his doctrine of energies and the triadological dogma shows that Bulgakov himself wanted to connect them, to correlate the reality of Sophia with the hypostatical being of God.

Bulgakov formulates his own version of the Trinitarian theology in his *Chapters on Trinity*, published in 1928, soon after his "Palamitic" *The Burning Bush* (1927), but some time before the "non-Palamitic" *The Lamb of God* (1933). In this work Bulgakov solves the issue of the correlation of essence and hypostases in God. It is solved in such a way that nature, understood as "potentiality," present as "the bosom of being" and "unlit darkness" in the created "I," in relation to God, in whom there can be nothing potential, but everything is actual, loses all features of independent reality, becoming completely en-hypostasized and coinciding with the hypostatical element: "there is no nature which is not hypostatical or out-of-hypostasis; on the contrary, all life of the Divinity is en-hypostasized (ἐνυπόστατος)."[41] "Attempts to look beyond personality to see substance behind it, are inappropriate here. It is true that in the Divinity there is no hypostasis without essence, as well as no essence without hypostasis, for in the Divinity they are perfectly fused and inseparable, and differ only by conditional human abstraction."[42] And further on: "the contra-distinction of hypostasis and essence appeared as an auxiliary logical means in the age of Arian controversy and the very notion ομοουσιος has a negative meaning first of all."[43]

This is Bulgakov's way of understanding the problem of correlation between essence and hypostases in God radically influenced his sophiological conception, provoking its distancing from the Palamite model. In the main text of the *Chapters on the Trinity* the subject of Sophia is not present, but in the initially unpublished draft manuscripts,[44] which act as a continuation of the *Chapters,*

---

41 Sergii Bulgakov, *Trudy o troichnosti* (Moscow: OGI, 2001), 88.

42 Ibid., 131.

43 Ibid., 132, note.

44 See Anna I. Reznichenko, "'Vse vremennoe est' splav iz nichto i vechnosti': eshche raz o trinitarnoi ontologii prof. prot. Sergiia Bulgakova (k 150-letiyu so dnia rozhdeniia)," *Philosophy. Sociology. Art History* 4 (2021), 19: "The first publication of the 'Chapters' took place in the pages of the Parisian magazine 'Orthodox Thought' in 1928 and 1930, with comments by the author. A reissue of the 'Chapters' was already undertaken in

Sophia reappears in the context of Bulgakov's thoughts on the question of God's relation to the world. Here, considering the definition of the Trinity as *unum universorum principum*, adopted at the Fourth Lateran Council, Bulgakov argues that it cannot be attributed to the Trinity as such, but only to its Divine world, via which the Trinity is facing creation. Bulgakov distinguishes between the inner unity of the Holy Trinity, which can be thought of as *ousia* (or "the triune Divine Subject himself in His life"[45]) and the unity of the Holy Trinity in the creation of the world. This second unity is the very "content of this divine Life, the condensed cloud of God's self-revelation or the Glory of God,—the Divine Sophia, the Divine world, the one Origin of Creation in God."[46] At the same time, according to Bulgakov, the second not only does not coincide with the first, but in no way comes from the first. Now we have two separate kinds of Divine unity: "the unity of the world,—writes Bulgakov—is not based on the unity of the divine *ousia* that is common to three hypostases (as follows from the Catholic understanding), because this *ousia* is not revealed in its unity except in the life of three hypostases [...] The unity of the world is based on the fact that the unified, although tri-hypostatic God, also has a unified revelation of His Own (the Divine World — Sofia, *L. P. note*)."[47] Thus, Sophia is no longer understood by Bulgakov as a revelation of the transcendent divine essence on the model of the Palamite energy, but acts as some independent principle of world unity, rooted in the unity of the divine world.

In the later works published after the *Chapters on the Trinity* in the thirties, Bulgakov no longer understands Sofia as energy, and gradually its conceptualization approaches the concept of the divine essence, replacing it with itself. He speaks about Sophia as essence for the first time in *Icon and Veneration of Icons* (1931),[48] and the sophiological ontology of the further works, *The Lamb of God* and *The Bride of the Lamb*, is predominantly built on identifying Sophia and *ousia* (essence). As Natalia Vaganova notes, "in 'The Lamb of God' Bulgakov

     post-Soviet Russia. Only in 2009, in the Sergius Bulgakov Foundation in the Archive of the St. Sergius Institute in Paris, we discovered a continuation of the 'Chapters' (with some failure in the numbering of sub-chapters), and only at the end of 2021 did this text finally see the light."

45   S. N. Bulgakov: *Pro et contra, anthology.* St. Petersburg: RHGA, 2021, 168.

46   Ibid., 168.

47   Ibid., 169.

48   See Sergii N. Bulgakov, *Pervoobraz i obraz: sochineniia v dvukh tomakh. T. 2. Filosofiia imeni. Ikona i ikonopochitaniie. Prilozheniia* (St. Petersburg: Inapress, Moscow: Iskusstvo, 1999), 263: Sophia is "the Divinity of God and the Divinity in God, and in this sense she is also the Divine world before its creation."

uses the model of correlation between hypostasis and nature in the Divinity, which he developed in 'Chapters on Trinity,'"[49] and this model happened to be definitive: "the proposition that the nature is hypostatized in God," Bulgakov writes, "has a fundamental significance for sophiology."[50]

Evidently, if Sophia is *ousia*, it is not energy anymore, for, according to Gregory Palamas, though energy is uncreated, it is different from essence. Complete en-hypostasizedness of the Divine nature and its reduction to the status of an auxiliary logical means bereaves the basic Palamite ontological judgment ("essence and energy") of one of its conjuncts, thus destroying it and depriving it of its distinctness. Sophia cannot be energy anymore, for as such, not having essence, it has nothing to differ from. At the same time, the very notion of energy, which in Bulgakov's understanding is the "active voice in relation to passive voice,"[51] disintegrates. If "energy is the action of nature, nature in action,"[52] then in relation to the Divine reality, which cannot be ascribed anything "passive," the notion of energy loses its predicate and essential attribute. Indeed, considering the Christological debate of St. Maximus the Confessor with the Monothelites (in which Maximus correlated will with nature, while the Monothelites regarded will as an attribute of hypostasis), Bulgakov concludes: "From our present perspective this dispute appears to be academic. In essence, both sides are wrong. Both will and energy are manifestations of the life of the spirit, contained in itself and revealing itself for itself (or ad extra). But the spirit is the living and inseparable unity of person and nature, so that in concreto there is no impersonal nature or natureless personality; they can be separated and even opposed only in abstract."[53]

The "anti-essentialist" move by Bulgakov, according to whom "personality is essence and, vice versa, essence is personal principle,"[54] turns the notion of energy into as an "auxiliary logical means," as the notion of essence. And, as usually happens to means, its necessity falls off simultaneously with the disappearance of the field of its application. Understanding God as the "inseparable unity of person and nature" makes the assumption of "natural energy" in him redundant and the vacant space is occupied by the reality of Sophia, who, in her "Divine form," combines *ousia* and the uncreated energy, and in her second,

---

49   Vaganova, *Sofiologiia*, 336.
50   Bulgakov, *The Lamb of God*, 97, note.
51   Ibid., 106.
52   Ibid., 75.
53   Ibid., 77.
54   Bulgakov S. N. *Trudy o troichnosti*, 130.

"cosmic" form, retains Bulgakov's Platonic intentions in explaining the foundations of the created world. We will omit the question of how well-founded and necessary was the affirmation of the reality of Sophia as the essence and energy in God. What appears quite clear is that Bulgakov's refusal to follow the logic of Palamism in his sophiological conception was connected to the incompatibility of the ontological disposition, posed in his trinitarian doctrine, with Gregory Palamas' basic thesis about the distinction between the Divine essence and energies.

Still, even in the later period of his work Bulgakov discovers in Gregory Palamas' theology something akin to his own intuitions, lying beyond any particular terminology. In *The Lamb of God*, formulating the thought that the notion of God is relative, for the relation to the world is contained in it from the very beginning, Bulgakov notes that Palamas's distinction between οὐσία and ἐνέργεια is connected to this correlation between God and the world:

> In practice, God exists only as energy, whereas God in Himself, Deus absconditus, simply does not 'exist.' In Himself, He is the darkness of the Absolute, to which even being is inapplicable. But in God's energy, His *ousia* is known; His *ousia* begins to exist only in relation. Thus, Palamas' fundamental schema is the idea of God as the Absolute-Relative, the inclusion of relation (but of course not relativity) in the very definition of God."[55]

Here Bulgakov detects behind the Palamite dichotomy of essence and energy something close to the pair of notions "essential" and "existential": if energy is the manifestation of the Divine essence, then the predicate of existence can be applied only in relation to it, for "to exist is to be for another."[56]

It is evident that the character of the reception of Palamism in Sergii Bulgakov's Sophiology in the course of its development is heterogeneous: a period of convergence, connected with the application of notion tools of Gregory Palamas's theology, is succeeded by a period of critical distancing. These "oscillations" are apparently connected to Bulgakov's search for a more adequate expression for his initial sophiological intuitions. Bulgakov was interested in Gregory Palamas's theology not as such but almost exclusively to the extent in which it was able to open the way to overcoming the contradictions between understanding God personally, which is essential for Christianity, and the Platonic intuition of the divinity and unity of the cosmos. As a consequence, the

55   Bulgakov S. *The Lamb of God*, 122, note 2.
56   Ibid., 121.

point where the explaining resources of the Palamite model come to an end happens to be the borderline for its application in Sergii Bulgakov's sophiological conception.

Building the House of Wisdom
DOI 10.17438/978-3-402-12189-4

An Unfinished Dispute. How is it Possible to Criticize Bulgakov's Sophiology at the Present Time?

Natalia Vaganova

Bulgakov's sophiology has been generating heated controversy for more than a hundred years. It was Evgenii Trubetskoi who first undertook a critical attack on this doctrine, long before the famous "Paris dispute." In 1918, immediately after the publication of Bulgakov's book *The Unfading Light*, E. Trubetskoi, in his book *The Meaning of Life*, pointed out what he considered to be Bulgakov's principal mistake: "He thinks of Sophia in a gnostic way, portrays her as an independent eon."[1] No exchange of views followed Trubetskoi's speech, and this was hardly possible under the well-known historical circumstances.

E. Trubetskoi's critical remarks were purely philosophical and were addressed to Bulgakov's main philosophical work. In emigration, after Fr. Sergius turned to theology and began to develop his teaching on theological grounds, the controversy, accordingly, acquired a theological character. This stage is perfectly documented, its chronological outline is well known,[2] and there is con-

---

1   Evgenii N. Trubetskoi, *Smysl zhizni* (Moscow: Respublika, 1994), 99–100.
2   See Vladimir N. Losskii, *Spor o Sofii: "Dokladnaia zapiska" prot. S. Bulgakova i smysl Ukaza Moskovskoi Patriarkhii* (Paris, 1936) (republished: Vl. Losskii, *Spor o Sofii. Stat'i raznykh let* (Moscow: Sviato-Vladimirskoe Bratstvo, 1996); Vladimir N. Losskii "Spor o Sofii" in *V. N. Losskii. Bogovidenie* (Moscow: ACT, 2006)); Iurii P. Grabbe, *Korni tserkovnoi smuty. Parizhskoe bratstvo Sv. Sofii i rozenkreitsery* (Belgrade, 1927); Pavel N. Grabbe, *O parizhskikh "bogoslovakh"* (Rovno, 1937); Nikolai Arsen'ev, *Mudrovanie v bogoslovii?* (Warsaw, 1936); Sergii Bulgakov, prot., "Eshche k voprosu o Sofii, Premudrosti Bozhiei. Dokladnaia zapiska mitr. Evlogiiu. Ianvar' 1936," *Prilozhenie k zhurnalu "Put'"*, no. 50 (1936): 1–24; Gennadii (Eikalovich), igum., *Delo prot. Sergiia Bulgakova. Istoricheskaia kanva spora o Sofii* (San Francisco, 1980); Modest A. Kolerov. "Bratstvo Sv. Sofii: "vekhovtsy" i evraziitsy (1921–1925)," *Voprosy filosofii* 10 (1994), 159–62; "K voprosu o tak nazyvaemom "edinolichnom mnenii" mitropolita Sergiia," *Simvol* 39, Iiul' (1998), 151–85.

siderable research literature. A recent study by Andrei K. Klementiev, based on a number of documents, reveals the history of the "Paris disputes" completely.[3]

Twenty five years after Bulgakov's death, Protopresbyter John Meyendorff stated that sophiological problematics had been exhausted as a scientific issue and would no longer be able to awake any interest among new generations of researchers.[4] This conclusion, as we can see, has proved to be premature. Not only Bulgakov's doctrine, but also the sophiological project as a whole, has recently received renewed attention. Sophiology research has reached a new stage, attracting more and more interest. Nevertheless, a suspicious shadow of heresy still lies over this religious and philosophical teaching. Therefore, a new appeal to this criticism of Bulgakov's teachings seems quite important. We need a critical revision of the very criticism of sophiology, that is, we need criticism of the criticism—those positions, arguments, and accusations that we have heard before. Such a "methodological shift" is necessary in order to move on to a substantive criticism of sophiology, which means the separation of the *living* from the *dead* in this teaching and the identification of both the internal moment of the theological and philosophical *crisis* and possibilities of finding a positive way out of the current situation. The purpose of this article is to outline some possible approaches to dealing with this problem.

Let me begin with theological aspects. First of all, we have to admit that criticism of Bulgakov's sophiology from the theological perspective *has completely failed*. The overwhelming majority of its blows missed the target; therefore, despite a number of very serious accusations, this criticism did not inflict *the slightest* damage on Bulgakov's doctrine (except, perhaps, his reputation). To put it simply, Bulgakov's opponents forced an open door, without affecting the essence of the doctrine. If we briefly list what exactly Bulgakov was accused of during the "Paris dispute," we will see a very variegated and rather chaotic picture. Bulgakov's sophiology proves to be a unique teaching that does not correspond to anything.

They pointed out the discrepancy between sophiology and the key provisions of Orthodox dogmatics, an "archaeological" attitude towards the tra-

---

3   See Andrei K. Klement'ev, "Materialy k istorii polemiki o tvorchestve professora protoi-ereia Sergiia Nikolaevicha Bulgakova (1924–1937 gg.)," *Vestnik Ekaterinburgskoi dukhovnoi seminarii* 2, no. 26 (2019), 275–370.

4   See John Meyendorff "Orthodox Theology Today" in *John Meyendorff. Living Tradition: Orthodox Witness in the Contemporary World* (Crestwood, NY: St. Vladimir's Seminary Press, 1978), 167–87 (first published: St. Vladimir's Theological Quarterly, 13, no. 12 (1969), 77–92).

dition of the Church, the deviation into Catholicism, a sympathetic attitude towards Origenism, Nestorianism, Appolinarism, etc. Particular criticism was caused by Bulgakov's alleged "introduction" of the "fourth hypostasis" into the Holy Trinity. Along with accusations of Gnostic dualism, the doctrine was defined as emanative-pantheistic. They pointed to impersonalism, determinism, mythologism, rejection of the principles of apophatic theology, insufficient detachment from purely philosophical methods and rational techniques of cognition that impudently invade the "sanctuary of faith"—and, at the same time, excessive "creative imagination" in theological constructions.

According to Fr. Sergius Chetverikov, Bulgakov disdained "preserving ecclesiastical like-mindedness" and rated "the freedom of his individual theological creativity"[5] above it. Metropolitan Sergius (Stragorodskii) and Vladimir Lossky were convinced that Bulgakov's sophiological synthesis is faced with unsolvable contradictions in the construction of Triadology and Christology, and that, in general, "the main principle on which all his teaching about Sophia is built—the Wisdom of God [...] is not church-grounded, and the system built on it is so independent that it can either replace the teaching of the Church, or succumb to it, but cannot merge with it."[6]

The "new doctrine of Sophia" was condemned as heresy in the definitions of the Sremski Karlovtsy Synod, especially with respect to everything that concerned the "feminine principle in God," called "a special being or hypostasis, although not consubstantial with the Holy Trinity, but not completely alien to It," or "not the Hypostasis, but only [...] the hypostatisity, which, however, is capable of being hypostasized, that is, becoming the Hypostasis," as well as "a being that surpasses Mother of God," or identified with the Mother of God.[7] The works of Archbishop Seraphim (Sobolev) were rigorously condemnatory. Metropolitan Evlogii (Georgievskii), in a private letter to Bulgakov, describes the method of argumentation used in these works as follows: with a large amount of collected material, these works are markedly simple, even primitive. It seems like a list of references written according to the following

---

5   Quoted by Andrei K. Klement'ev, "Materialy k istorii polemiki o tvorchestve professora protoiereia Sergiia Nikolaevicha Bulgakova (1924–1937 gg.)," *Vestnik Ekaterinburgskoi dukhovnoi seminarii* (2019), 310.

6   Vladimir N. Losskii "Spor o Sofii," in *V. N. Losskii. Bogovidenie* (Moscow: ACT, 2006), 24.

7   See "Okruzhnoe poslanie Arkhiereiskogo Sinoda Russkoi Pravoslavnoi Tserkvi Zagranitsei," *Tserkovnye vedomosti. Sremski Karlovtsy* 17/18 (1927), 2–4 (Klement'ev, "Materialy k istorii polemiki o tvorchestve professora protoiereia Sergiia Nikolaevicha Bulgakova," 287).

method: "Here is the teaching of Holy Fathers, and here is a completely different teaching of S. Bulgakov."[8]

More temperate voices urged that Bulgakov's doctrine be treated as an ec-
clesiastically acceptable theologumen (Zen'kovskii); they proposed considering the issue in a broader sense—in terms of the freedom of theological-dog-
matic research and the possibility (or impossibility) of dogmatic development
in general (Kartashev). The professors of the St. Sergius Institute (Vysheslavt-
sev, Fedotov, Veidle, Zander) supported Bulgakov; however, it should be noted
that, with the exception of Zander, they did not defend Bulgakov's teachings,
but rather defended his flawless pastoral reputation and good name.

It may be stated that the entire "trial" of the "Bulgakov case" was largely
due to the internal Church political situation, to the clarification of relations
between various Church groups in Russian Orthodoxy. In particular, the accusations of theological modernism on the part of the Karlovtsy group were in
fact directed rather against Metropolitan Evlogii and the church community
of the diaspora, and in this sense Bulgakov's teaching served as the most con-
venient model.

Thus, despite their wide range, the specific accusations did not add up to
a systemic picture. The opponents refuted the doctrine without touching its
essence. They disputed the particulars but overlooked the synthesis. Such critical attitudes did not allow them to capture the theological and philosophical system created by Bulgakov as an integral system (although this integrity
was indirectly confirmed by the above statement about the incompatibility of
sophiology and Orthodoxy)—only then could one proceed to challenge the
particular issues. In this regard, there is no particular difference between the
arguments of such different people as Archbishop Seraphim and Lossky.

The final text of the conference assembled by Metropolitan Evlogii was
not an official document.[9] This text noted in particular that "the doctrine of
Fr. S. Bulgakov has nothing to do with either Gnosticism or pantheism," and
that the conclusions of the Karlovtsy group, following Archbishop Seraphim,
incorrectly determined its origins. Meanwhile, Bulgakov's doctrine was nothing more than a theological hypothesis, the construction of which had yet to be
completed—and, since Bulgakov's works "have not yet been sufficiently studied

---

8   Quoted by Andrei K. Klement'ev, "Materialy k istorii polemiki o tvorchestve professora
     protoiereia Sergiia Nikolaevicha Bulgakova (1924–1937 gg.)", *Vestnik Ekaterinburgskoi
     dukhovnoi seminarii* 2, no. 26 (2019), 296.
9   The conclusions were published not in the diocesan publication, but in the newspaper
     (see Klement'ev, "Materialy k istorii polemiki," 314–15).

[...] an authoritative opinion of the Church authorities has not yet been expressed about them." Therefore, "grave accusations of heresy" were premature. Bulgakov was advised to

> revise his theological teaching about St. Sophia with all care, to clarify the disputable passages of his teaching in generally accessible forms, to bring them closer to the Orthodox understanding and to remove from them everything which confuses ordinary souls, those who do not have special theological and philosophical thinking.[10]

As we know, Father Sergius did none of this. Bulgakov began to explain his teachings in the text *The Wisdom of God: A Brief Summary of Sophiology* (1937), but this explanation did not contain any revisions or deletions.

In Metropolitan Evlogii's document, the concept of "theological hypothesis" seems to be of special interest. It is characteristic that, in searching for a solution to this situation, Bulgakov's doctrine was qualified with phrases not found in the toolkit of theological definitions (at least in the Orthodox theological tradition)—such as *dogma, theologumenon, private theological opinion*, or *heresy*.[11] This definition ("theological hypothesis"), which seemed a unique

---

10   Gennadii (Eikalovich), igum., *Delo prot. Sergiia Bulgakova. Istoricheskaia kanva spora o Sofii*, 33–35 (Klement'ev, "Materialy k istorii polemiki," 314).

11   In Russian theological scholarship, the triad "dogma, theologumenon, private theological opinion" was first proposed by Vassilii Bolotov (see "Thesen über das 'Filioque'. Von einem russischen Theologen," in *Internationale Theologische Zeitschrift* 24 [1898], 681–712; Vasilii V. Bolotov, *K voprosu o filioque* [Saint Petersburg, 1914], 30–36) and was widely used, including in theological teaching literature (see Sil'vestr [Stoichev], arkhim., *Dogmaticheskoe bogoslovie* [Kiev: Izdatel'skii otdel Ukrainskoi Pravoslavnoi Tserkvi, 2016], 121–26). "The area of dogma is *necessaria*, the area of theologumenun is *dubia*: In necessariis unitas, in dubiis libertas!" (Bolotov, 31). According to Bolotov, the distinction between the former (true) and the latter (probable) is not as significant as that between theologumenon (the private theological opinion of the Holy Fathers) and the "non-authoritative" private theological opinion of a "mere theologian." Bulgakov does not enter into a direct polemic with Bolotov, but clearly does not accept his scheme. In a text printed in the midst of the dispute (1937, see Sergii Bulgakov, prot., "Dogmat i dogmatika," in *Zhivoe predanie. Pravoslavie v sovremennosti* [Moscow, 1997], 8–25) he argues that dogmatics is broader than dogmas; it continues in "dogmatic facts" (ibid., 9). These are, for example, the sacraments, the whole liturgical tradition, prayer, etc. They are not formulated in dogmas, but have the same (binding) significance in the life of the Church as dogmas themselves. Furthermore, the boundaries of the authoritative sacred tradition are not defined, and "the 'church fathers,' before they became

innovation, was, in fact, a proposal for a compromise. Since this definition goes beyond the scope of the list of theological terms and does not mean any of them, it can be considered a successful and rather witty finding. But is it productive? In a sense, yes, it is, because it correctly reflects the basic intuition of Bulgakov's teaching, namely, theologizing not based on theological sources. As we can see now, the incorrectness of qualifying the origins of Bulgakov's teachings was rightly noted: theological criticism of Bulgakov's doctrine at this stage was definitely doomed to failure, since it could not undermine its foundations.

This state of affairs is determined not by the "weakness" of theology, but by other factors. Although Bulgakov's doctrine in emigration took a theological direction and a corresponding genre-stylistic design, while very large-scale it was only a logical and ontological continuation of his philosophical system. Therefore, criticism on behalf of theology was forced here to play on a foreign field. The indication that sophiology has no church foundation is based on general theological intuition, but the latter cannot in any way be resolved in adequate formulations, since it does not have the tools for revealing the existing contradictions.

It is a matter not of particular discrepancies, but of fundamental principles. If we discard all imaginary accusations (Gnosticism, etc.) and focus on the main thing, the question can be posed in this way: is Bulgakov's system an attempt to synthesize some aspects of Platonism and Palamism—or is it a fusion of two incompatible ontological models? It is clear that the answer to the second part of the question can be obtained only as a result of a thorough study of the first part, in other words, when we find out how successfully Bulgakov was able to "palamize" the Platonic elements of his teaching. The difficulty of this task is determined by the fact that, as a philosophical teaching, Palamism has not been completed. In fact, in Bulgakov's works we see an attempt to complete the Palamas's apophatics in the direction of philosophical kataphatics.

Now let me return to the philosophical criticism represented by Evgenii Trubetskoi. As already mentioned, it sounded before Bulgakov's transition to theology. Indeed, the entire critical part of Trubetskoi's book *The Meaning of*

---

such, were also theologians searching for the truth." Hence "in dogmatics a place must be given to dogmatic enquiry" and "the dogmatic treatment" of its material can be presented "in theologeme or hypothesis" (ibid., 19). In "The Sophiology of Death", written in the 1940s, Bulgakov uses the expression "auxiliary theological hypothesis" once (Sergei N. Bulgakov, "Sofiologiia smerti" in *Sergei N. Bulgakov. Tikhie dumy* [Moscow: Respublika, 1996], 274). It is likely that Metr. Evlogii takes the concept of "theological hypothesis" from Bulgakov.

Life is directed "against the Gnostic understanding of Sophia." Yet it is not Soloviev's sophiology that is considered here to be gnostic, although it really is close to Gnosticism, but the Platonic aspects of the sophiology in Bulgakov's *Unfading Light*. However, Trubetskoi, contrary to the real state of affairs, argues that Soloviev's Gnosticism is only rudimentary and, therefore, excusable, while Bulgakov's Gnosticism determines the nature of his entire teaching.

Trubetskoi's main argument is as follows: in his constructions, Bulgakov relies on the teachings of Spinoza, and hence, in his sophiology, the world of divine ideas (i. e. Sophia) is related to the created world like *natura naturans* is related to *natura naturata*.[12] This results in the identification of Sophia and creature, which is not in accordance with Christian doctrine and must be rejected as a deviation into Monophysitism.[13]

Indeed, in Bulgakov's *Philosophy of Economy* and in *Unfading Light* among the many definitions of Sophia there is the Spinozist one represented by the terms *natura naturans* and *natura naturata*. However, the definition that Trubetskoi considers the only true one—Sophia is the Platonic world of ideas— is also there. Meanwhile, Vladimir Soloviev already considered Spinoza's principle to be a delusion and proposed to overcome it with the help of Kant's critical idealism, which showed that between the absolute essence and the world of phenomena there is certainly a subject of knowledge.[14]

Having realized that understanding Sophia as a special metaphysical entity in the divine Universe is futile, Bulgakov (in his *Philosophy of Economy* and of course in *Unfading Light)* began to clarify her status as a subject: the subject of cognition, activity and culture, and her relation to the Kantian transcendental subject. Here, of course, it should be noted that, using Kant's terminology, Bulgakov gives it a specific and largely "non-Kantian" meaning. He points out that his "transcendental subject," in contrast to the Kantian "scheme of the mind," is a real and living actor.

The religious question, then, arises in the unprejudiced mind, in the phenomenological field of spontaneous, undetermined religious experience. Religion, according to Bulgakov, is in this sense such a universal fact of human life that it cannot be denied. It is precisely *experience* that cannot be denied, which is realized as the experience of the unprecedented and unstoppable entrance of *the other* into the concrete-personal. In religious experience a direct *tangible*

---

12   Trubetskoi, *Smysl zhizni*, 99.
13   Ibid.
14   See Vladimir S. Solov'ev, "Poniatie o Boge. V zashchitu filosofii Spinozy," *Voprosy filosofii i psikhologii* VIII, 3 (38) (1897), 383–414.

experience of other worlds is *given*, an experience of a higher divine reality, an *experience* of the nearness of God, and not generally, but in concreto, just for *this* person, which imperatively requires him to respond by entering into the realm of the divine. Bulgakov calls this a sophian feeling, which, in turn, raises the question of Sophia as its source. To conceive of her as some kind of special metaphysical being would be fantastic, or, at worst, would reduce religious experience to a mystical visionary of Soloviev's type, which is not only not of universal significance, but not at all obvious. But at the same time, since Sophia is the source of the personal-religious, it is impossible to think of it as something generally impersonal and extrapersonal, just as it is impossible to imagine the philosophizing person as an impersonal "transcendental subject," "which is only a regulative idea, a cut through consciousness, a methodological fiction, though perhaps a fruitful one."[15] Bulgakov's idea of Sofia was thus to find, in its definition as a concrete and universal subject of religious and all other activities (economy, knowledge, culture), a possibility that would equally avoid both the fantasy of the "metaphysical being" and the "fiction" of the Kantian transcendental subject.

Having captured this perspective, Trubetskoi calls Bulgakov's teaching "deeply unsatisfactory."[16] The only possible solution to the problem of Sophia, which would correspond to Christianity, Trubetskoi sees in her identification with the Platonic world of divine ideas. Let me note in parentheses that E. Trubetskoi—quite sincerely, however—is inclined to present his own interpretation of Plato's metaphysics as a "Christian teaching" of the Wisdom of God. At the same time, he distinguishes between Plato, who discovered "the only way," and Plato-pagan, whom, in his opinion, Bulgakov follows—for example, in the rapprochement of Sophia with the demiurge from the dialogue "Timaeus." Therefore, Trubetskoi sees in Bulgakov's teachings traces of Gnosticism that has not been overcome, of the Platonic or even the Schelling type. It should be noted that in Paris, during the dispute about Sophia, Bulgakov was accused of Gnosticism, monophysitism, and pantheism at the same time.

It is not the substantial understanding of Sophia that Trubetskoi considers illegal, but the introduction into Sophia of the properties of becoming and change—in other words, subjectivity and psychologism. According to Trubetskoi, who was looking for the unity and absolute synthesis of "all that is conscious and thinking" in an all-unified consciousness as absolute thought, the introduction of Sophia-*subject* into "God's plan for what should be" seemed

---

15   Trubetskoi, *Smysl zhizni*, 78.
16   Ibid., 99.

to be a deviation from Christianity (if, of course, under the Christian teach-ing of Wisdom we understand the generalized scheme of the purest and most unsophisticated Platonism, which, with references to patristic authority, Trubetskoi reproduces).

The Christian understanding of Sophia, according to Trubetskoi, makes us "think of the relationship between this force and the world created in time as the relationship of two natures, essentially different and therefore not merged, but at the same time forming an inseparable unity [...] the relationship be-tween Sophia and this world is in no way, nor can it become, an identity. The inseparable unity of two natures seems possible and proper here, but not their merging into one."[17] The philosopher's attempt to present Sophia in the para-digm of Chalcedonian definitions is obvious, but is it possible in principle to combine the Christological dogma with the Platonic realism of ideas? Was it not the unsolvability of this very problem that later prompted Bulgakov to move away from Platonism?

The striving for a purely Christian understanding of Sophia inevitably leads Trubetskoi to a transcendental problem—in the formulation as it has been called for in Russian philosophy: how—not only theoretically, but also practi-cally—can the limit to a human's individual consciousness be removed in order to " [...] fill my consciousness with a sobornal consciousness"?[18]

Trubetskoi, quite in the Russian manner, hopes to solve the transcendental question in a non-transcendental way. Another book, published almost at the same time as *The Meaning of Life*, had a very characteristic title, *Metaphysical Presuppositions of Knowledge*, and an even more characteristic subtitle: "An attempt to Overcome Kant and Kantianism." Here Trubetskoi criticizes Kant for not completing the transcendental question, for he did not pose and, as a result, did not solve the problem of the *unconditional foundation* to the repre-sentations and concepts of the subject.[19] The consequence was the dogmatism of the *Critique of Pure Reason*, which manifested itself, in particular, in the inadequacy of the anthropological justification of knowledge: if, according to Trubetskoi, a priori concepts cannot be justified outside the subject, they will not have a universal and objective value.[20] At the same time, the ontological sta-tus of the subject does not play a role, no matter if it is connected only with *my*

---

17   Trubetskoi, *Smysl zhizni*, 99.
18   Ibid., 97.
19   Evgenii N. Trubetskoi, *Metafizicheskie predposylki poznaniia. Opyt preodoleniia Kanta i kantianstva* (Moscow, 1917), 13.
20   Ibid.

own self, with "universal consciousness," or even with the "world soul"[21]—the
subject as the bearer of a specific empirical psyche cannot be a priori. Hence,
Trubetskoi finds the main contradiction of Kantian transcendentalism: no psychological subject, be it a human person or *any other being,* can provide the
a priori function of transcendental apperception in such a way that sensory
representations have a universal character. And if it is not conditioned by such
a subject, then the problem in the Kantian sense does not exist at all. Trubetskoi
believes that the question of the possibility of a priori knowledge is the basis of
all knowledge in general, and this must necessarily lead us to overcoming Kant
and Kantianism by going metaphysically beyond the limits of Kant's teaching.[22] So, perhaps, Trubetskoi's rejection of Bulgakov's sophiology was not at
all caused by his imaginary Gnosticism, but by the fact that Bulgakov demonstrates a more sympathetic tendency towards Kant? Calling Kant an *asophian*
philosopher, Bulgakov, nevertheless, declares that the transcendental problem
of religion is completely analogous to those basic problems that were raised
and studied by Kant in his three "critiques." The content of the *third* critique is
closest to the problem of religion.[23]

Trubetskoi would like to find "such a being" that would be able to become
the subject of perception of the fullness of universal revelation. It wholly "co-
feels" and "co-realizes" Sophia as the All-Unity. However, in that version of
the development of metaphysical idealism, to which Trubetskoi was committed, he could not find such a subject under any circumstances. In the book
Metaphysical Presuppositions of Knowledge (written at the same time as *The
Meaning of Life*) Trubetskoi tries to "overcome Kant and Kantianism." Kant,
according to Trubetskoi, does not complete the transcendental question to the
very end, since he does not point to the *unconditional foundations* of the ideas
and concepts of the subject. This requires a metaphysical transcendence of the
limits of Kant's teachings. As a result, we see that Trubetskoi balances between
awareness of the transcendental problem and unwillingness to include in the
sophiological synthesis theoretical reflection more loyal to Kant's thought,
while Bulgakov offers an attempt to synthesize Kant's transcendentalism in
the understanding of Sophia as a universal subject of cognition and activity.

21 Trubetskoi, *Metafizicheskie predposylki poznaniia,* 13.
22 Ibid., 14.
23 See Sergei N. Bulgakov, *Svet Nevechernii* (Moscow: Respublika, 1994), 8–9. See Nata-
    lia Vaganova, "Transtsendental'nyi ideal Kanta i sofiologiia Bulgakova," in *Sofiologiia
    i neopatristicheskii sintez,* ed. Konstantin Antonov and Natalia Vaganova (Moscow:
    PSTGU, 2013), 65–85.

Interestingly, Trubetskoi's general attitude against Bulgakov's sophiology was largely determined by circumstances of personal character. In fact, Trubetskoi ascribed to Bulgakov's doctrine all those "sins" that are actually characteristic of Vladimir Soloviev's sophiology. In his effort to cleanse the latter of Gnostic and even occult moments, Trubetskoi, in fact, accused Bulgakov of them. However, when Trubetskoi turns to his own sophiological constructions, we can easily ascertain that his teaching on the "positive potentials of Sophia" as the foundations of the emerging world is a rather eclectic *locus communis* of Sophiology which included both Soloviev's intentions and some of Florenskii's propositions, and, of course, Bulgakov's ideas.

For example, Trubetskoi postulates the non-identity of Sophia and the created world. But even though the world is "other," it still has its beginning in Sophia as a possibility and reality. He provides a general scheme of antinomism: the "other" world denies the divine Sophia, but the contradiction will be overcome in eternity. And as for the "other" world, quite in Bulgakov's style, Trubetskoi defines it as relative non-being (μη όν, as distinct from absolute non-being, ούκ όν), as *potential* Sophia.[24] This world is striving for an actual, realized all-unity, which is Sophia in her completeness,[25] etc.

Indeed, a great deal of Trubetskoi's ideas do not just remind the reader of *Unfading Light*, but literally repeat its formulations in a slightly modified form. Of course, he does not take the formulations which were presented in *The Meaning of Life* as gnostic (and in fact they correspond to Soloviev's thought), but those that satisfied Trubetskoi's desire to see Sophia immaculately Orthodox, unsuspicious for an Orthodox reader—both a metaphysician and a dogmatist.

However, the question as to how Trubetskoi understood the synthesis of individual consciousnesses, these "all-unities in possibility," into the all-unity in reality, obviously goes beyond the scope of philosophical and theoretical analysis and leads us to completely different speculations. Kant refused to cross this line. Spurred on by his refusal, not only Trubetskoi, but also other representatives of Russian philosophy rushed to this line, which often forced them to move from philosophy to theological problems.

To sum up, the specific formulation of the transcendental problem on the basis of Russian philosophy in Bulgakov's system showed that the subject cannot freely "hypostatize" the objective worlds, which was of great interest for

---

24   Trubetskoi, *Smysl zhizni*, 109.
25   Ibid.

Russian social thought.[26] Reasonable and spontaneous at the same time, sobornal and particular, the subject is immersed in a laborious, active, continuous, growing, and essentially beneficial effort to transform chaos into cosmos, into the creation of life as an organic synthesis of two ontologies ("God" and "world"). In this process, *not yet being* ("hypostatisity", in Bulgakov's terminology), becomes *being* ("hypostasis"), which is most clearly achieved throughout human culture as a combination of material, social, and spiritual projections of human being. All in all, Bulgakov's sophiological theology constitutes a single and indivisible continuum with the philosophical part of his system. His sophiology, regardless of its theological "good quality," has demonstrated the demand for the idea of building an Orthodox theological and philosophical synthesis. Bulgakov himself, while claiming that "belief never establishes prohibitions for reason in its *proper* domain,"[27] considered the positive theological teaching of Sophia to be an unresolved task and a matter of the future.

Translated by Julia Rost
The article was prepared within the framework of the project "The Religious Subject of the Modern Age and its Reflexive Practices in Russian Culture of the Late XIX—First Half of the XX Century" with the support of PSTGU and the Foundation for the Development of Science, Education and Family "Living Tradition."

---

26 See Natalia Vaganova, "Russian Sophiology and the Problem of the Subject in Modern Philosophy," in: *Beyond Modernity. Russian Religious Philosophy and Post-Secularism*, ed. Artur Mrowczynski-Van Allen, Teresa Obolevitch, Pawel Rojek (Eugene: Pickwick Publications, 2016), 86–96.

27 Sergius Bulgakov, *The Lamb of God*, trans. Boris Jakim (Grand Rapids: W. B. Eerdmans, 2008), 184.

Building the House of Wisdom
DOI 10.17438/978-3-402-12190-0

Sophiology, Ascesis and Prophecy

Joshua Heath

Evaluations of Bulgakov's life and work have consistently insisted upon his spiritual integrity. Memoirs from the time of his final illness and death famously record the transfiguration of his face and the manifestation of the uncreated light. He was known for his skill as a confessor and spiritual director. And then there are Alexander Schmemann's 'three images' of Bulgakov and, perhaps chief among them, the image of Bulgakov celebrating the Divine Liturgy. Schmemann recalls the intensity of Bulgakov's celebration, the sense that 'there was accomplished here something involving the whole created world, something of the pre-eternal, the cosmic,'[1] before going on to assert the profoundly liturgical character of Bulgakov's theology. This chimes with Bulgakov's own explicit articulation of the inspiration of theology: 'the deepest origins of the theologian's inspiration must be nourished from the altar.'[2] Yet for someone like Schmemann, Bulgakov's seemingly excessive speculative tendencies cannot be so easily reconciled with his liturgical devotion.

> In Fr. Sergii it was as if two people were joined together and did not fully merge: one 'experiential' [...] and the other 'scholarly' [...] It seems to me that the way to solving the 'riddle' of Fr. Sergii, his lived and creative tragedy, lies here. This tragedy ultimately consists in the fact that his system (namely his 'system,' and not the infinite richness of all that it 'systematises') does not correspond to his experience.[3]

---

1   Alexander Schmemann, 'Tri obraza,' *Vestnik R. H. D.* 101–02 (1971): 9–24.
2   Quoted in Andrew Louth, 'Sergii Bulgakov and the Task of Theology,' *The Irish Theological Quarterly* 74, no. 3 (2009), 243–57 (246).
3   Schmemann, 'Tri obraza,' 20–21.

Notwithstanding Bulgakov's own discomfort with the description of his thought as a 'system,'[4] we can further isolate the central tenet of his 'sophiology' as a significant source of discomfort amongst his critical readers. 'Sophiology is a question about the power and significance [...] of the divine-humanity as *the unity of God with the whole created world*.'[5] This assertion of the unity of God and the world has been a consistent focus of critique, with the late Russian thinker Sergei Horujy summarising the primary metaphysical and moral concerns that such an assertion allegedly poses. Horujy's metaphysical critique echoes those made by Lossky and others: namely, that such a unity fails to accommodate the radical, 'ontological difference' between God and creation that is affirmed in the Christian theological doctrine of creation *ex nihilo*.[6]

But more significant for our purposes is Horujy's moral critique of sophiology. The events of the twentieth century rule out a complacent picture of an abiding unity between the divine and the human, in which the history of the world unfolds according to a divine plan 'independently of any sobriety or effort.'[7] For Horujy, Russian sophiology fails to take seriously human responsibility within history, being seduced by 'illusions and starry-eyed idealism.'[8] By contrast, recognition of the *discontinuity* between God and creation, which for Horujy is expressed in the Essence–Energies distinction, also entails an affirmation of the necessity of human action in securing the adherence of the world to God: 'Orthodox ascesis, having attained on the basis of experience the *energetic* nature of the relation between God and the human, issues this warning from the fourth century: this relation is maintained only through steady and unwavering effort; it offers no good guarantees.'[9] But is Horujy (and indeed, Schmemann) right to posit such a discontinuity between sophiological theory and spiritual practice?

---

4   See Sergius Bulgakov, *The Unfading Light*, trans. Thomas Allan Smith (Grand Rapids: W. B. Eerdmans, 2012), xxxviii. 'The ideas guiding this philosophising are united not in a "system" but in a certain *syzygy*, an organic articulation.'
5   S. N. Bulgakov, 'Tsentral'naia problema sofiologii,' in idem, *Tikhie dumy* (Moscow: Respublika, 1996), 269.
6   Sergei S. Horujy, 'Imiaslavie i kul'tura serebrianogo veka: fenomen moskovskoi shkoly khristianskogo neoplatonizma,' in idem, *Opyty iz russkoi dukhovnoi traditsii* [Experiments from the Russian Spiritual Tradition], 296–98.
7   Sergei S. Horujy, 'Pereput'ia russkoi sofiologii,' in idem, *O starom i novom* (Saint Petersburg: Aleteiia, 2000), 166.
8   Ibid.
9   Ibid. I suspect 'fourth century' should read 'fourteenth century,' i.e., when Palamas definitively articulated the Essence–Energies distinction.

Andrew Louth has argued for a greater continuity between Bulgakov the 'systematiser' or 'sophiologist' and Bulgakov the man of prayer. He argues not only that Bulgakov's overall approach to theology is liturgical because it takes as its starting point 'the human being who comes to know by standing before God in prayer, primarily liturgical prayer,'[10] but also that the very structure of Bulgakov's major dogmatic trilogy carries the shape of the anaphora of St John Chrysostom.[11] For Louth, we ought to understand Bulgakov's sophiological account of the unity of creation with God (and indeed, of the unity of God with God in the 'Divine Sophia'), as likewise emerging from his liturgical devotion: 'for Bulgakov, to celebrate the Eucharist entails that creation belongs to God, that it is not alien to him, that to be a creature is already to be graced [...] it is this intuition that lay at the heart of his sophiology.'[12] In its *intuition* at least, for Louth, Bulgakov's sophiology was likewise formed by his priestly life.

I want to take further this emphasis on the continuity between Bulgakov's scholarship, on the one hand, and his devotional life, on the other. Louth has convincingly shown how Bulgakov's immersion in the liturgy inspired his speculation. But can we see Bulgakov's speculative thought, his writing, as itself a spiritual exercise, an act of ascesis? In order to make this case, much of this chapter will be devoted to Bulgakov's own writing on ascesis. We will see how Bulgakov is perennially concerned with articulating a form of Christian ascesis that has at its heart a commitment to the world and its history. We will see how Bulgakov ends up joining the concept of ascesis with that of prophecy, such that authentic Christian self-transcendence becomes inseparable from an orientation toward the future. We will then briefly consider the indicators throughout Bulgakov's corpus that he understood his own writing in such ascetic-cum-prophetic terms, with the aim of fostering a hopeful, rather than fearful, attitude within the Church toward the future.

***

In his 'primer' on sophiology for a Western audience, Bulgakov makes clear the centrality of *ascesis* to his project. 'Sophiology contains within itself the nexus of all the dogmatic and practical problems of contemporary Christian dogmatics and asceticism.'[13] And again in the same work: 'we need a true Christian

---

10   Louth, 'Sergii Bulgakov,' 253.
11   Ibid., 253–54.
12   Ibid., 256–57.
13   Translation my own. Based on the forthcoming German–Russian edition of this text, prepared by the Sergii Bulgakov Centre of the University of Fribourg. English trans-

ascesis in relation to the world.'[14] Likewise, in his short text 'The Central Problem of Sophiology,' Bulgakov's theoretical assertion of a unity between God and
the world, manifest in the Divine Humanity, is inseparable from ascesis: 'the
Divine Humanity is a dogmatic summons to spiritual ascesis and creativity, to
salvation from the world and salvation of the world.'[15] Once we attend to the
consistent ascetic emphasis of Bulgakov's sophiology, it becomes clear that this
unity between God and the world is not primarily asserted as a 'given' [*dan-
nost'*] (although it is that), but as a 'proposal' [*zadannost'*] that humanity must
accomplish in the face of the tragic diremption of history.

Bulgakov was pre-occupied with the nature of Christian ascesis throughout his career, from a cluster of articles on the theme in the first decade of the
twentieth century, through the major dogmatic trilogy and on to his final work
on the Apocalypse of John. Throughout his writings on asceticism, Bulgakov
notes within asceticism what he considers a quasi-Manichean hostility to the
world of history. This concern is not original to Bulgakov. For Vladimir Soloviev, a cardinal influence on Bulgakov and his fellow thinkers of the 'Silver
Age,' the Christian ascetical tradition, with its hostility to the body, was at best
a superseded moment in the development of Christianity's self-consciousness.
Its continued prominence within the life of the Church, however, was an active
impediment to Christianity's present, providential task: 'the joining together
of spirit and body.'[16] We find a Solovievian position on Christian asceticism
reproduced somewhat uncritically in Bulgakov's essay 'On the Economic Ideal' (1903), where he asserts that 'the ascetical view of the world is at no point
more alien to contemporary consciousness than in [its] denial of history and
social ethics.'[17]

But as late as 1944, Bulgakov will continue to have reservations about this
perceived tendency in Christian asceticism. Thus, he will write that the 'feeling
of life' is 'lost and even denied by an *ascetically* understood Christianity with

---

lation: Sergei Bulgakov, *Sophia: The Wisdom of God: An Outline of Sophiology* (Hudson,
N. Y.: Lindisfarne, 1993), 21.

14   Ibid., 20.

15   Bulgakov, 'Tsentral'naia problema,' 270.

16   Patrick Lally Michelson, *Beyond the Monastery Walls: The Ascetic Revolution in Russian Orthodox Thought, 1814–1914* (Madison, Wisconsin: University of Wisconsin Press,
2017), 169.

17   S. N. Bulgakov, 'The Economic Ideal,' trans. Rowan Williams, in idem, *Sergii Bulgakov:
Towards a Russian Political Theology* (Edinburgh: T&T Clark, 1999), 38.

its transcendentalism.'[18] But the most concentrated articulation of Bulgakov's concerns with this tradition comes in his preface to *The Lamb of God* (1933). There, Bulgakov describes a conviction 'that Christ has abandoned the world and that His Kingdom, which is not of this world, will never be realized in this world.'[19] This conviction has resulted in a tendency 'simply to flee—in fact or in spirit, ascetically or theologically—from this world into the desert of nihilism [...] for the world exists only to be rejected ascetically, to be relegated to fire.'[20] This theological-ascetical rejection of the intrinsic value of creation is a principle adversary of Bulgakov's own intellectual efforts.

The attempt to articulate an *alternative* account of Christian ascesis is therefore present from the earliest moments of Bulgakov's engagement with asceticism. The most well-known, early example of this effort is Bulgakov's essay 'On Heroism and the Spiritual Struggle,' published in the 1909 collection *Landmarks*. Commentators have rightly noted the prominence in this essay, not of the Russian '*asketizm*' or '*askeza*' (calques of 'asceticism'), but rather the terms '*podvig*' and '*podvizhnichestvo*', even in the article's title.[21] Whilst *asketizm* will continue to be an object of varying evaluation in Bulgakov's theological career, *podvig* will consistently denote what he considers the 'authentic' form of self-transcendence to which the Christian is called. Through the essay's organizing opposition between the heroic revolutionary and the Christian ascetic, Bulgakov develops an understanding of ascesis as an exercise of situating oneself within (and not apart from) the course of human history. Unlike the heroic revolutionary, the ascetic 'does not set himself to do the job of providence,

---

18 Sergii Bulgakov, *The Apocalypse of John: An Essay in Dogmatic Interpretation*, trans. Mike Whitton and rev. Michael Miller (Münster: Aschendorff, 2019), 259. My emphasis.

19 Sergius Bulgakov, *The Lamb of God*, trans. Boris Jakim (Grand Rapids: W. B. Eerdmans, 2008), xiv.

20 Ibid.

21 See, for instance, Ruth Coates, 'Feuerbach, Kant, Dostoevskii: The Evolution of "Heroism" and "Asceticism" in Bulgakov's work to 1909,' in *Landmarks Revisited: The* Vekhi *Symposium 100 Years On*, ed. Robin Aizlewood and Ruth Coates (Boston: Academic Studies Press, 2013), 287–307. Alongside Max Weber (discussed below), an important influence on the conceptual apparatus of Bulgakov's text is Ernst Troeltsch. Troeltsch presents 'heroism' and 'asceticism,' not as an opposition, but as an expression of two complementary elements of the Church's life, in his *The Social Teaching of the Christian Churches and Groups* (1908–1910). For a discussion of Troeltsch's text in relation to Bulgakov's essay, together with locations where Bulgakov cites Troeltsch, see Nikolai Plotnikov, 'Zametki o "Vekhah" [Remarks on *Landmarks*], *Issledovaniia po istorii Russkoi mysli*] 6 (2003): 562–71 (esp. 562–65). My thanks to Regula Zwahlen for drawing my attention to this.

and so does not link the destiny of history or humanity to his or anyone else's individual efforts.'[22] Instead, 'his attention is concentrated on his immediate task, his concrete obligations.'[23]

Moreover, *podvizhnichestvo* is characterised not only by a reduction in scale, from the historic to the immediate, but also by a movement inwards. Whereas the efforts of the revolutionary are 'entirely expended on the struggle to improve the environment,' the Christian ascetic is engaged in 'the ethical development of personality.'[24] This development of personality is a matter of 'unwavering self-discipline, endurance and perseverance [...] faithful performance of one's duty, bearing of one's own cross, repudiation of self.'[25] Such a discipline, Bulgakov observes, is characteristic of the 'physician and the engineer, the professor and the political activist, the manufacturer and his workers' in their 'fulfilment of their duties.'[26] Here, Bulgakov acknowledges the influence of Max Weber's notion of 'inner-worldly ascesis' [*innerweltliche Askese*] on his own account of Christian asceticism.[27] Indeed, Weber's description of the worldly ascetic as one who participates 'within the institutions of the world but in opposition to them,' focusing on 'the alert, methodical control of one's own pattern of life and behaviour,'[28] seems apt for the 'citizen-ascetics' that populate Bulgakov's essay.[29] Likewise, Weber's emphasis on the ascetic as an 'instrument of God' precisely through this inward, ethical transformation[30] is how Bulgakov will secure the ascetic's relationship to history. For the ascetic's attention to the particular is the means by which he 'reorders his personal will' so that it is 'wholly permeated by the will of God.' The ascetic's concentration on the immediate therefore secures the participation of their individual actions within the divine, providential direction of history. The apparent indifference of the

22   S. N. Bulgakov, 'Heroism and the Spiritual Struggle', trans. Rowan Williams, in idem, *Sergii Bulgakov*, 97.
23   Ibid., 93.
24   Ibid., 95.
25   Ibid., 98.
26   Ibid., 99.
27   Ibid. The influence of Weber on Bulgakov, not only with respect to the nature of 'asceticism,' but also more broadly, is discussed in Josephien van Kessel, 'From Secular Sociology to Orthodox Sophiology: Max Weber's Influence on Sergei Bulgakov's Christian Social Theory,' *Transcultural Studies* 4 (2008): 43–56.
28   Max Weber, *Economy and Society*, ed. Guenther Roth and Claus Wittich (New York: Bedminster Press, 1968), vol. 2, 542–44.
29   Coates, 'Feuerbach, Kant, Dostoevskii,' 303.
30   Weber, *Economy and Society*, 543.

saint to the wider fortunes of world history thus belies a profound involvement in the course of those fortunes.

Despite the predominantly 'civic' characterisation of asceticism in this essay,[31] the monk is nonetheless a presence in the text. Bulgakov gathers the qualities of the ascetic or *podvizhnik* together under the term 'obedience' [*poslushanie*], recognising the origins of this 'very fine expression' in 'monastic practice.'[32] Later in the essay, Bulgakov approvingly describes 'the light that burned in the monastic houses, where the *people* have flocked across the ages, seeking moral nurture and instruction.'[33] One monastic figure whom Bulgakov identifies at multiple points in this essay is Saint Sergii of Radonezh. In particular, Saint Sergii instantiates the joining of the inward and socio-historical dimensions of asceticism: 'when Dmitri Donskoi set out with the blessing of St Sergii to fight the Tatars, this was a revolutionary action in the political sense [...] but at the same time it was, I believe, an act of Christian spiritual achievement.'[34] In a later watershed in Bulgakov's thinking on asceticism, Sergii of Radonezh takes centre stage, as a paradigm of the ascetic's engagement with the fate of the world. Indeed, this watershed text is a 1926 lecture on the legacy of Saint Sergii. Bulgakov begins this lecture by observing that the saint was born at a nadir in Russia's historical fortunes. 'The Lord stirred up his chosen one in the arduous time not only of our people's outward enslavement, but also of inward degeneration.'[35] The young monk's pursuit of the hermetic path may seem to indicate indifference to this wider historical picture. Yet, through his reform and propagation of cenobitic monasticism in Russia, Sergii 'set out upon the work of building the City of God, in which the stones are human hearts, he set out to gather souls, to create fraternity, to initiate into the Church, so that all may be one, in the image of God, in the image of the Holy Trinity.'[36] In this gathering together and dispersal of communities in new monasteries, Sergii became 'the spiritual gatherer of Rus', and the centuries after the life of Sergii 'are the Sergievskaya epoch in the history of the Russian spirit and creativity.'[37] We find instantiated in Sergii the coincidence of an intensely inward asceti-

31   Williams, *Sergii Bulgakov*, 63.
32   Bulgakov, 'Heroism and Spiritual Struggle,' 99.
33   Ibid., 106. On this monastic thread in the text, see Coates, 'Feuerbach, Kant, Dostoevskii,' 302–04.
34   Bulgakov, 'Heroism and Spiritual Struggle,' 98.
35   Bulgakov, 'Blagodatnye zavety prep. Sergiia russkomu bogoslovstvovaniiu,' *Put'* 5 (1926): 3–19 (11).
36   Ibid.
37   Ibid., 12.

cism—since above all 'he fulfilled the ascesis of *sobornost*' in the hiddenness of his heart, conquering self-love, sacrificially renouncing himself'[38]—and a thorough involvement in human history and culture. Sergii of Radonezh thus becomes the figure of the world-affirming ascesis that Bulgakov is concerned to secure.

Moreover, this lecture on St. Sergii of Radonezh brings Bulgakov's thinking on asceticism together with his Trinitarian thought, articulated most fully in his works of the 1920s. It is true that the impulse to think Christian asceticism or *podvig* in Trinitarian terms predates this lecture. In *The Unfading Light* (1916), for instance, Bulgakov writes of the ascetic or saintly virtue of *tselomudrie*, whose common translation is 'chastity' but which can also be rendered as 'integral wisdom' or 'the wisdom of the whole,' as a realisation of the Trinitarian image in human beings:

> by sacrificing their hypostasis, by going beyond themselves in love, in the likeness of the trihypostatic God, human beings find their being within themselves. For them the law of life becomes the wisdom of wholeness and the wholeness of wisdom—*tselomudrie*, which is at once the condition and consequence of love.[39]

This Trinitarian framing of ascesis is also present in 'Hypostasis and Hypostaseity' (1925), where Bulgakov writes that 'the experience of the saints, as the bearers of chastity [*tselomudrie*], is qualitatively different from the wisdom of this world [...] to the illumined eye of the ascetic, the world presents itself as the living *riza* of the Godhead, as his Word, clothed in the Holy Spirit.'[40] In these texts, ascesis takes on a Trinitarian shape because of Bulgakov's interpretation of the *imago Dei* as an *imago Trinitatis*. This is especially clear in the passage from *The Unfading Light*, where ascesis is defined as a particular mode of the human being's realisation of themselves as an *hypostasis* or person.

In the 1926 lecture on Saint Sergii of Radonezh, this Trinitarian shape of Christian ascesis, asserted briefly in *The Unfading Light* and 'Hypostasis,' is presented more fully through the phenomenological-cum-grammatical analysis of subjectivity that is most fully set out in 'Chapters on Trinitarity' and *The*

---

38   Bulgakov, 'Blagodatnye zavety,' 12.

39   Bulgakov, *The Unfading Light*, 319.

40   Sergii Bulgakov, 'Hypostasis and Hypostaseity: Scholia to *The Unfading Light*,' trans. Anastassy Brandon Gallaher and Irina Kukota, *St Vladimir's Theological Quarterly* 49, no. 1–2 (2005): 5–46 (38).

Tragedy of Philosophy, as well as in *The Philosophy of the Name*.[41] In this lecture, Bulgakov abbreviates this analysis to his demonstration of the presupposition of both the second-person *You* and third-person *(S)he* in the first-person *I*, such that the individual, created subject is in fact a triune *We*; an image of the Trinity. What is presented in the other texts (*Tragedy* and 'Chapters') as the *given structure* of personal life is here participation in the death and resurrection of Jesus Christ: 'does the *I* not feel itself to be a singular, absolute, self-asserting, self-loving centre of being? [...] And yet suddenly we have its humble immersion of itself into the *we*, the death of the *I* and its resurrection. *We* testifies to the extent of the self-revelation and self-consciousness of the *I* and the depth of its establishment in its reality.'[42] Here, the degrees of ascetic achievement are nothing other than the degrees of the subject's self-realisation as a person. Ascesis has no other goal than the full realisation—not negation—of self-consciousness. Moreover, the affinity of Saint Sergii of Radonezh with the natural world affirms what is asserted theoretically in 'Chapters' and *Tragedy*: namely, that full personhood involves a recognition of the world as one's own proper nature. As such, in this lecture Bulgakov is able to ground his vision of ascesis as a commitment to the world and its history, through his Trinitarian account of created personhood. For the 'sacrifice of one's hypostasis' or 'going beyond oneself in love' is a commitment to live in history, understood as the common self-determination of other hypostases and the hypostasised (if not hypostatic) natural world.

This interweaving of the Trinitarian shape of Christian ascesis, and the Christian commitment to the world and history, finds definitive expression in *The Comforter* (1936). The Trinitarian shape of Christian ascesis and, more broadly, of personhood is inevitably foregrounded here, insofar as the spiritual life is discussed within the context of pneumatology. 'The human spirit is neither closed nor impenetrable. It is created in the image of Divine spirit, which, being one and trihypostatic, is thus "communal" and transparent.'[43] The realisation of this Trinitarian image is the goal of *podvig*. Indeed, in *The Comforter*, we find a more schematic distinction between *askeza* and *podvig*. Asceticism

---

41   I can only present this linguistic, Trinitarian account of subjectivity in highly compressed form here. Interested readers should consult the contributions of David Bentley Hart, John Milbank and Rowan Williams to this volume, as well as my own 'Sergii Bulgakov's Linguistic Trinity,' *Modern Theology* 37, no. 4 (2021): 888–912, and 'On Sergii Bulgakov's *The Tragedy of Philosophy*,' *Modern Theology*, 37, no. 3 (2021): 805–23.

42   Bulgakov, 'Blagodatnye zavety,' 8–9.

43   Sergius Bulgakov, *The Comforter*, trans. Boris Jakim (Grand Rapids: W. B. Eerdmans, 2004), 301.

as *askeza* is a *negative* discipline, a codifiable set of practices for the restraint of the appetitive ego: 'efforts of the spiritual life […] have a predominantly *negative* character—the character of struggle with oneself, ascesis.'[44] This struggle admits of codification because in its fallenness, the human spirit possesses a consistency across differing historical periods.[45] Therefore, the parameters and instruments of this struggle find enduring expression in such texts as the *Philokalia*, and asceticism thus understood is the particular preoccupation of monastic Christianity, although nonetheless a responsibility for all Christians. The purpose of such a discipline is to produce *humility*, which Bulgakov glosses as 'a certain state of readiness of the human spirit for communion with God,'[46] i. e., for the 'actualisation' of the divine image in humanity.

Asceticism is therefore one *wing* of the wider process of self-transcendence, *podvig*, by which Christians go out of themselves into history, where the image of the Trinity is realised. The other wing of *podvig* is *creativity* [*tvorchestvo*], whose centrality to Bulgakov's understanding of the human long predates the dogmatic trilogy. But what is perhaps the most distinctive feature of Bulgakov's treatment of the spiritual life in *The Comforter* is the pairing of 'creativity' with 'audacity' or 'daring' [*derznovenie*], as well as prophecy. Bulgakov's use of *derznovenie* has scriptural warrant: it is taken from the Acts of the Apostles (an obvious object of interest in a book on the Holy Spirit), where it occasionally characterises the apostolic preaching. 'Both Paul and Barnabas spoke out *boldly* [*s derznoveniem skazali*]' (Acts 13: 46), whilst Peter and John, together with the other gathered disciples, 'were all filled with the Holy Spirit and spoke the word of God with boldness' (Acts 4: 31). 'Audacity' and 'creativity' become two faces of the same activity of *podvig*, as when Bulgakov writes that 'the two paths—ascetic humility and *creative audacity*, obedience and the acceptance of responsibility—are antinomically harmonized in spiritual life.'[47]

Whereas the procedures of asceticism [*askeza*] can be expressed in an abiding tradition or canon, 'there is nothing like this in the case of creative activity and audacity: there is no tradition and no repetition; everything is unique and individual, new and original.'[48] The course of creative human action is history itself[49] and is therefore oriented towards a future that, whilst

---

44   Bulgakov, *The Comforter*, 302.
45   Ibid., 312.
46   Ibid.
47   Ibid., 308.
48   Ibid., 312.
49   'If one would like to have a spiritual map of this path, it is universal history.' Ibid., 313.

undetermined, nonetheless remains under the care of Providence: 'man [...] feels himself called to live in the human race with its history, in this world, where the Kingdom of God is being realised.'[50] In this determination of *podvig* as oriented toward the future, *prophecy* emerges as the fundamental figure of creative Christian action. We have already seen how 'boldness' characterises the apostolic preaching or prophecy in the Acts of the Apostles. But Bulgakov also writes, with respect to the gifts of the Holy Spirit: 'what is essential for prophesying is Christian activity, to consider history as a creative act and task. The gift of prophecy, as a general gift of Pentecost, signifies that, henceforth, Christian man makes history in an inspired and creative manner.'[51] By gathering all authentic Christian action under the heading of prophecy, *The Comforter* represents the consummation of Bulgakov's endeavour to render Christian ascesis a commitment to the world and its history, as the place where 'the Kingdom of God is being realised.'

There is one other feature of Bulgakov's account of Christian ascesis that should be mentioned: its Christological (and especially cruciform) shape. Already in *The Lamb of God*, Christ is presented as a model of *podvig*, particularly in his devotion to prayer.[52] Through his 'unceasing' prayer, Christ's consciousness as the Son of the Father is realised: 'his prayer to the Father [...] was returned to Him as His own divine consciousness.'[53] Further, it is through this *unity* of the Persons of the Father and the Son in the consciousness of Christ that the unity of the divine and human in the life of Jesus is also realised: 'the entire experience of His earthly life, from the beginning of His ministry to Golgotha, corresponds to this consciousness of self as the affirmation of the will of the Divine Sonhood and presents Him with growing possibilities for the self-renunciation that constitutes the very essence of the Divine love for the world, as well as of the Divine Sonhood.'[54] In terms familiar from the preceding discussion, Christ's *podvig* is a generative ('*growing* possibilities') process of Trinitarian self-determination that culminates in the Cross. In *The Comforter*, Bulgakov returns to this understanding of the way of the Cross as a creative undertaking, as well as an act of self-abnegation in the sense of *askeza*: 'the Cross is not only passive reception, but an active taking hold, creative self-definition

50 Bulgakov, *The Comforter*, 309.
51 Ibid., 294.
52 Bulgakov, *The Lamb of God*, 279.
53 Ibid., 280.
54 Ibid., 265.

and daring [*derznovenie*].'[55] As well as being the consummation of a singular process of creative, vital self-definition, the Cross also opens a future of such creativity in the spiritual life of the Church, standing as the figure of all Christian self-determination: 'Christian asceticism is a cross in the image of the Cross of Christ and the Holy Spirit only descends upon this Cross.'[56]

In this understanding of the Cross as the heart of Christian creativity (or should we say signification?), we unexpectedly find a distant, Orthodox articulation (albeit less direct) of Maurice de la Taille's famous dictum that in the Incarnation, 'He [Christ] placed Himself in the order of signs.' In particular, Bulgakov's account of the Cross resonates with the ways in which twentieth-century British theology has developed the implications for creative activity of de la Taille's maxim.[57] Certainly, Bulgakov himself understood the Cross as the figure of his own writing. In the preface to *The Unfading Light*, Bulgakov presents the 'miscellanies' that make up the book as a refusal of 'flight from spiritual fate, from my historical cross.'[58] Earlier in the same preface, he describes the work as 'a creative act of the spiritual life: a book, but no longer a book, not only a book.'[59] As Bulgakov describes his writing in terms redolent of the discussion of creativity and *podvig* in *The Comforter*, he encourages his readers to interpret his work in terms of authentic Christian ascesis, as an act of his own self-determination. In yet another anticipation of his thinking on creativity and prophecy in *The Comforter*, Bulgakov articulates the ambition of *The Unfading Light* as at once an assumption of the full weight of the present *and* a cultivation of hope for the future: 'even if the spiritual essence is ulcerated by problems and perforated with doubts, still in its heart faith does not grow scarce and hope still shines.'[60] Indeed, Bulgakov intimates that his task in this work is an eschatological transformation of present awareness: 'all our problems with their presentiments and portents are the shadow cast by the one who

---

55   Bulgakov, *The Comforter*, 306.

56   Ibid., 305.

57   Three crucial texts in this development are David Jones' 'Art and Sacrament,' in idem, *Epoch and Artist* (London: Faber and Faber, 2017), Rowan Williams' exposition of Augustine's account of signification, and particularly Scriptural meaning, in terms of the Cross in his 'Language Reality and Desire,' in ibid., *On Augustine* (London and New York: Bloomsbury, 2016), 41–58, and, of course, Catherine Pickstock's seminal thesis that the transubstantiation is the condition of all meaning in *After Writing* (Oxford: Blackwell, 1998).

58   Bulgakov, *The Unfading Light*, xxxvii.

59   Ibid.

60   Ibid., xxxviii.

comes.'[61] In the light of the preface, it becomes difficult not to read Bulgakov's discussion of prophecy in *The Comforter* as self-reflective, a description of his self-understanding as a writer and thinker: 'prophesying, as creative activity and inspiration, is directed toward the future, not above but through the present, which is pregnant with the future.'[62]

Strikingly, Bulgakov will continue to employ the genre of authorial preface to set his highly speculative works within such a prophetic frame. In the prefaces to each of the volumes in the major dogmatic trilogy, Bulgakov situates his works on the threshold of a particular vision of the world, of the *future* of the world. This is particularly true of the final volume, where he describes the events of the first half of the twentieth century as 'paling' in comparison to what is to be revealed.[63] But in the preface to *The Lamb of God* also, there is a summons to the Church to remember its faith in what is to come and the commitment to the world that flows from that faith.[64] The implication is that these essays, which present Bulgakov's 'sophiological' vision of the *unity* of God and creation, human history and Divine Providence, have as their goal the stimulation of a renewed engagement of the Church in the world, in view of the fulfilment of all things. In each of these prefaces, then, Bulgakov invites his readers to understand his texts in terms of the accounts of ascesis, creativity and prophecy that they contain.

For we see that the articulation of that sophiological vision is itself a *labour*, a discipline of proclaiming Christ as the 'one in whom all things cohere', in defiance of the 'disbelief in Christ's royal ministry' that the tragedies of history provoke.[65] A concrete instance of this comes in Bulgakov's exegetical-speculative reflections on the figure of Judas. In the concluding section of those essays, Bulgakov declares his motivation in undertaking this meditation on the apostle-traitor: an effort to understand Russia's own betrayal of Christ in the Bolshevik Revolution. By interpreting Judas' betrayal as an act of misdirected *love* for Christ and *hope* for the future, thus holding open the possibility of Judas' redemption, Bulgakov likewise seeks to make Russia's apostasy a moment within the development of its religious consciousness:

---

61 Bulgakov, *The Unfading Light*, , xxxviii.
62 Bulgakov, *The Comforter*, 296.
63 Bulgakov, *The Bride of the Lamb*, xvii.
64 Bulgakov, *The Lamb of God*, xv.
65 Ibid.

in the rejection of Christ and his betrayal by the Russian people, we are also dealing with a religious aberration, which emerged [...] with an apocalyptic intensity of faith in the future and a genuine desire to realise it. And we can hope that this will toward the future will not be displeasing and hateful to God.[66]

The essay on Judas is an effort to transform Bulgakov and his reader's perspective on both the present predicament and future destiny of Russia. So with the major trilogy, we might say that Bulgakov's sophiology, the cosmic vision of the inherence of Creation in God, the co-ordination of history and Providence, is an attempt to secure at the highest level of generality a transformation of perspective, according to which the future becomes something not to be dreaded, but longed for.

This is how we ought to understand Bulgakov's final work: his dogmatic exegesis of the Revelation to St. John. Indeed, there is a telling beauty in Bulgakov's final work being devoted to such an audacious expansion of the horizon of human history and activity. For in this work, Bulgakov is insistent on interpreting the prophecies of Revelation in millenarian or chiliastic terms, as Antoine Arjakovsky has discussed in his contribution to this volume. The dominant opinion 'that the prophecy of the first resurrection and the thousand-year reign of Christ on earth does not relate to a *new* event and revelation of the Church in earthly history,' is for Bulgakov 'outright war not only against the prophecy [...] but yet more against its fundamental meaning.'[67] Instead, Bulgakov maintains that 'the thousand-year reign is a definite era in the history of the Church with a beginning and an end.'[68] The understandable, instinctive response of readers to this text may be to see it as yet another instance of Bulgakov being 'unable to help himself' in asserting a controversial reading of a settled text. After all, was Origen's allegorical interpretation of the thousand-year reign not—as Henri de Lubac has insisted, following Newman—a crucial moment in securing a stable Christian orthodoxy?[69]

But there is a difference between the self-consciousness of the early Church and that of the Church in the twentieth century. 'The first Christians had such a living recollection of Christ's presence in the world [...] they were waiting for Him and calling upon Him, they spoke and thought of His advent as something

---

66   Sergii Bulgakov, 'Iuda Iskariot: Apostol-Predatel' (II),' *Put'* 27 (1931): 3–42 (40).

67   Bulgakov, *Apocalypse*, 180–81.

68   Ibid., 183.

69   Henri de Lubac, *Histoire et esprit: l'intelligence de l'Ecriture d'après Origène* (Paris: Aubier, 1950), 103–04.

that would happen the next day."[70] Whilst 'ugly exaggerations and perversions [that] arose out of this feeling' needed to be corrected, a need that excuses the 'neutralisation' of the prophecy concerning the millennium, a graver deformity in the Church's life has taken hold. Namely, a loss of hope, an inability to join with the early Church in its prayer 'even so, come, Lord Jesus.'[71] Bulgakov's chiliastic interpretation of the Revelation to St. John finds its justification in the restoration of the early Church's anticipation of the future, an anticipation which for Bulgakov is the condition (and outcome) of authentic Christian ascesis. Indeed, in keeping with Bulgakov's fondness for antinomic resolutions to theological problems, his 'chiliastic' interpretation of the thousand-year reign combines a valorisation of human action with an insistence on the eschaton as a second creation, or direct act of the Father upon the created order. This is consistent with the eschatology developed in *The Bride of the Lamb*, where the eschaton is at once the outcome of an immanent process—the 'ripening' of creation, fostered by human endeavour—and a transcendent 'catastrophe.'[72]

Bulgakov concludes the first and last of the volumes of his major trilogy with the prayer that closes the Revelation to St. John: 'even so, come, Lord Jesus.'[73] This is the very prayer that the Church of the present cannot bring itself to say, paralysed as it is by fear of the Last Judgement and disbelief in the presence of Christ in history. This is the prayer that the Church must learn to say again: 'it must become not only an object of particular prayerful attention, but a new spiritual orientation.'[74] Is the placement of this prayer at the *end* of these volumes a mere rhetorical flourish? Or does this placement signify that the culmination of these texts is the *restoration* of the possibility of such a prayer, the restoration of Christian hope? 'We are concerned with nothing more nor less than a new (and at the same time primordial) feeling of life, which must be born again in Christianity, and this must be a spiritual and prayerful turning-point in the life of the Church.'[75] My contention in this chapter is that sophiology does not merely *reflect* such a feeling, justified or not, on the part of

---

70 Bulgakov, *Apocalypse*, 257–58.
71 Ibid., 276–77.
72 On the eschaton as simultaneously 'ripening' and 'catastrophe,' see *The Bride of the Lamb*, 322. 'The transfiguration of the world, with the coming of its "end", is, of course, determined not only by its internal structure but also by the direct action of God upon the world, by a new creative act of God.' See also the editors' introduction in Bulgakov, *Apocalypse*, xi.
73 It is, of course, not the last word of the book, which is instead the apostolic blessing.
74 Bulgakov, *Apocalypse*, 277.
75 Ibid.

its author. Rather, taking my cue from Bulgakov's own self-understanding as a writer, we should understand both the writing and reading of Bulgakov's works as efforts in the cultivation of the second theological virtue: hope. We need only look at our own present time to see that, understood in this light, Bulgakov's sophiology is as needed now as when it was first put to paper.

Building the House of Wisdom
DOI 10.17438/978-3-402-12191-7

Mariology as Personalized Sophiology.
Sergii Bulgakov's Chalcedonian Theology

Dario Colombo

"The heart and the soul, the personal center of creation, is the Virgin Mother"[1]—a very provocative sentence in Bulgakov's work *The Bride of the Lamb*, especially for me as a Christian of Protestant origin. This article attempts to show why Mariology is not only central to Christian theology, but necessary. That said, I hope I don't meet the same fate as Bulgakov, who was not allowed to speak about Mary at the First World (Ecumenical) Conference on Faith and Order in Lausanne 1927. He did it anyway and so will I.[2] In this contribution I will argue that in a Christian theology that starts from God incarnate, we cannot ignore Mary.

The Book *The Bride of the Lamb* "is the third and concluding volume of a theological trilogy devoted to the study of *Divine-humanity*, a fundamental truth of Christianity."[3] By 1939, *The Bride of the Lamb* was fully prepared for printing but had to be postponed due to the outbreak of the Second World War. Bulgakov did not live to see the publication of what he himself called the most

---

1   Sergius Bulgakov, *The Bride of the Lamb*, trans. Boris Jakim (Grand Rapids: W. B. Eerdmans, 2002), xviii.

2   Cf. Barbara Hallensleben, *Ökumene als Pfingstgeschehen bei Sergij N. Bulgakov.* In: *Ökumene. Das eine Ziel—die vielen Wege*, ed. Iso Baumer and Guido Vergauwen 1995, 156–58. Bulgakov says in his report on this conference: "But first the question must be posed, directly derived from the acceptance of the Nicene Creed, of the meaning and power of the veneration of the Godmother [...]. This is the question that most divides the Christian world, and the treatment of it must be brought to full clarity. All this presupposes a long and difficult road of study, discussion, and debate. However, the disputants are no longer enemies, but friends, seeking to understand one another." Sergii Bulgakov, *K voprosu o Lozanskoi konferentsii*, in: *Put'* 13 (1928), 71–82: 82. That long road is taken here, with the attempt to understand a friend.

3   Bulgakov, *The Bride of the Lamb*, xvii.

important part of his work on Divine-humanity. In view of the horror of the war, Bulgakov emphasizes:

> The truths contained in the revelation of Divine-humanity, particularly in its eschatological aspect, are so unshakable and universal that even the most shattering events of world history, which we are now witnessing, pale and are nullified in their ontological significance in the face of these truths insofar as we perceive these events in the light of that which is to come. And that which is to come is the Church in its power and glory, together with the transfiguration of creation.[4]

Ecclesiology and Eschatology mean hope for the world, which is founded not in chaos, but in God who became human (Christology) to redeem the world in and through the Holy Spirit (Pneumatology). In this act of God, humanity is involved. What role does Mary play in Divine-humanity? To answer this question, we must first clarify how Bulgakov develops his theology.

In the preface to the first part of Bulgakov's trilogy, *The Lamb of God*, he outlines his way of doing theology: In order to formulate a doctrine of Divine-humanity, one must "develop a Chalcedonian theology."[5] The question which he is trying to answer is the following: "How is the incarnation of God possible, what does it presuppose and what does it include?" In his argumentation, he intends to avoid the one-sidedness of both pantheism and transcendentism.[6] In order to achieve this, a *Chalcedonian theology* is needed: Jesus Christ is *one* person in *two* natures, perfect in divinity and perfect in humanity.[7] Within a non-Chalcedonian theology, Jesus is viewed as *only* God (or *only* seemingly human) or *only* human. The first way leads to pantheism, the second to transcendentism. Only a Chalcedonian theology does not fall into a one-sidedness. I will argue that Bulgakov's Chalcedonian theology is of utmost importance for the Mariological question.

In my view, this is an important addition to Walter Nunzio Sisto's book about Bulgakov's Mariology: *The Mother of God in the Theology of Sergius Bul-*

---

4   Bulgakov, *The Bride of the Lamb*, xvii–xviii.
5   This statement comes from Bulgakov's preface to the book *The Lamb of God*. However, this preface was omitted by the English translator in the edition otherwise used here.
6   In *The Bride of the Lamb*, Bulgakov speaks more of cosmism and dualism.
7   Peter Hünermann, Heinrich Denzinger (DH), *Compendium of Creeds, Definitions, and Declarations on Matters of Faith and Morals*. 43rd ed. (San Francisco: Ignatius Press, 2012), 301–02.

gakov. The Soul of the World (New York: Routledge, 2018).[8] He has taken too little time to point out the Chalcedonian disputes, which does not explain well enough why, according to Bulgakov, Mary must be called the heart and soul, the personal center of creation. Apollinarius, for example, who plays a central role in Bulgakov's investigation, is not mentioned at all. Therefore, I am trying to fill a gap regarding that matter.

I will argue that a Chalcedonian theology leads directly to Sophiology. If Jesus is fully God and fully man, something is thereby said about creation. God and the world cannot be understood as fundamentally different from each other. I will also argue that a Chalcedonian theology leads to Mariology. The divine Logos is the person of Christ and thus cannot be understood as a created person. Who, then, is God's human and created counterpart? According to the Bible, it is the people of Israel. In this context, Mary must be understood as the culmination of this narrative, for she conceives and gives birth to the God who becomes man. Therefore, I want to bring Mariology back into the conversation of a Chalcedonian theology. Or put the other way around: A Chalcedonian theology always leads to Sophiology and Mariology.

Chalcedonian Theology

The possibility of the incarnation always was and remains the most fundamental problem of Christology: How can the infinite God become a finite human without giving up his divinity and without humanity being subsumed into divinity? The first attempts to answer the unification of divinity and humanity in Christ were proposed by Irenaeus († around 200) and Athanasius († 373) with a soteriological argument: "God assumed the whole man in order to save and deify him."[9] While this emphasizes the union of divinity and humanity in Jesus Christ, the question of how this union *is possible* has not been answered.

---

8   Sisto's conclusion on Bulgakov's Mariology: Mary is the pneumatophoric hypostasis. Mary is the first human hypostasis (person) to be fully deified. Mary illustrates the human side of the divine-human synergy of the economy of salvation. That means: God involves a created human hypostasis in the salvation of the world. Mary is the New Eve and the heart and the soul of the world, the complete personification of Sophia in its feminine and creaturely form. Sisto calls Bulgakov's Mariology *anticipated eschatology*—in her womb she receives salvation itself. That is why meditation on the role of Mary in salvation history ultimately sheds light on what incarnation means.

9   Sergius Bulgakov, *The Lamb of God*, trans. Boris Jakim (Grand Rapids: W. B. Eerdmans, 2008), 3. Cf. Irenaeus, *Adversus Haereses* III,19,1; Athanasius, *De incarnatione Verbi*, 54.

According to Bulgakov, Apollinarius asked this question in its radicality for the first time.[10] The question is not only that of the union of divinity and humanity in Christ, but rather about how this is thinkable without contradiction. The basic axiom of Apollinarius is that "two perfect [complete] principles cannot become one."[11] Therefore, if the perfect God were to unite with the "perfect" human, there would be two perfect principles existing in two natures. The question is: If the divine and human natures were to become one, would the human nature not be destroyed? Apollinarius therefore speaks of "mixing" (*synkrasis*).[12] This is where the central problem of Christology becomes clear:

> How can one understand the *union* of the divine essence and the human essence in the God-Man without transforming this union into a duality, into nothing more than a certain harmonization [...]? In other words, how can one assure their real unification while preserving the authenticity and autonomy of each of the essences without the absorption of the one by the other [...]?[13]

According to Bulgakov, Apollinarius has posed the real question of Christology: How is the unification of divinity and humanity conceivable? His heresy claims a composite nature of Christ,[14] which ultimately negates the freedom of humanity, because the perfect divine nature dominates the defective human nature and can thus only perfect it at the price of its annulment: "The [human nature] must therefore be subjugated, made subordinate to the divine nature [...] and therefore it cannot be perfect, that is, complete."[15]

Bulgakov takes up the crucial Christological question of Apollinarius, as he was misunderstood and condemned because of it. This led to the essential question's being suppressed and only resurfacing when Nestorius, Bishop of Antioch († 451), began to deny the title *Theotokos* for Mary.[16] Nestorius did not reject the title completely, but wanted it interpreted and limited in a certain

---

10   "Apollinarius was the first to consider a fundamental problem of Christology: What is
      the Divine-Humanity? Or, how is the Incarnation possible? What does it presuppose?"
      Bulgakov, *The Lamb of God*, 4.
11   Bulgakov, *The Lamb of God*, 5.
12   Cf. ibid., 6.
13   Ibid., 7.
14   Ibid., 10.
15   Ibid., 5. For a brief summary of the meaning of Apollinarius, see ibid., 17 f.
16   Cf. ibid., 40 f.

way.[17] He was interested not in a Mariological question, but in a Christological. He wanted to maintain both the divine and the human natures of Christ. If Christ assumed humanity wholly, then human nature must also remain as such. Bulgakov traces Nestorius' thought through his work *Liber Heraclidis* (*LH*). In it, Nestorius uses the vague term *prosopon* and develops it further to be able to state unity and duality in Christ. It is important to point out a major difficulty in the development of early Christology, indeed of theology as a whole: *the problem of terms*. Not only the bilingualism of Latin and Greek, but also the different use of the same terms in the same language and their change of meaning over time make it difficult to clearly determine the meaning of a theological position. The very terms *prosopon, ousia, hypostasis, physis*, etc. can sometimes denote different things and sometimes the same thing, depending on who is using them and in what context.[18]

A literal translation of *prosopon* is 'face, countenance, mask'. The problem is that Nestorius uses the term *prosopon* to express both unity and duality in Christ. He speaks of a *natural prosopon* and a *prosopon of union*. Nestorius thus uses the term *prosopon* (as *natural prosopon*) on the one hand to designate the peculiarities of two natures which remain distinct even after unification. Thus, the need for redemption belongs to the peculiarity of human nature, holiness to divine nature. On the other hand, Nestorius uses *prosopon* (as *prosopon of union*) to express unity in Christ. This *prosopon of union* belongs to each of the two natures, which in turn have their corresponding *prosopa*. In Bulgakov's words:

> In *The Bazaar of Heracleides*, Nestorius insistently and repeatedly develops the idea that the two natural *prosōpa* constitute one *prosōpon* of union, Christ.[19]

According to Bulgakov, Nestorius' great achievement is to have clearly stated the duality of natures in Christ. However, he was unable to explain their union.[20] If the complete man is to be assumed, then the human nature must not be dissolved in divinity. Nestorius thus keeps the duality of natures, as Chalcedon later will do too: *Jesus Christ* has *two natures*, one fully divine and

---

17 Nestorius "only insisted that it be defined more precisely. In a polemic against a particular Christological doctrine, he proposed, as more precise, the term 'Theodokos' (bearer of man and of God)." Bulgakov, *The Lamb of God*, 41.
18 Cf. ibid., 3 f.
19 Ibid., 43.
20 Cf. ibid., 45.

one fully human. Nestorius did not see that the unity of the person is already implied in this statement. As soon as the same term *(prosopon)* is used both for the distinction of the *two natures* and for the *unity*, no clarity is achieved. In the end, the term does not matter: Nestorius could have already anticipated Chalcedon if he had said that Christ is one *prosopon* in *two natures* without also using the term prosopon to distinguish the two natures. For it is also possible to use terms like person and hypostasis, not only to express the unity, but also to distinguish the two natures.[21] In this way, these terms would also lead to a heretical Christology, because they simultaneously express the unity and duality in Christ.

In contrast to this is the position of Cyril of Alexandria (†444). Cyril is particularly disturbed by the weak term union *(sunapheia)* that Nestorius uses to express the unity in Christ.[22] He rejects it because it does not sufficiently express the oneness of Christ and thus gives rise to a two-sons doctrine. In his view, the duality in Christ must be carried by unity: The *hypostasis* bears the two natures. He thinks of this union so radically that he speaks of a completely united nature in Christ. Thus, Cyril emphasizes the other side of Christology to which Chalcedon will adhere: *Jesus Christ* is *one hypostasis* bearing a perfectly unified nature. Cyril, however, falls into the one-sidedness complementary to Nestorius and does not see clearly enough how the duality of natures must be co-stated. According to Bulgakov, Cyril owes his opponent the answer as to how this union is to be understood. He saves himself in the "paradox of faith":

> In the final analysis, St. Cyril ends the theological debate by an appeal to the authority of faith: "Do not inquire, I ask you, into this matter […] such a union [of soul and body] is unexplainable. […] Soul and body are inseparable from Divinity." His argument is purely soteriological: From the religiously indisputable fact of the reality of our existence and our salvation, it follows that if the Word had not become flesh and had not suffered by trials and temptations, He would not be able to help those who are tried and tempted, and His sufferings would not do us any good. "Does a shadow suffer?"[23]

---

21 This is also alarmingly evident in modern Christology. I refer to Aaron Riches' book *Ecce homo. On the Divine Unity of Christ* (Grand Rapids: W.B. Eerdmans, 2016), in which he proves the ecclesiastical-theological affirmation of the oneness of Christ dogma-historically.

22 Cf. Bulgakov, *The Lamb of God*, 41.

23 Ibid., 31 f.

Nestorius and Cyril thus accuse each other of negating the reality of salvation in the incarnation. Nestorius accused Cyril of fusing natures, and Cyril accused Nestorius of doubling the persons.[24] Both emphasize a necessary side of Christology. Jesus Christ must be one person (hypostasis/prosopon). In this respect, Cyril emphasizes a truth: It is not possible to speak of two centers of unity in Christ, because otherwise God would not have become human, but would only have settled in an already existing person. Nestorius also emphasizes such a truth: This one-person Jesus Christ must preserve in himself the two natures—the divine and the human—because otherwise humanity would be dissolved into divinity.

This dispute found a temporary end in the dogmatic formula of the Council of Chalcedon:

> Following therefore the holy Fathers, we unanimously teach to confess one and the same Son, our Lord Jesus Christ, the same perfect in divinity and perfect in humanity, the same truly God and truly man [...] We confess that one and the same Lord Jesus Christ, the only begotten Son, must be acknowledged in two natures, without confusion or change, without division or separation. The distinction between the natures was never abolished by their union but rather the character proper to each of the two natures was preserved as they came together in one Person [...][25]

The truth about Christ can only be formulated if *one person* and *both natures* are affirmed. This is the theological root of a concept that Bulgakov uses over and over: the *antinomy*. An antinomy consists of two contradictory statements, each of which is necessary and must therefore be held. Chalcedonian theology can thus be described as an antinomian form of theology: Jesus is fully God and fully human. The antinomy binds divinity and humanity together in the one-person Jesus Christ. A one-sided emphasis on the divinity or humanity of Jesus always becomes heresy (pantheism or transcendentism). It is about a theology in which thesis and antithesis are not dissolved in a higher synthesis, but are *held together in* a higher synthesis, without confusion and without separation.

According to Bulgakov, even the Chalcedonian formula does not solve the Christological problem, but represents a new birth, insofar as the formula is neither the result of Antiochian-Nestorian nor Alexandrian-Cyrillic theology:

---

24 Cf. Bulgakov, *The Lamb of God*, 41.
25 DH 301–02.

The Definition of Chalcedon is the *synthetic* resolution of the dialectical antithetics that we have in the Christology of the schools of Antioch and of Alexandria. In a certain sense, this definition says both "yes" and "no" to both schools, raising them to a higher unity.[26]

Bulgakov tries to show the dialectical structure of early church history. The thesis of Cyril is the unity of the God-Man, which finds its heretical expression in Monophysitism, Monotheletism and Monoenergism. The antithesis of Nestorius is the duality of natures in the God-Man, which finds its heretical expression in Ditheletism and Adoptionism. The doctrine of Chalcedon embraces both: "the thesis and the antithesis, the bi-unity of the God-Man and the unity of the hypostasis in the duality of the natures [...]".[27] *Chalcedonian theology is antinomian theology.*

That Jesus Christ is *one* person in *two* natures is essential for understanding the importance of Mariology. But before this can be examined, we must take another step. As already emphasized, Chalcedon leaves us above all with a conceptual tension: How does one interpret this conceptual tension? How does one do theology after Chalcedon? Is an antinomian theology even possible? This tension, according to Bulgakov, can be endured only with Sophiology.

Sophiology as the Natural Foundation of Theology

Bulgakov is not simply concerned with *the relationship between divinity and humanity in Jesus Christ.* He further asks: *How is the unification of divinity and humanity in Jesus Christ possible?* The formula of Chalcedon shows that this question is self-evident:

The negative formula of the Council of Chalcedon cannot be understood as a *prohibition* against positive definitions; it can be understood only as a *preliminary* definition, incomplete, inexhaustive, awaiting continuation.[28]

---

26 Bulgakov, *The Lamb of God*, 56 f.
27 Ibid., 18. I am aware that in the logic of my presentation Nestorius should have formulated the thesis and Cyril the antithesis. Cyril, however, is chronologically earlier, which is why in Bulgakov's account he is also the one who formulates the thesis. However, I chose Nestorius first because the real dispute about Christology only begins with his rejection of a certain way of using the title of Theotokos.
28 Ibid., 195 f.

The Chalcedonian formula answers the question as to the relationship between divinity and humanity in Jesus Christ, and thereby raises the question of the God–world relationship: How is it possible that Jesus is fully God and fully human and what must creation be like, to enable the incarnation? In other words: the Christological question becomes a sophiological question:

> The central point from which Sophiology proceeds is that of the relation between *God* and *the World*, or, what is practically the same thing, between *God* and *humanity*. In other words we are faced with the question of the meaning and significance of Divine-humanity—not only insofar as it concerns the God-human, the incarnate Logos, but precisely insofar as it applies to the theandric union between God and the whole of the creaturely world, through humanity and in humanity.[29]

The Chalcedonian formula answers the question as to the relationship between divinity and humanity in Jesus Christ. Bulgakov asks in his Sophiology how this relationship is possible. The Christian doctrine of the incarnation becomes the decisive starting point. The belief in the incarnation of God "presupposes the existence of absolutely necessary dogmatic assumptions in the doctrine of God and humanity."[30] These presuppositions are unfolded in Sophiology. In Christ, an original unity is presupposed, which bears this duality. The one-person Jesus bears the two natures perfectly, "without confusion or change, without division or separation." In this way, incarnation and the Chalcedonian formula presuppose certain conditions for the God-world relationship:

> *It is no alienation for God to enter a community of life with humanity and the world. Or: God can become human without giving up his divinity and humankind can receive God without losing their humanity.*

This is what Sophiology in its core means and only in this way can the Chalcedonian formula be taken seriously. Sophiology thus is a Chalcedonian antinomy for the whole of theology: *Sophiology is Chalcedonian theology.* This has considerable implications for the doctrine of creation. Sophiology arises from the reflection on the dogmatic presuppositions that necessarily follow from a Chalcedonian theology: If Jesus Christ is fully God and fully human, it cannot be an alienation or even a contradiction for God himself to enter a community of life with his creatures. On the contrary, humanity, indeed ulti-

---

29 Sergei Bulgakov, *Sophia. The Wisdom of God* (Hudson: Lindisfarne Press, 1993) 14.
30 Bulgakov, *Sophia*, 18.

mately the whole of creation, was created for the reception of God. These are dogmatic presuppositions that a Chalcedonian theology necessarily requires: Creation cannot be thought outside of or in contradiction to God. In a certain sense we must speak of creation in God, or rather of creation as a part-giving of God's life.

This idea can be explored by the Christian doctrine of *creatio ex nihilo*. Bulgakov emphasizes: "Nothingness" does not exist. We only know the concept because we derive it from being. We cannot think "nothing" because we know nothing only as a negation of being, that is, as a conceptual deduction from the concept of being. Therefore, creation out of nothing cannot mean: God creates "something" out of "nothing". This "nothing" does not exist. In Bulgakov's words:

> In fact, such an extra-divine nothing simply does not exist. It is by no means the limit to divine being. Divine being is limitless. Nothing is by no means like an ocean that flows around this being. Rather, it is divinity itself that is an ocean without any shores.[31]

If creation out of nothing cannot be understood as creation out of something that is next to God, it must be said that God creates "out of himself" to give space to creation in himself: The eternal-being God is with his essence (his "nature") the foundation of the finite-temporal creature. Creation out of nothing thus only means "that the world exists in God and only by God, for the world does not have within itself the ground of its own being."[32] Bulgakov calls this foundation of creation in God: *Sophia*. God is the fullness of being and therein the foundation of creation. Everything comes from God and has its foundation in God. In Bulgakov's words:

> The creation of the world is included in God's sophianic self-positing and consists in the fact that the Divine being in Sophia receives *another being in the world*. The Divine Sophia exists in a dual mode: in her own mode, which belongs to her in eternity; and in the creaturely mode, as the world. Only such an identification of the two modes of Sophia, with their simultaneous differentiation, can explain why, although God is the Creator, this does not change his divinely sophianic being or introduce in the latter a non-divine or extra-divine principle.[33]

---

31   Bulgakov, *The Bride of the Lamb*, 43 f.
32   Ibid., 6.
33   Ibid., 52.

Creation should neither be understood monistically as God, nor dualistically outside of God, but in an antinomy that holds together both the eternity of God and the finitude of creation:

> The fullness of the truth compels us to affirm both the one and the other: The world is eternal in God, for in Him all is eternal, as in its eternal prototype, the Divine Sophia; and the world exists, as such, as a creation, in temporality or becoming. The two are incompatible abstractly-logically, but, ontologically, they mutually condition each other.[34]

Chalcedonian theology leads to Sophiology: The antinomy of Jesus Christ as fully God and fully human has its foundation in the antinomy of God and its creation. A theology that takes the Chalcedonian formula as its starting point becomes Sophiology, that is, a doctrine of God-humanity, a doctrine of the God–world relationship. And that is why we must ask the question about Mary. After all, she is the one who has the most intimate relationship with God.

Mariology as Personalized Sophiology

So far, the Chalcedonian formula has been examined in regarding the antinomy between the *two natures* of Christ: Jesus Christ bears the two natures perfectly. This statement has significant Christological and Anthropological consequences: In Jesus Christ there is no separate human person, but the divine Logos is the person of Jesus Christ. Jesus Christ is the divine Logos who became human: "The Word became flesh" (Joh 1:14). The presupposition of a human person alongside the divine person in Christ becomes—as is evident in Nestorius—a two-sons doctrine, which annuls the unity of Christ and thus negates the incarnation of God. In Christ, God himself assumed humanity—that is, the nature of humanity—and approached human beings personally.

This raises the question as to a personal counterpart: In Jesus Christ, it is not humanity that personally says yes to God, but God personally says yes to humanity. This confronts us with the fundamental question of salvation: If Jesus Christ is not the counterpart of God, if he is not a created person, but God incarnate, that is, the uncreated divine person as human, how does salvation personally arrive at humanity?

At this point it becomes clear why the Virgin Mother is the heart and the soul of creation: Mary is the one who personally says yes to God, conceives and

---

34   Bulgakov, *The Bride of the Lamb*, 70.

gives birth to the incarnating God. If theology is to hold on to the personal counterpart of humanity to God, Mary and thus Mariology must form the intersection of theology. If God became human, then no greater devotion can be imagined than that expressed by Mary in her response to Gabriel: "Let it be to me according to your word" (Lk 1:38). If God became human, then Mary is the highest possible form of union between a created person and God. Christ is the God-Man who has fully assumed humanity, and Mary is the one who has realized God-humanity as a human being in the highest way. In short: *Mary is the personal center of creation.* If this is not taken seriously, as Bulgakov accuses Protestantism of doing, then "the Virgin Mary is only an instrument for the Incarnation, inevitable, but still something external, an instrument which is laid aside and forgotten when the need has passed".[35] Thus, it is not possible to hold on to "the sanctification and the glorification of human nature."[36] Only in Mary does it become apparent what God-humanity means for human beings, because the God-humanity of Christ is and remains the God-humanity of God who became human. Mary's God-humanity is the creaturely personal side of the God-humanity of humanity, to which every human being is called.[37]

This leads us to the question of history: So far, no attention has been paid to Mary's connection to the rest of humanity—a danger that is only too evident in Mariology. If one were to stop at this personal relationship between God and Mary, it would in any case become incomprehensible why the history of Israel, that is, God's salvation-history with his people, exists at all. The time of the Incarnation would become an arbitrary point in time, and the question why this did not already take place *in principio*, would pose a lot of problems for any theodicy. Bulgakov accuses the Catholic dogma of the Immaculate Conception of this flawed understanding which does not take seriously the fullness of time (Gal 4:4), because through this dogma

the whole human side of the preparation for God's incarnation becomes insubstantial and unimportant. Essentially the meaning of *the genealogy* of Christ the Saviour

35   Sergius Bulgakov, *The Orthodox Church*, trans. Lydia Kesich (Crestwood, New York: St Vladimir's Seminary Press, 1988), 116.
36   Ibid., 116.
37   At this point, the question of the human nature of Jesus Christ in relation to his person would have to be further reflected. But here there is only space for a short sophiological hint: The entire creation, that is, every smallest speck of dust participates in God's essence (nature), and it is precisely this creation that God accepted in a natural way in his incarnation (kenosis) and deified in his resurrection (theosis). In short: The unified God-human nature of Christ is the divine and creaturely Sophia fallen into one.

is cancelled. In fact, given such an understanding this act of restoration of *iustitiae originalis* could have come at any moment of history, and not in the fullness of time, and generally speaking, history as the *common task* of humanity, as the sole and coherent act which has the incarnation as its centre, does not even exist in such an understanding.[38]

Whether this applies to the dogma is not the subject of this article. However, it is essential to note that Mary relates to the history of Israel, as the Magnificat expresses:

> For he who is mighty has done great things for me [...] He has helped his servant Israel, in remembrance of his mercy, as he spoke to our fathers, to Abraham and to his offspring forever. (Lk 1:49, 54–5; ESV)

Mary is the culmination of God's history with his people, with Israel, and therefore Mary is the personal center of creation: All human beings are called to be a counterpart to God. This began in the history of Israel (Abraham, Moses, etc.). But so far, the full union has only taken place once: in Mary, the mother of God. In its essence, Mariology is therefore about indicating the historical-personal place where the God-humanity of human beings has already become reality: namely in *Mary*. *Mariology is thus personalized Sophiology*: The antinomy of the divinity and humanity of Jesus Christ, which is revealed in a Chalcedonian theology and outlined as Sophiology, can only be held together in Mariology.[39] Recently Aaron Riches has stated a similar thesis:

> Here I claim that the Jesus-Mary relation is so integral to the incarnational fact, and therefore to a coherent Christocentrism, that a Christology without a full Marian account fails to be incarnational in any meaningful way and is reduced to mere abstraction.[40]

---

38 Sergius Bulgakov, *The Burning Bush. On the Orthodox Veneration of the Mother of God*, trans. Thomas Allan Smith (Grand Rapids: W. B. Eerdmans, 2009), 51.

39 Sisto makes the same point: "Mary is Sophia inasmuch as she is the actualization of Godhumanhood from the perspective of humankind (i. e., she demonstrates how God involves humankind in God's revelation and saving work)". Sisto, *The Mother of God in the Theology of Sergius Bulgakov*, 113. But what should be clearer in this article is the Chalcedonian foundation of this statement.

40 Riches, *Ecce homo*, 17. What is missing in Riches is the reference to Sophiology (or something like it) as the basis or presupposition for the incarnation. Of course, Sisto stresses this point too: "Mariology provides a corrective function for Christology against

Only Mariology allows there to be a human-personal counterpart to God that is not lost when the infinite God appears on the stage of finitude. There is no better way to express this than to say: "The heart and the soul, the personal center of creation, is the Virgin Mother."

Conclusion

A Chalcedonian theology, as I have tried to show here, will unfold on two sides. On the level of nature, it leads to Sophiology. That Jesus Christ possesses both natures has its foundation in the theology of creation: God and the world are neither the same nor opposed to each other, but God is the one who sustains the world in himself. On the level of the person, it leads to Mariology. That the divine Logos is the person of Christ leads to the question of a created human counterpart to God and this is found in the history of Israel, in the history of the Church, and, of course, in Mary.

Since God became human, Mariology should be understood as personalized Sophiology: The God-humanity of humanity, which is realized in Mary. Without Mary, there is no counterpart to God at the climax of salvation. Without Mariology theology remains incomplete. Positively formulated: Only in Mary and in the reflection on her can the relationship between God and humankind be held together, by which humanity is truly accepted. Only with Mary as the personal center of creation can the title of Bulgakov's greatest work be understood: *The Bride of the Lamb*.

What happened in the case of Mary, was that God himself entered the world and this is the vocation for the entire creation. Because ultimately it is the entire church, the Bride of the Lamb, that awaits its wedding. In this respect Mariology is hope for the world, because the coming one comes not as an oppressor but as the Lord of love. He comes as the one who can assume humanity without forcing and destroying it. He comes as the same one who has already walked, is walking and will walk the path of history with the persons of humanity, and it is precisely through this that God enables humanity to realize Divine-humanity:

> And in the face of this Coming Church, the prayer of faith, love, and hope should cry out again and again in one's heart: "And the Spirit and the bride say, Come! And let him that heareth say, Come! [...] He which testifieth these things saith, Surely I come quickly! Amen. Even so, come, Lord Jesus!" (Rev. 22:17, 20).[41]

non-Chalcedonian theology. How we view Mary is the litmus test to determine if our Christology is orthodox." Sisto, *The Mother of God in the Theology of Sergius Bulgakov*, 156.
41 Bulgakov, *The Bride of the Lamb*, xviii.

Building the House of Wisdom
DOI 10.17438/978-3-402-12192-4

The Training for Dying and Death: A New Reading of Bulgakov's Sophiology

Paul L. Gavrilyuk[1]

> *The one aim of those who practice philosophy in the proper manner*
> *is to train for dying and death.*
> (Plato, Phaedo 64a3–4)

Sergii Bulgakov's vast theological system is commonly presented under the general heading of "sophiology" or the teaching about Sophia, the Wisdom of God. For the Russian theologian, sophiological teaching provided a framework for addressing the central problem of God's relation to the world by extending the Chalcedonian dogma about Christ's two natures into the general principle of Godmanhood. Without rejecting this widely accepted reading of Bulgakov, this paper proposes that the central inspiration of Bulgakov's system was a set of revelatory experiences that he had while confronting mortality in various forms. I show how the encounter with mortality and dying shaped Bulgakov's worldview from his early childhood experiences to his struggle with throat cancer towards the end of his life. My contention is that Bulgakov's central theological intuition—that all things are "in God"—stems from his earth-shattering experiences of witnessing the deaths of those close to him, which were accompanied by an equally powerful sense of the reality of eternal life and resurrection.

---

1   First publication: Paul Gavrilyuk, "The Training for Dying and Death: A New Reading of Bulgakov's Sophiology," in *Christian Dying: Witnesses from the Tradition*, ed. Matthew Levering and George Kalantzis (Eugene, OR: Wipf & Stock Publishers https://wipfandstock.com/9781532630965/christian-dying/, 2018), 160–78.

In order to make my case, I examine the sources that are often neglected in the discussions of Bulgakov's theology: his *Autobiographical Notes*, *Spiritual Diary*, and the essay "The Sophiology of Death."[2] Having established the importance of the *memento mori* theme in Bulgakov's spirituality, I consider its implications for his theological system. I reach the conclusion that eternity revealed through death is an existential axle of Bulgakov's sophiology.

Sergii Bulgakov (1871–1944) grew up in the family of a Russian priest who was attached to a cemetery chapel in the provincial town of Livny and whose livelihood depended upon officiating at funeral services. As a boy, Sergii would find himself regularly participating in a solemn Easter procession, singing "Christ is risen" outside the cemetery chapel amidst the old graves.[3] The encounters with death and dying, sanctified by the solemnity of the Orthodox services for the departed, were a part of the young Bulgakov's everyday existence. Years later Bulgakov would write about his childhood home: "I do not recall any weddings; but I do recall numerous funerals."[4] In this house, one by one, most members of his large extended family expired, beginning with his grandfather. As Bulgakov reminisced years later:

> With his departure, death for the first time entered into my young mind (I was 12).
> I was, on the one hand, mystically shaken, and on the other hand, defended myself
> with animal self-love. Funerals in Livny were done right: it was some sort of Egypt.
> And first of all, there was no fear of death. The relatives, first of all women, arrived
> to dress the departed, to pray for him, and to help with the household chores with

---

2   These works were written during different periods of Bulgakov's life. The first part of
     Autobiographical Notes, entitled "My Motherland," was written in the beginning of
     1938 during Bulgakov's trip to Athens; the surviving entries of the *Spiritual Diary* date
     to 1924–1926; finally, the first part of "The Sophiology of Death" was written in 1939,
     sometime after Bulgakov underwent two surgeries to treat his throat cancer in the May
     of the same year, while the second part comes from a diary of 1926. The editions cited
     here are as follows, in my own translation: "Avtobiograficheskoe," in *S. N. Bulgakov:
     Pro et Contra* (St. Petersburg: RKhGI, 2003), vol. 1: 63–111; *Dnevnik dukhovnyi* (Moscow: Obshchedostupnii Pravoslavnii Universitet osnovannii Aleksandrom Menem,
     2008); "Sofiologiia smerti," *Vestnik Russkogo khristianskogo dvizheniia* 127 (1978), [I:]
     18–41; 128 (1978), [II:] 13–32. Meanwhile, the latter two works have become available
     in English translation: Sergius Bulgakov, *Spiritual Diary* (Brooklyn, NY, 2022), trans.
     Roberto De La Noval and Mark Roosien; Sergius Bulgakov, *The Sophiology of Death.
     Essays on Eschatology: Personal, Political, Universal* (Eugene, OR, 2021), trans. Roberto
     De La Noval.
3   Bulgakov, "Avtobiograficheskoe," 69.
4   Ibid., 65.

a joyous, solemn feeling. Then came the funeral in the church with the carrying of the coffin around town accompanied by the ringing of the bells, the giving of the body back to the earth, the veneration of the tomb, and prayer-filled memory. They bury well in Livny. If it is possible to speak of the sophianicity of a funeral, then it could be said that the burial was sophianic, bearing a mark of eternity, a triumph of life, and a union with nature. "Dust thou art and unto dust shalt thou return." [Gen 3: 19, KJV][5]

While these words reflect Bulgakov's much later interpretation of his childhood encounter with the reality of death, it is plausible that even as a child he could experience as vague calls of the heart those things that would with time grow into deeply rooted convictions: the absence of the fear of death, the awareness of the presence of God, the triumph of eternity over time, and a sense of passing into another world in order to reach a greater state of union with the cosmos.

After the death of his grandfather, "the angel of death unceasingly stood before our house,"[6] remarked Bulgakov, reflecting on the deaths of five of his siblings, two dying in infancy, one in early childhood, one in adolescence, and one in young adulthood. Perhaps the most profound impact was that of the death of his younger brother Mikhail, of consumption:

> Even now, after 40 years, my eyes are filled with tears when I recall his holy, beautiful death. Before he departed this world, he was sent like an angel to pour the treasure of his death into my soul. This was at night. It was evident that his agony had begun. All stood up, surrounded him, and my father began to read the service for those about to die (everybody felt that this was quite natural). "Is this a service for those about to die?"—asked Mikhail and began to say farewell to everybody, kissing everyone for the last time. He kissed me so [...] He particularly wanted me to be near him, when I was so full of myself, only of myself [...] He left peacefully and the mystery of death was filled with light. His hands, as the hands of those dying of consumption, were white. The sun was breaking out, my brother Lelia and I went into the garden, and my heart was filled with heavenly music, with a celebration that is made possible by tender, quiet, faithful death, which opens up the heavens and angels [...] Yes, death was our educator in this household so full of death.[7]

---

5   Bulgakov, "Avtobiograficheskoe," 72–73.
6   Ibid., 75.
7   Ibid., 74.

Not all deaths in Bulgakov's family caused him to humbly acquiesce in the inevitable. Bulgakov's recollection of the death of his infant brother Kos'ma was quite chilling: "I remember the night with the dead body of my infant brother at home and my mother's howling cries at night [...] This event has crept into my heart as a call and dread and awe-inspiring memory of eternity."[8] Bulgakov noted that he had a similar experience on the occasion of his grandfather's death in his household. "Awe-inspiring memory of eternity" remained an existential constant of his subsequent confrontations with human mortality, animating and shaping his theological thought.

The loss of his five-year-old brother Nikolai was a deeply wounding and fearful experience, filling Bulgakov's household with grief and lament. Years later, in 1909, Bulgakov would have to endure the agony and death of his own three-year-old son, Ivan, similar to his parents' suffering through the death of Nikolai and other children. For Bulgakov, Ivan's death was not only a bleeding wound, a scar upon his family that would never heal completely, but also a profound epiphany of love. He describes the revelatory character of confronting Ivan's death in *The Unfading Light* (1917), a book that is generally regarded as marking a theological turn in his thinking:

> My holy one, before the holy shrine of your relics, near your pure body, my white one, my light-filled boy, I have learned *how* God speaks, I understood the meaning of the words "God said!" And my heart was granted a new, previously unknown clairvoyance as the heavenly joy came upon it and together with the darkness of Godforsakenness, God came to reign in it. My heart opened itself to the pain and torment of other people and their previously foreign and closed hearts opened up to me with their pain and grief. For a single moment of my life I came to understand what it meant to love with the love of Christ, rather than with the love that was human, selfish and seeking its own. It is as if the veil that separated me from others fell and all the darkness, bitterness, hurt, anger, and suffering of their hearts was revealed to me. Unspeakably elated, ecstatic, self-forgetting, I spoke then—you remember this, my white one!—I spoke: *God said to me*, and, hearing you, with equal simplicity added, *you spoke to me too*. And God spoke to me then and you spoke to me! Presently I again see only in darkness and cold and, hence, can speak of these things only from memory, but I have learned the meaning of the words *God said*. [...]

---

8   Bulgakov, "Avtobiograficheskoe," 75.

Listening to the Epistle Reading [in the church] about the resurrection and about the general sudden transformation [...] I came to understand for the first time that it would happen *for certain* and *how* it would happen.[9]

As Bulgakov was praying at the deathbed of his son, something new and profound had happened. We might recall that, according to his own admission, he defended himself emotionally from the death of his grandfather with "animal self-love" and that he persevered in being "full of" himself when his dying brother Mikhail reached out to him in the last embrace of love. But in the death of Bulgakov's son, it is as if the "the veil that separated him from others fell off" and he was given an epiphany of complete, all-consuming love for others, love that had enabled him to enter experientially into the grief and pain of others like never before. In the encounter with his son's death, Bulgakov was also given to understand and experientially enter into the reality behind Paul's words in 1 Cor. 15: 51–53: "Listen, I will tell you a mystery! We will not all die, but we will all be changed, in a moment, in the twinkling of an eye, at the last trumpet. For the trumpet will sound, and the dead will be raised imperishable, and we will be changed. For this perishable body must put on imperishability, and this mortal body must put on immortality." The death of his son had lifted the veil of his self-love and given him a new, more profound taste of transfigured humanity. In light of these deeply formative and ego-shattering experiences, Bulgakov could write: "One's Motherland is only where there is death. This is why the last word about the Motherland is about death."[10]

The epiphany received in 1909 would continue shedding its light upon Bulgakov's priestly ministry, especially his care for the dying and his sense of the participation of the saints in the Eucharistic communion. I would also suggest that this epiphany gave him peace and spiritual strength in the times of extreme adversity and accounted for the eschatological thrust of his sophiology.

Following a calling common to the six generations of his ancestors, Bulgakov became a priest in June 1918, less than a year after the Bolshevik coup d'état in Russia. The price that Bulgakov immediately paid for his ordination was the loss of a university post in Moscow for his perceived opposition to the atheist regime. During the time of the Civil War, he found himself serving at a provincial parish in Crimea not dissimilar to his father's parish in Livny. Here Fr. Sergii would witness with great anguish how some of his parishioners would starve to death and he felt guilty for remaining alive, although he was

9   S. N. Bulgakov, *Svet Nevechernii* (Moscow: Respublika, 1994), 18.
10   Bulgakov, "Avtobiograficheskoe," 77.

gradually deprived of basic means of existence. But the Soviet authorities could not rest until they quashed all opposition to their power. In 1922, Bulgakov was arrested and had to watch his fellow prisoners being shot by the drunken officers of the Red Army. In early 1923, the regime expelled Bulgakov on one of the "Philosophy Steamers" along with other prominent religious thinkers and philosophers of his time. Bulgakov put the matter astringently: "As she was herself rotting in a casket, Russia expelled me as useless, having branded me with the mark of a slave."[11] The experience of expulsion and deracination was both traumatic and stimulating. Not unlike Bulgakov's encounter with death and bereavement, which was at once heartbreaking and transforming, the experience of dying to his own country was a both blow and a providential opportunity. Among many burdens of émigré life—the loss of most of his Russian-speaking audience, the challenges of leading the St. Sergii Orthodox Theological Institute against much strife and opposition, financial instability, and finally the advent of fascism and World War II—none was as emotionally draining as the permanent separation from his elder son, Fedor (1902–1991), who was left behind the Iron Curtain in 1923, never to be seen by his parents again. Bulgakov often agonized over the fate of his son, especially when for long stretches of time he did not receive any letters from him. After World War II, Fedor was able to travel abroad for the first time in order to visit his parents' graves at Sainte-Geneviève-des-Bois near Paris.

Bulgakov's *Spiritual Diary*, which he kept from 1924 to 1926 during his first years in Paris, is a unique testament to his life with God. The main thrust of the diary is vertical, rather than horizontal. Bulgakov is primarily addressing God and his soul, as he stands *coram Deo*. He is brutally honest with himself, functioning as his own harshest judge, sometimes to the point of being quite self-effacing. He registers his human interactions, but rarely reveals many particulars. The diary is a testament to Bulgakov's profoundly Christocentric and Mariological piety. While sophiological motifs appear, Sophia is never made an object of prayer or private adoration, as in Vladimir Soloviev. Whatever one might claim about Bulgakov's theological "modernism," his spiritual life was profoundly grounded in his childhood experiences of death and dying, as well as his attendance at the Orthodox services, especially those of the feasts of Easter and the Dormition of the Theotokos (an Orthodox equivalent of the Assumption of the Blessed Virgin, celebrated on August 15). The diary contains Bulgakov's own Akathistos (hymn of praise) to Mary, in which he speaks of

11   Bulgakov, "Iz dnevnika," in *Tikhie dumy*, ed. V. V. Sapov and K. M. Dolgov (Moscow: Respublika, 1996), 351.

her as "bringing consolation at the hour of death"[12] and "making death a joy-ous feast by her light."[13] Bulgakov is strikingly traditional and conventional, almost pre-modern, in his piety, especially if one considers the prominence of the *memento mori* theme in his diary. In fact, his observation that "life must be a constant dying for the Lord"[14] could serve as the diary's epigraph. The prevailing tone of the diary reminds one of the spiritual sobriety and clarity of St. John of Kronshtadt's *My Life in Christ*. Bulgakov speaks of the love of God, of prayer, of humble acceptance of suffering, and of being mindful of God, and of his own failures with remarkable honesty and simplicity. The theosophic motifs, associated with the period when he was influenced by Pavel Florenskii, are conspicuously absent from the diary, as are sophiological speculations.

Bulgakov reflects on mortality in the context of dying and parting with the dead in several diary entries. For example, in the entry dated October 7(20), 1924, he writes:

We are created for eternity, it is not here below that we are called to live—this becomes evident when the most precious person departs for the other world but the lover remains here, in this world. How does one save love from powerlessness, how does one save the soul from despair? [One can do so] only by God and in God, only through prayer. The wings of prayer will carry us into another world, they will give us an invisible connection with the beloved, they will carry us closer and closer to him until the hour of our own call and until the light of our eyes goes out too.[15]

In his capacity of father confessor and parish priest, Bulgakov attended to the needs of those approaching the hour of death, following in the steps of his own father. At times he speaks of this ministry with poetic lyricism. Here, for example, is the beginning of his diary entry dated January 23 (February 5), 1925:

I witnessed a striking and touching picture of a young maiden's departure to God. The Lord brought me to her deathbed not long before her end. Christ visited her and communed her of His Body and Blood by my sinful hand. Then her soul took flight to the Bridegroom as a bird flying into the blue abyss of the sky. And heaven appeared in that room of sorrow, the Lord was close, granting the miracle of divine

12   Bulgakov, *Dnevnik dukhovnyi*, 48.
13   Ibid., 49.
14   Ibid., 89.
15   Ibid., 53–54.

mercy. She lay quietly, clearly and plainly, having known everything that we do not know here below. And around her everything was prayerful and solemn.[16]

Tending to the needs of the dying meant that for Bulgakov *memento mori* was not a solitary exercise, as it was often the case for the ascetics of the past, but an experience of entering compassionately into the sorrow of another person's encounter with death: "I was at the deathbed of a young girl dying of consumption and my soul was burning as I was overwhelmed by pity at the sight of this flower cut off from life."[17] For Bulgakov this compassion was hard-earned, for it was the death of his own son Ivan that lifted up the veil of his self-love and broke down the boundaries separating his self from those of others. Death was more than a revelation of human brokenness; it was also a revelation of love, joy, and eternity. In Bulgakov's own words:

> For the first time in my life I have learned by experience that death is the greatest joy that *awaits* each human being, because the Theotokos and her love, the angels, the saints, the relatives and the loved ones, and the Lord await him. This encounter is full of awe and trepidation, but it is also full of boundless joy. The desire "to depart and be with the Lord" [Phil 1:23]—these words of the apostle have become a living truth for the first time.[18]

Death is more than parting with this life, it is entering into the joy of the Lord, into the communion of the saints. In this context, Bulgakov speaks of love that is "strong as death" (Cant. 8:6) and, boldly asserts that "love is death and death is love," intending to convey the point that the revelation of true love becomes possible at the threshold of death.

In Bulgakov's own life, two experiences that left him hovering on the brink of death were profoundly transformative. The first occurred during his first serious illness in January 1926, when for several days, if not weeks, he burned with high fever. He described his experience in the second part of his essay "The Sophiology of Death," published posthumously. While he was feverish, Bulgakov "lost the consciousness of being in a limited place in space and time," "the consciousness of having a body that rests on a bed," and "lost awareness of the boundaries of the self, which became 'we,' a plurality into which my 'I'

16　Bulgakov, *Dnevnik dukhovnyi*, 124.
17　Ibid., 10.
18　Ibid., 39.

entered as an indefinite point."[19] At the same time, "my spiritual 'I' achieved a greater sharpness and consciousness. It was an unadorned judge of my life. I was seized by fear and trembling. It was as if my soul underwent the trials of hell in which the burning wounds of my soul were being opened up. At that time the Lord spared me and protected me from the visions of the demonic. But fever coupled with the spiritual pangs created a fiery furnace [...] This experience taught me the meaning of burning in the furnace of blazing fire without burning down" [Dan. 3: 23–27]. The transformation brought about by this hellish experience was most extraordinary:

> Suddenly—after this burning—cool and consolation penetrated the fiery furnace of my heart. How can I relate this miracle of God's mercy, of forgiveness? With all my being I felt its boundless joy and lightness. My guardian angel, who was with me ceaselessly, put this into my heart. I suddenly felt that nothing separated me from the Lord for I had been redeemed by the Lord [...] Even during confession I felt that I already had forgiveness. I had a feeling that my sins had been burned away, that they were no more.
>
> But this mystery of forgiveness was revealed to me only in conjunction with the mystery of death, for I felt at the same time that my life had ended and that I was dying. But where was the fear of death? Only the joy of death was there, the joy of the Lord. Heavenly joy, which cannot be expressed in human language, filled all my being.[20]

Bulgakov goes on to say that during his illness he had periods of being terrified of death primarily because he despaired of leaving his family without his care. But this feeling was a passing weakness which was soon replaced by the sense of entering into the communion of the saints and of the breaking of the boundary between the living and the dead. This experience was accompanied by an equally potent feeling of being reunited with his deceased son, Ivan, and of "the presence of God reigning over everything. I have learned forever that only God and his mercy exist, that we must live only for God, love only God, and seek only the kingdom of God, and that everything that blocks God is a delusion."[21] The sense of the abiding presence of God coupled with the liberation from the fear of death is present with great consistency in Bulgakov's earlier accounts of his encounters with death and dying. The novel element in the experience

19   Bulgakov, "Sofiologiia smerti," II: 13.
20   Ibid., 14.
21   Ibid., 15.

of 1926 is that of profound assurance of forgiveness. While such experience is sanctioned by the Orthodox Church in the sacrament of confession, the matter of assurance is not generally emphasized, as it is in Pietism, Methodism, and other Christian movements. Elsewhere, Bulgakov speaks more concretely of being relieved from his fascination with the particularly dubious forms of theosophy and from the Gnostic elements in his sophiology.[22] Whatever the particulars of this experience, the effect was purgative and profoundly freeing. The experience only reinforced the conviction with which Bulgakov continued to theologize *sub specie aeternitatis*.

One may also find in these experiences the wellspring of Bulgakov's remarkable tranquility in the face of the Sophia Affair, which cast a long shadow of ecclesiastical condemnation upon his theological system and threatened to subject his life's work to *damnatio memoriae*. In 1935, as the theological opposition to sophiology began to mount in the Orthodox Church, Bulgakov demonstrated extraordinary intellectual tenacity in upholding his views and developing his system with an even greater speculative depth rather than maintaining silence in order not to provoke his numerous detractors. It could be said that Bulgakov showed more tolerance towards his theological enemies than some of his close friends, who rose rather passionately to his defense. In his memoirs he attributes this attitude to his aversion to fighting and cowardice, while one might be more disposed to ascribe Bulgakov's reaction to the nobility of his spirit and gentleness.

In 1939, Bulgakov was diagnosed with throat cancer and endured a second encounter with death during his surgery. It was the experience of living through the operation and its aftermath that occasioned his writing the first part of "The Sophiology of Death" the same year. In this essay, Bulgakov's description of his near-death experience reaches a new level of sincerity and immediacy. He does not gloss over the parts of the experience that do not fit into the canons of conventional piety. His description is more direct, sober, and free from rosy sentimentality. He paints on the canvas of his soul with the assurance of a man who has glimpsed into eternity and who no longer has anything to hide either from others or from himself. It is in this essay that Bulgakov offers his most nuanced theological analysis of dying.

He had two surgeries during which his throat was cut up without a general anesthetic. Since he was conscious throughout, he could see the implements with which the cancerous growth was being removed from his body. The main physiological state that he described was that of suffocation in which he was

---

22 Bulgakov, Letter to G. Florovsky, 8 (21) February 1926, GFP PUL, Box 12, f. 11.

no longer capable of praying. Bulgakov was hovering on the brink of death and was exhausted by the sufferings of his body to the point of being unable to experience what he had previously experienced on several occasions, namely, the joy of death as entering into the light-filled life with God. Instead, this experience was a new revelation of co-suffering and co-dying with the crucified Christ:

> Christ died our human death in order to accept through it the death of the God-man. This is why our dying, as co-dying with Him, is a revelation about Christ's death, although not a revelation about His glory. I have come to know the meaning of the apostle's words "always carrying in the body the death of Jesus, so that the life of Jesus may also be made visible in our bodies. For while we live, we are always being given up to death for Jesus' sake, so that the life of Jesus may be made visible in our mortal flesh. So death is at work in us, but life in you" (2 Cor. 4: 10–12). And also, "the whole creation has been groaning in labor pains until now; and not only the creation, but we ourselves, who have the first fruits of the Spirit, groan inwardly while we wait for adoption, the redemption of our bodies" (Rom. 8: 22–23).

Pondering the matter further, Bulgakov noted that

> Dying was not resolved in a death, but remained a revelation about the way of death, which, after Christ, awaits each man, whether he wishes it or not. Mortality is contained in the fallen human nature that was assumed by Christ in his mortal human being. Each illness is an awareness of mortality, its revelation, which nobody can avoid. Its measure is determined by the strength of illness, by how close it brings us to death. Objectively, I was at a hair's length from death during the first part of my illness, subjectively I was nearly completely enveloped by mortality and came to know it for this reason. I came to know my mortality as the Lord's cruciform dying in his Godforsakenness even to death, from "why have You forsaken me" to "into Your hands I command my spirit." Dying does not contain a revelation about death itself, such revelation is given only to those who have tasted death and thereby have left this world without return. Behind the threshold of death there follows a revelation of life after death as the beginning of new existence; the experience on this side of death has nothing to tell us about this reality. Dying knows nothing of the revelation of the life after death and of the resurrection.[23]

---

23   Bulgakov, "Sofiologiia smerti," I: 41.

It is remarkable that Bulgakov's last recorded and analyzed experience of confronting his mortality was a revelation of his co-dying with Christ, rather than the revelation of entering into the communion of the saints and the life with God. While the two revelatory experiences were closely related and followed one upon the other, Bulgakov sought to differentiate them as clearly as possible, for this very differentiation was not solely a matter of theoretical speculation, but the content of a divine disclosure. In the same essay he admitted that even in dying it was possible, by the grace of God, to receive a foretaste of the joy of the resurrection, as he himself had done during his purgative illness of 1926, and as he had received on other occasions when he witnessed the death of those dear to him. But in the revelatory experience of 1939 it was the sorrow of Godforsakeness, rather than the joyous foretaste of the resurrection, that was disclosed to him.

Throughout his life, Bulgakov remembered and carefully recorded his encounters with death and dying. In his childhood experiences, the predominant motif was the acceptance of the reality of death within the framework of Orthodox beliefs and practices, which his family took for granted. His grandfather's death left Bulgakov "mystically shaken," yet the experience itself was solemn and filled with a sense of God's abiding presence and even beauty. Of the siblings that he lost while he was still a child, his most vivid memory was that of the death of his younger brother, Mikhail. Strikingly, Bulgakov speaks of this experience without any lingering bitterness or rebellion; the dominant feeling is that of humbly accepting human fragility and mortality. There is also a lingering regret that this death did not break his self-centeredness. Only years later, when his own son Ivan died, did Bulgakov experience a shattering of his selfish defenses and experienced this particular loss as a revelation of compassionate love, indeed as a divine call to selfless love. In his priestly ministry, Bulgakov often attended to the needs of the dying. Again, the dominant hue of these experiences is the sorrowful joy of sending a soul to God, purified and released of its burden. The experiences of 1926 and 1939 distinguish themselves from the rest as Bulgakov's confrontations with his own mortality rather than that of others. The experience of 1926 brought about the assurance of having his sins purged in the fiery furnace of suffering. With this assurance also came a profound sense of Christ's victory over the power of death and the joy of the resurrection. The experience of 1939 enabled Bulgakov to enter into the mystery of co-dying with Christ.

The Revelatory Character of Death in Bulgakov's Sophiology

Such a profound and frequent confrontation with mortality had a deep impact on Bulgakov as a churchman and as a thinker. It would be naïve to claim that the causal connection was unidirectional, that the experiences influenced theology and not vice versa. It would be safe to assume instead that he came to interpret his experiences in light of his theological assumptions and that his theological views were in turn shaped and deepened by his experiences. One undisputable example of Bulgakov interpreting the phenomenological content of his *childhood* experience in light of his later theological views is his discussion of the "sophianic" character of death in his *Autobiographic Notes*. Obviously, as a twelve-year-old child he could not possibly think of the solemn acceptance of death received within the context of the Orthodox funeral service in terms of his later teaching about Sophia, the Wisdom of God. It is also significant that during the period when he lived through the deaths of his grandfather and his five brothers he turned away from the faith of his parents, rebelled against traditional Christianity by embracing nihilism and materialism in a Marxist form. But his fifteen-year rebellion, lasting approximately from 1888 to 1904,[24] does not surface in his much later recollections (1938) of how he reacted to the deaths of his relatives. Was the trauma of so many deaths in the family also a factor in his temporary loss of his childhood faith? One would search in vain for any such connection in Bulgakov's writings. His existential crisis seems to have been caused by a failed system of state-sponsored theological education rather than by the anguish of losses.

What was, then, the relationship between Bulgakov's sophiology and his experiences of death? Did such experiences factor at all into his theological thinking? What existential impulses gave birth to his thought? A commonly accepted answer to the last question is that the main driving force of his sophiological teaching is his lifelong effort to resolve the metaphysical problems surrounding cosmology, especially the problem of an intermediary between God and creation. His solution was to extend the Chalcedonian dogma of Christ's two natures into a general metaphysical principle of Godmanhood, or divine-human unity, along the lines proposed earlier by Vladimir Soloviev. This is a plausible interpretation of the central impulse behind sophiology, corroborated by ample evidence from Bulgakov's writings. Nevertheless, I would propose more controversially that the central intuition of sophiology—that all things find their eternal ground in God and that God is present in all things—

---

24 Bulgakov, "Avtobiograficheskoe," 78.

also has a crucial *existential* dimension conveyed by the experiences of death and dying.

This claim becomes more plausible if we examine *how* the earth-shattering experience of his son's death is introduced in *The Unfading Light*. At the beginning of the book, Bulgakov sets out to show, in a quasi-Kantian fashion, what makes religion possible. For Bulgakov, the main factor is experiential: people reporting to have an encounter with the divine. While claims to have religious experience could be challenged on various skeptical grounds, in the final analysis the skepticism does not do justice to the world-orienting value of such experiences. As one example, Bulgakov mentions his confrontation with the reality of his son's death as a moment when his selfish ego was shattered and his heart was flooded with compassion for all who were suffering and wounded. More importantly, he received these truths not upon reflection, but as a prophetic word, as God speaking directly into his heart. In his later writings Bulgakov consistently placed a very high cognitive premium on private revelations received while facing death and dying. While he had a rich and complex mystical life, and no less complicated spiritual evolution, Bulgakov had never trifled with the concept of prophetic speech and did not appeal to direct divine speaking on other occasions. Clearly, the experience of Ivan's death was a cognitive breakthrough that directed and animated his thought, even if the final shape of his speculative system appeared as a result of much deliberation.

A different way of casting the same point would be to say that Bulgakov regarded the sense of the abiding presence of God in all of creation, eternity underlying time, to be the final truth of human existence and that any construal of the world that ignored that truth was a profound distortion. He expresses this point rather forcefully in his *Spiritual Diary*: "Only God exists!", which is to say that the foundation of reality is eternal life with God rather than mortality and contingency. While the sense of the presence of God could be in principle available everywhere — and Bulgakov's enduring interest in "nature mysticism" could be viewed as an important aspect of the "sophianicity of the world" theme — its most concentrated revelation is granted in the experience of passing from this world, in which God's existence is often dubious, into another world, in which it is an evident and overwhelming reality. Death itself (as distinct from dying) was for Bulgakov a revelation of love and joy precisely because death marked an entrance into the communion of the saints and, more importantly, into the communion with God. For these reasons, I would submit that the world-orienting experience underlying sophiology was that of the encounter with death. Like the knight in Ingmar Bergman's film *The*

Seventh Seal, Bulgakov met death at the dawn of his life and continued to have transformative encounters with death and dying throughout his life.

In his theological investigations Bulgakov explored the dual nature of death at great length. Death was at once the end of earthly life and the beginning of the new life. As an end of this life, death had the effect of severing vital human bonds and for that reason brought sorrow, misery, and hopelessness; as a beginning of the new life, death could be joyous, peaceful, and liberating. Bulgakov's lifelong acquaintance with death supplied the experiential knowledge of both states. It was this tasted knowledge that fueled Bulgakov's theological investigations into the nature of death.

"The Sophiology of Death" was Bulgakov's second and most definitive exploration of the nature of death, written *after* his cancer surgery of 1939. In the 1930s, sometime before the experience of 1939, Bulgakov also explored a similar set of issues in the seventh chapter of his book, *The Bride of the Lamb*, which had been completely finished by 1939, but could be published only posthumously, in 1945, because of the troubles with Bulgakov's health and World War II.[25] The book is the last volume of his major trilogy on Godmanhood, the previous two volumes dealing with Christology (*The Lamb of God*) and pneumatology (*The Comforter*). *The Bride of the Lamb* covers the doctrine of creation, ecclesiology, and eschatology, to which the seventh chapter "On Death and the State after Death" provides an introduction.

In the introductory chapter, Bulgakov raises two central questions: What is death? and What does it mean for Christ to die? He answers the first question within the framework of the threefold division of human nature into spirit, soul, and body. Bulgakov writes that "death is a release of the soul from the bonds of the body and is a great consecration, a revelation of the spiritual world," adding that "this revelation of the spiritual world in death is a great joy and unspeakable celebration for those who were separated from it in this life but craved it, and an inexpressible terror, hardship, and turmoil for those who did not want this spiritual world, did not know it, and rejected it."[26] Bulgakov's numerous experiences of death and dying underlie this succinct statement of a revelatory dimension of death.

Bulgakov notes that death is a result of the original sin. Because of the original sin human life is surrounded with decay and dying from the very beginning. Yet, life is not sunken in death, does not emerge from death, as the

---

25 Bulgakov, *Nevesta Agntsa* (Moscow: Obshchedostupnyi pravoslavnyi universitet osnovannyi Aleksandrom Menem, 2005), 374–402.

26 Ibid., 383, 384.

materialists hold; on the contrary, death is a passing state of life, it has to be understood as a passing from one form of life here below into another form, in the kingdom above. Death is a threshold between two lives.

Bulgakov questions the presupposition of traditional Christian eschatology that there could be no spiritual change in the life after death. He argues that the spirit cannot remain inactive and that the spirits of the dead remain receptive both to God and to the prayer of the living.[27] According to Bulgakov, the souls of the dead are capable of spiritual growth, which takes the form not only of joy and delight, but also of judgment, as the soul comes to recognize its short-comings and failures in its earthly life. In his reflections, Bulgakov attempts to maintain a dual character of otherworldly experience, a change that presup-poses a reevaluation of one's previous life and a deepening of one's orientation towards God and divine things. He emphasizes that the strongest bond that will continue to exist in the life of the age to come is that of prayer and love.[28] For this bond to be effectual, it has to have some bearing upon the fate of the souls in the intermediate state. Bulgakov leaves open the possibility of a profound spiritual transformation in the life of the age to come without overdetermining the precise form that such a transformation might take.

The second central question that he raises is how to understand the death of Christ. What does it mean for the Godman to die? Does such a death entail a separation of the Logos from his human nature? In *The Bride of the Lamb*, Bulgakov answers negatively, for such a separation would have implied dis-in-carnation (*razvoploshchenie*), which is impossible, since the unity of Christ's divine and human natures is inseparable and endures even in death. In "The Sophiology of Death," he gives a more profound and extended answer: "The death of Christ is included in the general divine kenosis as His voluntary self-abasement and self-emptying."[29] For the sake of human salvation, "God accepts death freely and sacrificially."[30] "The revelation of the Godman for us is inevitably also a revelation of His *death* in us and we have to comprehend His measureless sacrificial love for us in His co-dying with us. This is only possible through our co-dying with Him."[31] Here Bulgakov speaks through the prism of his experience of co-dying with Christ in 1939. It is noteworthy that the theme

27   See Paul Gavrilyuk, "Universal Salvation in the Eschatology of Sergii Bulgakov," *The Journal of Theological Studies* 57 (2006), 110–32.
28   Bulgakov, *Nevesta Agntsa*, 389.
29   Bulgakov, "Sofiologiia smerti," I: 18.
30   Ibid., 20.
31   Ibid.

of Christ's co-dying with those who die is absent from *The Bride of the Lamb*, which was finished before his battle with throat cancer.

According to Bulgakov, the kenosis of the Son of God renders not only the human nature but also the divine nature of Christ accessible to death, although in different respects. The divine Logos accepts human death into himself in order to conquer death, for mortality can only be overcome by God. This overcoming is achieved through the act of self-sacrificial and self-emptying love, rather than through an omnipotent act of creation.[32] God empties himself in the life of Christ by rendering the union of his nature with the lowly human nature possible. For Bulgakov kenosis consists in God's acceptance of all conditions and deprivations of human mortality, including fatigue, hunger, thirst, cold, and so on. Following an influential trope in patristic theology, Bulgakov insists that it is possible to speak of the death of the Godman. Death does not mean annihilation. Death means the acceptance of human mortality into the life of God, God's co-dying with man. The death of each individual human being is included in the death of Christ because his human nature is at once individual and universal, and includes all humanity. In the death of Christ, God temporarily withholds the power of the resurrection from human nature, while remaining God. Bulgakov insists that such withholding also happens in the case of the death of all human beings, since God could spare them from death by his power. It is in this specific sense that each human death is co-dying with Christ.

The kenosis of the crucified Christ also has a trinitarian dimension, of the Father co-suffering with the Son in sending the Son to death (Bulgakov does not seem to be concerned about the Patripassian connotations of this claim), of the Son's obedience to the salvific will of the Father, and of the Holy Spirit's kenotic withdrawal from the Son. God takes human dying into his divine nature in order to draw human nature into the life of resurrection, into eternity.

Bulgakov's reflections on divine kenosis are not always clear or consistent.[33] He is aware of the range of speculative alternatives available in German and British kenoticism. His project is to include the valid insights of the nineteenth- and twentieth-century theologians without overturning the classical trinitarian doctrine and Chalcedonian Christology. Whether he succeeds in the latter undertaking is somewhat questionable. What cannot be doubted, however, is that in "The Sophiology of Death," Bulgakov's own experience of co-dying

---

32   Bulgakov, "Sofiologiia smerti," II: 19.
33   See Paul Gavrilyuk, "The kenotic theology of Sergius Bulgakov," *Scottish Journal of Theology* 58, no. 3 (2005), 251–69.

with Christ comes to bear upon his theology. Bulgakov's theology achieves a seamless fusion of lived mystical experience and speculative theology, which constitutes a distinguishing mark of any authentic Orthodox theology. While one might question various individual elements of Bulgakov's thinking—and he never intended his thinking to become church dogma—one cannot doubt his genuineness. The revelatory experiences of death constitute an experiential kernel of his sophiology. Philosophical theology was for Bulgakov the Christian Platonist what philosophy was for Plato: "a training for dying and death."[34]

Bulgakov died in 1944, about four years after completing "The Sophiology of Death." His final agony, which brought about his death, was not something he had an opportunity or need to analyze. As he passed into the realm beyond all words, those witnessing his last moments reported different things. One witness noticed the signs of profound spiritual struggle on his face, a struggle that remained to the end. Another witness, a nun present at his deathbed, saw an expression of unutterable joy and exclaimed: "Fr. Sergii is approaching the throne of God and is being surrounded by the light of His Glory!"[35]

34   Plato, *Phaedo* 64a4, cf. 67e.
35   Nun Elena, "Professor protoierei Sergii Bulgakov," *Bogoslovskie trudy* 27 (1986), 101–78.

CREATION AND ONTOLOGY

Building the House of Wisdom
DOI 10.17438/978-3-402-12193-1

Sergii Bulgakov's Early Marxism:
A Narrative of Development

Caleb Henry

Russia's pre-Revolutionary landscape was dotted with various and competing Marxisms usually schematized around two or three axes: Necessitarian (Populist) Marxism, Legal (Critical) Marxism, and Revolutionary (Orthodox) Marxism.[1] Within such schemes Sergii Bulgakov's earliest writings fall within the second designation, that of Legal or Critical Marxism.[2] The "legal" descriptor is phenomenological, indicating the historic tendency of this brand of Marxism to disseminate its ideas within legal publications and—in general—to promote political, social, and economic change through already existing (legal) structures. The "critical" descriptor is more conceptual in nature, indicating this type of Marxism's admixture with Immanuel Kant's critical project.

The most defining conceptual characteristic of Bulgakov's early Marxism, then, is this: his seemingly idiosyncratic intermingling of Marxist materialism with Kantian critical philosophy, a peculiarity not lost on Bulgakov himself, who retrospectively acknowledges the influence of Kant on these early works. "I considered it necessary to verify Marx with Kant and not the other way

---

1 Cf., Andrzej Walicki, *The Flow of Ideas: Russian Thought from the Enlightenment to the Religious-Philosophical Renaissance*, ed. Cain Elliott, trans. Jolanta Kozak and Hilda Andrews-Rusiecka, vol. 7, Eastern European Culture, Politics and Societies (New York: Peter Lang Edition, 2015), 665–720. See also, Andrzej Walicki, "Russian Marxism," in *A History of Russian Philosophy, 1830–1930: Faith, Reason, and the Defense of Human Dignity*, ed. G. M. Hamburg and Randall A. Poole (New York: Cambridge University Press, 2010), 305–25. Leszek Kolakowski combines Walicki's first and third categories together, resulting in two groupings: Legal Marxism and Revolutionary/Orthodox Marxism (*Main Currents of Marxism: Its Rise, Growth and Dissolution*, trans. P. Falla [New York: Oxford University Press, 1978], II.3).
2 For a brief overview of Critical Marxism, see Richard Kindersley, *The First Russian Revisionists: A Study of "Legal Marxism" in Russia* (Oxford: Clarendon Press, 1962).

around," he writes, and again, "I could never accept economic materialism in its raw form, without clarification from Kantian philosophy ..."[3] Within and alongside Bulgakov's early Marxism, then, lies an equally operative Kantianism.

The correlation between Marx and Kant, however, took many different forms and arrangements amongst the representatives of Critical Marxism, often giving rise to fierce disagreement between them. Bulgakov's Critical Marxism, as will be demonstrated, is a correlation between Marxist materialism (conceived as an ontological unity) and Kant's transcendental unity of apperception (conceived as an epistemological unity) wherein the latter is perceived to grant philosophical veracity to Marxist materialism while the former provides ontological cogency which Kant's transcendental unity is depicted as deriving from and gesturing toward. Ultimately, Kant's epistemological unity (apperception) and Marx's ontological unity (materialism) are—for Bulgakov—two sides of the same coin. The remainder of this paper will be devoted to unpacking these observations while outlining the consequences this correlation has upon Bulgakov's evolving understanding of materialism itself.

The Kantian component of Bulgakov's Marxism is most clearly seen in his early attempts to differentiate his Critical Marxism from that of Rudolf Stammler and Peter Struve's similar proposals. His 1896 essay "On the Regularity of Social Phenomena" was written in response to Stammler's *Economics and Law according to the Materialist Conception of History*. "Just as the recognition of the universal applicability of the law of causality and universal regularity is a condition for our knowledge of nature," Stammler had written, "so the regular knowledge of social life in advance sets some conditions for knowing, accepting in advance the existence of the regularity of social phenomena."[4] The epistemological transcription of the discussion does not go unnoticed by Bulgakov, and he summarizes Stammler's position quite accurately: "Whoever wishes to establish the laws of human social life must first understand the general conditions of knowledge under which all social science must stand with its own special features."[5] Any "knowledgeable person," Bulgakov continues, "will not be left in doubt as to who inspired this perspective of social philosophy ...

---

3   Sergei Bulgakov, *Ot marksizma k idealizmu: Sbornik Statej (1896–1903)* (SPb: "Obshest-
     vennaia pol'za," 1903), xi, xii.

4   Rudolf Stammler, *Wirtschaft und Recht nach der materialistischen Geschichtsauffassung:
     eine sozialphilosophische Untersuchung* (Leipzig: Veit & Comp., 1896), 6; as quoted in
     Sergej N. Bulgakov, "O zakonomernosti sotsial'nykh iavlenii," in *Ot marksizma k idea-
     lizmu*, 2.

5   Bulgakov, "O zakonomernosti sotsial'nykh iavlenii," 5.

the powerful influence of Kant and critical philosophy in general is evident."[6] Far from decrying this Kantian influence or the Kantian sublimation of the sociological question at hand, however, Bulgakov lauds the same as Stammler's "masterly application of the principles of critical philosophy to social science," and he considers it Stammler's "great merit," entitling him to the "appreciation of science."[7]

The disagreement between Stammler and Bulgakov rests not with a generalized Kantian-Marxist conjunction but, rather, with the pragmatic outworking or interpretation of Kant in relation to Marx, and this coalesces around divergent readings of Kant's notion of the transcendental unity of consciousness/apperception. Both Stammler and Bulgakov are in agreement that

> Kant established the unity of transcendental consciousness as an unavoidable condition for the possibility of experience. On it is based the unity of space and time, hence the unity of the object, the unity of the law, and the unity of the world order. If the unity of consciousness and the identity of the knowing self are destroyed, no experience is possible. "The permanent and abiding self (of pure apperception) is the correlate of all our representations."[8]

Kant's critique of knowledge and his unity of transcendental consciousness remain just as "essential" and "unquestioned" for Bulgakov as it does for Stammler. The disagreement consists in Bulgakov's discomfort with Stammler's construction of "two contradictory points of view" (e. g., antinomic dualities of necessity and freedom, causality and teleology, knowledge and will, etc.) existing simultaneously and, at least in Bulgakov's estimation, irreconcilably within the same Kantian transcendental consciousness.[9] Such a philosophical construction, Bulgakov argues, yields not only two different "directions" of consciousness but two different bundles or unities of representations. Since these unities of representations are contradictory and exclusionary, what Stammler is perceived as proposing is two different transcendental consciousnesses altogether, and this, Bulgakov charges, remains fundamentally irreconcilable with the Kantian notion of the identity (or unity) of consciousness.[10] The debate

---

6   Bulgakov, "O zakonomernosti sotsial'nykh iavlenii," 6.

7   Ibid.

8   Ibid., 23.

9   Ibid.

10   If, on the other hand, these two directions remain asymmetrical or one subordinate to the other, then Bulgakov argues, "there is nothing new in [Stammler's] whole con-

concerning materialism, moreover, hinges on these divergent readings of Kant, and Bulgakov's position is quite clear: "The unity of [Kant's] transcendental consciousness cannot tolerate two irreconcilable and at the same time equal points of view."[11] As such, Stammler's position is characterized by Bulgakov as "epistemological nonsense."[12]

Bulgakov's alternative proposal, of course, is a retrenched position of materialism which he argues possesses greater explanatory power by introducing "unity and regularity into the chaos of the constantly changing phenomena of social history."[13] Such unity and regularity is accomplished by means of "causality," and Bulgakov describes his program of social determinism accordingly, without feeling the need to broaden or include other idealistic principles except by means of subordination:

> Thus, the principle of social determinism is as follows: the whole of social life is a unity that is known on the basis of the laws of world mechanics, i. e., under the category of causality; the regularity of social life is the regularity of economic phenomena; the knowledge of this regularity is the knowledge of the causal origin of

---

cept" (ibid.). While eventually conceding much of the debate to Stammler within a few short years, Bulgakov remains persistent in his criticism regarding Stammler's alleged dualism (cf. "Zadachi politicheskoj ekonomii," in *Ot marksizma k idealizmu*, 321). In its place, Bulgakov prefers a more-Schellingian "philosophy of identity" already presciently formulated with his Kantian notion of an "identity of consciousness." (See Bulgakov, "O zakonomernosti sotsial'nykh iavlenii," 23; and especially, Sergei N. Bulgakov, "Osnovnye problemy teorii progressa," in *Ot marksizma k idealizmu*, 141; 141–42 (fn 1); "Basic Problems of the Theory of Progress," in *Problems of Idealism: Essays in Russian Social Philosophy*, ed. and trans. Randall A. Poole [New Haven: Yale University Press, 2003], 107; 122 [note 33]). The Kantian notion of an "identity of consciousness," initially brought forward here in 1896, is referenced again in 1912 in explicit association with Schelling's *Identitätsphilosophie* (cf., Sergei N. Bulgakov, *Filosofiia Khoziaistva. Chast' Pervaia: Mir kak khoziaistvo* [Moscow: Put', 1912], 181); *Philosophy of Economy: The World as Household*, ed. and trans. Catherine Evtuhov (New Haven: Yale University Press, 2000), 175].

11   Bulgakov, "O zakonomernosti sotsial'nykh iavlenii," 23.

12   Ibid. On a proleptic note, once Kant's notion of the transcendental unity of apperception has been retooled in Bulgakov's thought via Soloviev's influence, Bulgakov will charge Kant with a similar failure. With the publication of "Basic Problems of the Theory of Progress" (1902), Bulgakov begins to accede to Stammler's interpretation of Kant, yet far from offering a Kantian substantiation of Stammler, Bulgakov extends his critique of Stammler's ontological dualism to Kant himself (cf. "Osnovnye Problemy Teorii Progressa," 140–41; "Basic Problems of the Theory of Progress," 106–07).

13   Bulgakov, "O zakonomernosti sotsial'nykh iavlenii," 6.

economic phenomena. In the sense of the complete rule of the law of causation, social development is a natural process, like all other processes of nature.[14]

What is important to note, once again, is that Bulgakov is careful to argue that this conception remains not only in full agreement with Kant's critique of reason, but the fullest expression thereof: "[A] unity of law corresponds to a unity of object, which in turn is conditioned by the unity of space and time," all of which correlates with Kant's transcendental unity of consciousness, which Stammler—and not Marx!—is said to violate.[15] Accordingly, the theory of social development derives from social materialism's monism of causality rather than from two different directions as Stammler's antinomy of causality and teleology suggests.

Bulgakov's criticism of Stammler, however, quickly drew the attention of Peter Struve, the hallmark representative of Russian Critical Marxism, who remained unpersuaded and unimpressed with Bulgakov's materialist retrenchment. Once applied to history, Struve argued in his rebuttal published the following year, Bulgakov's conception of regularity becomes extended beyond its proper bounds, trespassing into the domains of goals (teleology), ideals, and—most importantly—freedom, all of which remain "directly contrary" to the idea of necessity.[16]

For Bulgakov, Struve's rebuttal was little more than a representation of Stammler's earlier idea of two contradictory directions within the same transcendental consciousness, and he issued his defense, "The Law of Causation and the Freedom of Human Actions," the same year.[17] On the one hand, Bulgakov doubles down on his materialist position. On the other, he offers two interrelated emendations, both precipitating from a clear demarcation between primary and secondary principles strongly reminiscent of Vladimir Soloviev's early, synthesizing period.[18]

---

14 Bulgakov, "O zakonomernosti sotsial'nykh iavlenii," 7.

15 Ibid.

16 C. B. Struve, "Svoboda i istoricheskaia neobkhodimost': Po povodu knigi Shtamlera i stat'i S. N. Bulgakova (Voprosy Filosofii i Psikhologii, Noiab.—Dek., 1896)," *Voprosy Filosofii i Psikhologii* VIII, no. 1 (36) (1897): 120.

17 Cf., "Zakon prichinnosti i svoboda chelovecheskikh deistvii," in *Ot marksizma k idealizmu*, 35–52.

18 Cf., Vladimir S. Solov'ev, *Krizis zapadnoj filosofii (Protiv pozitivistov)* (Moscow: V" Universitetskoj tipografiia (Katkov" i k), 1874); *The Crisis of Western Philosophy: Against the Positivists*, trans. Boris Jakim (Hudson, NY: Lindisfarne Press, 1996); and Vladimir S. Solov'ev, *Kritika Otvlechennykh Nachal* (Moscow: Univ. tip., 1880).

First, a secondary (or psychological) antinomy between freedom and necessity is acknowledged, yet this is still placed within a larger framework of causal monism. In contradistinction to Stammler and Struve's alleged dualistic proposals (characterized by irreconcilable antinomies such as freedom and necessity), Bulgakov insists that the idea of a strict regularity of human actions, "proclaimed by Spinoza and critically established by Kant," only "apparently" or "fictitiously" comes into conflict with psychologically perceived notions of human freedom.[19] Stammler and Struve, he observes, correctly recognize this "psychological contradiction," yet they mistakenly transpose it into a logical contradiction.[20] This confusion, he argues, remains the "source of [their] corresponding theoretical constructions … which desire to somehow, and at all costs, defend the freedom of human action and thereby escape from the inexorable law of causation."[21]

Bulgakov's argument is that goals and ideals, representing the noumenal pole within Stammler and Struve's constructed antinomies, "are mere motives in human consciousness and provide as such only a special kind of causation—psychological."[22] This remains only an apparent contradiction for Bulgakov, for the antinomic poles under investigation have been relegated to a secondary position, unified within the larger rubric of causation. The "ideals" in question are not given by science, Bulgakov concedes, yet materialism nonetheless is said to offer the clearest explanation "of those interests and feelings which encourage [humans] to set certain ideals."[23] This is because, as Bulgakov explains, interests and feelings are entirely borrowed from one's surrounding environment, regardless of their psychological modification and combination in forming certain qualities.[24] On the one hand, Bulgakov's allowance of "freedom" in antinomic relation to "necessity" amounts to little more than denial by absorption, for the end result, as Bulgakov himself is not shy in noting, is that "freedom turns out to be unnecessary and superfluous."[25] Both are unified under the primary law (or meta-principle) of causality. On the other hand, Bulgakov does

---

19   Bulgakov, "Zakon prichinnosti," 36.
20   Ibid., 36–37.
21   Ibid.
22   Ibid., 39.
23   Ibid., 51.
24   Ibid., 50.
25   Ibid.

admit for the first time that those ideals noted by Stammler and Struve are not given by science … at least not directly.[26]

Most importantly, Kant's unity of apperception—which prohibits contradictory directions or dualistic juxtapositions between freedom and necessity—is perceived to derive from and gesture toward a more fundamental ontological unity which excludes the same contradiction. The ontological unity of materialism and the epistemological unity of Kant's apperception presuppose one another, and this conjunction is then measured against Stammler and Struve's proposals with unsurprising results. Bulgakov not only determines their notion of contradictory directions in a single consciousness yields two contradictory consciousnesses (as previously argued), but these are now described as deriving from and pointing to two irreconcilable ontological bundles or unities as well. Stammler and Struve, he charges, are ontological dualists.

The same primary–secondary-differentiating logic can be seen in Bulgakov's second emendation, which attempts to broaden understandings of history while continuing to argue for the unity of the same via notions of causality. In response to Struve's criticism of materialist understandings of history, which purportedly cannot account for human ideals and freedom, Bulgakov adds an epistemic clarifier to his previous position. He argues that the unifying logic of necessity and causality (as an *ontological* principle) becomes *epistemically* manifest *a posteriori*. "Both Stammler and Struve," he writes, "mistakenly imagine history as being limited to a single present moment," with the setting of goals and ideals (along with their accompanying sense of freedom) being likewise limited to the present.[27] Bulgakov's materialistic understanding of history, however, is "an attempt to introduce the history of humanity into the system of scientific experience."[28] Viewed microscopically—and cordoned off from both the past and the future—Stammler and Struve's construal of history-as-present lends itself to the allowance of free human actions, but this is only a psychological façade, one produced by the limitations of scientific human knowledge as circumscribed within the present. On the contrary, and using the analogy of waves hitting a beach, Bulgakov insists that one cannot "doubt that each

26 Bulgakov's attempt to unify these antinomic poles within "different states of consciousness" will be abandoned shortly thereafter (cf. Sergei N. Bulgakov, "O sotsial'nom ideale," in *Ot marksizma k idealizmu*, 291 (fn 1)). And his full capitulation to Stammler and Struve's argument that ideals are not given by science, either directly or indirectly, is fully affirmed the same year (Bulgakov, "Zadachi politicheskoi ekonomii," 321 (fn 1); and *Ot marksizma k idealizmu*, xi).

27 Bulgakov, "Zakon prichinnosti," 39.

28 Ibid.

individual wave hits the shore according to the laws of mechanics, although one cannot [at present] determine the regularity of each impact."[29] However inadequate the analogy between human freedom and waves hitting a beach may be, Bulgakov's point is clear: Although human actions might appear free, these are only "appearances" of freedom derived from a limited perspective, a temporal slice of history psychologically masquerading as the whole of the same. History—including individual human history[30]— is an ontological unity (past-present-future) established by causality. Though this unity may not always be perceived by human knowledge due to its temporal limitations, it will undoubtedly be revealed as such in the future. Unbeknownst to Bulgakov, this second emendation in defense of Marx quite dramatically circumscribes the latter's socially predictive power, a consequence Bulgakov will not fully realize until three years later.[31]

As with his 1896 interaction with Stammler, what is interesting in Bulgakov's response to Struve is not the details of his argument in favor of social materialism but the mediating and even substantiating role Kant plays within them. In both interactions Kant emerges as the sole protagonist in this *tour de force* between friends, with Marx's name hardly appearing at all. While acknowledging that Stammler's teaching is also constructed in the spirit of Kant (which Bulgakov holds as "quite indisputable") and, while acknowledging that he and Struve share a similar Kantian epistemology, Bulgakov's main objective in these early essays is to demonstrate that both Stammler and Struve fundamentally misunderstand Kant, and that it is precisely this misunderstanding which precipitates their criticisms of Marxist materialism. The fulcrum of the debate in both instances hinges on Kant's unity of transcendental consciousness.

In his response to Struve, Bulgakov introduces a clear distinction between hierarchical unities, that is, between primary and secondary principles:

> Struve recognizes the unity of experience *while denying the unity of pure or transcendental consciousness* upon which the unity of experience, according to Kant, is grounded. But if you eliminate this unity of the pure self, on what, then, is the unity

---

29 Bulgakov, "Zakon prichinnosti," 36.
30 Bulgakov is quite clear this extends all the way to the "highest products of psychic activity," namely science and art (ibid., 37 [fn 1]).
31 This will be Bulgakov's powerful conclusion as formulated for the first time in *Capitalism and Agriculture* (cf. *Kapitalizm i Zemledelie* [S.-Peterburg: Tipografiia i litografiia V. A. Tikhanova, 1900], especially 442–58).

of experience founded? ... "No knowledge can find a place in us," says Kant, "no connection and unity between its separate parts without that unity of consciousness which precedes all given views, and only in relation to them, to which every conception of objects is possible."[32]

For Bulgakov, it is Kant's unity of apperception which "creates, out of all possible phenomena that can only occur side by side in experience, the unity of all these representations on the basis of laws," and this, to continue Bulgakov's argument, "eliminates the possibility that 'the unity of experience is not identical with the unity of transcendental consciousness," for "this latter unity is the basic and necessary condition for the unity of experience."[33] Here, a tiered, double-unity construct (e. g., primary and secondary principles) is quite discernible. While Bulgakov concedes Stammler and Struve's observed antinomy or contradiction occurs at the secondary level, he maintains that the only means of unifying the disparate, side-by-side phenomena of experience is their grounding in a more primordial principle, represented epistemologically by Kant's unity of apperception and ontologically by Marxist materialism. Despite this unity being purchased with the currency of causality, it is worth noting that Bulgakov's reading of Kant already signals a post-Kantian rupture in the vein of Fichte, Schelling, and Soloviev, all of whom read Kant's critical project as intelligible only if one presupposes a real, ontological unity undergirding it. Regardless, Stammler and Struve's fundamental problem is said to be their indiscriminate conflation of primary and secondary principles, and it is this failure, Bulgakov continues, which leads to the violation of the irreducible center of Kant's entire epistemology, the notion of the unity of apperception and/ or transcendental consciousness.

Struve retaliates by charging Bulgakov with infidelity to Kant in bypassing the latter's notion of antinomy and the possibility of contradictions in pure reason. Bulgakov counters by repeating his position that the unity of experience is dependent upon the unity of transcendental consciousness, so any perceived Kantian antinomy found within pure reason, far from presupposing two different directions of consciousness, necessarily requires the unity of the same.[34] Struve's accusation of Bulgakov's "infidelity to Kant" is reversed as Bulgakov goes on the counter-offensive: Struve—and by extension Stammler—are the ones unfaithful to Kant:

---

32   Bulgakov, "Zakon prichinnosti," 41 (emphasis added).
33   Ibid., 41, 42.
34   Ibid., 42.

> I [Bulgakov] spoke not of the absence of contradiction in pure reason, but of the impossibility of two contradictory directions in a single consciousness … In this I perfectly follow Kant. Struve is wrong when he says that the theory of Stammler concerning the two directions of consciousness … is unquestionably contained in Kant's main thought. It would be strange to suggest such a contradiction in Kant, and in fact Kant does not have it … . It must be recognized that Kant does not establish two directions of consciousness in the world of experience … . In this, Stammler does not follow Kant at all.[35]

Within a few short years, of course, Bulgakov will cede much of the Kantian debate to Stammler and Struve (although it is important to note this derives not from their respective arguments but from Soloviev's influence). The substance of the debate, however, will remain much the same, and Bulgakov's eventual acceptance of Stammer and Struve's portrait of Kant will result not in the Kantian substantiation of either antagonist but in the extension of these same criticisms and their redeployment against Kant himself.[36]

Bulgakov's predilection for distinguishing primary and secondary principles in circumventing criticisms against Marx, however, quickly begins unraveling his understanding of materialism itself. This is clearly seen in "Economy and Law" (1898), wherein Bulgakov tackles the thorny issue of describing the relation between economy and law, which had long preoccupied Critical Marxists.[37] Economic materialists, he observes, give priority of expression to economy, whereas lawyers give preponderance to law, each subordinating the other principle within itself. Moderate authors, he continues—undoubtedly alluding to both Stammler and Struve—espouse equal influence to each, constructing a dialectic or contradiction between the same.[38] Bulgakov's proposal, however, is to relativize and unify both antinomies within an overarching grammar of "social life."[39]

The positive relation between "economy" and "law" remains far less important to Bulgakov than the architectonic solution he proposes, which relegates both to secondary principles sublimated within the primary principle

---

35 Bulgakov, "Zakon prichinnosti," 42–43.
36 The criticisms of Kantian dualism begin surfacing in 1902. See fn 12 above.
37 Bulgakov, "Khoziaistvo i Pravo," in *Ot marksizma k idealizmu*, 53–82.
38 Ibid., 53 f.
39 It is perhaps worth noting that similar to the Kantian notion of the transcendental unity of apperception, the notion of "life" will eventually become one of Bulgakov's earliest conceptual identifications of Sophia (cf. Bulgakov, *Filosofiia khoziaistva*, 1–48 and 109–59; *Philosophy of Economy*, 29–76 and 123–56).

of "social life."[40] "Social life," he writes, is "a kind of trunk from which both phenomena under study [e. g., economy and law] grow."[41] Quite importantly, however, "social life" is still characterized by causality and regularity, and—while Bulgakov's preferred nomenclature in 1898 is clearly "social life"—he still interchanges it frequently with "social materialism."[42] The main development in 1898, then, is that Bulgakov's primary-secondary scheme has now fragmented his understanding of materialism: Social materialism continues as the primary principle, yet this is maintained only by bifurcating this materialism from economic materialism, demoting the latter to a secondary principle. This is a notable departure from Bulgakov's 1896 essay, in which social materialism, economic materialism, and historical materialism were explicitly equated with one another.[43]

With this distinction in place, Bulgakov now charges Marx's critics—echoing his earlier arguments against Stammler and Struve—with confusing one type of materialism for another, that is, conflating primary and secondary principles, and his deflections are quite humorous in this regard. Accusations that materialistic investigations into history are characterized by "one 'economic' explanation in everything … explain[ing] the whole history by narrow, egoistic, and economic calculation" are dismissed as having "nothing to do with *social* materialism."[44] Similarly, accusations that "materialism … 'reduces' all human life to economic activity" are forthwith dismissed with the assertion that such a desire "has never existed among the *social* materialists."[45] Thus, by 1898 Bulgakov's defense of Marxism and materialism has clearly resulted in the relativization of economic materialism. Writing five years after the publication of "Economy and Law," Bulgakov recounts that with its publication he "was already accused of betraying Marxism," and he further confesses this was "unsurprising" given the nuanced version of Marxism espoused therein.[46]

Bulgakov's subsequent Marxist writings are best described as successively tumbling dominos. In 1899 the Solovievian language of "social organism" is

---

40 Bulgakov writes that he certainly has in mind the relation between "any other parties or 'factors' of social life," not just that between "economy" and "law" ("Khoziaistvo i pravo," 55). See also his disregard of this particular relation when setting forth his larger argument (cf. ibid., 62).

41 Bulgakov, "Khoziaistvo i Pravo," 54.

42 Ibid., 62.

43 Cf. Bulgakov, "O zakonomernosti sotsial'nykh iavlenii," 1 (footnote 2).

44 Bulgakov, "Khoziaistvo i pravo," 64 (emphasis added).

45 Ibid.

46 Bulgakov, *Ot marksizma k idealizmu*, xii.

introduced alongside that of "social life" and "socialism," and the process of disassociating these terms from "social materialism"—already begun in 1898—becomes increasingly palpable.[47] This process will culminate in 1901 (if not 1900) as Bulgakov's defense of Marx collapses altogether. Under the influence of Soloviev, all variants of materialism are once again gathered together under the single rubric of "philosophical materialism" which is itself positioned as a secondary or—to use Soloviev's preferred diction—an abstract principle.[48] In short, Bulgakov's 1896 and 1897 notion of materialism as a primary principle fragments in 1898 (with social materialism and economic materialism resting on either side of the divide), and by 1900/1901 the various species of materialism are once more unified, yet now demoted to a secondary position. This movement signifies materialism's failure—in Bulgakov's mind—to provide the ontological unity as originally promised. It now continues only as a one-sided or abstract unity.

Capitalism and Agriculture (1900)—Bulgakov's empirical substantiation for what he conceptually formulated in 1898—publicly announces this failure. The important development here is that Bulgakov includes Marx in his polemic for the first time, purportedly defending the truth of Marxism from the "non-Marxism" of Marx himself. The fundamental problem as identified by Bulgakov—and one which recapitulates his argument against Stammler in 1896, Struve in 1897, and Marxism's unnamed critics in 1898—is that Marx indiscriminately conflates a secondary principle/unity with the primary principle/unity undergirding it. The result is that economic materialism (as a secondary principle) spills outside its defined boundaries and usurps what does not belong to it. This is so, Bulgakov argues, temporally/diachronically (with respect to Marx's inability to reliably forecast the future with scientific precision) and spatially/synchronically (with respect to Marx's inability to account for the peculiarities of economic activity in its fullness, much less all of reality).[49] All of this evidences very little philosophical development, and it is worth noting

---

47 Cf., Sergei N. Bulgakov, "K voprosu o kapitalisticheskoi èvoliutsii zemledeliia," *Nachalo* I, no. 2/3 (1899): 1–21; 25–33.
48 Cf., Sergei N. Bulgakov, "Ivan Karamazov (v romane Dostoevskogo "Brat'ia Karamazovy") kak filosofskii tip," in *Ot marksizma k idealizmu*, 109.
49 Bulgakov is primarily concerned with the latter transgression and Marxism's inability to account for agrarian development, yet he is also concerned with the first transgression, as his concluding sentences make clear: "Therefore, as for predictions of the future, we prefer honest ignorance to social medicine or charlatanism. The veil of the future is impenetrable. Our sun illuminates only the present, casting an indirect reflection on the past. This is enough for us ... But we gaze in vain at the horizon beyond which our

that many of the gaps in Marxist theory he identifies in *Capitalism and Agriculture* were already noted in his earliest published writing from 1895, a review of Marx's third volume of *Capital*.[50] Nevertheless, his 1900 criticism of Marx and materialism—cogently articulated here for the first time—will remain largely unchanged throughout the next decade. Once materialism (as a secondary principle) masquerades itself as a primary principle, a whole host of ethical, idealist, and religious beliefs (lying outside materialism's one-sidedness) must be uncritically presupposed by the same. Once this occurs, Bulgakov observes, following Soloviev, a malignant positivism ensues. Bulgakov's anti-Marxist writings after the turn of the century—without too much reductionism—are perhaps best described as his continued attempt at uncovering and exposing Marxism's uncritical presuppositions.

Kant and Marx are united together in Bulgakov's Critical Marxism, and as such, they fall together. And this is precisely what happens at the close of the nineteenth century as Bulgakov determines that neither Kant's transcendental unity of apperception nor Marx's materialism can provide the unified vision of reality as originally promised. Bulgakov will begin new searches for new solutions at the dawn of the new century, and he will encounter new influences in the process. But that is a subject for another story; here concludes the present one.

---

setting sun is sinking, lighting a new dawn for the coming, unknown day" (*Kapitalizm i zemledelie*, II, 464).

50 Bulgakov, "Tretii Tom 'Kapitala' K. Marksa," *Russkaia Mysl'* 16, no. III (1895): 1–20.

Building the House of Wisdom
DOI 10.17438/978-3-402-12194-8

Creatio ex sapientia in Bulgakov's *Unfading Light*: The Influence of F. W. J. Schelling

Taylor Ross

Throughout his career, Sergei Bulgakov plays heir to the apophatic tradition in Christian theology, even as he strikes his own path. For instance, he shares with his forbears the conviction that God cannot be counted among things that exist. Hence the opening gambit of *Unfading Light* (1917), for which Bulgakov marshals plenty of patristic and medieval evidence: "we have to admit that it is impossible to affirm even being about the transcendent."[1] But he proves more assiduous than, say, Gregory of Nyssa, Dionysius the Areopagite, or John Scotus Eriugena in distinguishing this "Divine Nothing" from the source of *creatio ex nihilo*.[2] Whence, of course, the well-known taxonomy of "nothing" Bulgakov gleans from three Greek particles: the ἀ privative, οὐκ, and μή.[3] If those concepts are familiar to Bulgakov's readers, their source is somewhat less so. The present chapter argues that his initial account of *creatio ex nihilo* cannot be understood apart from F. W. J. Schelling's own attempts to chart a middle course between emanation and creation by means of the very same meontological distinctions.

Three Varieties of „Nothing" in *Svet Nevechernii* (1917)

Less a concept than an apophatic placeholder, the alpha privative stands in for the "absolute NOT" of negative theology: "a gesture, a surge, a motion,

---

1   Sergius Bulgakov, *Unfading Light: Contemplations and Speculations*, trans. Thomas Allan Smith (Grand Rapids: W. B. Eerdmans, 2012), 108.

2   Cf. Gregory of Nyssa, *De hominis opificio* 23; Dionysius the Areopagite, *De Divinis Nominibus* 4.7; John Scotus Eriugena, *Periphyseon* 3.5–6.

3   Hereafter transliterated (i. e., alpha privative, *ouk*, *mē*) to match the English translation of Bulgakov's text.

not a thought, not a word."[4] It is a verbal icon of the fundamental antinomy of religious consciousness, if you like: a literal window onto that which language itself cannot express. Such a transcendent sort of negation cannot be correlated to "being," to be sure, but neither can it correspond to "non-being." Otherwise, the absolute negation of negative theology becomes the contingent negation of a dialectical process. The sort of unsaying proper to the alpha-privative must be distinguished from *ou* and *mē*, in other words, "[f]or both *mē* and *ou* are for the *alpha privative* of negative theology already some sort of positive expressions about being, and thereby they relate to the immanent, diurnal, cosmic consciousness that distinguishes the light of being and the shadow of nonbeing, the manifestation of forms and the twilight of potentiality."[5] If the alpha-privative implies an absolute form of negation, once more, *ou* and *mē* are relative terms.

Which is another way of saying that both *ou* and *mē* represent "creaturely" forms of nothing in contradistinction to the "Divine Nothing" towards which the alpha-privative gestures.[6] But these terms themselves can be distinguished further still: "the first [*ou*] corresponds to full negation of being—*nothing*, while the second [*mē*] corresponds only to its nonmanifestation and nondefinition—*something*."[7] Whereupon the question immediately follows: when Christians confess the world was created "out of nothing," as indeed they must, what exactly do they mean? Bulgakov assures his readers that the only "admissible" possibility is creation out of *ouk on*—out of the "full negation of being," that is, in contradistinction to the *mē on* from which monists of various stripes attempt to derive the world's existence. For if the world simply gives form to some hidden potential within the depths of the Absolute, it thereby spells the logical elision of the alpha privative and *mē on*, the confusion of divine nothing and creaturely nothing. Bulgakov knows the provisos of his patristic forebears well enough to hold the line when it comes to the qualitative distinction between creation and emanation: "If we allow that the world arose out of divine *mē on*, this will mean that it is not created at all, but is *engendered* or *emanated*, generally speaking that it was realized in God in one way or another." At which point, he warns, "[t]he border between the world and God is erased."[8] Once again, the dogmatic formula of *creatio ex nihilo* must mean creation from *ouk*

---

4   Bulgakov, *Unfading Light*, 109.
5   Ibid., 108–09.
6   Ibid., 186.
7   Ibid., 188–89.
8   Ibid., 189.

on, lest the antinomic disjunctions on which Christian dogma itself depends give way to a dialectical identity between God and world.

Nonetheless, Bulgakov also insists that the "investment" of *ouk on* with *mē on* "was the first, fundamental, and essential act of creation." Indeed, he says the "conversion of *ouk on* into *mē on* is the fashioning of the common matter of creatureliness, of the Great Mother of the whole natural world."[9] Or again, if "*mē on* is pregnancy" and "*ouk on* is sterility," then the latter must "overcome its emptiness and be freed from its sterility." Simply put, "*ouk on* must become *mē on.*" It can only do so, however, when the Absolute "self-bifurcates" and becomes "absolute-relative," thereby "placing in itself another center."[10] Apart from this act in and through which the Absolute becomes "the Father of all," the "nothing, the nonexistent basis of creation" cannot become "the Mother, the *mē on* containing everything."[11]

But once it does, Bulgakov can even praise the monists he otherwise maligns—Baruch Spinoza, Jakob Böhme, G. W. F. Hegel—for stressing the inseparability of being and nonbeing, yes and no, determination and negation. For all of their dialectical insights readily apply to creation once *ouk on* becomes *mē on,* once "nothing" becomes "nonbeing." Indeed, the *Science of Logic's* "brilliant formula"—that "there is nothing that is not a middle state between being and nothing"—becomes the basis for Bulgakov's own definition: "Creatureliness is above all and in its essence *mē on,* being-nonbeing ..."[12] So long as *mē on* doesn't imply some unactualized potency within the Absolute itself, the term is practically synonymous with creation. Hence, "[t]he concept of creation [...] is *broader* than the concept of emanation," Bulgakov says, for "it includes the latter in itself, since creation is emanation *plus* something that is created by the creative *let there be!*"[13] That initial "something" is non-being—meonal "potency," as he likes to put it—but it's crucial to Bulgakov's thought in *Unfading Light,* at least, that God creates even such "non-being" out of "nothing."

All of which implies that the "nothing" (*ouk on*) in the dogmatic formula of *creatio ex nihilo* functions as something like an apophatic safeguard against confusing creaturely being-nonbeing and divine nothing—a mediator between *mē on* and the alpha-privative. But what *is* it? Does it even make sense to ask whether nothing "is," much less "what" it might be? Even if "*ouk on* cannot be

---

9   Bulgakov, *Unfading Light,* 189.
10 Ibid., 184–85.
11 Ibid., 195.
12 Ibid., 191.
13 Ibid., 183.

conceived directly but only indirectly, by a certain 'illegitimate judgment'—
hapton logismōi tini nothōi, according to Plato's famous expression about
matter,"[14] does the misbegotten attempt to think it nonetheless yield a bastard
thought?

Creatio ex nihilo in the late Schelling

Though he buries the confession in a footnote, Bulgakov actually credits
Schelling with the very distinction on which his doctrine of creation rests. "In
modern philosophy," he says, "the development between *mē* and *ou* is most
distinctly of all expressed by Schelling in his *Darstellung des philosophischen
Empirismus* [1836]" when he observes that "*mē on* is the not-existing which
only *is* the not-existing, with respect to which only actual existence is rejected,
but not the possibility of existing," while "*ouk on* is fully and in every sense that
which does not exist ..."[15] What's more, Bulgakov actually praises the aforementioned text for claiming "the world is created by God out of nothing in the
sense of *ouk on*, and not *mē on*," even though he also chides the late Schelling
for "not entirely remain[ing] faithful to it in *Philosophy of Revelation* [1841–43]
where he develops the idea of the creation of the world out of itself by God,
although in a covert and complicated way ..."[16] Setting aside the question of
the philosopher's alleged development on the issue for now—but nonetheless
noting our theologian's obvious disapproval of it—a brief glance at the text
Bulgakov elsewhere calls "one of [Schelling's] latest and most profound works"
confirms their agreement on the question of creation from *ouk on*.[17]

For we find in the *Darstellung des philosophischen Empirismus* a similar effort to safeguard the Absolute from any causal relationship to the world—even
one couched in terms of an as yet unactualized "potency" within the divine
life—which thereby issues in a philosophical reinterpretation of the dogmatic
formula of *creatio ex nihilo*.[18] "The highest concept of God, and thus the highest
concept as such, is not the concept of cause," Schelling observes, but rather one

---

14 Bulgakov, *Unfading Light*, 190.
15 Ibid., 469n9.
16 Ibid., 470n9.
17 Sergei Bulgakov, *Philosophy of Economy: The World as Household*, trans. and ed. Cath-
    erine Evtuhov (New Haven: Yale University Press, 2000), 299, n. 23.
18 For discussion of these passages, see Emilio Brito, "La creation 'Ex Nihilo' selon Schell-
    ing," *Ephemerides theologicae Lovanienses* 60, no. 4 (1984): 298–324; Walter Kasper, *Das
    Absolute in der Geschichte: Philosophie und Theologie der Geschichte in der Spätphiloso-
    phie Schellings*, Gesammelte Schriften 2 (Freiburg: Herder, 2010), 343–49.

"in and through which he is determined to be absolutely independent (*absolut Selbständiges*), i. e., the concept of substance."[19] It follows that such "freedom (*Freiheit*) will be absolute and unconditional only if God is not already the creator directly (*unmittelbar*) by virtue of his concept, only if there is a concept of God in which there might be no reference whatsoever to even a possible (*mögliche*) creation."[20] Hence, "[h]e is only absolutely free when he not only posits the principles, i. e., potencies (*Potenzen*), insofar as they are already in act (*in Wirkung*), but also insofar as he posits the potencies *as* potencies, so that they would not even be potencies (i. e., possibilities of a future being) without his will."[21] Just so, the late Schelling's voluntarism replaces not only a "correlation theory" (*Korrelattheorie*) that would make God and world mutually constitutive terms but also a "doctrine of potencies" (*Potenzenlehre*) according to which creation is supposed to lie dormant in the divine ideas.

With these two models of cosmogenesis off the table, the traditional Christian doctrine recommends itself quite readily, for the plain reading of "[c]reation out of nothing (*creatio ex nihilo*) can mean nothing other than *creatio absque omni praeexistente potentia*—creation without any already existing potency that has not been posited at first by the will of the creator himself."[22] Despite the various objections[23] one might pose to the religious "picture-thought" (*Vorstellung*) preserved by the dogmatic formula, he says, it nonetheless points the way to a "third possibility," whereby God would be "absolutely free, to create or not to create …"[24] One such objection to the doctrine might worry at the "ambiguity" (*Zweideutigkeit*) of the operative term, Schelling notes.[25] Whereupon he introduces the aforementioned distinction between "non-*being*" (nicht *Seiende*) and "*non*-being" (*nicht* Seiende), between μὴ ὄν and οὐκ ὄν. It's clear, as Bulgakov himself claims, that Schelling means to say that *creatio ex nihilo* must signify creation out of οὐκ ὄν, i. e., "that from which not merely the *actuality* of being, but also being in general, even its possibility, has been denied."[26] For this alone secures a concept of God from which even the "potency"

---

19   F. W. J. Schelling, *Darstellung des philosophischen Empirismus*, in *Schellings Münchener Vorlesgungen*, ed. Arthur Drews (Leipzig: Verlag von Felix Meiner, 1902), 254–55 [Sämtliche Werke X, 279]. Hereafter *Darstellung*. All translations of this text are mine.

20   Schelling, *Darstellung*, 257 [SW X, 281–82].

21   Ibid., 258 [SW X, 282].

22   Ibid.

23   Ibid., 259 [SW X, 282].

24   Ibid., 257 [SW X, 282].

25   Ibid., 258 [SW X, 283].

26   Ibid., 259 [SW X, 283].

of creation has been stricken, a concept of God according to which he would be free to bring about such "potency" if he so pleased. Even so, what Bulgakov does not quite say is that Schelling also concedes an interpretation of creation out of "nothing" that includes its emergence from μὴ ὄν, i. e., "non-being, that which only is not, from which only actually existing being has been negated."[27] Said otherwise, Schelling believes *creatio ex nihilo* means both "that God made the world out of nothing" and "that he pulled it from nonbeing."[28]

Consider the following statement: "The true doctrine of creation out of nothing also knows this *Néant* [i. e., μὴ ὄv],[29] this nothing, but it takes it to be something that itself originated from nothing (*de rien*); this [μὴ ὄv] is the immediate possibility of actual being (*unmittelbare Möglichkeit des wirklichen Seins*), but [the true doctrine of *creatio ex nihilo*] does not claim that this potency (*Potenz*) was in any way already existing."[30] Just like that, Schelling recuperates his "doctrine of potencies," without thereby implicating the Absolute in a dialectical process. Such was the stated aim of his late distinction between "negative" and "positive" philosophy, between a logical derivation of the world from the concept of God and a voluntary recognition of reason's limits before the sheer fact of existence. Hence the "metaphysical empiricism" to which the work's title alludes.[31] Setting aside a longer summary of his "philosophy of revelation," though, it suffices here to note that Schelling introduces the distinction between μὴ ὄv and οὐκ ὄv in order to maintain his own commitment to creation's emergence from a prior state he variously calls "non-being" (*nicht Seiendes*), "unbeing" (*Unseiendes*), "shapeless matter" (*materia informis*), "unmediated stuff" (*unmittelbarer Stoff*), "not yet something" (*noch nicht Etwas*), "blind and unbounded being" (*blindes und grenzloses Sein*), and even "that which should not be" (*nicht sein Sollendes*).[32] All of these can be synonymous with the "immediate possibility of actual being" only to the extent that such a "potency" emerges from "nothing," not "the concept of God."[33] So long as μὴ ὄv itself originates from οὐκ ὄv, that is, being as such can be defined by the "con-

---

27   Schelling, *Darstellung*, 259 [SW X, 283].

28   Ibid., 260 [SW X, 285].

29   Cf. ibid., 260 [SW X, 284–85].

30   Ibid., 261 [SW X, 285].

31   Cf. F. W. J. Schelling, *The Grounding of Positive Philosophy: The Berlin Lectures*, trans. Bruce Matthews (Albany, NY: State University of New York Press, 2007), 179. Hereafter *Grounding*.

32   Schelling, *Darstellung*, 260–61 [SW X, 285].

33   Cf. Kasper, *Das Absolute in der Geschichte*, 344.

stant overcoming" (*beständige Überwindung*) of nonbeing.[34] Indeed, *creatio ex nihilo* can mean both creation out of μὴ ὄν and creation out of οὐκ ὄν, given the right interpretation of each term.[35]

With this qualified affirmation of creation out of μὴ ὄν in view, return to Bulgakov's summary of the *Darstellung*: "According to Schelling's own thought, which is defended in the treatise cited, the world is created by God out of nothing in the sense of *ouk on*, and not *mē on*."[36] He's only half-right, of course. But what makes this misrepresentation of Schelling more than a curious oversight is Bulgakov's proximity to the position he suppresses. For he too recuperates the *mē on* as creation's source on the very same condition that "non-being" itself be created from "nothing." According to Bulgakov, recall, "the world is created out of nothing in the sense of *ouk on*," but he immediately adds that "its [i. e., *ouk on*'s] investment with *mē on* was the first, fundamental, and essential act of creation," the ineffable decision whereby the Absolute first brings "the common matter of creatureliness" into "being-nonbeing."[37] Much like Schelling, moreover, Bulgakov also maintains that the Absolute "becomes its own potency (or 'meon') by giving in itself and through itself a place to be relative, but without at the same time forfeiting its absoluteness."[38] To do so, Bulgakov must presuppose a recalcitrant "nothing" in the divine life from which "meonal being" itself springs, just as Schelling must entertain a certain "non-potency" in God himself: *creatio ex nihilo* "stipulates only that the potencies are not in him as *potencies*," the latter claims, "but it does not say that they are not in him as *non*-potencies (*Nichtpotenzen*), sheer *differences* (*Unterschiede*) as such, which he freely treats and regards as potencies (as possibilities of another being) only because it pleases him."[39] Contextualizing this concept of "non-potency" in Schelling's corpus reveals just how close he actually comes to Bulgakov's own position, regardless of whether the latter was willing to admit it.

Despite his development, the idea of "non-potency" is a vestige of Schelling's middle period (ca.1805–ca.1815). Students of Schelling know this "non-potency" (*Nichtpotenz*) as the more familiar but no less impenetrable notion of the "non-ground" (*Ungrund*). Both terms imply a state of exception from the principle of sufficient reason, even as they point up the paradoxical relation

---

34 Schelling, *Darstellung*, 261 [SW X, 285].
35 Cf. Brito, "La Creation 'Ex Nihilo' Selon Schelling," 315.
36 Bulgakov, *Unfading Light*, 470, n. 9.
37 Ibid., 189.
38 Ibid., 185.
39 Schelling, *Darstellung*, 261 [SW X, 286].

such an "excluded term" still bears to the dialectic of cause and effect. Consider, for instance, Schelling's introduction of the term in the *Freiheitsschrift* of 1809: "there must be a being *before* all ground and before all that exists, thus generally before any duality—how can we call it anything other than the original ground [*Urgrund*] or the non-ground [*Ungrund*]?" For if this "being" is neither "ground" nor "existence," and this because it precedes them both in equal measure, "it can only be described as the absolute *indifference* [*Indifferenz*] of both." Which is to say "nothing else than their very non-existence [*Nichtsein*]."[40] The negative prefixes attached to these terms—*Un-grund, In-differenz, Nicht-sein*—signal an exemption from the "duality" in which they would otherwise traffic: the "original ground" (*Urgrund*) must be "ungrounded" (*Ungrund*) because it "grounds" (*begründen*) the very opposition to "existence" (*Existenz*) that defines "ground" (*Grund*) itself, must be "indifferent" (*Indifferenz*) because it "differs" (*differieren*) from the dialectic of "identity" (*Identität*) and "difference" (*Differenz*) on which the latter trades, must be "non-existence" (*Nichtsein*) since it "pre-exists" (*schon vor sein*) both "being" (*Seiendes*) and "non-being" (*Nichtseiendes*) alike.

Precisely because this point of "indifference" is itself "ungrounded," moreover, there can be no logical progression from non-existence to non-being, much less being itself: "the Other [i.e., the world] cannot be posited by that eternally commencing nature in a continuous series [...] as a potency that belongs to it," since "it is outside and above all potency, a lack of potency in itself (*das an sich Potenzlose*)."[41] Rather, existence itself must be the result of a groundless "de-cision" (*Ent-scheidung*) from this "abyss" (*Abgrund*) of possibility. Schematized in terms of the "doctrine of potencies" (*Potenzlehre*) from the slightly later *Weltalter* of 1815, "nothing" (non-potency) must first posit itself as "that which does not have being" (first potency) before its subsequent idealization as "something" (second potency) can become "that which should actually be, that which truthfully and in itself has being" (third potency).[42] For the middle Schelling, moreover, this "unprethinkable decision" (*unvordenkliche Entscheidung*) on the part of "nothing" is coterminous with the "personal-

---

40   F. W. J. Schelling, *Philosophical Investigations into the Essence of Human Freedom*, trans. Jeff Love and Johannes Schmidt (Albany, NY: State University of New York Press, 2006), 68. Translation altered. Hereafter *Freedom*.

41   F. W. J. Schelling, *The Ages of the World*, trans. Jason M. Wirth (Albany: SUNY Press, 2000), 23. Hereafter *Ages*.

42   Ibid., 13.

ization" of God himself.[43] Notice the parallels between the following passage and his description of the "non-ground" quoted above: "What then could be thought above all Being, or what is it that neither has being nor does not have being?" Schelling's answer: "It certainly is nothing, but in the sense that the pure Godhead is nothing … in the way that pure freedom is nothing …"[44] Or again, this "nothing" is "not so much God itself, but the Godhead, which is hence, above God …"[45] From which it follows that the "groundless" decision by which the Godhead contracts itself into the "non-being" at the "ground" of existence is not only the materialization of creation out of "nothing" but also the emergence of the "living God"[46] from the "eternal freedom to be" (*die ewige Freiheit zu sein*).[47]

Simply put, the middle Schelling betrays no interest in distinguishing a category like οὐκ ὄν from the divine nature itself.[48] The latter serves as the "dark ground" (*dunkler Grund*) of both God and world, the "indivisible remainder" (*der nie aufgehende Rest*)[49] at the basis of both creation as well as its Creator: "The attracting force, the mother and receptacle [!] of all visible things […] eternal force and might itself, which, when set forth, is seen in the works of creation."[50] Indeed, the *Weltalter* (1815) even glosses *creatio ex nihilo*[51] as the world's emergence from "first potency," thereby implying that the "nothing" in the dogmatic formula is something more like the exteriorization of the "non-ground" than the sheer absence of being as such.[52] Which is to say, μὴ ὄν: a self-revelation of the same "infinite lack of being" (*der unendliche Mangel an Sein*) in the heart of God itself.[53] For the middle Schelling, the "doctrine of potencies" (*Potenzlehre*) is just as much a theogony as it is a cosmogony, and this because not only "non-being" but the "non-existent" itself comes "to be"

43 Schelling, *Ages*, 12.

44 Ibid., 24.

45 Ibid., 25.

46 Cf. ibid., 17, 26–27, 47.

47 Ibid., 23.

48 Cf. Jason Wirth, *Schelling's Practice of the Wild: Time, Art, Imagination* (Albany, NY: State University of New York Press, 2015), 63.

49 Schelling, *Freedom*, 29–30.

50 Schelling, *Ages*, 31.

51 Ibid., 14.

52 Cf. Sean McGrath, *The Dark Ground of Spirit: Schelling and the Unconscious* (London: Routledge, 2011), 14.

53 Cf. F. W. J. Schelling, *Sämtliche Werke* vol. II/2, 49.

in the process: "God leads human nature down no other path than that down which God himself must pass."[54]

The late Schelling has given up such "historical immanentism"[55] for a notion of "pure act" completely exempt from temporal development—compare, for instance, his comment that the concept of God must be "absolutely free from the world, completely detached from the world"[56] in the *Darstellung* (1836) with his recurring claim in the *Weltalter* (1815) that God only becomes fully conscious of himself[57] when creation has come to fruition in third potency—but he nonetheless retains the notion of the "non-ground," now under the heading of "non-potency." Indeed, the contemporaneous *Grundlegung der positiven Philosophie* (1842) equates the latter term with the *actus purus* itself: "the potency, which is not a potency, but is rather itself the *actus*, does not exist via the transition *a potentia ad actum*."[58] Even if his final attempts at a philosophical system insist more strenuously than the works of his middle period that such a "transition" can only occur by an unprethinkable "act" of the divine will, the late Schelling is no less committed to the idea that "non-being" (first potency) exteriorizes a "dark ground" (non-potency) in God himself: "while the later Schelling abandons theogony, he still maintains the claim of the Freedom essay that the ground of God is in God but not identical to God, that is, that there is a distinction in God, something in the divine, which the divine depends upon for being, which is not God."[59] No matter his subsequent breakthroughs regarding the priority of actuality to potency, Schelling never abandons the hard-won insight that "all personality rests on a dark ground."[60]

Such is the background against which one must read Schelling's otherwise puzzling remark in the *Darstellung* that *creatio ex nihilo* "stipulates only that the potencies are not in [God] as *potencies*," but does not thereby say "that they are not in him as *non*-potencies (*Nichtpotenzen*), sheer *differences* (*Unterschiede*) as such, which he freely treats and regards as potencies (as possibilities of another being) only because it pleases him."[61] Again, the comment means to prescind from any possible relationship to creation, to secure a concept of divinity "com-

54 Schelling, *Ages*, 101.
55 Cf. McGrath, *The Dark Ground of Spirit*, 6–11.
56 Schelling, *Darstellung*, 257 [SW X, 282].
57 Cf. Schelling, *The Ages of the World*, 88.
58 Schelling, *Grounding*, 199.
59 Cf. Sean. J. McGrath, *The Philosophical Foundations of the Late Schelling: The Turn to the Positive* (Edinburgh: Edinburgh University Press, 2021), 92.
60 Schelling, *Freedom*, 75.
61 Schelling, *Darstellung*, 261 [SW X, 286].

pletely detached from the world" as we know it.[62] It should be clear by now, however, that Schelling can only do so at the cost of retrojecting a recalcitrant "nothing" into the divine life itself. For these "non-potencies" occupy the same (il)logical space as the οὐκ ὄν out of which God freely elects to bring μὴ ὄν. But precisely because the late Schelling insists upon God's absolute independence from the world while nonetheless maintaining that "God is only God as the Lord, and he is not the Lord without something over which he is Lord," his final system must presuppose something "in" God other than the "potencies" themselves, over which he might exercise such lordship.[63] As he puts the point in the last cycle of his *Philosophie der Offenbarung* (1854) lectures, "there must be something in the middle," between God and the potencies, as it were, since "without such a mediator the world can only be thought of as an immediate and therefore necessary emanation of the divine essence."[64] According to the *Darstellung*, that liminal being can be called "non-potency," or indeed "nothing." Whence, of course, the text's recuperation of *creatio ex nihilo*: the dogmatic formula itself becomes a testament to this "mediator" (*Mittelglied*) the late Schelling's concept of God requires.

But the *Philosophie der Offenbarung* proposes other names: "original potency" (*Urpotenz*), "original possibility" (*Urmöglichkeit*), "original contingency" (*das Urzufällige*), "wet nurse of the world" (*Weltamme*), "mother of the world" (*Weltmutter*), "matter of the world to come" (*die Materie der künftigen Welt*), even "wisdom" (*Weisheit*).[65] Indeed, the figure of *Chokhmah* (חכמה) becomes the operative term in this text, not least because of several important scriptural references. Schelling is especially drawn to Wisdom's own speech in Proverbs 8:22, which he renders thus: "The Lord had me at the beginning of his ways, before his works, *from then on*. From eternity I was appointed, from the beginning, *before* the earth ..."[66] His italics betray the connection Schelling descries between this biblical sketch of Wisdom and the "mediator" he seeks. For she is clearly "distinguished" (*unterschieden*) from the Lord in this passage, but still present to him from eternity: "although she is not herself God, she is nevertheless not a creature either, not something brought forth, and so she thereby represents the middle ground (*das Mittel*) between God and creation—just the mere possibility (*die bloße Möglichkeit*), the first distant material (*der erst*

---

62 Schelling, *Darstellung*, 257 [SW X, 282].
63 F. W. J. Schelling, *Sämtliche Werke* vol. II/3:, 291. All translations of this text are mine.
64 Ibid., 292.
65 Ibid., 294–95.
66 Ibid., 295.

entfernte Stoff) of future products."⁶⁷ This is not to say Wisdom competes for logical priority, since she is something God has always "overcome" (überkam) to establish his lordship. "He does not presuppose her; she presupposes him," to be sure. "But just as he is," Schelling continues, "she is there and presents herself to him as something he can either will or not will (*das er wollen oder nicht wollen kann*), something he can either take up with his will (*in seinem Willen aufnehmen*) or not,"⁶⁸ for she offers God a "mirror" (*Spiegel*) in which to see "that which could actually be in the future, if he wills it."⁶⁹ It's precisely because God perceives in her the highest possibility of creation that Schelling is willing to call "Wisdom" that which he otherwise labels "nothing." Even if the term properly belongs to "the consciousness that knows all things in their coherence, grasping together beginning, middle, and end," he concedes, "there is nothing wrong with assuming that [...] this principle should be named after that which it will be."⁷⁰ So it is, at any rate, that Schelling attempts to find a place for the "non-potencies" in God that compromises neither his freedom nor his personality. Proleptically speaking, he suggests, *creatio ex nihilo* is *creatio ex sapientia*, but not exactly *creatio ex deo*.

Conclusion

By means of an all too brief commentary on Schelling's late interpretation of *creatio ex nihilo*, we've nearly backed our way into Sophiology. Which makes it all the more strange, once again, that our Russian theologian both misrepresents the *Darstellung des philosophischen Empirismus* despite praising its distinctions and distances himself from the *Philosophie der Offenbarung* for supposedly defaulting on those same insights. For not only is there substantial agreement between these two works, but each sheds light on Bulgakov's own concept of *creatio ex nihilo*. They do so in at least three ways.

First, it bears repeating that Bulgakov not only borrows Schelling's distinction between οὐκ ὄν and μὴ ὄν but also endorses the latter's idea that μὴ ὄν represents the "the immediate possibility of actual being," so long as "non-being" itself "originated from nothing."⁷¹ Despite failing to disclose his proximity to Schelling on this point, in other words, Bulgakov also insists that "*ouk on*

---

67   Schelling, *Sämtliche Werke*, 301.
68   Ibid.
69   Ibid., 302.
70   Ibid., 295.
71   Schelling, *Darstellung*, 261 [SW X, 285].

must become *mē on*," that "it must overcome its emptiness and be freed from its sterility."[72] Otherwise, it remains a vacant womb, much like "prime matter" in Plato's myths: "naked potentiality," but not yet a "potency" in its own right.[73] Hence the late Schelling's use of "non-potency" to describe that which Bulgakov calls "pure possibility."[74] In either case, οὐκ ὄν represents the sufficient condition on which the world rests, without it thereby implying that creation is the necessary product of a transition from potency to act in God's own life.

Second, the Bulgakov of *Unfading Light* agrees that a transition from οὐκ ὄν to μὴ ὄν—from "non-potency" to "first potency," as the late Schelling puts it—can only be the result of a supra-rational "decision" on the part of the Absolute. "[I]t is impossible *to comprehend* by what manner *mē on* arises in *ouk on*,"[75] says Bulgakov, and this because the "self-bifurcation of the Absolute as absolute-relative forms the ultimate antinomic limit for thought."[76] We are thus given to know *that* the Absolute "becomes thereby its own potency ('meon') by giving in itself and through itself a place to the relative," but not *how* this has come about.[77] Likewise, the late Schelling's "positive" philosophy turns on his recognition of the "unprethinkable" act by which God not only creates the world but thereby becomes the Creator of Christian revelation—the "living God," as he likes to put it.[78] For him, too, the dogmatic formula of *creatio ex nihilo* ultimately safeguards the freedom of God's decision to create or not. It "stipulates only that the potencies are not in him as *potencies*," recall, "but it does not say that they are not in him as *non*-potencies (*Nichtpotenzen*), sheer *differences* (*Unterschiede*) as such, which he freely treats and regards as potencies (as possibilities of another being) only because it pleases him."[79] Such is the late Schelling's solution to the relationship between that which Bulgakov dubs the alpha privative, οὐκ ὄν, and μὴ ὄν.

Finally, the fact that Schelling ultimately treats this "non-potency" under the heading of "Wisdom" offers the most salient point of contact with Bulgakov's first account of *creatio ex nihilo*. For it not only provides a precedent for his attempt to find a "mediator" between God and world in the figure of Sophia,

---

72 Bulgakov, *Unfading Light*, 189.
73 Ibid., 191.
74 Ibid.
75 Ibid., 189.
76 Ibid., 184.
77 Ibid., 185.
78 Cf. F. W. J. Schelling, *Die Philosophie der Offenbarung 1831/32 (Paulus Nachschrift)*, ed. Manfred Frank (Frankfurt am Main: Suhrkamp, 1977), 191.
79 Schelling, *Darstellung*, 261 [SW X, 286].

but also anticipates the Russian tradition's characteristic tendency to distinguish her from the second person of the Trinity. By contrast with Bulgakov's later efforts to suture his Sophiology to Christology—and this by interpreting "the two forms of the one Wisdom of God" as "the two natures in Christ,"[80] thereby indexing "the inclusion of creation in God's own life" to Sophia's "dual mode,"[81] recall—his work prior to the Great Trilogy still treats her as a "fourth hypostasis," straddling the line between time and eternity.[82] Or again, "[o]ccupying the place *between* God and the world," says Bulgakov, "Sophia abides between being and super-being; she is neither the one nor the other, or appears as both at once."[83] But it's precisely Schelling's influence that explains why Bulgakov should assign such a mediating role to οὐκ ὄν as well: "Between God and creature, between the Absolute and the relative, there lay *nothing*."[84] Bearing in mind the philosopher's claim that "non-potency" should be called "Wisdom" *per anticipationem*—from the perspective of the fully actualized creature it will become in "third potency," that is—Bulgakov's elision becomes somewhat clearer. The provenance of "nothing" in the middle Schelling's notion of "non-ground" makes sense of why Bulgakov might claim that Sophia is "free of being submerged in the nothing which is proper to worldly being"[85] while nonetheless insisting that "a certain *intelligible matter* [...] forms the basis of corporeality in Sophia herself."[86] It sheds light on why he might say "nothing, nonbeing, *apeiron*, emptiness"[87] finds no place in Sophia proper, while nevertheless protesting that "*apeiron* proves to be not weakness or defectiveness" but rather "that matter thanks to which Sophia becomes *ens realissimum, ontos on*, and not an idealist phantom."[88] Simply put, it may be the case that Bulgakov is never more Schellingian than when he suggests that Sophia is a "person," for he seems to be no less committed than his German predecessor to the idea that

---

80 Sergei Bulgakov, *Sophia: The Wisdom of God*, trans. Rev. Patrick Thompson, Rev. O. Fielding Clarke, and Xenia Braikovitc (Hudson, NY: Lindisfarne Press, 1993), 95.

81 Sergius Bulgakov, *The Bride of the Lamb*, trans. Boris Jakim (Edinburgh: T&T Clark, 2002), 45.

82 Bulgakov, *Unfading Light*, 217.

83 Ibid., 219.

84 Ibid., 186.

85 Ibid., 219.

86 Ibid., 258.

87 Ibid., 219.

88 Ibid., 258.

"personality rests on a dark ground," even if the "nothing" in question has been always already overcome.[89]

The full story of Schelling's influence on Bulgakov has yet to be written. He is certainly not the only philosophical source of Bulgakov's sophiological gloss on creation. A more exhaustive treatment of the topic would have to include Plato himself, Plotinus, and Jakob Böhme, especially. But then again, each of these figures already plays a significant role in Schelling's own philosophy of creation. Rather than treating each of the sources in his vast "storehouse of wisdom" on their own terms, it may behoove scholars of Bulgakov to reconsider the extent to which his reception of past figures was mediated by modern authors. Pride of place among such privileged guides should belong to Schelling.

---

89   Schelling, *Freedom*, 75.

Building the House of Wisdom
DOI 10.17438/978-3-402-12195-5

Sergii Bulgakov's Chalcedonian Ontology and the Problem of Human Freedom

Brandon Gallaher

Bulgakov's Doctrine of Creation, Pantheism and *creatio ex nihilo*

Bulgakov's sophiological account of creation is one of the most obscure, contradictory and controversial parts of his work because in it he characteristically weaves together, but simultaneously holds apart, God and creation.[1] This blurring of the uncreated/created distinction forces us to look at the limits of orthodoxy, what constitutes on a basic level an orthodox doctrine of creation: faith in the creation of the world by God out of nothing (*creatio ex nihilo*). Creation out of nothing is reenvisioned as a distinct form of active and creatively directed emanation out of God which ultimately can be understood as in or within God with God self-positing himself as both Creator and creation, with all creaturely being said to mirror Christ in being uncreated-created. We shall suggest, therefore, that Bulgakov's account of creation and creation out of nothing, by blurring the uncreated-created distinction, surprisingly, does not necessarily fall into pantheism, but, through elaborating it, he puts forth a position that both remains within the ambit of a doctrinally orthodox vision of creation and states a highly original radically Christocentric doctrine of the same: creation embodies a difference-in-unity of God and the created, the divine and creaturely being, uncreated and created, underwritten by God himself, without mingling, without change, indivisibly and undividedly. I call

---

1   For commentary see Robert Slesinski, 'Bulgakov's Sophiological Conception of Creation,' *Orientalia Christiana Periodica*, 74.2 (2008), 443–54 and Paul Gavrilyuk, 'Bulgakov's Account of Creation: Neglected Aspects, Critics and Contemporary Relevance,' *International Journal of Systematic Theology*, 17, no. 4 (October 2015), 450–63.

this Bulgakov's Chalcedonian ontology and this study will attempt to sketch the position in brief.

Theological Orthodoxy and Creation Out of Nothing

However, first, there is a theological elephant in the room that needs to be acknowledged directly: pantheism. Does Bulgakov's teaching on creation risk pantheism or can we see a more benign 'panentheism' at work in sophiology? To answer this we need to return to the very notion of a Christian understanding of creation, God and the world he creates out of nothing. But what are the basic lines of an orthodox position on creation out of nothing? In its most basic form we affirm in *creatio ex nihilo* that God is *not* the world and the world is *not* God. The world was created out of nothing into being by a free act of God's will and is very good. It is not eternal, that is, it was not created out of some pre-existent matter, being co-eternal and over against God. Creaturely being is finite and temporal, in contradistinction from divine being, which is infinite and eternal. However, this doctrinal minimum does not mean 'creation out of nothing' is wholly explicated. It still remains, without a theory of or detailed Christian teaching concerning creation, which might save the appearances of faith, highly ambiguous.

It is for this reason that there exist multiple orthodox theological accounts creation out of nothing: Is creation an eternal act, being an action of the eternal God, or an eternal act in time by which time and the creaturely comes to be? What is the 'nothing' out of which creation is created by God? Is it an eternal primordial reality that somehow co-exists with God—a divine nothingness that is coextensive with the divine life of free love or a reality God does not will and which he rejects and which lives by his rejection of it? Or are we speaking when we use the term 'nothing' not of a pure potentiality, a 'not yet something' (*me on*) (or 'not-yet-being'),[2] but a radical blank, an 'absolute nothingness' (*ouk on*) that simply asserts that creation has no foundation in itself and is held in being at each moment by God and comes from an act of God? Lastly, is creation out of nothing a freely willed emanation from God as its first cause, with creation being an effect that, while not a distinct actuality *in* God before its coming into existence, pre-exists (in some sense) virtually in and reflects

2 See Regula M. Zwahlen, 'Different concepts of personality: Nikolaj Berdjaev and Sergej Bulgakov,' *Studies in Eastern European Thought*, 64, no. 3–4 (November 2012), 183–204, at 189 (and espec. 189–95).

in likeness the cause from which it came?[3] Or, in contrast, is creation out of nothing a sort of thrusting by God's will into being of a reality from the abyss of absolute nothingness, which, since it did not exist in any sense prior to creation, nor was potentially or implicitly in God, being neither an emanation nor transformation of a pre-existing reality, has no likeness in being to the being of God, who created it?[4]

Christian orthodoxy generally is able to embrace these multiple ways of parsing creation out of nothing, as long as one keeps a distinction between the eternal God and his contingent creation he freely wills, the uncreated and the created. Theological controversy has more often focused on the minutiae of right teaching in Christology and Trinitarian theology as the determination of orthodoxy in the doctrine of creation, with the dangers of Gnosticism and Neo-Platonism being a distant memory, was long taken to be a given. However, the predominant strain of modern Orthodox theology,[5] neo-patristic synthesis, is an exception here, and, for almost a century, it has maintained, arguably in reaction to Bulgakov and sophiology, that there is only one legitimate way to understand creation out of nothing and this position is presupposed in Orthodox circles as basic. Creation out of nothing, it is alleged, always must mean a) there is between God and creation an infinite divine abyss such that creaturely being is effectively alien to divine being and in no way resembles it and we can never say that creation is created out of or from God; b) when we say God created the world and that it began to exist that this means that it might not have existed and is *radically* contingent and always threatened by an abyss of pre-creation nothingness or non-being, seen above all in death as annihilation, which it might tumble back into; and c) when God creates the world he creates an "Other" over "against" him and "outside" him, making for a sort of divine-creaturely ontological dualism.

---

3   See Daniel Soars, 'Creation in Aquinas: *ex nihilo* or *ex deo*,' *New Blackfriars*, 102, no. 1102 (November 2021), 950–66.

4   See Julius J. Lipner, 'The Christian and Vedāntic Theories of Originative Causality: A Study in Transcendence and Immanence,' *Philosophy East and West* 28 (1978), 53–68, at 54, cited in Soars, 'Creation in Aquinas,' 951–52.

5   For an overview see Paul Ladouceur, *Modern Orthodox Theology: "Behold, I Make All Things New"* (London and New York: T&T Clark, 2019), 193–229.

Bulgakov's Sophiological Account of Creation: A Reconsideration

Here I am summarizing the basic position of Georges Florovsky and Vladimir Lossky,[6] but it is followed by such theological luminaries as John Zizioulas and John Meyendorff, reiterating and often creatively building on the basic position of their teachers. Florovsky and Lossky arguably developed their doctrines of creation in reaction to Bulgakov's sophiology. Bulgakov held in his sophiology that there was one Sophia in two forms related to one another in an antinomy: the uncreated and eternal divine Sophia and the created and temporal creaturely Sophia. Sophia is, as I have written elsewhere, a 'living antinomy'.[7] Bulgakov blurred the uncreated/created distinction by arguing that the uncreated eternal Divine Sophia (the *ousia* of God) and the created temporal Creaturely Sophia (creation but sometimes the world soul) were not ultimately two radically different realities but one reality in two different modes of being. The Creaturely Sophia or creation he held to be a special revelatory or theophanic *mode or image* of the Divine Sophia in becoming and temporality which had as its uncreated and eternal foundation that of the Divine Sophia. In this context, Bulgakov uses the term *obraz*, a key technical term, seen especially clearly in his theological aesthetics,[8] which can mean 'image' (sometimes, 'icon'), 'type' or 'representation' but also 'mode' or 'means of' as well as 'form'.

Let us quickly sketch the main moments of Bulgakov's complex theology/doctrine of creation. Bulgakov held that every created thing is simultaneously uncreated-created: uncreated in its guiding root or base (Bulgakov talks about 'divine seeds' or *logoi*) and creaturely in its mode of becoming or existence. This 'sketch' will be inevitably dense. We shall return to these points later in more detail and, hopefully, with somewhat more clarity. In Bulgakov's theology, we shall see multiple (ultimately spatial) metaphors for the act of creation and creation itself as a uncreated-created reality. These include creation as kenotic self-emptying and creation as limitation (a sort of divine contraction and unfolding) as well as creation as God self-positing or placing himself as 'creation' beyond himself as a divine reality.

---

6   For more detailed discussion see Brandon Gallaher, 'God With Us: A Contemporary Sophiological Reading of Nicaea,' in *Nicaea, Conciliarity and the Future of Christianity*, eds. Aristotle Papanikolaou and George Demacopoulos (New York: Fordham University Press, Forthcoming 2025).

7   Gallaher, *Freedom and Necessity in Modern Trinitarian Theology* (Oxford: Oxford University Press, 2016), 46 ff.

8   See Brandon Gallaher, 'Sergii Bulgakov's Theology of Beauty,' *The Wheel*, 26/27 (Summer/Fall 2021), 42–49.

Between God and creation, therefore, for Bulgakov, there is a) difference but also simultaneously continuity and even identity, for one must 'simultaneously unite, identify and distinguish creation and God's life, which in fact is possible in the doctrine of Sophia, Divine and creaturely, identical and distinct';[9] b) the Divine and Created Sophias, God as uncreated and creation as created, are one Sophia, a united reality so there is strictly speaking no being outside divine being or there is no extra-divine being; c) creaturely being or the Created Sophia is a divinely posited and divinely mediated form of divine being or the Divine Sophia, which is the result of God kenotically limiting himself ontologically or by God positing himself as Creator, which Bulgakov sometimes describes as God positing the world outside God as a 'creatively, initiatively directed and realized emanation—relativity as such'[10]; d) by creating through the means of limiting himself or acting in the mode of Creator facing himself in the mode of world/creation in self-positing, God relates to a part of himself as other than himself ontologically, whereby we can say creation exists and God is the Creator towards it; e) in limiting himself God is said to create out of nothing or create from himself (which is the same thing) but this is fundamentally a relatively new self-relation *in* himself whereby he both relates to himself as relative being or as freely self-alienated and self-sacrificed being and this relative being presupposes 'nothing' as a new divine self-relation (creation and nothing being different aspects of the divine self-relationship of Creator to creation so creation and nothing are both posited by God); f) that creaturely modality of the divine being has a self-existence and autonomy apart from God, with God freely kenotically binding himself by creation's free distinctness and potential opposition; and g) God is unable to omnipotently swamp the creaturely in its divinely mandated unique ontological self-existence in God and control it but only able to interact with it through persuasion and cooperative synergy.

As one can see, Bulgakov's understanding of creation out of nothing has as its core a divine and eternal self-relationship of God as Creator to God-self as created and temporal (though as Bulgakov talks about is as 'self-positing', it also appears to be a relatively novel self-relation). Bulgakov simply could not accept

---

9   Sergii Bulgakov, *Nevesta Agntsa* (Paris: YMCA-Press, 1945), 52 and see 40 [*The Bride of the Lamb*, abridged trans. and ed. Boris Jakim (Grand Rapids: W. B. Eerdmans, 2002), 44 and see 33].

10   Sergei Bulgakov, *Svet Nevechernii: Sozertsaniia i Umozreniia* [1917] in *Sergei Bulgakov: Pervoobraz i Obraz: Sochineniia v Dvukh Tomakh* (Moscow and St. Petersburg: Iskusstvo/Inapress, 1999), Vol. 1: 166 [*Unfading Light: Contemplations and Speculations*, trans. and ed. Thomas Allan Smith (Grand Rapids: W. B. Eerdmans, 2012), 183].

that the world could exist in any other sense than *in* God himself (or even *as* God himself) if God was infinite and eternal being. God is, for Bulgakov, 'everywhere present and filling all things' (as a famous Orthodox prayer to the Holy Spirit puts it) for 'Whither shall I go from thy Spirit? Or whither shall I flee from thy presence? If I ascend to heaven, thou art there! If I make my bed in Sheol, thou art there!' (Psalm 139:7–8). Moreover, 'if God is the Creator, He is the Creator from all eternity [*ot veka*: unto the ages]' or, put differently, 'God is the Creator and the Creator is God.'[11] Ontology, for Bulgakov, must follow theology and theology must follow revelation and we know nothing but God as Father, Son and Holy Spirit *as Creator* always now and ever and unto ages of ages.

I have previously argued that Bulgakov, at least in his works before his posthumously published *The Bride of the Lamb* (1945), does keep open (like Barth) the abstract antinomic possibility that God might not have created and redeemed the world, might not have been Creator and Redeemer.[12] Even in his late work, there is some sense (though not explicit) of what might be called "levels of eternity", not unlike Barth with the problem of election,[13] with God eternally self-determining himself as Creator, and so being in relation to a portion of himself as created, which implies there is at least some abstract eternal status quo ante prior to creation as an eternal act. Whatever the case may be on God eternally being Creator, Bulgakov refused to see creaturely being and the creature as fundamentally other than God-self if that meant the creature was ontologically alien to God or apart from or outside him (made from some separate source of being). The creaturely modality was a divine eternal intra-modality of temporal otherness but that temporal creaturely otherness existed not outside the eternal God but in God-self. As we shall see later, he explicitly argued that this was 'panentheism' and not pantheism and need not lead to the collapse of God and creation.

Florovsky and Lossky, it is not surprising, feared that Bulgakov's doctrine of creation risked pantheism and monism by allowing ontological continuity and identity between the Creator and his creatures, the uncreated and the created. I have had these same concerns for the last twenty years but I now have changed my mind and feel one must go beyond neo-patristic synthesis and risk pantheism for the gain of an overall more inclusive and agile theology able to respond to a creation and society alienated from God and the Church.

---

11   Bulgakov, *Nevesta*, 53, 57 [*Bride*, 45, 49].
12   See Gallaher, *Freedom and Necessity*, 92–93.
13   Ibid., 134–35.

This contribution forms a *qualified* retraction of my previous critiques of Bulgakov's alleged pantheism[14] and attempts to begin thinking through this issue theologically.

It is 'qualified' as I still have some remaining concerns, as will become apparent below, concerning Bulgakov's eschatology, which, I think, is deterministic and *runs the risk* of swamping human freedom by the triumph of God's necessary drive to be all in all. But every great theologian has tensions within their theological work as they grasp over time in multiple works towards a coherent vision when faced with theological ambigua. This need not lead to the view—exemplified by Alexander Schmemann[15] but also seen in his students—

---

14 The earliest being Brandon Gallaher, "'… Tam Svoboda": Problema Bozhestvennnoi Svobody i Neobkhodimosti Liubvi u K. Barta i S. Bulgakova,' in *Russkoe Bogoslovie v Evropeiskom Kontekste: S. N. Bulgakov i zapadnaia religiozno-filosofskaia mysl'*, ed. Vladimir Porus (Moscow: Bibleisko-bogoslovskii institut sv. apostola Andreia, 2006), 40–81 but see also especially 'Antinomism, Trinity and the Challenge of Solov'ëvan Pantheism in the Theology of Sergij Bulgakov,' *Studies in East European Thought* 64, no. 3–4 (2012), 205–25. I have now moved closer to the position long defended by my colleague Dr Regula Zwahlen. See her ground-breaking monograph: Regula M. Zwahlen, *Das revolutionäre Ebenbild Gottes: Anthropologien der Menschenwürde bei Nikolaj A. Berdjaev und Sergej N. Bulgakov* (Vienna/Berlin: LIT, 2010), 355, n. 154 (and more broadly 350–57) and in the English summary see 'Different concepts of personality: Nikolaj Berdjaev and Sergej Bulgakov,' 189–95.

15 'From this experience and vision, by which he really lived with complete wholeness or integral character and without any sort of division, Fr Sergii decided to build a complete and all-encompassing theological system. And now, I do hope he forgives me, if I, having owed him so much, truly being unworthy to untie the thong of his sandal, in all good conscience say honestly that in this desire of his for a 'system' I see for him a personal *fall* of sorts. It seems to me that Fr Sergii fell here into a kind of 'temptation.' Reading his works, especially the late ones, which are the most systematic in character, I wanted often to tell him in a sort of reverie about what the good-natured doctor Samoylenko in Chekhov's 'The Duel' says to the over-confident idealist-systematician Von Koren: 'Dear Fr Sergii, the Germans have ruined you!' The Russian intelligentsia came to believe in this 'German' western 'systematic character' as the main condition for 'scientific character' but they did it in a completely Russian way: with an unrestrained enthusiastic maximalism that made it almost into a sort of idol. In the mean time, on the one hand, the concept of '*integrality*' or '*complete wholeness*' and, on the other hand, the concept of *systematic character* can scarcely be considered synonyms. The theology of the Fathers, for example, is integral or completely whole, 'catholic', and in this consists its eternal and imperishable value, but it is scarcely possible to deduce from it a smooth and definitive 'system.' But it actually seems to be the very opposite: the more 'integral' or 'completely whole' the experience from which thought is born, the deeper will be the vision, the less it gives way to 'systematization' and the more obviously a

that sophiology is not a logically coherent system and that we must face the inevitable breakdown of any attempt to capture Bulgakov's theology in purely systematic terms as sophiology is and was less about constructing a systematic theology than a practical, cultural and existential raid on the unspeakable best expressed in poetry and liturgy.[16] This type of critique of Bulgakov ignores the fact that he attempted to present a coherent theological vision, that is, he aimed to construct a theological system, even if that system was *by design* unsystematic at many points and one which constantly pointed beyond reason by utilizing antinomism as its methodology. It is a view, furthermore, that also might just as well be made towards the theology and philosophy of multiple modern thinkers whose work is infused with the paradoxical, weaving together mystical, pastoral and the artistic threads within a complex scheme of conceptual argument and architecture—such as Kierkegaard, Berdyaev, Buber, Balthasar and Weil—though for some reason Bulgakov and sophiology are considered to be exceptional in this regard. Thus, this essay will continue to attempt to 'make sense' of sophiology on its own terms while acknowledging its multiple ambiguities, some of which may be ultimately purposefully irresolvable.

'reduction' is happening in it [in the systematization]: a simplification, a hardening and even a distortion of the experience. Maybe this is why the Orthodox East did not give rise to any dogmatic 'systems', similar to the 'Summae' of Thomas Aquinas, and did not canonize, as did some western confessions, a special category of 'symbolic books.' But in Fr Sergii there are combined, and to the very last not amalgamated, two men: one man is a 'man of experience', a seer of the mysteries of God's glory and joy, revealed in the Church, and the other man is 'a learned man', a professor who aspired not only to communicate or to explain these mysteries he had seen but also to set them forth as one might say 'without remainder' in a philosophical-theological system, translating from a 'doxological' language into a discursive language. It follows also that there is a kind of 'stylistic' failure of Fr Sergii: these two languages of his do not mix and are not converted into one language, into a sort of organic witness. The experience convinces and subdues you, shining in his writings, but often they do not convince but instead raise doubts and even objections, concerning words and definitions. And it is here, it seems to me, where lies the path to the solution of the 'riddle' of Fr Sergii, his life and creative tragedy. This tragedy, in the end, is that his system (precisely, the 'system' and not the infinite wealth of all that it is 'systematizing') does not correspond to his experience' (Alexander Schmemann, 'Tri Obraza,' *Vestnik Russkogo Studencheskogo Khristianskogo Dvizheniia*, no. 101–02 (III–IV 1971), 9–24 at 20–21).

16 Ibid., 18–19.

Bulgakov's Sophiology: Pantheism or Panentheism?

But let us return to Bulgakov's theology of creation and unpack in detail his teaching on creation out of nothing. Here we see a very different approach to the doctrine of creation than his neo-patristic contemporaries. He too affirms, as orthodoxy dictates, creation out of nothing and the difference between God and creation, but he arrives at the same place as Lossky and Florovsky through a quite different ontology and understanding of *creatio ex nihilo*. Here he builds on the Patristic tradition, and most certainly various Neo-Platonic and Romantic sources, and argues that creation out of nothing is identical to creation out of and even in God. The claim made by his critics is that his sophiology leads to a collapse of God and creation. I myself have written that his sophiology is a 'divine love monism, a free love that must necessarily create the world to love, swallowing up creation and negating human and divine freedom'.[17] But is this actually the case?

What comes up repeatedly in Bulgakov's account of creation is that one must avoid the twin dangers of Monism and Dualism. The dualistic position, say of Manichaeism, would argue that there are two gods: the all-knowing Father and an evil demiurge whose creative act explains the evil in creation.[18] Such a position is self-negating as two gods 'mutually annul each other', for in the very idea of God is uniqueness and absoluteness.[19] Yet the difficulty with dualism is not just seen in Gnosticism, but in all forms of anti-cosmism, which put an 'impassable gulf' between God and the world, making the existence of the incarnation or Godmanhood impossible.[20] This type of ontological dualism can arguably be seen in the case of neo-patristic synthesis, where we are faced with visions of creation out of nothing that see creation not as an act of love but as the product of an ungrounded and even capricious exertion of the divine will, with creation separated by an abyss from the Creator.[21] Moreover,

---

17   Gallaher, Freedom and Necessity, 111.
18   Bulgakov, *Nevesta*, 9–11 [*Bride*, 5–7].
19   Ibid., 9 [Ibid., 5].
20   Bulgakov, *Sophia, The Wisdom of God: An Outline of Sophiology*, trans. revd. Christopher Bamford (Hudson, NY: Lindisfarne Press, [1937] 1993), 14.
21   See Georges Florovsky, 'Creation and Createdness' [1928], trans. Alexey Kostyanovsky, in *The Patristic Witness of Georges Florovsky: Essential Theological Writings* , ed. Brandon Gallaher and Paul Ladouceur (London and New York: T&T Clark, 2019), 36–38; Compare Vladimir Lossky, *The Mystical Theology of the Eastern Church*, trans. The Fellowship of St Alban and St Sergius (London: St Vladimir's Seminary Press, 1976 [1944]), 92 (quoting the same passage of Met. Philaret from Florovsky in the text above), John

the world comes to be seen in dualism as a reality that is so completely alien to God that there is no point of contact in it to reach out to God—'the Charbydis of abstract cosmism in which the world's being loses its connectedness with divinity'[22]—unless God himself seizes it and it comes to seem as if it were another quasi-divine reality forever opposing God.

But more importantly still in understanding Bulgakov's theology of creation is his critique of monism or Spinozism. He argues that the idea that the world is simply the emanation of the Absolute sacrifices plurality and results in the 'suicide of the relative',[23] which is 'the Scylla of pantheism, in which the world is in danger of sinking into the ocean of divinity'.[24] To say all relative being is, simply speaking, the aggregate of modes of the Absolute is to risk falling into the position that creation is but an illusion. But is this God's own illusion or do we end up negating the absoluteness of God himself?[25] Thus Bulgakov is very clear in articulating that his position is not monism and that pantheism is something that must be wholly avoided although, he argued, for panentheism, which he considered to be something entirely different.[26]

What Bulgakov wanted to assert is that creation is neither (*pace*, neo-patristic synthesis) radically other than God, nor need it be collapsed back into him. Creation is, in some sense, distinct, but yet dwelling *in* God. Thus, by "panentheism", he understood 'the truth that all is in God or of God'[27] or 'the

Meyendorff, 'Creation in the History of Orthodox Theology,' *St. Vladimir's Theological Quarterly*, 27, no. 1 (1983), 27–37, John D. Zizioulas, *The Eucharistic Communion and the World*, ed. Luke Ben Tallon (London: T & T Clark, 2011), 158–62 and 'Christology and Existence: The Dialectic of Created and Uncreated and the Dogma of Chalcedon' in *Synaxis: An Anthology of the Most Significant Orthodoxy Theology in Greece in the Journal ΣΥΝΑΞΗ from 1982 to 2002, Vol. I: Anthropology-Environment-Creation* (Montreal: Alexander Press, 2006), 23–35 (with subsequent responses by Zizioulas and Philip Sherrard: 37–61).

22 Bulgakov, *Nevesta*, 41 [*Bride*, 34].
23 Bulgakov, *Svet Nevechernii*, 166 [*Unfading Light*, 182].
24 Bulgakov, *Nevesta*, 41 [*Bride*, 34].
25 Bulgakov, *Svet Nevechernii*, 166–67 [*Unfading Light*, 182–83].
26 See Bulgakov, 'Ipostas' i Ipostasnost' (Scholia k *Svetu Nevechernemu*) [1925] in *Sergii Bulgakov: Pervoobraz i Obraz*: Vol. 2, 313–23, at 317 ['Protopresbyter Sergii Bulgakov: Hypostasis and Hypostaticity: Scholia to the *Unfading Light*,' revised trans., ed. and intro. of A. F. Dobbie Bateman by Brandon Gallaher and Irina Kukota, *St Vladimir's Theological Quarterly*, 49, no. 1–2 (2005), 5–46, at 26–27; *Uteshitel'* (Paris: YMCA, 1936), 245 [*The Comforter*, abridged trans. and ed. Boris Jakim (Grand Rapids: W. B. Eerdmans, 2004), 199–200]; *Sophia*, 71–73, 147; and *Nevesta*, 231–32, 249 [*Bride*, 212, 228]].
27 See Bulgakov, 'Ipostas," 317 ['Hypostasis,' 27] and see *Sophia*, 71–73 and 147.

world is that which is not God [*ne-Bog*] existing in God, God is that which is not the world [*ne-mir*] existing in the world. God posits the world outside of Himself, but the world possesses its Being in God.'[28] Bulgakov, in opposing dualism, argues that one must say that there is nothing apart from God, no separate reservoir of being (divinely willed) apart from him, who is limitless, and that 'Only the divinity of the existent God *is*, and there is nothing apart from or outside of divinity.'[29] Put otherwise, creaturely being, the created Sophia, is a special modality of divine being or the divine Sophia. Yet this need not necessarily lead to the equally dangerous error of pantheism, because one affirms that God creates out of nothing. Creation out of nothing does not mean, as many neo-patristic writers affirm,[30] that there is a reality alongside, outside and apart from God; rather, it implies that the 'whole power of the world's being belongs to divinity' since 'God created the world out of Himself.'[31]

Creation out of nothing, if it was interpreted as creating a sort of otherness of being apart from the being of God, separated by an abyss, might run the risk of being said to complete or supplement divine being.[32] Absolute nothing, *ouk on*, simply does not exist in itself,[33] so to say something is created out of nothing is to simply say it is related or turned in being to God as Creator, from which it finds its origin and reality: 'the directedness [*obrashchennost*': orientation/conversion] of the world toward God, for createdness is precisely this relationship.'[34] Alternatively, to be created is for God to turn to himself in a new non-divine modality. Absolute nothing is no thing, then, not something. It is the presupposition of God's intra-relationship to himself in a creaturely modality. Everything which exists in creation positively 'belongs to divinity', as only God exists, as there is nothing beside him; no being exists but different modalities of divine being. The divine 'receives in creation extra-divine being, otherness of being [*inobytie=Anderssein*], which precisely constitutes creation and creatureliness.'[35]

28 Bulgakov, *Ikona i Ikonopochitanie* [1931] in *Sergii Bulgakov: Pervoobraz i Obraz*: Vol. 2, 241–310 at 262 (my translation). [See *The Icon and Its Veneration* in *Icons and the Name of God*, trans. Boris Jakim (Grand Rapids: W. B. Eerdmans, 2012), 32].

29 *Nevesta*, 51 [*Bride*, 43]; 'Only God exists and there is nothing outside of God" (ibid., 128 [ibid., 117]).

30 e. g. Florovsky, 'Creation and Createdness,' 36–38.

31 Bulgakov, *Nevesta*, 52 [*Bride*, 44].

32 See ibid., 128 [ibid., 117].

33 Ibid., 51 [ibid., 44].

34 Ibid., 12 [ibid., 7].

35 Ibid., 128 [ibid., 117 (revised translation)].

In writing of 'extra-divine being' as 'otherness of being', I think Bulgakov was, like Karl Barth,[36] playing with the ideas of Hegel, or 'Hegeling',[37] as he tried to come to terms with the Christian understanding of creation out of nothing.[38] The Hegelian concept Bulgakov is adapting is that of *Anderssein* (otherness/ otherness of being) where, for Hegel, Spirit (as what is in itself) grasps itself 'out of itself' as an object that is other to itself.[39] For Hegel, the infinite absolute idea or Spirit when it is externalized, freely self-alienated, can be said to exist as nature which has otherness of being.[40] In Hegel, this movement of the infinite God into otherness presupposes the logic which is thought's autonomous self-determination of itself, grasping itself as a totality, and this requires the conceptualization of difference from what is other than itself, a radically

---

36   See Brandon Gallaher, '"A Supertemporal Continuum": Christocentric Trinity and the Dialectical Reenvisioning of Divine Freedom in Bulgakov and Barth,' in *Correlating Sobornost: Conversations Between Karl Barth and Russian Orthodox Theology*, eds. John C. McDowell, Scott A. Kirkland, and Ashley J. Moyse (Minneapolis: Fortress Press, 2016), 95–133, at 112–30 and see Georges Florovsky on the links between Bulgakov and Barth in the archival paper of Florovsky by Paul Ladouceur, "Georges Florovsky and Russian Idealism: Two Unpublished Papers' ("The Renewal of Russian Theology—Florensky, Bulgakov, and the Others: On the Way to a Christian Philosophy"), *St Vladimir's Theological Quarterly*, 65, no. 1–2 (2021), 187–222, at 207–22, espec. 212–13.

37   'I myself have a certain weakness for Hegel and am always fond of doing a bit of "Hegeling". As Christians we have the freedom to do this [...] I do it eclectically' (Barth to W. Herrenbrück, 15 February 1952, cited Eberhard Busch, *Karl Barth: His life from letters and autobiographical texts*, trans. John Bowden (Philadelphia: Fortress Press, 1976), 387).

38   But for a very critical earlier reading of Hegel (denying that Hegel's dialectic, which is pantheist, could fathom the Christian notion of 'creation out of nothing') see Sergii Bulgakov, *Tragediia Filosofii (Filosofiia i Dogmat)* [1920–1921] in *S. N. Bulgakov: Sochineniia v Dvukh Tomakh*, 2 vols., vol. 1 (Moscow: Nauka, 1993), 309–518, at 459–89, espec. 478–80 [*The Tragedy of Philosophy (Philosophy and Dogma)*, trans. Stephen Churchyard (New York: Angelico Press, 2020), 171–205 at 193–94].

39   'Spirit becomes the object, for it is this movement of becoming an other to itself, which is to say, of becoming an object to its own self and of sublating this otherness' (G. W. F. Hegel, *Phenomenology of Spirit*, trans. and ed. Terry Pinkard (Cambridge: Cambridge University Press, 2018), § 36, 23).

40   See Hegel, *Encyclopedia of the Philosophical Sciences in Basic Outline, Part I: Science of Logic*, trans. and eds. Klaus Brinkman and Daniel O. Dahlstrom (Cambridge: Cambridge University Press, 2015), § 18, 46 and *Hegel's Philosophy of Nature*, vol. 1, trans. and ed. M. J. Petry (London/NY: George Allen and Unwin/Humanities Press, 1970), § 247, 205–08.

different other which is autonomous from thought: nature.[41] But the logic of essence which follows that of being is reciprocal in character and assumes a self-determining subject facing an other through which it *is* through being the other of its other.[42] To be other is to be oneself as differentiated from one's other insofar as that other is and is not, in some sense both being and nothingness in its becoming, or, to quote William Maker, 'differentiating [for Hegel] is now explicit as the truth of identity.'[43] To quote Hegel's *Science of Logic:*

> Each is itself and its other; for this reason, each has its determinateness not in an other but within.—Each refers itself to itself only as referring itself to its other [...] Each, therefore, simply is, first, to the extent that the other is; it is what it is by virtue of the other, by virtue of its own non-being; it is only positedness. Second, it is to the extent that the other is not; it is what it is by virtue of the non-being of the other; it is reflection into itself.[44]

Hegel gives multiple examples of self-differentiation as the determination of identity, including 'above and under', 'right and left' and 'father and son'. In Hegel's words: '"Father" is the other of "son" and "son" the other of "father," and each is only as this other of the other; and the one determination is at the same time only with reference to the other; their being is one subsisting. The father is indeed something for itself outside this reference to the son, but then he is not "father" but a "man" in general'.[45]

There exists the common academic view that Hegel's logic is deterministic and the consummate identity philosophy, like a snake swallowing its tail, driving that which is derived back to its ground. In this sense, to contend Bulgakov adapted Hegel would be, for some, proof positive that Bulgakov's alleged determinism, monism and pantheism find their noxious origin in German Idealism. Rather, it might be argued, on the contrary, that Hegel's logic assumes that determination and self-identification comes through a *pluralization* of differentiation[46] in nature and that divine freedom always already

---

41   William Maker, 'Identity, Difference, and the Logic of Otherness,' in *Identity and Difference: Studies in Hegel's Logic, Philosophy of Spirit, and Politics* (Albany, NY: State University of New York Press, 2007), 15–30, at 18.

42   Ibid., 22–23.

43   Ibid., 23.

44   Hegel, *The Science of Logic*, ed. and trans. George di Giovanni (Cambridge: Cambridge University Press, 2015), II.i.2, 368–69.

45   Ibid., 383.

46   Maker, 'Identity, Difference, and the Logic of Otherness,' 26–27 and see 15.

contains necessity within itself so does not necessarily have to grasp itself in and through creation.[47] At the close of the *Science of Logic* we are told, contrary to the view Hegel was a determinist, monist and pantheist, that the pure Idea of cognition, which was confined to subjectivity, is sublated and the last result, which is nature, free concrete existence, is the beginning of another sphere and science which is 'absolute liberation for which there is no longer an immediate determination [...] the form of its determinateness is just as absolutely free: the externality of space and time absolutely existing for itself without subjectivity.'[48]

But to what end is this "Hegeling" for Bulgakov in borrowing, as I think he was arguably doing, the Hegelian concept of "otherness" of being as creation? Bulgakov is adapting Hegel's idea of self-identity through differentiation to a) speak about creation as a freely and reciprocally determined otherness by God insofar as it is the result of a God who allows himself to become creation's Other as Creator and freely bestows otherness on creation by giving 'up in Himself a place for the relative by an inexpressible act of love-humility He posits it [the relative, creature] next to Himself and outside Himself, limiting Himself by His own creation';[49] and b) to emphasize that all creation has a 'non-creaturely-creaturely character' or has sophianic divine roots (the creaturely Sophia being a mode or image of the Divine Sophia) with God as its Other/Creator.[50] To express this otherwise, creation, for Bulgakov, is constituted by God as the other of itself as other (other of the other) and the otherness of being of creation is its divine roots, God as other of the other of creation, sophianicity as the Creaturely Sophia which is grounded in the Divine Sophia. Likewise, God is freely constituted as Creator, known by himself as such and later for creation, by the otherness of being in himself as the Divine Sophia or divine world of ideas that is then expressed as the Creaturely Sophia. This "move" from the Divine to the Creaturely Sophia is also expressed by Bulgakov as a transition of God as being Absolute to God as being Absolute-Relative or Creator.[51]

When God, therefore, for Bulgakov, freely creates or so relativizes himself in Being and one speaks of 'relative being', it is at this point that one can speak

47 I am indebted for this observation to Prof Justin Coyle.
48 Hegel, *The Science of Logic*, II.iii.3, 752–53.
49 Bulgakov, *Svet Nevechernii*, 192 [see *Unfading Light*, 214–15 (my translation)]; See discussion at Gallaher, *Freedom and Necessity*, 62–63, 84–94.
50 Bulgakov, *Nevesta*, 128 [*Bride*, 117].
51 I am indebted for these last observations to Dr Harry Moore and for his reference to the work of William Maker.

of 'relative nothing, *me on*' which is the half-shadow, nothingness (insofar as all becoming posits nothingness), included in the state of creaturely-relative being created by God.[52] Bulgakov at times identifies this meonic nothingness with *prima materia*.[53] In other words, creation and nothing (which go together) are both creations of the God who allows himself to become relativized as Creator and creation. For the world to exist (stated positively) is to have no other ground of being except as a 'special *modality*' of divine being, which is to exist in God and only by God, and (stated negatively) therefore the world has no ground in itself, being established literally on the abyss of nothing.[54] Creation out of nothing, therefore, means creation comes from God (*creatio ex deo*) and exists in him and has no independent foundation. Creation, Bulgakov contends, is broader than the neo-platonic notion of emanation. It is not a 'passive overflow' like 'foam in an overflowed cup'. Rather, creation contains emanation in itself; 'creation is emanation *plus* something new that is created by the creative *let there be!*', in that creation is an active and free 'creatively, initiatively directed and realized emanation'. God as Absolute contains the relative of the world in himself: 'the world rests in the bosom of God like a child in the mother's womb.'[55] In summary, *creatio ex nihilo* can be interpreted as in harmony with *creatio ex deo*, for we see both a continuity with God in creation (emanation) but also real novelty (out of nothing), and, though we do not have the space to elaborate this contention here, we see various canonical writers, including Gregory of Nyssa and Maximus the Confessor, treating creation out of nothing as being out of God himself in a fashion not dissimilar to Bulgakov.[56]

---

52 Bulgakov, *Nevesta*, 52 [*Bride*, 44].
53 Ibid., 75–76 [ibid., 66–67].
54 Ibid., 11 [ibid., 7].
55 Bulgakov, *Svet Nevechernii*, 166–67 [*Unfading Light*, 183 (revised translation)].
56 See Daniel Heide, 'The World as Sacrament: The Eucharistic Ontology of Maximos Confessor,' PhD diss., McGill University, November 2022, especially Chapter 4 (he quotes Maximus: "it must be accepted that all things have been created *from the eternally existing God from nothing* [ἐκ Θεοῦ τοῦ ἀεὶ ὄντος τὰ πάντα ἐκ τοῦ μὴ ὄντος γενέσθαι]' (*Amb.* 10.41, 1188B)), Harry Wolfson, 'The Identification of *Ex Nihilo* with Emanation in Gregory of Nyssa,' *Harvard Theological Review*, 63, no. 1 (Jan. 1970), 53–60 (see Gregory of Nyssa, *De Hominis Opficio*, 23, no. 4–5, PG 44 212B–C) and 'The Meaning of *Ex Nihilo* in the Church Fathers, Arabic and Hebrew Philosophy, and St Thomas,' in *Medieval Studies in Honor of Jeremiah Denis Matthias Ford*, eds. Urban T. Holmes and Alex J. Denomy (Cambridge, Mass.: Harvard University Press, 1948), 355–70.

Bulgakov, therefore, says that creation must be understood within the reality of God or *in* God: 'The roots of the world's creation lie in God's eternity.'[57] Creation, having divine otherness of being, is 'as the creaturely Sophia [...] uncreated-created'.[58] For this reason, Bulgakov, particularly in his late writing, articulates creation as the 'self-determination of intra-divine life' *in* God,[59] using a kaleidoscope of metaphors or multiple images: a) creation is said to be 'a self-positing of God'[60] in which God both 'coposit[s] the creation' with his own life as Divine Sophia and 'correlate[s]' his act of creating with his own self-determination precisely as Creator in a creaturely mode which is the Created Sophia[61] and so Bulgakov can claim that for God to be Creator is an eternal reality co-posited with his triunity; b) God is said to submerge himself in nothing in the form of the '*uncreated* forces and energies' of the Divine Sophia,[62] 'the very seeds of being' or Maximean *logoi*, comprising the eternal divine world, entering nothingness or are said to have been 'implanted in the meonal half-being of becoming'[63] and become the Creaturely Sophia, receiving 'a creaturely, relative, limited, multiple being for themselves and the universe comes into being';[64] c) God is said to create through revealing himself in creation insofar as the creaturely Sophia is 'only a special mode [*obraz*: image/representation, form, type] of the being of the Divine Sophia, the revelation of the Divine Sophia in the creaturely Sophia';[65] d) God as Trinity, the Absolute, who is an eternal movement of self-emptying and self-sacrificial love empties himself, sacrifices his own inner life by no longer possessing the world for itself and allows the world to have its own being in himself as relative, thereby making himself Absolute-Relative,[66] that is, 'The creation of the world by God, the self-bifurcation of the Absolute, is the sacrifice of the Absolute for the sake of the relative [...] The voluntary sacrifice of self-sacrificing love, the Golgotha of the Absolute, is the foundation of creation';[67] e) Creation is said to be 'the imparting of the

---

57 Bulgakov, *Nevesta*, 52 [*Bride*, 44].
58 Ibid., 72 [ibid., 63].
59 Ibid., 53 [ibid., 45].
60 Ibid., 54 [ibid., 46].
61 Ibid., 52–54, 63 [ibid., 44–46, 54].
62 Ibid., 72 [ibid., 63].
63 Ibid., 64 [ibid., 55].
64 Ibid., 72 [ibid., 63 (revised translation)].
65 Ibid., 69 [ibid., 60].
66 Ibid., 58 [ibid., 50]; For detailed discussion on God as Absolute and Absolute-Relative see Gallaher, *Freedom and Necessity*, 70–94.
67 Bulgakov, *Svet Nevechernii*, 168 [*Unfading Light*, 185 (revised translation)].

image [*obraz*: mode] of the Divine Sophia to the creaturely Sophia' in "'a pro-logue in heaven,'" whereby one might speak of a "co-being [*sobytie*: event, hap-pening]" in Sophia'[68] which is the eternal creation and beginning of creaturely being in God manifesting his life not only in the absoluteness of the Divine Sophia but in the becoming of the Creaturely Sophia; and f) God in creating 'releases' or 'lets be' creation from the depths of the Divine Sophia into 'self-ex-istence' or 'self-being', making a world out of nothing out of himself, his own divine life.[69] The reader will be forgiven if they are somewhat lost amidst this torrent of imagery, but, Bulgakov is, in these panentheistic matters, at the very edge of language. He is attempting, and frequently falls into contradiction and deep obscurity in the process, to articulate simultaneously how creation both is and is not God and how God is and is not creation.

Bulgakov and the Problem of Creaturely Freedom

Now, if creaturely life is God in becoming or (stated otherwise) equally if cre-ation somehow takes place *in God*, as there is nothing outside him, and, in some sense, all there is *is God* in different modes, and if 'God in His eternity encompasses in one supra-temporal act the fullness of being, with its spatiality and temporality', then, from this perspective, 'God himself does not become in the world, but the world becomes in God – the genesis of the relative happens in the absolute.'[70] This would seem, *prima facie*, despite all of my long defense, to lead to pantheism, monism and the complete negation of all freedom of the creature, especially with the addition of Bulgakov's notion of 'sophianic determinism'[71] thrown into the mix. However, I want to argue that this quite eccentric panentheistic doctrine of creation, which I have attempted to analyze and hopefully clarified at least a little for the reader, appears to be the basis of Bulgakov's account of synergy and human autonomy. It is only because there is divine being which creatures have a share in at their foundation that they can be given, by God's kenotic withdrawal, a certain independence apart from God.

---

68   Bulgakov, *Nevesta*, 73 [*Bride*, 63].
69   Ibid., 56 [ibid., 48].
70   Sergii Bulgakov, 'Iuda Iskariot—apostol-predatel'. Chast' vtoraia (dogmaticheskaia),' *Put'*, 27 (1931), 3–42, at 13–14 ['Judas Iscariot—Apostle-Betrayer. Second Part (Dog-matic),' trans. T. Allan Smith, 35] (I am grateful to Prof T. Allan Smith for use of his unpublished manuscript translation).
71   Bulgakov, *Agnets Bozhii* (Paris: YMCA-Press, 1933) 462 [*The Lamb of God*, abridged trans. and ed. Boris Jakim (Grand Rapids: W. B. Eerdmans, 2008), 435].

Creaturely freedom exists only because the creature is founded on the divine and is uncreated-created in character.

The world is not only a thing or object in God's hands but possesses, through God's self-limitation, its own proper being, nature and life, but this 'created nature does not remain outside God, because ontologically extra-divine being does not exist at all.' Creation abides in God although it is not God and the relationship of God to his creation is not one of 'unilateral action of God towards a world lying outside of Him and alien to Him' but a *cooperation* (*vzaimodeistvie*) or synergism of Creator with his creation, which is *in* him as uncreated-created. The only way that such a synergism, with its 'mutual connectedness and dependence', can happen is if not only God has a true 'reality and self-existence [*samobytnost*']' but creation also has such a reality but, Bulgakov contends, 'In order to become self-existent [*samobytnyi*], the world must be divine in its positive foundation.'[72] Thus, it is only because creation is first divine in its substratum that the 'the world maintains its self-existence in the eyes of God, although it is created from nothing', and then, secondarily, thanks to creatureliness it also maintains its independence of being, its 'unbridgeable difference' in God's eyes. The world ostensibly has a 'genuine reality' because it is both divine in its foundation and creaturely in its temporal becoming, determined by God for himself unto the ages but only because it exists both for God, being dependent on his life and being, and for itself, in the tightest cooperation, seen at its apex in Christ himself. The creation, then, has an independent self-existent status by the 'fullness of the divine ideas-energies, which, being submerged in non-being in the divine act of creation, acquired for themselves otherness of being [*inobytie=Anderssein*] in the world'.[73] Bulgakov describes this creaturely otherness of being of the divine, described above, which has its own autonomy, as we have seen, as a form of kenosis.[74]

Yet the creature cannot fall away from God and maintain its own independent self-existence. If it tips over the abyss then it—in some sense—ceases to be, as with the Fall when man exists in a sort of state of non-existence. In Christ, through his whole divine-human life, God embraces the world, freely diminishing himself, and through free cooperation brings it back into being. This all presupposes that the creature is 'created by God for God, for participa-

---

72   Bulgakov, 'Iuda,' 11; *Samobytnost*' and the synonym *samobytie* (with slight differences for cognate versions) might also be rendered 'autonomy', 'distinctiveness', 'uniqueness', 'self-sufficiency', 'integrality' and 'independence' (my translation).

73   Ibid., 11–13 (my translation).

74   Bulgakov, *Nevesta*, 69–70 [*Bride*, 60].

tion in the Divine life', but he was, despite having an uncreated-created foundation, 'created in himself and for himself', which is to say that the 'freedom of creation in its self-existence [*samobytnost'*] is indestructible for God':[75]

> The world is placed by God in non-being, it originated from nothing, it has a reality that is indestructible and insuperable even for God, who does not repent of his works and does not make non-existing what was created out of the non-existing, does not return into nothingness anything of what has been created by Him. This is why each human being and every creature [alternate translation: all creation] are real by the reality of God and in this sense equally real to God. But at the same time the reality of the world and the human being is not closed and impenetrable for God, who created it after His own image.
>
> ---
>
> God is not free in relation to the world, but is bound by its nature, its stagnation, its opposition. God cannot do everything with the world that he wants, having once already given the world its self-existence [*samobytie*]. Divine omnipotence is voluntarily self-limited by the self-existence [*samobytnost'*] of the world, and in order to save the world, God himself descends into it, becomes human, i. e. unites with the world indivisibly.[76]

But if this is so, then God can only ever cooperate with his creature and in regards to the freedom of the creature can only persuade (never coerce) it to work with him. He cannot coerce the creature into a synergy with him. God's synergism assumes that the mode of divine action is always persuasion, not coercion: 'Divinity can act upon the person only by interacting with him on the basis of creaturely freedom. God spares the person and protects him even from His own omnipotence. He acts without coercing; that is, He persuades, limiting His power to the measure of creaturely receptivity. This is precisely *synergism*, as the form [*obraz*] of Divine Providence with regard to human beings.'[77] God knows all the possibilities of creation, which can be enacted in creaturely freedom, as he created the world as a totality with them within it. The creature cannot surprise God by creating a new path for its freedom in the world. However, God effectively blinds himself kenotically as to which of these possibilities the creature will actualize in its freedom (including the possibility of the fall and rebellion against God himself) as its free creative contribution

---

75   Bulgakov, 'Iuda,' 14 [*Judas*, 36 (Smith translation—revised)].
76   Bulgakov, 'Iuda,' 14,23 [*Judas*, 35–36, 40 (Smith translation—revised)].
77   Bulgakov, *Nevesta*, 253 [*Bride*, 232 (revised translation)].

and awaits the choice humanity will choose, though always coaxing it forward towards the right choice in love:

> Although creation cannot be absolutely unexpected and new for God in the on-tological sense, nevertheless, in empirical ("contingent", i. e. by a free occurrence) being, it represents a new manifestation for God Himself, who is waiting to see whether man will open or not open the doors of his heart. God himself will know this only when it happens [...] Veiling His face, God remains ignorant of the actions of human freedom. Otherwise, these actions would not have their own reality, but would only be a function of a certain divine mechanism of things.[78]

Bulgakov's major claim is that humanity's freedom remains inviolable for God and that 'ontologically, man cannot get rid of freedom even if he so desires, for it is the mode of the creaturely spirit'.[79] He even goes so far as to say (claiming it is not the reiteration of the Origenist pre-existence of souls) that humans freely co-participate with God in their own creation, saying 'yes' to God's cre-ation of them in a sort of created eternity.[80] Thus, Bulgakov highly reverences creaturely freedom, but there are remaining difficulties, and here lie some of my continuing reservations concerning Bulgakov's sophiology.

What can we make of what Bulgakov called God's 'victory by persuasion'[81] or, alternatively, 'sophianic determinism'?[82] Bulgakov is very clear that the free-dom of the creature has definite limits to it and, in this sense, there is a definite divinely chosen end to creation. First of all, he argues that the world can never 'take a path of development completely opposed to the paths of God and divine

---

78   Bulgakov, *Nevesta*, 259–60 [*Bride*, 238–39 (revised translation)]; see Zwahlen, 'Different concepts of personality,' 195.
79   Ibid., 255–56 [ibid., 234].
80   Bulgakov claims (drawing on Fichte, Schelling and Schopenhauer) that in a supra-temporal created eternity prior to temporality and not yet the eternity of God, 'free entities, angels and humans, co-participate in their own creation and receive it by their freedom, and this participation of the human in his creation is the reflected light of his God-likeness, the image of God in him, permeating even his very origination, be-stowing actuality on him [...] We together with God pronounce *I* about ourselves at our creation and by this we say *yes* in response to His creative "let there be" (*fiat*) [...] The creature not only says its free *yes* to the creative call of God to being, but it speaks in the call's response to the concrete and definite individual acknowledgment' ('Iuda,' 19–20 [*Judas*, 38 (Smith translation); Compare to *Agnets*, 164–66 [*Lamb*, 142–43]).
81   Ibid., 456 [Ibid., 429].
82   Ibid., 462 [Ibid., 435].

concern', as this would be complete indeterminism. Despite its 'self-existence and freedom, a general divine determinability is proper to the world as an inner law and ontological norm of its being, and this is the *Sophianity of the world.*' Creation, he argues, may be self-existent but it is not autonomous.[83] All of creation is moving towards its fulfilment in Christ in God so that God will be all in all, that is, the 'cosmos', 'sophianic determinism' or 'dynamic pan-Christism'.[84] Second of all, human freedom and creativity for Bulgakov are defined by the reality of their foundation, which is sophianic. This reality is a givenness by which freedom is defined as a mode: 'Creaturely and human freedom is not absolute, its actuality refers only to the form of the realization of the givenness [*k obrazu osushchestvleniia dannosti*], while the path and the limits are predetermined by this givenness, and this predeterminability [*predeterminirovannost'*] of creation is determined by the [fact that] "God will be all in all"[1 Cor 15:28]'.[85] Only in God as Trinity do you encounter an absence of givenness and therefore pure freedom, which coincides with necessity.[86]

Strictly speaking, fallen human liberty cannot, Bulgakov says, echoing Maximus the Confessor on the gnomic versus the natural will,[87] even be called 'freedom'. Eventually, the creature will run out of (wrong) possibilities to choose between and enact, and will run the course of its rebellion, and naturally follow God by enacting its natural and determined path of being at one with God. It will, in some sense, cease to be free, in the creaturely sense of continuing to choose between opposed possibilities, and will be free as God is free (i.e. not 'free', as we know it). Creaturely freedom contains the possibility of its falling and rising ('the mutability [*udoboprevratnost'*] of the creature')[88] and as a further part of its modality of freedom 'contains in itself also the possibility of its own overcoming, of liberation from this creaturely freedom, an exit beyond it, along that side of it, towards the image of God.' Bulgakov even goes so far as to say that 'so that in a certain sense salvation too is the overcoming of freedom

---

83 Bulgakov ('Iuda,' 15 [*Judas*, 36 (Smith translation)].

84 Bulgakov, *Agnets*, 462–63 [*Lamb*, 435]; See discussion at Gallaher, *Freedom and Necessity*, 109 ff.

85 Bulgakov, 'Iuda,' 15 [*Judas*, 36 (Smith translation)].

86 For discussion see Gallaher, *Freedom and Necessity*, 75–76 and earlier at 46–47.

87 See Maximus the Confessor, *Opscule* 3, *Maximus the Confessor*, trans. and ed. Andrew Louth (London/NY: Routledge, 1996), 192–98.

88 *Udoboprevratnost'* is a neologism of Bulgakov and translated by Smith as 'predisposition.' It is more accurately rendered literally as 'susceptibility to change' or simply 'changeability.' (Thanks to Dr Harry Moore for his insights on this term).

as mutability.'[89] In other words, to be saved is to transcend the susceptibility to change or changability of one's freedom, going beyond the gnomic will that is variant to the natural will that follows what it was created for by God and choosing between this possibility and that possibility.

Yet Bulgakov's theology of creaturely freedom does seem to be at odds with itself. On the one hand, creation, insofar as it is freely shares in a sort of portion of divinity, cannot be involuntarily overwhelmed by grace, since God considers it inviolable as he encounters a portion of his own freedom and must limit himself. Here only talk of 'persuasion' reigns and Bulgakov frequently speaks in this vein concerning divine-human synergism. But, on the other hand, creation, for Bulgakov, is also said to be sophianic in its foundation and its ultimate freedom is *determined* by the givenness of its own nature, which is the Divine Sophia and that uncreated-created base of its nature will eventually become all in all. The creaturely will eventually become overwhelmed by its own divine roots, and it will finally attain its full sophianization as complete divinization, ceasing (it seems) to be created. No one can hold out from the love of God unto ages of ages. God will triumph even over the stoniest of hearts turned away from him: 'Freedom is not an independent power in itself; it is impotence in its opposition to Divinity.'[90]

Nevertheless, Bulgakov simultaneously refuses to see divinization as a de-creation, a collapse of the uncreated and the created, and the end of the free synergistic relation between God and man. Such would be the end of the 'mystery of createdness' and the synergism of God's love for creation, maintaining its self-existence as creature, and its free loving creaturely response (or not) to God: 'Creation is not abolished, is not consumed in divine fire, does not drown in the ocean of divine depths, is not annihilated before God's magnificence. It remains in its creaturely self-existence [*samobytnost'*: Jakim has 'identity'], for it is posited to being by God and it itself posits itself to being in its freedom.'[91]

The problem in this context of the ontology of freedom would seem to be with Bulgakov's eschatology, which will not allow him an eternal hell and an eternally rebellious creature and because of this he forces his ontology and doctrine of creaturely freedom into a deterministic groove. God cannot be 'all in all', the divine Sophia meeting with the creaturely, if there is the remaining possibility that the creature could *eternally* turn its face away from God and that he will not be able to persuade it to cooperate with him. Bulgakov cannot counte-

89   Bulgakov, 'Iuda,' 17 [*Judas*, 37 (Smith translation)].
90   See Bulgakov, *Nevesta*, 521–22 [*Bride*, 491].
91   Ibid., 334 [ibid., 308 (translation revised)].

nance the possibility that a creature could eternally freely reject divine love, an act which is, for him, the very definition of an eternal hell. And given that all being is divine being for Bulgakov, a creature (as uncreated-created) who eternally rejects God would eternally import hell into God. God would never be at one with himself. He would never be all in all. Bulgakov notes that Gregory of Nyssa indicates that evil 'does not have the creative power of eternity and therefore cannot extend into eternity.' It is 'incapable of infinite self-creative activity.'[92] In the Parousia, 'God's being is the dominant, all-conquering certainty, as "all in all"', overwhelming all militant atheism, theomachy, blasphemy, demonic possession and all rebellion against God. This is 'triumphant truth, all-conquering love, irresistibly attractive and salvific beauty' because there is nothing but God or, rather, the reality that God is everything is revealed: 'In the future age, God is the universal and absolute given: in general, there is only God, and there is nothing outside of God, against God, apart from God. This is not contradicted by the proper being of creation, since it is grounded in God and exists in Him.' But Bulgakov, perhaps realizing that he has now gone too far, remembering all his earlier talk of synergism, then describes this divine tsunami, this swamping of creation by grace as persuasion, albeit an all-conquering one (the oxymoronic, 'irresistible persuasiveness'). Once again, the creature is saved from being free as a choice between possibilities and attains divine freedom as a synthesis of freedom and necessity which Bulgakov calls 'free necessity'. Man can now never fall away from God and becomes 'set' in his will like the angels.[93] Yet, it might be argued, this is not divinization as dehumanization but simply humanity's natural eschatological angelization because angels, for Bulgakov, are 'co-human', and humans are co-angelic, both related to one another but different.[94]

Nevertheless, it is arguable that Bulgakov's theology of human freedom wishes to give human autonomy a divine, almost sacrosanct foundation in God. He wants to say that God freely limits himself at the walls of his own image in the human being and will not bypass even the creature's most stubborn rebellion. Yet the very same theology must also argue that all things, insofar as they are divine, must realize themselves only through becoming united with

---

92 Bulgakov, *Nevesta*, 517 [*Bride*, 486].
93 See ibid., 522–23 [ibid., 491–92 (revised)].
94 See Bulgakov, *Lestvitsa iakovlia* (Paris: YMCA-Press, 1929), 194–216 [*Jacob's Ladder: On Angels*, trans. and ed. Thomas Allan Smith (Grand Rapids: W.B. Eerdmans, 2010), 139–54]; For discussion see Gleb S. Tikhon Vasilyev, *Christian Angelology in Pseudo-Dionysius and Sergius Bulgakov*, DPhil thesis, University of Oxford, 2019.

God and to be united with God (one risks saying) one sheds, as one becomes divinized/sophianized, the creaturely, including freedom itself, in any finite sense of the term. But a Parousia that would risk the collapse of the creaturely and the divine or perhaps the dropping of all illusions that the creaturely is anything but part and parcel of the divine down to its very toes, though it may not know it, would be no real liberation of the creature. The creature, as a distinct free and finite being glorifying God, would cease to exist. The problems with Bulgakov's account of creation being uncreated-created lie less in its incipient pantheism than in the conclusions he draws about creaturely freedom given the need to uphold his eschatology, his deterministic form of universalism, now newly trendy.[95]

Nevertheless, I have changed my mind on Bulgakov. It is no longer apparent to me that an antinomic account of creation, arguing that creation is founded on the divine, necessarily leads to sophianic determinism. Such an account holds together if one continues to maintain the principle that God eternally limits himself and potentially forever is open and even locked into an activity towards its rebellious creatures in the mode of persuasion—a divine persuasion that is non-triumphant, cross-like, refusing to conquer the creature turned away from God, but always in love turning the other cheek, as the creature slaps its Creator unto ages of ages. Upon this panentheistic vision of creation and creaturely freedom, although we do not have the space to elaborate this point here, we have a sure basis for a contemporary restatement of sophiology.

Bulgakov's Chalcedonian Ontology: The Logic of Panentheism

But why would Bulgakov go to such trouble to elaborate this panentheistic doctrine of creation? One could reply that he simply saw his account of creation as the most plausible articulation of creation out of nothing which did not fall into either monism/pantheism or dualism/anti-cosmism. But do we not have a clue in his own expressed Chalcedonian methodology? Bulgakov's whole Major Trilogy, *On Godmanhood*, which begins with his volume on Christ, goes on to the Spirit and ends with the creation, the Church and eschatology was, as is well known, the search for a sufficient common basis for the union of the two natures of Christ. Put otherwise, Bulgakov was searching for a principle that might account for both the suitability of the divine hypostasis in hypostatizing human nature, in becoming its own proper hypostasis, and, conversely,

---

95 See David Bentley Hart, *That All Shall be Saved: Heaven, Hell and Universal Salvation* (New Haven/London: Yale University Press, 2019).

what makes human nature appropriate, ontologically capable for its assumption by the Logos.[96] Chalcedon, for Bulgakov, is absolutely fundamental for all of theology, not just Christology, but, he saw its negative expression in the four a-privatives of its *horos* as *preliminary*, and so awaiting its continuation in a truly positive (not simply apophatic) definition.[97] Apollinarius, he argued, was badly misunderstood because his account of the composition of the God-Man not only anticipated the scheme of Chalcedon but also in some ways provided intimations of the beginning of a positive definition, an answer to "how" the union might be possible.[98] For Apollinarius, believes Bulgakov, sensed that the union of the divine and the human natures in the Logos was not an arbitrary external act of two utterly alien realities. Rather, the basis for the descent of the Logos to man is the fact that he already eternally is in some sense human, that is, the Logos possesses an eternal heavenly humanity (being the Second Adam, the man from heaven) and it is after this image that the earthly man or first Adam was created.[99] The whole of Bulgakov's *The Lamb of God* (1933) can be viewed as an attempt, drawing on the intimations of Apollinarius but without falling into his errors, to express Patristic Christology positively.

Yet cannot we argue the same for the whole of *On Godmanhood* and indeed Bulgakov's whole late corpus? Is it not an attempt to express all of theology from creation through redemption to the second and glorious coming again through a new positive divine-human principle? "Sophia", for Bulgakov, is the missing piece of the puzzle that explains not only how the divine and the human can be united in Christ but how humanity is related to its Creator and, more broadly, how God and creation are in relation. Sophia explains how we can understand the link between the uncreated and the created, as seen in creation, which is uncreated-created with the creature's freedom being founded upon the divine (as we have argued at length). In Christ, the divine and the human are capable of a 'living identification' in the one life of the hypostatic union precisely because there is 'something mediating or common which serves as the unalterable foundation for their union', which is the *'sophianicity'* of both the Divine world, i. e., of Christ's Divine nature, and of the creaturely world, i. e., of His human nature'.[100] In another passage, Bulgakov argues that the human I or human hypostatic spirit 'has a divine, uncreated origin from "God's

96 Bulgakov, *Agnets*, 89–91, 211, 220–23 [*Lamb*, 69–71, 188, 195–97].
97 Ibid., 79–80, 220–21 [ibid., 61–62, 195–96].
98 Ibid., 9–30 [ibid., 2–19].
99 Ibid., 27–28 [ibid., 16–17].
100 Ibid., 222 [ibid., 196–97].

breath." This spirit is a spark of Divinity [*iskra Bozhestva*] which is endowed by God with a creaturely-hypostatic face in the image of the Logos and, through him, in the image of the entire Holy Trinity, insofar as the trihypostatic Face can be reflected in the creaturely consciousness of the self."[101]

Humanity is marked, as it were, with the image of the creaturely Sophia, which is hypostatized in him, thereby making man the 'sophianic hypostasis of the world',[102] and, through his spirit, humanity communes with the Divine essence, the Divine Sophia, and 'is capable of being deified.'[103] Therefore, a mediation or third term exists between God and the creature and this third term is Sophia, insofar as 'creaturely sophianicity is only the bridge for, or the objective possibility of, the movement of God and the creature toward one another.'[104] Once again, we see a correlation between the divine and creaturely worlds between the eternal and creaturely Sophias, since they are 'identical in their foundation', but different in 'their mode [*obraz*] of being'.[105] In the Creator and in his creation in God, 'Sophia is the bridge that unites God and man; and it is this *unity* of Sophia that constitutes the Chalcedonian "yes", the foundation of the Incarnation.'[106]

Ontology is itself Christoform insofar as it involved a perfect union in difference between God and creation. I have described this as Bulgakov's 'Chalcedonian ontology'.[107] In Christ, one has the absolute, hypostatic and unique pinnacle of a process of personal embodiment or concretion that undergirds all that is with the uncreated and created (so the Chalcedonian definition) united without mingling, without change, indivisibly and undividedly. Bulgakov's panentheistic account of creation simply is one more version of a vision of how *in* God, the Creator and the created are 'simultaneously unite[d] and separate[d], identif[ied] and oppos[ed]' as 'two modes of being: divine-absolute and creaturely-relative'.[108] All creaturely being bears in itself, as uncreated-created,[109] a trace of the reality of Jesus Christ. He is—pre-eternally—the heart of the cosmos and has a pre-eternal relationship to creation and was in it even before his

101 Bulgakov, *Agnets*, 209 [*Lamb*, 186 (translation revised)].
102 Ibid., 210 [ibid., 187].
103 Ibid., 209 [ibid., 186].
104 Ibid., 249 [ibid., 220–21 (translation revised)].
105 Bulgakov, 'Agnets Bozhii (Avtoreferat)' ['The Lamb of God (a Synopsis)'], *Put*, 41 (1933), 101–05 at 102 [*LG*, 444–45].
106 Ibid., 103 [ibid., 445].
107 Gallaher, *Freedom and Necessity*, 91.
108 Bulgakov, *Nevesta*, 40 [*Bride*, 33].
109 Ibid., 72 [ibid., 63].

advent in the flesh. Creation and Incarnation, for Bulgakov, are—unto ages of ages—peculiar to the Logos, who is the 'cosmourgic [lit. world-creating/-building: *mirozizhditel'nyi*] and incarnate hypostasis'.[110] God's 'ways of His general relation to the world', including creation, also 'include the Incarnation', and 'this Incarnation precisely of the Second hypostasis has its foundation in the pre-eternal sonhood of the Word', for 'The Incarnation cannot be understood in the sense that, decided in the Divine counsel, it could be the work of any other hypostasis except the Second, since it follows precisely from the personal property of this hypostasis, sonhood, both in relation to the world and in relation to God. Imprinted in the world is the Face of the Logos, who in the fullness of time descends from heaven to earth in order to be "in-humanized" [*vochelovechit'sia*] in it'.[111] One is reminded here of Maximus the Confessor and how the *logoi* are in the Logos and the Logos in the *logoi*, for, as Jordan Daniel Wood has argued, 'created being itself is fully Christological',[112] insofar as the *logoi* are the cosmic Incarnation of the Logos or creation is, in some sense, Incarnation, as arguably Maximus hints in places when speaking of their role in deification.[113] We can now see why, with Bulgakov's Chalcedonian ontology, he could describe divine being (*ousia*) revealed eternally to God by God as Father, Son and Holy Spirit, the divine Sophia (*ousia*-Sophia), as eternally *Godmanhood*. The divine being, as Godmanhood, contains forever creation as humanity in union with divinity. In this sense, then, Bulgakov's sophiology is, as he himself claimed, a positive working out of the a-privatives of the Chalcedonian definition,[114] touching on all doctrines (especially creation) but beginning with ontology as a tacit Christology.

---

110 Bulgakov, *Agnets*, 218, n. 1 [*Lamb*, 193, n. 8].

111 Bulgakov, *Agnets*, 218 [*Lamb*, 193].

112 Jordan Daniel Wood, 'Creation is Incarnation: The Metaphysical Peculiarity of the *Logoi* in Maximus the Confessor,' *Modern Theology*, 34, no. 1 (January 2018), 82–102, at 100 and in more detail see his magisterial *The Whole Mystery of Christ: Creation as Incarnation in Maximus the Confessor* (Notre Dame, IN: University of Notre Dame Press, 2022). See the review essay, Brandon Gallaher, 'Going Beyond the "Calculus of the Infinite": The Uncreated/Created Distinction and Jordan Daniel Wood's Reading of Maximus,' *Logos: A Journal of Eastern Christian Studies*, forthcoming 2024.

113 See Maximus the Confessor, *On Difficulties in the Church Fathers*, 1: *Amb. 7* (PG 91.1084C–D), 104–07.

114 Bulgakov, *Agnets*, 79–80, 220–21 [*Lamb*, 61–62, 195–96].

A Radically Christocentric Vision of Creation and Redemption

In conclusion, we can now see why Bulgakov insists on his panentheistic account of creation: it is the vehicle for a radically Christocentric vision of creation and redemption where it is absolutely inconceivable that God would not have become one with us in Jesus Christ. For every doctrine in Bulgakov speaks the name of Jesus from the nature of God being Godmanhood to creation reflecting Christ in being an uncreated-created reality in God, to the Incarnation and redemption in the Church as an extended Incarnation and divinization, whereby not only can we say God becomes all in all in the eschaton but God in Christ becomes everything for everyone. Furthermore, Bulgakov's panentheistic sophiological account of creation, if it is shorn of its deterministic eschatological excesses, remains plausible as an orthodox vision of creation. It not only keeps the distinction and unity between God and the world, but maintains the orthodox affirmation that creation is created not out of eternal matter but out of nothing, having no foundation in itself but only being founded on God. Where it is different from some other modern theologies of creation is in understanding creation as an intra-self-determination of God. This does not lead necessarily to determinism if we hold with Bulgakov that God is not free in relation to creation's opposition to him but that his omnipotence is freely limited by the self-existence of the world which exists in him. All of creation is held together in Christ for Bulgakov and the world has interest in itself as it is made to be divinized. At every point, behind every facet and curve and edge of the creaturely, we face Jesus Christ, who is the perfect hypostatic union of the uncreated and the created. The world is infinitely precious, infinitely interesting in itself from ethics to science to economics because that world is the creaturely Sophia, which is itself in a unity in difference with the Divine Sophia, without mingling, without change, indivisibly and undividedly.

Building the House of Wisdom
DOI 10.17438/978-3-402-12196-2

Sergii Bulgakov: Between Kenotic Theology of the Event and Trinitarian Ontology

Antonio Bergamo

To approach the figure and thought of Sergii Bulgakov means to engage with both a theological method and a hermeneutical horizon of the Christian *novum* that has a generative value; it means to listen to the data by welcoming them in their overall complexity and their epistemological development.

In a global framework, we can identify the two emerging and interrelated polarities which are typical of Bulgakov's thought: the kenotic theology of the event and the Trinitarian ontology.[1]

In this contribution we will try to outline the reception of his work in the Italian theological context, insisting on the main conceptual points that give it its singularity. In the first part we will try to describe the hermeneutical starting point of the Russian thinker, based on the criticisms made against him. In the second part, we will return to the reception of Bulgakov's work, based in particular on the reflection of the theologian Piero Coda, who has highlighted some of its potential. In the third part, we will outline the conceptual framework that could result from this development based on correct foundations.

---

1   See Piero Coda, Maria Benedetta Curi, Massimo Donà, Giulio Maspero, *Manifesto. Per una riforma del pensare* (Rome: Città Nuova, 2021); Piero Coda and Lubomir Zak, eds., *Abitando la Trinità. Per un rinnovamento dell'ontologia* (Rome: Città Nuova, 1998); Piero Coda, *Dalla Trinità. L'avvento di Dio tra storia e profezia* (Rome: Città Nuova, 2011); Massimiliano Marianelli, *Ontologia della relazione. La "convenientia" in figure e momenti del pensiero filosofico* (Rome: Città Nuova, 2008); Massimo Donà, Piero Coda, *Dio-Trinità. Tra filosofi e teologi* (Milan: Bompiani, 2007); Giulio Maspero, *Essere e relazione. L'ontologia trinitaria di Gregorio di Nissa* (Rome: Città Nuova, 2003); Carmelo Meazza, *La scena del dato. Materiali per una ontologia trinitaria* (Rome: Inschibboleth, 2019); Maria Benedetta Curi, "Sulla storia dell'ontologia: introduzione e origini," *Sophia*, IX, no. 1 (2017), 77–86; Emanuele Pili, "L'ontologia trinitaria. Cosa 'non' è ?," *Sophia*, IX, no. 1 (2017), 47–56.

1. Criticism of Bulgakov's Thought

Since the 1970s, Western Catholic theology has reserved a space and attention for the thought of Sergii Bulgakov that now seems well established, albeit not without occasional criticism or reservations.[2] The originality of this author's kenotic perspective is to be found in the relationship between Christology, Trinity, and ontology.

If an initial skepticism rather pointed out the limits of the apparent subjectivism attributed to the Russian theologian, Hans Urs von Balthasar was the first to identify the positive aspects of his thought.[3] However, if on the one hand the latter had understood the central role of relationality in the understanding of kenosis as the hermeneutical horizon of the Trinitarian event, he also pointed out the limits which, according to him, were the result of a latent Gnosticism in Bulgakov's other conceptual pole, namely, the sophiological pole.

In fact, Bulgakov's revival of the Chalcedonian perspective seems to refer to an intrinsic relationality in which—from a global vision, simultaneously from above and below—it is possible for the human subject to apprehend reality, through a kind of refraction of the view, in the light of the Trinitarian Christological event.

We therefore see how Balthasar welcomes Bulgakov's kenotic perspective while rejecting his sophiological perspective, which he interprets with reference to Russian theology, by which Bulgakov is certainly influenced, but from which he differs in the conclusions to which the maturation of his thought leads him. The reservations expressed by the Swiss theologian thus seem to have influenced the initial reception of Bulgakov's works, especially in the Italian context.

It was the Italian theologian Marcello Bordoni who came up with the intuition of a fundamental unity of these two poles, based on the event of revelation in its paschal summit.[4] This was in 1986. He highlights a dynamic asymmetry between the three divine Persons as well as in the strong relationship they establish with creation, a dynamism of reciprocal directionality, not aggressive

2   Cf. Lubomir Zak, "La croce fonte della teologia in S. N. Bulgakov," in Gennaro Cicchese, Piero Coda, and Lubomir Zak, *Dio e il suo avvento. Luoghi, momenti, figure* (Rome: Città Nuova, 2003), 283–314; Piergiuseppe Bernardi, Ninfa Bosco, Graziano Lingua, "Storia e storiografia bulgakoviane," *Filosofia e Teologia* 2 (1992), 236–52.
3   Hans Urs von Balthasar, *Teologia dei tre giorni* (Brescia: Queriniana, 1990), 45–46.
4   Marcello Bordoni, *Gesù di Nazaret Signore e Cristo. Saggio di cristologia sistematica*, vol. 3 (Rome: Herder, Università lateranense, 1986), 423.

and assimilative but diachronic. The kenotic perspective should be read not in isolation but from the hypothesis of the relation as an ontological category. This intuition seems to be the basis of the positive reception of Bulgakov's work in Italy and its singular deployment in the light of the agapic principle.

2. The Reception of Bulgakov's Thought in Italy

The reception of Bulgakov's thought in Italy will be presented in two steps. First we will deal with the progressive translation and publication of his works, before focusing on their philosophical and theological reception and on their global hermeneutics.

The first phase was the 1970s.[5] During this decade, the publishing house Jaca Book published two collections of essays and in 1971 Dehoniane Editions published the first translation of *Il Paraclito* (*The Comforter*). After a pause in the 1980s, a second phase began in which writings related to ecumenism, social commitment and religious idealism were published by Russia Cristiana, but above all by Marietti. In a third phase, in the 1990s, interest seems to shift towards a more strictly theological production. In 1990, Città Nuova published *L'Agnello di Dio* (*The Lamb of God)* and in 1991 Dehoniane published *La sposa dell'agnello* (*The Bride of the Lamb*).[6] With regard to the reception of his theological thought, a solid contribution has been made by Piero Coda, in particular, with *L'altro di Dio* (1998).[7] In several essays that precede this volume,[8] the Italian theologian proposes a global approach to the double sophiological and kenotic perspective, against the background of the Trinitarian event, which

---

5   Cf. Lubomir. Zak, "Visione di Dio e visione del mondo nella sofiologia di S. Bulgakov," *Nuova Umanità* XXI (1999/1) 121, 129–55.

6   Sergii Bulgakov, *Il Paraclito*, trans. F. Marchese (Bologna:EDB, 1971); ibid., *L'Agnello di Dio. Il mistero del Verbo incarnato*, trans. O. M. Nobile Ventura (Rome: Città Nuova, 1990); ibid., *La Sposa dell'Agnello*, trans. C. Rizzi (Bologna: EDB, 1991).

7   Piero Coda, *L'altro di Dio. Rivelazione e kenosi in Sergej Bulgakov* (Rome: Città Nuova, 1998).

8   Piero Coda, "Lo Spirito come 'in-mezzo-Persona' che compie l'unità nella teologia di S. Bulgakov," *Nuova Umanità* IX (1987), 52–53, 72–93; "Un' introduzione storica e metodologica alla cristologia di S. Bulgakov, in *Lateranum*, 2 (1989), 435–69; "Cristologia della kenosi e della gloria. La sintesi 'sofiologica' di S. Bulgakov. Introduzione all'edizione italiana," in S. N. Bulgakov, *L'Agnello di Dio. Il mistero del Verbo incarnato* (Rome: Città Nuova, 1990), 11–35; "Per una rivisitazione teologica della sofiologia di Sergei N. Bulgakov," *Filosofia e teologia* 2 (1992), 216–35; "Trinità, sofiologia e cristologia in S. Bulgakov," *Lateranum* 49 (1993), 97–142.

allows us to understand its hermeneutical circularity, as well as its fundamental limits. This elaboration is systematically explained in *L'altro di Dio*.

As for the epistemological approach, to which we shall return, it seems that the best point of reference for correctly interpreting the Russian theologian is a prior understanding of the Trinitarian mystery. The life of the three divine Persons is grasped in the tri-unity that characterizes it, as a concrete correlation between the Father, the Son and the Holy Spirit. Bulgakov's particularity is to be faithful to the Orthodox tradition, to its attention to the monarchy of the Father, while interpreting it in dialogue with the Western tradition, especially Augustine. The New Testament statement "God is love" (1 Jn 4:8) constitutes an ontological awareness of the divine being in its intimate mutual relationship and in its fulfillment outside itself. Thus, according to Coda, Bulgakov follows the solid Orthodox theological elaboration of the fifth century, present in particular in Athanasius and the Cappadocian Fathers: the *equidivinity* (*homousianism*) makes possible the mutual interiority of the three persons. However, Bulgakov perceives the limit of the causal character of the Aristotelian categories to which these Fathers refer. By accepting the Augustinian originality, and applying it as a corrective, the Russian theologian emphasizes the unique *ousia* at the basis of the original relationships. It is with Augustine, in fact, that the Trinity is apprehended as love, although one can reproach it—as Bulgakov himself does—with a certain impersonality. It is therefore a question of crossing the Eastern and Western viewpoints for a simultaneous reading, *essentialiter* and *personaliter*, of the Trinitarian event, based on the intimacy of God.

Piero Coda underlines that it is through this type of simultaneous reading of Bulgakov that it is possible to link the sophiological perspective and the kenotic perspective in a mutual relationship, for a global hermeneutic. This makes it possible to overcome a dissociated reading that could lead to gnostic excesses in sophiology and to an extrinsic reading of the kenotic perspective, in the relationship to the created real. For Coda, the centre of gravity of this holistic reading of Bulgakov can be found in a third perspective that acts as a backdrop, namely God as an absolute subject. If Bulgakov's debt to modern idealist philosophy, in particular Hegel, is clear, he brings out new elements that allow us to go beyond the limits and aporias of the latter.

For the Italian theologian, it is clear that, in Bulgakov's thought, the Trinitarian God is a tri-hypostatic subject. God is therefore an absolute subject in the sense that there is an intimate correlation between the divine Persons that is deployed in the dynamic of tri-hypostatic self-revelation. This dynamic implies a certain hierarchy: the monarchy of the Father, the revelatory hypostasis, and then the subordinate *taxis* of the Son and the Holy Spirit which follows from it.

The only absolute subject is self-revealed in the divine Sophia as tri-hypostatic love, defined by a kenotic dynamic that personally characterizes the Father, the Son and the Spirit. The Spirit is this hypostatic "between" and his *kenosis* consists in a kind of self-emptying.

Salvation history, the elevation of creaturely *theantropy* to the life of divine *theantropy*, unfolds according to this intimate Trinitarian logic. Bulgakov has elaborated this overall vision by revisiting the contribution of Gregory Palamas, which he puts into dialogue with the Western tradition. In this elevation, *kenosis* is the fundamental principle that illuminates the dynamics of creation and salvation: salvation and creation are works of love. There is thus a certain asymmetry between the polarities involved, which protects from extrinsic retouching and expresses both the ontological link in the intra-trinitarian life, the gift of this life in creation and in history, and the reception, in it, of the created reality.[9]

The place where the human and the divine meet is the Incarnate Word. Through the Incarnation, the Word looks to the Father from his humanity, which presupposes the work of the Holy Spirit made possible by the fiat of Mary. The Incarnation finds its culmination in the paschal event, in which the kenosis of the Holy Spirit's action takes over from the personal kenosis of the Son and continues it through the divinization of the human being. In this sense, the Spirit is "the transparent environment in and through which the Logos is seen."[10]

The human being is thus guided, in freedom, to enter into the divine life and to participate in this kenotic movement, supported by the Holy Spirit, through the renunciation of self for love. It is realized in the love that not only gives it being, but also challenges it.

Based on this simultaneous reading of the sophiological perspective and the kenotic perspective, setting out from the reality of God as an absolute Subject, a tri-personal love, Coda exposes three principles from Bulgakov's thought. 1) The *principle of the divine tri-unity* which translates into ecclesial pluri-unity—which allows one to go beyond the Hegelian monological reductionism based on the ontological affirmation of God's love. 2) The *principle of panentheism*, in which the immanence and transcendence of the Trinity are asymmetrically related in history and in creation. Sophiology is situated here, asking the question—as Coda points out—as to the relationship between nature and

---

9   Antonio Bergamo, *Essere, Tempo e Trinità. Paradigmi e percorsi ermeneutici* (Rome: Città Nuova, 2021), 117–20.

10   Sergii Bulgakov, *Il Paraclito*, 396.

person in God, between unity and multiplicity in creation, between incarnation and divinization. 3) The *principle of intra-trinitarian and historical-salvific kenosis*, which allows the articulation of the reciprocal relationship of otherness between the Creator and creation.

The approach favored by Coda can be found in various works published in Italy over the years whose purpose is to investigate one or other aspect of Bulgakov's work and thought, among them Graziano Lingua's study of Bulgakov's sophiology. The author approaches the theme of sophiology from the category of creation. Sophiology, he writes, is "a *Weltanschauung*, a Christian worldview."[11] In 2001, Arvydas Ramonas published a study on eschatology in Bulgakov. Bulgakov is presented as "one of the most brilliant representatives of Russian eschatological thought, the first in the religious tradition of his country to have systematically elaborated an Orthodox eschatological theology."[12] In 2004, a study by Andrea Pacini[13] addressed the pneumatological theme in Bulgakov, with particular emphasis on its ecumenical impact.[14] In these pages, the author takes up the Russian theologian's critique of the principle of causality, as well as the centrality of the category of revelation and the intratrinitarian agapic act for the purposes of a personological hermeneutic of the Trinity.

In 2006, Luigi Razzano argued that "the intuition of the aesthetic principle [...] underlies all of Bulgakov's theological thought and its understanding is revealed in the light of the category of the Sophia." Sophiology is thus that "category which interprets the intimate and ineluctable relationship of the world with its origins, in a constant process of recapitulation and synthesis between experience and eternity."[15] In 2017, Graziano Lingua published a solid essay in which he compares the first Bulgakov, an attentive specialist in socio-economic issues and Marxism, with the second Bulgakov, the one of the great trilogy.[16] Lingua identifies a common thread that links them. It is to be found in the

---

11   Graziano Lingua, *Kénosis di Dio e santità della materia. La sofiologia di Sergej N. Bulgakov* (Naples: Edizioni Scientifiche Italiane, 2000), 189.

12   Arvydas Ramonas, *L'attesa del Regno. Eschaton e apocalisse in Sergej Bulgakov* (Rome: Mursia, 2000), 416.

13   Andrea Pacini, *Lo Spirito Santo nella Trinità. Il filioque nella prospettiva teologica di S. Bulgakov* (Rome: Città Nuova, 2004).

14   See Piero Coda, Alessandro Clemenzia, *Il Terzo persona. Per una teologia dello Spirito Santo* (Bologna EDB, 2020), 253–72.

15   Luigi Razzano, *L'estasi del bello nella sofiologia di S. N. Bulgakov* (Rome: Città Nuova, 2006), 68, 76.

16   Graziano Lingua, "Una salvezza per tutti rispetta la libertà dell'uomo? Libertà, storia ed escatologia in S. Bulgakov," *Annuario filosofico*, 33 (2017), 378–408.

Russian theologian's theology of history and proves that there is indeed an intrinsic speculative continuity in him and not a radical rupture, as a classical interpretation sometimes suggests.

3. Between Kenotic Theology of the Event and Trinitarian Ontology

Piero Coda, in *L'altro di Dio*, points out that it is in the light of the paschal event, indispensable access to the Trinitarian mystery, that the interpretative horizon of reference of reality opens up, in which the human being experiences God and finds the traces of his passage as well as an openness to his advent in history.[17] The relationship between the Father and the Son within the Trinity and its reflection in the light and power of the Spirit are in fact the keystone of Bulgakov's speculative system. For the Russian theologian, the cross is the hypostasis of God the Father. Following the Fathers of the Church, in particular Gregory of Nazianzus, he realizes that in the paschal event, the Father and the Spirit suffer as much as the Son, although in different ways. Thus, the relationship on the cross between Christ, the incarnate Son of God, and the Father, who lives his kenosis, is the foundation of all fatherhood.

The *kenosis* thus expresses on the one hand the dynamic of the Trinitarian life of God and on the other hand its reverberation in creation. Indeed, creation also expresses itself as the *kenosis* of God, God who is a mystery of love. Bulgakov invites us to understand in ontological terms the mystery of the unity of the three divine persons and the Trinitarian nature of the One, a love that gives itself and finds its culmination and its gateway in the paschal event.

In this framework, Coda perceives in Bulgakov the outline of a Trinitarian ontology,[18] or rather of an ontology *tout court* and, consequently, of an anthropology, which emerge in the light of the proprium of the Christological and Trinitarian Revelation.

If Pavel Florenskii established the basis of a fundamental ontology on the basis of antinomy,[19] Bulgakov goes one step further. He correlates the antinomy with the Chalcedonian dogma. Thus, a patristic/theological approach is taken,

---

17 Cf. Vincenzo Di Pilato, *Discepoli della via. Questioni e prospettive sul metodo della teologia* (Rome: Città Nuova, 2019), 190–92.

18 Piero Coda, *Sergej Bulgakov* (Brescia: Morcelliana, 2003), 65–66.

19 Pavel Florenskij, *La colonna e il fondamento della verità* (Milan: Rusconi, 1998), 210–11; Lubomir Zak, "P. A. Florenskij: progetto e testimonianza di una gnoseologia trinitaria," in *La Trinità e il pensare*, ed. Piero Coda and Andreas Tapken (Rome: Città Nuova, 1997), 193–228.

not only from above or from below, but from both simultaneously. The paschal event, as a Trinitarian event, sheds light on reality in a retrospective, inaugural and prospective way. From the Christological event emerges an ontological structure that configures reality from the original creative act of God, so that the incarnation is an affirmation of the divine-human form of creation.[20]

The Russian theologian thus overcomes the obstacle of both Hegelianism and theism. Sophia is the content of God's self-revelation in the Spirit, creation is a kenosis of love, and the created Sophia is characterized by a vocation to participate in the Trinitarian life. Bulgakov thus recovers the authentic patristic meaning of *oikonomia* as the providential order and divine government of the world. In this horizon, immanence and transcendence are interlaced: transcendence is, from the beginning, grafted into history through creation and immanence is inhabited by the divine, which makes it open to the beyond itself.

The beginnings of a Trinitarian ontology that we find in Bulgakov thus seem to be characterized by Spirit, freedom and intersubjectivity. The paschal event opens up 1) the *place of the Spirit* given and open to the participation of creatures so that they can draw on the Trinitarian life, despite an eschatological gap. 2) The *place of true freedom* grounded in the gift of self. 3) The *place of reciprocity* in interpersonal relationships. In the humanity of the Incarnate Word—who lives the dynamic of kenosis up to its paschal summit—it is the whole of humanity, the whole of the flesh which, in the flesh assumed by the Son, is joined in the light and strength of the Spirit by the love of the Father. The Risen One is the Living One who, in the Church, introduces us into the unfathomable mystery of the Father, in the light and power of the Spirit.

4. Concluding Reflections

Without pretending to be exhaustive, the brief outline of the reception of Sergii Bulgakov's works and thought in Italy offers the image of a progressive interest that has grown according to a particular approach, and whose merit can be attributed to the recognition of the *methodos* of the Russian thinker's theology.

Piero Coda's position is based on an understanding of the relationship between sophiology and *kenosis* in Trinitarian terms. While grasping the limitations of Bulgakov's reflection, it highlights its positive potential. The key to reading sophiology, he points out, works only if one adds the Christological key, even if the latter is not so obvious in Bulgakov. They can only be understood from an originally Christian perspective, as an attempt to think the on-

---

20   Graziano Lingua, *Una salvezza per tutti*, 387–91.

tology of the Trinitarian mystery according to a specifically Trinitarian logic: as much for what concerns the Being of God in itself (the immanent Trinity, to refer to Karl Rahner's terminology), as for what concerns the relationship between the Uncreated and the Created, made of creation and redemption/ divinization in the crucified/resurrected Christ and in the Spirit of Pentecost.[21]

The overcoming of the Platonic dualism between created and uncreated *Sophia* could be overcome, according to Coda, by taking seriously the fact that creation "takes place in the Incarnate Word" and that, therefore the content of creation—as Bulgakov intuited—is nothing other than the created projection of God's unique nature, "without, however, implying a doubling of the uni-multiplicity in God (in the Word and in the Spirit) and the multiple unity of/in creation. In Christ, the unity of the Word of God becomes the hypostatic form of the multiplicity of creation, summarized and expressed in the multiplicity of human persons, which gives reality (in Christ, through the action of the Spirit, a divine reality) to the infinite richness and participatory invitation of the Uni-Trine God."[22]

Bulgakov's theological method makes the Trinitarian event not only the content but also the form of the believer's opening to the whole of reality, according to a global perspective; this, while safeguarding human subjectivity in its ontological consistency, situates this subjectivity in a constitutive and emergent relationship with the One and Triune God who places in being what it is, and—through grace—accompanies reality and transcends it. The Christological axis is thus joined to the pneumatological axis in order to overcome the dichotomy between East and West, which Bulgakov had intuited. If the Christian event is read in the West with a certain primacy of the Christological, which underlines the aspects of visibility, institutionality, centrality and conceptual rationality, in the East there emerges a certain primacy of the pneumatological which highlights the mystery, communion, collegiality and apophatic symbolism.[23] The Russian theologian, who breathes with two lungs, with a double hermeneutic, proposes instead an interweaving of vertical reciprocity (that of intratrinitarian life) and horizontal reciprocity (that of the Trinitarian life that happens between human beings in reality), proposing a specific reading of the paschal event.

---

21 Piero Coda, *L'altro di Dio*, 150.
22 Ibid., 152.
23 Piero Coda, *Il Logos e il nulla. Trinità—Religioni—Mistica* (Rome: Città Nuova, 2003), 250.

The history in which each human being lives is not closed in an intra-temporal process, it is not flatly linear, but divine-human. On the one hand, history experiences the presence of evil and its aggressiveness as an anti-sophistic force; on the other hand, each individual, open to the transcendence that breaches immanence, contributes to the positive movement of history in a human-divine synergy following a kenotic rhythm.[24]

Moreover, as Coda suggests again, it is a question of "rereading [...] the perspective of *Sophia* with an emphasis that is not only protological, which Bulgakov tends to do, but more resolutely eschatological: thus, Sophia would be nothing other than creation recapitulated in Christ, through the work of the Spirit, where God becomes 'all in all.'"[25]

Bulgakov's life and thought are therefore not only a formidable speculative performance, but also an exercise in *auditus temporis*, that is, in listening attentively to reality, aiming to give concrete translation to the instances of fullness of life that inhabit the human being and that mark out history according to a Trinitarian rhythm in which the gift of God becomes the source and summit of existence.

24 Graziano Lingua, *Una salvezza per tutti*, 401–07.
25 Piero Coda, *L'altro di Dio*, 153.

Building the House of Wisdom
DOI 10.17438/978-3-402-12197-9

From Social Trinity to "Linguistic Trinity": Sergii Bulgakov's Contribution to Analytic Theology

Nikolaos Asproulis

Since the mid-twentieth century a revival of the interest in Trinitarian theology has taken place, initially spurred on by theologians from different Christian traditions[1] and most recently by analytic philosophers of religion[2] who by employing various metaphysical or logical arguments try to provide their own rational reconstruction of the doctrine of the Trinity. At the same time, increasing scholarly interest in the person and work of Sergii Bulgakov is clearly evident today not only in the English-speaking world, but more widely, which draws our attention to a possible direct or indirect encounter on this crucial topic.

In his *Philosophy of the Name*[3] and *The Tragedy of Philosophy*,[4] Bulgakov exploits a Trinitarian approach to reality, starting out from a tripartite understanding of the proposition "I am A"=subject–copulapredicate. In this chapter, an attempt is made to use this logical-grammatical exploration as a means to struggle with the "logical problem of the Trinity." After briefly describing the major views on the Trinity (e.g., the Greek/social and the Latin), the chapter

---

1   Cf. for instance: Giulio Maspero and Robert Wozniak, eds., *Rethinking Trinitarian Theology. Disputed Questions and Contemporary Issues in Trinitarian Theology* (London/ Oxford: Bloomsbury, 2012).

2   Cf. for instance: Melville Stuart, ed., *The Trinity. East/West Dialogue* (Springer/Science + Business Media, BV, 2003); William Hasker, *Metaphysics and the TriPersonal God* (Oxford: Oxford University Press, 2013); Michael Rea, ed., *Oxford Readings in Philosophical Theology*, vol. I (Oxford: Oxford University Press, 2009); Beau Branson, "The Logical Problem of the Trinity," (PhD diss., Graduate Program in Philosophy, Notre Dame, IN, 2014).

3   Sergii Bulgakov, *Philosophy of the Name*, Cornell University Press, 2022.

4   Sergij Bulgakov, *The Tragedy of Philosophy (Philosophy and Dogma)*, trans. Stephen Churchyard, intro. John Milbank (Brooklyn, NY: Angelico Press, 2020).

focuses on Bulgakov's "linguistic trinity"[5] in dialogue with the "Material Constitution" theory as represented by Michael Rea and Jeffrey Brower, in order to justify his view as a valuable, albeit unintended, Eastern Orthodox contribution to contemporary philosophy of religion.

The Patristic-historical Background: A Brief Overview

Let us now provide a brief overview of the patristic-historical and contemporary analytical account of Trinitarian theology.

Since the early post-apostolic era, the Church has been challenged by the question as to how to make sense of the affirmation that there are three persons and still one God, in other words, how to combine two seemingly contradictory claims. In line with Brower and Rea, this philosophical, or rather "logical problem" consists in the following assertion:

> On the one hand, it affirms that there are three distinct Persons—Father, Son, and Holy Spirit—each of whom is God. On the other hand, it says that there is one and only one God. The doctrine therefore pulls us in two directions at once—in the direction of saying that there is exactly one divine being and in the direction of saying that there is more than one.[6]

Throughout the centuries, various theories have been formulated towards a solution to this philosophical problem. Most of them, however, proved erroneous if not dangerous. This was the case with *modalism*, according to which the three divine persons are not really distinct from each other, with *subordinationism*, which claims that not all the Trinitarian persons are divine, or *polytheism*, according to which there is more than one God.

It was not until the fourth century that an adequate terminology became available, without however, providing a definite solution to the debate. While the West considered the Greek *hypostasis* (particular) as synonymous with the Latin substance (concrete universal), this was not the case with the East, which eventually ended up with a distinction between substance (a generic essence, abstract universal) and *hypostasis* (particular instances of essence) and an identification of the latter (a clearly ontological term) with the person (a

---

5   I take the term from and base much of the discussion on Joshua Heath's article "Sergii Bulgakov's Linguistic Trinity," *Modern Theology* 37, no. 4 (2021), 888–912.

6   Jeffrey Brower and Michael Rea, "Material Constitution and the Trinity," in *Oxford Readings*, 127.

relational term).[7] It was the merit of the Cappadocians in the East to "ascribe to the three divine hypostases the properties constitutive of personhood, such as mutual knowledge, love, volition …,"[8] leading to an *ontological* understanding of personhood. At the same time, Augustine, in his *De Trinitate*,[9] by making use of psychological analogies of the individual human mind, followed a different path, by highlighting the unity of Godhead and understanding person as subsisting relations, that is, in a *logical* way. Although recent studies[10] of the works of certain Eastern and Western patristic thinkers (like Gregory of Nyssa, John of Damascus, etc.) as well as Augustine (or Boethius) show that a shared understanding might be at work, rather than a deep rift between their views, the personalistic ontology in the East (premised on the diversity of the three divine persons) over against the substance ontology in the West (premised on unity) became, in the subsequent centuries, a "controlling schema" for Trinitarian theology.

The year 1892 saw the Jesuit Theodore de Régnon publish his monumental work under the title *Études de théologie positive sur la Sainte Trinité*.[11] In this study, by employing the dialectic between person and nature, de Régnon offered a binding (albeit schematic) understanding of Trinitarian theology which accounts for a clear-cut division between Eastern and Western Trinitarian theologies. As the still normative story goes, the East, mainly following the Cappadocian Fathers, begins with the diversity of the persons, thus emphasizing the Trinity (de *Deo trino*) of persons, while the West, in line with Boethius, Augustine and Aquinas, starts with the divine essence, focusing on the unity of God (*de Deo uno*). The so-called "de Régnon paradigm" has recently been boldly criticized for relying too much on historical generalizations.[12] Yet, a

---

7   For such an interpretation see John D. Zizioulas, *Being as Communion* (Crestwood, NY: St. Vladimir's Seminary Press, 1985).

8   J. P. Moreland and W. L. Graig, "The Trinity," in *Oxford Readings*, 29.

9   For a discussion see: Michalis Philippou, "Η τριαδική θεολογία του De Trinitate του Αγίου Αυγουστίνου και οι κριτικοί της," in Stavros Zoumboulakis & Pierre Salembier, Η ελληνική και ευρωπαϊκή συμβολή στον Ευρωπαϊκό πολιτισμό (Athens: Artos Zoes, 2019) 115–56.

10 Cf. for instance, Richard Cross, "Two Models of the Trinity?," in *Oxford Readings*, 108–26.

11 Théodore de Régnon, *Études de théologie positive sur la Sainte Trinité* (3 vols. Paris: Viktor Retaux, 1892–98).

12 Michel René Barnes, "De Régnon Reconsidered," *Augustinian Studies* 26 (1995): 51–79; D. Glenn Butner, "For and Against de Régnon: Trinitarianism East and West," *International Journal of Systematic Theology* 17, no. 4 (October 2015): 399–412. In contrast see

considerable number of contemporary theologians still took it for granted in their discussion of the Trinity (K. Rahner, C. Gunton, V. Lossky, J. Zizioulas, S. Bulgakov, R. Jenson, C. Gunton, etc.), following the alleged deep dichotomy between a Greek and a Latin Trinitarian view.[13]

Social Trinity vs. Latin Trinity: An Archaic but Modern Debate

Does this very complex doctrine still make sense today? While Enlightenment thinkers boldly questioned the validity of any religious authority in general and Christian doctrine in particular, today numerous Christian philosophers have attempted to re-conceptualize the doctrine of the Trinity in a philosophically and logically defensive manner. This renewed interest in solving the "logical problem" of the Trinity arose especially with the attempt by analytic philosophers and theologians to defend the logical coherence of Christian doctrine. Echoing "de Régnon's paradigm," with its one-sidedness, these intellectuals have been led to identify two basic Trinitarian models with their variations under the rubric of *social trinitiarianism* ("three self" theories) and *Latin trinitarianism* ("one self" theories).[14] Schematically, the former amounts to the Greek/Eastern patristic view, giving priority to the diversity of the Trinitarian persons, the latter to the Latin/Western, stressing the unity of God. This distinction, although useful, is still misleading, to the extent that it does not take into account several figures of both currents like Athanasius of Alexandria, Tertullian, Hilary of Poitier, John of Damascus, Peter Lombard, etc., who could be easily classified in the opposite camp.[15]

The central commitment of social trinitarianism, exemplified mainly by the Cappadocians, lies in the fact that there are three distinct centers of self-consciousness in God (following a more contemporary conception of the person;

Kristin Hennessy, "An Answer to De Régnon's Accusers: Why We Should Not Speak of 'His' paradigm," *Harvard Theological Review* 100, no. 2 (2007): 179–97.

13   See for instance, Karl Rahner, *The Trinity*, trans. Joseph Donceel (New York: Crossroad Publishing Company, 1997); Vladimir Lossky, *The Mystical Theology of the Eastern Church* (Cambridge: James Clarke & Co, 1957), who extensively draws on de Régnon; John Zizioulas, *Communion and Otherness: Further Studies in Personhood and the Church* (New York: T. & T. Clark, 2006); Colin Gunton, *The Promise of Trinitarian Theology* (New York: T. & T. Clark, 2003).

14   For a general, comprehensive and critical overview of all the different models and theories, cf. D. Tuggy, "Trinity," *Stanford Encyclopedia of Philosophy*, accessed March 23, 2019, https://plato.stanford.edu/entries/trinity/ (access 2024/01/26).

15   Cf. Cross, "Two Models"; Moreland-Graig, "The Trinity."

cf. the distinction between humanity in general and Peter, Paul, Mary, etc. in particular) with a danger of resulting in tritheism, while in Latin trinitarianism, championed primarily by Augustine and Aquinas, there is only one God, not compromised by the diversity of persons (Augustine is hesitant to speak of "three persons"), possibly leading to a classic version of modalism (as is the case with K. Barth or K. Rahner).[16]

Three major sub-models of social trinitarianism have been identified: a) functional monotheism, b) group mind monotheism and c) trinity monotheism, each of them often being developed in different directions, yet keeping close to the basic assumption of the plurality in God.[17]

Functional monotheism proposes a "harmonious [...] interrelated functioning"[18] of the three persons as the basis of their unity. Richard Swinburne, for instance, drawing on Richard St. Victor's "trinity of love" model (in which love is understood as perfect, fully mutual and total sharing) and distinguishing between God and divine, holds that each of the three "is God" in the sense that each possesses all divine attributes, while he intends to overcome previous accusations that an overemphasis on causal intra-trinitarian relations makes the Son a sort of divine creature (drawing a distinction between "ontological and metaphysical necessity"[19] or his more nuanced account of "dependent and independent necessity"[20]).

The *group mind model*, (represented by, among others, Champion, Bartlett, and Williams)[21] claims that Trinity is a group mind composed by the (sub) minds of the three persons in the Godhead.[22] In this respect the mind of the Trinity itself should not be understood as a self-conscious self in addition to

16 For a critical survey, see Moreland-Graig, "The Trinity," and Tuggy, "Trinity."
17 Cf. Moreland-Graig, "The Trinity," and Tuggy, "Trinity."
18 Moreland-Graig, "The Trinity," 35.
19 Richard Swinburne, *The Christian God* (New York: Oxford University Press, 1994), 88.
20 Richard Swinburne, "The Social Theory of the Trinity," *Religious Studies* 54, no. 3 (2018): 419–37.
21 Cf. John Champion, *Personality and the Trinity* (New York: Flemming H. Revell Co, 1935); Charles Barlett, *The Triune God* (New York: American Tract Society, 1937); C. J. F. Williams, "Neither Confounding the Persons nor Dividing the Substance", in *Reason and the Christian Religion: Essays in Honour of Richard Swinburne*, ed. A. G. Padgett (New York: Oxford University Press, 1994), 227–43.
22 Brian Leftow, "Anti Social Trinitarianism," in *The Trinity*, ed. Stephen T. Davis, Daniel Kendall, and Gerald O'Collins (Oxford: Oxford University Press, 1999), 221; Moreland-Graig, "The Trinity," 36; Michalis Philippou, "Θέματα Αναλυτικής Χριστιανικής θεολογίας," in *άλλες μελέτες στην αναλυτική φιλοσοφία της θρησκείας*, ed. St. Virvidakis, M. Philippou (Athens: Artos Zoes, 2018), 463ff (in Greek); Tuggy, "Trinity."

the three sub-minds, an understanding that would amount to Quaternity. For this model to become more intelligible, Leftow[23] employs quite controversial thought experiments involving surgical operations in human beings so as to conceptualize the relation between the sub-minds in the group-mind.

Trinity monotheism (championed by D. Brown, K. Yandell, L. Graig, J.P. Moreland, et.al.)[24] holds that although the three divine persons are divine, it is the Trinity as a whole that can be properly called God. In this regard "the Trinity is the sole instance of the divine nature."[25] This part–whole understanding of the divinity of the persons again relies on an ambivalent understanding of the concept of "God" (the Trinity is God; Father, Son, and Spirit are divine persons). Peter van Inwagen,[26] by employing the concept of "relative identity" (the Father is the same being as the Son; the Father is not the same person as the Son) indirectly attempts to defend the coherence of this model.

On the contrary, Brian Leftow,[27] a strong critic of the *social* theory and a basic advocate of *Latin trinitarianism*, on the basis of the Athanasian Creed, the Council of Toledo (675), Thomas Aquinas, and the analogy of time travel, makes use of the concept of the "trope" (an individualized case of an attribute; "the Persons have the same trope of deity")[28] so as to conceptualize his understanding of God as "living three life-streams," by famously referring to the "Radio City Music Hall Rockets."[29] Following his argumentation, God's life naturally runs in three streams; that is, "God's life consists of three non-overlapping lives going at once."[30] To secure the diversity of the Persons and avoid the thread of modalism, Leftow perceives Aquinas understanding of relational properties in terms of "acts/events" which constitute the Triune life.

23 Leftow, "Anti Social Trinitarianism," 221.
24 David Brown, *The Divine Trinity* (London: Duckworth/Open Court, 1985); Keith Yandell, "The most brutal and inexcusable error in counting?: Trinity and consistency," *Religious Studies* 30, no. 2 (1994): 201–17; J.P. Moreland and W.L. Craig, *Philosophical Foundations for a Christian Worldview* (Downers Grove, Illinois: InterVarsity Press, 2003); W.L. Craig, "Trinity Monotheism Once More: A Response to Daniel Howard-Snyder," *Philosophia Christi* 8, no. 1 (2006): 101–13.
25 Moreland-Graig, "The Trinity," 39; Philippou, "Topics of Analytic Christian Theology," Θέματα Αναλυτικής Χριστιανικής θεολογίας," 459.
26 See his "Three Persons in One Being: On Attempts to Show that the Doctrine of the Trinity is Self-Contradictory," in Rea, *Oxford Readings*, 61 ff.
27 Brian Leftow, "A Latin Trinity," in Rea, Oxford Readings, 77 ff.
28 Leftow, "A Latin Trinity," 77.
29 Ibid., 79 ff. In contrast see William Hasker, *Metaphysics and the Tripersonal God* (Oxford: Oxford University Press, 2013), 109 ff.
30 Leftow, "A Latin Trinity," 86.

A nuanced version of "one-self theory," put forth by the two "Karls," Barth and Rahner, suggests a different reception of the term person as "modes of being"[31] or "manners of subsisting"[32] so as to remain faithful to biblical monotheism. Yet, serious problems arise with regard to the coherence of this doctrine, which amounts to a revival of the Sabelianism of old, to the degree that the different modes might be considered "strictly sequential,"[33] or in logical and not ontological terms.

Another quite interesting new theory classified in between social and Latin trinitarianism is the Brower/Rea "Material Constitution" model of the Trinity.[34]

Having sketched in brief the variety of models which try to conceptualize the Trinitarian doctrine, we must ask in which model one can classify Bulgakov's trinitarianism. One can certainly relate Bulgakov's theology to social trinitarianism in general and the Trinity monotheism sub-model in particular. Although he makes use of various philosophical tools in his attempt to build his system, Bulgakov is more at ease with the Eastern patristic tradition, which seeks to interpret it through the lens of his much-contested and sometimes obscure sophiology. According to Bulgakov Divine Sophia, is considered "the pleroma, the divine world, existent in God and for God."[35] In other words, Sophia (as far as it concerns the divine being), while it "is nothing other than God's nature," is more than this, since it is the very self-revelation of the entire Holy Trinity; it is the divine world within which the divine ousia is revealed and hypostasized in the three hypostases. As he puts it, "Sophia [...] as the divine world, exists in God and [...] is present before God."[36] To paraphrase a definition used before, "Sophia [in the place of The Trinity] is the sole instance of the divine nature." By making use of the Sophia concept, Bulgakov seeks to move beyond bygone conceptual bipolarities that give priority either to *ousia* or *hypostasis* in the Trinity—which according to him do not successfully elucidate God's trinitarian being. In this vein, he tries to give an active role to each one of the divine persons in God's self-revelation as Trinity. Through then the

---

31   Karl Barth, *Church Dogmatics*, I, i2, trans. G. T. Thomson, and Harold Knight, ed. G. W. Bromiley and T. F. Torrance (Edinburgh: T. & T. Clark, 1956).

32   Rahner, *The Trinity*, 42–5, 103–15.

33   Tuggy, "Trinity."

34   Jeffrey Brower and Michael Rea, "Material Constitution and the Trinity," in Rea, *Oxford Readings*, 128 ff.

35   Sergius Bulgakov, *The Lamb of God*, trans. Boris Jakim (Grand Rapids: W. B. Eerdmans, 2008), 103.

36   Sergius Bulgakov, *The Bride of the Lamb*, trans. Boris Jakim (Grand Rapids: W. B. Eerdmans, 2002), 30.

ad intra relationships of the divine persons, God the Trinity is actualized. As Papanikolaou puts it:

> All that God is, which is the self-revelation of God to Godself, is actualized in the eternal being of God and this actualization is the work of the Holy Spirit, whose relationship to the Son is such that the Holy Spirit actualized the content that is the Son, and in so doing, brings to completion the self-revelation of Absolute Spirit.[37]

Sophia appears then to function as the conceptual background of Bulgakov's firm Trinitarian ontological view of the whole reality (divine world and the created realm). In this vein, it is not an exaggeration to argue that the so-called "Linguistic Trinity" is nothing other than the Sophia–Trinity account, being "actualized" in the realm of language, as the "I am A" [= subject–copula–predicate] proposition (and vice versa).

The "Material Constitution theory" and Bulgakov's "Linguistic Trinity"

In this section, by exploring the model of *Material Constitution* as it was initially proposed by Michael Rea and Jeffrey Brower, along with certain comments suggested by William Hasker,[38] I seek to show that Bulgakov's "Linguistic Trinity" can possibly fit into this scheme so as to provide a possible way out of the logical problem of the Trinity.

a) What is the meaning of the "material constitution" theory. In Brower's and Rea's words:

> This problem arises whenever it appears that an object *a* and an object *b* share all of the same parts and yet have different modal properties. To take just one of the many well-worn examples in the literature: Consider a bronze statue of the Greek goddess, Athena, and the lump of bronze that constitutes it. On the one hand, it would appear that we must recognize at least two material objects in the region occupied by the statue for presumably the statue cannot survive the process of being melted

---

37   Aristotle Papanikolaou, "Why Sophia? Bulgakov the Theologian," *The Wheel* 26–27 (2021):17. For a detailed account of Bulgakov's Trinitarian metaphysics, see Brandon Gallaher, *Freedom and Necessity in Modern Trinitarian Theology* (Oxford: Oxford University Press, 2016).

38   Hasker, *Metaphysics and the Tripersonal God*, 129 ff.

down and recast, whereas the lump of bronze can. On the other hand, our ordinary counting practices lead us to recognize only one material object in the region.[39]

In their view the problem of material constitution should be understood in the light of Aristotle's notion of "accidental sameness." According to the Greek philosopher,

> familiar particulars (trees, cats, human beings, etc.) are hylomorphic compounds— things that exist because and just so long as some *matter* instantiates a certain kind of *form*. Forms, for Aristotle, are complex organizational properties, and properties are immanent universals (or, as some have it, tropes). The matter of a thing is not itself an individual thing; rather, it is that which combines with a form to make an individual thing.[40]

Following this line of argumentation, a hylomorphic compound is constituted by *matter* and *form*, or in the paradigmatic example of a living organism which is preferred by Aristotle, the same hylomorphic compound is now constituted by a substance (in the place of matter) and an accidental property (in the place of form).

By virtue of various, and sometimes "kooky" paradigms (like the one referring to the "seated-Socrates" and Socrates)[41] Aristotle would agree with the common sense that there is only one material object that fills, in this respect, a particular place, as is the case, for instance, in the kooky paradigm of Socrates and seated Socrates. The two "objects" then, while they share all of the same parts, have different modal properties, meaning that they are no longer two different objects, a fact that would contradict common sense, since it is impossible for two objects to occupy one and the same place. In this perspective Aristotle would argue that the relation between the two objects is not one of identity but is a variety of "numerical sameness," that is, two objects (Socrates and seated Socrates) are "one in number but not in being."[42] If one thinks that this example is too "kooky" for serious reflection, one could take into account another more common example, that of the bronze statue and the lump of bronze:

---

39 Brower and Rea, "Material Constitution," 127.
40 Brower and Rea, "Material Constitution," 131.
41 Ibid., 132–33, referring particularly to Gareth Matthews, "Accidental Unities," in *Language and Logos*, ed. M. SchoWeld and M. Nussbaum (Cambridge: Cambridge University Press, 1982).
42 Brower and Rea, "Material Constitution," 132–33.

Thus, one can continue to believe that there are bronze statues and lumps of bronze, that every region occupied by a bronze statue is occupied by a lump of bronze, that no bronze statue is identical to a lump of bronze (after all, statues and lumps have different persistence conditions), but also that there are never two material objects occupying precisely the same place at the same time.

Indeed, if one reflects on the relationship between a lump of bronze, a bronze statue and the statue, one should admit that the one and the same place is still occupied by one single object, the statue, while at the same time one can identify three different objects (the bronze statue, the lump etc.), to the extent that common sense does not always "count by identity." In spite of any welcome reservations that one might have or any similarities with the Relative Identity theory outlined above, it seems that the "material constitution" theory provides us with the general framework and the appropriate conceptual tools for seeking a solution to the logical problem of the Trinity.

b) In this respect, Sergii Bulgakov is not an ordinary thinker.[43] Well known for his quite controversial sophiology, he widely authored on various philosophical and theological topics with remarkable creativity for a contemporary Orthodox intellectual. It is not my purpose here to either focus on Sophia or to fully deal with his rich and multilevel work. In contrast, and having briefly referred to his Sophia account, special attention will be paid to two quite important works of his, little known because they remained untranslated until recently, but highly valuable for the discussion of the "logical problem of the Trinity." By doing so I do not argue that Bulgakov can be considered an analytic thinker *per se* in the modern sense of the term, or that the above described "Material Constitution theory" is but a sequel of his overall philosophical explorations. However, as it will become clear, his speculations on language and consciousness present interesting and valuable points of convergence with this theory which can certainly be utilized in the discussion.

It was the atmosphere of his early period that led him to join the debate about the nature and the limits of language in God-talking. Bulgakov has been intensely involved in the well-known "imiaslavie (name-worshipping)" contro-

---

43   For an overview of his legacy and thought see the special double issue 26–27 of *The Wheel* including contributions by Rowan Williams, Aristotle Papanikolaou, Brandon Gallaher, Andrew Louth, Regula Zwahlen, etc.

versy[44] that broke out around the relationship of the Name of God to God on Mount Athos. Following eminent colleagues and friends like Pavel Florenskii, Bulgakov sided with those who asserted that God is contained and present in the Name.[45] An output of this historical adventure was the book *Philosophy of the Name* (1917–1921), where Bulgakov seems to provide a preliminary sketch of what could be called a "trinitarian ontological view" (that is, Being is trinitarian in itself). In this respect he focuses on language, as a revelationary means through which we obtain knowledge of the surrounding world. In an otherwise quite paradoxical assertion, in which one can discern a hidden theological concern that recalls the modern animal studies, Bulgakov claims that "God brought all the animals to Adam, in order to see [...] how they named themselves through him and in him." In this vein, language in general and names in particular take on an ontological aspect, not being merely functional words without relevance for reality; they rather "function as modes of being and acting of that which is named."[46] If this is the case, the Name of Jesus is not an abstract name, but Jesus himself. Being well informed about patristic theology, Bulgakov couples this view with the famous Palamite distinction between divine essence and energies, so as to further substantiate the ontological character of language, as it is clearly expressed in a single proposition (subject/ copula/predicate–name). As Bulgakov himself put it in his *Philosophy of The Name*, the subject of the proposition points to the essence while the predicate/ name is understood as the energy: "the pronoun expresses by itself the ousia, the name [...] is the revelation of a thing [...] because in the name its [...] energeia is made manifest."[47] Clearly, Bulgakov is a realist in his metaphysical vision, an element which can be coupled with a certain "materialism" in his religious view, in opposition to any philosophical or religious idealism, evident in many of his counterparts of the time, not only in religion but also in philosophy.

According to Heath, what is distinctive for Bulgakov, is not that he just makes use of the Palamite distinction (a common gesture of most of the contemporary Orthodox theologians and scholars), but that he approaches the

---

44 For a general account see Scott M. Kenworthy, "The Name-Glorifiers (Imiaslavie) Controversy", in *The Oxford Handbook of Russian Religious Thought*, eds. Caryl Emerson, George Pattison, and Randall A. Poole (Oxford: Oxford University Press, 2020), 327–42.

45 Joshua Heath, "Sergii Bulgakov's Linguistic Trinity," 3.

46 Ibid., 4.

47 *Filosofiia Imeni* [*The Philosophy of the Name*], 50, 61, as cited in Heath's "Sergii Bulgakov's Linguistic Trinity."

proposition in clear Trinitarian terms, a move that will be fully expressed, and I would say completed, in his *The Tragedy of Philosophy*. Besides, as has been argued recently, "these works represented the beginning of Bulgakov's final transition to the mature works of theology."[48]

Thus, in *The Philosophy of the Name*, Bulgakov argues that the subject of a proposition counts for "the first hypostasis of being in which is generated the second hypostasis, the word, and which, perceiving its bond with the verbal expression [...] accomplishes its third hypostasis (the copula)."[49] Following at some point his predecessor Vladimir Soloviev,[50] Bulgakov would clearly see in language a revelation of the trinitarian structure that underlies the whole reality. As Heath observes again, a weak point in this vein is that Bulgakov does not discern between a clear personal or an impersonal nature of the proposition: For him the subject can easily be an "it", not necessarily a He or She. By no means can this be seen as an inadequacy of his thought. Rather, it can be better understood as an initial and perhaps immature understanding of the trinitarian structure of the proposition which needed to be further developed and nuanced in his later work.

Thus, this line of thought would be further advanced in his *The Tragedy of Philosophy*. In this more or less mature sequel to his early linguistic explorations, Bulgakov would more clearly connect the inherent trinitarian structure of reality with the Holy Trinity. According to Heath, the "fundamental form of the proposition is not 'A is B' but rather 'I am A'."[51] Not an impersonal tripartite structure but a personal one, which now is clearly bound to the Holy Trinity.

Since a proposition always consists of three basic elements, that is, the "subject, a predicate, and a copula," Bulgakov argues for the trinitarian foundation of the whole reality, the Substance, Being. As he clearly puts it, "Substance is a living proposition consisting of a subject, a predicate, and a copula,"[52] the three in one at once, a sentence which can be considered a response to the diachronic philosophical question about the relationship between the One and the many, which often prioritizes unity/monism over otherness or multiplicity, in our case, triunity. In his latter book Bulgakov finds the opportunity to provide a

---

48   John Milbank, "Introduction" to Bulgakov's, *The Tragedy of Philosophy*, trans. ibid., xl.

49   Filosofiia Imeni [The Philosophy of the Name], 50, as cited in Heath's "Sergii Bulgakov's Linguistic Trinity."

50   Cf. his *Lectures on Divine Humanity*, ed. and trans. Boris Jakim (Hudson, NY: Lindisfarne Press, 1995).

51   Heath, "Sergii Bulgakov's Linguistic Trinity," 5.

52   Bulgakov, *The Tragedy of Philosophy*, 236.

certain misreading in the history of philosophy, which tends to absolutize one of the elements of the proposition over against the triunity of the reality. As he himself argues: "Substance" exists not only "in itself," as a subject, but also "for itself," as a predicate, and, moreover, "in and for itself," in the copula, as existence," so as to confirm the triune nature of reality. And he continues by saying: "And these three beginnings are by no means merely dialectical moments of a unity, negating each other and being sublated into a synthesis; no, they are, simultaneously and with equal dignity, three, like three roots of being which in their joint result make up the life of substance."[53] Bulgakov will also provide a scheme by which he tries to clarify the relationship between these three poles:

> In this way, substance is like an equilateral triangle

> whose angles may be placed in any order, but in which each of the three necessarily presupposes both of the others.[54]

In contrast to *Philosophy of the Name*, in this work Bulgakov is more confident and clear in connecting the proposition not with an abstract dialectic trinity but with the trinitarian doctrine: "The subject, the hypostasis, is the first; the predicate, the εἶδος [eidos], the second; the copula, existence, φύσις [phusis], the third. Yet it is impossible to say that the third element is thereby in any sense the synthesis of the first and the second, or that the first is the thesis to the second's antithesis. In general, these three moments are by no means of a logical nature, of the kind which necessarily characterizes dialectical contradictions. On the contrary, they stand for ontological relationships.[55]

Bulgakov's insistence on the triune character of Substance, meaning of the whole reality, has tremendous importance for our discussion here. Without being involved in all the details of his complex thought and for the sake of our argumentation in this respect, I would try to merely rephrase the material constitution theory, as described above, so as to show Bulgakov's relevance for contemporary analytic, philosophical thought.

53   Bulgakov, *The Tragedy of Philosophy*, 11.
54   Ibid., 18.
55   Ibid., 18–19.

Consider then instead of the bronze statue of the Greek goddess, and the lump of bronze that constitutes it, the fundamental proposition "I am A." On the one hand, it would appear that we must recognize at least three "elements" (subject, predicate and copula) in the proposition. At the same time, our ordinary counting practices lead us to recognize only one proposition/Substance. The three "objects" then, while they share all of the same parts, have different modal properties (e. g. being subject, predicate or copula), meaning that they are no longer three different "objects", a fact that would contradict common sense, since it is impossible for three "objects" to occupy the same place at once. In this perspective, Aristotle would argue that the relation between these three "objects" is not one of identity (consider here Bulgakov's reservations about the predominant tendency of philosophy towards monism) but is a variety of "numerical sameness," meaning that three "objects" (I, am, A) are "one in number but not in being." If one thinks that the example of "Socrates and seated Socrates," much used by analytic thought today, is too "kooky" to be taken seriously, let us reflect closer on the bronze example to further justify Bulgakov's primordial assumption of the triune character of Substance.

Returning again to the previous analysis of the "material constitution" theory, one can continue to believe that there are bronze statues and lumps of bronze, in our cases that there is a subject, a predicate and a copula, which together constitute one and the same proposition, one Substance while no subject is identical to its predicate or copula (after all, subjects and predicates have different persistent conditions), but also that there are never three "objects," occupying precisely the same place at the same time, but just one proposition/Substance.

Indeed, if one looks more carefully at the relationship between the subject (say, a lump of bronze), the predicate (the bronze statue) and the copula (the statue), one should admit that the one and the same place is still occupied by one single object, the one proposition/Substance (the statue), while at the same time one can clearly identify three different objects (the subject, the predicate and the copula), to the extent that common sense does not always "count by identity." Linguistic Trinity then, this primordial structure as it has been described by Bulgakov, appears to fit well the theory that in my view is the most adequate, that of "material constitution," ready to offer valuable insights into the analytic discussion of the logical problem of the Trinity.

If we would like to offer a preliminary practical application of Bulgakov's linguistic Trinity (encapsulated in the following verses: "Substance" exists not only "in itself," as a subject, but also "for itself," as a predicate, and, moreover, "in and for itself," in the copula, as existence" and "Substance is a living proposition consisting of a subject, a predicate, and a copula"), then one could set out two of the central tenets of the doctrine of the Trinity, where his view perfectly fits:

Thesis 1: Father, Son and Holy Spirit are not identical (which amounts to the personal otherness in the Trinity: subject/predicate/copula);

Thesis 2: Father, Son, and Holy Spirit are consubstantial (which amounts to the one divine substance: one proposition/Substance).

What is lacking here is the special role attributed—according to certain authors –[56] by the Greek Fathers to the hypostasis of the Father as the cause of existence of the other two hypostases, which in traditional terms is known as the *monarchia* of the Father.

By Way of a Conclusion

This is a chapter only introductory in character, seeking to read Bulgakov as an analytic thinker. My initial goal was to deal with Bulgakov's more philosophical work, showing how valuable a resource it can be for the ongoing discussion taking place in analytic (but also continental) philosophy with respect to the trinitarian doctrine. Despite the hesitancy on the part of the Orthodox due to their apophatic overemphasis on working with analytic tools and reason or language in their God-talk, Bulgakov's explorations in language have much to contribute to the deepening of our understanding of the fundamental Christian paradoxical question that is how to combine the One and the Three in the Holy Trinity. Much work remains to be done with respect to certain aspects of Bulgakov's thought, such as how one can incorporate his understanding of Sophia in his "analytic" vision, or what its role is, if it plays a role at all, of the *monarchia* of the Father, a basic axiom of doctrinal orthodoxy, or the relationship between personhood and nature in this scheme.

---

56   Cf. in particular Zizioulas, *Communion & Otherness.*

Building the House of Wisdom
DOI 10.17438/978-3-402-12198-6

Sergii Bulgakov: From Grammar to Wisdom

John Milbank

1. Introduction: Bulgakov and the German Legacy

Increasingly, Sergii Bulgakov is regarded as one of the major voices of Twentieth Century theology that sounds even more resonantly in the Twenty-First than that of most of his contemporaries.

One of his most decisive and earlier philosophical works, alongside *Unfading Light* and *The Philosophy of the Name*, is *The Tragedy of Philosophy*.[1] It can be interpreted, as its title suggests, as a theological critique of all philosophy as such, but more specifically it is a critique of German Transcendental Idealism and its three greatest exponents: Fichte, Hegel and Schelling, besides being a critique of the thinker who made this philosophy possible, Immanuel Kant. In these respects, Bulgakov sustained, deepened and intensified the first major Russian critique of Western thought, written by the founder of the Sophiological tradition in which he stood: Vladimir Soloviev's *The Crisis of Western Philosophy*.[2]

As passages in *Unfading Light* indicate, Bulgakov also conceived this exercise as part of his specifically Russian response to German culture as a whole.[3] His attitude to that was thoroughly ambivalent. Negatively, he regarded it as half-barbaric, whereas Russia and the Eastern Church for him sustained a continuous link to the ultimate Greek sources of Western civilisation. By contrast,

---

1 Sergij Bulgakov, *The Tragedy of Philosophy*, trans. Stephen Churchyard (New York: Angelico, 2020). This chapter is a re-written version of John Milbank's introduction to this English translation of *The Tragedy of Philosophy*.

2 Vladimir Soloviev, *The Crisis of Western Philosophy: Against the Positivists*, trans. Boris Jakim (Hudson MY; Lindisfarne Press, 1996).

3 Sergius Bulgakov, *Unfading Light: Contemplations and Speculations*, trans. Thomas Allan Smith (Grand Rapids: W. B. Eerdmans, 2012).

the Latin West, and still more the Teutons, had half-mangled this legacy, which contained at its core an anthropocentric art and a Platonic philosophy that interpreted this art as epiphanic.

The Teutonic mangling is connected in the Russian theologian's mind with the Arian heresy which had especially appealed to the northern barbaric tribes. Thus he accuses the German tradition of being marked by an 'Arian monophysitism'. A failure to correctly grasp the dogmas of the Trinity and the Incarnation has supposedly engendered opposite and yet complicit tendencies both to a Faustian exaltation of the Human ego and to a pantheistic spiritualism, reducing God to nature. Moreover, this has too frequently taken pessimistic forms, which Bulgakov thinks is connected to a barbaric refusal of a refined sensuality, of sexuality and of the feminine—variously exemplified by Martin Luther, Jacob Boehme and Richard Wagner. German civilisation has either lured us into the echo-chamber of the self or has grimly celebrated blind forceful striving, unilluminated by the disclosures of the beautiful.

All this was surely thought and written not without awareness of the disasters into which Prussian nationalism had led Europe at the time of the First World War.[4] On the other hand, Bulgakov was of course equally aware of the catastrophe engulfing his own country during the same period. The Russian tradition is mainly castigated by him for an overly Oriental world-refusal which had taken variously quietist and hysterically ecstatic forms over the centuries. In his own epoch, this had dialectically encouraged an unprecedently appalling reversal: an immanentism that was sheerly arid, atheistic and mechanical, reducing not only religion but also art to economics.

In the face of these Russian diseases, the West and even specifically the German tradition offered for Bulgakov after all, if not a remedy, then at least a salve. As *Unfading Light* relates, it had to some degree rightly celebrated life in this world: the beauty of nature, participation in politics and the practice of art. Furthermore, it had seen all these things as suffused with the divine. Much of Bulgakov's work can be interpreted as an attempt to do justice to the German sense of immanence while avoiding what he saw as the German descent into a gloomy pantheism, for which the totality of everything discloses literally nothing. It is equally and inversely the case that he attempts to do positive justice to the Western and most of all the German sense of anthropocentrism and subjectivity. Faust was not just to be condemned by the Russian master, but also to be redeemed. It is by no means irrelevant here to think of the great

---

4   See James Hawes, *The Shortest History of Germany* (London: Old Street, 2018).

novelistic gloss upon Goethe written by his remote relative Mikhail: *The Master and Margherita.*

Of course, this double attitude towards German culture contains considerable delusion besides great insight. Too much is projected backwards in terms of a supposed continuity of Teutonic character: thus, in *Unfading Light* Eckhart is excessively read through the lens of Jacob Boehme, whose mode of mysticism specifically follows Luther (though one could suggest that too many German scholars have themselves made the same mistake). And a pantheistic tendency is traced ultimately and again falsely to the Irish theologian of Aachen: John Scotus Eriugena. Yet in both cases it can seem as if Bulgakov goes on to reproduce different Russian versions of doctrines that he has repudiated in their 'German' guise.

For example, he condemns Eckhart's notion of a *Gottheit* beyond the God/Creation contrast, but then speaks himself of a deeper 'Absolute' that only becomes 'God' in relation to the world. Or again, he denounces Eriugena's talk of Creation as 'Created God', but then himself proposes *Sophia* for a similar and problematically liminal role.[5] He notably situates the divine ideas within Sophia rather than within the original Trinitarian Godhead, just as Eriugena places them with the immanent *primalitates*.

One can also observe that Bulgakov somewhat disguises the way in which he is developing (albeit with brilliance) *German* Romantic critiques of German Idealism—especially the thoughts of Jacobi, Hamann, Herder, Novalis, Friedrich Schlegel and Wilhelm von Humboldt. To a degree he wants to claim all the 'romance' for the Russian steppes and birchwoods, rather than the Rhineland, the Black Forest and the Baltic coast.

2. Why Fichte?

This ambiguity towards German theology and philosophy is most strikingly apparent in terms of Bulgakov's attitude towards Johann Gottlieb Fichte in the *Tragedy of Philosophy*. His appropriation and critique of this philosopher lies surely at its core. This can seem strange insofar as the thesis of the book is that philosophy inevitably falls into error and contradiction by ignoring the dogmas of revelation and specifically the doctrine of the Trinity. It is well-known that

---

5   See, for example, Sergius Bulgakov, 'The Sophiology of Death,' in *The Sophiology of Death*, trans. Roberto J. De La Noval (Eugene OR: Wip and Stock, 2021), 117: 'Man, and in him all creation, in uncreated-created Sophia, created divinity, a created god by grace'.

both Hegel and Schelling try to incorporate this doctrine into their respective philosophies: indeed, it is impossible to comprehend them unless one takes this into account. By comparison, Fichte does no such thing: he does not mention the Trinity at all, even when writing at length about religion. For this reason, Bulgakov says that Fichte was in effect the philosopher of a Jewish God, of a pure monotheism.

And yet, it is apparent in this text and in later ones towards the end of his career that Bulgakov much more derives his proposed Trinitarian ontology from an engagement with Fichte than with Hegel or even with Schelling.[6] Why should this somewhat surprising fact be the case?

First, and very simply, it is because he can more think of Fichte as offering an 'Old Testament' that is nearer to being acceptable so far as it goes. By comparison, Hegel and Schelling are seen as articulating highly heterodox versions of Trinitarian metaphysics.[7]

But in the second place, there is something much more crucial which takes us back to the issue of the Faustian. Certainly, for Bulgakov, Fichte is the 'Luciferian' thinker *par excellence*, trying, like Jonathan Swift's spider in *The Battle of the Books*, to weave all of reality out of his own selfhood. Bulgakov observes that this endeavour in effect goes in the opposite direction from all of philosophy hitherto, including even that of Kant: instead of trying to situate the subject amongst objects or things, or to locate subjectivity in being, it tries to position all things and all of beings within the scope of the knowing self, taken as the 'truly existing'. However, the Russian thinker does not only regard this attempt as demonically perverse (though he does that); he also thinks that in a way this attempt is in continuity with the specifically Christian cultural and conceptual revolution which newly elevated *personhood*. Thus, any metaphysics true to the Bible and to credal faith ought indeed to place the personal subject at the ontological outset. For this reason, Bulgakov *retains* the Fichtean understanding of the self as the 'truly existing'.

What is more, this understanding can be thought of as in keeping with the greater Eastern Christian insistence on the 'monarchic' primacy of the hypostasis of the Father, which Bulgakov, like so many Orthodox theologians, considered to have been too often obscured in the west by a primacy of essence in the Trinity, and by the added *filioque* clause in the Western creed that was in danger of suggesting a secondary and equally potent hypostatic origin in the Godhead. In consequence, the West had been in peril at once of reducing God

---

6   Bulgakov, *The Tragedy of Philosophy*, 207–36.
7   Ibid., 24–51, 171–205.

to an impersonal essence and yet also of taking a tritheistic approach to the Trinitarian persons. This latter danger had been compounded by a tendency (running counter to an emphasis on their co-relational definition, which Bulgakov supports) to identify the persons with particular psychological faculties.[8]

It is against this background that Bulgakov was inclined to take Fichte very seriously. Other factors were involved also: in particular, his awareness of the proximity of neo-Kantian thought to the Fichtean legacy. In a contemporary philosophical landscape from which neo-Kantianism has long vanished, this can seem to be no longer of relevance and one can readily suppose that Bulgakov's philosophical concerns were already outdated. He makes scarcely any mention, or rarely shows very much awareness, of either Analytic philosophy or Phenomenology.

However, contemporary scholarship (in part based on more detailed textual research) sometimes suggests that Fichte is the most crucial of all modern Continental philosophers: his problematic not only anticipated phenomenology, but also foreshadowed its deconstruction and the more recent Continental turn back towards metaphysics.[9] It not only took Idealism to a new extreme, but also suggested how neither Idealism nor Realism seem to be entirely coherent. Much of neo-Kantianism, especially the work of Hermann Cohen, can be seen as implicitly a re-engagement with this Fichtean legacy. Moreover, Bulgakov's own simultaneous linguistic reworking and yet critique of Fichte is not without echo in some exponents of the Analytic philosophy of language.

For these reasons, it may be that perhaps only today, in the first quarter of the Twenty-First Century, can we newly appreciate the relevance of Bulgakov's philosophy. What is more, when we realise that Bulgakov was revisiting the problematics that Fichte was trying to resolve in the wake of the critique of Kant, then we can get a sharper sense of the degree to which he proposed a novel and specifically theological philosophy of his own. Indeed, his degree of philosophical inventiveness is perhaps unsurpassed amongst other modern systematic theologians.

---

8 Bulgakov, *The Tragedy of Philosophy*, 131–55. In reality, Bulgakov ascribes to the whole of Western Trinitarian theology exaggerations which tended to appear only in the High to Later Middle Ages.

9 See, for example, Walter E. Wright, 'Introduction,' in J. G. Fichte, *The Science of Knowing: J. G. Fichte's 1804 Lectures on the* Wissenschaftslehre (New York: SUNY, 2005), 1–20 and Andrea Bellantone, *La métaphysique possible: Philosophies de l'esprit et modernité* (Paris: Hermann, 2012), 191–220.

3. Fichtean Complexities

If Bulgakov now appears after all prodigious rather than belated in foregrounding Fichte, then that is primarily because he was aware of the key ambiguities in Fichte's thought, long before they have been more regularly stressed. For a start, he grasped that Fichte's shift beyond Kant to a more absolute idealism was also and paradoxically a move back towards constitutive metaphysical realism. This concerns initially the role of the knowing 'I' in philosophy.

Kant had spoken of a 'transcendental apperception' on the part of the subject as accompanying all of its 'judgements of experience' and Bulgakov commends Kant's awareness that in all our judging we are always dimly aware of ourselves as knower.[10] However, he also agrees with Fichte that this insight does not go far enough. For it is not possible merely to say, with Kant, that we assume our own knowing reality as a logical condition of the possibility of knowing anything whatsoever. This pretends to lock our awareness into a mutually referential circle of the self-conscious cognition of mere appearances, such that it is supposed that our real, ontological and 'noumenal' self is concealed from us. But in reality this is absurd; everything is the other way around. We only know anything besides ourselves because we are, as Descartes said, directly aware of our own reality as thinking beings, aware of our existential insertion in a manner that exceeds the conceptual knowledge of objects. Everything else that is thought is thought 'for us', 'posited' by us as a mode of our own directly experienced and felt self-thinking, else we would not be able to think it at all.

Moreover, Bulgakov points out that Kant falls suspiciously silent even about transcendental apperception at a crucial point in the *Critique of Pure Reason*: namely with respect to his transcendental aesthetic, which argues that space and time are transcendental assumptions of sensory awareness which allow the 'schematisation' of sensory information through the application of rational categories of the understanding.[11] By not, in this specific context, pointing out that we are also apperceiving ourselves when we apprehend space and time, Kant is suppressing the degree to which the self only knows itself as something that actually transcends, in some measure, both space and time, inevitably intuiting itself as eternal, since it is always able to imagine itself elsewhere and in another moment, while being unable to think of itself in its simultaneously experiencing and experienced selfhood as dead.

---

10   Bulgakov, *The Tragedy of Philosophy*, 91–121.
11   Ibid., 159–70. See also Père Serge Boulgakov, *La Philosophie du Verbe et du Nom*, trans. Constantin Andronikoff (Paris: L'Age d'Homme, 1991), 85–112.

By ignoring this, Kant can suggest that the theoretical self is 'trapped' in spatial and temporal perspectives, even while contradictorily regarding them as 'merely subjective'. Bulgakov's subtle Fichtean point here is that if Kant had considered apperception also in relation to *aesthesis*, if he had more allowed that space and time are encountered experientially always in terms of our sense of selfhood, then he could *also* have seen that, since the self thereby transcends space and time, in consequence space and time rather more objectively and realistically confront the self as something somewhat alien and external to it.

Instead of doing that, Kant tries to secure the merely phenomenal reach of all our theoretical categories by the fact of their supposed schematic applicability only to finite and specifically Newtonian space and time, which are already taken to be sheerly subjective frameworks. Thereby, as Bulgakov argues, the comprehensible is arbitrarily restricted by Kant to the temporarily sequential and spatially relational, not allowing for the equal objectivity of holistic coherence (as with the belonging of accidents to substance—which Kant reduces to an extrinsic relation) that can be readily imagined, as with selfhood, as extending to infinity.

Because he perceived the inadequacy of the doctrine of transcendental apperception, never mind its inconsistent application, Fichte consciously and explicitly returned to Descartes behind Kant. He grounded knowledge not in an 'as it were' subject that is only apparent through his knowing of this or that, but in a directly perceived and fully real subject that is existentially 'absolute' in the sense that it transcends any particular content.[12] This is not in any way to speak of an illusory Lockean 'punctual' self, taken outside and before social and linguistic instantiation, but merely to note that the subject can indeed 'ironically' stand back from any particular content—imagine herself as born elsewhere, undergoing totally other experiences, re-locating across the seas, learning completely different languages etc., which sometimes she may indeed actually do. It is for this reason that we have a sense of the universality of our subjectivity which allows us readily to say 'we' alongside other people, who are the existential possessors of quite different contents of experience.

The paradox of Fichte's position is that this direct realism about the subject is also the basis for his attempted absolute idealism. He argued that we have intuitive insight into the noumenal realm in terms of our own subjectivity: what we are, we also immediately act and will. We are not just 'given' to ourselves,

---

12   J. G. Fichte, *The Science of Knowing; The Science of Knowledge*, trans. Peter Heath and John Lachs (Cambridge: CUP, 1997); *Introductions to the Wissenschaftslehre and Other Writings*, trans. Daniel Breazeale (Indianapolis IN: Hackett, 1994).

but are given as self-posited and as 'self-made' in the sense that we cannot stand back from ourselves, cannot refuse to 'go' with ourselves or not play our own part, whatever role this may assume. We are never an object to ourselves, because as soon as we try to look at ourselves we displace ourselves by being exhaustively the self who is doing this looking. To be a self is ineluctably to perform the self—we can assume a role, tell a lie, but it is always 'I' who is doing so.

This is the self as *Tathandlung* as Fichte puts it. By token of the subject's *real* transcendence of any objectivity, we can never exit our own circle: we can always go somewhere else, but only by being ourself somewhere else. Subjectivity is a permanent metaphysical sentence of absolute lockdown, as it were. For this reason, it further follows that we cannot affirm or 'posit' the reality of anything save as a mode of our own self-awareness, or as in some sense a derivation from our own self-understanding. I cannot know the clock as a clock outside the accompanying reflexive awareness of myself using it to tell the time.

Moreover, we have no reason, as with Kant, to suppose that hidden essences or 'things in themselves' lurk behind phenomena. This is all the more true, since in the instance of our self-awareness we now have a direct insight into the noumenal, which Fichte has extended from Kant's practical to his theoretical reason, while somewhat fusing the two—since to 'be' oneself is also immediately to 'enact' oneself.

These two theoretical shifts, in combination, give the basis for Fichte's absolute idealist project. While he returned from Kant to Descartes and so to a certain realism about the self, he still entertained and sought to extend Kant's 'critical' project, which would found certainty in knowledge and not being, and so in a subjective starting point, not in being in general—as, for example, with Spinoza. It then follows that the 'critical' knowledge possessed by the subject, if it is to be certain knowledge and to overcome sceptical doubt as to its import, must now be an absolute knowledge of things in their appearance as being how they really are. One sees how, in this respect, Fichte can be regarded as a proto-Phenomenologist.

Moreover, since pre-Kantian speculation is still refused, the only way to ground this knowledge with certainty is to see these things in their very manifestness as derived from the subject. It is not that Fichte denied their external reality (as Berkeley is supposed to have done, on the usual mistaken reading), but rather that he affirmed that all of their knowability was derived from the knowing subject. This subject does not actually make things, but he does entirely posit them insofar as they can be known. There is a certain anticipation of both Husserlian bracketing and Husserlian intentionality involved here.

All the same, and as with the neo-Kantians and Husserl in his later phase, the loss of the *Dinge an sich* seems to reduce things to our awareness of them. However, and again as with Phenomenology, there is some ambiguity: just because there is no longer any sceptical gulf between phenomena and noumena, phenomena start to assume a greater quasi-ontological weight than is the case with Kant.

And in fact, a reversion to realism after all goes further than this in the case of Fichte.

From the very outset of his reflections, although the self as absolute must be assumed, and assumed as prior to the contrast of subject and object, I and Not-I—in order that it may be a final ground, that is taken to be more or less the immanent presence of God—Fichte also considers that this self can never directly appear to us, but remains, as it were, unconscious. Thus, for him, *sum ergo sum* precedes even *cogito ergo sum*. As soon as we have started to enact ourselves consciously we are involved with the objective 'Not I' with which we are in a co-constitutive relation. The Not-I or the object is for this reason really just as fundamental as the I, even though it *prevents* there being any absolute foundation after all.

Furthermore, since the I only first knows itself in encountering the Not-I, and yet the Not-I is only there at all as grounded in the ultimate and inaccessible *sum ergo sum*, it follows (in a very proto-postmodern manner) that the self is from the outset divided from itself, unable because of a primordial fall into reflection ever fully to know itself or existentially to be at one with itself.

In this way, realism eats deconstructively into the very heart of Fichte's idealism, which is 'absent' just to the degree that it is absolute. But equally, even though he tries to 'deduce' all the structures of our knowing of external things from the conditions of our self-awareness, he admits that this attempt is never complete, rather in the way that phenomenological description will later prove 'an infinite task'. At the core of what we posit is always something that is obstinately just 'there', confronting us in all its irreducible density, including Being as such. The latter cannot after all be spun out of our *Dasein*, with a pre-echo of Heidegger's philosophical dilemmas.

Since these given appearances are for Fichte no longer floating on a sea of noumena with which they may have no intrinsic connection, his position at this point becomes *evidently more realist than that of Kant*. And he says so. The Not-I is bafflingly posited as irreducible for the I, as just given for it in an alien mode. Also, in contrast to Hegel, there is no logical route from the I to the Not-I in Fichte and this is part of why he appealed more to Bulgakov. Nor is this difference between the two poles, subjective and objective, engulfed in a vitalist sea of nature, as (supposedly) for Schelling. Again, this was attractive to the Russian thinker.

Therefore, we can see how the Fichtean *Anstoss*, or 'push-back' of objective appearances involves much more genuine practical exteriority than the Kantian *noumena*.

All the same, there is nothing straightforward here, and nothing, from Bulgakov's perspective, that clearly overcomes Jacobi's charges of nihilism and atheism as consequent upon the Fichtean attempt (again anticipating Husserl) to turn philosophy into a strict science. Fichte was always trying to overcome these charges, while not surrendering to Jacobi's perceived 'fideism'.[13] Indeed, as scholarship has now shown, his work was driven as much by Jacobi's simultaneous critique of both Kant and Spinoza as by his attempt to deepen the Kantian critique itself.

Jacobi had charged that any rational foundationalism, in trying to suppress pre-rational presuppositions, tends to deny reality altogether in favour of an empty self-reference or an infinite regress. In order to meet this challenge, Idealism was forced to try to show that the rational subject could indeed do justice to and encompass all of the actually real, including both the subject and the object, both freedom and necessity (beyond Spinoza), both culture and nature, in a complete system.[14]

Bulgakov correctly perceived that Fichte's system remained nonetheless thoroughly aporetic, in part because the latter grasped the radicality of Jacobi's challenge. For Fichte, the knowing subject is self-grounded and absolute. In consequence, the drive of philosophy towards full comprehension of everything has to be idealist in character. The recognition of a reality that cannot be subsumed is indeed the recognition of a blockage for philosophy as such, even though it intrudes from the very outset of philosophical investigation. The self must seek to overcome this obstacle even in order to achieve an unproblematic self-recognition, but it cannot do so.

---

13   Friedrich Heinrich Jacobi, 'Jacobi to Fichte,' in *The Main Philosophical Writings and the Novel* Allwill, trans. George di Giovanni (Montreal-Kingston: McGill/Queen's UP, 1994), 497–536. Bulgakov in places accuses Jacobi of producing a surrogate of religious faith as ontological trust, yet surely makes the same move himself. Jacobi is rarely given his due because he wrote in an amateurish, journalistic idiom that makes other more professional thinkers consistently reluctant to admit the devastating direct brilliance of his insights and their crucial role in the later unfolding of all modern philosophy.

14   See Paul W. Franks, *All or Nothing: Systematicity, Transcendental Arguments and Scepticism in German Idealism* (Cambridge MA: Harvard UP, 2005).

Fichte 'resolves' this cognitive and existential conundrum by declaring, somewhat like Kant, though in an altered way, the primacy of practical reason over theoretical. The practical will involves an endless drive to assert its own all-encompassing self-willing and free all-comprehending or positing of all that it knows. Ethics is grounded in this will to absolute and uninhibited self-assertion.

Nonetheless (and here Bulgakov is arguably not quite fair to Fichte and somewhat disguises his more surreptitious borrowings from him) the real barriers that this subjective drive constantly come up against include our encounters with other selves, whose equal absoluteness we are able to acknowledge just because we experience our own subjectivity as something undetermined and so potentially shared in common: the always latent sense of the 'we'. It is for this reason that Fichte faintly sustained (after Jacobi) some sense of the interpersonal or of an 'I–Thou' consciousness. Yet the need to mediate between equally absolute subjective poles gives rise in Fichte to the advocacy of a politics at once extremely liberal and resolutely totalitarian, as the British Hegelian Gillian Rose was fond of pointing out. Nothing can connect such subjective poles save a doctrine of private rights and nothing can guarantee our non-interference with each other's liberties save the most continual state surveillance and policing.[15] Ultimately then, in practice, it would seem that, for Fichte, the shared 'we' is the unlimited political state committed to what Bulgakov would have understood as a total 'economising' of all human life where practical regulation, and not art and culture, is what we thereby fundamentally share in common.

4. Bulgakov's Critique of Fichte

It is, however, already at the gnoseological and ontological level that Bulgakov finds Fichte to be unsatisfactory. He is not content with the theoretically unresolved *aporia*. It is in this respect that he notes that, while Fichte proposes something like a shadow of the human imaging of the Second Person of the Trinity in terms of the 'Not-I', which can also be seen as the inescapable 'predicate' required to establish any reflective and effective 'subject', that he lacks altogether (unlike Hegel and Schelling) any inkling of the Third Person or of the grammatical copula. The I and the Not-I are not conjoined by Being or by an

---

15   J. G. Fichte, *Foundations of Natural Right*, trans. Michael Baur (Cambridge: CUP, 2000).

existential judgement, because they always just kick against each other, being caught up in an endless and always unresolved agonistic tussle.[16]

Bulgakov refuses this agonism in its ontological import, rather than as a constant but contingent mark of our fallen propensities. He does so essentially by re-instating against Fichte the proto-Romantic and Romantic critiques that were levelled against him and to which he was constantly seeking to respond.

These critiques were basically threefold. First, as we have seen, Friedrich Heinrich Jacobi had suggested in relation to both Fichte and Kant that philosophy always arrives too late to secure any rational foundation of thought in subjective self-awareness. By the time we start to reflect, we are already existentially and culturally situated, have already embarked on a thousand ungrounded assumptions that we nonetheless require in order to be able to think at all. Taking ourselves on trust, we equally take on trust and with an equal certainty the real world that surrounds us.

Fichte, with great intellectual respect, half-conceded Jacobi's point, and as we have seen, allows that we cannot really catch up with our absolute selfhood. Yet, unlike Jacobi, he continued to insist that our subjectivity, which we have to assume from the outset, must *in principle* be fully self-transparent and thinkable, even though our doomed failure to do so results in an irresolvable antinomy that we cannot just push to the margins, as with the antinomies of Kant.

Significant here is Fichte's attitude towards religion. Jacobi had suggested that, since we inhabit the real world necessarily 'by faith', actually religious and mythical pre-comprehensions of our subjectivity cannot be displaced and must, to some degree, be trusted. Fichte instead thought that the only revelation that could be accepted was one which did not violate our *a priori* criteria for what a true revelation would be: namely one that did not contradict our absolutely given rational philosophical understanding.[17] In consequence, for Fichte, God is really the finite and unblocked realisation of the Absolute ego: indeed a pure monotheism with no Trinitarian inflection. Arguably, a kind of acosmism seems to ensue, since if the independence of the Creation can in any way 'count' for God, he would be himself caught up in the agonistic tussles of understanding that Fichte had disinterred. It is this latter, Behmenist route that Hegel and Schelling were indeed variously to explore.

It is apparent here that Bulgakov in effect sides once more with Jacobi. Before human beings ever get to philosophy they have already made elective exis-

---

16   Bulgakov, *The Tragedy of Philosophy*, 223–34.

17   J. G. Fichte, *Attempt at a Critique of All Revelation*, trans. Garrett Green (Cambridge: CUP, 2012).

tential choices which they express in terms of myths and dogmas. Just because we can never catch up with ourselves, these shared decisions are unavoidable. The Idealist claim to surmount them or surpass them is deluded: either, as with Fichte's honesty, one runs into a cognitive *impasse*, or one succumbs to alternative and heterodox religiosities, as with Hegel and (supposedly) Schelling: gnostic mythologies which hover between acosmism and pantheism, or agonistically combine both at different moments.

For this reason, Bulgakov thinks that no philosophy really escapes from religion: in reality every philosophy is an attempt to think more clearly through various different religious presuppositions. This is what he claims for his own Christian philosophy: it is a reflection on Christian 'myths' and 'dogmas'—in the sense of primordial written teachings or cognitive reflections that have liturgically acquired such a collective status. Given his statement that philosophy is the *ancilla* of religion and not of theology, one can validly conclude that Bulgakov in reality abolished the entire distinction between philosophy and theology. He is arguably the very greatest modern theologian just because he realised, like the Church Fathers, both Greek and Latin, and much later like Meister Eckhart, that the only real Christian theologian is one who directly assumes the philosophical task in the light of the Holy Scriptures.

In another vital and linked respect, Bulgakov effectively agrees with Jacobi against Fichte. If the knowing subject is fully real, as for Descartes, and not just 'transcendental' as for Kant, then we no longer have any warrant for staying with Kant's 'critical' subjectivism. To know ourself as a real living and thinking self is to know ourself as situated in a world alongside other things and other selves with the same immediacy of cognitive trust. For this reason, we need not see the always already co-given 'Not-I' as a contradictory blockage to our understanding, nor even our divided self-hood as entirely irresolvable. We can, instead, think in more originally relational terms of a natural if selective blending of self with other and of different moments of our own self-hood in terms of a narrative coherence (as for Paul Ricoeur or Alasdair Macintyre), albeit one that it is never finitely complete.

This means that we must engage with the neglected *copula*, ignored by Fichte. At this point, we can invoke the second, crucial proto-Romantic critique of Idealism that Bulgakov explicitly appeals to in *The Philosophy of the Name* and that is equally important for *The Tragedy of Philosophy*. This is the charge that Kant had ignored the philosophical import of language.

In relation to Fichte this means that Bulgakov suggests that everything becomes much clearer if we replace the supposed primacy of *logic* with the real existential primacy of *grammar*. Again and again the Russian theologian suggests that the over-extension of logic in German Idealism from Kant through to Hegel leads to all sorts of argumentative *legerdemain*, of which he is as disdainful from the Eastern margins of Europe as the British tend to be from the Western.[18] One should not pretend to be able to deduce even the knowledge of objects from our subjectivity, as Fichte seeks to do, nor imagine that any proposed deduction of ontological categories can be anything more than a 'rhapsody' of classification, rationalistically abusing the categories of Aristotle.

Yet this is now, for Bulgakov, for a more than Aristotelian reason: it is because, prior to any classification of things into substance, accident and relation (these being the crucial extremes of Aristotle's ten categories), lies the already-lived grammatical arrangement of things into subject, predicate and copula. Every predicate is, for Bulgakov, a kind of universal idea, and the hypostatic subject is still more universal and open in character. There exists for him no simple priority between the two, and so the subject no longer plays any straightforward role of substance to which things just accidentally attach. For there can be no real, living subject prior to received and selected attachments, and in consequence any unproblematic sifting between substance and attribute, or between external and constitutive relations, is grammatically disturbed from the outset. Therefore, the *Tragedy of Philosophy* concludes in its very last sentence that 'Substance is a *living proposition* consisting of a subject, a predicate, and a copula'.[19]

Bulgakov's case, explicitly following Hamann, Herder and Humboldt, is that philosophy goes astray if it seeks to transcend or escape the cultural, because linguistic mediation of nature. In a sense he reads Fichte as half-conceding this, because the German philosopher had rightly concluded that when we say, for example, 'the table is in the dining room,' we are really saying 'I can see that the table is in the dining room', in such a way that only by imbuing the table in a certain sense with our own subjectivity are we able to see the table at all. However, Bulgakov adds to Fichte that this circumstance reveals that we inevitably subscribe to a *grammatical ontology* that we cannot seriously refuse without lapsing into incoherence. The subject–predicate–copula structure of all human language reveals indeed that we can only perceive the world at all by symbolically animating it—and for this reason, in *Unfading Light*, Bulgakov cautiously endorsed 'occultist' and esoteric natural philosophies.

---

18   Though of course one must note that other central European traditions from Bolzano through Frege to Tarski have been equally disdainful.

19   Bulgakov, *The Tragedy of Philosophy*, 236.

However, this ontological 'propositionality' also for him tells against Idealism and against Fichte. In a kind of admitted exacerbation of Fichtean insights, which the first fully Romantic current, that of the self-named actual 'Romantics', Novalis and Friedrich Schlegel, had already sketched, we need to see that the only available subjectivity that we can inhabit is, in later Lacanian terms, 'the subject of the statement' and not the sublimely inaccessible, though always assumed 'subject of enunciation', which is somewhat like Fichte's *sum ergo sum*.[20] If we do admit this beginning always already with the linguistic subject as the only available 'I', then more drastically than Fichte we will see that we have to also admit the equal co-reality from the outset of the 'Not-I', now taken in the mode of the predicate. For it is not just that the predicate always blocks our advance, requiring our integral retreat into ironic subjective reserve, it is also the case (as Fichte already in effect admitted) that without adopting some attachment to predicates, without appropriating them as properties of our selfhood—without, as Bulgakov sees it, *naming* ourself—we will not enter into subjectivity at all. We surpass negative irony, as Friedrich Schlegel taught, when we positively embrace flashes of linguistic 'wit' that are fragments of revelatory and participatory disclosure. Then our lives and the reality we inhabit can turn into continuous symbolic allegories.[21]

From such a perspective, there is in fact no easy distinction to be made between the subject and predicate positions, either in grammar or in reality. Thus, in *The Philosophy of the Name*, Bulgakov stresses that every word as an 'idea' is transcendentally prior to its grammatical position as a part of speech. This also means for him that the inflection of a word is genetically prior to linguistic structure, and that for this reason the older languages are the inflected ones. There is a wholesale fluidity between absolutely individual substance and the universal qualities that attach to it—they can always confusingly change places because they so radically require each other, just as a noun may turn into a verb or vice-versa.

Indeed, Bulgakov maintains that the claimed identity between subject and predicate that allows us to make sense at all, is nonetheless grounded in an apparent nonsense that transcends the Law of Non-Contradiction. In order to achieve *any* locatable identity in the first place, the human subject or the

---

20 Novalis [Friedrich von Hardenberg], *Fichte Studies* (Cambridge: CUP, 2003); *Philosophical Writings*, trans. Margaret Mahony Stoljar (New York: SUNY, 1997).

21 Friedrich Schlegel, *Philosophical Fragments*, trans. Peter Firchow (Minneapolis MN: Minnesota UP, 1997). See also Catherine Pickstock, *Repetition and Identity* (Oxford: OUP, 2013), 17—92.

thing taken in the subject-position has to claim that something also *is*, without reserve, what it is not. The table is round and brown etc.; it also is neither of those things and yet without them it cannot really be there at all. Likewise, I am not my name, my history, my location etc. and yet without these things I likewise simply vanish.

In terms of such considerations, Bulgakov declares that *any* name is at once both proper and empty and yet descriptive and universal, with only a series of relative variations of respective emphasis. One could well wonder if this approach does not entirely outflank that of Saul Kripke and his successors.

In terms, therefore, of the three fundamental grammatical and ontological positions, Bulgakov considers that he has exceeded and corrected Fichte.

First, the mysteriously fundamental subject, whose circle we can never exit, is nonetheless a co-situated subject in a sense less inherently problematic than it was for the German philosopher. If it has absolute depths coinciding with the divine presence, then this is not a problematic implied identity with God that we must ceaselessly and hopelessly endeavour to realise, but a given participation in his infinity mediated to us by symbolic nature and by the inspired signs and allegories of revealed religions.

Secondly, predicated objects are radically external to us and yet even their resistance is a gift of shared community in being. Our ceaseless advance towards the perspective of the divine Father is therefore also a quest for the perfectly answering and supplementing other. The Christian revelation has astonishingly shown us that this need not imply a quandary whereby we alternatively lose the world in the absolute divine subjectivity, or else abandon transcendence through an attempted pantheistic dilation. For now we realise that God himself is the infinitisation of our grammatical circumstance: he is only an absolute Paternal hypostasis because he is also Filial and Spiritual subjectivity.

Thus where philosophy seeks to overcome grammar by absolutising one or other of the grammatical poles: either the Subject (Fichte), the logical predicate (Hegel) or yet again the vital being of their combination (Spinoza, Schelling— for Bulgakov—and the pre-Socratics), Christian theology keeps them all in play. The truth is not a logical displacement of our ontological grammar, which already embodied a mode of faith: it is rather the doctrine revealed to religious faith that this grammar and so finite reality remains fully in triple play because it is a participation in an infinite triunity.[22]

Thus thirdly, the spiritual moment in God also infinitises the copula. For Bulgakov, the linkage between subject and predicate is neither aporetic (Fichte)

---

22 Bulgakov, *The Tragedy of Philosophy*, 123–30.

nor governed by logical negation (Hegel) nor yet either fated or darkly willed by nature (Schelling on one reading). Instead, the linkage is one of natural creativity and of specific art in the case of human beings. In all of nature the immanent and actively receptive hypostasising power of God as Sophia is at work to link subject and predicate together as ineffable beauty and to overcome the ugliness of extrinsic matter (as opposed to intrinsic body) that is the result of the Fall. In human beings, as described especially in *Unfading Light*, this is simultaneously the work of conscious self-creation and assisted recreation of nature in anticipation and prospective enabling of the final resurrection.

Our selfhood is not entirely and tautologically self-made as with Fichte, as from the very outset we co-create ourselves alongside our environment, and all of this process is but a participated if active reception of the divine creative act. Nor do we just 'posit' external things according to an intentionality that is merely an 'internal' imaginative creativity which half-accepts these things as resisting us and half tries to deduce them from pre-given *a priori* structures of subjectivity. The only external creativity involved in this Fichtean conception is a sheerly arbitrary attempt to reduce the impact of all external obstacles, to simply will them away, economically to master and control them.

By contrast, Bulgakov's sophiological and more Romantic vision actually *increases*, beyond Fichte, and with Novalis and Schlegel, the sense of an external creativity over things which even, as with Novalis, is granted a kind of 'magical' reach. Thus, we do more than posit those things with which we identify: in re-shaping them and bringing them under our purposive and spiritual (not instrumental) control, we actually 'bring them to birth' in participation of the eternal Paternal generation of the Son.

The somewhat difficult point to grasp here is that the Romantic switch to a greater realism *also* allows a greater external reach for a human creativity which is neither the operation of a pre-given logic, nor merely the assertion of will, but rather the realisation along with things of a shared teleology only intuited in the very process of co-construction. In the very long term one can venture (with some simplification) that Idealism is the remote offspring of Plotinus, who stressed the internal creative action of the soul on the body (which is not to be denied) and Romantic Realism the remote offspring of the later neoplatonists after Iamblichus, who stressed also the creative action of soul-plus-body on the surrounding cosmos as a ritual action which allowed the synergic or 'theurgic' working of the divine descent through ritual.

Bulgakov explicitly understood himself as lying within this legacy via the Christian mediation of Dionysius and Maximus, though he distinguished (however problematically) between the 'sophiurgic' operation of art and the more humanly passive and solely divine theurgic operation of the liturgy or *Opus Dei*. The redeemed Faust is for him a much more effective, if purely white *magus*, one might say.

5. The Mystery of the Name

It is indeed the theurgic dimension which serves to link Bulgakov's critique of philosophy to his specific mode of Christian piety. *The Philosophy of the Name* is a long and extremely sophisticated defence of the Russian 'Name worshippers' in terms of a complete philosophy of language. It is legitimate, Bulgakov thinks, to say that 'the Name of Jesus is God', though not, like the more extreme onomaphiles (Rasputin?) to say that 'God is the name of Jesus', because this is to confuse Subject with predicate. We should not say that the absolute Paternal hypostasis is exhaustively the name any more than he is the incarnate God-Man, or even the Second Person of the Trinity. Nevertheless, the predicate position is not straightforwardly subordinate to the subject position and can even be raised to co-hypostasicity, as most perfectly achieved within God himself—since there it is paradoxically required to exist as a co-subject out of the existence of the primal subject itself. Similarly, I am not my name and yet without my name in the widest sense I am not me at all. Unidentified, I am so lost that I do not really exist, for existence or 'being' is not, as for Hegel, an empty starting point identical with nothing, but instead always arises as the third position of habitual attachment.

To be is for something to be this or that in various modes or degrees. *Not*, for Bulgakov, in the Kantian sense that being is a mere existential copula that is not a predicate, but rather in the sense that the copula is always a judgement as to the real holding in place of the predicate or not—such that one could infer that, for the Russian thinker, 'possible' or fictional Thalers (Kant's famous example) do in fact really exist in some measure or other. For Bulgakov being is indeed not directly a predicate, but it is never detached from the judgement of predication.

Since, as we have seen, a name, for Bulgakov, is indeterminately general or proper, descriptive or vacuously nominative, he insists after Plato's *Cratylus* that no word and no name is ever *purely* arbitrary. Language (following Hamann and explicitly disagreeing with Gregory of Nyssa) cannot have been simply invented by human beings, because everything human already presupposes its existence and we cannot really imagine a world outside our articulation of it.[23] For Bulgakov, it is literally the world that speaks through us, and all language is originally poetic manifestation. Every word is really a disclosure of the 'idea' behind things which things themselves cannot fail to proclaim. In consequence, a defence of the Platonic sense of the universal goes along with a defence of the primacy of language. A forest is not a manifold exemplification of an abstract idea of a tree, nor is it plausibly an accidental evolution. Instead, it is actually more rigorous to think of every tree as really striving to realise one single, absolutely named most proper tree with which it is somehow identical. For were trees only realising a blueprint, then one might ask why they so constantly vary and alter or why they generate in time at all. Similarly, Bulgakov thinks that the Bible is right to speak of languages as fragments of one lost language, rather than being various attempts to express a shared conceptuality.[24] Outside language, such a conceptuality is meaningless, so the fact that translation is possible suggests a constant struggle to reunify language and recover a lost shared tongue—which attempt he thinks was initially realised on the day of Pentecost.

It follows that for him the name Jesus is the name of names and the word of words which unites us to the eternal Word and begins to usher in the eschatological and more final reversal of Babel. Just as the Incarnation is only an abstract affirmation unless Christ continues to be manifest to us through the shape of ritual and sacred images (which themselves bear named inscriptions), so it must also be conveyed through specific language. The name Jesus Christ, like all names, sustains a complex freight of association, including both acquired and buried onomatopoeic resonance. This is why, in the Bible, God names the world into being and throughout its texts naming and re-naming are clearly regarded as ontological and revelatory events.

6. Trinitarian Ontology

All this, for Bulgakov, suggests a Biblical metaphysics, pre-intimated by Plato, which in exalting naming or the proposition exceeds mere rational or logical

23 See John Milbank, 'The Linguistic Turn as a Theological Turn,' in *The Word Made Strange: Theology, Language, Culture* (Oxford: Blackwell, 1997), 84–120.
24 Other Russian contemporaries of Bulgakov, like the symbolist poet Andrey Bely, spoke of the partial survival of the pre-Babel tongue in the mythical sacred dialect of *Senzar*, in which all the great sacred revelations of the world were supposed to have been first given. See Andrey Bely, 'The Magic of Words', in *Selected Essays*, trans. Steven Cassedy (Berkeley CL: California UP, 1985), 96.

classification. Reality as such, spoken into being by an infinite subject, is itself linguistic or propositional. It is surely highly significant that, somewhat before Bulgakov, the Italian priest-philosopher Antonio Rosmini had come to a similar conclusion in his massive *Teosofia*, also in part through a reflection on Fichte, and also in explicit connection with the elaboration of a Trinitarian ontology.[25]

In terms of such an ontology however, one might conceivably detect ambiguities in Bulgakov. Is he not too Fichtean after all? In the later long article *Capita de Trinitate* he even speaks of God as a single hypostasis appearing in three subjective moments.[26] So is there a lurking modalism here, not so unlike that of the also Fichte-influenced Karl Barth? This, however, would be not to understand Bulgakov's radical purposes.

Throughout his *opus*, one of the intentions of his focus on the divine Wisdom is to undercut any too simplistic a duality of hypostasis and essence, whether in the case of the Trinity or of Christology. Yes, in either case, the difference of the terms is trying to indicate two incommensurable and therefore non-competitive planes, but this must not be allowed to override their nonetheless paradoxical fusion, on pain of impairing the divine simplicity.

Therefore, Bulgakov toys with a certain conceptual inversion: although it is less true than the reverse orthodox formula, it is not quite untrue that Christ is also two persons (as he is an 'atomic' human individual, as Aquinas eventually allows)[27] in one divine nature, since God cannot be divided. Likewise, though it is less true than orthodoxy, it is not quite untrue that God is one hypostasis in three natures. Here Bulgakov notably pleads the Cappadocian doctrine of *tropes* in his favour: in some ineffable way the three divine persons possess three different though not divided 'characters', which implies a certain incomprehensible variation of 'kind'. Conversely, the unity of nature cannot be thought of as anything other than the original and absolute hypostaticity of the Father. In a sense, the Persons of the Son and the Spirit are not 'new' persons, but necessary co-original manifestations of one and the same Personhood.

To a degree, indeed, Bulgakov remains Fichtean here—the I itself requires the Not-I and its linkage to it. But as we have seen, he has abandoned Fichtean self-making of the I and mere positing of the Not-I in favour of a relational

25   Antonio Rosmini, *Teosofia* (Milan: Bompiani, 2011).
26   Sergius Bulgakov, '*Capita de Trinitate*,' [in three instalments] in *Internationale Kirkliche Zeitschrift* 26, no. 3 (1936), 144–67; no. 4 (1936), 210–30, 35, no. 1–2 (1945), 24–55.
27   See Aaron Riches, *Ecce Homo: On the Divine Unity of Christ* (Grand Rapids: W. B. Eerdmans, 2016).

self-making through a creative giving birth to the other which still 'surprises' in its upshot its originator—just as a human parent is always amazed by their new baby and it is as if he or she had always been there.

It is for this reason that, in Bulgakov's theology, the divine essence as Sophia is not exactly impersonal, even if it is not precisely a 'fourth hypostasis', except when God reflects on his own essence as 'loving love' in an action that is co-terminous with the external creation. The result of this initial reflection and initial ecstatic giving is the bringing into being of the Plotinian sphere of the intellect or *nous*, which for Bulgakov is identical with Sophia as the world-soul—rather as for Augustine it was identical with the heavenly Jerusalem.

But what prevents, in Bulgakov, an unambiguous hypostasisation of Wisdom, either within God or within the Creation, is his important grammatical *qualification* of any outright personalism that would despise the blind witness of *things* and so of sacramentality. It is in this respect very important that his primary *vestigium trinitatis* is *not* social and relational, even though he builds up to that—such that the ultimate 'predicate' is the *Thou* and the ultimate copula is the 'he', which then allows the sophiological shared essential, but personal 'we' to come into being. Rather, his consistently very high valuation of the bodily, the sensual, the sexual, the feminine (as he sees it) and the sacramental, requires him to insist that the personal cannot emerge at all without a sort of sublimated fetishistic attachment to things, which alone supplies us with any 'character' or operable content. Adam, he declares, was lost in Eden, which lacked for him any charm till the arrival of the disclosive Eve. He required not simply a companion, but rather an ultimate attachment to another freely self-expressive 'thing' like himself, with which he could be corporeally united.

In a lesser way, all our speaking involves a continuous appropriation of things, including of those things that are spoken of in terms of their appropriation by other things, like the inclusion of the table in the dining room. For this reason, Bulgakov declares that the whole of a human life is actually one long string of propositions, or alternatively one long continuous proposition. But this is not just a process of realisation; it is also a further disclosure of the world through its further poetic re-creation. It is ontology as autobiography and shared history, because reality itself is both autobiographical and historical.

In consequence, the second, predicamental moment is first impersonal before it is personal and is even identified with *essence*, with which the primary hypostasis of the self must identify if it is to become a real person at all. This means that, perhaps rather surprisingly, Bulgakov consistently associates essence, both divine and created, with the Second Person of the Trinity, including its created echo. One might say that for him, and in very Johannine terms, we have to see that the Son is the complete Word and utterance *before* we can grasp the complete import of his personhood and eternal birth.

The essential rather than the purely personal also matters to Bulgakov insofar as, according to Trinitarian doctrine, it is essence, albeit a personifying, sophianic essence, that is *one*, whereas the hypostases are in principle plural. The lurking and somewhat disturbing emptiness of our self-hood witnesses to us that there can be other selves, in a way that the continuity of the earth, air, sea, sky and light does not, nor inversely the absolute specificity of *this* rock, beach, cottage or jug and so forth.

The problem with philosophy, to reiterate, is that it tries to escape this solidarity of grammar with ontology, whereas the Incarnation of the Word in person reminds the Universal Adam, and so all of us, of the primacy of the propositional judgement. The point here is not simply to rebuke philosophy, to say that it is all a terrible mistake, since even a philosophy that has tried impossibly to shake off its religious moorings, still nonetheless bears a negative and providential witness when it is foundering in the immanentist sea.[28] If it is a *tragic* endeavour, then so too for Bulgakov are human art and human economy. The artist is always, like the great poet Pushkin, prey to melancholy, as he realises that he cannot ever produce the work that is within him to bring forth. The economist is equally so prey, because he is always half-aware that what Bulgakov calls his 'gray magic' is an often meaningless substitute for the white Adamic magic of powerful naming, while only half-avoiding the black magic of demonic control of natural forces for the mere sake of such control. As the 'art of concepts', philosophy shares in both frustrations, but can begin to be redeemed insofar as it becomes also an exposition of Christian dogma.

7. Conclusion: Beyond the Critical Turn

As we have seen, Bulgakov's understanding of Fichte is pivotal for his work in both philosophy and theology. His attitude towards the German idealist is at once extremely positive and extremely negative. What does this double stance imply for Bulgakov's attitude towards the modern 'critical' turn in philosophy as such? If the foregoing analyses are correct, then he does not really accept it, and only finds it to be of value to the degree that he can subvert it and turn it metacritically against its own assumed intentions.

---

28 See Stephen Churchyard, 'Translator's Introduction' to *The Tragedy of Philosophy*, xxxv–lviii.

He finds it to be of value, to reiterate, to the degree that it exalts the human, the subjective and so the personal. But the Russian theologian refuses the post-Kantian assumption that to emphasise the subject is to turn critically away from metaphysics and towards the primacy of epistemology. To the contrary, he emphasises both in *The Tragedy of Philosophy* and in *Unfading Light* that metaphysics itself *first appeared* as a break with the 'physics' and monism of pre-Socratic philosophy, when Socrates started to enquire into himself and linked this inquiry to transcendent, theological origins.

It would then follow that the later deepening of such enquiries from Augustine through Kierkegaard to Bergson are naturally linked (as indeed these three thinkers variously supposed) to a renewed insistence on the metaphysical in an explicitly Platonic or neoplatonic sense. In this context, Descartes is a profoundly ambivalent thinker (as scholarship increasingly attests) who can be read either in terms of a deepening of the metaphysical or of a modern turn to the epistemological. As we have seen, Bulgakov construes Fichte's critique of Kant as a return to the metaphysical import of the Cartesian *cogito* which Kant had incoherently suppressed, while at the same time refusing Fichte's clinging to an absolute subjective foundationalism which inconsistently tries to erect metaphysics within a purely epistemological space that has already been called into question.

That is to say, once I admit that I am, as a knowing subject, fully real, and not just (as for the theoretical Kant of the First Critique) real as knowing, then it is indeed a kind of Satanic delusion to then try to suppress after all the secondariness of knowing to existence (which Fichte embraced to a still greater degree than Descartes, as we have seen) and to ignore the co-primacy in reality of all things and other people around me. For one now lacks even Kant's sceptical excuse to be a sad spider, spinning away in a dusty library corner.

Instead of claiming Bulgakov as a modern, post-critical thinker, one can rather situate him. alongside Augustine and the other named thinkers, as another great Christian theorist who, by re-emphasising subjectivity, also insisted on the primacy of a constitutive metaphysics as a holistic speculation which our very existential perplexity cannot honestly evade.

However, he does this in a novel way which is metacritical as well as pre-critical, since he rounds upon critical thought by stressing the primacy of language beyond the remit of most medieval thinking. Quite simply, the primacy of the modern knowing subject, or the subject of enunciation, is trumped by pointing out that this is always also the grammatical subject, or the subject of the statement. But with the primacy of the statement comes also the co-primacy of the predicated thing and its copulative link to the subject.

This Romantic and metacritical neo-realism is not just identical with pre-critical realism, to the extent that, first of all, it emphasises that our only access to the external real is through expressive appropriation. And secondly, to the extent that it realises (like the early G. E. Moore and Alfred North Whitehead)[29] that it cannot actually think any reality whatsoever outside the assumption that all of nature approaches in its structures the subjective and the propositional.

This is not then, a matter of our fated and self-deluded propensity to project. To the contrary, the fluidity of words, as between subjects and predicates, identified by Bulgakov, rather shows that we only begin to be as subjects at all by identifying with predicates already bearing within themselves some mode of subjectivity. A kind of totemism is at work here: I do not wrongly see the stream as a nymph; I only begin to have any sense of self in the first place by partly identifying with the stream, as with stone and tree and plant and bear and so forth.

All this amounts to an implicit claim in Bulgakov that a real linguistic turn *returns us* to metaphysical speculation rather than deepening the Kantian epistemological project. This then constitutes his challenge to Analytic philosophy at least in its Fregean and Wittgensteinian modes.

It is also clear that Bulgakov's preference for Fichte over Kant arises because Fichte's hyper-critique of Kant in one dimension points back towards realism. And following Hamann and Herder, the Russian thinker also applied his linguistic critique to Kant himself. The latter is accused of falsely trying to distinguish 'judgements of appearance' as merely subjective, from 'judgements of experience' taken as objective, in the sense that they fall under shared categories of understanding, especially of causality.[30] Thus 'I feel sad' is for this outlook subjective, but not 'he has fallen over' or even 'Mary has caused John to feel sad by spurning his love'. Bulgakov argues that, to the contrary, the fact that we can take simply 'he feels sad' as objective suggests that objectivity is already sufficiently secured by propositional grammar and not by a supposed placing of sensory or affective information under *a priori* conceptual categories. Because all of our understanding is linguistic, every appearance is already, if reflexively, judged as an experience, and nothing not already schematised or categorised by language ever appears to us at all. We have therefore no warrant for distinguishing the purely empirical from the purely rational, the *a posteriori*

---

29   See Fraser MacBride, *On the Genealogy of Universals: the Metaphysical Origins of Analytic Philosophy* (Oxford: OUP, 2018).

30   Bulgakov, *La Philosophie du Verbe et du Nom*, 85–112.

from the *a priori*, or the synthetic from the analytic. In consequence, a more 'internal' event of feeling is just as objective as a more external event of falling over, and the latter is no more certain or purely factual in character.

It can therefore be concluded that Bulgakov's critique of modern, non-religiously-based philosophy by no means accepts its 'critical' starting point, which for him is identical with this bracketing of religion. Instead, he offers us a Trinitarian ontology which newly accentuates the place of the subjective person only because it also newly accentuates the importance of things, of community and of creativity with respect to all of nature, with Humanity as its crown.

Inspired by Bulgakov, a more Biblically-infused philosophy can, in the future, lead us through grammar to wisdom, since the lesson of both is that personhood and essence are to be distinguished, yet never divided.

ECUMENICAL PERSPECTIVES

Building the House of Wisdom
DOI 10.17438/978-3-402-12199-3

Father Sergii Bulgakov's "Karamazov's excursus"

Pavel Khondzinsky

1.

As we know, Father Sergii Bulgakov took a keen interest in the legacy of Blessed Augustine, the pre-revolutionary book *Two Cities* (*Dva Grada*) containing some allusions to his works. In his triadological research, Fr. Sergii criticizes Augustine's concept of the Trinity, although ultimately he turns out to be not far from this concept himself. Moreover, to the final part of his major trilogy, *The Bride of the Lamb*, Bulgakov attaches a special excursus, "Augustinianism and Predestination," dedicating it to the problem of the relationship between grace and freedom. Not only criticizing (as we may guess) the position of the Western Church fathers, but also substantiating his own alternative point of view, Bulgakov in this excursus recalls Karamazov's revolt against "world harmony." We will try to establish how legitimate the reproach of Ivan Karamazov is, if addressed to Blessed Augustine.

2.

To begin with, let me briefly recall the main theses of Fr. Sergii. The excursus consists of three sections: "The Teaching of Blessed Augustine on Freedom and Predestination," "Toward a Characterization of Augustinianism," "On Predestination According to the Apostle Paul: Romans 8:28–30 and Ephesians 1:3–12 in Blessed Augustine's Interpretation."

In the first section, Father Sergii develops the idea that the "anti-Pelagian" doctrine of Blessed Augustine is centered on the thought of election (*electio*), which is entirely based on the will of God and has nothing to do with personal merits and faults. "Accordingly, the *donum perseverantiae* is given (or not given) not corresponding to merits but rather *secundum ipsius secretissimam, eamdemque justissimam, sapientissimam, beneficentissimam, voluntatem*."[1]

Any other point of view leads to the conclusion that grace is given according to merits, but this, as Augustine insists, does not agree with the thought of St. Paul. Grace always precedes, and that is why the Church prays for the conversion of the infidels.[2] The elect are chosen "'by that predestination by which God has foreknown His future works.'"[3] Although Bl. Augustine does not speak about predestination to perdition ("Clearly, Bl. Augustine is himself horrified by his own logic"[4]), this inevitably follows from his doctrine. Like Bl. Augustine, Thomas Aquinas and the Council of Trent (as well as the Orthodox Patriarchs in their famous epistle[5]) stopped halfway on this issue, whereas Jansenius and Calvin should be considered consistent in this respect. At the same time, "the question becomes especially burning concerning the salvation of infants who die at an early age, both those elect for salvation through Holy Baptism and those who are rejected for lack of it. [....] Their fate proved a quasi *experimentum crucis* for his entire theory, from which Augustine does not shrink (and, following him, neither has the entire Western Church, compared to which the East has the advantage only of not having defined the issue)."[6]

The second section, "Toward a Characterization of Augustinianism," expounds the ideas already mentioned. First, the duality of Augustine's position gave rise to mutually exclusive interpretations of his ideas. Catholics put an emphasis on the Church "as an organization of life in grace" outside of which salvation is impossible. Protestants focus on salvation by grace through faith. However, both of these approaches place an exaggerated emphasis on the importance of grace in human life, and "abolished anthropology along with its attendant teaching on Divine–Humanity."[7] In this sense, Orthodox theology, being free of the Augustinian past, has every opportunity to "lay bare the contradictions" of Augustinianism "and to intensify the problematic, which is exactly what is most important and valuable in this system.[8] With extreme

---

1   Sergii Bulgakov, "Augustinianism and Predestination," trans. Roberto J. De La Noval, in *Journal of Orthodox Christian Studies* 2.1 (2019), 69–99, 74.
2   Ibid., 72.
3   Ibid., 75.
4   Ibid., 80.
5   Cf.: *Dogmaticheskie poslaniia pravoslavnykh ierarkhov XVIII–XIX vekov o pravoslavnoi vere* (1900) (Moscow 1900), 172–73.
6   Bulgakov, "Augustinianism," 77.
7   Ibid., 82.
8   Ibid., 83.

tension Augustine raised the question of the opposition and incomparability of the divine and the human, taken in the complete omnipotence of the first, and the complete abjection of the second.[9] But he did not give an answer to this question. The answer in turn consists solely in the idea of Divine-Humanity (Godmanhood), "Divine and created Sophia."[10] Hence all of Augustine's hesitations on the issue of freedom of the will. More likely, Bl. Augustine "teaches not freedom but rather the unfreedom of the will."[11] Moreover, it still remains incomprehensible how this transition from the original freedom of man to unfreedom took place, because Augustine does not explain in any way how humanity (and a particular person) can be charged with original sin.[12]

In order to evade the answer, Augustine refers to the incomprehensibility of the Divine will; however, the motivation of this will, inaccessible to us, makes us recall the *deus ex machina*.[13] Anthropomorphism and rationalism are other consequences of Augustinian predestination. Anthropomorphism (clearly inspired by the anthropomorphic language of Paul the Apostle in Romans VIII, 28–30[14]) reveals itself in the fact that "the matter is presented as if God, before creating the world, thought things over, predestined them, and afterwards created the world according to the previously decided plan which He then implements."[15] The second consequence of Augustine's predestination (rationalism) consists in the attempt to provide answers to all questions, so that the unfathomability of the Wisdom of God turns into "the despotism of election, and in this arbitrary character there remains nothing of mystery."[16] An attempt to justify God in this way is reminiscent of Job's friends and "can satisfy only those who are already satisfied and hypnotized in submissiveness. *But then in others this theodicy provokes this Karamazovism: 'It's not God that I do not accept, but I do not accept His world'*" (italics mine—PK).[17] Meanwhile, in contrast to Bl. Augustine, St. John Chrysostom says, "But when he says, '*Which He prepared for glory,*' he expresses by this that not everything happens by God alone, because if this were the case, then nothing would prevent Him

---

9   Bulgakov, "Augustinianism," 83.
10   Ibid., 84.
11   Ibid.
12   Ibid., 84–85.
13   Ibid., 85.
14   Ibid., 89.
15   Ibid.
16   Ibid., 90.
17   Ibid., 89–90.

from saving all. And although the greater part belongs to God, nevertheless we add something small from ourselves."[18]

Finally, in the last section of the "Excursus," Fr. Sergii first criticizes Augustine's exegetical approaches in more detail, and then offers his own interpretation. The ancient interpreters ("beginning already with the Pelagians and Chrysostom"[19]) tried to find a way out by separating foreknowledge (referring it to human freedom) from predestination (which is a consequence of the former). However, "Bl. Augustine insists—implacably and not without certain formal grounds—that God's foreknowledge is also His pre-destination and is thus identical with it in one pre-eternal act."[20] This identity arises due to the fact that Paul the Apostle "in a deliberately anthropomorphic manner" inserts the pre-eternal acts of God "into the temporality of the world, into its past ages."[21] Meanwhile, these expressions are only a verbal form for expressing the love of God, which extends to everyone. "They do not in any way contain that limiting sense which was put into them by Bl. Augustine [...]. On the contrary—here the Apostle Paul speaks of (pre)-election and (pre)-determination in general, as the common foundation for both the creation of the human being and for the relationship of God to the world."[22] In other words, the *election* of God should not be related to "a limited number of the elect but to humanity as a whole, or, more accurately, to Divine–Humanity, which is precisely the pre-eternal foundation of created humanity."[23]. Esau and Jacob's example is purely historical.[24] The example of clay and a potter indicates only one side of the relationship between God and man,[25] the creaturehood of the latter. At the same time, all those who are rewarded with being are thus rewarded with the love of God, and the comparison of vessels for an honorable and shameful use, "in no way need be understood *in malam partem*, as an expression of the exaltation of some and the disdainful humiliation of others. Here it could not be more appropriate to recall the other comparison from the Apostle Paul concerning the different members of the body of the Church, equally important and necessary in all their differences (1 Cor. 12:14–26)."[26] In general, the text 11:33–36 should be con-

---

18   Bulgakov, "Augustinianism," 89 fn. 65.
19   Ibid., 91.
20   Ibid., 92.
21   Ibid., 93–94.
22   Ibid., 94.
23   Ibid., 95.
24   Ibid., 96.
25   Ibid., 97.
26   Ibid.

sidered a semantic center of the Epistle to the Romans. "If we can find here a teaching on pre-destination (within, at least, generally acceptable limits), then we must do so not with respect to an Augustinian-Calvinistic predestination of some for salvation and the abandonment of others for rejection, but rather predestination for universal mercy."[27]

3.

The first question that we may raise now is the question of how correctly Sergii Bulgakov was reading the works of Bl. Augustine. On the one hand, we must admit that Fr. Sergii really "exacerbated the problematics," focusing mainly on the theses about the death of innocent children as the main argument, which proves the absurdity of the Augustinian concept. We should say that Augustine really has all these theses. On the other hand, it seems that Fr. Sergii did not know Augustine very well. First, he did not use the last chapters of "The Gift of Perseverance," which could confirm his position. In these chapters, Augustine explains how the truth of predestination should be preached so as not to confuse believers. He thereby implicitly admits that in its straight form, it looks confusing to say the least. Second, Augustine can be much criticized for his theory of original sin as a punishment (*reatus*), which is removed only by baptism, even if a person (foremost a child) does not have personal sins, but we cannot say that he does not have this theory as Fr. Sergii insists.

Third, it would be appropriate to quote here a profound remark of Harnack's, whose works Fr. Sergii, of course, knew. Harnack writes: "When Augustine wanted to clarify nature, world history and the history of the individual, he fell into many contradictions and came to easily refutable assumptions. But there are things that, viewed from the outside, are false, while viewed from the inside they are true. This is the Augustinian teaching on grace and sin. As an expression of psychological and religious experience it is true, but when reflected in history it turns out to be false."[28]

Augustine's thought was indeed based on his pastoral and human experience, facing the facts that are difficult to explain. Why do the children of pious parents sometimes die unbaptized, while the children of impious parents have time to receive the sacrament before they die? Why does a righteous man fall into sin before his death, and the omniscient Lord does not take him away before his fall, just as some of the baptized babies do not die right away, but

---

27 Bulgakov, "Augustinianism," 98.
28 Adolf von Harnack, *Dogmengeschichte* (Tübingen: Mohr 1914), Vol. 3, 311.

grow up to end their lives badly? And are the babies who die after baptism those of whom the Lord foresaw that they would subsequently sin? These and similar examples and questions are often found on the pages of the treatises "On the Predestination of the Saints" and "The Gift of Perseverance," since Augustine faced them in his pastoral experience at every step. Namely, these questions and examples compel Augustine to construct the theory of predestination, which, in his opinion, is the only theory that can satisfactorily explain them. And if we agree with Harnack that this theory explains them "from the outside" and not in the best way, then does the theory of Fr. Sergii explain them better? He is merely silent about them in his text. It is not correct to reproach Augustine for identifying the concepts of foreknowledge and predestination, not in the sense that this reproach has nothing to do with him, but in that it would be necessary to criticize his concept of divine simplicity as a whole. According to this concept, he really believes that the properties of God, which are called various things in human language, are in fact identical.[29] In addition, while formulating the very concept of predestination in theory very harshly, from a practical point of view Augustine emphasized the completely Christian idea that no one can be sure of their salvation until the last hour of their life:

> Keeping this hope, *serve the Lord with fear and rejoice with trembling* (Ps. 2:11), since no one can be sure of the eternal life that the non-lying God promised to the sons of promise before eternal times, before this life of this man, which is a *temptation on earth* (Job .7: 1), is completed. But may the One to whom we say every day: 'Do not lead us into temptation (Matthew 6:13)' make us remain in Him until the end of this life.[30]

As for this text we can say in the words of Fr. Sergii: "The first half of the text addresses human will and freedom, and the second speaks of the Divine activity within us."[31]

It is also characteristic that Bulgakov, in his exegesis of the words of Paul the Apostle, refers only to modern Western researchers, and the reference he once quoted in the text to St. John Chrysostom does not speak in his favor, especially if we turn now to the broader context of the latter's words.

---

29   Cf.: Augustinus Hipponensis, *De Trinitate*. VI. 6.
30   Augustinus Hipponensis, *Antipelagianskie sochineniia pozdnego perioda* (Moscow: AS-TRAST 2008), 444.
31   Bulgakov, "Augustinianism," 99.

4.

Bl. Augustine, as we remember, assumed the notion of the guilt of original sin extending to the entire human race, of the incomprehensibility of the election of the elect (the foreknown and predestinated) and of the inevitability of death for those who were not chosen. St. John Chrysostom also touches on these issues. Although he recognizes mortality as the first consequence of original sin, he regards it not only as damage to nature, but also as a punishment which at first glance may even seem unjust: "It seems not quite fair for one to be punished (κολάζεσθαι), through the fault of the other, but for one to be saved through the other—this is more decent and consistent with reason. If the first is true, then the second should be true especially."[32] A little later, he again returns to this question and again wonders whether not only mortality, but also sinfulness extends to everyone, because by the disobedience of one, many have become sinful, and to be sinful "means people [are] subjected to punishment (τὸ ὑπεύθυνοι κολάσει) and condemned to death."[33] Much to our regret, the Apostle does not explain why this happened. However, despite this, we can derive considerable benefit from mortality itself, since because of mortality, for example, sin in us is not immortal.

In its turn, the question of foreknowledge and predestination in the Augustinian sense does not interest John Chrysostom at all. He recognizes the same problem as Augustine, although he resolves it differently: "God alone knows the worthy, and none of the people do, although they think that they know something well but they are wrong in their conclusion. He who knows secrets already clearly knows who is worthy of crowns, and who is worthy of punishment and torment. Therefore He punished many of those who, in the opinion of men, were good, by reproving them, and He crowned many who were considered vicious, and testified that they were not like that."[34] In other words, election is incomprehensible only for people who are deceived in their judgments, but in fact for Divine Wisdom it is quite consistent and logical. The apophatic theology of Providence in Augustine's works gives way here to a rather cataphatic approach. Assuming that Jacob and Esau differed in the foreknown virtues and vices, Chrysostom at the same time pays attention to the fact that "all Jews committed the same sin, namely, they made a molten calf. However, some were punished while others were not. That's why God said: "I

---

32 John Chrysostom, *Tvoreniia*, vol. 9 (Pochayiv Lavra 2005), 619 (On Rom 10.2).

33 Ibid., 621 (On Rom 10. 3).

34 Ibid., 727 (On Rom 16. 6).

will have mercy on whom I will have mercy, and I will have compassion on whom I will have compassion." For it is not yours to know, O Moses, who deserves My love of man, but leave this to Me. But if Moses had no right to know, much less have we."[35] John Chrysostom maintains that he speaks not about denial of free will but about full obedience and submission to God: "For as the potter (he says) of the same lump makes what he pleases, and no one forbids it; thus also when God, of the same race of men, punishes some, and honors others, be not thou curious nor meddlesome herein, but worship only, and imitate the clay. For He works nothing at random, or mere hazard, though thou be ignorant of the secret of His Wisdom."[36] Besides, St. John is not confused by the idea of the possible death of many people: "Do you see that according to Isaiah, not everyone will be saved, but only those who are worthy of salvation? I am not afraid of the multitude, says (God), and I am not afraid of the generation that has multiplied so much, but I save only those who are worthy of it."[37]

Thus, based on the absolute goodness and wisdom of the Creator and at the same time on the incomprehensibility of His decisions, to which we can only submit without reasoning, St. John protects both the freedom of human will and the foreknowledge, if not of deeds, then of the inner dignity of the elect for salvation. However, St. John gets away from these hard questions of Augustine's, and if one of the two lacks a consistent teaching on original sin, then, of course, it is more likely that it is John Chrysostom, not Augustine. Yet it is not necessarily a drawback.

5.

From everything that has been said before, we may assume that Fr. Sergii was reading Bl. Augustine from a somewhat predetermined point of view. Hence we must also raise the question of the origin of this point of view. At first glance, it is quite simple: Fr. Sergii needs to "exacerbate the problematics" in order to emphasize (as he often did on other occasions) that the only way out of the arising aporia is to apply for the services of sophiology. Sophiology, as he writes, is grounded in the idea of Divine-Humanity. Here we should remember that long before Bulgakov, Prince Evgenii N. Trubetskoi (in his dissertation dedicated to Bl. Augustine) opposed the idea of the independent value of Divine Humanity to Augustine's teaching on the two cities and the omnipotence

---

35   Chrysostom, *Tvoreniia*, 730 (On Rom 16. 7).
36   Ibid., 732 (On Rom 16. 8). Cf. ibid., 731 (On Rom 16. 8).
37   Ibid., 735 (On Rom 16. 9).

of Divine Providence. "The Kingdom of God," he wrote, "as it appears in the teaching of Augustine, does not reconcile humanity with Itself, for humanity is not content with the role of a means of a providential plan alien to it and wants to be its very aim in it."[38] Here we will also meet other motives, famous for us from Fr. Sergii's excursus, for example, criticism of Augustine for justifying the death of infants by the goals of Providence[39] or for the image of the Church as a world organization[40] etc. However, it seems more interesting for us that in his later work *Smysl Zhizni* (The Meaning of Life) Prince Trubetskoi reproaches not Bl. Augustine, but Sergii Bulgakov for underestimating the significance of human freedom and suppressing it with the idea of predestination. Let us dwell a little more on this unexpected turn of the topic.

According to E. Trubetskoi, Sergii Bulgakov mixes the Divine plan for man (the idea of a particular person) with his nature. "If the Divine plan about me is my substance or nature, I cannot but be a manifestation of this nature. Whether I want it or not, I am what God intended me to be and all my actions, whether good or bad, are the product of this nature, the phenomenon of Divine Sophia."[41] Besides, this leads to the assertion that Sophia, on the one hand, is the power of God, inseparable from God, but on the other hand, the substance of the world that is developing and sinful in its freedom. Trubetskoi believes that there is only one way out of this situation—to consider that "the idea of each created being is not his nature, but another reality, different from him, which he may or may not be combined with. The idea is that image of a coming, new creation, which must be realized in freedom."[42] On the one hand, the choice of the creature is predetermined by this image, so to speak, by the irrevocable task of God, but, on the other hand, this creature can either work on its implementation or refuse it.[43] In the latter case, "a free being affirms its selfhood against the idea, loses completely this image and likeness of God."[44] However, this assertion of selfhood in opposition to the predetermined image of God leads, on the contrary, to its loss, because "a being who has finally severed all connection with eternal life becomes, as a result of this rupture, an empty phantom with

---

38 Evgenii N. Trubetskoi, *Mirosozertsanie blazhennogo Avgustina* (Moscow 1892), 259. Cf. Chrysostom, *Tvoreniia*, 213, 245.

39 Cf. ibid., 206.

40 Cf. ibid., 101, 161.

41 Evgenii N. Trubetskoi, *Smysl zhizni* (Moscow 1994), 99.

42 Ibid., 103.

43 Ibid.

44 Ibid., 104.

no selfhood at all."[45] Thus, "*in eternity*, evil ceases to be real: phantoms without selfhood do not fight, because they do not live: therefore, their life is not the present, but the past that has perished forever."[46] This, however, does not mean that in this case the eternal Divine idea remained unfulfilled, since "eternal divine ideas are not only God's plans but they are living creative forces. If man refuses to be a co-worker and bearer of these creative forces, he will be replaced by another co-worker: whether he wants it or not, the fullness of divine life must come true."[47]

For the sake of justice, it should be noted that Trubetskoi in *The Meaning of Life* criticizes Bulgakov's *The Unfading Light* and *Philosophy of Economy*. Those who read *The Bride of the Lamb* (to which the excursus about Augustinianism is appended) may think at first that here Bulgakov's position has become much closer to that of Trubetskoi. Indeed, Father Sergii also says that each created individuality has its own idea, which he calls a "theme."[48] This theme-idea is a given, within which variations of created freedom or self-creation of creatures can be realized: "In creaturely creativity, we have, on the one hand, an inner *causa* lying in the depths of personal being, a *causa* as the ontological boundary and theme of being. On the other hand, we have in it the free, creative execution of this theme, its 'original development,' creaturely creativity, as the actualization of a new possibility."[49] This novelty is rather relative: as the themes-ideas themselves and the possibilities contained in them are always known to God, the creature cannot bring anything ontologically new into the world. At the same time, "in empirical ("contingent") being," the concrete actualization of these possibilities "represents a new manifestation for God Himself, who is waiting to see whether man will open or not open the doors of his heart. God Himself will know this only when it happens."[50]

The difference between individuals, which results from this, is not only empirical but also metaphysical, since each person enters the world, having already determined himself about the theme given to him.[51] Father Sergii says in one of his works that man can vary the implementation of his "existential

---

45   Trubetskoi, *Smysl zhizni*, 104.

46   Ibid., 105.

47   Ibid., 106.

48   Sergius Bulgakov, *The Bride of the Lamb*, trans. Boris Jakim (Grand Rapids: W. B. Eerd-mans, 2002), 96.

49   Ibid., 140.

50   Ibid., 238.

51   Ibid., 233, also fn 23.

theme," as well as that he may not accept it.[52] However, it is not very clear how this is consistent with the statement he insisted on earlier: "there cannot be a hypostasis without a specific theme, or an empty I, so to speak, an I that does not have its own individually colored nature."[53] But what is really more important is that "failure" in the implementation of this theme in life is not final, since there are no people who are so sinful that "the power of the sophianic image of God is totally annulled and who are completely incapable of good"[54] (that is, they would obviously turn out to have completely rejected their theme). Freedom, as absolute arbitrariness, is not given to man precisely because of a predetermined personal theme. Therefore, "the state of hell must be understood as an unceasing creative activity, or more precisely, self-creative activity, of the soul, although this state bears within itself a disastrous split, an alienation from its prototype."[55] Ultimately, there is every reason to believe that this alienation will be overcome "in the ages of ages."[56]

This last point seems to reveal the fundamental difference between Trubetskoi and Bulgakov. According to Trubetskoi, the number of Divine ideas is finite (similar to the finite number of the righteous in Augustine), but the number of created attempts to implement these ideas is infinite, since created persons who refuse to implement the idea are annihilated in non-existence and others take their place.

In Bulgakov's view, the number of ideas-themes is also determined by the Divine pleroma, but the metaphysical connection between the theme and the person who has accepted it cannot be broken even in hell. Therefore, either we must recognize in God a double predestination: to eternal bliss and eternal torment, or we must come to apocatastasis, for which the most risky variations of created freedom are of no essential importance, since the idea posited in the Divine Sophia cannot but come true.

As we have seen, Father Sergii is inclined to this idea in his interpretation of the Apostle Paul. However, he does not notice that in this way he himself is provoking Karamazov's revolt. Ivan protested precisely against the universal harmony in which a tortured child and his mother would embrace their tor-

52 Bulgakov, *The Bride of the Lamb*, 342.
53 Ibid., 96.
54 Ibid., 498.
55 Ibid.
56 Ibid., 499.

mentor, and that is why he said "It is not God that I don't accept, but I do not accept His world."[57]

Conclusions

1. Augustine's excursus completes the entire "Major Trilogy," and in a sense it is the final apology of its key message—the idea of Divine-Humanity. It is no coincidence, of course, that Bl. Augustine appeared on the stage in the epilogue. The idea of Divine-Humanity, which was put forward by Russian religious thought, had the concept of *De civitate Dei* as its global alternative, although it is not mentioned in the excursus.

2. Unleashing all the power of his philosophical genius on the teachings of Bl. Augustine on predestination, Fr. Sergii nevertheless makes a number of mistakes. Firstly, he does not know the works of Augustine thoroughly. Secondly, referring to St. John Chrysostom, he does not notice that St. John's position is not at all identical with his own, and in some respects (in particular, in recognizing the impossibility of giving a reason for the actions of Providence or in agreeing that a certain number of people are doomed to eternal death) is much closer to Augustine's position than to his own.

3. Father Sergii, apparently, does not notice that his own concept of universal predestination for salvation is no less destructive for existential ideas about human freedom and is no less fraught with Karamazov's revolt than the concept of Bl. Augustine.

4. To sum up, we may assume that, by completing the "Major Trilogy" with "An Excursus on Predestination," Father Sergii wanted not only to speak about the most important things for him, but also wanted to vie once again with Augustine, who obviously did not give him rest. It may be due to the opposition of beliefs, or it may be due to the equal greatness of both, or because of the excessively close and therefore annoying similarity, which the creator of sophiology (spilling *lux ex Oriente*) could not or did not want to put up with.

English translation by Julia Rost.

---

57   Fedor Dostoevskii, *Polnoe sobranie sochinenii v tridtsati tomakh*, Vol. XIV (Leningrad 1976), 223.

Building the House of Wisdom
DOI 10.17438/978-3-402-12200-6

Ships in the Theological Night?
Sergius Bulgakov and Liberation Theology

Graham McGeoch

Sergius Bulgakov is widely regarded as among the most influential Orthodox theologians of the twentieth century. His reputation has been enhanced in recent years by translations of his work into different languages (particularly English), and by his reception in the Anglo-American world, or Western theology, through contributions from the likes of Rowan Williams and John Milbank.[1] Bulgakov's influence is evident, too, in other worlds and other theologies. There is still no translation of Sergius Bulgakov's major work into Portuguese, although some work has appeared in Spanish.[2] Despite this language limitation, aspects of his theology can be found in Latin American Liberation Theology.[3] In what follows, I will explore some aspects of Sergius Bulgakov's theology that appear in Liberation Theology and highlight some major theological themes that Bulgakov and Liberation Theology share. I will also consider the 'silences' in Liberation Theology towards Bulgakov, all the more surprising because Bulgakov's contemporary, friend and intellectual foil—Nikolai Berdiaev—exerts a strong influence on early Liberation Theology.

---

1   Regula M. Zwahlen. "Introduction," *Studies in East European Thought*, vol. 6, no. 3–4 (2012), 159.

2   Francisco José López Sáez has translated and published *El Paráclito*, Sígueme, Salamanca 2014. He is currently translating *The Bride of the Lamb*.

3   In the remainder of this chapter, I will refer to Liberation Theology meaning Latin American Liberation Theology. I am aware that Liberation Theology is no longer exclusive to the Latin American region, or indeed to Christianity.

Sergius Bulgakov in Translation

Orthodox theologians like Brandon Gallaher acknowledge that Bulgakov's growing influence is, in part, due to the translation into and dissemination of his work in English.[4] Bulgakov's work appeared in academic journals in Europe and North America during his lifetime, but translations of his major trilogy only appeared in the twenty-first century in English. Two major translation initiatives of the Orthodox Church in Latin America largely overlook Bulgakov, giving preference to the work of Paul Evdokimov, Georges Florovsky, Christos Yannaras and John Zizioulas.[5] Some of the work of Paul Evdokimov and John Zizioulas has been translated into Portuguese and Spanish, respectively, by Roman Catholic publishing houses.

Paul Valliere has noted, "The Latin Americans showed little interest in Russian thought."[6] The reasons for this lack of interest include language and ideology. For example, Sonia Maria de Freitas claims there is an "academic silence" in the literature about Russian Émigrés in Latin America.[7] She attributes this to ideology. Russia was committed to communism in the twentieth century, while dictatorships in many Latin American countries were anti-communist. Furthermore, the Brazilian academic journal *Teoliteraria* dedicated a whole edition to Russian Theology & Literature in 2018. The edition hoped to explore Christianity without 'Western' constructs.[8] Articles reflected on the work and contributions of Fyodor Dostoevsky, Mikhail Bulgakov, Sergius Bulgakov, Paul

---

4   Brandon Gallaher, "Antinomism, Trinity, and the challenge of Solov'ean pantheism in the theology of Segij Bulgakov," *Studies in East European Thought*, vol. 6, no. 3–4 (2012), 206.

5   www.fatheralexander.org and www.ecclesia.org.br/biblioteca (access 2024/01/26).

6   Paul Valliere. "The Influence of Russian Religious Thought on Western Theology in the Twentieth Century," in *The Oxford Handbook of Russian Religious Thought*, ed. Caryl Emerson, George Pattison, and Randall A. Poole (Oxford: Oxford University Press, 2020), 660–76: 671.

7   Sonia Maria De Freitas, "Identity, Religion and Resistance of Russian people in Brazil," in *Migration and Public Discourse in World Christianity*, ed. Afe Adogame, Raimundo Barreto, and Wanderley Pereira Rosa. (Minneapolis: Fortress Press, 2019): 99–116: 99. Sonia Maria de Freitas is a Brazilian historian. Her work is perhaps symbolic of some of the work now just beginning in Latin America in relation to Orthodox Christianity. Normally, we can find some ethnographical or historical studies of 'foreign national' communities—Russian, Greek, etc.—which may or may not make explicit the study of religion within these communities.

8   Alex Villas Boas, Antonio Manzatto, Marcio Fernandes, Lubomir Zak, "Teologia e Literatura Russa: Editorial," *Teoliteraria*, vol. 8, no. 16 (2018), 4–10: 8.

Evdokimov, Andrei Tarkovskii, Pavel Florenskii and Nikolai Berdiaev[9]. Despite the mention of Sergius Bulgakov in the Editorial, reference to his work only appears in a footnote in one of the articles.[10]

Language is obviously a barrier. Yet, it is important to remember that the first generation of Liberation Theologians all studied in Europe or North America.[11] Language was not necessarily a limitation to accessing theological work. Furthermore, some of the most influential Liberation Theologians trained in France, Bulgakov's place of exile and creativity.[12] Notable Liberation Theologians who studied in France include Juan Luis Segundo, Gustavo Gutierrez (they both met for the first time in 1950s Francophone Europe[13]), Camilo Torres, Pablo Richard, Enrique Dussel, and Ronaldo Muñoz, not to mention the French-speaking Belgian theologian José Comblin. In a later generation, Elsa Tamez also studied in France. (Leonardo Boff studied in Germany.) There is no doubt that these first-generation Liberation Theologians are schooled in the French *nouvelle theologie* under the influence of Henri de Lubac, and in the Paris salons of Christian Humanism influenced by the work of Jacques Maritain and the intellectual discussions that engaged Roman Catholics, Protestants and Orthodox.

During this period, Nikolai Berdiaev emerges as an important influence on Liberation Theologians. Juan Luis Segundo is a major interpreter of Berdiaev's ideas, basing many of his books on an exploration of the key Berdiaev categories of 'personhood' and 'freedom'. In *El Hombre de hoy ante de Jesus de Nazaret,*

9   Boas et al., "Teologia e Literatura Russa", 9.
10   Lubomir Zak, Marcio Fernandes, "O romance como teologia: reflexões em diálogo com Fiódor Dostoiévski," in *Teoliteraria*, vol. 8, no. 16 (2018), 11–32: 18. Moreover, the footnote refers to an Italian translation of Bulgakov's work: *Lo spirituale della cultura* (2006).
11   Furthermore, the Liberation Theologian and journalist, Frei Betto spent extended periods in the USSR in the 1980s.
12   We are speaking about a period roughly from the late 1940s to the 1970s. After the 1970s, with the exceptions of those persecuted by the military dictatorships in the region, there is a turn to regional or national theological formation in Liberation Theology mirroring the import substitution policy followed by Latin American governments. For a classic account of this process in Latin America see F. H. Cardoso and E. Faletto. *Dependency and Development in Latin America* (Berkeley: University of California Press, 1979).
13   Gustavo Gutierrez, "Uma Amizade para Toda Vida," in "Dialogando com Juan Luis Segundo," ed. Afonso Maria Ligório Soares, *Ciberteologia—Revista de Teologia & Cultura* II, no. 3 (2006), 239–41. Both Gutierrez and Segundo studied for periods in France and Belgium in the 1940s and 1950s.

Segundo asks a question inspired by his interpretation of Berdiaev, "how are we to establish one goal above all the rest? That is the question. But it is obvious that this goal cannot really be known as the satisfactory one ahead of time by any empirical means. Therefore, every human being must take a chance on life, choosing as his or her supreme goal something whose value is not known in a personal, experiential way".[14] This question reappears in different forms in Segundo's subsequent work, even his most well known work in the English language, *The Liberation of Theology*, when he considers the freedom *from* and freedom *to* (for) discussion through the lens of Protestant contributions (Martin Luther and Paul Lehmann) and the shifts in Marxist thought, particularly under the influence of Eric Fromm.[15] Segundo is above all concerned with the fact that 'freedom' must be put into practice if it is to be liberation, but he recognizes that the moment it is practiced it has concrete historical limitations.

Sergius Bulgakov is interested in this discussion, too. He explores 'freedom' and 'necessity' in the *Philosophy of Economy*, particularly in relation to historical materialism. Bulgakov's rejection of historical materialism[16] is one of the major differences between him and early Liberation Theologians. I will discuss this further at another point in this chapter.

Bulgakov and Berdiaev, in different ways, broach similar themes. Segundo, and other Liberation Theologians, appear to be unaware of Bulgakov's writings on these themes. Instead, Liberation Theologians consistently turn to Berdiaev when discussing human freedom. In addition to Juan Luis Segundo and Rubem Alves, José Comblin became a late convert to theme of human freedom in Liberation Theology.[17] Previously Comblin had misconceived human freedom as restricted to a bourgeois concept.[18] When Comblin does turn to the theme of human freedom—over thirty years after Segundo—he turns to the example of the Zapatista uprising in Mexico[19] and to work of Nikolai Berdiaev.[20] In between the publication of the books by Alves and Segundo, and Comblin, theological students in the region—both Protestant and Roman Catholic— read Berdiaev (mainly in French) trying to find a Christian response to the

---

14   Juan Luis Segundo, *El Hombre de hoy ante de Jesus de Nazaret* (Madrid: Cristandad, 1982), 16.
15   Juan Luis Segundo, The Liberation of Theology (Maryknoll: Orbis Books, 1976), 150.
16   Sergei Bulgakov, *Philosophy of Economy* (Yale: Yale University Press, 2000), 278.
17   Rubem Alves, *A Theology of Human Hope* (Washington: Corpus Books, 1969).
18   José Comblin, *Vocação para a Liberdade* (São Paulo: Paulus, 1998), 181.
19   Ibid., 7.
20   Ibid., Vocação para a Liberdade, 15.

military dictatorships in the region. (Libraries of Dominican and Protestant seminaries discreetly held copies of Berdiaev's work).

Political Theology

Sergius Bulgakov's theology is a political theology. He was active in Russian politics before his exile.[21] After entering the Church, he produced a number of political theology reflections, including on the nature of the Church in relation to politics and polities, the experience of God in the modern world, and personhood. His reflections on personhood will prove important to Orthodox theology in the twentieth and twenty-first centuries. Indeed, personhood makes helpful preliminary distinctions between individual rights and human dignity—Bulgakov presents an altogether more social and communal understanding of the human being[22]—which have rumbled on through theological and political discussion of human rights into the twenty-first century.

Bulgakov's political theology advanced an example of Christian socialism independent from a Church which was, in his view, in collaboration with an imperial state. Bulgakov advocated for a Christian conception of politics independent of clericalism and Church interests. He developed a theological focus of reaching the poor and working classes in Russia, harbored a deep suspicion and offered a critique of nationalisms in Church and theology, and explored human freedom [liberation] rooted in love.[23] In this respect, the recent work by Robert F. Slesinski is worthy of note. Slesinski pays attention to Bulgakov's preaching, not only his scholarship.[24] This helps to place Bulgakov in the liturgical setting of Orthodoxy, but it also underlines the importance of the being of the Church as a political and theological praxis for Bulgakov, something crucial to Liberation Theology.

---

21 It is beyond the scope of this chapter, but Catherine Evtuhov's study of the Russian Silver Age ("a spiritual and cultural movement of great intensity") reflects on Sergius Bulgakov's contributions and commitments. *The Cross and the Sickle: Sergei Bulgakov and the Fate of Russian Religious Philosophy, 1890–1920* (Ithaca: Cornell University Press, 1997).

22 Bulgakov, *Philosophy of Economy*.

23 For a fuller discussion of these aspects of Sergius Bulgakov's theology, see Aristotle Papanikolaou, *The Mystical as Political: Democracy and non-Radical Orthodoxy* (Notre Dame: University of Notre Dame Press, 2014), 36–40.

24 Robert F. Slesinski, *The Theology of Sergius Bulgakov* (New York: St Vladimir's Seminary Press, 2017).

Bulgakov's political theology is an Eastern theology. His Eastern roots, and rejection of Western theological constructs, is clearly presented in *The Comforter*, his dogmatic exploration of the Holy Spirit.[25] This Eastern theology distances Bulgakov from some premises of Liberation Theology. Early Liberation Theologians are Western. I use the term 'Western' here to denote theologians from the Latin Church (either Roman Catholic or Protestant). I am aware that reading this first generation of Liberation theologians—mostly trained in Europe, and grappling with issues internal to Western theology—in this way is now highly contested. Indeed, it is rejected by some of those who interpret Liberation Theology as a decolonial theology or epistemology of the South.[26] While Sergius Bulgakov and Liberation Theology differ due to their Eastern or Western roots, they are quite similar in their critique of Western rationalism in theology. Bulgakov uses sophiology to advance this critique, while Liberation Theology uses the 'option for the poor'.

More importantly, Sergius Bulgakov and Liberation Theology are major contributors to the political theology of Christianity and Marxism. Olivier Clement noted that Liberation Theology faces "the problem of the contemporary encounter between Christianity and Marxism—or rather, very concretely, the encounter of Christians and Marxists in a 'Third World' suffering from the shock of adjustment to modern civilization."[27] One of the consequences of this encounter in Liberation Theology is the use of the Marxist concept of history (historical materialism) to articulate salvation history[28]. This sets Liberation Theology on a quite different course of political theology to Bulgakov.

Sergius Bulgakov changed his mind about historical materialism as a political theory of history. In the *Philosophy of Economy*, he decisively abandoned

---

25 Sergius Bulgakov, *The Comforter*, trans. Boris Jakim (Grand Rapids: W.B. Eerdmans, 2004).

26 I maintain that the early Latin American Liberation Theologians are Western in terms of theology due to their formation in Europe and the US, and due to the bibliographies that underpin their early works. For example, Rubem Alves' book *A Theology of Human Hope* (1969), while later promoted (particularly by Protestants in the region) as the first publication of Liberation Theology, actually engages extensively with the theology of Karl Barth and the philosophy of language of Ludwig Wittgenstein. Likewise, the pioneering work of Gustavo Gutierrez, *A Theology of Liberation* (1971), is firmly rooted in a theological dialogue with Johann Baptist Metz, Karl Rahner and Jurgen Moltmann, among others.

27 Olivier Clement, "Notes and Comments: Some Orthodox Reflections on Liberation Theology," *St Vladimir's Theological Quarterly*, vol. 29 (1985), 63–72: 64.

28 Gustavo Gutierrez, *A Theology of Liberation* (London: SCM, 2001), 151.

the Marxist concept of history in favor of a Christian theory. Bulgakov was increasingly ill at ease with the lack of human freedom in the Marxist concept of history. His development of Sophiology as an alternative to historical materialism is one of Bulgakov's major political theology contributions to human freedom. Bulgakov's is a freedom from determinisms. Liberation Theology's is a freedom from oppression.

Sergius Bulgakov and Liberation Theology

Aristotle Papanikolaou sees in Bulgakov's theology an anticipation of themes circulating in Liberation Theology.[29] Specifically, he identifies a struggle for justice on the side of the poor (and the need for Christians to engage with trade unions and be involved in education of the poor), and the need for theology to use the social sciences to engage in policy and political discussions with wider society.[30] According to Papanikolaou, Bulgakov is also keen to develop a Christian vision to counter the atheism underpinning some Marxist analysis related to human freedom (or personhood).

Papanikolaou's first two observations relating to the struggle for justice on the side of the oppressed is also recognized and interpreted as a key element in Liberation Theology by two other Orthodox theologians, Athanasios N. Papathanasiou and Pantelis Kalaitzidis. Papathanasiou distinguishes between social critique and social action in the life of Gregory of Palamas, in a reflection on Patristics and Liberation Theology.[31] The former is present, the latter absent from the theology of Palamas. Therefore, according to Papathanasiou, Palamas offers a possible form of Liberation Theology that stops short of Christian praxis. Liberation Theology would not accept this interpretation. Liberation Theology is first an action, and secondly a critique. This is why Papanikolaou's earlier additional observation, *on the side of the oppressed*, becomes so important in any discussion of social justice/option for the poor in Liberation Theology.[32]

Pantelis Kalaitzidis links the emergence of Orthodox political theology with Patristic traditions, and with specific contexts in Russian theology in the early

---

29 Papanikolaou, *The Mystical as Political*, 38.
30 Ibid., 39.
31 Athanasios N. Papathanasiou, "Liberation Perspectives in Patristic Thought: an Orthodox Approach," *Scientific Review of Post-Graduate Program 'Studies in Orthodox Theology*, vol. 2 (2011), 419–38.
32 Papanikolaou, *The Mystical as Political*, 38.

twentieth century.[33] He highlights the contributions of Bulgakov and Berdiaev, noting, like Papanikolaou, that political theology emerged in Orthodox theology long before the debates of the 1960s in Western and Liberation Theology. The attempts of Bulgakov and Berdiaev to articulate a Christian socialism certainly predates the 'Christians for Socialism' movement in the 1970s in Chile.[34]

Kalaitzidis also notes that Bulgakov develops a political theology independent of Church and State—something key to Liberation Theology. Although Kalaitzidis notes that Bulgakov does this with some degree of reticence.[35] Bulgakov's decision to appeal to theology and Christianity as the basis of a more authentic understanding of the human being and society in the face of historical materialism in Marxism most clearly distances him from Liberation Theology. The decision by Liberation Theology to deploy 'social analytic mediation'—and thereby Marxist analysis of society, at least in the early writings—moves it discreetly in the opposite direction to Bulgakov.[36] Bulgakov finds historical materialism (and Marxism) unconvincing in its understanding of the human being and human freedom. Liberation Theology finds historical materialism (and Marxism) convincing as a tool of social analysis. It is the different stance taken by each in relation to historical materialism (albeit with different subject matter in mind: Bulgakov on the human being, Liberation Theology on society) that enables us to perceive why 'Christians for Socialism' throughout Latin America, and Liberation Theology do not necessarily turn to Bulgakov's work. His contribution is bypassed.

Bulgakov's critique and practice of social justice did include reaching out to the poor, as a Christian praxis. Liberation Theology calls this 'the option for the poor'. The work of the Protestant missionary Richard Shaull is a good example of this Christian vision in Liberation Theology.[37] Shaull was elected to a Trade

---

33 Pantelis Kalaitzidis, "Eastern Orthodox Thought," in *The Wiley Blackwell Companion to Political Theology*, eds. William T. Cavanaugh and Peter Manley Scott. (London: John Wiley & Sons Ltd, 2019), 97–110.

34 Teresa Donoso Leoro, *Historia de los Cristianos por el Socialismo en Chile* (Santiago: Editorial Vaitea, 1975). This book documents the story of the movement in Chile. Notable in the movement is a focus on a critique of capitalism as a false God (based on the critique of Walter Benjamin). Notable too is the complete absence of reference to the work of Bulgakov and Berdiaev.

35 Kalaitzidis, "Eastern Orthodox Thought," 105.

36 Clodovis Boff, *Teologia e Prática* (Petrópolis: Vozes, 1982).

37 Richard Shaull was a North American missionary working in Latin America. On completing his studies at Princeton in 1941, under the influence of John Mackay, he was sent to Colombia by the Board of World Missions of the Presbyterian Church USA

Union Chapter in a periphery of Sao Paulo and he lived in a communal house in a working class neighborhood with seminary students and manual workers, where, in addition to group bible study, the house provided adult literacy classes to manual workers.[38] He had previously done something similar while a missionary in Colombia. Latin America is littered with examples like Shaull in the twentieth century. However, Shaull's Christian praxis, while committed to the struggles for justice and the use of the social sciences, was actually rooted in the theology of Karl Barth. Shaull's Christian praxis, sometimes erroneously interpreted as a form of Christian socialism, is in fact the proposal of a 'third way'—a Christian way—between capitalism and socialism.

Instead of bringing Sergius Bulgakov and Liberation theologians together—as Papanikolaou 'anticipates'—the question of Christian socialism as a viable and tenable vision is deeply contested within Liberation Theology. Shaull's example and theology contest it. Moreover, it is also deeply contested, in part, due to the third factor identified by Papanikolaou, namely the atheist premise underpinning some Marxist (and Christian) visions of humanism and human freedom. Furthermore, it is deeply contested in some parts of Liberation Theology because it is a 'Western' import into the region.

The use of the social sciences—heavily advocated by Liberation theologians—is technically known as 'social analytic mediation'. It is always recognized as the *a priori* to the theological task proper. However, there is considerable confusion about the relationship between theology and the social sciences in Liberation Theology today, and the role of the social analytic mediation played by the social sciences in the theological task. This confusion is not unique to Liberation Theology and is perhaps indicative of wider symptoms troubling theology today.

Pantelis Kalaitzidis attributes the reticence of Orthodox Theology to engage with the social sciences as a direct consequence of the dominant paradigm of "Return to the Fathers" (a form of de-Westernization) in twentieth-century Orthodoxy at a time when other theological trends were grappling with modern

---

(PCUSA). He worked for eight years in Colombia amidst rural and urban poverty, finally settling in a favela in Barranquilla. From there he organized workers in factories, developed a national literacy course, and built houses in rural areas. He left Colombia (reluctantly) in 1950 and then decided to study at Union Theological Seminary in New York under Reinhold Niebuhr, completing his doctorate at Princeton under Paul Lehmann. Shaull attributes his interest in Latin America to John Mackay, and his interest in social revolution to the theology of Paul Lehmann. He was Rubem Alves' teacher.

38   Richard Shaull, *Surpreendido pela Graça*. (Rio de Janeiro: Record, 2003), 120–22.

biblical studies, social sciences, hermeneutics, and contextual theologies.[39] In other words, Orthodox Theology turns from the Sophiology of Soloviev and Bulgakov to the neo-Patristic synthesis of Florovsky and Lossky at the same time that Liberation Theology is turning from Scholastic theology to the social sciences. Does Bulgakov simply fall between the cracks of both movements?

Yes and no, is probably the answer to this question. Bulgakov clearly conceives of theology differently from Liberation theologians. Bulgakov foregrounds the study of specific doctrines in his trilogy—*The Lamb of God, The Bride of the Lamb*, and *The Comforter*—addressing Christology, Ecclesiology, and Pneumatology on the basis of sophiological insights.[40] Christology, Ecclesiology and Pneumatology are favorites of Liberation Theology, too, with notable contributions from Jon Sobrino and Leonardo Boff.[41] However, for the most part, Liberation theologians do not foreground the study of specific doctrines. This is because of 'the option for the poor', or emphasis on Christian praxis. Nor do they base theology on sophiological insights. Rather, Liberation Theology foregrounds the 'non-person' and it sets out to describe the experience of God based on the 'non-person'.[42]

This different conception of theology has not prevented fruitful engagement between Sergius Bulgakov's theology and Liberation Theology. Bulgakov's influence is often subtle, and is mainly derived 'second-hand' by way of Paul Evdokimov's theology. Paul Valliere notes that Leonardo Boff engages with Bulgakov's sophiology and Evdokimov's use of Bulgakov's sophiology in articulating the *theotokos*. Boff's book, *The Maternal Face of God*, reflects on the feminine revelation and salvation of God—a discussion that he frames as *theotokos*.[43] It is clearly partly derived from Evdokimov's discussion in his book, *La Mujer y la Salvacion del Mundo*.[44] It is less clear from Boff's engagement

---

39   Pantelis Kalaitzidis, *Orthodoxy and Political Theology* (Geneva: WCC Publications, 2012), 76.

40   Sergius Bulgakov. *The Lamb of God*, trans. Boris Jakim (Grand Rapids: W. B. Eerdmans, 2008); Sergius Bulgakov. *The Comforter* (ibid., 2004) and Bulgakov, *The Bride of the Lamb* (ibid., 2001).

41   Jon Sobrino, *Christology at the Crossroad* (Eugene: Wipf & Stock Publishers, 2002) and Leonardo Boff, *Igreja: Carisma e Poder*. (Petropolis: Vozes, 1981). Specific discussions of the Holy Spirit normally appear in reflections on Spirituality. Hugo Assmann, Leonardo Boff, Segundo Galileu, Ivone Gebara, Pablo Richard, and Jon Sobrino, amongst others, have contributed to a vast literature on Liberation Spirituality.

42   Gustavo Gutierrez, *A Verdade vos Libertará* (São Paulo, Loyola, 2000), 22.

43   Leonardo Boff, *The Maternal Face of God* (London: Collins, 1989).

44   Paul Evdokimov, *La Mujer e la Salvacion del Mundo* (Salamanca: Sigueme, 1980).

with Evdokimov that he is in any way directly aware of Bulgakov's sophiology influencing Evdokimov's discussion.[45]

Silences

The silence in Liberation Theology with regard to Sergius Bulgakov does not indicate an absence, as the previous section demonstrated. However, the silence is surprising for a number of reasons. Firstly, there is an established Russian diaspora in Latin America. Russian literature (in translation) circulates widely in the region with Dostoevsky being a particular favorite among the Latin American cultural elites. Secondly, while Bulgakov is often overlooked, Berdiaev's works are influential in political and theological circles in Latin America. Thirdly, Bulgakov's political theology discusses themes widely resonant in Liberation Theology.

The silence is not surprising if Juan Lios Segundo's Liberation Theology is the framework. He intentionally produces a 'theology for atheists'. Bulgakov's theological intent—a religious solution to the ills besetting Russia—is of no interest to a theologian like Segundo, who lives in the most atheist society in Latin America.[46] Bulgakov, of course, after flirting with Marxism, developed a theology decidedly absent of 'atheist premise', instead rooted in the Divine-Human ideas of Pseudo-Dionysius, Maximus, the Confessor, John of Damascus, and given expression in the Sophiology of Vladimir Soloviev. Segundo moves his theology in a decidedly different direction in Latin America: "I will not hide from the reader that I feel seduced by the idea to revisit—with more logic and method, if possible—the task proposed by Milan Machovec: to write a Jesus for atheists. In other words, to tear from religion or its theoretical interpretation (theology) the monopoly of interest and explanation about Jesus."[47]

Segundo's silence is indicative of the wider silence in Liberation Theology with regard to Sergius Bulgakov.[48]

---

45 Boff, *The Maternal Face of God*, 78.

46 For the avoidance of doubt, the theology of J. L Segundo has no interest in re-Christianizing Uruguay, or bringing religion back to Uruguay.

47 Juan Luis Segundo, *A História Perdida e Recuperada de Jesus de Nazaré* (São Paulo. Paulus, 1997), 8. My translation. In the English translation of Machovec's book, the title is "Jesus for Marxists". In Latin America—in both Spanish and Portuguese—the title is changed slightly to "Jesus for Atheists". For this reason, Juan Luis Segundo writes about Jesus for Atheists.

48 The silence is even more intriguing due to the "French connection" in the formation and experience of many of the first generation of liberation theologians. It is also sur-

The silence on the sophiology of Bulgakov is worthy of note. Based on Soloviev's sophiology—where the Sophia is sometimes she, sometimes he, sometimes it—the recent Feminist and Queer Liberation theologies would be enriched by engaging Bulgakov's sophiology. For Liberation Theology, exploration of the body of God and the human body have been fundamental.[49] However, largely, with the exception of Juan Luis Segundo and later Marcella Althaus-Reid, Liberation Theology assimilated Western philosophical groundings of personhood (French existentialism) and continues to make use of social analytic mediation to critique Phallocentric Theology. Bulgakov's sophiology offers an altogether unexplored theological theme for Feminist and Queer Liberation Theologies.

Conclusion

In this short chapter, I have pointed to themes from Sergius Bulgakov's theology that appear in Liberation Theology. I have also indicated where some Liberation Theologians have engaged with Bulgakov in a more direct (or mediated) way. The work of Paul Evdokimov and Nikolai Berdiaev being of special note for Liberation Theologians. Despite the overlap of theological themes, the theological methodology of Bulgakov and Liberation Theology appear quite distinct. In particular, while Bulgakov appears concerned to offer a specifically Christian response to modernity, Liberation Theology opts to adopt and integrate aspects of modernity, including atheism, into its theological project. This places Liberation Theology firmly within the Western sphere of theology, even as a decolonial theology. Bulgakov's approach is Eastern, and at varying moments of his work, he is not shy in commenting on Western theology and its deficiencies. Those critiques would largely apply to Liberation Theology too.

However, it would be wrong to dismiss the links between Bulgakov's theological endeavors and Liberation Theology's praxis. Indeed, I think that Sergius Bulgakov and Liberation Theology can appear as ships in the theological night.

---

prising because liberation theologians are aware of Russian theology and appear to read Russian theology even if they do not always quote Russian theologians in their own work. For example, pastoral agents working with the poor translated *The Russian Pilgrim* into Portuguese, and José Comblin introduces the translation. Furthermore, the Dominican theologian (and journalist) Frei Betto (more recently anti-poverty advisor to President Lula da Silva in Brazil) spent extensive time in Russia studying and networking during the 'Cold War'.

49   Marcella Althaus-Reid, *From Feminist Theology to Indecent Theology* (London: SCM, 2004).

Not as ships passing each other silently in opposite directions, but ships sailing silently in the same theological waters (in parallel) in isolation of each other. Ripples are felt now and again, but neither ship is sure of where those ripples come from. Both conceive the theological night differently and therefore each ship can easily misread the stars that chart the course as they make their way towards the Divine reality.

Building the House of Wisdom
DOI 10.17438/978-3-402-12201-3

"Your Labor Is Not in Vain."
Sergii Bulgakov's Sophiology as a Key to a (Protestant) Theology of the Kingdom of God

Oliver Dürr[1]

'Synergy' and 'Mediation': Challenges for Contemporary (Protestant) Theology

This chapter examines the centrality of the notion of 'synergy'[2]—i. e., the (or at least some) possibility of divine-human cooperation—in the process of shaping creation towards God's eschatological kingdom. Modern theologies, in many cases, are critical of the concept of synergy,[3] but by the same token they appear to lack the metaphysical foundation to affirm what Paul makes clear in his first letter to the Corinthians: namely that "we are labourers together with God [θεοῦ γάρ ἐσμεν συνεργοί]" (1 Cor 3,9)[4] and that therefore our "labour is not in vain in the Lord" (1 Cor 15,58). The reason for theological reticence

---

1   I am grateful to the Forschungsstelle Sergij Bulgakov at the University of Fribourg as well as Harris Manchester College, Oxford for providing me with the resources and support for writing this chapter.

2   The term is used here specifically not in a heresiological sense, always already designating an 'unorthodox' position, but as a concept to be positively appropriated by contemporary theology and spirituality. I have developed a more detailed account of this in Oliver Dürr, *Homo Novus. Vollendlichkeit in Zeitalter des Transhumanismus. Beiträge zu einer Techniktheologie* (= Studia Oecumenica Friburgensia 108) (Münster: Aschendorff, 2021), 403–53.

3   I will argue below that this statement is not true across the board. Ultimately it reflects popular and polemic interpretations, somewhat forgetful of the theological traditions taking up positively the notion of 'synergy' even within Protestantism (see, e. g., Rowan Williams, *Christ the Heart of Creation* [London: Bloomsbury Publishing, 2018], 127–218).

4   All biblical citations are taken from the revised King James Bible, Greek quotations from Eberhard Nestle, Barbara Aland, *Novum Testamentum Graece* (Stuttgart: Deutsche Bibelgesellschaft, 28th ed., 2014).

concerning the idea of divine-human cooperation is that many theologians find it difficult to positively relate God's work within creation to human action. Therefore, issues like creativity and prayer strike at the metaphysical 'Achilles' heel' of decidedly modern accounts of theology that is the unresolved question of 'mediation'.[5] By this, I mean an unclarity concerning the ontological relationship of the Creator and creation, questions of transcendence and immanence, how the Infinite and the realm of finite beings relate to one another, and finally, insecurity regarding the relationship of divine and human freedom.[6] This unclarity leads to torturous debates about the 'efficacy' of prayer and the weight of human 'works' in God's kingdom.

Fr. Sergii Bulgakov's (1871–1944) sophiology is a helpful approach to the ontological question of mediation and, therefore, a fruitful background for a positive account of how human beings can substantially contribute to and even freely co-create God's future in the Spirit.[7] The late Dietrich Bonhoeffer (1906–1945) shows significant consonances with the sophiological intuitions of Bulgakov and Vladimir Soloviev (1853–1900) and therefore provides elementary points of departure for a (Protestant) theological metaphysics in appreciation of synergy.

Competitive Modes of Modern Theology

There are two extreme views, ultimately incompatible with an Orthodox theological account of 'synergy': 'univocity' and 'equivocity'. Both tendencies are simplified here and construed as types that will not do justice to most modern theologians. Furthermore, they are deliberately not associated with particular names, since the aim here is not polemic but to develop the contours of a metaphysical problem and its consequences for human self-understanding.[8]

The first of the two view refers to a tendency to understand God's being as univocal to created being, which results in a theology that will only accept as meaningful speech about God, cast in terms that are fully intelligible to human beings. For modern (Protestant) theologians, this is further corroborated by

---

5   'Mediation' is used here primarily in an ontological and not a soteriological sense.
6   As will be argued below, this pertains specifically to the questions raised by the existence of Jesus Christ himself.
7   N. T. Wright provides helpful biblical-theological perspectives that account for human cooperation with God in the Spirit but circumvent the metaphysical questions (see Nicholas Thomas Wright. *History and Eschatology. Jesus and the Promise of Natural Theology* [London: SPCK, 2019]).
8   For a more detailed account, see Dürr, *Homo Novus*, 479–91.

the way the scriptures speak of God's actions and personal interactions with his people in history. Such an approach locates Creator and creation in an ontic continuum and consequently has them wrestling for metaphysical space in a kind of competition. Where God wants to act, he must 'overrule' human freedom and the autonomy of creation; wherever he does not perform such 'miraculous' deeds, he is considered absent. Such theology cannot picture God's transcendence in ways that substantially differ from the distance of a deist God.

The second extreme is a theology conceiving of God's being as entirely equivocal to finite being. God in his true being is 'wholly other'—utterly different from and incomprehensible for human understanding. In an attempt to guard the 'sovereignty', 'power', and 'transcendence' of God, many modern theologians tend to stress the dichotomy between God and the world (i.e., Creator and creation) in such a way. This equivocal perspective—though from another angle—runs into similar ontological difficulties as the first: One can only understand God's transcendence as absence, and by the same token, God is banned from the world—rendering him again a deist God. Moreover, his self-revelation, presence, or even action within creation can only be conceptualized as a metaphysical act of violence—of a God forcefully breaking into creation.

In both extreme cases, the notion of synergy has to be considered metaphysically incoherent and cannot be consistently affirmed. Both (1) conceptualize Creator and creation as two clearly distinct entities in opposition to each other, (2) understand their respective being as mutually exclusive, and (3) see their respective wills as somehow competing. Both cases rule out from the start the metaphysical possibility of the God-Man Jesus Christ because for them, 'God' and 'the world' have become—in Soloviev's terms—abstract principles asserted in exclusivity.[9]

Back to the Beginnings: an Alternative Approach

Christian theology, in its historical beginnings, on the other hand, originated from the interaction with and reflection on the life, death, and resurrection of

---

9   Wladimir Solowjow, "Kritik der Abstrakten Prinzipien [1877–1881]" in *Kritik der Abstrakten Prinzipien und Vorlesungen über das Gottmenschentum* (= Deutsche Gesamtausgabe der Werke von Wladimir Solowjew 1) (Freiburg im Breisgau: Wewel Verlag, 1978), 13–519, here: 14. Soloviev's critique of abstract principles of thought is applied here to the relationship of God and humanity in Christology. Bulgakov follows Soloviev in this critique.

Jesus Christ.[10] It was after the fact of the incarnation of the eternal Logos that the great doctrinal disputes—which culminated in the symbols of faith—tried to grapple with the reality of Divine-Humanity as experienced in first-century Palestine and then handed on to posterity. Thus Christology begins—in Bonhoeffer's terms—with the givenness of the God-Man.[11] From these Christological reflections arose a different methodological approach to theology and metaphysics: If the infinite transcendent God can no longer be severed from Jesus Christ—though also not confused—then the revelation of the incarnated Logos must become the foundation for thinking through the relationship of creation and Creator in terms of a 'non-competitive'[12] Christian metaphysics (to use Kathryn Tanner's phrase).[13] Bulgakov saw this very clearly when he wrote about the need to both "connect" and "separate" the "divine-absolute" and the "creaturely-relative"[14] and suggested that this relationship can only be conceived in such a way if it is determined in terms of creation—which for him was the positive connection of Divine-Humanity that likewise sustains the ontological difference between uncreated and created nature.[15] The transcendence of the Creator God turns out to be a "transcendence of even the traditional

---

10 See Oliver Dürr. *Auferstehung des Fleisches. Umrisse einer leibhaftigen Anthropologie* (= Studia Oecumenica Friburgensia 91) (Münster: Aschendorff, 2020); Rowan Williams. *Resurrection. Interpreting the Easter Gospel* (London: Darton, Longmand & Todd Press, 2nd ed., 2014).

11 See Dietrich Bonhoeffer, "Christologie," in *Theologie—Gemeinde. Vorlesungen, Briefe, Gespräche 1927 bis 1944* (= Gesammelte Schriften 3) (Munich: Kaiser, 1966), 166–242, here: 181: "[H]ier [in Christology, *author's note*] steht nicht das Verhältnis eines isolierten Gottes zu einem isolierten Mensch in Christus zur Debatte, sondern das Verhältnis des vorgegebenen Gott-Menschen."

12 See Kathryn Tanner, *God and Creation in Christian Theology: Tyranny or Empowerment?* (Oxford: Blackwell, 1988) and Kathryn Tanner, *Jesus, Humanity and the Trinity: A Brief Systematic Theology* (Minneapolis: Fortress Press, 1998). Williams is right to assert: "The logic of finite and infinite overall has to be repeatedly clarified for the sake of affirming both divinity and humanity in their proper integrity" (Williams, *Christ*, 120).

13 Bonhoeffer writes: "Die Gegenwart Christi erzwingt den Satz: Jesus ist ganz Mensch—und sie erzwingt den anderen Satz: Jesus ist ganz Gott" (Bonhoeffer, *Christologie*, 180).

14 See Sergius Bulgakov, *The Bride of the Lamb* [1945], trans. Boris Jakim (Grand Rapids: W. B. Eerdmans, 2001), 33–56.

15 Bulgakov's sophiology, in short, can be understood precisely as a non-competitive metaphysics mediated in the unity of the divine and creaturely Sophia.

metaphysical demarcations between the transcendent and the immanent."[16] Thus God does not at all need to distance himself from finitude and mutability, and hence it is nothing intrinsic to creatureliness that separates creation from its Creator—instead, true transcendence can allow the utmost intimacy. This becomes apparent in the life of prayer and creativity: God can be both *superior summo meo* and *interior intimo meo*. The transcendent God's infinite act of being can—in the idiom of Nicholas of Cusa—be understood as *non-aliud* to every act of finite being because in the light of the God-Man, their difference turns out to be a *coincidentia oppositorum*.[17] Jesus Christ, as the self-revelation of God, manifests the ontological relation of Creator and creation and shows it to be one of harmonious hypostatic unity in the life of love. Bonhoeffer makes this point well: Because Jesus Christ is human, he is present in space and time, and because he is divine, he is in an eternal presence. Thus, Christ can be considered the "Heart of Creation."[18] Around him, everything falls into place and from him flows—through the Spirit—the life that carries the mystical intuitions, spiritual experiences, and the sacramental life of the Church to this day.

Sophiological Perspectives on Mediation and Synergy

The sophiology of Bulgakov seems to be, at its core, precisely this: An intuition of the dynamic intimacy of God and creation that—in Bulgakov's case—originated in mystical experience[19] and was sustained by his participation in the li-

---

16 David Bentley Hart, "Impassibility as Transcendence: On the Infinite Innocence of God," in *The Hidden and the Manifest: Essays in Theology and Metaphysics* (Grand Rapids: W. B. Eerdmans, 2017), 167–90, here: 169–70. This is explained in more detail in David Bentley Hart, *The Experience of God. Being, Consciousness, Bliss* (New Haven: Yale University Press, 2013).

17 See Nikolaus von Kues, "De non-aliud" in *Nikolaus von Kues* (= Die philosophisch-theologischen Schriften 2) (Darmstadt: Wissenschaftliche Buchgesellschaft, 2014), 443–556 and Nikolaus von Kues, "De venatione sapientiae" in *Nikolaus von Kues* (= Die philosophisch-theologischen Schriften 1) (Darmstadt: Wissenschaftliche Buchgesellschaft, 2014), 1–190, here: 62–68, see also David Bentley Hart, "From Notes on the Concept of the Infinite in the History of Western Metaphysics" in *The Hidden and the Manifest: Essays in Theology and Metaphysics* (Grand Rapids: W. B. Eerdmans, 2017), 165–66.

18 See Williams, *Christ*.

19 I am speaking here of the three mystical experiences he had: upon the death of his son Ivan, in contemplating the Caucasian mountains and with Raffael's Sistine Madonna in Dresden (see Sergij Bulgakov. *Aus meinem Leben. Autobiographische Zeugnisse* [= Sergij Bulgakov Werke 2] [Münster: Aschendorff, 2017], 55–64 and 106–15). On this mystical context of theology, see also Michael Martin. *The Submerged Reality: Sophi-*

turgical and sacramental life of the Church and then fleshed out by the attempt
to think both along with and through the dogmas of the great ecumenical
councils.[20] Bulgakov characterized his approach as a "Chalcedonian theology"
and was thinking through (as creational preconditions) the metaphysical implications of the mystery of the God-Man, which is "Divine-Humanity [...] the
perfect union of Divinity and Humanity in Christ, and then in general of God
and the world."[21] To be sure, such talk of the "union" of divinity and humanity
only confirms the greater dissimilarity (*maior dissimilitudo*) between creation
and the Creator, as Bulgakov states again and again.[22] When reflected upon in
terms of the intellect, this divine-human unity is comprehended "through a
glass, darkly" (1 Cor 13,12)[23]—this refers to the necessary apophatic qualification of his positive metaphysics of all-unity in the life of Sophia.

---

ology and the Turn to a Poetic Metaphysics. (Kettering, Ohio: Angelico Press, 2015),
specifically: 156–68, which spells out Bulgakov's approach to theology in light of his
mystical intuitions. I agree with Martin when he writes: "Sophianic insight—though
always informed by scripture, liturgy, and the traditions of the Church—is arrived
at experientally, mystically, [and] artistically" (Martin, *Reality*, 140). Nevertheless it
is vital to note that Martin's statement that Bulgakov "understands Sophia as [...] a
kind of fourth hypostasis" (Martin, *Submerged Reality*, 159) applies only to Bulgakov's
very early philosophical-theological thought (see, e.g., Sergius Bulgakov, *Unfading
Light: Contemplations and Speculations*, trans. Thomas Allan Smith [Grand Rapids:
W.B. Eerdmans, 2012]) but does not do justice to his developed thought after his essay
Hypostasis and Hypostaticity of 1925 (see Sergius Bulgakov, "Hypostasis and Hypostaticity: Scholia to the Unfading Light [1925]," *St Vladimir's Theological Quarterly* 49, no.
1–2 [2005]: 5–46).

20   Sophiology is, in Bulgakov's terms, a *Weltanschauung* (see Sergij Bulgakov. "Zur Frage
     nach der Weisheit Gottes," *Kyrios: Vierteljahresschrift für Kirchen- und Geistesgeschichte
     Osteuropas* 1 [1936], 93–101), a lens through which one perceives reality—and the pro-
     cess of thinking through what one sees and experiences mystically and sacramentally,
     based on the perspective of the great dogmas of the church, which themselves go back
     to the apostolic and scriptural testimony of the earliest Christians (on this see Aar-
     on Riches. *Ecce Homo: On the Divine Unity of Christ* [Grand Rapids: W.B. Eerdmans,
     2016], here: 61–62, note 21), and trying to explicate the metaphysics implicated by these
     formulae.
21   Sergius Bulgakov, *The Lamb of God* [1933], trans. Boris Jakim (Grand Rapids: W.B. Eerd-
     mans, 2007), here: 443 and Bulgakov, *Weisheit*, 97.
22   Bulgakov consistently and explicitly distances himself from any pantheistic confusion
     of the creation with its Creator (see, e.g., Bulgakov, *Bride*, 3f.). See also Riches, *Ecce
     Homo*, 247.
23   See Bulgakov, *Bride*, 37.

The sophiological habit of returning to the historical origins of Christian theology privileges life in the real world and historical experience over abstract conceptual thought.[24] Only secondarily can these personal and historical experiences be discursively systematized through rational thought and imagination. Bulgakov himself stressed the importance of 'personal life' in *The Lamb of God*: The "initial dogmatic axiom of Christology is the *unity of life* of the God-Man in His Divine-human I and the manifestation of the two natures, which are joined but not combined: not only two natures but also one life."[25] This "life of the spirit [...] is the living and inseparable unity of person and nature so that in concreto there is no impersonal nature or natureless personality; they can be separated and even opposed only in the abstract."[26] Unity in the personal life of a hypostatic spirit is thus, in short, one direction in which Bulgakov speaks about the "yes" implied in the "no" of Chalcedon.[27] It is one way for him to transpose the antinomic and paradoxical language of two natures, two wills, and two energies into a positive discourse about unconfused union: They are all "manifestations of the life of the spirit."[28] Man is neither separated from God nor fused or identified with him. He is rather "united in his life with God; he is correlated with God, interacts with Him, as the creaturely Sophia with the Divine Sophia, as a creaturely hypostatic spirit with a divine hypostatic spirit."[29] Such interaction and correlation take place in the relational life of hypostasis[30]—here designating the whole person as "realized action, the specific phenomenon or ensemble of phenomena in which a set of 'natural' or generic possibilities becomes concrete."[31] The sophiological language of hypostatic life thus binds theology back to the creaturely world of space, time, matter, and spirit—it is an incarnational (even practical) notion seeking the unification of Creator and creation in history and experience—and this includes laboring for the kingdom. As it was at the origin of the Christian faith when the God-Man was seen, heard, and touched (see 1 John 1,1), still today, the reality of Divine-Humanity is experienced in spiritual intuition, mystical prayer, and

---

24 I see Bulgakov here as less of a platonic dualist than others. The focus here lies not on the tension between an ideal world above and the mutable world below, but between abstractly excarnated thinking and concretely incarnated living.

25 Bulgakov, *Lamb*, 221, emphasis added.

26 Bulgakov, *Lamb*, 77.

27 See Bulgakov, *Lamb*, 44.

28 Bulgakov, *Lamb*, 77.

29 Bulgakov, *Bride*, 226.

30 See Rowan Williams, "Bulgakov's Christology and Beyond," above p. 25 ff.

31 Williams, *Christ*, 119.

sacramental life: They all testify to the mediatedness *in vivo* of Creator and creation.

Bulgakov made clear that such divine-human life is only understandable in the light of synergism (that is, the sophiological union in the act as revealed in the God-Man).[32] However, synergism requires not only a non-competitive ontology but, more specifically, a non-competitive understanding of divine and human freedom. In Christology, the notion of synergy is commonly associated with the doctrine of the incarnation and the life of Jesus Christ in the union of his two wills and energies (paradigmatically in the prayer at Gethsemane).[33] With regard to creativity, prayer and the transformation of creation in the kingdom of God, this can be spelt out in light of Jesus' resurrection. It is no coincidence that Paul's encouragement that human "labour is not in vain in the Lord" concludes his lengthy discussion of the resurrection. It is precisely there, in 1 Cor 15, that the apostle also presents his model of synergy: "by the grace of God I am what I am: and his grace which was bestowed upon me was not in vain; but I laboured more abundantly than they all: yet not I, but the grace of God which was with me [ἡ χάρις τοῦ θεοῦ [ἡ] σὺν ἐμοί]" (1 Cor 15,10; see also Gal 2,20 and Phil 2,12 f.). So, while the incarnation allows a Christian metaphysics to speak of the ontological possibility of divine-human synergy, the resurrection and subsequent outpouring of the Spirit ground theology with a cooperative theopraxis that realizes these possibilities in the act.[34] Through participation in the resurrection life of Jesus, humanity is graciously enabled to anticipate the kingdom of God in the free and dynamic act of life that is interpersonal love.[35]

For Bulgakov, both this possibility and its realization converge in Sophia, which is "the living [...] self-revelation of God in creation" and thereby the

---

32   See Bulgakov, *Bride*, 240. It is vital to note here that 'synergy' itself is not an exclusively sophiological notion—a positive notion of synergy is part of almost all reputable modern Orthodox theology, but not always presented sophiologically or indeed necessarily sophiological. (I would like to thank the external reviewer who brought the need for this clarification to my attention). Sophiology does, however, provide an elaborate and helpful framework for a coherent account of synergism.

33   See for example Riches, *Ecce Homo*, 128–52 and 177–91; specifically, 138–42.

34   Bonhoeffer makes a similar point: "Es ist der tote Christus, der wie Sokrates und Goethe *gedacht* werden kann. Allein der Auferstandene ermöglicht erst die Gegenwart der lebendigen Person und gibt die Voraussetzung für die Christologie, nicht mehr aufgelöst in historische Energie oder ein angeschautes Christusideal" (Bonhoeffer, *Christologie*, 180, *emphasis added*).

35   See Dürr, *Homo Novus*, 361–477.

"foundation for the unification of love for God and love for the world in the unity of the Divine Sophia and the creaturely Sophia."[36] In this sense, Bulgakov understands the kingdom of God as the full realization of the relationship of love between God, Man and all of creation: "God, all in all, the divine all in creaturely being, the Divine Sophia in the creaturely Sophia."[37] Moreover, this is to be achieved precisely through free divine-human cooperation in the life of the Spirit. The theandric task of the co-creative shaping of a world in which "God may be all in all" (1 Cor 15,28) is for Bulgakov at once the "task of man's sophianization by grace"[38] and creation's sophianization in and through man.[39] Thus a Christological model of synergy is inseparably linked with the doctrines of creation and eschatological consummation—and can stress both unity and continuity. It is precisely the realization that creation is not at all alienated from the Creator simply by virtue of its finitude and mutability that leads to a new realization of the ontological liberty of created nature itself.[40] It needs not overcome creatureliness; rather, it mirrors the transcendent God by more fully becoming what it already is.[41] Because man "is irrevocably rooted in a world that has become the kingdom of God," for Bulgakov, even "the life of the future age will consist in creative activity in the world."[42] For this, humanity is not to be taken out of the natural world but will be eternalized in and with it:[43]

---

36 Bulgakov, *Bride*, 521.

37 Ibid., 521.

38 Ibid., 226.

39 See Sergij Bulgakov. *Philosophie der Wirtschaft. Die Welt als Wirtschaftsgeschehen* [1912] (= Sergij Bulgakov Werke 1) (Münster: Aschendorff, 2014), here: 87–125. There is significant proximity here to the eschatological vision of Soloviev (see Oliver Dürr. "Christus oder Antichrist. Zur Frage nach der Kontinuität in Vladimir Solov'ëvs Eschatologie des vollendeten Gottmenschentums," *FZPhTh* 66, no. 2 [2019], 539–58).

40 See Hart, *Impassibility*, 170.

41 "Jesus Christus, der Mensch, das bedeutet, dass Gott in die geschaffene Wirklichkeit eingeht, dass wir vor Gott Menschen sein dürfen und sollen." (Dietrich Bonhoeffer. *Ethik* [Gütersloh: Gütersloher Verlagshaus, 2010]). Of course, this thought is further qualified by the crucifixion and resurrection (see Bonhoeffer, *Ethik*, 140 f.; see also Dietrich Bonhoeffer. *Widerstand und Ergebung: Briefe und Aufzeichnungen aus der Haft* [Gütersloh: Gütersloher Verlagshaus, 2005] here: 144; 204 / English version: Dietrich Bonhoeffer. *Prisoner for God. Letters and Papers from Prison*, trans. Reginald Fuller [New York: The Macmillan Company, 1959] and Günter Thomas. *Neue Schöpfung. Systematisch-theologische Untersuchungen zur Hoffnung auf das 'Leben in der zukünftigen Welt'* [Neukirchen-Vluyn: Neukirchener Verlagshaus, 2009], here: 352–54).

42 Bulgakov, *Bride*, 520.

43 See Bulgakov, *Bride*, 523 and Dürr, *Auferstehung*, 15–61; 127–58.

[T]he glory of resurrection [...] extend[s] to the world. [...] Therefore, although the future age is separated by the present one by a universal catastrophe of being, this catastrophe does not rupture the continuity between them. Human history is included in the life of the future age, continues beyond its proper limits, into meta-history. All that has been accomplished in human history thus acquires a new significance in the single stream of life flowing from the Lord.[44]

Divine-human synergy is not only the model of present human fulfillment but also its eschatological horizon.

Bulgakov and Bonhoeffer: Sophiology as a Key to Modern Theology?

Significant parallels can be drawn between Bulgakov's sophiological model of synergy and the reflections of the late Bonhoeffer, but they can only be outlined briefly here. In his 1933 lectures on Christology, Bonhoeffer—similar to Soloviev and Bulgakov—already made clear in terms of his 'negative' or 'critical Christology' that the Chalcedonian dogma sets a limit to the human intellect.[45] Its characterization of the relationship of Godhood and Manhood in Jesus Christ as without confusion and without separation is to be understood as an antinomic and paradoxical statement guarding a mystery (*asylum mysterii*) that cannot be penetrated fully by conceptual reasoning.[46] One cannot understand it in a detached mode of theorizing that speaks of divine and human nature as if they were distinguishable things.[47] For Bonhoeffer, the relationship between the two is a personal one that has become a fact in Jesus Christ—and Christian theology is speaking about God *post factum Christi*.[48] As Rowan Williams has convincingly shown, Bonhoeffer refuses to treat "finite and infinite as comparable forms of a single reality" and thereby shows forth a "basic theological clarity about the 'Godness' of God, and thus affirms the

---

44 Bulgakov, *Bride*, 519.
45 See the beginning of Part II of the lectures: "Hier handelt es sich um jenen Teil der Christologie, in dem die Unbegreiflichkeit der Person Christi begreiflich gemacht werden soll. Das Begreifen jedoch soll hier darin bestehen, das Unbegreifliche stehen zu lassen. [...] Die kritische Christologie hat zum Ziel, den Raum abzustecken, innerhalb dessen das Unbegreifliche stehen gelassen werden muss." (Bonhoeffer, *Christologie*, 205).
46 Bonhoeffer, *Christologie*, 205–06.
47 See Bonhoeffer, *Christologie*, 230; see also 179–82 and 199–200.
48 See Bonhoeffer, *Christologie*, 230–31.

classical belief that God can have no territory or interest to defend over against the created order."[49] Bonhoeffer increasingly makes clear in his prison letters that any God that can be pushed out of the world by man is not, after all, the God of the Christian faith.[50] With this crucial understanding of the Creator's transcendence, he did not need to shy away from talking about God's intimacy with creation. In one of the last letters, he wrote:

> Our relationship to God [is] not a religious relationship to a supreme Being, absolute in power and goodness, which is a spurious conception of transcendence, but a new life for others, through participation in the Being of God.[51] [...] [T]ranscendence consists not in tasks beyond our scope and power, but in the nearest thing to hand.[52] God in human form [Gott in Menschengestalt!]."[53]

Here Bonhoeffer articulates the rudimentary approaches of a Protestant model for what above has been termed 'synergy': A human being living "for others"—following the model of Christ—becomes "der aus dem Transzendenten lebende Mensch."[54] He is living the life of Jesus Christ and does human things divinely,[55] as the God-Man did divine things humanly.[56]

Bonhoeffer stands here within a longer tradition of Protestants thinking constructively about the relation between divine and human action and causality.[57] Two standard works within the Reformed tradition can be cited to illustrate this point: First, Herman Bavinck (1854–1921) writes in his *Reformed*

---

49 Williams, *Christ*, 169–217, here: 197. Bonhoeffer's argument can be summarized with Williams: "If God is wholly for us in Christ, God is never seeking to displace our createdness in order to win for Godself a space in the world; thus faith can never be a matter of securing territory within the world, over against some alternative space of human action and aspiration" (Williams, *Christ*, 170).
50 See Bonhoeffer, *Widerstand*, 140–44; 179–80; 182 f.; 186 f., and 191–96.
51 Bulgakov in comparison speaks of a "living participation" of creaturely life in the divine life (Bulgakov, *Bride*, 87).
52 See also Bonhoeffer, *Widerstand*, 96.
53 Bonhoeffer, *Prisoner*, 179 = Bonhoeffer, *Widerstand*, 204. He writes: "Das Jenseitige ist nicht das unendlich Ferne, sondern das Nächste [The transcendent is not the infinitely remote, but the close at hand]" (Bonhoeffer, *Widerstand*, 200 = Bonhoeffer, *Prisoner*, 175).
54 The English translation reads: "A life based on the transcendent," which does not fully capture the German rendition.
55 See Bonhoeffer, *Ethik*, 325: "[I]n der Liebe leben und zunehmen heißt ja in der Versöhnung und Einheit mit Gott und dem Menschen leben, heißt das Leben Jesu Christi leben."
56 I am adapting Aaron Riches's phrase (see Riches, *Ecce Homo*, 15).
57 On this wider context, see Williams, *Christ*, 127–218.

Dogmatics: "In relation to God the secondary causes [i. e., within creation] can be compared to instruments [...]; in relation to their effects and products they are causes in the true sense. [...] There is no division of labor between God and his creature, but the same effect is totally the effect of the primary cause as well as totally the effect of the proximate cause."[58] Secondly, Otto Weber (1902–1966) took up the same thread after Bonhoeffer and criticized competitive construals of the relationship between divine and human activity as if they belonged to the same realm of being.[59] Both show forth similar sensibilities with regards to the question of God's relationship to creation.

To conclude: Bonhoeffer probably would not have approved lightly of the positive formulations and style of Bulgakov's sophiology.[60] Nevertheless, his negative and critical approach to Christology resembles the apophatic critique of abstract principles that characterizes Bulgakov's approach.[61] Moreover, Bonhoeffer's considerations in the prison letters, qualified by his understanding of God's transcendence, suggest the possibility of a model of Divine-Human cooperation in the "life for others" that approximates unsystematically, and from the bottom up, Bulgakov's sophiological model of synergy. Finally, the clarity about the relationship between the infinite Creator God and his finite creation—that both Bulgakov and Bonhoeffer show—results in the courage to affirm Paul's vision from 1 Corinthians 15: Human beings actually are God's coworkers, and in God's kingdom, their labor is not in vain.

---

58 Herman Bavinck, *Reformed Dogmatics*, vol. 2, ed. John Bolt and John Vriend (Grand Rapids: W. B. Eerdmans, 2004), here: 614; see also Heinrich Heppe, *Die Dogmatik der evangelisch-reformierten Kirche*. (Neukirchen-Vluyn: Neukirchener Verlag, 2nd ed., 1958), here 200–01; 209–11 and J. Todd Billings, *Calvin, Participation, and the Gift. The Activity of Believers in Union with Christ*, Oxford 2007, 47–48.

59 See Otto Weber, *Grundlagen der Dogmatik*, Neukirchen-Vluyn, 4th ed., 1972, vol. 1, p. 570.

60 Assessing this and more generally to which degree Bonhoeffer's late theology is compatible with a robust, developed, Bulgakovian Sophiology would be a fruitful task for future research.

61 To be clear: This 'negative' approach is part of every sound theological approach and it is a strength of Protestantism to keep it alive. But this negative way should not be self-contained, or else it paradoxically enforces the Godlessness of the world and the wordlessness of God. Against such a tendency Bulgakov's positive assertions retain an apophatic shape and Bonhoeffer's negative approach remains dynamically open to the affirmative—in reflection and praxis.

Building the House of Wisdom
DOI 10.17438/978-3-402-12202-0

Sergius Bulgakov and Modern Theology

Paul Ladouceur

Sergius Bulgakov is a theological giant of modern Christianity. The originality, scope, and volume of his theological writings are breathtaking. As of 2023, some twenty-five books by Bulgakov (about 5,500 printed pages) have been published in English translation, covering most aspects of systematic theology. With other articles and essays already available in English, or in the translation–publication pipeline, about 8,000 pages of Bulgakov's writings will soon be available in English.

Yet Bulgakov's theology is little known or appreciated in theological circles, both Orthodox and Western, for three reasons. First, Bulgakov suffers from the general neglect of Orthodox theology in Western Christianity; typically, Orthodox thinkers are at best considered marginal to central theological concerns in the West. Secondly, Bulgakov wrote almost entirely in Russian, and until relatively recently, few of his major works were available in English. This has now been largely rectified with the publication of translations of most of his monographs and many minor works. Finally, key aspects of Bulgakov's theology are infused with the theology of Divine Wisdom or sophiology, a theology contested in certain Orthodox circles, and often bewildering for non-Orthodox theologians.

This essay advances ideas for an assessment of the influence or impact of Bulgakov's theology on Orthodox theology and, more tentatively, on broader Christian theology. Important methodological considerations surround the assessment of an author's influence. "Influence" in intellectual history is at best a slippery concept, with no clear definition or means of measuring the "influence" of one theologian on others. Some objective indicators are available, such as an author's recognition of another author, perhaps revealed in positive citations in publications. But often leading theologians do not provide such direct indicators of their sources; rarely do major theologians consciously recognize the influence of other contemporary theologians.

Faced with the paucity or non-existence of such indicators, more typically influence must be assessed qualitatively, deduced from indicators such as the adoption of ideas, vocabulary, or definitions by one writer from another—but both writers may have arrived at the same conclusions or concepts independently, and may even be oblivious to the other's theology. An external observer can only note similarities in ideas, without being able to discern direct influence.

Influence or "impact" may be both positive, the conscious adoption of a theologian's ideas by others, or negative, the rejection of this theology, at least on specific issues. For example, Georges Florovsky was certainly "influenced" by Bulgakov, not in the adoption of Bulgakov's ideas (at least not overtly), but in Florovsky's struggle for much of his career against aspects of Bulgakov's theology.

In a similar vein, Dumitru Stăniloae engaged extensively with Bulgakov's theology. Stăniloae visited Paris in 1928 while working on Gregory Palamas, although there is no clear evidence that he met Bulgakov. Stăniloae learned Russian to read Bulgakov and in Stăniloae's book *Iisus Hristos sau Restaurarea omului* (Jesus Christ or the Restoration of Man) (1943)[1] and in several other writings, he critiques aspects of Bulgakov's theology. In particular, Stăniloae distances himself from sophiology and other aspects of Bulgakov's theology such as Christology and anthropology, and considers Bulgakov's sophiology pantheistic.[2]

While many Orthodox theologians, such as Florovsky and Stăniloae—and non-Orthodox—report on and critique aspects of Bulgakov's theology, few actually appropriate his ideas. Simple mention of an author is insufficient to demonstrate influence, since many theological publications are historical theology, reporting on, analyzing, and critiquing the theology of others, rather than adopting, refining, or extending previous ideas to advance theological reflection. These factors come into play in the assessment of the impact of

---

1   Dumitru Stăniloae, *Iisus Hristos sau Restaurarea omului* (Sibiu, 1943; Bucharest: Basilica, 2013).

2   See Stăniloae, *Iisus Hristos*, 69, 105, 110, 118. Stăniloae's engagement with Bulgakov is understudied, but see Vasile-Ciprian Burca, "The Holy Trinity as the Source of the Unity of the Church in the Creative Theological Vision of Fr Dumitru Staniloae," doctoral thesis, University of Winchester, 2015, 30–42; and his unpublished paper "Wrestling with the Angel: Dumitru Staniloae and Sergius Bulgakov."

Bulgakov's theology on other Orthodox theologians and on wider Christian theology.

Is Bulgakov a Major Christian Theologian?

Important aspects Bulgakov's theology may be well known, if frequently criticized, in Orthodox theological circles, but this is much less true in broader Christian circles. This is demonstrated in Bulgakov's visibility in classic surveys of modern Christian theology, such as the five discussed here.

In the thirty-two essays (none of them by an Orthodox theologian) in the *Blackwell Companion to Modern Theology* (2004),[3] there are only a few passing references to Orthodox theology, mainly concerning Trinitarian theology. Almost all references to "orthodox" in the book are synonymous with "traditional" or "fundamentalist" theology. Among Orthodox theologians, only Florovsky is mentioned for his theology of redemption; Lossky and Zizioulas are relegated to brief references in footnotes, and Bulgakov is not mentioned at all.

The Modern Theologians: An Introduction to Christian Theology Since 1918 (2005) approaches modern Christian theology from three main perspectives: individual theologians; themes in theology; and "particular" theologies or ecclesial clusters in Christianity. Eleven of the forty-two chapters are devoted to individual theologians; none are Orthodox. Orthodox theology features mainly in a fine essay by Rowan Williams.[4] Williams focuses on Bulgakov, Lossky, and Florovsky, with briefer attention to other major figures. Except for Zizioulas, Orthodox theologians are hardly mentioned elsewhere in the book, and Lossky and Florovsky not at all. Zizioulas features in three essays, but Bulgakov only in one, with an upbeat, if isolated compliment in John Milbank's essay on Henri de Lubac, where Milbank ranks, without elaboration, de Lubac "along with Sergei Bulgakov, one of the two truly great theologians of the twentieth century."[5] Nor will an Orthodox theologian have a dedicated chapter in the forthcoming fourth edition of *The Modern Theologians* (2024).

---

3   Gareth Jones, ed., *The Blackwell Companion to Modern Theology* (Oxford, Blackwell, 2004).

4   Rowan Williams, "Eastern Orthodox Theology," in David F. Ford and Rachel Muers, eds., *The Modern Theologians: An Introduction to Christian Theology Since 1918* (Oxford: Blackwell, 3rd ed., 2005), 572–88.

5   Ford and Muers, eds., *The Modern Theologians*, 88.

Orthodox theology and theologians rank significantly higher in a similar book, *Key Theological Thinkers: From Modern to Postmodern* (2013).[6] Separate introductory surveys cover Protestant, Catholic, and Orthodox theology[7] in the twentieth century, and ten of the fifty-two chapters are devoted to Orthodox authors: Bulgakov; Florovsky; Afanasiev; Lossky; Stăniloae; Schmemann; Matta El-Meskeen; Emilianos Timiadis; Zizioulas; Yannaras. The selection is somewhat hit and miss; one wonders why major figures such as Berdiaev, Evdokimov, Florenskii, Meyendorff, and Ware do not merit a chapter. As in *The Modern Theologians*, Orthodox theologians figure little outside their respective chapters; Bulgakov is mentioned only in passing in the general introduction.

Orthodoxy, especially the patristic period, features reasonably well in in Alister McGrath's *Christian Theology: An Introduction* (2017).[8] But individual Orthodox theologians receive only passing references—except for Vladimir Lossky with four (compare Barth, with over fifty). McGrath refers to Bulgakov once, with Khomiakov, concerning *sobornost* in a discussion on catholicity in the church; sophiology is not mentioned. The related *Christian Theology Reader* edited by McGrath contains short extracts from a wide range of ancient and modern authors. The ancient Fathers of the Church are well represented, as are six modern Orthodox theologians (Lossky, Schmemann, Zizioulas, Meyendorff, Stăniloae, George Dragas, and David Bentley Hart)—but not Bulgakov (nor Florovsky).[9]

This brief survey of an admittedly small sample of general theological works illustrates the problem of assessing the impact of modern Orthodox theologians, including Bulgakov. Unless the author or editor(s) has a particular interest in Orthodoxy—as is the case in *Key Theological Thinkers*—modern Orthodox authors are unlikely to feature significantly (as in the case of McGrath), or be relegated mostly to an "Orthodox chapter" (*The Modern Theologians*).

Quantitative indicators of the importance or influence of Bulgakov, and of Orthodox theology in general, produce disappointing results, but indicate that Orthodox theology, including Bulgakov, carries little weight in wider Chris-

---

6 Staale Kristiansen and Svein Rise, eds., *Key Theological Thinkers: From Modern to Postmodern* (Burlington, VT: Ashgate, 2013).

7 Aristotle Papanikolaou, "Orthodox Theology in the Twentieth Century," *Key Theological Thinkers*, 53–62.

8 Alister McGrath, *Christian Theology: An Introduction* (Oxford: Wiley Blackwell, 6th ed., 2017).

9 Alister McGrath, *The Christian Theology Reader* (Oxford: Wiley Blackwell, 5th ed., 2017).

tian theological circles, despite a century of significant exposure to Orthodox theology in the West. Qualitative approaches may yield more positive results.

Some Qualitative Assessments

In a 2020 essay, Paul Valliere tracks the influence of the Russian religious renaissance in modern theology in six Western theological milieux: Karl Barth and later evangelical Protestants; liberal Protestants; Anglicans; Yves Congar and Roman Catholic ecumenism; *nouvelle théologie* and *ressourcement*; and liberation theology and feminism.[10] Despite pockets of influence of Russian religious thought in these areas, overall impact is limited, but perhaps strongest, among Catholics and Anglicans, in key figures such as Yves Congar, Henri de Lubac, Hans Urs von Balthasar, Louis Bouyer (a Lutheran who became Catholic), Michael Ramsay, and Rowan Williams, and more limited in some major Protestant theologians, especially Paul Tillich, Reinhold Niebuhr, and Jaroslav Pelikan (a Lutheran who became Orthodox). Although Karl Barth was acquainted with some Russian theologians, notably Bulgakov and Florovsky, in his vast *Church Dogmatics* he does not refer at all, as Valliere wistfully notes, "to modern Orthodoxy's greatest dogmatic theologian."[11]

Valliere identifies Bulgakov's influence especially in Paul Tillich's adoption of "panentheism" to sum up his vision of the consummation of all things (which Bulgakov also uses for his sophiology); Rowan Williams on social and political theology and on kenotic personalism; Yves Congar on *sobornost*, hierarchy in the church, and pneumatology, especially Bulgakov's consideration of the *filioque* as a *theologoumenon* rather than a heresy; Henri de Lubac on synergy as the reconciliation of divine grace and human freedom; Hans Urs von Balthasar on kenotic Trinitarianism; and Louis Bouyer in his focus on God–world relations and the structure of his writings (three theological trilogies).

The impact of Russian religious thought, especially Bulgakov, is especially evident in three major twentieth-century Catholic personalities: Louis Bouyer, Thomas Merton, and Hans Urs von Balthasar.

Louis Bouyer (1913–2004), an important French Catholic theologian in the late twentieth century, was strongly influenced by Bulgakov, whom he met in

---

10 Paul Valliere, "The Influence of Russian Religious Thought on Western Theology in the Twentieth Century," in Caryl Emerson, George Pattison, and Randall A. Poole, eds., *The Oxford Handbook of Russian Religious Thought* (Oxford: Oxford University Press, 2020), 660–76.

11 Valliere, "Russian Religious Thought," 663.

the 1930s. Bouyer adopted sophiology as a key motif in his theology, reflected in numerous monographs. He was struck especially by Bulgakov's sophiology as an insight into God's presence in creation, largely setting aside ontological issues in sophiology to focus on its practical applications in God-world relations: "The main characteristic of divine Wisdom is that it is an eternal thought of God concerning creation as a whole."[12] Bouyer finds sophiology interpreted as divine presence in creation throughout Christianity, from the Old Testament to St. Paul, Athanasius, Augustine, Maximus, Aquinas, and Eckhart, then in the mystical lineage from Jakob Boehme to the German idealists, and thence to the Russians. Bouyer adopts many of Bulgakov's sophiological themes, such as uncreated/created Wisdom, and the dedication of churches to Holy Wisdom and their association with the Mother of God. Bouyer interprets sophiology basically as panentheism, as did Bulgakov himself (see below). In a glowing eulogy of Bulgakov, Bouyer cites approvingly from Bulgakov's account of his visit to Hagia Sophia in Constantinople in 1923, where Bulgakov writes of Sophia as "the real unity of the world in the Logos, the co-inherence of all with all, the world of divine ideas."[13]

The monk and spiritual writer Thomas Merton (1915–1968), in the last decade of his life, was also strongly influenced by sophiology, from the works of Soloviev, Bulgakov, Berdiaev, and Evdokimov[14] (although the last two cannot be considered "sophiologists"). Merton's actual acquaintance with Bulgakov's writings was likely very limited, most probably to the two books available to Merton in English, *The Orthodox Church* (1935) and especially *Sophia: The Wisdom of God* (1937). Merton was struck, like Bouyer, by the sophiological perception of the divine presence in creation, conveyed in Bulgakov's notion of "Created Wisdom," which Merton perceived as the principal insight of sophiology: "[God] speaks to us gently in ten thousand things, in which his light is one fulness and one Wisdom," writes Merton in his prose poem "Hagia Sophia" (1962); "Thus he shines not on them but from within them. Such is the lov-

---

12 Louis Bouyer, "An Introduction to the Theme of Wisdom and Creation in the Tradition," *Le Messager orthodoxe* 98 (1985), 154. For a more extensive treatment of Bouyer's cosmology, see his *Cosmos: The World and the Glory of God* (Petersham, MA: St. Bede's Publications, 1988). Bulgakov and John Henry Newman are the most cited theologians in this work.

13 Louis Bouyer, "La personnalité et l'œuvre de Serge Bulgakov (1871–1944)," *Nova et Vetera* 53 (1978): 144; Sergius Bulgakov, "Hagia Sophia," in James Pain, Nicolas Zernov, eds., *Sergius Bulgakov: An Anthology* (London: SPCK, 1976), 13.

14 See Christopher Pramuk, *Sophia, The Hidden Christ of Thomas Merton* (Collegeville, MN: Liturgical Press, 2009).

ing-kindness of Wisdom."[15] For Merton, the writings of Bulgakov and Berdiaev transmit "the light of the resurrection and theirs is a theology of triumph"; they dared "to say something great and worthy of God."[16] Merton united Bulgakov's Divine Wisdom with the *logoi* of things of Maximus the Confessor, and incorporated into his perception of creation other key notions of Bulgakov, writing, for example, that the Blessed Virgin Mary "can be said to be a personal manifestation of Sophia, who in God is *Ousia* rather than Person."[17]

Thomas Merton's theopoetic assimilation of sophiology focuses, like Bouyer, not on the ontological mechanics of Divine Wisdom, but rather on the re-enchantment of creation manifesting God's presence and glory as Creator and Sustainer of all—when God will be "all in all" (1 Cor. 15:28), as Bulgakov constantly reiterates. In this, Merton is also close to related notions in Schmemann and Zizioulas, such as "the world as sacrament" and humanity as priests of creation, offering to God God's own creation.[18]

Hans Urs von Balthasar (1905–1988) studied Soloviev, Berdiaev, and Bulgakov. Jennifer Newsome Martin concludes that for Balthasar, Berdiaev strays "beyond the boundaries of licit theological speculation"; Soloviev gets a better rating as "a genuinely Christological thinker informed mostly deeply by Scripture and the Fathers"; but Bulgakov is "absolutely formative for Balthasar [...] Balthasar incorporates many of Bulgakov's reflections into the heart of his own theology." Martin summarizes Bulgakov's themes assimilated by von Balthasar: his unusual interpretation of Christ's descent into hell, sustained attention to the theology of Holy Saturday, interest in the universality of human salvation, Trinitarian understanding of the symbol of Ur-kenosis that includes within it the creation of the world as the exteriorization and kenotic expression of God, dyadic action of Son and the Spirit, the apocalyptic symbol of the Lamb as though slain from the book of Revelation, and the decisive turn to pneumatology.[19]

---

15 Thomas Merton, "Hagia Sophia," in Pramuk, 303.

16 Merton's Dairy, 25 April 1957, cited in Pramuk, 11.

17 Merton, "Hagia Sophia," 305.

18 The first edition of Alexander Schmemann's *For the Life of the World: Sacraments and Orthodoxy* was entitled *The World as Sacrament* (Darton, Longman & Todd, 1966); John Zizioulas, "Man the Priest of Creation: A Response to the Ecological Problem," in Andrew Walker and Costa Carras, eds., *Living Orthodoxy in the Modern World: Orthodox Christianity & Society* (Crestwood, NY: St. Vladimir's Seminary Press, 1996), 178–88.

19 Jennifer Newsome Martin, *Hans Urs von Balthasar and the Critical Appropriation of Russian Religious Thought* (Notre Dame, IN: University of Notre Dame Press, 2015), 206–07. See David Bentley Hart's reading of Martin: "Martin and Gallaher on Bulga-

Bulgakov's sophiology also features in the Radical Orthodoxy movement. John Milbank, the most well-known exponent of Radical Orthodoxy, considers that sophiology is "perhaps the most significant theology of the two preceding centuries."[20] Despite this high praise, sophiology, even in its panentheistic mode, does not feature in the theological foundations of Radical Orthodoxy; neither Bulgakov nor sophiology are mentioned in the key publication *Radical Orthodoxy: A New Theology* (1999).[21]

The remainder of this essay surveys three theological areas where Bulgakov's influence is most visible, especially in the Orthodox context.

Panentheism

Although Bulgakov's sophiology has not found much echo among Orthodox and non-Orthodox theologians beyond historical theology, Bulgakov also placed sophiology within the philosophical notion of panentheism. To distance himself from Soloviev's subtly pantheistic philosophical-theological system, Bulgakov emphasizes God's transcendence to creation and God as Creator, while maintaining the prime panentheist affirmation that God is in creation and creation in God: nothing can exist apart from God; all created beings are constantly sustained by the divine will and hence are somehow "in God."[22] Even the notion that God creates *ex nihilo* is not absolute, since creation has a form of existence in God before it is actualized.[23]

Bulgakov's cosmology fuses panentheism and sophiology, into which he also assimilates the patristic notion of the divine energies, in a complex and not entirely coherent system that seeks to maintain an antinomic balance between God as utterly transcendent and yet radically immanent. He defines his theology as panentheist, defending it against the accusation of pantheism

---

kov," *Theological Territories* (Notre Dame, IN: University of Notre Dame Press, 2020), 55–64.

20 John Milbank, "Sophiology and Theurgy: The New Theological Horizon," in Adrian Pabst and Chistoph Schneider, eds., *Encounter Between Eastern Orthodoxy and Radical Orthodoxy: Transfiguring the World Through the Word* (Burlington, VT: Ashgate, 2009), 45.

21 John Milbank, Catherine Pickstock, and Graham Ward, eds., *Radical Orthodoxy: A New Theology* (London: Routledge, 1999).

22 See for example, Sergius Bulgakov, *Judas Iscarioth, L'Apôtre félon* (1931) (Geneva: Syrtes, 2015), 102–04.

23 Sergius Bulgakov, *Sophia, the Wisdom of God: An Outline of Sophiology* (1937) (Hudson NY: Lindisfarne Press, 1993), 63–64, 72.

brought against Soloviev: "But is this not a pantheism, an impious deification of the world, leading to a kind of religious materialism? Yes, it *is* a pantheism, but an entirely pious one; or more precisely, as I prefer to call it in order to avoid ambiguity, it is a panentheism."[24] Bulgakov summarizes his panentheism as "the truth that all is in God or of God (panentheism),"[25] and: "the world is the not-God existent in God; God is the not-world existent in the world. God posits the world outside of himself, but the world possesses its being in God."[26]

Other modern Orthodox theologians identify themselves as panentheists, including Metropolitan Kallistos Ware, Fr Andrew Louth, Alexei Nesteruk, and Christopher Knight. All participated in a symposium on panentheism in December 2001.[27] But rather than linking panentheism to sophiology as Bulgakov does, they associate panentheism with the *logoi* of things in Maximus the Confessor and the divine energies in Gregory Palamas, bypassing sophiology altogether. None of the four invokes Bulgakov, yet their project relating the doctrines of Maximus and Palamas to panentheism is akin to Bulgakov's affirmation that his sophiology was panentheism, not pantheism, and that it is consistent with Palamas's divine energies.

Orthodox critics of panentheism are not lacking. Georges Florovsky saw Bulgakov's panentheism as little more than Soloviev's pantheist wolf disguised

---

24 Sergius Bulgakov, *The Comforter* (1936) (Grand Rapids: W. B. Eerdmans, 2004), 199–200. See Brandon Gallaher, "Antinomism, Trinity and the Challenge of Solov'ëvan Pantheism in the Theology of Sergij Bulgakov," *Studies in East European Thought*, 64 (2012), 215–18. Gallaher concludes here that Bulgakov falls into the same pantheist difficulties as Soloviev. In his contribution to this book, however, Gallaher discharges Bulgakov from the accusation of pantheism and affirms that Bulgakov "remains within the ambit of a doctrinally orthodox vision of creation." Gallaher accepts Bulgakov's own identification of his sophiology as panentheistic. See Brandon Gallaher, "Sergii Bulgakov's Chalcedonian Ontology and the Problem of Human Freedom," 381 ff.

25 Sergius Bulgakov, "Hypostasis and Hypostaticity: Scholia to the *Unfading Light*" (1925), *St Vladimir's Theological Quarterly*, 49:1–2 (2005), 5–46: 27.

26 Sergius Bulgakov, *Icons and the Name of God* (1931) (Grand Rapids: W. B. Eerdmans, 2012), 32.

27 Philip Clayton and Arthur Peacocke, eds., *In Whom We Live and Move and Have Our Being: Panentheistic Reflections on God's Presence in a Scientific World* (Grand Rapids: W. B. Eerdmans, 2004): Christopher Knight, "Theistic Naturalism and the Word Made Flesh: Complementary Approaches to the Debate on Panentheism" (48–61); Kallistos Ware, "God Immanent yet Transcendent: The Divine Energies according to Saint Gregory Palamas" (157–68); Alexei Nesteruk, "The Universe as Hypostatic Inherence in the Logos of God: Panentheism in the Eastern Orthodox Perspective" (169–83); Andrew Louth, "The Cosmic Vision of Saint Maximos the Confessor" (184–96).

in a theistic sheepskin. But rather than waging a frontal battle against Soloviev and Bulgakov, Florovsky attacked them indirectly. In his seminal 1928 essay "Creation and Createdness," Florovsky posits the patristic doctrine of creation *ex nihilo* as the true Christian theology of relations between God and the world.[28] Florovsky attaches creation to the divine will, but ironically, his willingness to admit, however reluctantly, that creation has some form of eternal existence in the divine will can be considered a form of panentheism. Florovsky speculates that the idea of creation existed in God's mind from all eternity but its realization occurs in time. His solution is not entirely satisfactory, since it seems to run counter to his own categorical assertion that "Nothing created can ever be part of God,"[29] and involves introducing time into eternity: "God's idea of the world, his plan and intention are without any doubt eternal, but in some sense they are not co-eternal with him, as they are 'separated' from his 'essence' by the exercise of his will."[30]

Florovsky further muddles his own argument that there are two types of eternity by citations from Gregory of Nazianzus, Augustine, John of Damascus, and Maximus the Confessor that there was some form of eternal divine pre-contemplation of creation before its actual realization.[31] Unlike Bulgakov and later theologians, Florovsky is unwilling to call a spade a spade—to recognize intimations of panentheism in the ancient Fathers—but in the end his solution appears to be panentheist in all but name.

Florovsky's main target in "Creation and Createdness" is sophiology but panentheism suffers collateral damage for being too closely interwoven with sophiology in Bulgakov and ultimately reducible, thinks Florovsky, to pantheism. Whereas Florovsky sees panentheism as a sub-species of pantheism (hence unacceptable), Bulgakov and other Orthodox theologians regard panentheism as a sub-species of theism (hence acceptable). Considering the totality of Bulgakov's theology, with the overwhelming evidence that he was a Christian theist, it is not possible to sustain a claim that his theology was pantheistic, even if his own theological system grounded in sophiology breaks down under close analysis.

---

28   Georges Florovsky, "Creation and Createdness," in Brandon Gallaher and Paul Ladouceur, eds., *The Patristic Witness of Georges Florovsky* (London: T&T Clark, 2019). See Paul Gavrilyuk, *Georges Florovsky and the Russian Religious Renaissance* (Oxford: Oxford University Press, 2013), especially 106–11 and 145–50.

29   Florovsky, "Creation and Createdness," 45.

30   Ibid., 43.

31   Ibid., 45–46.

Nicolas Lossky was another strong critic of sophiology and panentheism. In his comments on Soloviev's cosmology, Lossky speaks of its "pantheistic flavor," and he also implicitly rejects panentheism, affirming that only the doctrine of creation ex nihilo in an absolute sense resolves the question of the connection between God and the world; God does not employ "for this creation any material either in himself or outside."[32]

Nicolas Lossky, like Florovsky, finds that Bulgakov was unable to prevent his sophiology from slipping into pantheism: "the non-divine aspect of the world proves to be so characterless that his theory must be regarded as a peculiar variety of pantheism."[33] Lossky considers that the basic flaw in Bulgakov's system is that he blurs if not eradicates the ontological gulf between God and creation: "All his theories connected therewith [God and creation] contain too great an ontological approximation of the world, and especially of man, to God [...]. That is logically incompatible with the teaching about God expounded by negative theology [...]."[34] Lossky's specific objections to Bulgakov's panentheism overlap with his critique of sophiology: the ideas that God creates from within himself minimizes divine creativity, and that Bulgakov's argument suggests that humanity is consubstantial with God, are untenable. Lossky also concludes that panentheism is unable to give a reasonable explanation of the presence of evil in the world, the freedom of created agents, and their capacity for independent creativity.[35]

Panentheism is widely diffused in modern Christian theology, but it is difficult to make a connection with Bulgakov. Paul Valliere finds that from Paul Tillich's early engagement with Russian thought and his subsequent move away from it, there may nonetheless be an affiliation with Bulgakov in Tillich's expression "eschatological pan-en-theism" to characterize his understanding of the consummation of all things, a theology close to Bulgakov's.[36] Bulgakov may rightly be considered an Orthodox pioneer in placing his theology under the panentheist umbrella, but this does not diminish suspicions in some Orthodox quarters that his sophiology is implicitly pantheist.

---

32 Nicolas Lossky, *History of Russian Philosophy* (London: George Allen & Unwin, 1952), 128.
33 Lossky, *Russian Philosophy*, 229.
34 Ibid., 228.
35 Ibid., 228–31.
36 Valliere, "Russian Religious Thought," 665.

Personalism

The Russian religious thinkers vigorously applied the notion of "person" to human existence. Their starting point was the Biblical and patristic teaching that humans are made in the image of God. Just as God exists as three Persons, so humanity exists as a multiplicity of persons. Personalism in modern Orthodox thought originated in the Slavophiles of the mid-nineteenth century, but it was the main figures of the Russian religious renaissance, in particular Florenskii, Bulgakov, and Berdiaev, who affirmed the uniqueness and hence the absolute value of the human person, applying the theological understanding of divine personhood and of love as the foundation of intra-Trinitarian relationships to human existence. Their personalism constituted a Christian response to the impersonal, positivist, reductionist, and nihilist philosophies, especially Marxism, competing for the Russian soul prior to the revolution. Olivier Clément writes: "It is, it seems to me, to the honor of Russian theology and religious philosophy in the nineteenth and twentieth centuries to have realized this approach, by distancing themselves as much from individualism as from mystical and totalitarian fusions."[37]

Personalist theology achieved a fuller expression in the work of the Russian thinkers in exile and in later leading Orthodox theologians such as Yannaras, Zizioulas, and Kallistos Ware. There is a remarkable continuity in the development of ideas on what it means philosophically and theologically to be a person. Olivier Clément, referring to Berdiaev, Bulgakov, and Vladimir Lossky, says: "These men conflicted with each other on other subjects. But they concur entirely concerning the person. I would not dare say: *consensus patrum*—but perhaps one should, because the Spirit is not exhausted, especially in times of distress and of lucidity."[38]

Among the leading members of the Russian religious renaissance, Berdiaev is the pre-eminent philosopher of the person: "From beginning to end, Nicolas Berdiaev's thought is a thought of the person," writes Clément.[39] Both Florenskii and Bulgakov sought to express the basis of the uniqueness of the

---

37   Olivier Clément, "Aperçus sur la théologie de la personne dans la 'diaspora' russe en France,"in *Mille Ans de christianisme russe 988–1988* (Paris: YMCA-Press, 1989), 303.

38   Clément, "Aperçus," 304.

39   Olivier Clément, "Le personnalisme chrétien dans la pensée russe," *Contacts* 40:143 (1988), 305. Berdiaev's thinking on human personhood is found notably in *The Destiny of Man* (London: Geoffrey Bles, 1937), and *Slavery and Freedom* (London: Geoffrey Bles, 1943).

person, emphasizing in particular that the person is above any rational catego-ry, making the person philosophically "incomprehensible," not irrational, but beyond rationality, in the realm of mystery.[40] In *Unfading Light* (1917), Bulga-kov re-iterates personalist ideas similar to Florenskii's, and, perhaps more than other Russian theologians, Bulgakov stresses the apophatic nature of human personhood: "What is a person? What is the I? No answer can be given to this question other than with a gesture that points inward. *A person is indefinable*, for it is always being defined with everything, remaining however *above* all of its conditions or determinations."[41]

Berdiaev, more than Bulgakov, stresses the distinction between person and individual as an essential aspect of a robust Orthodox theology of the human person. While in ordinary parlance "person" and "individual" are often synon-ymous, the theological distinction between them is a powerful affirmation of the uniqueness of the human person created in the image of the Persons of the Trinity.[42] Whereas "individual" emphasizes a human in isolation, the "person" must exist in relation to others.

What Florenskii, Bulgakov, and Berdiaev sought to characterize as the es-sence of personhood, Vladimir Lossky pithily articulated by appealing to the patristic categories of nature and person, in a formula which may be summa-rized as the irreducibility of person to nature: "It will be impossible for us to form a concept of the human person and we will have to content ourselves with saying: 'person' signifies the irreducibility of man to his nature."[43]

Zizioulas reiterates this idea: "I have excluded every possibility of regarding the person as an expression or emanation of the substance or nature of man (or even of God himself as 'nature')."[44] Modern Orthodox anthropology would be inclined to say that human personhood is the highest aspect of the divine

---

40 Pavel Florenskii, *The Pillar and Ground of the Truth: An Essay in Orthodox Theodicy in Twelve Letters* (1914) (Princeton, NJ: Princeton University Press, 1997), 59–60.

41 Sergius Bulgakov, *Unfading Light: Contemplations and Speculations* (1917) (Grand Rapids: W. B. Eerdmans, 2012), 290 (Bulgakov's italics).

42 Berdiaev, *The Destiny of Man*, 54–58; and Berdiaev, *Slavery and Freedom*, 21.

43 Vladimir Lossky, "The Theological Notion of the Human Person," in *In the Image and Likeness of God*, ed. John H. Erickson and Thomas E. Bird, intro. John Meyendorff (Crestwood, NY: St Vladimir's Seminary Press, 1974), 120. Lossky says much the same thing in *The Mystical Theology of the Eastern Church* [1944] (Crestwood, NY: St Vladi-mir's Seminary Press, 1976), 122.

44 John Zizioulas, *Being as Communion: Studies in Personhood and the Church* (Crest-wood, NY: St Vladimir's Seminary Press, 1985), 59.

image in humanity, which Yannaras aptly characterizes as the "personal mode of existence" and "being-as-person."[45]

Modern Orthodox theology of human personhood illustrates theological influence among Orthodox theologians. Few acknowledge this influence beyond occasional hints, but Aristotle Papanikolaou put the question directly to Yannaras and Zizioulas:

> There are those [...] who would not necessarily agree that Lossky's and Zizioulas's interpretation of 'person' is explicitly patristic. This dispute becomes important in considering how much Zizioulas actually owes to Lossky for his theology of person. Though Zizioulas criticizes Lossky, giving the impression of radical break with his thought, the similarities in their theology of "person" raises the query of whether such similarities result from the clarity of the patristic texts or whether Lossky's thought formed the basis for Zizioulas's understanding of person. Such is the case with Christos Yannaras, who has also developed a theology of personhood similar to that of Lossky's and Zizioulas's, and who admitted to me that one of the starting points for his thought was Lossky's theology of person. In a personal conversation with Zizioulas, he indicated to me that one of the influences for his ontology of personhood was Yannaras. In then suggesting to Zizioulas that perhaps Lossky influenced him indirectly, Zizioulas was willing to admit that may be the case, but added that the influence would be slight given the substantial differences between their theologies.[46]

We have here a golden chain of insight from Lossky to Yannaras to Zizioulas. Because Lossky's personhood was mediated through Yannaras to Zizioulas, Zizioulas is likely closer to Lossky on personhood than Zizioulas himself recognizes. And this chain of insight does not begin with Lossky; Lossky did not "invent" his theology of human personhood *ex nihilo*. Rather, he drew on ideas of his predecessors and contemporaries, especially Berdiaev and Bulgakov. Lossky does not acknowledge his sources among his fellow Russian intellectuals, but analysis shows that Lossky follows the strong personalist philosophies and theologies received not only from Berdiaev and Bulgakov, but also Dostoevskii, Florenskii, Semen Frank, and Viktor Nesmelov.[47]

---

45   Christos Yannaras, *Person and Eros* (Brookline, MA: Holy Cross Orthodox Press, 2007), 19.

46   Aristotle Papanikolaou, *Being with God: Trinity, Apophatism, and Divine-Human Communion* (Notre Dame, IN: University of Notre Dame Press, 2006), 198, n. 4.

47   Clément, "Aperçus," passim.

Because of his stature in the first half of the twentieth century, Bulgakov was a key link in the chain of transmission of theological personalism from the Slavophiles through the religious renaissance to neopatristic theology. But it is difficult to extract Bulgakov's particular contribution from those of other leading personalities in this chain of transmission. Lossky provided the essential liaison between the Russians and the Greeks, even if he does not acknowledge his sources. Even less obvious is Bulgakov's influence on Yannaras, Zizioulas, and other modern Orthodox personalists such as Metropolitan Kallistos Ware—except as mediated through Lossky.

Eschatology and Universal Salvation

Modern Orthodox thinking on the possibility of universal salvation (*apocatastasis*) occurs in three main strands. One, perhaps the strongest, found notably in theological manuals typical of "academic theology," stresses that the four "last things" (death, judgment, heaven, and hell), revolve around divine judgment of humans for their success or failure in heeding divine commandments, followed by eternal reward (heaven) or eternal punishment (hell). This emphasizes divine justice, with an absolute barrier between the two possible eternal outcomes. A second strand, recognizing that this juridical approach to the finality of human existence downplays divine mercy and forgiveness, maintains a hope and prays that "all will be saved" despite human sinfulness, but accepts that universal salvation is not the teaching of the church, and that the historical record of the condemnation of Origen's doctrine of apocatastasis is at best ambiguous. The third strand argues that universal salvation is a doctrinal certitude. Florenskii, Bulgakov, and Berdiaev are in the "universalist" camp.

Bulgakov's eschatology, especially as developed in *The Bride of the Lamb*, is the most complete exposition in modern Orthodox theology. Cyril O'Regan writes: "Eschatology is not simply a theme in Bulgakov's writings, but at once its central energy and milieu."[48] Bulgakov's eschatology revolves around universal salvation, following closely themes from Origen, Gregory of Nyssa, and Isaac the Syrian.

The starting point of Bulgakov's eschatology is a move away from an emphasis on a juridical view of "the last things," focusing on divine judgment and eternal reward or eternal punishment, to a consideration of the finality of hu-

---

48   Cyril O'Regan, endorsement in *The Sophiology of Death: Essays on Eschatology: Personal, Political, Universal*, trans. Roberto J. De La Noval (Eugene, OR: Cascade Books, 2021).

man (and cosmic) existence in relation to God's own existence, and especially divine love—a move characterized as "from predominantly forensic to ontological categories."[49] For Bulgakov, a juridical approach to eschatology, grounded in "rationalism and anthropomorphism,"[50] reduces limitless divine love and mercy to the constraints of human legal systems, with a decided emphasis on divine justice simplistically interpreted as reward for good and punishment for evil. Bulgakov stresses instead that the eschaton represents the completion of God's creation, when God will be "all in all" (1 Cor. 15:28), a key phrase in Bulgakov's eschatology.[51]

A second key feature of Bulgakov's eschatology is that the resurrection is universal, simultaneous and permanent, since it is grounded in Christ's resurrection: "The God-man is the all-man, and his resurrection is ontologically the universal resurrection […] the *parousia is* also the universal resurrection, and the universal resurrection is the *parousia:* the two are identical and inseparable."[52]

Distinct from much Christian theology, including Orthodox theology, that the deceased are only passive subjects of after-life processes, Bulgakov argues that the deceased have an active role in their evolution after death. Divine-human collaboration (synergism) in salvation does not end with this life, but continues into the next. Bulgakov sees this synergism in the collaboration of the righteous in their own resurrection, the recomposition of the resurrected body, and self-judgment.[53] This judgment occurs in relation to each person's "own eternal image in Christ, that is, before Christ. And in the light of this image, he will see his own reality, and this comparison will be the judgment."[54] Thus, the last judgment is not so much external, as in human jurisprudence, but internal, as each sees his or her failings in relation to the ideal that God intended.

This self-judgment leads not to eternal self-condemnation, but to a process of purification as humans shed their negative qualities prior to entering divine bliss; hell is not eternal retribution for evil, but purgative and therapeutic, and

---

49   Paul Gavrilyuk, "Universal Salvation in the Theology of Sergius Bulgakov," *Journal of Theological Studies* 57:1 (2006), 110–32: 115. The presentation of the highlights of Bulgakov's eschatology here is inspired by Gavrilyuk's essay.

50   Sergius Bulgakov, *The Bride of the Lamb* (1945), trans. Boris Jakim (Grand Rapids: W.B. Eerdmans, 2001), 382.

51   St. Paul's expression that God will be "all in all" occurs over thirty times in *The Bride of the Lamb.*

52   Bulgakov, *The Bride of the Lamb*, 429.

53   Ibid., 430; 434; 446; 457.

54   Ibid., 457.

hence temporary. Bulgakov refers to his teaching as "universal purgatory,"[55] with awareness of divine love—"fire"—as the key agent of the purgative process.

The practitioners of neopatristic theology eschewed soteriological universalism, and indeed generally avoided eschatology beyond emphasizing, like the early Fathers, the resurrection of the body. Kallistos Ware summarizes the approaches of Origen, Gregory of Nyssa, and Isaac the Syrian, without endorsing their views, but advocating, in keeping with earlier tradition, that the church hopes and prays "for the salvation of all."[56]

David Bentley Hart inherits Bulgakov's mantle as a strong Orthodox proponent of the theology "that all shall be saved," the title of his powerful book on eschatology.[57] Hart follows much the same general arguments as Bulgakov, invoking mainly Origen, Gregory of Nyssa, and Isaac the Syrian as patristic authorities supporting universalism. Hart mentions Bulgakov only in passing (and Florenskii and Berdiaev not at all), although strongly praising him: "Sergei Bulgakov, the most remarkable Christian theological mind of the twentieth century, was perhaps the nearest modern Orthodox thinker in sensibility to Gregory of Nyssa (and, really, to all the greatest of the early church fathers)."[58]

The main thrust of Hart's defense of universalism, like Bulgakov's, is to demonstrate that the notion of eternal punishment for sin is incompatible with divine goodness and mercy, with divine love. Both marshal similar arguments against the eternity of hell: God created rational creatures not for punishment, but for love and bliss; the disproportion between evil committed in time and punishment for eternity; the possibility, indeed necessity, of continued human progress towards God after death; the inconceivability that with perfect knowledge and perfect freedom, any would reject God; punishment would serve no purpose if there is no possibility of redemption after death.

Both Bulgakov and Hart appeal to Isaac the Syrian in arguing against hell as a physical punishment, although the image of fire is relevant, since "the torments of hell are the burning love for God [...] the eternal source of love for Christ is revealed together with the torment caused by the failure to actualize this love in the life that has passed" (Bulgakov); "the fires of hell are nothing

55 Bulgakov, *The Bride of the Lamb*, 3061, 375.
56 Kallistos Ware, "Dare We Hope for the Salvation of All? Origen, St Gregory of Nyssa and St Isaac the Syrian," in *The Inner Kingdom* (Crestwood, NY: St. Vladimir's Seminary Press, 2001), 193–215.
57 David Bentley Hart, *That All Shall Be Saved: Heaven, Hell, and Universal Salvation* (New Haven, CN: Yale University Press, 2019).
58 Hart, *That All Shall Be Saved*, 195.

but the glory of God [...] [which] will inevitably be experienced as torment by any soul that willfully seals itself against love of God and neighbor" (Hart).[59]

Bulgakov, consistent with Orthodox teaching, argues that purification after death is necessary before the enjoyment of the beatific vision of God (theosis). This appears close to the contemporary Catholic doctrine of purgatory, although Orthodox thinking, as expressed vigorously by St. Mark of Ephesus at the Council of Ferrara in 1439–40, does not accept notions such as purgatory being a "place," or that purification resembles physical suffering.[60] Bulgakov follows the Orthodox teaching of purification as a sort of "universal purgatory'"—all, even recognized saints, undergo a process of purification from evil. This conception of "hell" as purification is thus temporally limited; sooner or later, hell will be "empty"—as the Orthodox Paschal liturgy celebrates Christ's freeing humanity from the bonds of death.

Bulgakov's soteriological universalism may prove to be one of his most enduring contributions to modern Christian thought. Here Bulgakov is consistent with his ecclesiological universalism: both are cut from the same cloth, a cloth reflecting light, hope and love, a seamless garment woven from the Incarnation of the Son of God who deifies all humanity and indeed all creation. Just as Bulgakov considered all humanity, all creation, as belonging to the one Church of God, so all humanity and indeed all creation will be deified as the fulfillment of God as Creator, when "God will be all in all."

Conclusion

Eight decades after his death, Sergius Bulgakov's stature as a major Christian theologian has yet to be sufficiently recognized. This is due in part to the unavailability until recently of his major works in English. His two books *The Orthodox Church* and *The Wisdom of God*, together with a handful of shorter pieces, mainly on ecclesiology and ecumenism, that appeared in English prior to World War II were not representative of the range and depth of his theology. It was only with the publication in English translation of the major and minor trilogies, and key works such as *Unfading Light*, between 1990 and 2010 that it was possible to appreciate Bulgakov's stature as a major theologian. In some areas, such

---

59   Bulgakov, *The Bride of the Lamb*, 459; Hart, *That All Shall Be Saved*, 16. See Isaac the Syrian, *The Ascetical Homilies*, 28 (Brookline, MA: Holy Transfiguration Monastery, 1984), 141.

60   See Paul Ladouceur, "Orthodox Theologies of the Afterlife," *St Vladimir's Theological Quarterly* 62, no. 1 (2018), 51–72.

as *sobornost*, personalism, synergy, kenosis, even panentheism, and especially sophiology, Bulgakov represents and in some areas culminates the thinking of the Russian religious renaissance rather than expressing a unique perspective.

Several important stumbling blocks prevent a full appreciation and appropriation of Bulgakov's theology by both Orthodox and non-Orthodox theologians. One is the frequent opacity of Bulgakov's writings, and another is the at times tiresome repetition of ideas. Translations may help to smooth otherwise rough patches in Bulgakov's writing, but the unfamiliarity and complexity of the many ideas that Bulgakov brings to play may deter some Western theologians who have difficulty situating Eastern Christian notions in typical Western theological frameworks.

Perhaps more important is continuing unease with the theology of Divine Wisdom underpinning much of Bulgakov's thought. It is the same unease that affected Bulgakov's contemporaries in the 1920s and 1930s—among the conservative elements of the Russian Orthodox Church, which resulted in the "sophiology affair" of the mid-1930s; among the Anglicans in the Fellowship of Saint Alban and Saint Sergius, who never warmed to sophiology and were more at home with the more biblical, liturgical, and patristic orientations of other Orthodox, such as Florovsky, Lev Gillet, and Vladimir Lossky; and among many of his fellow Orthodox, especially his strongest critics, the Losskys (Nicolas and Vladimir, for different reasons) and Florovsky.

But just how dependent is Bulgakov's theology on sophiology? Much of his writing contains few references to sophiology, except for an occasional obeisance, often in the form of remarks on this or that theological notion as a manifestation of divine or uncreated Wisdom or of created wisdom. To tie Bulgakov's theology too closely to sophiology is to relegate Bulgakov largely to the domain of historical theology, a fascinating byway of Orthodox and Christian theology, but to which few Orthodox theologians subscribe. By way of contrast, Maximus's theology of the *logoi* of things and Palamas's divine energies receive much more enthusiastic support as approaches to understanding relations between God and creation.

Bulgakov's adherence to panentheism may have more staying power than unadorned sophiology, with its tendency to personalize Divine Wisdom as a semi-autonomous entity, amidst lingering intimations of a shadowy "fourth hypostasis," even if Bulgakov himself explicitly rejected this in his 1924 essay "Hypostasis and Hypostasticity." Considering Bulgakov's thought apart from the substrate of sophiology reveals the depth of his insights across a very broad range of theological issues and should continue to be pursued, as we have sought to present in this essay.

Building the House of Wisdom
DOI 10.17438/978-3-402-12203-7

The Vision of Unity. The Ecumenical Thought of Fr. Sergii Bulgakov

Adalberto Mainardi

Father Sergius Bulgakov is acknowledged as one of the most important Orthodox theologians and probably one of the greatest of the twentieth century. His ecumenical thought is strictly linked to his ecclesiology. Although the latter depends on his sophiological views, nonetheless it mirrors and reacts to questions, problems, and issues that arose in the ecumenical debate. Bulgakov's insights anticipate themes and questions still crucial for Christian unity. In this paper I will try to enlighten the shaping of his ideas on the unity of the Church. First, we will consider his views on the unity of the Church in relation to the historical situation of the Russian Orthodox Church in the aftermath of the Revolution (§ 1), then his engagement in ecumenical bodies such as Faith and Order and the Fellowship St. Alban and St. Serge (§ 2); the two final paragraphs enlighten the ecumenical implication of Bulgakov's ecclesiology regarding the question of the veneration of the Mother of God and the Communion of saints (§ 3) and that of the sacramental boundaries of the Church (§ 4).

Raising the Question of Church Unity

As a member of the local council of the Russian Orthodox Church, Bulgakov pleaded for the restoration of the patriarchate. In his conception, the Russian patriarch would be an organ of the ecumenical consciousness of the Church, and the Local Council of the Russian Orthodox Church a prelude of an Ecumenical Council, in which the question of the division between the Eastern and Western Churches would be posed. At that time, Bulgakov felt that the Russian Church and indeed all Christianity was "on the eve of a great dogmatic movement";[1] he understood the historical crisis of the Russian revolution as a revelation of the consequences of the Great Schism in Christianity between East and West in the eleventh century, but also as a chance for its healing.[2]

The task of the ecclesial consciousness expressed in the local council was to seize the _kairòs_, the call of God in human history: "If it should please Providence that the historic hour has finally come, when the nearness of the miracle of new peace in the Universal Church will be felt, then we must be ready, our loins girded and our torches burning."[3] The local council, in fact, did devote a commission to the question of church unity, focused on the relations with Old Catholics and Anglicans; however Bulgakov was not one of its members.[4]

In the aftermath of the Revolution, as the collapse of the last Christian Empire put an end to the Constantinian era in Christianity and questioned the narrowness of the national Churches, he still felt a rapprochement between East and West was on the way:

> Differences of dogma never really had any vital importance in the question, and they can and must be solved amicably, with a sincere and loving desire for mutual understanding. Neither Catholicism nor Orthodoxy are quite the same as they were. Something visible to only a few is happening here: a new sense of an ecumenical Church is coming to life. If this consciousness grows and spreads, all the endless

---

1   Bulgakov alludes to the dogmatic aspects of the controversy on the Name of God on Mount Athos (1912–1913), to which he would devote his posthumous _Philosophy of Name_: Sergii Bulgakov, "Afonskoe delo," _Russkaia mysl'_ 9 (1913), 37–46; ibid., _Filosofiia imeni; Ikona i ikonopochitanie_ (Moscow: Iskusstvo—Saint Peterburg: Inapress, 1999). Cf. Antoine Nivière, _Les glorificateurs du nom. Une querelle théologique parmi les moines russes du mont Athos (19071914)_ (Geneva: Éditions des Syrtes, 2015); Robert Slesinski, "The Enigma of the Name in the Philosophy of Language of Sergius Bulgakov," _St Vladimir's Theological Quarterly_ 58 (2014), 417–40.

2   Sergii N. Bulgakov, "Smysl patriarshestva v Rossi. Prilozhenie I k Deianiiu 31," in _Dokumenty Sviashchennogo Sobora Pravoslavnoi Rossijskoi Tserkvi 1917–1918 godov._ V, _Deianiia Sobora s 1-go po 36-e_, ed. Aleksii Kolcherin and Aleksandr Mramornov (Moscow: Izd. Novospasskogo monastyria, 2015), 706–11.

3   Ibid., 711.

4   Cf. Günther Schulz, "Der Ausschuß für die Vereinigung der Kirchen des Landeskonzils der Orthodoxen Kirche in Rußland 3./16.8. bis 7./20.9.1918," _Kirche im Osten_ 39 (1996), 70–100; Aleksandr I. Mramornov, "Voprosy mezhdunarodnykh i mezhtserkovnykh otnoshenii na Sviashchennom Sobore Pravoslavnoi Rossiiskoi tserkvi 1917–1918 gg.," _MGIMO Review of International Relations_ 66 (2019), 176–201 (DOI 10.24833/2071-8160-2019-3-66-176-201).

disputes, together with the vast literature on the subject, will quietly disappear. All else will fade before the irresistible longing for reunion in Christ.[5]

Here Bulgakov was still under the influence of the prophetic vision of Soloviev's *Three Dialogues*. The unity of the Church is an undeniable fact that transcends historical limitations: Orthodoxy is not identical with Byzantinism. Even the philosophical speculations of the Slavophiles are very often biased for political reasons:

> Insofar as the Church is the Church, we cannot deny its unity, although in history this unity appears more as a mysterious vocation still in becoming than as an accomplished fact. The historical, militant Church needs exterior forms of union, it looks for them. And once you possess these forms of life, it seems that the unity is something natural: on this basis, the Slavophiles started speculating about unity in love, without realizing that this unit was brought about by the iron power of the autocracy.[6]

Bulgakov himself at a certain point (*Diary of Jalta* 1921–1922)[7] cheered the idea of joining the Roman Catholic Church: although he was later bitterly disappointed by the Catholics he met in Constantinople and regarded this idea as a "temptation", he never gave up the conviction that the question of the division of the Churches, as hopeless as it could seem to the human judgment, should be his task and his mission.[8] And this was perhaps the first inner step of his personal engagement in the burgeoning ecumenical movement.

---

5   Sergius Bulgakov, "At the Feast of the Gods: Contemporary Dialogues. Dialogue the fifth," *The Slavonic Review* 1/3 (1923), 616–18. Cf. Adalberto Mainardi, "Conflicting Authorities. The Byzantine Symphony and the Idea of Christian Empire in Russian Orthodox Thought at the Turn of the Nineteenth and Twentieth Centuries," *Review of Ecumenical Studies* 11, no. 2 (2018), 170–85 (DOI: 10.2478/ress-2018-0014).

6   Sergii Bulgakov, *U sten Khersonisa* (Sankt-Peterburg: Dorval, Liga, Gart, 1993), 37. Bulgakov never published these Dialogues.

7   First published by Nikita Struve: Sergii Bulgakov, "Ialtiiskii dnevnik," *Vestnik Russkogo Khristianskogo Dvizheniia* 170 (1994), 28–66.

8   Ibid., 53 (entry of 24 April 1922).

Involvement in Ecumenical Bodies

Contacts with Protestants and the disinterested funding of the Orthodox Theological Institute of St. Serge by different Christian associations,[9] made Bulgakov gradually aware that the Holy Spirit had not denied His gifts to Western
Christians and that it was not given to theologians to delimit the frontiers
of the Church. In 1927 Bulgakov, together with Metropolitan Evlogii (Georgievskii), then head of the provisional administration of the Russian parishes
in Western Europe, attended the first world conference on Faith and Order in
Lausanne. In the January of the same year, in the cathedral city of St. Albans in
Hertfordshire, there took place the first of a long series of conferences among
Orthodox (mainly teachers and students of St. Serge in Paris) and Anglicans
(mainly clergy and ordinands at the Universities of Oxford and Cambridge).
This marked the beginning of the Fellowship of St. Alban and St. Sergius (of-
ficially founded the following year, 1928), in which Bulgakov played a major
role. As the history of these ecumenical bodies is well known,[10] we will focus
on Bulgakov's theological contributions as a member of both.

Bulgakov's main speech in Lausanne was devoted to the ordained ministry. He looked at it through the lens of the idea of *sobornost'*, borrowed from
Khomiakov, which he claimed to be untranslatable. (It means "conciliarity"
and at the same time "catholicity.") The theology of ordained ministry is in
fact a crucial ecumenical issue: on the one hand it concerns the question of
Apostolic succession and the recognition of Anglican orders (which was then
on the agenda of Orthodox–Anglican relations); on the other hand, it implies
an assessment of the hierarchical structure of the Church, in dialectical con-
traposition with the Roman Catholic model. The point made by Bulgakov was

---

9   Such as the Appeal for the Russian Clergy and Church Aid Fund, presided over by the
     bishop of Birmingham Russell Wakefield, and the Young Men's Christian Association,
     presided over by John Mott. See Donald A. Lowrie, *Saint Sergius in Paris: The Orthodox
     Theological Institute* (London: SPCK, 1954).

10 Tissington Tatlow, "World Conference on Faith and Order," in Ruth Rouse, Stephan
     C. Neill, *A History of the Ecumenical Movement. 1517–1948*, vol. I (London: SPCK,
     1954), 405–41; Luca Ferracci, "Charles Brent and the Faith and Order Project: From Its
     Origins to the Lausanne Conference of 1927," in *A History of the Desire for Christian
     Unity. Ecumenism in the Churches, 19th–21st Century*, vol.1, *Dawn of Ecumenism*, eds.
     Alberto Melloni, Luca Ferracci (Leiden: Brill, 2021), 615–39; on the Fellowship see now:
     Dimitrios Filippos Salapatas, *The Fellowship of St Alban and St Sergius. Orthodox and
     Anglican Ecumenical Relations 1927–2012* (Newcastle upon Tyne: Cambridge Scholars
     Publishing, 2018); Nichols Aidan, *Alban and Sergius: The Story of a Journal* (Hereford-
     shire: Gracewing, 2018).

that it was necessary to subordinate canonical questions to the broader problem of the dogmatic foundations of ecclesiology. Priesthood could be properly understood dogmatically only in the context of a proper theology of the people of God, that is, in other terms, of the "sobornost". He said:

> Priesthood within the Church is related inseparably to the laity, and the relationship is not merely that of ruler to subject: it is also a relation of mutual help and of unity within the *sobornost*. The priest requires the co-operation of the laity in the administration of the sacraments, and the laity take their share in service and sacrament through singing, responses, and prayers.[11]

The bishop is not above his local church, but he is the guardian of communion with the other Churches:

> [The bishop] does not impose his opinion upon his church but gives authoritative expression to the voice of the whole Church: and an episcopal council expresses not the sum of the personal views of the bishops assembled (which, in that case, would have binding force) but the harmony of the views of the local churches.[12]

Bulgakov still looks at ecclesiology through the lens of the romantic theology of the Slavophiles: ecclesial relationships are not to be understood in terms of public law as "representative and constitutional," but as "a spiritual reciprocity, a union in love, a oneness in thought," that is in terms of *sobornost'*, which is "an organic rather than an organised principle."[13] A new perspective, namely that of Eucharistic ecclesiology, seeing the Church as the gathering together of the local community around the bishop celebrant in the mystery of the Eucharist, would have helped assess the relationship between hierarchical and charismatic principles in the structure of the Church, a topic which Bulgakov later felt crucial to the dogmatic question underlying ecumenism as a historical *and* charismatic movement.

The Lausanne Conference marked the Orthodox involvement in the ecumenical movement.[14] Bulgakov considered it a sort of revelation: the movement towards the Christian unity was a historical event provoked by the Spirit,

---

11 Herbert Newell Bate, ed., *Faith and Order: Proceedings of the World Conference, Lausanne, August 3–21, 1927* (London-New York: George H. Doran Company, 1928), 259.

12 Ibid., 260.

13 Ibid.

14 Cf. Stefan Zankow, "Die Orthodoxe Kirche und die Bewegung für die Vereinigung der Kirchen," *Una Sancta: Zeitschrift des Hoch-Kirchlich-Oekumenischen Bundes* 3 (1927),

the Church authority should recognise it, the theologians rethink it theologically, and the entire Church live out its consequences: "Something happened
and those who took part in it are responsible for the memory of this spiritual
event."[15] Lausanne was a spiritual experience infinitely surpassing the modest
theological results of the meeting, because there "it was perceived in a new
way and with a new strength that the whole Christian world believes and loves
Jesus the Lord, […] is spiritually nourished by the holy Gospel and the Word of
God, with the Holy Spirit living in it."[16] The ecumenical movement as a spiritual
experience is born on a Trinitarian foundation.

At Lausanne Bulgakov held that "the priest is above all an offerer of sacrifice."[17] The ecumenical question is inextricably intertwined with the participation at the one Eucharistic chalice. Whereas the movement of Faith and Order
took as its starting point the doctrinal questions, the Fellowship of St. Alban
and St. Sergius since its very beginning was essentially a society of common
prayer. At Bulgakov's proposal (1927), its members began to celebrate on alternate days the Anglican and Orthodox Eucharist on the same altar. Bulgakov
himself, however, made his most momentous and controversial proposal some
years later, in June 1933, when he first proposed partial intercommunion between the Anglican and Orthodox members of the Fellowship. After a couple
of years of debates inside the Fellowship, in which the divide crossed confessional borders, the final version of Bulgakov's proposal was ultimately rejected
in June 1935 by the Fellowship council, with particularly strong opposition by
Georges Florovsky. The history of these discussions has recently been assessed
by scholars.[18] I will briefly summarize their results and make some observations.

290–97; Nicolas Arseniew, "Gedanken über Lausanne", ibid., 397–400; ibid., "Lozans-
kaja konferencija," *Vestnik RSChD* 3 (1928), 1–5.

15   Sergii Bulgakov, "K voprosu o Lozannskoj konferentsii (Lozannskaia konferentsiia i
entsiklika Piia XI *Mortalium animos*)," *Put'* 13 (1928), 71–82; ibid., "The Papal Encyclical
and the Lausanne Conference," *The Christian East* 9 (1928), 116–27.

16   Bulgakov, "K voprosu," 72.

17   Bate, ed., *Faith and Order*, 260.

18   Anastassy Brandon Gallaher, "Bulgakov and Intercommunion," *Sobornost* (2002),
9–28; ibid., "Great and Full of Grace: Partial Intercommunion and Sophiology in Sergii
Bulgakov," in *Church and World*, ed. William C. Mills (Rollinsford: Orthodox Research
Institute, 2013), 69–121; Bryn Geffert, *Eastern Orthodox and Anglicans, Diplomacy, Theology, and the Politics of Interwar Ecumenism* (Indiana: University of Notre Dame Press,
2009), 158–83; Nichols, *Alban and Sergius*, 191–208; Salapatas, *The Fellowship*.

The theological and spiritual basis for the sharing of the Eucharistic chalice among the members of the Fellowship, according to Bulgakov, was given on the one hand by the achievement of "a substantial dogmatic agreement with one another," "more complete than that which exists within the Anglican Church itself"; and on the other hand by the fact that a certain "spiritual communion" was already in existence, and it would have been spiritually dangerous to leave this sprout of unity fruitless: "nothing comes from nothing," and the prophetic gesture of partial inter-communion within the Fellowship would also have facilitated dogmatic and canonical agreement. The Fellowship itself was not a canonical body, but in fact it existed, "and not without a silent blessing of both authorities—the Anglican and the Orthodox."[19] Reunion would come not "through tournaments between the theologians of the East and of the West, but through a reunion before the Altar."[20]

The dogmatic implications of the Athonite controversy over the Name of God (1913),[21] had convinced Bulgakov of the sacramental nature of the Name of Jesus, which already achieved an invisible but real union between those who invoked it with faith. Bulgakov was not thinking of achieving a partial union despite the division between the two Churches (Anglican and Orthodox), but of responding with a new "sacrament of reunion" to what he considered to be a call of the Holy Spirit. The Church had to respond to a new historical situation with a creative act, in obedience to the Holy Spirit, certainly respecting the canons, but without being held back by situations inherited from the past (i. e., the divisions of the past). The fact that at that time there already existed an "economic" intercommunion between the two Churches (in extreme cases Orthodox and Anglican laity were blessed by their bishops to partake of one another's sacraments) was an encouraging premise.

Bulgakov's basic idea—as it was refined in the context of common discussion—was that of a mutual episcopal 'sacramental blessing' of Orthodox and Anglican Fellowship members, both ordained and lay, to partake of communion at one another's altars at Fellowship conferences. There was a fact that overcame divisions by the power of God: communion at the one cup. A dogmatic minimum was sufficient, while open questions were not such as to prevent communion. Jurisdictional and canonical questions would have to

---

19 Fellowship of St Alban and St Sergius, Minutes, Fellowship Archives, 16 February 1934, 3.

20 Sergei Bulgakov, "By Jacob's Well," *Journal of the Fellowship of St. Alban & St. Sergius* 22 (1933), 11, quoted in Geffert, Eastern Orthodox and Anglicans, 159.

21 See footnote 1.

be resolved in view of unity: nevertheless, their relevance was not underestimated, and it was therefore entrusted to the bishop (through the blessing)[22] to discern this seed of unity in an experience limited in space and time: it would have been an initial cell, a "sacrament of reunification", a living epiclesis for the unity of the two Churches.

The strongest opposition to Bulgakov's proposal on the Orthodox side came from Fr. George Florovsky, who objected that *"communio in sacris* can never be private action. It is always Catholic action, the sacrament of Catholic Unity. Realised privately it is an open contradiction."[23] But objections also arose on the Anglican side.[24] Michael Ramsey, the future archbishop of Canterbury, felt that rushing to intercommunion could compromise the theological (and Catholic) understanding of the Eucharist as "the act of Christ in His one Body."[25] On the contrary, Walter Frere deemed Bulgakov's proposal worthy of further study, considering that confessional diversity was a richness that averted rigid narrow-mindedness.[26]

On the Orthodox side, in favour of intercommunion were Anton Kartashev (intercommunion was a creative act in response to a new situation), Nicolas Zernov, and Lev Zander. However, reservations prevailed. Archbishop Evlogii himself, Bulgakov's mentor, eventually judged his proposal for intercommunion to be "completely false," as such an issue could not possibly be applied to a single organisation without involving the entire hierarchy.[27] The Fellowship finally decided not to go ahead with the proposal.

Bulgakov's scheme proved to be too radical a proposal and was eventually shelved. Still, it revealed an important ecclesiological issue. What was here at stake were in fact two ecclesiological models: a universalistic (catholic) hier-

---

22	Bulgakov himself wrote the blessing: "The grace divine [...] cleaveth through the laying on of hands on the priest N. for intercommunion with the Orthodox members of the Fellowship of St Albans and St Sergius. Therefore, let us pray for him that the grace of the all-Holy Spirit may come upon him. *Choir:* God, have mercy": Gallaher, "Bulgakov and Intercommunion," 15.

23	Fellowship of St Alban and St Sergius, *Report of Conference held at High Leigh, June 26–28, 1934,* Fellowship Archives, 6.

24	Cf. O. F. Clarke, "The Healing of Schism," *The Journal of the Fellowship of St Alban and St Sergius* 25 (1934), 3–7.

25	Nichols, *Alban and Sergius,* 204.

26	Ibid.

27	*Le chemin de ma vie. Mémoires du Métropolite Euloge.* Rédigés d'après ses récits par Tatiana Manoukhina (Paris: Presse Saint Serge—Institut de théologie orthodoxe, 2005), 493.

archical model in Florovsky, and the "decentralised ecclesiology", as Brandon Gallaher calls it, which underlaid Bulgakov's proposal, and which implied a radical questioning of the traditional doctrine of the boundaries of the Church, as the canonical did not necessarily coincide with the pneumatical.

The Mother of God and the Communion of Saints

The ecumenical implications of Bulgakov's ecclesiological conception may be illustrated by his insistence on the veneration of the Mother of God, a topic which he raised in Lausanne, and which the president of the session considered quite scandalous. Bulgakov insisted that one "cannot separate the humanity of our Lord from that of His mother, the unspotted *Theotokos*."[28] It was not just a matter of devotion. Church's faith expressed in worship was at stake:

> The Church has a rich and growing treasure of liturgical worship, a treasure which the Orthodox Church has guarded faithfully as an inspired well-spring of faith. She desires a great Christian unity in worship but hopes for it not so much through the common acceptance of liturgical forms as through the energy of love, drawn out by the irresistible attraction of spiritual beauty.[29]

As a member of the Continuation Committee, Bulgakov asked that the "Communion of Saints" should be a part of the agenda of the Conference of Faith and Order in Edinburgh (1937), including "a special question on the Blessed Virgin." For Bulgakov this point of the programme was so important that it should "not to be swallowed in general expressions," and he suggested a clearly ecclesiological ground for its inclusion: "The theology of the relation between the militant on earth (*the Church in Paradise and Purgatory*, that particular point, I think, is *not necessary*, perhaps is better to be *excluded as not prepared*) and the Church triumphant in Heaven. Here I propose to add: *The Communion of Saints*."[30]

Bulgakov explains his conviction "that the question of the veneration of Our Lady and its importance for the Orthodox Church might be explained *not for a discussion, but for the information*, as a 'witness to what the worship and life of the Church mean' to the orthodox people. I have a firm conviction that

---

28 Bate, ed., *Faith and Order*, 208.
29 Ibid., 208–09.
30 Letter by Bulgakov to Canon Hodgson, 10/07/1935, in Genève, WCC Archives 23.4.020/1 (autograph), emphasis in the original.

the right understanding of this side of worship of Orthodoxy would be helpful for the Protestant world. In contrary [sic] the exclusion of this point from the program may make a painful impression in the whole orthodox world, what is in any case to be avoided".[31]

In his intervention at the first congress of Orthodox theology (Athens 1936), devoted to the doctrine of the Church, Bulgakov stressed the intimate link between the Church as "the leading bearer of holiness in the world," expressing "the true divinisation of humanity," and "her personification is the Most Holy, Most Pure Virgin Mother of God, who belongs to our world and humanity and at the same time, in her Dormition [...] already belongs to the glorified humanity of Christ."[32] The Mother of God reflects the twofold nature of the Church, human and divine, which Bulgakov explained in the light of his sophiology as the mysterious union of created and uncreated Sophia.[33]

The Boundaries of the Church

In 1937 Bulgakov took part in both conferences of Life and Work and Faith and Order in Edinburgh. At the latter he was one of the leading Orthodox speakers. He urged the assembly to tackle the problem of the Church, which was not included as such in the conference programme. "In dogmatics—he maintained—the chief universal problem is that of the Church—ecclesiology."[34] The polemical character of the definitions of the Church coming from post-Reformation era, he observed, was "one of the chief obstacles to our finding a way of reconciliation."[35] In his eyes the task of theologians was to promote a deeper understanding of the doctrine of the Church that could make clear "the difference between dogmatic definitions which are obligatory and definitions concerning doctrinal differences on other points which are often too much exaggerated."[36] In no way was truth to be sacrificed, but "in all matters

31   Ibid. Emphasis in the original.
32   Hamilcar S. Alivisatos, ed., *Procès-Verbaux du premier congrès de théologie orthodoxe à Athènes, 29 Novembre—6 Décembre 1936* (Athens: Pyrsos, 1939), 133–34.
33   Cf. Andrew Louth, "Father Sergii Bulgakov on the Mother of God", *St Vladimir's Theological Quarterly* 49 (2005), 145–64.
34   Leonard Hodgson, ed., *The Second World Conference on Faith and Order held at Edinburgh, August 3–18, 1937* (London: Student Christian Movement Press, 1938), 67.
35   Ibid.
36   Ibid.

where we are not bound by obligatory definitions, we must look for possibilities of reconciliation."[37]

As was the case in his proposal of partial intercommunion, Bulgakov takes as starting point not an abstract definition of the Church, but the reality itself of the Church as realised in the sacraments, specifically the Eucharist. As he stated in the last part of his major theological trilogy, *The Bride of the Lamb*, published posthumously, "every sacrament opens the way to the depth, to the noumenal being, and is thereby in its action indefinable and inexhaustible."[38] The ontological nature of the Eucharist, in fact, questioned the very idea that the canonical boundaries of the Church delimited her mystical nature as well. In the first case, the Church, as a particular confessional organisation, has clearly circumscribed boundaries. In this case Cyprian's sentence that outside the Church there is no salvation (*extra ecclesiam nulla salus*) applies. But such a definition—Bulgakov argues—"appears inapplicable in relation to the Church as the Body of Christ and to all humanity received by it, especially to the whole ecclesial world. This is expressed in the fact that the Church recognises—albeit to different degrees—the validity of the ecclesiastical sacraments, which also took place outside Orthodoxy."[39] In this mysterious non-coincidence of the canonical and the mystical boundaries of the Church consisted for Bulgakov the dogmatic basis "of the present ecumenical movement, which strives to recognise and realise this actual unity of the ecclesial and to bring to fullness what is lacking in its being."[40]

Bulgakov was conscious that the spirit of militant proselytism, which penetrated every confession confirming its own truth, was one of the main obstacles

---

37   Ibid.

38   Serge Boulgakov, *L'Épouse de L'Agneau. La création, l'homme, l'Église et la fin* (Lausanne: L'Age d'Homme, 1984), 211–12.

39   Alivisatos, ed., *Procès-Verbaux*, 133. As early as 1926/1927, in an address given at the Orthodox & Anglo-Catholic Conference, Bulgakov devoted a careful study to the canonical and patristic tradition of the first centuries which showed the recognition of sacraments outside the Church in various degrees; this in turn implied that "non-Orthodoxy also belongs to Orthodoxy, all that is truly valuable and holy in it is also Orthodox, in spite of its un-Orthodoxy or notwithstanding it": *Outlines of the Teaching about the Church. Address given at the Orthodox & Anglo-Catholic Conference by Father S. Boulgakoff*, December 1926/January 1927. Fellowship archives, accessed August 25, 2023, https://fsass.org/shop/archives/fr-sergius-bulgakovs-outlines-of-the-teaching-about-the-church/ (access 2024/01/26); Sergius Bulgakov, "Outlines of the Teaching about the Church—The Church and Non-Orthodoxy," *American Church Monthly* 30, no. 6 (1931), 411–23 and 31, no. 1 (1932), 13–26.

40   Alivisatos, ed., *Procès-Verbaux*, 133.

to the path towards Christian unity. Since every confession considers itself the One Holy Catholic Church, "ecumenism in this case naturally means an impossibility (a contradiction), or even apostasy."[41] But for Bulgakov the ecumenical movement was a phenomenon dictated not by a contingent political situation, but a prophetic call rising from the depths of Christian consciousness:

> The very nature of Church being, which transcends any ecclesiastical organisation, even though it lies at its foundation, can be detected and seen along with the closeness and exclusiveness of separated Church organisation and even notwithstanding it.[42]

Bulgakov was especially critical of the Roman Catholic stance against the ecumenical movement (particularly after *Mortalium animos* stigmatised participation in it by Catholics). A turning point in Bulgakov's ecclesiology was his historical appraisal of the Council of Florence (1439). The historical weight of the evolution of the papacy in the West weighs on possible reconciliation in the present: Bulgakov deemed papal infallibility and universal jurisdiction as affirmed in Vatican I were the central issue for the reunification of the Church.[43] Later, Bulgakov himself recognised that "the Vatican Council did not give a precise definition of the episcopate, which therefore remains to be dogmatically clarified in Catholicism. It is to be hoped that this imprecision will open constructive future developments."[44] One might observe here that these were precisely the developments of the doctrine of the episcopacy brought about by the second Vatican Council (*Lumen Gentium* 21–27).

The fact that the Orthodox and the Catholics were very close to re-establishing communion, and only a different conception of their respective hierarchical structure and a different historical practice of conciliarity hindered them, was another argument that convinced Bulgakov that "the hierarchical-sacramental organisation is not an adequate or absolute phenomenon of the Church," but a relative though legitimate historical datum, which does not extend to the noumenal level:

---

41   Sergii Bulgakov, "*Una Sancta.* (Osnovaniia ekumenizma)," *Put'* 58 (1938/39), 3–14 (quotation 10).

42   Ibid.

43   Sergii N. Bulgakov, "Ocherki ucheniia o Tserkvi IV. O Vatikanskom dogmate," *Put'* 15 (1929), 39–80; 16 (1929), 19–48; see Adalberto Mainardi, "Vzgliad s Vostoka. Osmyslenie Florentiiskogo sobora (1438–1439 gg.) v russkoi istoriografii i bogoslovii XIX–XX vv.," *Istoriia* 12/5 (2021). DOI 10.18254/S207987840015718-8.

44   Bulgakov, *L'Epouse*, 453, n. 183.

This relativisation does not at all detract from the full power and significance of the Church as a hierarchical-canonical establishment, nor does it shake the divinity of this establishment in history, but it surely testifies to a certain non-conformity of the Church as a noumenal or mystical phenomenon with its institutional one. It generally means that the power of the Church can extend, or better, cannot fail to extend beyond the institutional Church: *ecclesia extra ecclesias*.[45]

This was the foundation for the special being of the Church as an ecclesial reality which is not hierarchically subordinated or regulated:

> This is the *Una Sancta*, as the incarnation of God always taking place and Pentecost always continuing, the effective Presence of God in the world and in man, the Divine Sophia as 'invisible', that is, transcendent to the identification of the Church, whose action is visibly revealed as the Mystery being revealed.[46]

Here lay for Bulgakov also the foundations and at the same time the paradox of ecumenism: a new breath of the Holy Spirit, which is at work in the depth of the Church, unrestricted and unbound by the facets of Church organisation, and at the same time a patient historical and theological work to be done in obedience to call of the Spirit, a theological duty, a task and at the same time a gift which we are not allowed to refuse.

> "That they all may be one; as thou, Father, art in me, and I in thee, that they also may be one in us (Joh 17:21)." This unity is not the unity of a hierarchical organisation, that is, only its exterior detection, but above all the unity of the life which is contained in its divine source. This unity is present in the Church as its Divine depth and strength, but at the same time it needs to be found, as a task for the historical life. This is the primary task for our time, the whetstone by which are now sharpened Christian conscience and will.[47]

A call and a duty still before us.

---

45   Bulgakov, *L'Epouse*, 226.
46   Ibid.
47   Bulgakov, "*Una Sancta*," 14.

List of Contributors

Antoine Arjakovsky, co-director of the Politics and Religions Research Department at the Collège des Bernardins in Paris.

Nikolaos Asproulis, Dr., deputy director of the Volos Academy for Theological Studies and lecturer at the Hellenic Open University.

Antonio Bergamo, Professor of Theological Anthropology and Eschatology at the Apulian Theological Faculty and at the Higher Institute of Religious Sciences "don Tonino Bello" (Lecce), of which he is also the Director.

Deborah Casewell, Ph. D., Lecturer in Philosophy at the University of Chester.

Dario Colombo, MA, doctoral candidate and graduate assistant at the University of Fribourg in Switzerland.

Justin Shaun Coyle, Ph. D., Associate Dean and Assistant Professor of Church History, Theology, & Philosophy at Mount Angel Seminary in St Benedict, Oregon.

Oliver Dürr, Dr., PostDoc Researcher at the Institute for Hermeneutics and Religious Philosophy at the University of Zurich and a scientific collaborator at the Center for Faith & Society at the University of Fribourg, Switzerland.

Catherine Evtuhov, Professor of History, Department of History, Columbia University in the City of New York.

Brandon Gallaher, Associate Professor of Systematic Theology at the University of Exeter.

Paul Gavrilyuk, Aquinas Chair in Theology and Philosophy at the Theology Department of the University of St. Thomas, Saint Paul, Minnesota, and the Founding President of the International Orthodox Theological Association (IOTA).

Barbara Hallensleben, Professor of Dogmatic Theology and Theology of Ecumenism, member of the Institute for Ecumenical Studies and director of the Study Centre for Eastern Churches at the University of Fribourg in Switzerland.

David Bentley Hart, Collaborative Research Fellow, The University of Notre Dame, USA.

Joshua Heath, Junior Research Fellow in Russian Studies at Trinity College, Cambridge.

Caleb Henry, Ph. D. (Toronto), Adjunct Professor in Religious Studies and Theology, Canisius University (Buffalo, New York).

Austin Foley Holmes, doctoral candidate at Boston College in the Theology Department.

Ivan Ilin, doctoral student, Faculty of Theology, University of Fribourg, Switzerland; research assistant and visiting lecturer, HSE University, Moscow.

Pantelis Kalaitzidis, Director, Volos Academy for Theological Studies (Greece), member of the Executive Committee of the European Academy of Religion.

Pavel Khondzinsky, Dean of Faculty of Theology of St. Tikhon's Orthodox University, d. h. (Theology), Associate Professor of St. Tikhon's Orthodox University, Moscow.

Nikos Kouremenos, Ph. D., Research Associate, Volos Academy for Theological Studies.

Alexei P. Kozyrev, Dean and Associate Professor of the Faculty of Philosophy, Chair of History of Russian Philosophy, Lomonosov Moscow State University.

Paul Ladouceur, Dr, Orthodox School of Theology at Trinity College, University of Toronto; Faculté de théologie et de sciences religieuses, Université Laval (Québec).

Sarah Livick-Moses, doctoral candidate in Systematic Theology at Boston College.

Adalberto Mainardi, Ph. D. student at the Italian National Doctorate in Religious Studies; scientific secretary of the International Ecumenical Conferences on Orthodox Spirituality of the Monastery of Bose from 1994 to 2020.

Graham McGeoch, Dr., Associate Professor, Theology and Religious Studies at Faculdade Unida de Vitória, Brazil and collaborates with UNIperiferias in the favela Maré, Rio de Janeiro.

Mark McInroy, Associate Professor of Theology and Founding Co-Director of the Claritas Initiative on Beauty, Goodness, and Truth at the University of St. Thomas, Saint Paul, Minnesota.

John Milbank, Emeritus Professor in the Department of Theology and Religious Studies at the University of Nottingham, President of the Centre of Theology and Philosophy.

Aristotle Papanikolaou, Professor of Theology, Archbishop Demetrios Chair in Orthodox Theology and Culture, and Co-Founding Director of the Orthodox Christian Studies Center, Fordham University, New York.

Jack Pappas, Ph. D. candidate in systematic theology and philosophy of religion at Fordham University in New York City.

Liubov A. Petrova, doctoral student in Philosophy in theological studies, Faculty of Theology, University of Fribourg; Senior Researcher, Sociological Institute, Federal Center of Theoretical and Applied Sociology, Russian Academy of Sciences, St. Petersburg.

Taylor Ross, Ph. D., Instructor in the Theology department at Fordham University.

Dionysios Skliris, Ph. D., Teaching Fellow, Hellenic Open University.

Natalia Vaganova, Lecturer of Philosophy at the Theological Faculty, St. Tikhon's Orthodox University, Moscow.

h. **Tikhon Vasilyev,** MPhil, DPhil (Oxon), Lecturer at the Institute of Theology, St Petersburg State University.

Rowan Williams, Master of Magdalene College, Cambridge (2013–2020), Archbishop of Canterbury (2002–2012).

Nathaniel Wood, Ph. D., Associate Director, Orthodox Christian Studies Center, Managing Editor, Journal of Orthodox Christian Studies, Fordham University, New York.

Regula M. Zwahlen, Dr. phil., Scientific Director of the Sergii Bulgakov Research Center at the University of Fribourg, Switzerland.